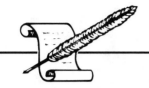

HISTORIC

DOCUMENTS

OF

1989

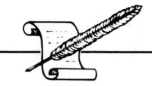

HISTORIC
DOCUMENTS
OF
1989

Cumulative Index, 1985-1989
Congressional Quarterly Inc.

Congressional Quarterly Inc.
1414 22nd St. N.W., Washington, D.C. 20037

The following have granted permission to reprint copyrighted material: From the *Journal of the American Medical Association*, November 3, 1989, vol. 262, pp. 2395-2401, © 1989, American Medical Association. From *The Chronicle of Higher Education*, June 21, 1989, pp. A29-A30, © 1989, The Chronicle of Higher Education. From MacNeil/Lehrer Newshour, June 9, 1989, show #3450, © 1989, Educational Broadcasting Corporation and GWETA.

The Library of Congress cataloged the first issue of this title as follows:

Historic documents.   1972—
    Washington. Congressional Quarterly Inc.

    1. United States — Politics and government — 1945— — Yearbooks.
2. World politics — 1945— —Yearbooks. I. Congressional Quarterly Inc.

E839.5H57   917.3'03'9205   72-97888

ISBN 0-87187-535-7

ISSN 0892-080X

Historic Documents of 1989

Editor: Hoyt Gimlin
Assistant Editors: Jamie R. Holland, Kerry V. Kern
Contributors: Mary Cooper, Carolyn Goldinger, James R. Ingram, John L. Moore, Richard C. Schroeder, Susanna Spencer, D. Park Teter, Margaret C. Thompson.
Indexer: Victoria Agee

Congressional Quarterly Inc.

Andrew Barnes *Chairman*
Richard R. Edmonds *President*
Neil Skene *Editor and Publisher*
Robert W. Merry *Executive Editor*
John J. Coyle *Associate Publisher*
Michael L. Koempel *Director of Information Services*
Robert E. Cuthriell *Director of Development*

Book Division

Patrick Bernuth *General Manager*

Book Editorial

David R. Tarr *Director, Book Department*
Nancy A. Lammers *Managing Editor*
Carolyn Goldinger *Senior Editor*
Margaret Seawell Benjaminson *Developmental Editor*
Ann Davies *Project Editor*
Colleen McGuiness *Project Editor*
Jamie R. Holland *Production Editor*
Nancy Kervin *Production Editor*
Ann F. O'Malley *Production Editor*
Jerry Orvedahl *Production Editor*
Virginia Johnson *Editorial Assistant*
Julie Mattes *Editorial Assistant*
Linda White *Administrative Assistant*

Book Marketing

Kathryn C. Suárez *Director, Book Marketing*
Jacqueline A. Davey *Library Marketing Manager*
Kimberley B. Hatton *Marketing Coordinator*
Leslie Brenowitz *Administrative Assistant*

Production

I. D. Fuller *Production Manager*
Michael Emanuel *Assistant Production Manager*
Jhonnie G. Bailey *Assistant to the Production Manager*

PREFACE

Publication of *Historic Documents of 1989* carries through the eighteenth year the project Congressional Quarterly started with *Historic Documents of 1972*. The purpose of this continuing series is to give students, librarians, journalists, scholars, and others convenient access to documents of basic importance in the broad range of public affairs.

Each document is preceded by an introduction providing background information and, when relevant, an account of following developments during the year. We believe that these introductions will become increasingly useful as memories of the current times fade in future years.

The year 1989 was exceptionally newsworthy, with epochal events occurring in the Soviet Union and Eastern Europe. At the year's beginning, few experts would have dared predict the speed with which political, economic, and social liberalization would take place in that part of the world. By the year's end, some scholars were calling 1989 the "Year of Revolution." Not since 1848, they said, had so many European countries been caught up in a wave of revolution. The salient features in 1989 as in 1848 were a quest for democracy and a reassertion of nationalism.

The transforming changes that Soviet president Mikhail S. Gorbachev initiated often appeared to race beyond his control in the Soviet Union itself, as well as in Eastern Europe. Poles, Hungarians, East Germans, Czechs, Slovaks, Romanians, and Bulgarians achieved measures of self-determination that were unthinkable only a short time earlier. Moscow made big concessions to the Baltic republics of Estonia, Latvia, and Lithuania but could not still their demands for outright independence. Those demands, together with ethnic strife on the Soviet empire's southern rim, seemed to threaten the USSR's very existence.

However, no event was more dramatic than the razing of the Berlin Wall, which for more than a quarter-century had symbolized the East-West divisions of the Cold War. Once the Wall and other physical barriers were punctured along the length of the Iron Curtain, people and ideas and money flowed freely into once forbidden territory. German reunification became a foregone conclusion.

In the United States, the bicentennial year of the American federal government was still new when George Bush took over the presidency from the retiring Ronald Reagan, the man he had served for eight years as vice president. Bush quickly charted a political course that differed in style from his predecessor's. The new Republican president stressed pragmatism instead of ideology and bipartisan teamwork instead of confrontation. He negotiated with a Congress that remained under Democratic control to reach a budget accord and to reconcile large areas of disagreement over America's involvement in Nicaragua.

Other news highlights of the year that are portrayed in this volume include: Congress's rejection of a key Bush nominee, John Tower, a former Texas senator, as secretary of defense; the trial and conviction of Oliver L. North for his involvement in the Iran-contra affair; lawmaking to deal with the savings and loan crisis; the Alaskan oil spill and its consequences; the Supreme Court's ruling that moved the longstanding fight over abortion mainly to the state legislatures; and the U.S. invasion of Panama that resulted in the capture of military strongman Manuel Noriega.

Such topics of national and international significance are presented in texts of official statements, Supreme Court decisions, reports, presidential news conferences, speeches, and special studies. In our judgment, the documents chosen for this volume will be of lasting interest. Where space limitations prevent reproduction of a full text, excerpts provide essential details and the flavor of the material.

Hoyt Gimlin, Editor
Washington, D.C., February 1990

How to Use This Book

The documents are arranged in chronological order. If you know the approximate date of the report, speech, statement, court decision, or other document you are looking for, glance through the titles for that month in the table of contents.

If the table of contents does not lead you directly to the document you want, turn to the index at the end of the book. There you may find references not only to the particular document you seek but also to other entries on the same or a related subject. The index in this volume is a five-year cumulative index of *Historic Documents* covering the years 1985-1989.

The introduction to each document is printed in italic type. The document itself, printed in roman type, follows the spelling, capitalization, and punctuation of the original or official copy. Where the full text is not given, omissions of material are indicated by the customary ellipsis points.

CONTENTS

January

President's Economic Report, Economic Advisers' Report
Text of the Economic Report of the President, submitted to
Congress January 10, 1989, by President Reagan, and a concluding section from the accompanying Annual Report of the Council
of Economic Advisers 3

President Reagan's Farewell Address
Text of President Reagan's last address to the nation, from the
White House, delivered on radio and television January 11, 1989   15

Paris Declaration on Chemical Weapons
Text of the declaration issued January 11, 1989, by an international conference in Paris on chemical weapons   25

Surgeon General's Review of Anti-Smoking Campaign
Excerpts from the Executive Summary of the surgeon general's
report, "Reducing the Health Consequences of Smoking: 25
Years of Progress," released January 11, 1989   31

President Bush's Inaugural Address
Text of President Bush's inaugural address as delivered January
20, 1989, from the West Portico of the U.S. Capitol   41

Episcopal Church Statements on Its First Woman Bishop
Text of the statement issued to the church January 24, 1989, by
the Rt. Rev. Edmond L. Browning, presiding bishop of the
Episcopal church, and the partial text of an ecumenical letter he
sent February 8 to the leaders of other churches, as released by
the Episcopal Church Center in New York City   49

February

State Department's Human Rights Report
Excerpts from the State Department's "Country Reports on
Human Rights Practices for 1988," submitted to the Senate
Foreign Relations and the House Foreign Affairs Committee and
publicly released February 7, 1989 57

Bush's Budget Address and Bipartisan Agreement
Texts of President Bush's budget address before Congress February 9, 1989, and of the Bipartisan Budget Agreement, signed
April 14 at the White House by the president and congressional
leaders 71

Report on the State of U.S. Education
Excerpts from the report, "Crossroads in American Education,"
prepared by the Educational Testing Service for the National
Assessment of Educational Progress of the U.S. Department of
Education and released February 14, 1989 85

Rushdie's Death Sentence
Text of the death sentence issued by the Ayatollah Ruhollah
Khomeini against Salman Rushdie, in English translation, as
broadcast February 14, 1989, on Tehran Radio 95

U.S. Tributes at Hirohito's Funeral
Excerpts from President Bush's remarks at news conferences at
the U.S. ambassador's residence in Tokyo on February 24 and
February 25, 1989, following the funeral of the Emperor Hirohito   99

Rejection of Tower as Secretary of Defense
Excerpts from the Senate Armed Services Committee's majority
report recommending against the nomination of John Tower to
be secretary of defense, and from its minority report supporting
the nomination, both issued February 28, 1989 105

March

Bicentennial Commemorations of Congress and Inaugural
Excerpts from speeches at the 101st Congress's joint session
March 2, 1989, commemorating the bicentennial of the First
Congress, as recorded in the Congressional Record; and excerpts
from the White House text of President Bush's speech in New
York April 30, 1989, at the reenactment of the nation's first
presidential inauguration 123

Brady Plan for World Debt Relief
Excerpts from Treasury Secretary Nicholas F. Brady's address to a conference on Third World debt, sponsored by the Brookings Institution and the Bretton Woods Committee, in Washington, D.C., March 10, 1989 137

Gorbachev's New Farm Policy
Excerpts from Mikhail S. Gorbachev's report to the Soviet Communist party's Central Committee, March 15, 1989, as translated by Novosti Press Agency Publishing House in Moscow and titled, "On the Agrarian Policy of the CPSU [Communist Party of the Soviet Union] in the Present Conditions"... 145

Toxic Waste Treaty
Excerpts from "The Basel Convention on the Control of Transboundary Movements of Hazardous Wastes and Their Disposal," as presented March 22, 1989.................... 153

Agreements on the Future of the Contras
Texts of the bipartisan accord on Central America, signed at the White House on March 24, 1989, by President Bush, House Speaker Jim Wright, D-Texas, Senate Majority Leader George J. Mitchell, D-Maine, Senate Minority Leader Bob Dole, R-Kan., House Majority Leader Thomas S. Foley, D-Wash., and House Minority Leader Robert H. Michel, R-Ill., and of the president's statement, issued the same day. These texts are followed by excerpts from the Tela Declaration, as translated from Spanish by the State Department. It was signed August 7 by the five Central American presidents............................. 161

Remarks on Soviet Election and Perestroika
Excerpts from translations of an election story published in Pravda March 26, 1989; of remarks by Communist officials at a Moscow meeting of the Central Committee, as quoted in Pravda April 27; and from a White House transcript of a speech by President Bush at Texas A&M University, May 12 173

Court Rulings on America's Cup Race
Excerpts from the ruling by Judge Carmen Beauchamp Ciparick of the New York Supreme Court, issued March 28, 1989, disqualifying the San Diego Yacht Club's *Stars & Stripes* as winner of the 1988 America's Cup and awarding the title to the *New Zealand*, the entry of the Mercury Bay Boating Club, and from the majority and dissenting opinions in the 4-1 reversal of her decision, issued September 19, by a panel of the court's Appellate Division.. 183

CONTENTS

Pleas for Higher Judiciary Pay
Excerpts from the report of the National Commission on the
Public Service, "Leadership for America: Rebuilding the Public
Service," issued March 29, 1989, and from a transcript of Chief
Justice William H. Rehnquist's testimony May 3, before the
House Post Office and Civil Service Committee   195

April

Kennan Observes End of Cold War
Text of George F. Kennan's statement to the Senate Foreign
Relations Committee, April 4, 1989.   207

Report on Black College Athletes
Excerpts from the report, "The Experiences of Black Intercollegiate Athletes at NCAA Division I Institutions," prepared by the
Center for the Study of Athletics and the American Institutes of
Research on behalf of the Presidents Commission of the National Collegiate Athletic Association, which publicly released
the report April 5, 1989   213

Congressional Hearing on Alaskan Oil Spill
Excerpts from the Senate Committee on Commerce, Science, and
Transportation hearing April 6, 1989, on the Exxon Valdez oil
spill   225

Ethics Committee Reports, Wright's Resignation Speech
Text of the House ethics committee's statement of April 13, 1989,
listing alleged violations of House rules by Speaker Jim Wright,
and Wright's farewell speech May 31   239

May

Statements on China's Protest and Repression
Text of a statement in support of the student prodemocracy
movement, signed by 500 faculty members of Beijing University
on May 16, 1989, as translated for *The Chronicle of Higher
Education*; President Bush's remarks and China-related questions at a White House news conference June 5, from an official
transcript; and excerpts from a speech by Chairman Deng
Xiaoping in Beijing June 9 to commanders of law-enforcement
troops   275

Secretary Baker's Policy Address on the Middle East
Excerpts from the State Department's transcript of Secretary of
State James A. Baker III's speech May 22, 1989, to the American
Israel Public Affairs Committee in Washington   289

President Bush's Proposal for Conventional Arms Cuts
Text of the White House transcript of President Bush's news
conference in Brussels, May 29, 1989   297

San Francisco Recognizes "Domestic Partnerships"
Text of the San Francisco domestic-partners ordinance, passed by
the city-county Board of Supervisors, May 30, 1989   305

June

Khomeini's Death, Hostages, and U.S.-Iran Relations
Text of the White House's statement on June 4, 1989, about
Ayatollah Ruhollah Khomeini's death; excerpts from a sermon
President Hashemi Rafsanjani preached in Tehran August 4, as
translated by the Foreign Broadcast Information Service, a U.S.
government agency, and remarks by President Bush to questions
at a White House news conference August 4   315

Supreme Court Rulings on Civil Rights Laws
Excerpts from the Supreme Court's majority and minority opinions in *Wards Cove Packing Co. v. Atonio,* June 5, 1989, that
made job discrimination more difficult to prove; and *Martin v.
Wilks,* June 12, enabling white firefighters to challenge a pay
and promotion plan for black firefighters in Birmingham,
Alabama   321

James Watt on Influence Peddling
Excerpts of James G. Watt's testimony before the House Government Operations Subcommittee on Employment and Housing,
June 9, 1989, and questions by subcommittee members, as taken
from a transcript of the "MacNeil/Lehrer NewsHour"   333

Hungary's Belated Eulogy for 1956 Uprising Heroes
Text of a declaration issued by the government of Hungary, June
14, 1989, as provided in English translation by the Hungarian
embassy in Washington   339

Court Ruling on Flag Burning
Excerpts from the Supreme Court's June 21, 1989, majority,

concurring, and dissenting opinions in the case of *Texas v. Johnson,* which tested the constitutionality of burning the American flag in a public political protest 343

Energy Secretary's Environmental Plan
Excerpts from the press conference conducted by Secretary of Energy James D. Watkins at the department's auditorium in Washington, June 27, 1989 355

July

Supreme Court's Decision in Webster Abortion Case
Excerpts from the Supreme Court's majority, concurring, and dissenting opinions issued July 3, 1989, in the case of *Webster v. Reproductive Health Services,* which gave the states more authority to impose restrictions on abortion................. 365

Sentencing of Oliver North
Text of Judge Gerhard A. Gesell's statement at his sentencing of Oliver L. North in U.S. District Court, Washington, D.C., July 5, 1989 391

Gorbachev's Vision of a Common Europe
Excerpts from Soviet president Mikhail S. Gorbachev's address to the Council of Europe's parliamentary assembly in Strasbourg, France, July 6, 1989, as translated by Tass, the official Soviet news agency 399

Bush's European Trip and Economic Summit
Excerpts from White House transcripts of President Bush's remarks July 11, 1989, at the Solidarity Workers Monument in Gdansk, Poland; his speech to students and faculty at Karl Marx University in Budapest, July 12; a news conference with the president conducted July 13 aboard Air Force One en route from Budapest to Paris; the final communiqué of the Paris economic summit conference, issued July 16; a Bush news conference in Paris at the summit's conclusion July 16; and the president's speech July 17 at Pieterskerk (St. Peter's Church) in the Dutch city of Leiden.. 411

Soviet Marshal Testifies to the U.S. Congress
Excerpts from the testimony of Soviet Marshal Sergei F. Akhromeyev before the House Armed Services Committee, July 21, 1989, as provided in translation by the committee........ 439

National Research Council Report on Black Americans
Excerpts from the National Research Council's report, "A Common Destiny: Blacks and American Society," released July 27, 1989 445

August

President Bush's Remarks on Signing S&L Bailout Bill
Excerpts from remarks by President Bush at the signing of the Financial Institutions Reform, Recovery, and Enforcement Act of 1989—the bailout bill—August 9, 1989, at the White House Rose Garden in the presence of several congressional leaders, Treasury Secretary Nicholas F. Brady, Secretary of Housing and Urban Development Jack F. Kemp, and members of the Federal Reserve Board, Council of Economic Advisers, and White House staff. 463

Baltic Freedom Statements
Excerpts from a statement issued August 23, 1989, by the Baltic nationalist movement, as provided in English translation by the Lithuanian Information Center in Washington, D.C., and from a statement issued August 26 by the Central Committee of the Soviet Communist party, as provided in English translation by the Soviet government 469

Statements on Banning Pete Rose from Baseball
Texts of statements by A. Bartlett Giamatti and Pete Rose, and the agreement they signed August 23, 1989, as issued by the major league baseball commissioner's office in New York City, August 24 477

September

Kohl on German Remorse at World War II Anniversary
Excerpts from the West German government's translation of Chancellor Helmut Kohl's speech at a Bundestag session in Bonn, September 1, 1989, commemorating the fiftieth anniversary of the German invasion of Poland and the start of World War II 487

Bush's Drug-War Speech, Colombian Leader's UN Appeal
Text of President Bush's address delivered on national television, outlining his plan for a "war on drugs," and a televised response by Sen. Joseph R. Biden, Jr., D-Del., on behalf of the Democratic

party—both on September 5, 1989—and Colombian President Virgilio Barco's address to the United Nations General Assembly, September 29, 1989 499

Navy Report on the USS Iowa Explosion
Excerpts from the navy's report, *Manual of the Judge Advocate General*, on the USS *Iowa* explosion April 19; the passages are in an August 31 memorandum from the chief of naval operations, Adm. Carlisle A. H. Trost, to the judge advocate general, released publicly September 7, 1989 517

Speeches Marking Poland's New Era
Excerpts from speeches by Polish prime minister Tadeusz Mazowiecki to the Sejm (legislative body), September 12, 1989, as translated from Warsaw Television Service by the U.S. State Department; and by Solidarity leader Lech Walesa to a joint session of Congress, November 15, as published in translation in the *Congressional Record* 523

Smithsonian Agreement to Return Indian Bones
Excerpts from remarks by Rep. Ben Nighthorse Campbell, D-Colo., opening a news conference at the U.S. Capitol on September 12, 1989, and from questions and answers that followed .. 539

South African President's Inaugural Address
Excerpts from the inaugural address of President F. W. de Klerk of South Africa, September 20, 1989, delivered outside the Capitol in Pretoria 545

Tennessee Court Decision in Frozen Embryo Custody
Excerpts from the decision of Judge W. Dale Young in Blount County, Tennessee, Circuit Court, September 21, 1989, granting temporary custody of frozen embryos to the woman from whom the ova were extracted 551

Statements at the Education Summit
Excerpts from President Bush's address at the University of Virginia September 28, during his meeting with the nation's governors for an "education summit," and the text of the final statement issued by Bush and the governors 561

October

Dalai Lama's Nobel Peace Prize Citation and Speech
Text of the Norwegian Nobel Committee's announcement Octo-

ber 5, 1989, that the Dalai Lama had been awarded the Nobel Peace Prize, and excerpts from his speech in Oslo on December 10, 1989, accepting the prize............................. 573

Congress Impeaches Two Federal Judges
Excerpts of a statement to the Senate from Sen. Arlen Specter, R-Pa., on the Hastings case, printed in the *Congressional Record,* October 20, 1989, and from Senate proceedings in the Nixon case giving portions of the summation of House impeachment articles by Rep. Don Edwards; and of Judge Walter L. Nixon's defense argument, November 1, as printed in the *Congressional Record*   583

Amnesty International's Report on Human Rights
Excerpts from Amnesty International's "Report 1989" on global human rights violations, released October 24, 1989.......... 597

November

Long-Term Study on Fitness and Health
Excerpts from the study, "Physical Fitness and All-Cause Mortality," conducted by Dr. Steven N. Blair and colleagues at the Institute for Aerobics Research and Cooper Clinic, Dallas, and published November 3, 1989, in the *Journal of the American Medical Association* 613

U.S. Catholic Bicentennial Observed in Baltimore
Excerpts from Archbishop William H. Keeler's homily at the bicentennial mass celebrated in Baltimore's Basilica of the Assumption, November 5, 1989 619

Statements on Berlin Wall and German Reunification
Text of the East German government's announcement, on November 9, 1989, as reported by the official news agency ADN, that it would open border crossings to the West, including the Berlin Wall; excerpts from the White House transcript of President Bush's reaction to that news, as expressed to reporters in his Oval Office, November 9; from an English-language translation of Chancellor Helmut Kohl's televised speech to the West German Budestag (National Assembly), November 28; and from a transcript of the response by Secretary of State James A. Baker III to Kohl's speech, November 29 625

Communist Concessions in Czechoslovakia
Excerpts in English translation from statements issued in Prague on November 29, 1989, by the Communist government and by

the political opposition—the Civic Forum and a counterpart
organization, Public Against Violence—spelling out the terms of
an agreement between the two sides on a political restructuring
in Czechoslovakia.   635

December

Bush-Gorbachev on Malta; Bush on NATO
Excerpts from White House transcripts of a news conference held
jointly by U.S. President George Bush and Soviet President
Mikhail S. Gorbachev at the conclusion of their meeting at
Malta, December 3, 1989, and from a news conference Bush
conducted December 4 at NATO headquarters in Brussels. . . .   643

Relief Effort in Hurricane, Earthquake Disasters
Text of the December 4, 1989, American Red Cross press release
describing its hurricane and earthquake relief efforts   667

Congressional Report on Discarded Children
Excerpts from the report, "No Place to Call Home," issued
December 11, 1989, by the House Select Committee on Children,
Youth, and Families, describing the plight of nearly 500,000
children in the United States.   671

Navigation Foundation Backs Peary's North Pole Claim
Text of the "Summary and Conclusion" section of the Navigation
Foundation's study, *Robert E. Peary at the North Pole,* issued
December 11, 1989   687

Army Denies Medal to Veteran for 1942 Combat
Text of the Army's review board recommendation denying a
Medal of Honor to David Rubitsky, as issued December 15, 1989,
by the Army Public Affairs Office in the Pentagon   697

Bush Announces Invasion of Panama
Text of President George Bush's televised address to the nation
on the morning of December 20, 1989, from the White House,
announcing the U.S. invasion of Panama   701

Bucharest Radio's Announcement of Romanian Ruler's Execution
Text of a Bucharest radio announcement December 25, 1989, as
reported in translation by the Western press, that Romanian
president Nicolae Ceausescu and his wife, Elena, had been tried
by a military court and executed for crimes against Romania and
its people.   709

January

President's Economic Report,
  Economic Advisers' Report   3

President Reagan's Farewell Address   15

Paris Declaration on Chemical Weapons...   25

Surgeon General's Review of
  Antismoking Campaign................   31

President Bush's Inaugural Address.......   41

Episcopal Church Statements on Its
  First Woman Bishop..................   49

PRESIDENT'S ECONOMIC REPORT, ECONOMIC ADVISERS' REPORT

January 10, 1989

In his final annual economic report to Congress, issued ten days before leaving office, President Ronald Reagan pointed with pride to what he described as the economic successes of his administration. The accompanying annual report by his Council of Economic Advisers (CEA) struck the same theme and elaborated on it.

In eight "short years," Reagan said, his administration had "reversed a fifty-year trend of turning to the government for solutions." By reducing taxes and regulatory bureaucracy, he said, "we have unleashed the creative genius of ordinary Americans and ushered in an unparalleled period of peacetime prosperity." The U.S. economy, he added, was entering a record seventh year of expansion. The length, strength, and resilience of the expansion, he continued, were "ample testimony" to the "wisdom" of the policies that had been pursued.

Reagan acknowledged that while his administration had "made progress" toward reining in government expenditures, "much still needs to be done." He did not mention the national debt, which more than doubled to nearly $3 trillion during his presidency under the impact of huge federal budget deficits. These deficits should be lowered by reduced spending rather than higher taxes, he said once again, repeating a central theme of his presidency.

Economic Advisers' Report

The Council of Economic Advisers, in their 267-page document, echoed Reagan's praise for a market-oriented economy and the nation's longest peacetime economic expansion. Since the 1981-1982 recession, they

3

reported, "real" (after inflation) economic growth had risen at an average rate of 3.0 percent a year, up from 2.1 percent in the 1973-1981 period. During the 1970s, the council said, high and rising inflation "distorted tax incentives," and burdensome regulation "snapped the productive energies" of the country.

The cure for those problems, the CEA said, "required nothing less than a fundamental refocusing" of federal responsibilities and policy initiatives. That "refocusing," the economists said, was the economic "legacy" of the Reagan administration.

Monetary Policy

The economists' report was signed by Beryl W. Sprinkel, the CEA chairman, and by Thomas Gale Moore, a member. The other member of the council, Michael L. Mussa, had resigned September 19 to return to the University of Chicago faculty. Sprinkel and Moore left office January 20, succeeded by President George Bush's new team of economic advisers, headed by Michael J. Boskin of Stanford University.

Sprinkel was of the monetarist school of economic thought, as expounded at the University of Chicago, which holds that change in the nation's money supply is the chief economic determinant. He had long been a critic of actions taken by the Federal Reserve Board. But the CEA report handed the board a mild compliment for keeping inflation from rising "[t]hus far in the current expansion."

Third-World Debt

In an analysis of problems created by the burgeoning debt of developing nations, the economists suggested that the roles of the International Monetary Fund (IMF) and the International Bank for Reconstruction and Development (World Bank) should be "appropriately reevaluated and redefined." The council said that almost one-third of an estimated $1.2 trillion worth of total debt owed by developing nations in 1987 had been subject to renegotiation in 1980-1987.

The report suggested that more active negotiating should take place between the debtors and creditors to reach market-oriented agreements on reducing debt. The increased responsibility of the IMF and World Bank to assist debtor countries had "blurred the traditional distinctions" between the two organizations and had "raised fundamental issues regarding their purpose and operations in today's world economy."

The Outlook

The economists predicted that the gross national product (GNP)—an accepted measure of economic strength—would rise 3.5 percent from the fourth quarter of 1988 to the fourth quarter of 1989, but that it would be outpaced by a 3.7 percent inflation rate. Real, or inflation-adjusted, GNP was up 3.9 percent in 1988, but the fourth-quarter increase was only 2.4 percent, which suggested that the economy was slowing down. Moreover, by the spring of 1989 inflation was running at an annual rate of more *than 5 percent. Unemployment, the advisers said, would fall slightly in 1989—to 5.2 percent of the labor force, down from 5.3 percent—but it, too, took an upward turn in the spring.*

Following is the Economic Report of the President, submitted to Congress January 10, 1989, by President Reagan, and a concluding section from the accompanying Annual Report of the Council of Economic Advisers:

ECONOMIC REPORT OF THE PRESIDENT

To the Congress of the United States:

It is with great pride in the accomplishments of the American people that I present my eighth, and final, *Economic Report of the President.* When I took office 8 years ago there was widespread doubt concerning the ability and resolve of the United States to maintain its economic and political leadership of the Free World. Political events abroad seemed to demonstrate the impotence of American power, while economic events at home raised concerns about the vitality of our system. Throughout most of the 1970s inflation raged at unacceptably high rates, and unemployment moved upward. Stagflation, a name invented for the era, and malaise were the words used to describe America.

Today, it is as if the world were born anew. Those who doubted the resolve, and resilience, of the American people and economy doubt no more. The tide of history, which some skeptics saw as ebbing inevitably away from Western ideals of freedom of thought, expression, and enterprise, flows in our direction. By strengthening our military posture and reaffirming our commitment to the cause of freedom throughout the world, we have restored respect for America and have achieved the first arms control agreement in history to eliminate an entire class of nuclear missiles. And by reducing taxes and regulatory bureaucracy, we have unleased the creative genius of ordinary Americans and ushered in an unparalleled period of peacetime prosperity. The world today is far safer, and more prosperous, than it was 8 years ago. And the America of today is, once again, brimming with self-confidence and a model for other countries to emulate. To be sure, there are challenges for the future, but I leave office confident that, with continued cooperation between the President and the Congress, America will meet these challenges and, in partnership with its allies, will continue to lead the world toward peace, prosperity, and freedom.

An Historical Perspective

Barely 40 years have passed since the end of World War II, but how the world has changed during that period. Man has walked on the Moon; products once unimagined are now commonplace; goods once considered luxuries are now necessities of life. Notwithstanding these enormous changes, the prime historical reality of this period has been the rivalry between two competing political and economic systems. One system operates by concentrating power in the hands of the few, by limiting personal freedoms, and by centralizing economic decisions. At its best, it is a system of state paternalism; at its worst, one of tyranny.

The other system believes that power emanates from the individual, not from the state; that the function of government is to serve, not dictate to, individuals. The great democracies recognize that political and economic freedom are indivisible; policies that threaten one of these freedoms inevitably undermine the other. These two divergent systems have vied, sometimes with words and sometimes with swords, for the hearts and minds of the rest of the world.

At the end of World War II the outcome of this competition was, to some, far from certain. Many intellectuals, looking back upon the experience of the depression in the interwar period, felt that the future was with communism. These people felt that capitalism, with its emphasis on the individual and decentralized decisionmaking, could not cope with the complexity of a modern economy. In the years that followed, some countries chose state planning and state ownership over the alleged chaos of the marketplace, while many more countries had this authoritarian system imposed upon them. Centralized control was especially attractive for many newly emerging economies, which felt themselves impoverished from, and were resentful of, their colonial experience. These countries turned inward, to highly regulated economies that shunned open markets and international trade as the path to prosperity, and instead sought self-sufficiency.

Today, few doubt which of these systems will emerge triumphant. Comparisons of economies with common cultures and people, such as North and South Korea, East and West Germany, or the People's Republic of China and Hong Kong or Taiwan, uniformly show that systems that emphasized individual initiative, open markets, and personal freedoms— as opposed to collective action—have prospered most. Developing economies have increasingly recognized the benefits of the market system as they have undertaken reforms to reduce the role of international trade. Most recently, this trend has even embraced the two largest proponents of state control, as first China and now the Soviet Union have reluctantly recognized that the true chains on individual fulfillment are an overbearing government that destroys motivation and freedom.

Viewed from the perspective of one who remembers well events of 40 years ago, the prosperity that we enjoy today is extraordinary. The economic growth experienced by countries that chose the path of economic and political freedom is virtually unparalleled in human history. This economic success is attributable to all nations that joined in pursuing market-oriented policies at home and in reducing barriers to trade among nations.

Americans can take a special pride in this postwar record. American aid to Western Europe and Japan helped rebuild those war-torn regions.

America took the lead in fostering negotiations that reduced trade barriers and created international institutions that promoted financial stability and reconstruction. Open American markets not only benefited consumers at home, but also sped recovery abroad. And America took the lead in preserving the freedoms and prosperity we all enjoy. As Winston Churchill said in 1952: "What other nation in history, when it became supremely powerful, has had no thought of territorial aggrandizement, no ambition but to use its resources for the good of the world? I marvel at America's altruism, her sublime disinterestedness."

The Role of Government

As I said in my first Inaugural Address, "If we look to the answer as to why for so many years we achieved so much, prospered as no other people on Earth, it was because here in this land we unleashed the energy and individual genius of man to a greater extent than has ever been done before." The central role of government must be to nurture this genius, not to shackle it in a morass of regulations or to tax away the incentives for innovation.

This is not to deny that there are vital functions that a government must perform, but it must always do so in the least intrusive and costly fashion. The guiding philosophy of my Administration has been to leave to private initiative all functions that individuals can effectively handle. Federal Government action should be reserved only for those functions that require national attention. In this way government will least interfere with private incentives and will be most responsive to the wishes of the people it serves.

The Federal Government, of necessity, must provide for the national defense. Only through strength can we maintain peace and secure freedom and prosperity for ourselves and all free nations. But we must ensure that our defense money is spent wisely, not on pork-barrel projects, such as maintaining military bases that are no longer necessary. This Administration, through its words and its deeds, has shown its commitment to protecting the health and financial security of our elderly. Similarly, the government must provide a safety net for the Nation's poor, but it must do so in a way that promotes individual initiative. Too often, government programs, created with the best of intentions, serve to prolong, rather than eliminate, poverty.

There are some limited circumstances in which government regulation of private activity may be beneficial. Few would doubt that some rules are needed to protect the Nation's water and air from pollution. However, it is imperative that all such rules and regulations be based on sound economic principles that minimize the intrusion on private decisions. Whether well or poorly designed, whether aimed at worthy or dubious objectives, these rules have one thing in common: They "tax" and "spend" billions of dollars of private funds, unconstrained by public budget or appropriations controls.

The main role of government is to provide a stable economic environment that allows each individual to reach his or her full potential. Individuals and businesses must be able to make long-run plans confident that the government will not change the rules halfway through the game. Government's drain on the economy, both through its use of resources that could be used more productively by the private sector and through taxes that destroy individual incentives, must be minimized. This Administration's long-term view of fiscal policy, which abandoned the outmoded emphasis on fine-tuning the economy, has set the basis for the record peacetime expansion we currently enjoy. This policy, in conjunction with responsible monetary policy, has led to a sizable decrease in both unemployment rates and inflation over the past 8 years. I am pleased to say that my Administration is the first in more than a generation that can lay claim to this accomplishment.

The government's economic role in the international sphere should be similarly circumspect. It is the primary responsibility of governments to promote sound and stable financial markets that encourage international commerce and to reduce barriers to trade at home and abroad. Reducing these barriers will allow markets, not governments, to determine the goods that society produces. Too often policies designed to preserve jobs in one industry reduce competitiveness and employment in other industries. A creative, competitive America is the answer to a changing world, not trade wars that close doors, create greater barriers, and destroy millions of jobs. We should always remember: Protectionism is destructionism. America's jobs, America's growth, America's future depend on trade—trade that is free, open, and fair.

The Record of the Past 8 Years

In my first Inaugural Address I stated, "The economic ills we suffer have come upon us over several decades. They will not go away in days, weeks, or months, but they will go away." After a shaky start, necessitated by the sorry state of the economy in 1980, we now have a peacetime economy entering an unprecedented 7th year of expansion. The length, strength, and resilience of this expansion are ample testimony to the wisdom of the policies that we have pursued.

During this expansion, real GNP has risen by more than 4 percent a year, nearly double the growth rate of the previous 8 years. The growth in employment and jobs has been phenomenal; nearly 19 million nonagricultural jobs have been created during this period, with nearly 3.5 million new jobs created in the first 11 months of 1988. Furthermore, this remarkable expansion has benefited all segments of the population. While civilian employment has increased by more than 17 percent, Hispanic employment has grown by more than 45 percent, black employment by nearly 30 percent, and female employment by more than 20 percent. The decline in unemployment rates is equally dramatic—the overall unemployment rate has been cut in half, down to levels not seen in 14 years. And, assertions to the contrary, the jobs created are good ones; over 90 percent of the new jobs are full-time, and over 85 percent of these full-time jobs are in occupations in which average annual salaries exceed $20,000.

Unlike previous experiences, this expansion has been accomplished without simultaneously fueling inflation. The average inflation rate during this period, as measured by the GNP deflator, has been barely one-third the rate of inflation that prevailed in 1980. The scourge of inflation, which served as a hidden tax on the American people and diverted productive resources to unproductive uses, has been brought under control here and in our major trading partners. This, in turn, has led to a dramatic decline in interest rates, which, while still high by historic standards, are far lower than they were in January 1981. In short, we have achieved the objectives that eluded us during the 1970s—rapid economic growth and declining inflation rates.

This record has been achieved not through alchemy, but by using that good old-fashioned recipe of reducing the role of government. Too often the government has sought to solve problems best left to the private sector; and too often these solutions have had devastating side effects. We have at least learned that more government is not the solution to our problem; often it *is* the problem.

Our New Beginning has restored personal incentives through a series of tax reforms and tax cuts. These reforms have reduced the top Federal marginal income tax rate to less than one-half the level that prevailed when we took office and decreased tax liabilities at all income levels. The Tax Reform Act of 1986 improved efficiency by eliminating many tax preferences that distort private decision-making. By reducing tax rates and tax loopholes, we have encouraged people to make money the old-fashioned way—by producing goods and services that people want, not by finding new ways to avoid taxes. The tax reforms have increased equity as well, as an estimated 4 million low-income individuals and families have been removed from the income tax rolls by 1988. If imitation is the sincerest form of praise, then the fact that many other major industrial powers have also cut their tax rates is praise indeed.

These tax reforms, combined with regulatory reforms, combined with regulatory reforms that will result in billions of dollars of saving over this decade, have helped spur productivity growth. Since 1981, manufacturing productivity has grown at an average annual rate exceeding 4 percent, triple the rate for the preceding 8 years and nearly 50 percent faster than that for the period 1948-73. This productivity growth, combined with exchange-rate changes, has led to a surge in U.S. exports that puts to rest the notion that U.S. industry is no longer competitive.

We have also made progress in reining in government expenditures, but much still needs to be done. We have reduced the rate of growth of Federal spending, and over the past 5 years government spending as a percent of GNP has fallen from 25.1 to 23.2 percent. Significant progress has also been made in reducing the budget deficit, both in absolute terms and as a percent of GNP, but further progress can be made only by reducing government spending. Tax increases would only threaten the enormous progress that has been made so far.

9

Our successes extend to the international sphere as well. The strong U.S. recovery, coupled with a weaker recovery abroad, helped create a sizable U.S. trade deficit. While the trade deficit has been significantly reduced during the past year as a result of our surging exports, it has served as an excuse for those seeking protection from foreign competition. Protectionism, like most forms of government intervention in the economy, serves only to enrich the few at the expense of the many. We have successfully resisted this protectionist pressure, while pursuing major trade liberalization efforts abroad.

The Israel-United States Free-Trade Agreement was the first such agreement entered into by the United States. The recently implemented Free-Trade Agreement with Canada represents an historic step forward for two staunch allies. In addition to creating the world's largest free-trade area between two countries and generating large benefits for both countries, it serves as a model of what can be accomplished in other negotiating forums. The United States remains committed to full multilateral liberalization, as reflected in the fact that we are the driving force behind the current Uruguay Round of multilateral negotiations under the General Agreement on Tariffs and Trade. While these negotiations are not scheduled to conclude until 1990, the results of the recent Mid-term Review indicate that they will result in significant reductions in trade barriers and a significant expansion in trade coverage.

Rather than succumbing to protectionist pressures at home, we have vigorously combatted unfair trade barriers abroad. This was the first Administration to seek, on its own initiative, changes in foreign trade practices that harmed American business. These policies have helped reduce foreign trade barriers and given American companies a chance to compete on equal terms.

The Challenges Ahead

As proud as I am of these and many other accomplishments, I will be the first to admit that the agenda is not yet completed. First, and foremost, is a need to reform the budget process and to bring Federal spending under control. The large budget deficit that this Nation faces is not a result of too few taxes, but too much spending. Strong economic growth and the base-broadening effect of tax reform have led to sizable increases in Federal receipts. According to current projections, these receipts will have increased by over $375 billion between fiscal years 1981 and 1989, but spending will have increased more rapidly—by more than $450 billion over this 8-year period. Projections indicate that Federal revenue will grow by more than $80 billion during the next fiscal year. All that is required to reduce the deficit is to halt, or moderate, the increase in expenditures.

Gramm-Rudman-Hollings is a first step toward bringing the deficit under control. However, further progress toward reform of the budget process is needed. Under current practice, funding for special-interest groups is combined with vital appropriations, leaving the President the choice between vetoing the entire package or accepting some funding that he knows is not in the national interest. To prevent this waste of taxpayers' money, the President needs what governors already have—a line-item veto and enhanced rescission authority.

Moreover, the current budget process places no real restraint on congressional appropriations, because expanded spending on one program does not require reduced spending on other programs. Too often the temptation is to raise taxes, not lower spending. A law that requires a super majority of the Congress to approve waivers of spending limits or tax limits would help ensure that taxpayers' hard-earned dollars are spent wisely, and that the temptation to increase tax burdens is resisted. Furthermore, reform of government credit operations is required to limit new subsidies and to guarantee that the true costs of these measures are not hidden from public scrutiny. These reforms, together with the balanced budget amendment that I have repeatedly endorsed, would guarantee the fiscal prudence that is needed to sustain the dramatic expansion of the past 6 years. Limiting government expenditures would also help stimulate the private investment that is required to ensure that the next generation of Americans can look forward to the same increase in living standards that previous generations have enjoyed.

Despite the enormous progress we have already made in bringing down inflation, there is still work to be done. Inflation is a hidden, insidious way of taxing the American people. Price stability, not merely lowered inflation, is the key to maintaining the vigor of the American economy and the strong international role of the dollar. Stable, predictable monetary policy can provide the type of price stability that benefits not only our own economy, but also provides significant benefits to those developing countries that are so dependent upon us.

Perhaps most importantly, the challenge for the future is to maintain and expand upon the progress we have made in taking economic decisions away from the government and returning them to the private sector, where they properly belong. Governments are notoriously bad at identifying "industries of the future," and efforts to have the government formulate and implement industrial policy must be strongly resisted. For decades, government policies throughout the world have distorted agricultural production and trade. Adoption of our bold proposal to phase out these policies in the United States and other major producing countries would result in enormous efficiency gains. And, while major deregulatory gains have been made, much more can be accomplished. Reduced regulation of vital sectors, including transportation, energy, and financial industries, has led to significant increases in productivity and to sizable gains for consumers. Further deregulation of the financial sector can help preserve this country's position as the financial capital of the world. Finally, we must resist pressure to increase government requirements for mandated benefits. These programs, while well-intentioned, increase costs, reduce labor market flexibility, and reduce productivity. They undermine the competitiveness of American business and they ultimately hurt the very people they are supposed to benefit.

11

Conclusion

In 8 short years, we have reversed a 50-year trend of turning to the government for solutions. We have relearned what our Founding Fathers knew long ago—it is the people, not the government, who provide the vitality and creativity that make a great nation. Just as the first American Revolution, which began with the shot heard 'round the world, inspired people everywhere who dreamed of freedom, so has this second American revolution inspired changes throughout the world. The message that we brought to Washington—reduce government, reduce regulation, restore incentives—has been heard around the world.

I leave office secure in the knowledge that these policies have worked, and confident that this great Nation will continue to lead the way toward freedom and prosperity for all mankind.

THE ANNUAL REPORT OF THE COUNCIL OF ECONOMIC ADVISERS

High and rising inflation, distorted tax incentives, and burdensome regulation sapped the productive energies of the Nation during the 1970s. Productivity and real income growth stagnated, U.S. competitiveness in world markets was severely eroded. The cure for these economic problems required nothing less than a fundamental refocusing of Federal Government responsibilities and policy initiatives. This refocusing of government policy is the legacy of this Administration.

The underlying tenet of economic policy in this Administration is that, with the proper incentives, private markets generally provide more efficient economic outcomes than are possible with direct government intervention. Thus, the Administration discarded social and economic policies that were wasteful and not incentive-based, and reversed activist aggregate-demand management policies. The Administration undertook efforts to establish and maintain a stable policy environment in which private initiative played the major role in providing desired outcomes. At the same time, the Federal Government continued to support basic public infrastructure investments and provide a social safety net.

Stable and incentive-based economic policies have served the Nation well in the past. Real incomes and standards of living improved rapidly between 1900 and 1913, during the 1920s, and between 1946 and 1965, when the money supply generally grew at a noninflationary rate and Federal Government spending was geared to providing basic services. On the other hand, economic performance deteriorated when such policies were not followed. For example, recession turned into depression during the early 1930s when the Federal Reserve allowed the money supply to fall by one-third between 1929 and 1933, and U.S. beggar-thy-neighbor trade policies incited retaliation and a consequent decline in world trade and income. Inflationary monetary policy, high tax rates and inflation-dis-

torted tax incentives, and a large and growing regulatory burden contributed to the stagflation of the 1970s.

The redefinition of fiscal policy under this Administration has been
aptly described as a fiscal revolution. This revolution has not overthrown
the Employment Act of 1946, which commits the Federal Government to
maintaining high levels of income, employment, and purchasing power. It
has overthrown a long entrenched view of the best way to achieve the goals
of the act. Gone are attempts to smooth fluctuations in aggregate demand
through frequent changes in government expenditure and tax policies and
efforts to find a balanced mix of fiscal and monetary actions. . . . [T]his
activist policy has generally failed to smooth aggregate fluctuations, and in
a few cases has actually increased the variability of aggregate demand.
Instead, this Administration has worked to establish and maintain stable
incentives for productive behavior by reducing marginal tax rates on
capital and personal income, indexing personal income tax rates to the rate
of inflation, eliminating wasteful tax preferences that distort incentives,
and controlling government outlays. Monetary policy has been used
principally to achieve and maintain a modest rate of inflation.

Another important element of the incentive-based policies of this
Administration was a commitment to flexible exchange rates and free
international trade. The rationale for this commitment . . . demonstrates
that international trade is not a zero-sum game, where an increase in the
exports of one country offsets a reduction in exports by other countries.
Free trade expands world trade and raises incomes of all nations.

Flexible exchange rates and free trade send a prompt and accurate signal
about the competitive position of a nation in world markets. The decline in
competitiveness of U.S. goods in world markets created by the stagflation
of the 1970s was laid bare during the first half of the 1980s, when U.S.
goods lost a considerable market share of world trade. The efficient
solution to this loss of competiveness was not, and is not, a shield
fashioned from tariffs, quotas, and other impediments to trade. Free trade
gave U.S. manufacturers an efficient, market-based incentive to compete
on the basis of the price and quality of their goods. . . . U.S. manufacturers
have lowered production costs and improved their productivity, and, with
help from a lower value of the U.S. dollar in foreign exchange markets,
they have seen a substantial rise in their world market share.

Flexible exchange rates and free trade impose a discipline on economic
policymakers worldwide, providing the incentive to implement sound,
market-based economic policies and to coordinate these policies with other
countries. A good example of this discipline appeared in the early 1980s,
when the U.S. dollar began to appreciate in foreign exchange markets. The
initial reason for this appreciation was the confidence in the part of U.S.
and foreign investors that the economic policies of the Administration
would contribute to strong economic growth and lower inflation in the
United States relative to the rest of the world. The U.S. dollar continued
to appreciate after the Administration's policies were implemented, and
these expectations were fulfilled. Foreign capital inflows into the United

13

States signaled to foreign governments that their own economic policies needed to be redirected in the same manner as in the United States. Other countries lowered their tax and inflation rates, and deregulated and privatized many of their key industries. As countries implemented these policies, their economic growth has increased and the U.S. dollar has depreciated in responses.

The challenge for the future is to sustain political and economic stability by maintaining a strong national defense and the commitment to market-based policies and price stability. Further efforts to deregulate domestic markets and international markets slated for upcoming negotiations under the General Agreement on Tariffs and Trade should be assigned high priority. Moreover, national governments worldwide must work to establish consistent monetary policies to achieve and maintain price stability. With these policies acting as the foundation, national economies can build on the achievements gained during this President's stewardship of the U.S. economy, and can continue to improve standards of living worldwide.

PRESIDENT REAGAN'S
FAREWELL ADDRESS
January 11, 1989

Leaving office with the highest popularity rating since opinion polls began measuring public approval of presidents, Ronald Reagan claimed for his eight years in the White House "two great triumphs." In his last televised address from the Oval Office, January 11, he said that the two things he was proudest of were the nation's "economic recovery" and its "recovery of morale."

Reagan sought with his parting speech to imprint on the public mind the philosophy that had guided his years as president. He concluded with a warning that the "resurgence of national pride" achieved during his presidency "won't last unless it's grounded in thoughtfulness and knowledge."

Reagan characteristically began his address with a personal touch, recalling the many times he had wanted to "reach out from behind the glass" of his speeding limousine to "connect" with a waving pedestrian. He then, also characteristically, used an anecdote to introduce his basic theme. He told how a refugee in a leaky boat in the South China Sea had called out to a rescuing American seaman: "Hello, American sailor. Hello, freedom man." The anecdote, the president explained, revealed "what it was to be an American in the 1980's," the years when Americans "rediscovered" that the nation stands for freedom.

This identification of freedom with the United States provided the philosophical basis of Reagan's military buildup and militant foreign policy. He saw a "new peacefulness around the globe" since America became "strong again after years of weakness and confusion."

Reagan saw not only peace but freedom increasing during his years in

15

the White House. "Countries across the globe," he observed, "are turning to free markets and free speech." Reagan had elaborated on this theme in a review of his foreign policy before students at the University of Virginia in Charlottesville. "These democratic and free-market revolutions are really the same revolution," he said. The main institutional barrier to human progress, he said, was government—in its attempts to encroach on freedom, "whether it be through political restrictions on the rights of assembly, speech or publication or economic repression through high taxation and excessive bureaucracy."

Reagan noted in the farewell address that high taxation also discourages production. He claimed for his economic program of tax cuts and deregulation "the longest peacetime expansion in our history." The president glossed over monumental budget deficits and ignored record deficits in international trade.

A New York Times-CBS opinion poll indicated that at the end of Reagan's tenure 68 percent of the public approved of his overall job performance. It reflected the highest popularity level of any departing president since such polling began at the time of Harry S Truman's departure in 1953. The next highest end-of-presidency score was Dwight D. Eisenhower's 59 percent. Richard Nixon, who resigned under the threat of impeachment, left office with the lowest rating (24 percent). Reagan was more popular with younger voters than with older ones, and more popular with men than with women, according to the poll. It recorded a 72 percent approval rating by white Americans but only a 40 percent approval rating by blacks.

Some historians suggested that Reagan's popularity was based more on sentimental attachment to the man himself than on critical evaluation of his policies. The Congressional Quarterly Weekly Report, in an appraisal on the Reagan presidency, said that "Reagan's two terms saw little authority accrue to his office." Despite his initial legislative successes, it said, he had lost power to Congress and handed over a weakened White House to Vice President George Bush. However, the New York Times-CBS poll indicated that 38 percent of the people said they could now trust the government "most of the time," an increase of sixteen points over 1980, the last year of Jimmy Carter's presidency.

Dissatisfaction, Dissent

The poll also reflected public dissatisfaction with some trends during the Reagan years. Although Reagan had recently claimed that "the poverty rate is down," 48 percent of those polled believed that it had increased, while only 14 percent said it had dropped. Statistics showed an improvement from the depth of the 1982 recession, but the poverty rate had worsened since the end of the Carter administration.

Three-fourths of those polled believed that crime had increased during the Reagan years, compared with 4 percent who thought it had fallen, and 54 percent felt that the administration had not done a good job of controlling illegal drugs. Education had deteriorated during the Reagan *presidency, according to 39 percent of those polled, while 21 percent believed it had improved. A decline in standards of ethics in government was seen by 33 percent; only 8 percent saw an improvement. Forty-eight percent said they favored bigger government, compared with 32 percent just before the Reagan era.*

The president's popularity did not deter negative assessments from longstanding critics. "The worst abuses we've ever seen of public trust and the environment in the history of the presidency," was the judgment of the organization Friends of the Earth. "The worst civil rights record of any administration in several decades," was the verdict of Ralph G. Neas, executive director of the Leadership Conference on Civil Rights. And consumer advocate Ralph Nader said the president had "led the nation in a drunken world-record spending binge while leaving millions of American workers, consumers and pollution victims defenseless."

The president's Democratic opponents in Congress avoided parting shots. A frequent critic, Sen. Patrick J. Leahy, D-Vt., said: "A lot of Democrats faced with a popular president have been willing to forgive him an awful lot."

Stephen E. Ambrose, a biographer of Eisenhower and Nixon and a professor of history at the University of New Orleans, observed that the American presidency had become "a symbol that is almost a monarchy." He added that "as the presidency becomes more imperial, more symbolic," the president is rated more on that basis.

President Reagan's farewell address urged that his "new patriotism" be made enduring through education that does "a better job of getting across that America is freedom." He feared that "younger parents aren't sure that an unambivalent appreciation of America is the right thing to teach modern children." To foster nationalism he urged "some basics: more attention to American history and a greater emphasis on civic ritual."

Following is the text of President Reagan's last address to the nation, from the White House, delivered on radio and television January 11, 1989:

My fellow Americans:

This is the 34th time I'll speak to you from the Oval Office and the last. We've been together eight years now, and soon it'll be time for me to go. But before I do, I wanted to share some thoughts, some of which I've been saving for a long time.

It's been the honor of my life to be your President. So many of you have written the past few weeks to say thanks, but I could say as much as you. Nancy and I are grateful for the opportunity you gave us to serve.

One of the things about the Presidency is that you're always somewhat apart. You spend a lot of time going by too fast in a car someone else is driving, and seeing the people through tinted glass—the parents holding up a child, and the wave you saw too late and couldn't return. And so many times I wanted to stop and reach out from behind the glass, and connect. Well, maybe I can do a little of that tonight.

People ask how I feel about leaving. And the fact is, "parting is such sweet sorrow." The sweet part is California, and the ranch, and freedom. The sorrow—the goodbyes, of course, and leaving this beautiful place.

You know, down the hall and up the stairs from this office is the part of the White House where the President and his family live. There are a few favorite windows I have up there that I like to stand and look out of early in the morning. The view is over the grounds here to the Washington Monument, and then the Mall and the Jefferson Memorial. But on the mornings when the humidity is low, you can see past the Jefferson to the river, the Potomac, and the Virginia shore. Someone said that's the view Lincoln had when he saw the smoke rising from the Battle of Bull Run. I see more prosaic things: the grass on the banks, the morning traffic as people make their way to work, now and then a sailboat on the river.

I've been thinking a bit at that window. I've been reflecting on what the past 8 years have meant and mean. And the image that comes to mind like a refrain is a nautical one—a small story about a big ship, and a refugee, and a sailor. It was back in the early eighties, at the height of the boat people. And the sailor was hard at work on the carrier *Midway,* which was patrolling the South China Sea. The sailor, like most American servicemen, was young, smart, and fiercely observant. The crew spied on the horizon a leaky little boat. And crammed inside were refugees from Indochina hoping to get to America. The *Midway* sent a small launch to bring them to the ship and safety. As the refugees made their way through the choppy seas, one spied the sailor on deck, and stood up, and called out to him. He yelled, "Hello, American sailor. Hello, freedom man."

A small moment with a long meaning, a moment the sailor, who wrote it in a letter, couldn't get out of his mind. And, when I saw it, neither could I. Because that's what it was to be an American in the 1980's. We stood, again, for freedom. I know we always have, but in the past few years the world again, and in a way, we ourselves—rediscovered it.

It's been quite a journey this decade, and we held together through some stormy seas. At the end, together, we are reaching our destination.

The fact is, from Grenada to the Washington and Moscow summits, from the regression of '81 to '82, to the expansion that began in late '82 and continues to this day, we've made a difference. The way I see it, there were two great triumphs, two things that I'm proudest of. One is the economic recovery, in which the people of America created—and filled—19 million new jobs. The other is the recovery of our morale. America is respected again in the world and looked to for leadership.

Something that happened to me a few years ago reflects some of this. It was back in 1981, and I was attending my first big economic summit, which was held that year in Canada. The meeting place rotates among the member countries. The opening meeting was a formal dinner for the heads of government of the seven industrialized nations. Now, I sat there like the new kid in school and listened, and it was all François this and Helmut that. They dropped titles and spoke to one another on a first-name basis. Well, at one point I sort of leaned in and said, "My name's Ron." Well, in that same year, we began the actions we felt would ignite an economic comeback—cut taxes and regulation, started to cut spending. And soon the recovery began.

Two years later another economic summit, with pretty much the same cast. At the big opening meeting we all got together, and all of a sudden, just for a moment, I saw that everyone was just sitting there looking at me. And then one of them broke the silence. "Tell us about the American miracle," he said.

Well, back in 1980, when I was running for President, it was all so different. Some pundits said our programs would result in catastrophe. Our views on foreign affairs would cause war. Our plans for the economy would cause inflation to soar and bring about economic collapse. I even remember one highly respected economist saying, back in 1982, that "The engines of economic growth have shut down here, and they're likely to stay that way for years to come." Well, he and the other opinion leaders were wrong. The fact is, what they called "radical" was really "right." What they called "dangerous" was just "desperately needed."

And in all of that time I won a nickname, "The Great Communicator." But I never thought it was my style or the words I used that made a difference: It was the content. I wasn't a great communicator, but I communicated great things, and they didn't spring full bloom from my brow, they came from the heart of a great nation—from our experience, our wisdom, and our belief in the principles that have guided us for two centuries. They called it the Reagan revolution. Well, I'll accept that, but for me it always seemed more like the great rediscovery, a rediscovery of our values and our common sense.

Common sense told us that when you put a big tax on something, the people will produce less of it. So, we cut the people's tax rates, and the people produced more than ever before. The economy bloomed like a plant that had been cut back and could now grow quicker and stronger. Our economic program brought about the longest peacetime expansion in our history: real family income up, the poverty rate down, entrepreneurship booming, and an explosion in research and new technology. We're exporting more than ever because American industry became more competitive and at the same time, we summoned the national will to knock down protectionist walls abroad instead of erecting them at home. Common sense also told us that to preserve the peace, we'd have to become strong again after years of weakness and confusion. So, we rebuilt our defenses, and this New Year we toasted the new peacefulness around the globe. Not only have the super-powers actually begun to reduce their stockpiles of nuclear weapons—and hope for even more progress is bright—but the regional conflicts that rack the globe are also beginning to cease. The Persian Gulf is no longer a war zone. The Soviets are leaving Afghanistan. The Vietnamese are preparing to pull out of Cambodia, and an Americanmediated accord will soon send 50,000 Cuban troops home from Angola.

The lesson of all this was, of course, that because we're a great nation, our challenges seem complex. It will always be this way. But as long as we remember our first principles and believe in ourselves, the future will always be ours. And something else we learned: Once you begin a great movement, there's no telling where it will end. We meant to change a nation, and instead, we changed a world.

Countries across the globe are turning to free markets and free speech and turning away from the ideologies of the past. For them, the great rediscovery of the 1980's has been that, lo and behold, the moral way of government is the practical way of government: Democracy, the profoundly good, is also the profoundly productive.

When you've got to the point when you can celebrate the anniversaries of your 39th birthday you can sit back sometimes, review your life, and see it flowing before you. For me there was a fork in the river, and it was right in the middle of my life. I never meant to go into politics. It wasn't my intention when I was young. But I was raised to believe you had to pay your way for the blessings bestowed on you. I was happy with my career in the entertainment world, but I ultimately went into politics because I wanted to protect something precious.

Ours was the first revolution in the history of mankind that truly reversed the course of government, and with three little words: "We the People." "We the People" tell the government what to do, it doesn't tell us. "We the People" are the driver, the government is the car. And we decide where it should go, and by what route, and how fast. Almost all the world's constitutions are documents in which governments tell the people what their privileges are. Our Constitution is a document in which "We the People" tell the government what it is allowed to do. "We the People" are free. This belief has been the underlying basis for everything I've tried to do these past 8 years.

But back in the 1960's when I began, it seemed to me that we'd begun reversing the order of things—that through more and more rules and regulations and confiscatory taxes, the government was taking more of our money, more of our options, and more of our freedom. I went into politics in part to put up my hand to say, "Stop." I was a citizen politician, and it seemed the right thing for a citizen to do.

I think we have stopped a lot of what needed stopping. And I hope we have once again reminded people that man is not free unless government is limited.

Nothing is less free than pure Communism, and yet we have, the past few years, forged a satisfying new closeness with the Soviet Union. I've been asked if this isn't a gamble, and my answer is no because we're basing our actions not on words but deeds. The détente of the 1970's was based not on actions but promises. They'd promise to treat their own people and the people of the world better. But the *gulag* was still the *gulag,* and the state was still expansionist, and they still waged proxy wars in Africa, Asia, and Latin America.

Well, this time, so far, it's different. President Gorbachev has brought about some internal democratic reforms and begun the withdrawal from Afghanistan. He has also freed prisoners whose names I've given him every time we've met.

But life has a way of reminding you of big things through small incidents. Once, during the heady days of the Moscow summit, Nancy and I decided to break off from the entourage one afternoon to visit the shops on Arbat Street, that's a little street just off Moscow's main shopping area. Even though our visit was a surprise, every Russian there immediately recognized us, and called out our names, and reached for our hands. We were just about swept away by the warmth. You could almost feel the possibilities in all that joy. But within seconds, a KGB detail pushed their way toward us and began pushing and shoving the people in the crowd. It was an interesting moment. It reminded me that while the man on the street in the Soviet Union yearns for peace, the government is Communist. And those who run it are Communists, and that means we and they view such issues as freedom and human rights very differently.

We must keep up our guard, but we must eliminate tension and mistrust. My view is that President Gorbachev is different from previous Soviet leaders. I think he knows some of the things wrong with his society and is trying to fix them. We wish him well and we'll continue to work to make sure that the Soviet Union that eventually emerges from this process is a less threatening one. What it all boils down to is this. I want the new closeness to continue. And it will, as long as we make it clear that we will continue to act in a certain way as long as they continue to act in a helpful manner. If and when they don't, at first pull your punches. If they persist, pull the plug. It's still trust, but verify. It's still play, but cut the cards. It's still watch closely. And don't be afraid to see what you see.

I've been asked if I have any regrets. Well, I do. The deficit is one. I've been talking a great deal about that lately, but tonight isn't for arguments. And I'm going to hold my tongue. But an observation: I've had my share of victories in the Congress, but what few people noticed is that I never won anything you didn't win for me. They never saw my troops, they never saw Reagan's regiments, the American people. You won every battle with every call you made and letter you wrote demanding action. Well, action is still needed. If we're to finish the job, Reagan's regiments will have to become the Bush brigades. Soon he'll be the chief, and he'll need you every bit as much as I did.

Finally, there is a great tradition of warnings in Presidential farewells, and I've got one that's been on my mind for some time. But oddly enough it starts with one of the things I'm proudest of in the past 8 years: the resurgence of national pride that I called the new patriotism. This national feeling is good, but it won't count for much, and it won't last unless it's grounded in thoughtfulness and knowledge.

An informed patriotism is what we want. And are we doing a good enough job teaching our children what America is and what she represents in the long history of the world? Those of us who are over 35 or so years of age grew up in a different America. We were taught, very directly, what it means to be an American. And we absorbed, almost in the air, a love of country and an appreciation of its institutions. If you didn't get these things from your family you got them from the neighborhood, from the father down the street who fought in Korea or the family who lost someone at Anzio. Or you could get a sense of patriotism from school. And if all else failed you could get a sense of patriotism from the popular culture. The movies celebrated democratic values and implicitly reinforced the idea that America was special. TV was like that too through the mid-sixties.

But now, we're about to enter the nineties, and some things have changed. Younger parents aren't sure that an unambivalent appreciation of America is the right thing to teach modern children. And as for those who create the popular culture, well-grounded patriotism is no longer the style. Our spirit is back, but we haven't reinstitutionalized it. We've got to do a better job of getting across that America is freedom—freedom of speech, freedom of religion, freedom of enterprise. And freedom is special and rare. It's fragile; it needs production [protection].

So, we've got to teach history based not on what's in fashion but what's important: Why the Pilgrims came here, who Jimmy Doolittle was, and what those 30 seconds over Tokyo meant. You know, 4 years ago on the 40th anniversary of D-Day, I read a letter from a young woman writing to her late father, who'd fought on Omaha Beach. Her name was Lisa Zanatta Henn, and she said, "We will always remember, we will never forget what the boys of Normandy did." Well, let's help her keep her word. If we forget what we did, we won't know who we are. I'm warning of an eradication of the American memory that could result, ultimately, in an erosion of the American spirit. Let's start with some basics: more attention to American history and a greater emphasis on civic ritual. And let me offer lesson number one about America: All great change in America begins at the dinner table. So, tomorrow night in the kitchen I hope the talking begins. And children, if your parents haven't been teaching you what it means to be an American, let 'em know and nail 'em on it. That would be a very American thing to do.

And that's about all I have to say tonight. Except for one thing. The past few days when I've been at the window upstairs, I've thought a bit of the "shining city upon a hill." The phrase comes from John Winthrop, who wrote it to describe the America he imagined. What he imagined was important because he was an early Pilgrim, an early freedom man. He journeyed here on what today we'd call a little wooden boat; and like the other Pilgrims, he was looking for a home that would be free.

I've spoken of the shining city all my political life, but I don't know if I ever quite communicated what I saw when I said it. But in my mind it was a tall proud city built on rocks stronger than oceans, wind-swept, God-blessed, and teeming with people of all kinds living in harmony and peace, a city with free ports that hummed with commerce and creativity, and if there had to be city walls, the walls had doors and the doors were open to anyone with the will and the heart to get there. That's how I saw it, and see it still.

And how stands the city on this winter night? More prosperous, more secure and happier than it was 8 years ago. But more than that; after 200 years, two centuries, she still stands strong and true on the granite ridge, and her glow has held steady no matter what storm. And she's still a beacon, still a magnet for all who must have freedom, for all the pilgrims from all the lost places who are hurtling through the darkness, toward home.

We've done our part. And as I walk off into the city streets, a final word to the men and women of the Reagan revolution, the men and women across America who for 8 years did the work that brought America back. My friends: We did it. We weren't just making time. We made a difference. We made the city stronger. We made the city freer, and we left her in good hands. All in all, not bad, not bad at all.

And so goodbye, God bless you, and God bless the United States of America.

PARIS DECLARATION
ON CHEMICAL WEAPONS
January 11, 1989

Completing a five-day conference in Paris January 11, delegates from 145 nations issued a declaration condemning the use of chemical weapons and calling for a treaty that would ban their development, production, and use. Moreover, signatory nations with existing stockpiles would be committed to destroy them. One hundred twenty-one nations had signed the 1925 Geneva Protocol, a treaty that bans the use but not the possession of chemical weapons. The declaration also expressed support for allowing the United Nations to conduct an investigation into suspected chemical weapons use.

Chemical weapons claimed more than 1 million casualties, soldiers and civilians, during World War I. The response to this devastation was the 1925 Geneva Protocol. The United States did not ratify the pact until 1975, after having used chemical defoliants such as Agent Orange—which would later be shown to be destructive to humans as well as vegetation—in Vietnam.

In acceding to the pact, the United States noted reservations, as many other nations had. It retained the right to the retaliatory use of chemical weapons and to permit certain military uses of herbicides. The United States resumed production of sophisticated binary weapons during the Reagan administration after an eighteen-year moratorium. (The chemical ingredients of binary weapons become poisonous gases in flight, after the projectile is fired.) However, in an October 1988 campaign speech, Republican presidential candidate George Bush pledged that, if elected, he would make it his "solemn mission" to bring about a "complete and total ban" of chemical weapons.

U.S.-Soviet Initiatives

President Bush said on September 25 that the United States would destroy most of its stocks of chemical weapons within eight years if the Soviet Union does the same. Speaking to the UN General Assembly, Bush said the United States would eliminate all of its chemical weapons only when every country now possessing them makes the same pledge.

Soviet Foreign Minister Eduard A. Shevardnadze, addressing the General Assembly the next day, advanced even more radical proposals: that the United States and the Soviet Union halt all chemical weapons production and immediately begin disposing of their existing arsenals. Each superpower conditioned its proposal on action by the other.

The United States and thirty-nine other countries are working on an international treaty to ban all chemical weapons within ten years. Negotiations on that treaty are moving fitfully in Geneva and probably will not be completed for at least another year or two.

In a major step toward U.S.-Soviet action on the issue, Secretary of State James A. Baker III and Shevardnadze on September 23 signed an agreement calling for an exchange of information and on-site inspections of each country's chemical weapons arsenals.

Bush suggested a three-step process by which the United States gradually would destroy its entire chemical weapons stockpile:

- *The United States would eliminate 80 percent of its chemical weapons even before the Geneva treaty is completed "if the Soviet Union joins us in cutting chemical weapons to an equal level." Bush said the two countries would have to agree on the conditions, including inspections, for destroying the stockpiles.*
- *During the first eight years of a chemical weapons treaty, the United States would destroy 98 percent of its chemical weapons stockpile "provided the Soviet Union joins the ban—and I think they will," the president said.*
- *Washington would destroy its chemical weapons "once all nations capable of building chemical weapons sign the total-ban treaty."*

Bush made no mention in his speech of the fact that the Pentagon already is required by law to dismantle 90 percent of its stocks of chemical weapons that were produced before 1969.

Later, the White House acknowledged a report in the Washington Post *on October 9 that Bush had secretly ordered U.S. diplomats to seek a major change in the chemical weapons treaty being negotiated in Geneva to allow countries to continue producing chemical weapons even after they sign the treaty.*

The current draft of the treaty, submitted in Geneva by Bush in April 1984, when he was vice president, would require each country to "cease immediately" all production of chemical weapons as soon as it becomes party to the treaty.

Each country also would have to reveal details of its chemical arms capabilities within thirty days after the treaty enters into force and would have to destroy all its chemical weapons within ten years. Some observers have predicted that the treaty could be completed within a year or two.

One State Department official said Bush's decision to continue chemical weapons production, despite the current wording of the Geneva treaty, was made during interagency bargaining over details of a proposal that Bush announced to the United Nations.

Bush made clear at the time that the United States would continue to produce chemical weapons for the immediate future. However, he did not say, either at the United Nations or in subsequent statements, that he was proposing to continue producing those weapons even after signing the Geneva treaty. Speaking to reporters on September 27, Bush rejected the Soviet proposal for an immediate halt to chemical weapons production.

Iraq's Use of Poison Gas

The main impetus for the Paris conference was Iraq's use of poison gas during its Persian Gulf war (1980-1988) with Iran and against its own rebellious Kurd tribesmen. In September 1988, the Reagan administration condemned the action as "abhorrent and unjustifiable." The United States, joined by Britain, Japan, the Soviet Union, and several European countries, requested that the UN secretary general send an investigative team to Iraq. Iraq denied the charges and kept out the investigators, terming the matter "an internal affair." A Senate Foreign Relations Committee inquiry reported "overwhelming evidence" that Iraq had subjected Kurdish villages to three days of poison gas attacks in August.

President Ronald Reagan made the issue of chemical weapons a centerpiece of his September 26, 1988, address to the UN General Assembly in New York. "It is incumbent upon all civilized nations to ban, once and for all, and on a verifiable and global basis, the use of chemical and gas warfare," he declared. Calling the use of poison gas in the Persian Gulf war an "ominous terror" and a "horror," the president said it had jeopardized the "moral and legal strictures that have held these weapons in check since World War I." In a speech to the same body three days later, President François Mitterrand of France said that wide-ranging sanctions should be imposed on any nation using chemical weapons against its own citizens or another country.

Meanwhile, negotiations continued at the Geneva Conference on disarmament on a comprehensive treaty, proposed by the United States in 1984, that would ban the possession and manufacture of chemical weapons. In an October 21, 1988, statement welcoming the convening of the January Paris meeting, the White House said, "The United States remains committed to the negotiations of a comprehensive, effectively verifiable, and truly global ban on chemical weapons. Such a ban would be the best solution to the threat posed by illegal chemical weapons use and proliferation."

27

Paris Conference Proceedings

During five days of often heated debate, delegates heard U.S. accusations that Libya was constructing a chemical weapons plant in the small town of Rabta, south of Tripoli. Libya denied the charge, claiming the plant was designed for pharmaceuticals. On January 1, U.S. officials reported evidence that a West German company assisted in building the Arabta facility for the manufacture of poison gas. West German chancellor Helmut Kohl initially said that there was no proof of the charge. But shortly after the Paris conference, his government disclosed that its own intelligence services had warned of possible participation by German companies in construction of the Libyan plant.

Addressing the conference on January 7, Secretary of State George P. Shultz alluded to the Libyan situation. "Terrorists' access to chemical and biological agents is another growing threat to the international community," he said. "There are no insurmountable technical obstacles that would prevent terrorist groups from using chemical weapons."

Soviet foreign minister Shevardnadze had announced to the Paris conference that the Soviet Union would immediately begin to eliminate its chemical weapons stockpiles. (Moscow had previously endorsed the idea of a comprehensive chemical weapons disarmament and agreed to inspections to verify compliance. The United States contended that the Soviets and their Afghan allies had used chemical weapons against their guerrilla foes in Afghanistan.)

The conference declaration represented a carefully crafted consensus. It did not endorse new export controls, proposed by the United States, on material required for chemical weapons production. India's foreign minister, Natwar Singh, echoed the sentiments of many Third World countries when he said that India could not accept an export ban because it would favor "certain countries," presumably the United States and Soviet Union, that already had "vast stocks of chemical arms." During the deliberations, Arab delegates argued that the conference should recognize their right to stockpile chemical weapons as long as Israel was presumed to have nuclear weapons, but their demand was rejected.

There was only a hint of imposing sanctions on nations that used chemical weapons. Throughout the conference, Iraq was rarely mentioned by name; the final document only noted "serious concern at recent violations" of the 1925 Geneva Protocol. At the conclusion of the conference, ten additional nations signed the 1925 protocol. William F. Burns, head of the U.S. delegation and director of the Arms Control and Disarmament Agency, said the conference had "forged a powerful global consensus." But he added, "It remains for the international community to translate this consensus into relevant actions toward these goals."

Following is the text of the declaration issued January 11, 1989, by an international conference in Paris on chemical weapons:

The representatives of States participating in the Conference on the Prohibition of Chemical Weapons, bringing together States Parties to the Geneva Protocol of 1925 and other interested States in Paris from 7 to 11 January 1989, solemnly declare the following:

1. The participating states are determined to promote international peace and security throughout the world in accordance with the Charter of the United Nations and to pursue effective disarmament measures. In this context, they are determined to prevent any recourse of chemical weapons by completely eliminating them. They solemnly affirm their commitments not to use chemical weapons and condemn such use. They recall their serious concern at recent violations as established and condemned by the competent organs of the United Nations. They support the humanitarian assistance given to the victims affected by chemical weapons.

2. The participating States recognize the importance and continuing validity of the Protocol for the prohibition of the use in war of asphyxiating, poisonous or other gases and bacteriological methods of warfare, signed on 17 June 1925 in Geneva. The States Parties to the Protocol solemnly reaffirm the prohibition as established in it. They call upon all States which have not yet done so to accede to the Protocol.

3. The participating States stress the necessity of concluding, at an early date, a convention on the prohibition of the development, production, stockpiling and use of all chemical weapons, and on their destruction. This convention shall be global and comprehensive and effectively verifiable. It should be of unlimited duration. To this end, they call on the Conference on Disarmament in Geneva to redouble its efforts, as a matter of urgency, to resolve expeditiously the remaining issues and to conclude the convention at the earliest date. All states are requested to make, in an appropriate way, a significant contribution to the negotiations in Geneva by undertaking efforts in the relevant fields. The participating States, therefore, believe that any State wishing to contribute to these negotiations should be able to do so. In addition, in order to achieve as soon as possible the indispensable universal character of the convention, they call upon all States to become parties thereto as soon as it is concluded.

4. The participating States are gravely concerned by the growing danger posed to international peace and security by the risk of the use of chemical weapons as long as such weapons remain and are spread. In this context, they stress the need for the early conclusion and entry into force of the convention, which will be established on a non-discriminatory basis. They deem it necessary, in the meantime, for each State to exercise restraint and to act responsibly in accordance with the purpose of the present declaration.

5. The participating States confirm their full support for the United Nations in the discharge of its indispensable role, in conformity with its Charter. They affirm that the United Nations provides a framework and an instrument enabling the international community to exercise vigilance with respect to the prohibition of the use of chemical weapons. They confirm their support for appropriate and effective steps taken by the

United Nations in this respect in conformity with its Charter. They further reaffirm their full support for the Secretary-General in carrying out his responsibilities for investigations in the event of alleged violations of the Geneva Protocol. They express their wish for early completion of the work undertaken to strengthen the efficiency of existing procedures and call for the cooperation of all States, in order to facilitate the action of the Secretary General.

6. The participating states, recalling the Final Document of the first Special Session of the United Nations General Assembly Devoted to Disarmament in 1978, underline the need to pursue with determination their efforts to secure general and complete disarmament under effective international control, so as to ensure the right of all States to peace and security.

SURGEON GENERAL'S REVIEW
OF ANTISMOKING CAMPAIGN
January 11, 1989

Exactly twenty-five years after Surgeon General Luther L. Terry issued his landmark warning against the dangers of smoking, the government examined the antismoking "progress" that had resulted since then. Dr. C. Everett Koop, a successor to Dr. Terry as the nation's chief public health official, issued a report on January 11 that said "tremendous changes" in the public's attitude toward cigarette smoking began to develop after that 1964 warning.

Koop characterized Terry's 1964 document, now referred to as the "Surgeon General's Report on Smoking and Health," as "America's first widely publicized official recognition that cigarette smoking is a cause of cancer and other serious diseases."

The 1989 report, the twentieth in a series on that subject issued by various surgeons general, is entitled "Reducing the Health Consequences of Smoking: 25 Years of Progress." A key finding was that half of today's adult Americans who once smoked have now quit despite tobacco's addictive nature.

"The ashtray is following the spittoon into oblivion," Koop said upon releasing his report. However, the document made clear that much work remained to be done. Although the prevalence of cigarette smoking among adults had declined, nearly three of every ten still smoked. Moreover, a decline in smoking among high school seniors leveled off in 1981, and children could easily acquire cigarettes despite restrictive laws in most states. "Given the prevalence of smoking, tobacco use is the nation's most widespread form of drug dependency," the report said. In May 1988 Koop released a report that likened nicotine's addictive

31

qualities to those of heroin and cocaine. (Report on Nicotine Addiction, Historic Documents of 1988, p. 309)

An outspoken public-health official, Koop informed President George Bush on May 5 of his intention to leave office in July, before his term expired in November. According to press reports, the surgeon general was angered that Bush did not ask him to stay in his administration.

Third-Leading Cause of Deaths

The 1989 report called cigarette smoking a major cause of strokes and the third-leading cause of deaths in the United States. It was also associated with cancer of the cervix. Noting that forty-three chemicals in tobacco smoke caused cancer, the report attributed smoking to unsuccessful pregnancies, low birthweights, and peptic ulcer disease. Smoking also contributed to cancer of the bladder, pancreas, kidney, and stomach.

In 1985, the last year for which estimates were available, 390,000 Americans died as a consequence of smoking, accounting for more than one-sixth of the deaths in the United States, the report said. It further estimated that between 1964 and 1985, 750,000 smoking-related deaths were "avoided or postponed as a result of decisions to quit smoking or not to start." The report predicted that 2.1 million additional lives would be saved between 1986 and 2000 for the same reasons.

Quarter-Century Smoking Decline

The prevalence of smoking among adults had declined steadily, from 40 percent in 1965 to 29 percent in 1987. The decrease was especially noteworthy among males in that period; the percentage who smoked declined from 50 to 32 percent. Proportionally there was more smoking among blacks, blue-collar workers, and less-educated persons than in the overall population.

The report said that, as of mid-1988, forty-two states and more than 320 communities had adopted laws or regulations restricting smoking in public places. Forty-three states and the District of Columbia restricted the sale of cigarettes to minors. But laxity in compliance and enforcement made tobacco products "relatively easy for children to obtain," the report said. It said a smoke-free society was attainable in the United States but the outlook was more pessimistic in many of the poor countries of the world. According to the World Health Organization, cigarette consumption exceeded population growth in all developing regions between 1971 and 1981.

Following are excerpts from the Executive Summary of the surgeon general's report, "Reducing the Health Consequences of Smoking: 25 Years of Progress," released January 11, 1989:

Exactly 25 years ago, on January 11, 1964, Luther L. Terry, M.D., Surgeon General of the U.S. Public Health service, released the report of the Surgeon General's Advisory Committee on Smoking and Health. That landmark document, now referred to as the first Surgeon General's Report on Smoking and Health, was America's first widely publicized official recognition that cigarette smoking is a cause of cancer and other serious diseases.

On the basis of more than 7,000 articles relating to smoking and disease already available at that time in the biomedical literature, the Advisory Committee concluded that cigarette smoking is a cause of lung cancer and laryngeal cancer in men, a probable cause of lung cancer in women, and the most important cause of chronic bronchitis. The Committee stated that "Cigarette smoking is a health hazard of sufficient importance in the United States to warrant appropriate remedial action."

What would constitute "appropriate remedial action" was left unspecified. But the release of the report was the first in a series of steps, still being taken 25 years later, to diminish the impact of tobacco use on the health of the American people.

This 1989 Report, the 20th in a series of Surgeon General's Reports on the Health Consequences of Smoking, spells out the dramatic progress that has been achieved in the past quarter century against one of our deadliest risks.

The circumstances surrounding the release of the first report in 1964 are worth remembering. The date chosen was a Saturday morning, to guard against a precipitous reaction on Wall Street. An auditorium in the State Department was selected because its security could be assured—it had been the site for press conferences of the late President John F. Kennedy, whose assassination had occurred less than 2 months earlier.

The first two copies of the 387-page, brown-covered report were hand delivered to the West Wing of the White House at 7:30 on that Saturday morning. At 9:00, accredited press representatives were admitted to the auditorium and "locked in," without access to telephones. Surgeon General Terry and his Advisory Committee took their seats on the platform. The Report was distributed and reporters were allowed 90 minutes to read it. Questions were answered by Dr. Terry and his Committee members. Finally, the doors were opened and the news was spread. For several days, the Report furnished newspaper headlines across the country and lead stories on television newscasts. Later it was ranked among the top news stories of 1964.

During the quarter century that has elapsed since that report, individual citizens, private organizations, public agencies, and elected officials have tirelessly pursued the Advisory Committee's call for "appropriate remedial action." Early on, the U.S. Congress adopted the Federal Cigarette Labeling and Advertising Act of 1965 and the Public Health Cigarette Smoking Act of 1969. These laws required a health warning on cigarette packages, banned cigarette advertising in the broadcast media, and called for an annual report on the health consequences of smoking.

In 1964, the Public Health Service established a small unit called the National Clearinghouse for Smoking and Health (NCSH). Through the year, the Clearinghouse and its successor organization, the Office on Smoking and Health, have been responsible for the 20 reports on the health consequences of smoking previously mentioned, eight of which have been issued during my tenure as Surgeon General. In close cooperation with voluntary health organizations, the Public Health Service has supported highly successful school and community programs on smoking and health, has disseminated research findings related to tobacco use, and has ensured the continued public visibility of antismoking messages.

Throughout this period, tremendous changes have occurred. As detailed in this Report, we have witnessed expansion in scientific knowledge of the health hazards of smoking, growing public knowledge of the dangers of smoking, increased availability of programs to prevent young people from starting to smoke and to help smokers quit, and widespread adoption of policies that discourage the use of tobacco.

Most important, these developments have changed the way in which our society views smoking. In the 1940s and 1950s, smoking was chic; now, increasingly, it is shunned. Movie stars, sports heroes, and other celebrities used to appear in cigarette advertisements. Today, actors, athletes, public figures, and political candidates are rarely seen smoking. The ashtray is following the spittoon into oblivion.

Within this evolving social milieu, the population has been giving up smoking in increasing numbers. Nearly half of all living adults who ever smoked have quit. The most impressive decline in smoking has occurred among men. Smoking prevalence among men has fallen from 50 percent in 1965 to 32 percent in 1987. These changes represent nothing less than a revolution in behavior.

The antismoking campaign has been a major public health success. Those who have participated in this campaign can take tremendous pride in the progress that has been made.

The analysis in this Report shows that in the absence of the campaign, there would have been 91 million American smokers (15 to 84 years of age) in 1985 instead of 56 million. As a result of decisions to quit smoking or not to start, an estimated 789,000 smoking-related deaths were avoided or postponed between 1964 and 1985. Furthermore, these decisions will result in the avoidance or postponement of an estimated 2.1 million smoking-related deaths between 1986 and the year 2000.

This achievement has few parallels in the history of public health. It was accomplished despite the addictive nature of tobacco and the powerful economic forces promoting its use.

The Remaining Challenges

Despite this achievement, smoking will continue as the leading cause of preventable, premature death for many years to come, even if all smokers were to quit today. Smoking cessation is clearly beneficial in reducing the risk of dying from smoking-related diseases. However, for some diseases, such as lung cancer and emphysema, quitting may not reduce the risk to the level of a lifetime nonsmoker even after many years of abstinence. This residual health risk is one reason why approximately 390,000 Americans died in 1985 as the result of smoking, even after two decades of declining smoking rates.

The critical message here is that progress in curtailing smoking must continue, and ideally accelerate, to enable us to turn smoking-related mortality around. Otherwise, the disease impact of smoking will remain high well into the 21st century.

Just maintaining the current rate of progress is a challenge. Compared with nonsmokers, smokers are disproportionately found in groups that are harder to reach, and this disparity may increase over time. Greater effort and resources will need to be devoted to achieve equivalent reductions in smoking among those whose behavior has survived strong, countervailing social pressures.

Today, thanks to the remarkable progress of the past 25 years, we can dare to envision a smoke-free society. Indeed it can be said that the social tide is flowing toward that bold objective. To maintain momentum, we need to direct special attention to the following groups within our society:

Children and Adolescents

As a pediatric surgeon, and now as Surgeon General, I have dedicated my career to protecting the health of children. In the case of smoking, children and adolescents hold the key to progress toward curbing tobacco use in future generations.

If the adult rate of smoking were to continue at the present level, the impact of smoking on the future health and welfare of today's children would be enormous. Research has shown that one-fourth or more of all regular cigarette smokers die of smoking-related diseases. If 20 million of the 70 million children now living in the United States smoke cigarettes as adults (about 29 percent), then at least 5 million of them will die of smoking-related diseases. This figure should alarm anyone who is concerned with the future health of today's children.

Two additional factors make smoking among young people a preeminent public health concern: (1) the age of initiation of smoking, and (2) nicotine addiction. As this Report shows, four-fifths of smokers born since 1935 started smoking before age 21. The proportion of smokers who begin smoking during adolescence has been increasing over time, particularly among women.

In the Teenage Smoking Survey conducted by the Department of Health, Education, and Welfare in 1979, respondents were asked, "What would you say is the possibility that five years from now you will be a cigarette smoker?" Among smokers, half answered "definitely not" or "probably not." This response suggests that many children and adolescents are unaware of, or underestimate, the addictive nature of smoking. The predecessor to this volume, *The Health Consequences of Smoking: Nicotine Addiction,* provided a comprehensive review of the evidence that cigarettes and other forms of tobacco are addicting and that nicotine is the drug in tobacco that causes addiction.

These two factors refute the argument that smoking is a matter of free choice. Most smokers start smoking as teenagers and then become addicted. By the time smokers become adults ... many have difficulty quitting. Today, 80 percent of smokers say they would like to quit; two-thirds of smokers have made at least one serious attempt to quit. Characteristically, people quit smoking several times before becoming permanent ex-smokers.

The prevalence of daily smoking among high school seniors leveled off from 1981 through 1987, at about 20 percent, after previous years of decline. Each day, more than 3,000 American teenagers start smoking. If we can substantially reduce this number, we will soon achieve a major impact on smoking prevalence among adults. Although research efforts in prevention are increasing, prevention programs are not yet reaching large numbers of young people. The public health community should pay at least as much attention to the prevention of smoking among teenagers as it now pays to smoking cessation among adults. Comprehensive school health education, incorporating tobacco use prevention, should be provided....

Women

Since release of the first Surgeon General's Report, the prevalence of smoking among women has declined much more slowly than among men. If current trends continue, smoking rates will be about equal among men and women in the mid-1990s, after which women may smoke at a higher rate than men.

The public health impact of this trend is already being seen. Lung cancer mortality rates are increasing steadily among women, and estimates by the American Cancer Society indicate that this disease has now overtaken breast cancer as the number one cause of cancer death among women. Smoking during pregnancy poses special risks to the developing fetus and is an important cause of low birthweight and infant mortality. Smoking and oral contraceptive use interact to increase dramatically the risk of cardiovascular disease. Women's organizations and women's magazines have paid scant attention to these issues.

The key to addressing this problem is the prevention of smoking among female adolescents. The disparity in smoking prevalence between men and women is primarily a reflection of differences in smoking initiation. Smoking initiation has declined much more slowly among females than among males. This difference is due, in large part, to increasing initiation rates among less educated young women. Among high school seniors, the prevalence of daily smoking has been higher among females than among males each year since 1977.

In summary, women, and especially female adolescents not planning higher education, are an important target group for prevention activities.

Minorities

Smoking rates are higher in certain racial and ethnic minority groups, many of which already suffer from a disproportionate share of risk factors and illness. In particular, smoking prevalence has been consistently higher among black men than among white men (41 and 31 percent, respectively, in 1987). In addition, the limited data available show higher rates of smoking among Hispanic men than among white men.

Trends in smoking initiation, prevalence, and quitting among blacks and whites show similar rates of change from 1974 to 1985. Thus, the gap in smoking prevalence between blacks and whites is not widening. However, to reduce the gap in smoking between blacks and whites, prevention efforts must focus on blacks more successfully. The public health community is only now beginning to address this problem. The urgency of the situation is greater because cigarette companies are increasingly targeting their marketing efforts at blacks and Hispanics.

Blue-Collar Workers

The prevalence of smoking has been consistently higher among blue-collar workers than among white-collar workers. In 1985, 40 percent of blue-collar workers smoked compared with 28 percent of white-collar workers. Again, blue-collar workers are a major target of cigarette company advertising and promotional campaigns. Worksite smoking cessation programs, employee incentive programs, and policies banning or restricting smoking at the workplace are effective strategies to reach this group.

Toward a Smoke-Free Future

Because the general health risks of smoking are well known, because smoking is banned or restricted in a growing number of public places and worksites, and because smoking is losing its social acceptability, the overall prevalence of smoking in our society is likely to continue to decline. The progress we have achieved during the past quarter century is impressive.

Equally impressive, however, are the challenges we face. During the next quarter century and beyond, progress will be slow, and smoking-related mortality will remain high, unless the health community more effectively reaches children and adolescents, women, minorities, and blue-collar workers. Organizations that represent these groups can contribute substantially to the antismoking movement. In large part, the future health of these populations will depend on the degree to which schools, educators, parents' organizations, women's groups, minority organizations, employers, and employee unions join the campaign for a smoke-free society. Here in the United States, such a society is an attainable long-term goal.

Unfortunately, the looming epidemic of smoking and smoking-related disease in developing countries does not encourage similar optimism. According to the World Health Organization, increases in cigarette consumption between 1971 and 1981 exceeded population growth in all developing regions: by 77 percent in Africa, and by 30 percent in Asia and Latin America.

The topic of tobacco and health internationally, although critically important, especially for developing nations, is beyond the scope of this Report. I can only hope that the lessons we have learned in the United

States, as detailed in this Report, will help other countries take the
necessary steps to avoid the devastation caused by use of tobacco. . . .

Highlights of Conclusions and Findings

Key New Findings

While this Report is designed to provide a retrospective view of smoking
and health over the past 25 years, several findings never previously
documented in a report of the surgeon general emerged during the process
of reviewing and analyzing the voluminous materials consulted for the
study. Discussed in detail throughout the Report, key new findings include
the following:

- Cigarette smoking is a major cause of cerebrovascular disease (stroke),
  the third leading cause of death in the United States.
- By 1986, lung cancer caught up with breast cancer as the leading cause
  of cancer death in women. Women smokers' relative risk of lung cancer
  has increased by a factor of more than four since the early 1960s and is
  now comparable to the relative risk identified for men in that earlier
  period. Gender differences in smoking behavior are disappearing;
  consistent with this, gender differences in the relative risks of and
  mortality from smoking-related diseases are narrowing.
- Cigarette smoking is associated with cancer of the uterine cervix.
- To date, 43 chemicals in tobacco smoke have been determined to be
  carcinogenic.
- In 1985, approximately 390,000 deaths were attributable to cigarette
  smoking. This figure is greater than other recent estimates of smoking-
  attributable mortality, reflecting the use of higher relative risks of
  smoking-related diseases for women and, especially in the case of lung
  cancer, for men. These higher relative risks were derived from the
  largest and most recent prospective study of smoking and disease,
  conducted by the American Cancer Society.
- Disparities in smoking prevalence, quitting, and initiation between
  groups with the highest and lowest levels of educational attainment are
  substantial and have been increasing. Educational attainment appears
  to be the best single sociodemographic predictor of smoking.
- There is growing recognition that prevention and cessation interventions need to target specific populations with a high smoking prevalence or at high risk of smoking-related disease. These populations
  include minority groups, pregnant women, military personnel, high
  school dropouts, blue-collar workers, unemployed persons, and heavy
  smokers.
- One-quarter of high school seniors who have ever smoked had their
  first cigarette by sixth grade, one-half by tenth grade. Associated with
  knowledge of this fact is a growing consensus that smoking prevention
  education needs to begin in elementary school.
- Whereas past smoking control efforts targeting children and adoles-

cents focused exclusively on prevention of smoking, the smoking control community has identified the need to develop cessation programs for children and adolescents addicted to nicotine.

- As of mid-1988, more than 320 local communities had adopted laws or regulations restricting smoking in public places. This compares with a total of about 90 as of the end of 1985, a more than threefold increase in 3 years. The number of new State laws restricting smoking in public places in 1987 exceeded the number passed in any preceding year.

- A growing body of evidence on the role of economic incentives in influencing health behavior has contributed to increased interest in and use of such incentives to discourage use of tobacco products. These include excise taxation of tobacco products, workplace financial incentives, and insurance premium differentials for smokers and nonsmokers.

- In marked contrast to the trends in virtually all other areas of smoking control policy, the number of legal restrictions on children's access to tobacco products has decreased over the past quarter century. Studies indicate that vendor compliance with minimum-age-of-purchase laws is the exception rather than the rule.

- The marketing of a variety of alternative nicotine delivery systems has heightened concern within the public health community about the future of nicotine addiction. The most prominent development in this regard was the 1988 test marketing by a major cigarette producer of a nicotine delivery device having the external appearance of a cigarette and being promoted as "the cleaner smoke."

- While over 50 million Americans continue to smoke, more than 90 million would be smoking in the absence of the changes in the smoking-and-health environment that have occurred since 1964.

- Quitting and noninitiation of smoking between 1964 and 1985, encouraged by changes in that environment, have been or will be associated with the postponement or avoidance of almost 3 million smoking-related deaths. That figure reflects ... three-quarters of a million deaths ... and an additional 2.1 million deaths estimated to be postponed or avoided between 1986 and the year 2000....

Limitations of Coverage

Despite the broad scope of this Report, certain limitations have had to be placed on coverage. Two in particular are worthy of mention here:

(1) The Report focuses primarily, but not exclusively, on cigarette smoking, reflecting its dominance among forms of tobacco use, in terms of both prevalence and disease impact. This focus also reflects the desire to represent the principal interest of the 1964 Advisory Committee in this 25th anniversary Report. Pipe and cigar smoking are much less prevalent than cigarette smoking but also carry significant health risks. Growing use of smokeless tobacco products (snuff and chewing tobacco), primarily by adolescent males, has

focused national attention on the prevalence and health consequences of using these tobacco products. This subject was recently
reviewed thoroughly by an advisory committee to the Surgeon
General and in a National Cancer Institute monograph.

(2) The Report concentrates on smoking in the United States. Both
within the United States and around the world, there is growing
concern about the spread of smoking, particularly in the world's
poorer countries. While per capital cigarette consumption is stable
or falling in most developed nations, it is rising in Third World
countries. Rates of smoking-related chronic diseases are also increasing rapidly, to the point that tobacco is expected to soon become the
leading cause of premature, preventable mortality in the Third
World, as it is at present in the developed world.

Concentration of this Report on smoking in the United States is no
reflection on the relative importance of the international situation. Rather,
it results from the principal objective of reviewing where this Nation has
come in its efforts to control smoking-related disease since the 1964 report
of the Surgeon General's Advisory Committee. The Public Health Service
hopes that this review, like its predecessors, will prove to be of value to
scientists, health professionals, and public health officials in countries
throughout the world. . . .

PRESIDENT BUSH'S
INAUGURAL ADDRESS
January 20, 1989

George Herbert Walker Bush took office January 20 as the nation's forty-first president. He was fresh from a decisive election victory at the head of the national Republican ticket but faced a Congress whose Democratic majority had actually been enlarged by the November voting. Bush and his vice-presidential choice, Dan Quayle of Indiana, captured 53.4 percent of the popular vote and carried forty states, taking 426 of the 538 electoral votes. However, it was an election that featured a 50.1 percent voter-turnout rate, the lowest since 1924, and the continuation of authority split between a Republican-controlled executive branch and a Democratic-controlled legislative branch.

The national mood as expressed by the election's low turnout and actual results muddled all attempts to discern which party's vision of America served as the governing outlook for the nation, and whether Bush held a leadership mandate to deal with a backlogged agenda of substantive issues carried over from the Reagan administration. These issues had been addressed only superficially in the 1988 election campaign by either Bush and Quayle or their Democratic rivals, Gov. Michael S. Dukakis of Massachusetts and his running mate, Sen. Lloyd Bentsen of Texas.

The new president came into office emphasizing pragmatism instead of ideology, and bipartisan teamwork instead of confrontation. He appealed not only for bipartisanship but for an end to the political cleavages opened by the Vietnam War. The new president offered olive branches all around—to blacks, young conservatives, hereditary Democrats, and, of course, Congress. In his inaugural address he called for cooperation with—and from—Speaker Jim Wright of Texas (who waved in response) and Senate Majority Leader George J. Mitchell of Maine (who smiled).

Bush said he wanted to be "president of all the American people," and that he would look for ways to get as close to them as possible. He took the oath not in formal attire but in a plain business suit. He got out of his limousine to walk portions of the inaugural parade route from the Capitol to the White House. And all comers were invited to the White House on January 21—the first such invitation in eighty years.

Continuing with a practice that Ronald Reagan began in 1981 at his first inaugural, Bush took the oath of office and delivered his address to the nation from the Capitol's grand West Portico. Bush referred to it as one great front porch, "a good place to talk as neighbors, and as friends."

A crowd estimated at 140,000 jammed the steps and lawn beneath the Capitol dome on an unseasonably balmy day. All spectators had encountered the tightest security ever at a swearing-in ceremony. Bush's uttering of the thirty-five-word oath of office had been timed to end exactly at twelve noon, the moment the Constitution specified for the new president to take office. But the ceremony ran several minutes late, meaning that Bush technically became president before taking the oath. Vice President Quayle preceded Bush by about eight minutes in being sworn in.

Rare Transfer of Power

Bush's inauguration was a rare event in American history: a friendly passing of power from one president to another of the same party. It had not happened since Herbert Hoover succeeded fellow Republican Calvin Coolidge in 1929. Except for reelections, every inauguration since then resulted either from the death or defeat of the incumbent. And for the first time since 1837, when Martin Van Buren followed Andrew Jackson into the Oval Office, had an outgoing president been succeeded by his vice president.

Bush and his transition team had worked since election day to convey a set of political messages. While his postelection remarks and appointments conveyed the firm notion that the new administration would be different from Reagan's, the inaugural planners took pains to portray continuity as well as change. George and Barbara Bush remained deferential to Ronald and Nancy Reagan; the departing Reagans seemed in no sense deposed.

After the swearing-in, the Reagans boarded a helicopter at the Capitol's East Front to begin the trip back to California. At the chopper's door, the outgoing president paused and saluted the new commander in chief. Bush returned the salute. The visual storyline was not the "changing of the guard" but the guarding of the change wrought by Reagan's eight years in office. Reagan, despite diminished effectiveness in his second term, left office with opinion polls showing his public-approval rating higher than 60 percent.

Much of the inauguration week events in Washington featured a blend *of glittering celebration and quiet expectation. Thousands of Republicans toasted the Reagan years of Republican rule, highlighted by tax cuts and economic expansion. They flew to the nation's capital, crammed its hotels, and zipped around town in chartered limousines on their way to dinners, dances, and other gala events. Nothing was cheap. Reagan's first inauguration was estimated to have cost about $10 million; the price of this one grew to more than $25 million—most of which came from donations and proceeds from expensive inaugural events.*

Bush Comes into His Own

The days preceding the inauguration amounted to a kind of getting acquainted for a nation unaccustomed to new faces in the White House. Reagan had been in the Oval Office longer than anyone since Dwight D. Eisenhower (1953-1961). Now, after years in semieclipse and a campaign year that featured his fighting side, it was time for the real George Bush to emerge.

This was the Bush now inevitably called "kinder, gentler"—words from his nomination acceptance speech echoed in his inaugural address, and repeated endlessly elsewhere. There were, of course, reminders of the recent electoral combat—a presidential campaign that was remembered chiefly for its negative character and scarcity of debate on substantive issues. A special train brought police units to the festivities from Boston and Springfield, Massachusetts—Dukakis's home state. Inauguration officials acknowledged the police were being thanked for their endorsement of Bush, which was used to underscore his attack on Dukakis as a governor "soft on crime."

In the book The Elections of 1988, *political scientists Francis E. Rourke and John T. Tierney said that from the outset "Bush's strategists recognized that their candidate drew a highly negative rating from voters, while Dukakis was viewed quite favorably. Their solution to this problem was to attack the Democrat's competence and character, a strategy that succeeded perhaps beyond their wildest dreams."*

Once victory was in hand, Bush turned to the themes of reconciliation. He was now a good-guy-grandfather with an awkward, spontaneous grin. He spoke of yearning for "an easy-goingness about each other's attitudes and way of life." He remained reticent about how he planned to run the government and dampened expectations of major domestic proposals, saying he would go slow on foreign initiatives. He mentioned balancing the budget, making "hard choices," and "looking at what we have and perhaps allocating it differently. . . ."

The new president inherited a $150 billion federal budget deficit that would require painful choices about spending and taxes. Since year-by-year deficit reductions were required by law, and Bush persistently vowed not to raise taxes, the choices focused essentially on what priorities to assign a host of defense and domestic programs. After five years of a massive arms buildup, military spending had slumped under the impact of federal budget constraints, requiring Bush and his defense chiefs to

43

decide where to cut costs without sacrificing national security. Bush promised no new public funds to redress the nation's social ills. Instead he sought an extension of private charity—a concept expressed in his campaign phrase, "a thousand points of light." "We have more will than wallet," he said, "but will is what we need."

Bush seemed more interested in taking his time than in taking the country by storm. "Some see leadership as high drama, and the sound of trumpets calling," he said. "But I see history as a book with many pages and each day we fill a page with acts of hopefulness and meaning." His first official act as president, in the ornate President's Room of the Capitol immediately after the inaugural address, was to proclaim January 22 a national day of prayer and thanksgiving.

Following is the text of President Bush's inaugural address as delivered January 20, 1989, from the West Portico of the U.S. Capitol. (The bracketed headings have been added by Congressional Quarterly to highlight the organization of the text.):

Mr. Chief Justice, Mr. President, Vice President Quayle, Senator Mitchell, Speaker Wright, Senator Dole, Congressman Michel, and fellow citizens, neighbors and friends.

There is a man here who has earned a lasting place in our hearts—and in our history. President Reagan, on behalf of our nation I thank you for the wonderful things that you have done for America.

I have just repeated word-for-word the oath taken by George Washington 200 years ago; and the Bible on which I placed my hand is the Bible on which he placed his.

It is right that the memory of Washington be with us today, not only because this is our Bicentennial Inauguration, but because Washington remains the father of our country. And he would, I think, be gladdened by this day. For today is the concrete expression of a stunning fact: Our continuity these 200 years since our government began.

We meet on democracy's front porch. A good place to talk as neighbors, and as friends. For this is a day when our nation is made whole, when our differences, for a moment, are suspended.

And my first act as President is a prayer and I ask you to bow your heads:

"Heavenly Father, we bow our heads and thank you for your love. Accept our thanks for the peace that yields this day and the shared faith that makes its continuance likely. Make us strong to do your work, willing to heed and hear your will, and write on our hearts these words: 'Use power to help people.' For we are given power not to advance our own purposes, nor to make a great show in the world, nor a name. There is but one just use of power, and it is to serve people. Help us to remember, Lord. Amen."

I come before you and assume the presidency at a moment rich with promise. We live in a peaceful, prosperous time, but we can make it better.

44

For a new breeze is blowing, and a world refreshed by freedom seems reborn; for in man's heart, if not in fact, the day of the dictator is over. The totalitarian era is passing, its old ideas blown away like leaves from an ancient lifeless tree.

A new breeze is blowing—and a nation refreshed by freedom stands ready to push on: There is new ground to be broken, and new action to be taken.

There are times when the future seems thick as a fog; you sit and wait, hoping the mists will lift and reveal the right path.

[A Door to Tomorrow]

But this is a time when the future seems a door you can walk right through—into a room called Tomorrow.

Great nations of the world are moving toward democracy—through the door to freedom.

Men and women of the world move toward free markets—through the door to prosperity.

The people of the world agitate for free expression and free thought— through the door to the moral and intellectual satisfactions that only liberty allows.

We know what works: Freedom works. We know what's right: Freedom is right. We know how to secure a more just and prosperous life for man on earth: through free markets, free speech, free elections, and the exercise of free will unhampered by the state.

For the first time in this century—for the first time in perhaps all history—man does not have to invent a system by which to live. We don't have to talk into the night about which form of government is better. We don't have to wrest justice from the kings—we only have to summon it from within ourselves.

We must act on what we know. I take as my guide the hope of a saint: In crucial things, unity—in important things, diversity—in all things, generosity.

America today is a proud, free nation, decent and civil—a place we cannot help but love. We know in our hearts, not loudly and proudly, but as a simple fact, that this country has meaning beyond what we see, and that our strength is a force for good.

But have we changed as a nation even in our time? Are we enthralled with material things, less appreciative of the nobility of work and sacrifice?

My friends, we are not the sum of our possessions. They are not the measure of our lives. In our hearts we know what matters. We cannot hope only to leave our children a bigger car, a bigger bank account. We must hope to give them a sense of what it means to be a loyal friend, a loving parent, a citizen who leaves his home, his neighborhood and town better than he found it.

And what do we want the men and women who work with us to say when we are no longer there? That we were more driven to succeed than anyone around us? Or that we stopped to ask if a sick child had gotten better, and

45

stayed a moment there to trade a word of friendship.

No President, no government, can teach us to remember what is best in what we are. But if the man you have chosen to lead this government can help make a difference; if he can celebrate the quieter, deeper successes that are made not of gold and silk, but of better hearts and finer souls; if he can do these things, then he must.

[Kinder and Gentler]

America is never wholly herself unless she is engaged in high moral principle. We as a people have such a purpose today. It is to make kinder the face of the nation and gentler the face of the world.

My friends, we have work to do. There are the homeless, lost and roaming—there are the children who have nothing, no love, no normalcy— there are those who cannot free themselves of enslavement to whatever addiction—drugs, welfare, the demoralization that rules the slums. There is crime to be conquered, the rough crime of the streets. There are young women to be helped who are about to become mothers of children they can't care for and might not love. They need our care, our guidance, and our education; though we bless them for choosing life.

The old solution, the old way, was to think that public money alone could end these problems. But we have learned that that is not so. And in any case, our funds are low. We have a deficit to bring down. We have more will than wallet; but will is what we need.

We will make the hard choices, looking at what we have, perhaps allocating it differently, making our decisions based on honest need and prudent safety.

And then we will do the wisest thing of all: We will turn to the only resource we have that in times of need always grows: the goodness and the courage of the American people.

And I am speaking of a new engagement in the lives of others—a new activism, hands-on and involved, that gets the job done. We must bring in the generations, harnessing the unused talent of the elderly and the unfocused energy of the young. For not only leadership is passed from generation to generation, but so is stewardship. And the generation born after the Second World War has come of age.

I have spoken of a thousand points of light—of all the community organizations that are spread like stars throughout the nation, doing good.

We will work hand in hand, encouraging, sometimes leading, sometimes being led, rewarding. We will work on this in the White House, in the Cabinet agencies. I will go to the people and the programs that are the brighter points of light, and I will ask every member of my government to become involved.

The old ideas are new again because they're not old, they are timeless: duty, sacrifice, commitment, and a patriotism that finds its expression in taking part and pitching in.

We need a new engagement, too, between the Executive and the Congress.

[An Offered Hand]

The challenges before us will be thrashed out with the House and Senate. We must bring the federal budget into balance. And we must ensure that America stands before the world united: strong, at peace, and fiscally sound. But, of course, things may be difficult.

We need compromise; we've had dissension. We need harmony; we've had a chorus of discordant voices.

For Congress, too, has changed in our time. There has grown a certain divisiveness. We have seen the hard looks and heard the statements in which not each other's ideas are challenged, but each other's motives. And our great parties have too often been far apart and untrusting of each other.

It's been this way since Vietnam. That war cleaves us still. But, friends, that war began in earnest a quarter of a century ago; and surely the statute of limitations has been reached. This is a fact: The final lesson of Vietnam is that no great nation can long afford to be sundered by a memory.

A new breeze is blowing—and the old bipartisanship must be made new again.

To my friends—and yes, I do mean friends—in the loyal opposition—and yes, I mean loyal: I put out my hand.

I am putting out my hand to you, Mr. Speaker.

I am putting out my hand to you, Mr. Majority Leader.

For this is the thing: This is the age of the offered hand.

And we can't turn back clocks, and I don't want to. But when our fathers were young, Mr. Speaker, our differences ended at the water's edge. And we don't wish to turn back time, but when our mothers were young, Mr. Majority Leader, the Congress and the Executive were capable of working together to produce a budget on which this nation could live. Let us negotiate soon—and hard. But in the end, let us produce.

The American people await action. They didn't send us here to bicker. They ask us to rise above the merely partisan. "In crucial things, unity"—and this, my friends, is crucial.

To the world, too, we offer new engagement and a renewed vow: We will stay strong to protect the peace. The "offered hand" is a reluctant fist; once made strong, it can be used with great effect.

There are today Americans who are held against their will in foreign lands, and Americans who are unaccounted for. Assistance can be shown here, and will be long remembered. Good will begets good will. Good faith can be a spiral that endlessly moves on.

"Great nations like great men must keep their word." When America says something, America means it, whether a treaty or an agreement or a vow made on marble steps. We will always try to speak clearly, for candor is a compliment. But subtlety, too, is good and has its place.

While keeping our alliances and friendships around the world strong, ever strong, we will continue the new closeness with the Soviet Union, consistent both with our security and with progress. One might say that our new relationship in part reflects the triumph of hope and strength over experience. But hope is good. And so is strength. And vigilance.

Here today are tens of thousands of our citizens who feel the understandable satisfaction of those who have taken part in democracy and seen their hopes fulfilled.

But my thoughts have been turning the past few days to those who would be watching at home—

To an older fellow who will throw a salute by himself when the flag goes by, and the woman who will tell her sons the words of the battle hymns. I don't mean this to be sentimental. I mean that on days like this, we remember that we are all part of a continuum, inescapably connected by the ties that bind—

Our children are watching in schools throughout our great land. And to them I say, thank you for watching democracy's big day. For democracy belongs to us all, and freedom is like a beautiful kite that can go higher and higher with the breeze. . . .

And to all I say: No matter what your circumstances or where you are, you are part of this day, you are part of the life of our great nation.

A President is neither prince nor pope, and I don't seek "a window on men's souls." In fact, I yearn for a greater tolerance, an easy-goingness about each other's attitudes and way of life.

There are few clear areas in which we as a society must rise up united and express our intolerance. And the most obvious now is drugs. And when that first cocaine was smuggled in on a ship, it may as well have been a deadly bacteria, so much has it hurt the body, the soul of our country. There is much to be done and to be said, but take my word for it: This scourge will stop.

And so, there is much to do; and tomorrow the work begins.

And I do not mistrust the future; I do not fear what is ahead. For our problems are large, but our heart is larger. Our challenges are great, but our will is greater. And if our flaws are endless, God's love is truly boundless.

Some see leadership as high drama, and the sound of trumpets calling. And sometimes it is that. But I see history as a book with many pages—and each day we fill a page with acts of hopefulness and meaning.

The new breeze blows, a page turns, the story unfolds—and so today a chapter begins: a small and stately story of unity, diversity, and generosity—shared, and written, together.

Thank you.

God bless you.

And God bless the United States of America.

EPISCOPAL CHURCH STATEMENTS ON ITS FIRST WOMAN BISHOP

January 24 and February 8, 1989

Amid controversy throughout the worldwide Anglican communion, the Episcopal church on February 11 consecrated its first woman bishop and—some assert—the first woman since the beginning of Christianity who claims divinely mandated authority as a successor to Christ's apostles.

The Rev. Barbara Clementine Harris, a black, fifty-eight-year-old former business executive from Philadelphia, was formally proclaimed the church's suffragan (assistant) bishop of Massachusetts. The same diocese, embracing eastern Massachusetts, broke another barrier twenty years earlier by choosing the church's first black bishop, the Rt. Rev. John Burgess.

Harris was consecrated in an elaborate—sometimes dramatic—three-hour ceremony in Boston's Hynes Auditorium. It was attended by fifty-five bishops of the church and more than seven thousand guests, including dozens of leaders of other religious denominations, Gov. Michael S. Dukakis of Massachusetts, and foreign delegations from as far away as Australia and New Zealand.

In the festive atmosphere, the ritualistic proceedings were often interrupted by spontaneous applause—and on two occasions by outspoken protests. These were voiced after the chief consecrator, the presiding bishop of the Episcopal church, the Rt. Rev. Edmond L. Browning, announced in the words of the ceremony: "You have been assured of her suitability and that the Church has approved her for this sacred responsibility. Nevertheless, if any of you know any reason why we should not proceed, let it now be made known."

Objections to the Consecration

John Jamieson, a representative of the church's conservative Prayer Book Society, which opposed the ordination of women both as priests and bishops, immediately went to a floor microphone and said the service was "a sacrilegious imposture." As the audience booed and Browning begged for silence, Jamieson was followed to the microphone by the Rev. James Hopkinson Cupit, Jr., rector of the Church of the Resurrection in New York City. He implored the presiding bishop not to proceed with a consecration "contrary to the unbroken tradition of 2,000 years of apostolic orders."

Hopkinson said Harris's election had caused "grievous division" in many of the Anglican churches, including the Episcopal church, which all follow the tradition of the Church of England. Some twenty-eight national churches, with seventy million members, form this communion. Only a few churches outside the United States—notably in Canada and Hong Kong—had ordained women priests and none had elected a woman bishop.

Many Episcopalians had never reconciled themselves to women priests. Some said the ordination of women was contrary to scripture. They objected especially in the Harris case to a woman who, as bishop, held authority to ordain priests.

Moreover, some opponents of Harris's elevation to bishop questioned her credentials, character, and politics during the four months that intervened between her election by the diocese of Massachusetts on September 24, 1988, and her approval by a majority of the 118 diocesan standing committees—composed of selected lay persons and priests— and of the bishops who head those dioceses. Majority approval was not granted until January 24, barely in time for the consecration to proceed.

Harris was accused, among other things, of "supporting members of terrorist groups" and "standing up for anti-American regimes." She had been active in the civil rights movement since the mid-1960s and was an outspoken critic of barriers within the church to blacks and women.

New Bishop's Background

In 1974, two years before the Episcopal church formally consented to the ordination of women, eleven women were ordained in an unauthorized ceremony in Philadelphia's Church of the Advocate. Harris, an active member of that church in a predominantly black section of north Philadelphia, carried a cross in the ordination service and eventually became a candidate for holy orders herself.

She was ordained a priest in 1980, although she was not a graduate of a theological seminary—which became a point of contention in her selection as bishop. Harris attended Villanova University in Philadelphia and studied theology in Sheffield, England. In addition, she was a graduate of the Pennsylvania Foundation for Pastoral Counseling.

After ordination, Harris served as priest-in-charge of a church in

Norristown, Pennsylvania, and as a chaplain in the Philadelphia County prisons. From January 1984 until becoming a bishop, she was executive director of the Episcopal Church Publishing Company in Philadelphia and interim rector of the Church of the Advocate.

An Obstacle to Reconciliation

On February 8, as the consecration approached, Bishop Browning sent an ecumenical letter to various churches in the United States and abroad, alluding to charges that the event was setting the Episcopal church apart from other Anglican churches—especially the Church of England—and raising new obstacles to reconciliation with the Roman Catholic and Orthodox churches.

The previous summer, as occurs every decade, the leaders of the various Anglican churches met in England for a Lambeth Conference, so named for the archbishop of Canterbury's palace in London. The expectation that a woman was about to be named a bishop became a divisive issue. Bishop of London Graham Leonard said he would consider himself "not in communion" with a woman bishop or with male bishops who participated in her consecration.

As summed up afterward by the archbishop, the Rt. Rev. Robert Runcie: "The Bishops at the Lambeth Conference gave overwhelming support to a resolution urging us to maintain courtesy and communication with any woman bishop. The Lambeth Conference also urged respect between the Provinces [national churches] of the Anglican Communion which come to different decisions about women bishops. . . ."

The conference created a Commission on Women and the Episcopate, which later recommended that male bishops also participate when any woman bishop ordains priests. This proposal was rejected by Anglican primates—the heads of the national churches—at a meeting in Cyprus in April 1989. Such a step would not be practical or appropriate, the primates said, and the requirement would question the validity of a woman's consecration and be demeaning to her.

The primates gave qualified endorsement to a controversial plan the Episcopal church adopted at its 1988 General Convention in Detroit. The plan, adopted as a compromise measure to prevent a schism, would allow a parish in a diocese headed by a woman bishop to request a male bishop from outside the diocese to perform certain functions in that parish. However, the primates said no bishop should undertake activities in another diocese without the consent of the local bishop.

Church's Rejection of Protests

At the ceremony in Boston, Bishop Browning said the protests he heard had already been aired in the preceding months, and that a majority of the Episcopal church's diocesan bishops and standing committees had affirmed Harris's election. "We shall proceed with the ordination," he proclaimed to the accompaniment of loud applause from the congregation. A few moments later, he asked, "Is it your will that we ordain

Barbara a bishop?" The crowd roared the traditional response, "It is our will."

Again there was applause when the presiding bishop asked, "Are you persuaded that God has called you to the office of bishop?" and she answered, "I am so persuaded." After a laying on of hands by fellow bishops and a prayer of consecration, Browning placed the mitre on Harris's head as the symbol of office.

Harris's mentor, the Rev. Paul Washington, the retired rector of the Church of the Advocate, preached the sermon. He said that as a black woman, the great-granddaughter of a slave, Harris stood symbolically as one "born in slavery." This is a woman, he said, "who has had to struggle." Then in words that echoed the Prophet Isaiah's lament for the suffering servant, Washington said: "She has been despised. She has been rejected." He recalled her record as an advocate of the downtrodden. Toward the end of his forty-five-minute sermon, Harris stood, as his comments became directed specifically to her, and she embraced him.

The next morning, in Boston's Cathedral Church of St. Paul, Harris preached her first sermon as a bishop. "If Jesus had played it safe, we would not have been saved," she said. "And if the diocese of Massachusetts had played it safe, I would not be standing here today clothed in rochet and chimere and wearing a pectoral cross."

> *Following is the text of the statement issued to the church January 24, 1989, by the Rt. Rev. Edmond L. Browning, presiding bishop of the Episcopal church, and the partial text of an ecumenical letter he sent February 8, to the leaders of other churches, as released by the Episcopal Church Center in New York City:*

STATEMENTS TO THE EPISCOPAL CHURCH

We have received in my office the necessary majority of consents from bishops with jurisdiction to the election and consecration of the Rev. Barbara C. Harris as Bishop Suffragan of the Diocese of Massachusetts. The consent process, as provided by Title III, Canon 21 of the Constitution and Canons, is completed. Therefore, I have taken order for the ordination and consecration for Saturday, February 11, 1989, in Boston, Massachusetts, and will serve as Chief Consecrator. Specific plans for the liturgy will be coordinated by the diocese of Massachusetts with my office.

This consecration will be both a momentous and a solemn occasion, and a time of great joy and celebration. The Rev. Barbara Harris will take her place among the bishops of the Church, and we will celebrate that new ministry with her and the people of Massachusetts. We will celebrate as well this particular recognition of the gifts of ordained women.

At the election of Barbara Harris on September 24, 1988, I asked the Church to offer in prayer our joys, our anxiety, and our commitment to unity. As the Presiding Bishop, I have been grateful to know that those prayers were offered throughout the Anglican Communion during the consent process. That process, with the participation of the standing committees of the dioceses and the bishops with jurisdiction, has also involved thoughtful discussion in this spirit of prayer.

I also asked the Church to be sensitive to the convictions and feelings of others. I have felt that sensitivity being expressed by the majority of the Church.

I do want to note that there have been some exceptions to the prevailing spirit of prayerful discussion and sensitivity. Unfortunately, these exceptions received disproportionate attention. We know that we have heard some angry words, some mean-spirited words, and some threatening words. I have found this both inappropriate to the process and diminishing to the sense of how we as the Church should conduct ourselves.

These days have not been easy, and I have had the opportunity to reflect more than once that growth does not come without pain. I believe that we, the Episcopal Church, are together in our growth and in the attendant struggles, and in our valuing of both our unity and our diversity.

As I personally rejoice with the Diocese of Massachusetts and Barbara Harris, it is my continued hope that the future days will be characterized by prayer, sensitivity, and discernment of God's will for us and the call to new life.

LETTER TO OTHER CHURCHES

... For twelve years, our Church has experienced the gifts of women in the priesthood. It is our hope, prayer, and clear expectation that we will have a similar experience with women in the episcopate. We believe that the incorporation of women in the catholic episcopate and priesthood as the Anglican Communion has received it, enhances the wholeness and the mission of the Church. I pray that their inclusion will come to be seen as a gift to the Church catholic and a contribution toward a deeper understanding of holy orders.

The Episcopal Church seeks to maintain and develop the highest possible degree of communion with partner churches. We have taken every reasonable step. Within our own Church, we have sought pastoral provisions for those who cannot accept women in the episcopate. Within the Anglican Communion, the Archbishop of Canterbury has appointed a commission to prepare guidelines to enable Provinces which differ on this issue to live together in one Communion. Ecumenically, we have consulted with the several partner churches through official dialogues.

We rejoice in the growth of communion in recent years with Orthodox, Roman Catholic, Lutheran, and Protestant Churches. Yet the road to Christian unity is not a straight line. The question of women's ordination, in the form in which it is put today, is a new one, and is still in an early stage of reflection and discussion among the churches. Given the complexity of the process which must take place, discussion will be difficult and lengthy. An essential part of the process will be the experience of a more active participation by women in the life and mission of the Christian community.

Our ecumenical dialogues will be driven to a deeper theological seriousness as a result of the ordination of women to the episcopate. In dialogues with churches that maintain the historic episcopate, we should concentrate on the serious theological reasons for opening the historic episcopate to women. In dialogues with Churches that do not claim to have the historic episcopate, we should show how teaching about the catholic episcopate is compatible with the ordination of women.

At this moment, our action brings rejoicing to some and anguish to others. The Lambeth Conference spoke directly to this situation when it resolved, "The Church needs to exercise sensitivity, patience, and pastoral care towards all concerned." We remember, too, that within the one holy catholic and apostolic Church some suffer pain because women are excluded from the episcopate and priesthood, and others suffer pain because they see ordination of women as a violation of God's will. I ask that we enter into one another's pain so that the fellowship of suffering may become, together with the fellowship of rejoicing, a sign of our deeper communion and a witness to the healing of the nations.

February

State Department's Human Rights
    Report 57

Bush's Budget Address and
    Bipartisan Agreement 71

Report on the State of U.S. Education 85

Rushdie's Death Sentence 95

U.S. Tributes at Hirohito's Funeral 99

Rejection of Tower as
    Secretary of Defense 105

STATE DEPARTMENT'S
HUMAN RIGHTS REPORT
February 7, 1989

In its annual report on human rights, released February 7, the State Department had cautious praise for progress made in the Soviet Union, but for the first time it was sharply critical of Israel's handling of the Palestinian uprising in the occupied West Bank and Gaza Strip, devoting 12 pages of its 1,560-page report on 169 countries to the situation there. The department's annual country-by-country analysis had been required by Congress since 1973. (1988 report, Historic Documents of 1988, p. 93)

Noting that it was possible to report on conditions in the occupied territories "by virtue of Israel's open and democratic society," the report nonetheless charged that the Israeli effort to control the Palestinian campaign of rockthrowing and civil disobedience—known in Arabic as the intifada—*had "led to a substantial increase in human rights violations," including "many avoidable deaths."*

The Israeli army had been "caught by surprise" by the outbreak of the intifada *in December 1987, the report said. The army, "untrained and inexperienced in riot control," often did not follow guidelines regarding the use of lethal force. "Soldiers frequently used gunfire in situations that did not present mortal danger to troops, causing many avoidable deaths and injuries."*

The report said that 366 Palestinians were killed in 1988, most of them by the army and some by Israeli settlers. More than 20,000 Arabs were wounded or injured. "At least 13 Palestinians have been reported to have died from beatings," the State Department report said. "By mid-April [1988] reports of deliberate breaking of bones had ended, but reports of unjustifiably harsh beatings continued."

The survey also criticized Israel's use of mass detention without trial, arbitrary arrest of many individuals "who have not engaged in or advocated violence," and deportations of alleged security offenders.

Arab-Israeli Reaction

James J. Zogby, executive director of the Arab-American Institute, said February 7 that for the first time "the State Department has fulfilled its mandate to tell the truth" about conditions in the occupied territories. He urged Congress to reduce the level of U.S. aid to Israel, currently $3 billion a year, the largest amount any country receives.

The Israeli Foreign Ministry said the report failed to consider the "overall context of events" and the "constant provocations" by "extremist elements." Deputy Foreign Minister Benjamin Netanyahu said Israeli soldiers "maintain as best they can, apart from a few exceptions, the standards of proper conduct that no country in the world could manage." Prime Minister Yitzhak Shamir said on February 8, "We're sorry about any loss of life, but there's no chance to put an end to violence without taking forceful means."

Other Nations' Practices

As it had in 1988, the State Department report noted "remarkable changes" in the Soviet Union. "We still cannot say that there has been a fundamental shift in the Soviet Union's approach to human rights," the report said, "but there is no doubt that the changes in evidence in 1988 have profound implications...." The report also noted "significant further advances in Hungary and Poland toward a more open society." Human rights abuses that were cited included:

- *Burma. The government systematically killed and detained student demonstrators seeking political freedom.*
- *Chile. Citizens were arbitrarily arrested under "vaguely defined and far-reaching state security laws." Moreover, "torture remains one of the most serious persistent human rights problems in Chile."*
- *Ethiopia. The regime used torture against opposition and separatist forces. "[T]here is no freedom of speech or press...." The government also used large-scale starvation as a political weapon.*
- *Iran. "Major human rights abuses continued ... in 1988," including "at least several hundred political executions ... and the use of torture in repressing political opposition."*
- *Iraq. The regime of Saddam Hussein had "an abysmal human rights record," particularly in its use of torture and poison gas against Kurdish separatists.*
- *Nicaragua. The Marxist-led Sandinista government carried out twenty-eight politically motivated murders.*
- *Philippines. "There were signs of deterioration in the human rights situation in 1988," with some members of the police and military allegedly having "resorted to extra-legal killing to combat" Communist insurgents.*

- *South Africa. The government's security forces and their right-wing sympathizers were "suspected of involvement" in the murder of Dulcie September and the attempted murder of Albie Sachs, two antiapartheid activists. Thousands of persons continued to be jailed without cause after a state of emergency was proclaimed in 1986.*

"Systematic violations of human rights" also continued in North Korea, Cambodia, and Laos, according to the report. Concerning China, the survey cited "some improvement" in the government's rights practices but criticized its subjection of Tibetan nationalists to "beatings and other forms of mistreatment." In El Salvador, the State Department said that the U.S.-supported government of President José Napoléon Duarte had worked to improve the rights situation but that killings and other abuses by the military, leftist guerrillas, and rightist forces continued.

Following are excerpts from the State Department's "Country Reports on Human Rights Practices for 1988," submitted to the Senate Foreign Relations and the House Foreign Affairs Committee and publicly released February 7, 1989:

Introduction

This report is submitted to the Congress by the Department of State in compliance with Sections 116(d)(1) and 502B(b) of the Foreign Assistance Act of 1961, as amended. The legislation requires human rights reports on all countries that receive aid from the United States and all countries that are members of the United Nations. In the belief that the information would be useful to the Congress and other readers, we have also included reports on the few countries which do not fall into either of these categories and which are thus not covered by the Congressional requirement. . . .

Any country-specific discussion of worldwide human rights developments in 1988 must start, as did our discussion of such developments in 1987, with an assessment of the remarkable changes in the Soviet Union. Last year we said that the changes which occurred in 1987 were more than cosmetic but less than fundamental. We still cannot say that there has been a fundamental shift in the Soviet Union's approach to human rights, but there is no doubt that the changes in evidence in 1988 have profound implications, as advocates of significant systemic reform appear to have gained strength. . . .

The year 1988 also saw significant further advances in Hungary and Poland toward a more open society.

As far as the positive side of the ledger in 1988 is concerned, we need to note that, abiding by the provisions of the Chilean Constitution, President Pinochet submitted his candidacy for continuation in office to popular referendum. In a free and fair plebiscite the decision of the voters went against him. There is hope that in 1989 we shall witness Chile's peaceful return to democracy.

On the Asian continent, the year 1988 also saw significant steps taken by the Republic of Korea, Taiwan, and Pakistan toward democracy and increasing respect for the rights of the individual. By contrast, in Burma a nationwide outpouring of sentiment in favor of free elections was brutally suppressed when the military systematically killed and detained student demonstrators and leaders.

The other most significant human rights violations of the year 1988, if measured by their severity and the numbers of persons affected, took place in the context of interethnic conflicts in Iraq, Burundi, and Sudan. In each of these situations innocent civilian bystanders died as a result of guerrilla warfare or reprisals for violence by others.

The Iraqi Government employed chemical warfare against a Kurdish insurgency, killing and injuring thousands of civilians and causing tens of thousands to flee their country. . . .

This year there are 169 separate reports. . . .

South Africa

. . .The human rights situation in South Africa continued to deteriorate in 1988 as the Government took additional harsh measures to repress opposition to apartheid, including nonviolent political activity. In February the Government effectively banned 17 antiapartheid organizations, including the United Democratic Front (UDF), a loosely organized national movement of more than 600 antiapartheid groups, and prohibited the largest union, the black-controlled Congress of South African Trade Unions (COSATU), from engaging in political activities; in 1988 a total of 32 organizations were banned. The state of emergency (SOE) was extended in June for the third consecutive year, with even tougher restrictions on antiapartheid groups and the media. These tight SOE restrictions further reduced available information about the current situation, including the number of detentions and the extent of political violence. Best estimates at the end of 1988 indicated the Government had used the emergency powers to detain hundreds of key nonwhite opposition leaders and organizers. At the end of the year, an estimated 1,500 people were being held without charge, down slightly from estimates at the end of 1987; hundreds of these have been held continuously since the imposition of the June 1986 SOE. While the number of detained children decreased in 1988, reports regarding torture of detainees, including some under age 18, continued. On the positive side, towards the end of the year the Government released several prominent political prisoners and commuted the death sentences of the Sharpeville Six, who had been convicted of murder for their presence in a crowd that had killed a township official. At the same time, commutations were granted to two white policemen convicted of murdering a black man while on duty.

There were waves of political violence emanating from various quarters, and overall political violence during 1988 appeared to be at or above 1987 levels, though still below 1984-86. The shadowy war between the African

National Congress (ANC) and South African Security Forces continued, with a disturbing increase in attacks on civilian targets. South African security forces and/or rightwing sympathizers were suspected of involvement in the unsolved killing of youth activist Sicelo Dhlomo, the assassination of ANC Paris representative Dulcie September, attacks on ANC targets in neighboring countries, including an attempt on the life of ANC theorist Albie Sachs in Maputo, and a series of mysterious political killings and bombings directed against antiapartheid groups. Their were, however, fewer instances in 1988 than in previous years of overt South African military intervention in neighboring countries. The ANC, with a major change in its military wing at the beginning of 1988, was suspected of involvement in numerous bomb explosions aimed at civilian targets, in part to disrupt the municipal elections held in October. In addition, violence between rival black organizations, e.g., clashes between UDF supporters and Chief Buthelezi's Zulu-led Inkatha movement, continued at a high level in Natal. While townships in the rest of the country remained quiet relative to the 1984-86 period, occasional attacks on black "collaborators" continued. Candidates in the October municipal elections were particular targets.

Nicaragua

The Sandinista National Liberation Front (FSLN) rules Nicaragua. The 1987 Constitution institutionalized Sandinista executive and party control over the country's military and security forces and central direction of the national economy. The FSLN has thus in 9 years transformed a popular uprising against the Somoza dictatorship into rule by a small elite which claims to be the vanguard of an irreversible revolution. The claimed legitimacy of Sandinista rule is widely challenged by civic opposition groups, as well as an armed Nicaraguan Resistance. However, the FSLN has suppressed peaceful opposition to its rule, claiming that such opposition constitutes collaboration with the armed Resistance and foreign aggression, and uses its monopoly of the security apparatus, the broad powers conferred upon the security forces by the Constitution, and coercive legislation, such as the law for the maintenance of order and public security, to neutralize independent groups, suppress opposition, and maintain its monopoly on power. . . .

In January [1988] the Central American presidents declared in San Jose, Costa Rica, that each country in Central America would unilaterally comply with the 1987 Guatemala accords, including implementation of democratization, political pluralism, and a general amnesty. Nicaragua lifted the state of emergency, restoring among other things the right to strike, and abolishing special tribunals to try persons suspected of counter-revolutionary activity. However, the Government maintained effective control of opposition activity through a combination of legal and extralegal tactics. In March [1988] a preliminary cease-fire agreement was reached between the Government and the Nicaraguan Resistance at Sapoa. The

Sapoa Accord called for compliance with the Guatemala agreement and Resistance participation in a national dialog on democratization. Although a truce remains in effect, a final cease-fire has not been achieved.

Since that time, the Sandinista regime gradually reduced the political opening available to the civic opposition, using intimidation and attack by government-controlled mobs to inhibit public demonstrations. On July 10, Sandinista police used force to break up a peaceful demonstration at the town of Nandaime, arresting a number of the demonstrators, and using their subsequent trial as a means of continued intimidation of the regime's critics. The United States Ambassador and seven other U.S. Embassy officers were expelled from Nicaragua on July 11 for allegedly orchestrating opposition activity.

Since July 10, the Government has refused permission for all outdoor opposition demonstrations. The independent newspaper La Prensa and a number of independent radio stations in operation for most of 1988 have also come under government pressure. Their owners have been threatened or assaulted by government officials, and they have been subjected to periodic suspensions for printing or broadcasting allegedly false reports critical of the Government.

In October the National Assembly reduced outside support for independent institutions through legislation making it a crime for any Nicaraguan entity to receive funds provided by specified U.S. Legislation. The Assembly also granted sweeping new emergency powers to the Nicaraguan President. On balance, the Guatemala, San Jose, and Sapoa agreements have resulted in only temporary and reversible improvements in human rights in Nicaragua. The 1987-88 report of the OAS Inter-American Commission on Human Rights (IACHR) noted "significant but precarious advances" for human rights in Nicaragua. With the situation exacerbated by the conflict between the Government and the Resistance forces, there continued to be charges against both sides of such human rights abuses as politically motivated killings, disappearances, torture, and illegal detentions.

Peru

...Peru's history has been punctuated by periods of military rule, most recently between 1968 and 1980. President Alan Garcia and his center-left American Popular Revolutionary Alliance (APRA) won the last general elections in 1985 by a large margin; representation in Congress ranges from conservative to Marxist. The next national elections are scheduled for 1990.

Public security responsibilities are shared by both the police and the military. The Interior Ministry and its police services have the primary counterterrorist role in Lima and those departments not under a state of emergency. The military leads the effort to combat subversion outside Lima in the 43 provinces now under a state of emergency. These states of emergency place all executive branch authority in the local military command, suspend restrictions on arbitrary detention and requirement for search warrants, and restrict rights to movement and assembly. A history of military coups has weakened civilian control over the military. There is little oversight of military activities in the emergency zones by civilian judges or prosecutors, and the constitutional rights of persons detained by the military are routinely ignored.

Peru has a mixed economy, and private property is generally respected. Strict price controls, higher wages, and restrictions on foreign debt repayment brought temporary growth to the Peruvian economy in 1986 and 1987. It became apparent by early 1988, however, that these policies were unsustainable. Export earnings fell, unemployment rose, central bank reserves plummeted, and the fiscal deficit fueled an inflationary spiral. Austerity measures instituted during 1988 will result in a further deepening of the recession and have already produced increased social unrest.

Since 1980 the Sendero Luminoso (Shining Path) Maoist guerrillas have been active proponents of terror to undermine democracy and the economy. Sendero is a major human rights violator and bears heavy responsibility for the rise in violence in Peru. In the face of minimal popular support for its vague revolutionary goals, it regularly assassinates development workers, teachers, police, soldiers, and ordinary citizens, principally Indian residents of the Andean highlands. Sendero violence escalated in 1988. As measured by the number of reported deaths, 1988 was the most violent year since Sendero announced its popular war in 1980. The group engaged in widespread economic sabotage and an increased level of assassinations, especially in rural areas. Sendero also operated in the major coca-producing area of Peru, the Upper Huallaga Valley, where it both defended peasant coca producers against traffickers and cooperated with traffickers to thwart law enforcement efforts. In addition, two other smaller terrorist groups are active. It is believed that at least 1,000 persons were killed in terrorist incidents in 1988.

Documented cases of human rights abuses by government security forces continued in 1988, even though it has become more difficult to carry out independent investigations of alleged summary executions and detentions by the military. Regional military commands deny access to the emergency zones where the vast majority of alleged human rights violations by both the military and Sendero occur.

Disappearances and summary executions appear to have increased in the past 2 years. Reliable human rights organizations reported 405 complaints alleging arbitrary detentions by security forces, of which 125 were resolved. These groups fear that most of the remainder are victims of summary executions. There are credible reports of the use of torture by the military. Trials of military personnel accused of human rights violations move slowly, and no military or security personnel were convicted of human rights abuses in 1988. Congressional investigations of alleged abuses have been severely criticized as inadequate. Independent investigations of alleged military killings have been impeded by military commanders.

The year also marked the emergence of an extralegal vigilante group calling itself the Rodrigo Franco Democratic Command. The group claimed responsibility for the murder of a prominent attorney and is also responsible for threats against an independent special prosecutor investigating alleged human rights violations by the military. There are reports that extremist members of APRA or the security forces may be using the group's name to conduct operations against suspected terrorists and sympathizers. . . .

Burma

For 26 years Burma was a single-party, Socialist dictatorship. In a popular, essentially nonviolent uprising unprecedented in the nation's history, millions of Burmese demanded in August and September 1988 that the regime step down in favor of a democratic system. On September 18-19, the old leadership reasserted control by a military takeover which lethally suppressed peaceful demonstrators all over Burma and returned the nation to formal military rule. . . .

The already poor human rights situation in Burma worsened significantly during 1988, as a result of regime efforts to quell its aroused population. Negative developments have included the killing of peaceful demonstrators, credible reports of arbitrary arrest and torture, compulsory labor, and the disappearance of political detainees. . . .

Although Burmese law prohibits summary executions and Buddhist tenets stress the sanctity of life, 1988 saw large-scale indiscriminate killings of Burmese citizens by the regime's security forces. Official versions of these incidents were widely at variance with numerous eyewitness accounts by foreign diplomats, journalists, and other observers. The regime admitted that in March [1988] 41 student demonstrators died by suffocation after being forced by police into an overcrowded paddy wagon. Government efforts to cover up this incident failed in the face of eyewitness accounts, photographs, and public pressures. Other students were killed or wounded by police or died in jail during the March disturbances, but government secrecy makes it impossible to arrive at a reliable estimate of casualties. Some responsible observers place the March death toll in the hundreds.

Observers estimate that in Rangoon several hundred were killed by police during antigovernment riots in June, although again it is impossible to confirm these figures. In one instance, police drove three trucks into a group of peacefully demonstrating high school students, killing four or five. Enraged crowds killed seven policemen in retaliation. During the March and June riots, students and workers destroyed some Government property. During August 8-13, troops opened fire on peaceful, unarmed citizens protesting Sein Lwin's ascension to power. Numerous eyewitness accounts confirm that troops chased and killed fleeing demonstrators and fired indiscriminately at onlookers and into houses. On August 10 troops fired into a group of doctors, nurses, and others in front of Rangoon

General Hospital, killing or wounding several doctors and nurses, who were pleading with troops to stop shooting. Thirty minutes later, the same troops returned and again opened fire. In other areas of Rangoon, eyewitnesses report soldiers bayoneted female students and kicked the bodies of teenage student victims. Four separate eyewitness accounts of an August 10 incident in North Okkalapa, a working class suburb of Rangoon, describe in detail how soldiers knelt in formation and fired repeatedly at demonstrators in response to an army captain's orders. The first casualties were five or six teenage girls who carried flags and a photograph of Burma's assassinated founding father, Aung San. All four eyewitnesses reported large numbers of dead and wounded and estimated several hundred casualties on the scene. Eyewitnesses report similar incidents throughout Rangoon during the August 8-13 period. Deaths probably numbered over 2,000, but actual numbers can never be known. In many cases as soon as they finished firing, troops carted off victims for surreptitious mass disposal in order to mask the extent of the carnage.

For security reasons, Burmese authorities did not allow U.S. and other diplomats to travel to areas of heavy insurgent activity. Therefore, U.S. officials were not able to gather directly information about human rights practices of the Burmese Government or of the insurgents in these areas. . . .

Republic of Korea

The South Korean Government describes the Republic of Korea (ROK) as a liberal democracy and, in fact, there were dramatic political changes in 1988. In February Roh Tae Woo became the first President directly elected by the people since 1971. At his inauguration, Roh proclaimed that his administration would be committed to democratic reform and political liberalization. In April National Assembly elections were held, and the opposition parties won control of the Assembly. The previous Chun Doo Hwan administration had come to power in a military coup in 1979 followed by an election held under strict martial law conditions and, many Koreans believe, maintained itself in power by strictly suppressing legitimate political dissent. As a result, the Chun regime suffered from a chronic lack of legitimacy in the eyes of most Koreans.

Determined to influence government policies, the current opposition-dominated Assembly played a much more independent role in domestic politics than had previous National Assemblies. In the fall, the Assembly held unprecedented televised hearings into alleged corruption and misdeeds of the former Chun Doo Hwan administration. Eventually, political pressure forced Chun to make a public apology on nationwide television, relinquish his wealth, and retire to the countryside. On November 26 President Roh asked the nation for leniency for Chun, promised to release political prisoners and restore their civil rights, compensate victims of past injustices, and amend the national security laws.

The security services have, for the first time in years, come under public criticism, and the opposition demanded that changes be made in their operations. However, in spite of some marginal changes—agents of the National Security Planning Agency (formerly the Korean CIA)) were evicted from their offices in the National Assembly—the Korean security forces remain pervasive. Police are generally well trained and disciplined. While there are still credible reports of the excessive use of force by the police, they appear to be more restrained than in the past. . . .

Following up on progress made during the last half of 1987, the overall human rights situation continued to improve. The press enjoyed much greater freedom, and articles criticizing the Government appeared frequently. No major cases of torture or politically related killings came to light during the year. The major remaining human rights problem is political prisoners. The Roh Government has shown itself willing to release political prisoners in small groups. However, continued arrests resulted in a stable or slightly increased number of prisoners during much of the year. The Government carried out a major release of prisoners on December 21 and at the same time restored civil rights to a number of former political detainees. In spite of the growing spread of Western-style, liberal democratic thought, Korean society still places great emphasis on the Confucian ideals of order and conformity. While the pace of positive political change is accelerating and the Roh Government's commitment to democratization seems firm, the evolution of South Korea's democracy is not yet complete. . . .

Soviet Union

. . .The limits of permissible dissent in 1988 continued to expand, perhaps most notably demonstrated at the XIX Communist Party Conference and by the massive national demonstrations in Armenia and the Baltic republics during the spring, summer, and early fall. While changes are still most evident in Moscow and Leningrad, an increasing number of informal organizations and publications are appearing in other cities, such as Sverdlovsk and L'vov. At the end of the year, however, Moscow cracked down on the Armenian National Movement, the Leningrad authorities launched an investigation under Article 70 (anti-Soviet agitation and propaganda), and local authorities brought charges under Article 190-3 (violating public order) against activists in Sverdlovsk and Georgia.

Reforms are taking place at the direction of the party; increased freedoms have come mainly as the result of political decisions. Most of the current reforms have yet to be reinforced by the adoption of laws, administrative regulations, and bureaucratic procedures that will ensure that rights of individual citizens. Moreover, the citizenry itself is unused to defending its rights against century-long traditions of state repression.

Emigration for selected groups—Jews, ethnic Germans, Pentecostals, and Armenians—continued to grow. By the end of 1988, monthly average departures for members of these groups compared favorably with the late 1970's. Jewish emigration was less than half of what it was in the peak year of 1979, but the total emigration from the Soviet Union was substantially above the 1979 figure. Emigration of members of other ethnic groups remained negligible. . . .

There was one report of suspected political killing in 1988. Dissident sources suspected KGB complicity in the murder of a Soviet activist of German descent, Vladimir Rayzev, in Kirgizia early in September. Rayzev reportedly knew so much about "KGB operatives" in Kirgizia that they were afraid of him. He had received exit permission from the Soviet Union and was planning to depart in mid-September. However, Rayzev's murder cannot be clearly labeled as a political killing. . . .

There have been no known instances of prolonged or permanent disappearance in recent years. . . .

Many Soviet prisoners suffer both mental and physical abuse and mistreatment during interrogation, trial, and confinement, according to a wide variety of reliable sources. Prisoners released in 1988 report that prison and camp conditions have not improved. Life in prison or labor camps continues to be marked by isolation, poor diet and malnutrition, compulsory hard labor, beatings, frequent incarceration in punishment cells for violations of camp rules, and inadequate medical care.

A decree of the U.S.S.R. Supreme Soviet Presidium in July rescinded a paragraph of the Soviet Penal Code stipulating reduced rations for labor camp inmates who undergo punishment in solitary confinement. This measure was issued apparently to bring Soviet domestic legislation into line with the U.S.S.R.'s commitments as a signatory of the International Convention Against Torture, to which it acceded in March 1987.

There were several instances of persons being confined in psychiatric hospitals for political reasons. Most were released within a few months. There continue to be reports of psychiatrists being called to militia stations to examine persons apprehended for political reasons. Reports indicate that conditions in psychiatric hospitals and the punitive administration of sedatives, antipsychotics, and other drugs have not changed significantly, except that beatings are fewer. . . .

Iran

. . .Although 10 years have passed since the ouster of the Shah in 1979 and the advent of the Islamic Revolution, the regime still considers itself revolutionary but must grapple with the need to revive the economy and operate political and social institutions, both new and old, in a productive manner. Although Iran is an oil-rich developing country, the disruptions of the revolutionary period and the burden of war have caused serious economic deterioration. Inflation and unemployment remain high, and corruption and black market activities continue to flourish.

The human rights situation continued to be affected by the Iran-Iraq war, despite the August ceasefire. Apart from its toll of hundreds of thousands of casualties, the war has resulted in large-scale destruction of cities and villages and massive population displacement, and in general has had a drastic impact on the quality of life of all segments of Iranian society which will continue to be felt for many years.

Major human rights abuses continued in Iran in 1988. These included at least several hundred political executions, continuing arbitrary detentions, the repression of freedoms of speech, press, and association, and the use of torture in repressing political opposition. Amnesty International (AI), in its 1988 Report covering 1987, described many of these abuses and detailed a wide range of particularly brutal forms of torture. A variety of observers in August and September alleged widespread executions of political prisoners. In October AI reported receiving more reports of political executions in Orumieh and Tabriz and elsewhere. . . .

Iraq

. . . Iraq's abysmal human rights record remained unacceptable in 1988. Political and individual rights continued to be sharply limited, and the news media remained largely under government control and subject to censorship. In addition to repressive domestic controls that predate the war with Iran, tight wartime controls remained in effect after the cease-fire. These included a decree which prescribes the death penalty for anyone who damages the country's military, political, or economic position. Wartime travel restrictions, which prevent most Iraqis from departing the country, also remained in force.

Most significant in 1988 were the grave human rights violations that occurred when the Iraqi armed forces moved to crush a longstanding Kurdish rebellion after the August 20 cease-fire with Iran. The campaign was marked by the use of chemical weapons against guerrillas and civilians alike. It marked an intensification of the program begun in 1987 to destroy villages and hamlets in Kurdish areas of northern Iraq, and to relocate approximately half a million Kurdish and Assyrian villagers to more easily controlled towns and cities. In addition, there are unconfirmed reports that tens of thousands of Kurds have been removed from their homes to camps located outside traditional Kurdish areas of northern Iraq. . . .

The Government's intensified efforts to crush a Kurdish rebellion in northern Iraq resulted in approximately 8,000 deaths, many of them civilians, according to Kurdish sources. The Iraqi armed forces made extensive unlawful use of chemical weapons against both military and civilian targets in Iran and Iraqi Kurdistan. In the course of a March 16 [1988] battle between Iraqi forces and Iranian Revolutionary Guards in and near the Kurdish city of Halabja in northern Iraq, an estimated 600 to 3,000 civilians were killed by Iraqi chemical weapons. The United States condemned Iraq's action as a particularly grave violation of the 1925 Geneva Protocol on chemical weapons, to which Iraq is a party, while noting that Iran also appears to have employed chemical weapons in the same battle. Several international teams, including a U.N. team and a team of Belgian doctors, confirmed the use of chemical weapons in this battle. Twice in 1988 the U.N. Security Council condemned use of chemical weapons in the Iran-Iraq War.

With the cessation of hostilities between Iran and Iraq in August, the Iraqi armed forces launched an offensive against Kurdish rebel forces. Combat troops from the Iranian front carried the battle to villages, which they claimed rebels were using for sanctuary. . . .

The Occupied Territories

The West Bank, East Jerusalem, the Golan Heights, and the Gaza Strip are areas occupied by Israel in the 1967 war which remain under Israeli occupation. The West Bank and Gaza continue under military government; Israel has unilaterally annexed East Jerusalem; and it has extended its civilian law, jurisdiction, and administration to the Golan Heights. . . .

Civilian unrest, reflecting Palestinian opposition to the occupation, has resulted in a number of outbreaks of violence during the last 21 years, which in turn have led periodically to sharp crackdowns by Israeli military forces. Beginning in December 1987, the occupation entered a new phase, referred to as the intifada, when civilian unrest became far more widespread and intensive than at any time heretofore. The active participants in these civil disturbances were primarily young men and women motivated by Palestinian nationalism and a desire to bring the occupation to an end. They gathered in groups, called and enforced strikes, threw stones and firebombs at Israeli security forces and civilian vehicles, or erected barricades and burned tires so as to interfere with traffic. The Israeli Government has regarded the uprising as a new phase of the 40-year war against Israel and as a threat to the security of the State. The Israeli Defense Forces [IDF], caught by surprise and untrained and inexperienced in riot control, responded in a manner which led to a substantial increase in human rights violations. . . .

In hundreds of confrontations between IDF troops and Palestinians throwing stones or Molotov cocktails or engaging in other forms of disorder, however, the IDF frequently responded with gunfire in which casualties resulted. Precise figures on casualties are not available and estimates vary depending on the source and counting criteria. Figures compiled from press, Palestinian, and Israeli government sources indicate that 366 Palestinians were killed in 1988 as a result of the uprising, most of them by the IDF, some by Israeli settlers. Thirteen Palestinians were killed by other Palestinians for suspected collaboration with Israeli authorities. Over 20,000 Palestinians were wounded or injured by the IDF. Eleven Israelis have been killed in the intifada. According to IDF statistics, approximately 1,100 Israelis have been injured.

Most Palestinian deaths resulted from the use of high velocity, standard service round bullets by the IDF during attempts to halt incidents involving stones, firebombs, or fleeing suspects. According to IDF regulations, live fire is permitted when soldiers' lives are in real and immediate danger. Only a specific attacker may be shot at; fire is to be directed at legs only; and it may be used against fleeing suspects only if a serious felony is suspected and as a last resort. Soldiers may fire only after exhausting all other means—including tear gas, rubber bullets, and warning shots. These guidelines were often not followed. Soldiers frequently used gunfire in situations that did not present mortal danger to troops, causing many avoidable deaths and injuries.

In September IDF policy was changed to allow the firing of plastic bullets in order to stop demonstrations or instigators of demonstrations in situations that do not threaten the lives of security forces and to increase injuries. The IDF claims plastic bullets are less lethal than lead bullets. While no precise figures are available, several deaths were attributed to plastic bullets, and nonlethal casualties increased after they were introduced. Other fatalities included at least 13 reported deaths by beating and at least 4 deaths from tear gas used by the IDF in enclosed areas. Exact figures are unavailable and estimates vary. There have been reports of several instances in which Palestinian wounded died because of IDF delays of ambulances or because, for whatever reason, there were delays in moving the wounded to a hospital. There were five cases in 1988 in which unarmed Palestinians in detention died under questionable circumstances or were clearly killed by the detaining officials.

Israeli authorities in some cases prosecuted or took disciplinary action against security personnel and [Jewish] settlers who killed Palestinians in violation of regulations. However, regulations were not rigorously enforced; punishments were usually lenient; and there were many cases of unjustified killing which did not result in disciplinary actions or prosecutions. . . .

Since the uprising began in December 1987, the number of Palestinian prisoners has risen from about 4,700 to about 10,000. According to IDF figures released November 28, 5,656 Palestinian were being held in prisons or detention centers. Seven military detention centers were added to two existing facilities, but there is serious overcrowding. Conditions at military detention facilities vary. Abuse of prisoners was particularly severe at the new facility at Dahariya, but conditions there improved after personnel changes were effected and disciplinary measures were taken. There was widespread beating of unarmed Palestinians in early 1988 in uprising incidents and of persons not participating in violent activities. . . .

BUSH'S BUDGET ADDRESS
AND BIPARTISAN AGREEMENT
February 9 and April 14, 1989

In a nationally televised address before a joint session of Congress on February 9, President George Bush outlined a fiscal agenda that had been virtually invisible during the 1988 presidential election campaign. He proposed a broad but thinly detailed set of revisions to the fiscal 1990 federal budget he had inherited from his predecessor, Ronald Reagan.

Bush called for increased spending for various education, antipoverty, antidrug, and environmental protection programs, and for a slightly lower level of military spending. White House budget officials projected overall expenditures of $1.16 trillion and a deficit of $91.1 billion, keeping within the $110 billion deficit ceiling that had been set for that year by the Gramm-Rudman Act. The law requires gradually smaller year-to-year deficits until a balanced budget is achieved in 1993.

The Bush budget set broad spending and revenue goals without spelling out exactly how they would be accomplished. He proposed $9 billion in defense cuts and asked the Pentagon to determine within sixty days where they should be made. While the president requested increased spending on a number of domestic programs, for all other domestic programs he offered only a lump sum of $136 billion—the same amount they received in fiscal 1989. That level of funding would not keep pace with inflation unless some programs were cut or eliminated. Bush suggested some trade-offs—cutting Amtrak and mass-transit subsidies to make up for nutrition and welfare increases, for instance—but otherwise remained silent on some eighty programs that Reagan wanted to discard.

"We must address some very real problems, we must establish some very clear priorities, and we must make a very substantial cut in the

71

federal budget deficit," Bush said. He then invited the Democratic-controlled Congress to negotiate the solutions with him. Many Democrats in Congress responded warmly to Bush's offer, but soon some became wary that he might attempt to take credit for increased funding of popular programs while leaving them the onus of making the hard cuts.

The Democratic leadership of the House and Senate, as well as the Republican leadership, engaged in more than a month of negotiations with White House officials. The participants included Richard G. Darman, director of the Office of Management and Budget, Treasury Secretary Nicholas F. Brady, House Majority Leader Thomas S. Foley, and the chairmen and ranking members of the House and Senate Budget and Appropriations committees.

The negotiations produced a skeletal plan for the 1990 budget. This agreement was signed by the president and a bipartisan contingent of Capitol Hill leaders in a White House Rose Garden ceremony on April 14. Bush called the written pact "a first manageable step" toward enactment of the budget.

Administration officials projected that the agreement would entail spending of $1.17 trillion and would produce a deficit of $99.4 billion in 1990, higher than the deficit forecast by the original Bush budget but still under the $110 billion limit. But the negotiators stayed under that limit only by using the rosy economic assumptions that underlay Bush's own budget. His budget drafters—headed by Darman—based their revenue figures on the expectation that the national economy would show a "real" (after-inflation) growth of 3.2 percent and that short-term interest rates would drop to 5.7 percent. At that time, they were about 8 percent.

In what was termed a "marriage of convenience" for both Democrats and Republicans, the House and Senate approved a budget resolution the week of May 15 that incorporated the agreement. However, the approval left many particulars to be addressed. A deadlock developed between Republicans opposed to any big tax increases and Democrats opposed to significant cuts in social programs. With the two sides unable to agree to final budget figures by the end of fiscal year, the Gramm-Rudman law triggered across-the-board budget cuts on October 1. On November 21, the eve of the 1989 session's adjournment, Congress passed a so-called reconciliation bill—the final product of the April 14 agreement—lumping together $14.7 billion in "real savings" with billions more that are expected to be illusory, in order to keep the budget under the $110 billion deficit ceiling. Democrats yielded to the cuts only after Bush abandoned his drive for lower capital gains taxes.

> *Following are the texts of the President Bush's budget address before Congress February 9, 1989, and of the Bipartisan Budget Agreement, signed April 14, at the White House by the president and congressional leaders. (The bracketed headings have been added by Congressional Quarterly to highlight the organization of the text.):*

BUDGET ADDRESS

Less than three weeks ago, I joined you on the West Front of this very building and—looking over the monuments to our proud past—offered you my hand in filling the next page of American history with a story of extended prosperity and continued peace. Tonight, I am back, to offer you my plans as well. The hand remains extended, the sleeves are rolled up, America is waiting, and now we must produce. Together, we can build a better America.

It is comforting to return to this historic Chamber. Here, 22 years ago, I first raised my hand to be sworn into public life. So tonight, I feel as if I am returning home to friends. And I intend, in the months and years to come, to give you what friends deserve: frankness, respect, and my best judgment about ways to improve America's future.

In return, I ask for an honest commitment to our common mission of progress. If we seize the opportunities on the road before us, there will be praise enough for all. The people didn't send us here to bicker. It's time to govern.

Many Presidents have come to this Chamber in times of great crisis. War. Depression. Loss of national spirit.

Eight years ago, I sat in that chair as President Reagan spoke of punishing inflation and devastatingly high interest rates, people out of work, American confidence on the wane. Our challenge is different.

We are fortunate—a much changed landscape lies before us tonight. So I don't propose to reverse direction. We are headed the right way. But we cannot rest. We are a people whose energy and drive have fueled our rise to greatness. We are a forward-looking Nation—generous, yes, but ambitious as well—not for ourselves, but for the world. Complacency is not in our character—not before, not now, not ever.

So tonight, we must take a strong America—and make it even better. We must address some very real problems. We must establish some very clear priorities. And we must make a very substantial cut in the Federal budget deficit.

Some people find that agenda impossible. But I am presenting to you tonight a realistic plan for tackling it. My plan has four broad features: attention to urgent priorities, investment in the future, an attack on the deficit, and no new taxes.

This budget represents my best judgment of how we can address our priorities, consistent with the people's view. There are many areas in which we would all like to spend more than I propose, but we cannot until we get our fiscal house in order.

Next year alone, thanks to economic growth, without any change in the law, the Federal Government will take in over $80 billion more than it does this year. That's right—over $80 billion in new revenues, with no increase in taxes. Our job is to allocate those new resources wisely.

We can afford to increase spending—by a modest amount, but enough to invest in key priorities and still cut the deficit by almost 40 percent in one year. That will allow us to meet the targets set forth in the Gramm-Rudman-Hollings law.

But to do that, we must recognize that growth above inflation in Federal programs is not preordained, that not all spending initiatives were designed to be immortal.

I make this pledge tonight. My team and I are ready to work with the Congress, to form a special leadership group, to negotiate in good faith, to work day and night—if that's what it takes—to meet the budget targets, and to produce a budget on time.

We cannot settle for business as usual. Government by Continuing Resolution—or government by crisis—will not do.

[The Budget Process]

I ask the Congress tonight to approve several measures which will make budgeting more sensible. We could save time and improve efficiency by enacting two-year budgets. Forty-three Governors have the line-item veto. Presidents should have it, too.

At the very least, when a President proposes to rescind Federal spending, the Congress should be required to vote on that proposal—instead of killing it by inaction.

And I ask for Congress to honor the public's wishes by passing a constitutional amendment to require a balanced budget. Such an amendment, once phased in, will discipline both Congress and the Executive branch.

Several principles describe the kind of America I hope to build with your help in the years ahead. We will not have the luxury of taking the easy, spendthrift approach to solving problems—because higher spending and higher taxes put economic growth at risk.

Economic growth provides jobs and hope. Economic growth enables us to pay for social programs. Economic growth enhances the security of the Nation. And low tax rates create economic growth.

I believe in giving Americans greater freedom and greater choice—and I will work for choice for American families, whether in the housing in which they live, the schools to which they send their children, or the child care they select for their young.

I believe that we have an obligation to those in need, but that Government should not be the provider of first resort for things that the private sector can produce better.

I believe in a society that is free from discrimination and bigotry of any kind. I will work to knock down the barriers left by past discrimination, and to build a more tolerant society that will stop such barriers from ever being built again.

I believe that family and faith represent the moral compass of the Nation—and I will work to make them strong, for as Benjamin Franklin said: "If a sparrow cannot fall to the ground without His notice, [can] a [great Nation] rise without His aid?"

And I believe in giving people the power to make their own lives better through growth and opportunity. Together, let's put power in the hands of people.

Three weeks ago, we celebrated the Bicentennial Inaugural, the 200th anniversary of the first Presidency. And if you look back, one thing is so striking about the way the Founding Fathers looked at America. They didn't talk about themselves. They talked about posterity. They talked about the future.

We, too, must think in terms bigger than ourselves.

We must take actions today that will ensure a better tomorrow. We must extend American leadership in technology, increase long-term investment, improve our education system, and boost productivity. These are the keys to building a better future. Here are some of my recommendations:

- I propose almost $2.2 billion for the National Science Foundation to promote basic research;
- I propose to make permanent the tax credit for research and development;
- I have asked Vice President Quayle to chair a new Task Force on Competitiveness;
- I request funding for NASA and a strong space program—an increase of almost $2.4 billion over the current fiscal year. We must have a manned space station; a vigorous, safe space shuttle program; and more commercial development in space. The space program should always go "full throttle up"—that's not just our ambition; it's our destiny.

I propose that we cut the maximum tax rate on capital gains to increase long-term investment. History is clear: This will increase revenues, help savings, and create new jobs.

We won't be competitive if we leave whole sectors of America behind. This is the year we should finally enact urban enterprise zones, and bring hope to our inner cities.

[Education: Top Priority]

But the most important competitiveness program of all is one which improves education in America. When some of our students actually have trouble locating America on a map of the world, it is time for us to map a new approach to education.

We must reward excellence, and cut through bureaucracy. We must help those schools that need help most. We must give choice to parents, students, teachers, and principals. And we must hold all concerned accountable. In education, we cannot tolerate mediocrity.

I want to cut the drop-out rate, and make America a more literate Nation. Because what it really comes down to is this: The longer our graduation lines are today, the shorter our unemployment lines will be tomorrow. So tonight I am proposing the following initiatives:

- the beginning of a $500-million program to reward America's best schools—"merit schools";
- the creation of special Presidential awards for the best teachers in every State—because excellence should be rewarded;
- the establishment of a new program of National Science Scholars, one each year for every Member of the House and Senate, to give this generation of students a special incentive to excel in science and mathematics;
- the expanded use of magnet schools which give families and students greater choice;
- and a new program to encourage "alternative certification"—which will let talented people from all fields teach in the classroom.

I have said I'd like to be "the Education President." Tonight, I ask you to join me by becoming "the Education Congress."

[The War on Drugs]

Just last week, as I settled into this new office, I received a letter from a mother in Pennsylvania, who had been struck by my message in the Inaugural address. "Not 12 hours before," she wrote, "my husband and I received word that [our] son was addicted to cocaine. [He] had the world at his feet. Bright, gifted, personable . . . he could have done anything with his life. [Now] he has chosen cocaine."

"Please," she wrote, "find a way to curb the supply of cocaine. Get tough with the pushers. [Our son] needs your help."

My friends, that voice crying out for help could be the voice of your own neighbor. Your own friend. Your own son. Over 23 million Americans used illegal drugs last year—at a staggering cost to our Nation's well-being.

Let this be recorded as the time when America rose up and said "No" to drugs. The scourge of drugs must be stopped. I am asking tonight for an increase of almost a billion dollars in budget outlays to escalate the war against drugs. The war will be waged on all fronts. Our new "Drug Czar," Bill Bennett, and I will be shoulder to shoulder leading the charge.

Some money will be used to expand treatment to the poor, and to young mothers. This will offer the helping hand to the many innocent victims of drugs—like the thousands of babies born addicted, or with AIDS, because of the mother's addiction.

Some will be used to cut the waiting time for treatment. Some money will be devoted to those urban schools where the emergency is now the worst. And much of it will be used to protect our borders, with help from the Coast Guard, the Customs Service, the departments of State and Justice, and yes, the U.S. military.

I mean to get tough on the drug criminals. Let me be clear: This President will back up those who put their lives on the line every day—our local police officers.

My budget asks for beefed-up prosecution, for a new attack on organized crime, and for enforcement of tough sentences—and for the worst king-pins, that means the death penalty.

I also want to make sure that when a drug dealer is convicted, there is a cell waiting for him. He should not go free because prisons are too full.

Let the word go out: If you are caught and convicted, you will do time.

But for all we do in law enforcement, in interdiction and treatment, we will never win this war on drugs unless we stop demand for drugs.

So some of this increase will be used to educate the young about the dangers of drugs. We must involve parents. We must involve teachers. We must involve communities. And my friends, we must involve ourselves.

One problem related to drug use demands our urgent attention and our continuing compassion. That is the terrible tragedy of AIDS. I am asking for $1.6 billion for education to prevent the disease—and for research to find a cure.

[Environmental Protection]

If we're to protect our future, we need a new attitude about the environment. We must protect the air we breathe. I will send to you shortly legislation for a new, more effective Clean Air Act. It will include a plan to reduce, by date certain, the emissions which cause acid rain—because the time for study alone has passed, and the time for action is now.

We must make use of clean coal. My budget contains full funding, on schedule, for the clean-coal technology agreement we have made with Canada. We intend to honor that agreement.

We must not neglect our parks. So I am asking to fund new acquisitions under the land and water conservation fund.

We must protect our oceans. I support new penalties against those who would dump medical waste and other trash in the oceans. The age of the needle on the beach must end.

In some cases, the gulfs and oceans off our shores hold the promise of oil and gas reserves which can make our Nation more secure and less dependent on foreign oil. When those with the most promise can be tapped safely, as with much of the Alaska National Wildlife Refuge, we should proceed. But we must use caution and we must respect the environment.

So tonight I am calling for the indefinite postponement of three lease sales which have raised troubling questions—two off the coast of California, and one which could threaten the Everglades in Florida. Action on these three lease sales will await the conclusions of a special task force set up to measure the potential for environmental damage.

I am directing the Attorney General and the Administrator of the Environmental Protection Agency to use every tool at their disposal to speed and toughen the enforcement of our laws against toxic waste dumpers. I want faster cleanups and tougher enforcement of penalties against polluters.

[A Compassionate Society]

In addition to caring for our future, we must care for those around us. A decent society shows compassion for the young, the elderly, the vulnerable, and the poor.

Our first obligation is to the most vulnerable—infants, poor mothers, children living in poverty—and my proposed budget recognizes this. I ask for full funding of Medicaid—an increase of over $3 billion—and an expansion of the program to include coverage of pregnant women who are near the poverty line.

I believe we should help working families cope with the burden of child care. Our help should be aimed at those who need it most—low-income families with young children. I support a new child care tax credit that will aim our efforts at exactly those families—without discriminating against mothers who choose to stay at home.

Now, I know there are competing proposals. But remember this: The overwhelming majority of all preschool child care is now provided by relatives and neighbors, churches and community groups. Families who choose these options should remain eligible for help. Parents should have choice.

And for those children who are unwanted or abused, or whose parents are deceased, I believe we should encourage adoption. I propose to re-enact the tax deduction for adoption expenses, and to double it to $3,000. Let's make it easier for these kids to have parents who love them.

We have a moral contract with our senior citizens. In this budget, Social Security is fully funded, including a full cost-of-living adjustment. We must honor our contract.

We must care about those in "the shadows of life," and I, like many Americans, am deeply troubled by the plight of the homeless. The causes of homelessness are many, the history is long, but the moral imperative to act is clear.

Thanks to the deep well of generosity in this great land, many organizations already contribute. But we in Government cannot stand on the sidelines. In my budget, I ask for greater support for emergency food and shelter, for health services and measures to prevent substance abuse, and for clinics for the mentally ill—and I propose a new initiative involving the full range of Government agencies. We must confront this national shame.

There is another issue I decided to mention here tonight. I have long believed that the people of Puerto Rico should have the right to determine their own political future. Personally, I favor statehood. But I ask the Congress to take the necessary steps to let the people decide in a referendum.

Certain problems, the result of decades of unwise practices, threaten the health and security of our people. Left unattended, they will only get worse—but we can act now to put them behind us.

Earlier this week, I announced my support for a plan to restore the financial and moral integrity of our savings system. I ask Congress to enact our reform proposals within 45 days. We must not let this situation fester.

Certainly, the savings of Americans must remain secure—insured depositors will continue to be fully protected. But any plan to refinance the system must be accompanied by major reform. Our proposals will prevent such a crisis from recurring. The best answer is to make sure that a mess like this will never happen again.

The majority of thrifts in communities across this Nation have been honest; they have played a major role in helping families achieve the American dream of home ownership. But make no mistake: Those who are corrupt, those who break the law, must be kicked out of the business; and they should go to jail.

We face a massive task in cleaning up the waste left from decades of environmental neglect at America's nuclear weapons plants. Clearly, we must modernize these plants and operate them safely. That is not at issue—our national security depends on it.

But beyond that, we must clean up the old mess that's been left behind—and I propose in this budget to more than double our current effort to do so. This will allow us to identify the exact nature of the various problems so we can clean them up—and clean them up we will.

[The Pentagon Budget]

We have been fortunate during these past eight years. America is a stronger Nation today than it was in 1980. Morale in our Armed Forces is restored. Our resolve has been shown. Our readiness has been improved. And we are at peace. There can no longer be any doubt that peace has been made more secure through strength. When America is stronger, the world is safer.

Most people don't realize that after the successful restoration of our strength, the Pentagon budget has actually been reduced in real terms for each of the last four years. We cannot tolerate further reductions.

In light of the compelling need to reduce the deficit, however, I support a one-year freeze in the military budget—something I proposed last fall in my flexible freeze plan.

This freeze will apply for only one year—after that increases above inflation will be required. I will not sacrifice American preparedness; and I will not compromise American strength.

I should be clear on the conditions attached to my recommendation for the coming year:

- the savings must be allocated to those priorities for investing in our future that I have spoken about tonight;
- this defense freeze must be part of a comprehensive budget agreement which meets the targets spelled out in the Gramm-Rudman-Hollings law without raising taxes, and which incorporates reforms in the budget process.

I have directed the National Security Council to review our national security and defense policies and report back to me within 90 days to ensure that our capabilities and resources meet our commitments and strategies.

I am also charging the Department of Defense with the task of developing a plan to improve the defense procurement process and management of the Pentagon—one which will fully implement the Packard Commission report. Many of the changes can only be made with the participation of the Congress—so I ask for your help.

We need fewer regulations. We need less bureaucracy. We need multi-year procurement and two-year budgeting. And frankly, we need less congressional micromanagement of our Nation's military policy.

[America and the World]

Securing a more peaceful world is perhaps the most important priority I'd like to address tonight. We meet at a time of extraordinary hope. Never before in this century have our values of freedom, democracy, and economic opportunity been such a powerful political and intellectual force around the globe.

Never before has our leadership been so crucial, because while America has its eyes on the future, the world has its eyes on America.

It is a time of great change in the world—and especially in the Soviet Union. Prudence and common sense dictate that we try to understand the full meaning of the change going on there, review our policies carefully, and proceed with caution. But I have personally assured General Secretary Gorbachev that, at the conclusion of such a review, we will be ready to move forward. We will not miss any opportunity to work for peace.

The fundamental fact remains that the Soviets retain a very powerful military machine, in the service of objectives which are still too often in conflict with ours. So let us take the new openness seriously. Let us step forward to negotiate. But let us also be realistic. And let us always be strong.

There are some pressing issues we must address: I will vigorously pursue the Strategic Defense Initiative. The spread and even use of sophisticated weaponry threatens global stability as never before.

Chemical weapons must be banned from the face of the Earth, never to be used again. This won't be easy. Verification will be difficult. But civilization and human decency demand that we try.

And the spread of nuclear weapons must be stopped. I will work to strengthen the hand of the International Atomic Energy Agency. Our diplomacy must work every day against the proliferation of nuclear weapons.

And, around the globe, we must continue to be freedom's best friend. We must stand firm for self-determination and democracy in Central America—including in Nicaragua. For when people are given the chance, they inevitably will choose a free press, freedom of worship, and certifiably free and fair elections.

We must strengthen the alliance of industrial democracies—as solid a force for peace as the world has ever known. This is an alliance forged by the power of our ideals, not the pettiness of our differences. So let us lift our sights—to rise above fighting about beef hormones to building a better future, to move from protectionism to progress.

I have asked the Secretary of State to visit Europe next week and to consult with them on the wide range of challenges and opportunities we face together—including East-West relations. And I look forward to meeting with our NATO partners in the near future.

I, too, shall begin a trip shortly—to the far reaches of the Pacific Basin, where the winds of democracy are creating new hope, and the power of free markets is unleashing a new force.

When I served as our representative in China just 14 years ago, few would have predicted the scope of the changes we've witnessed since then. But in preparing for this trip, I was struck by something I came across from a Chinese writer. He was speaking of his country, decades ago—but his words speak to each of us, in America, tonight.

"Today," he said, "we are afraid of the simple words like goodness and mercy and kindness." My friends, if we're to succeed as a Nation, we must rediscover those words.

In just three days, we mark the birthday of Abraham Lincoln—the man who saved our Union, and gave new meaning to the word opportunity. Lincoln once said: "I hold that while man exists, it is his duty to improve not only his own condition, but to assist in ameliorating [that of] mankind."

It is this broader mission to which I call all Americans. Because the definition of a successful life must include serving others.

To the young people of America, who sometimes feel left out—I ask you tonight to give us the benefit of your talent and energy through a new program called "YES," for Youth Entering Service to America.

To those men and women in business—remember the ultimate end of your work—to make a better product, to create better lives. I ask you to plan for the longer term and avoid the temptation of quick and easy paper profits.

To the brave men and women who wear the uniform of the United States of America—thank you. Your calling is a high one—to be the defenders of freedom and the guarantors of liberty. And I want you to know that the Nation is grateful for your service.

To the farmers of America, we appreciate the bounty you provide. We will work with you to open foreign markets to American agricultural products.

To the parents of America, I ask you to get involved in your child's schooling. Check on their homework. Go to school, meet the teachers, care about what is happening there. It is not only your child's future on the line, it is America's.

To kids in our cities—don't give up hope. Say no to drugs. Stay in school. And yes, "Keep hope alive."

To those 37 million Americans with some form of disability—you belong in the economic mainstream. We need your talents in America's work force. Disabled Americans must become full partners in America's opportunity society.

To the families of America watching tonight in your living rooms: Hold fast to your dreams, because ultimately America's future rests in your hands.

And to my friends in this Chamber, I ask for your cooperation to keep America growing while cutting the deficit. That is only fair to those who now have no vote—the generations to come.

Let them look back and say that we had the foresight to understand that a time of peace and prosperity is not a time to rest, but a time to push forward. A time to invest in the future.

And let all Americans remember that no problem of human making is too great to be overcome by human ingenuity, human energy, and the untiring hope of the human spirit. I believe this. I would not have asked to be your President if I didn't.

Tomorrow, the debate on the plan I have put forward begins. I ask the Congress to come forward with your proposals, if they are different. Let us not question each other's motives. Let us debate. Let us negotiate. But let us solve the problem.

Recalling anniversaries may not be my specialty in speeches ... but tonight is one of some note. On February 9, 1941, just 48 years ago tonight, Sir Winston Churchill took to the airwaves during Britain's hour of peril.

He had received from President Roosevelt a hand-carried letter quoting Longfellow's famous poem: "Sail on, O Ship of State! Sail on, Oh Union, strong and great! Humanity with all its fears, with all the hopes of future years, Is hanging breathless on thy fate!"

Churchill responded on this night by radio broadcast to a nation at war, but he directed his words to Roosevelt. "We shall not fail or falter," he said. "We shall not weaken or tire. Give us the tools, and we will finish the job."

Tonight, almost a half-century later, our peril may be less immediate, but the need for perseverance and clear-sighted fortitude is just as great.

Now, as then, there are those who say it can't be done. There are voices who say that America's best days have passed. That we are bound by constraints, threatened by problems, surrounded by troubles which limit our ability to hope.

Well, tonight I remain full of hope. We Americans have only begun on our mission of goodness and greatness. And to those timid souls, I repeat the plea—give us the tools; and we will do the job.

Thank you, and God bless you, and God bless America.

BIPARTISAN BUDGET AGREEMENT

White House Statement

In March 1989 the President, the Speaker of the House, the majority leaders of the Senate and House, the Republican leaders of the Senate and House, joined by the chairman and ranking Republican members of the Appropriations, Ways and Means, Finance, and Budget Committees, and by the Secretary of the Treasury, the Chief of Staff to the President, and the Director of the Office of Management and Budget, concurred in a recommendation to establish a special budget negotiating group. The group was charged to explore the possibility of reaching an agreement on a budget framework for fiscal year 1990 and to report upon its progress to the President and the joint leadership of Congress. The group was composed of the chairman and ranking Republican members of the Senate and House Budget Committees, the Majority Leader of the House, the Secretary of the Treasury, and the Director of the Office of Management and Budget. The attached agreement is the product of that negotiating group, as developed in accordance with the guidance of the leadership group.

Bipartisan Budget Agreement Between the President and the Joint Leadership of Congress

1. The elements of this agreement provide for deficit reduction amounts that, for fiscal year 1990, are currently estimated to meet the deficit target of the Balanced Budget and Emergency Deficit Control Reaffirmation Act of 1987.

2. The budget framework is approved by the President, the Speaker, and the Majority and Republican Leadership of Congress.

3. The President and the Leadership of Congress will carry out this agreement.

4. The following procedures will be utilized to implement this agreement: Congressional implementation will follow, as much as possible, the regular budget and legislative procedures. The House and Senate Budget Committees will each report a concurrent resolution on the budget for fiscal year 1990 consistent with this budget agreement. The budget resolution will contain reconciliation instructions and 302(a) allocations consistent with this budget agreement. The House and Senate Committees with jurisdiction over matters necessary to implement the agreement will be responsible for developing 302(b) allocations, legislation, and budget resolutions, appropriations bills, reconciliation legislation, and other measures will apply.

5. Congress shall present the revenue portion of the reconciliation bill to the President at the same time as the spending reduction provisions of the reconciliation bill.

6. Agreed-upon fiscal year 1990 budget levels are as follows for each of the three discretionary appropriations categories:

[in billions of dollars]*

Category	BA	O
Domestic	$157.5	$181.3
Defense (050)**	305.5	299.2
International Affairs	19.0	17.0

  * Congressional enforcement of these discretionary levels in the
  legislative process will be based on CBO scoring.
  ** Functional total includes mandatory spending.

7. The Budget Committees, CBO, and OMB shall use the "Scorekeeping Guidelines for the Bipartisan Budget Agreement of April 14, 1989," and shall work together to resolve any new scorekeeping issues that may arise.

8. Within the domestic discretionary amount, the budget resolution will provide sufficient funding for subsidized housing contract renewals (without prejudice to the form or length of such renewals).

9. Deficit reduction to be implemented in accordance with this agreement is specified in the attached "Deficit Reduction Plan." For both budget scorekeeping and Gramm-Rudman-Hollings, final scoring will necessarily depend on the review of legislation by the scorekeepers, as provided in the Congressional Budget Act and Gramm-Rudman-Hollings.

10. The specific measures composing the governmental receipts figure will be determined through the regular legislative and Constitutional process. Agreements reached between the Administration and the Congressional tax-writing committees on revenue legislation reconciled pursuant to this agreement will be advanced legislatively when supported by the President of the United States.

11. Neither the Congress nor the President shall initiate supplementals except in the case of dire emergency. When the Executive Branch makes such a request, it shall be accompanied by a presidentially-transmitted budget amendment to Congress.

12. Both the President and the Congress have addressed the need for additional domestic discretionary spending priorities for the fiscal year 1990 budget. It is agreed that any funding of priorities will be within the domestic spending levels set forth in paragraph 6 of this agreement.

13. The President and the Congressional Leadership will continue to consult closely to seek opportunities for further deficit reduction and to explore policy and process changes which would reduce the deficit to meet the deficit targets of the Gramm-Rudman-Hollings law and balance the Federal budget by fiscal year 1993. In order to facilitate progress toward that objective, the bipartisan Budget Committee Leadership, the Secretary of the Treasury, and the Director of Office of Management and Budget shall continue discussions in consultation with the bipartisan leadership of the appropriate committees of the House and Senate.

REPORT ON THE STATE
OF U.S. EDUCATION
February 14, 1989

In a report released February 14 entitled "Crossroads in American Education," the Educational Testing Service (ETS) stated that although American students had improved their basic knowledge over the past twenty years, few were able to apply that knowledge in real-life situations. The federally funded study—part of the Nation's Report Card project—was conducted by the testing service for the National Assessment of Educational Progress (NAEP) of the U.S. Department of Education.

It was the first comprehensive study published by the project under its 1969 congressional mandate. Previous reports focused on specific subject areas. The latest report contained no new data on student achievement. Rather, it was a compilation of reports issued by the testing service over the previous twenty years. (Reports on Math and Science Education, Historic Documents of 1988, p. 377)

In analyzing data collection since 1969 on 1.4 million students between the ages of nine and seventeen, researchers found that learning in the four basic areas of reading, writing, math, and science had improved since the 1970s. In addition, the gap in academic performance between white students on the one hand and blacks and Hispanics on the other had been "reduced by a considerable margin in some subjects."

However, substantial numbers of students lacked the ability to apply the information they had learned. In reading, 61 percent of the seventeen-year-olds who were tested could not understand complicated written information about topics they had studied in school. Thirty-five percent could not fill out an adequate job application form, and 79 percent could not produce a reasoned essay that would effectively convey a point of view. In math, 49 percent could not solve problems involving decimals, fractions, or percentages. In science, 93 percent could not infer relationships and draw conclusions using detailed scientific knowledge. Levels of proficiency in all subjects were clearly and consistently related to the amount of homework students did and to the number and level of courses they took, the report said.

Conclusion: Major Changes Needed

In his introduction to the report, ETS President Gregory R. Anrig said: "Recent improvements are evident and represent significant national accomplishment. But progress falls short of what the times require. Much more progress is needed for the economic development of our nation and the intellectual well-being of the next generation."

The report said that "fundamental changes in curriculum and instruction" are needed to produce graduates who could perform the complex jobs increasingly required if the nation is to compete successfully in the international economy. The education system, it continued, "needs to extend its focus from the teaching and learning of skills and content to include an emphasis on the purposeful use of skills and knowledge." The report recommended that schools develop new teaching methods to combine learning with practical applications, students be given more homework and more rigorous course work, and parents become more involved in their children's education.

A number of educators characterized the report's findings as a combination of good and bad news. Americans should "consider this report from the standpoint of shareholders in the largest endeavor in the nation," said Archie E. Lapointe, NAEP executive director. "If one views this report as a balance sheet on 20 years of American education, our assets clearly include strengthening students' basic skills and improving minority student performance."

"On the liabilities side of the ledger," he continued, "we find deficits in higher-order thinking skills, which means that large proportions of American students do not appear to be adequately prepared for college work, career mobility, and thoughtful citizenship."

Roger B. Porter, assistant to President Bush for economic and domestic policy, noted that the report's emphasis on the influence of the home environment paralleled the president's own philosophy. "Hands-on parents, which is what we need, need choices" about which schools their children attended, he said. Porter said stagnation in science and mathematics scores were "particularly disturbing." In an era of rapid technological advances, "if we're not moving forward, we're moving backwards," he said.

Related Studies

A report released January 31 by the ETS showed that U.S. students placed last in an international comparison of mathematics and science skills. The study, funded by the Department of Education and the National Science Foundation, compared the abilities of a representative sampling of thirteen-year-old students from the United States, South Korea, Great Britain, Ireland, Spain, and four Canadian provinces. In math, South Korean students outperformed those in all other countries surveyed. About 40 percent of the Korean students demonstrated an understanding of measurement and geography concepts, and 78 percent could use the intermediate skills to solve two-step problems. The comparative figures for American students were about 10 percent and 40 percent.

The international comparison was made public after a group of mathematical and scientific organizations called January 26 for sweeping changes in the way mathematics is taught in the United States. The report, entitled "Everybody Counts: A Report to the Nation on the Future of Mathematics Education," was released by the National Research Council, the research arm of the National Academy of Sciences. It called for revisions in elementary and secondary teaching methods to place less emphasis on rote learning and more on fundamental concepts, problem solving, and the creative use of calculators and computers. The report warned that the United States "was at risk of becoming a divided nation in which mathematics supports a productive, technologically powerful elite, while a dependent, semiliterate majority, disproportionately Hispanic and black, find economic and political power beyond reach."

Bush Education Budget

The NAEP report came at a time when George Bush was pledging to carry out his 1988 presidential campaign promise to be the "education president." He outlined legislation on April 5 to create more than $400 million worth of new school programs, in addition to the existing $21.9 billion education budget request for fiscal year 1990. The proposal met with a cool reception among some key congressional Democrats and education groups, who argued that more needed to be done. "[T]he Bush administration has not stopped the spending erosion that has taken place over the past eight years," said Rep. Augustus F. Hawkins, D-Calif., chairman of the House Education and Labor Committee.

Following are excerpts from the report, "Crossroads in American Education," prepared by the Educational Testing Service for the National Assessment of Educational Progress of the U.S. Department of Education and released February 14, 1989:

Overview

... Findings from recent NAEP assessments provide evidence of progress in students' academic achievement. Results from the 1984 and 1986 assessments indicate that, on the average, students' proficiency in reading has improved across time, and proficiency in writing, mathematics, and science has improved in recent assessments after earlier declines. In addition, there is evidence that some strides have been made toward equity: Gaps in average academic performance that have historically existed between Black students and their White peers and between Hispanic students and their White peers have been reduced by a considerable margin in some subjects.

Despite these positive signs, the remaining challenges are many. Not all ground lost during the 1970s and early 1980s has been regained, and there was considerable concern even at the time of the first assessments about the quality of student learning. In addition, a closer examination of the NAEP data indicates that recent gains in student performance have occurred primarily at the lower levels of achievement. For example, students have improved in their ability to do simple computation, comprehend simple tests, and exhibit knowledge of everyday science facts. However, too few students develop the capacity to use the knowledge and skills they acquire in school for thoughtful or innovative purposes. And too few students learn to reason effectively about information from the subjects they study. . . .

Trends in Academic Achievement

. . . A study of the timing of declines and recoveries for each age group across subject areas reveals some interesting patterns. The NAEP mathematics results indicate that students born in 1965 declined in performance at ages 13 and 17 compared to students born earlier. Further, those students born four years later (in 1969) showed gains at ages 13 and 17 compared to students born in 1965. Thus, it appears that the recent declines and improvements at age 17 may reflect declines and improvements made by this group of students when they were 13, suggesting that the recent improvements at age 17 are not simply the result of changes currently being made to strengthen high-school graduation requirements. Similar patterns of performance by birth-year cohorts were evident in the science and reading assessments.

The improvements in achievement reflected in the assessment data also may reflect the positive impact of a variety of recent efforts to reform education. Cumulatively, these efforts seem to have halted earlier declines in each subject and begun to bring proficiency levels back to where they were in the early 1970s.

Signs of Equity

In the last 20 years, one of the major goals of educational reform has been to improve the performance of minority populations historically at risk of school failure. A variety of programs have been introduced to accomplish this goal, from preschool and day-care programs to targeted classes providing additional instruction as part of the regular school day. Given that achievement levels have begun to improve somewhat for the nation as a whole, how well have members of these minority groups done during this period?

... In general, it appears that the performance gaps, as measured by differences in average proficiency, have narrowed across time, particularly for Black students. Decreases in the disparities in reading and mathematics performance are the most consistent among the subject areas across time, with the gap decreasing gradually, while the gaps in science performance are the least stable. For Hispanic and Black students alike, the gap in science achievement relative to White students increased until 1962, before narrowing between 1982 and 1986.

Levels of Learning

... Although most students appear to have learned the basics in core subject areas, the discrepancy between curricular goals and actual performance in these subjects widens as students progress through school. For example, a considerable percentage of 9-year-olds (approximately one-quarter) did not have beginning skills and understandings in mathematics ... and did not understand simple scientific principles. ...

Thirteen-year-olds fell even farther behind expected levels of performance. In mathematics, more than one-quarter of these middle-school students failed to demonstrate an adequate understanding of the content and procedures emphasized in elementary school; moreover, a majority (84 percent) did not display a grasp of mathematics material generally introduced during the seventh and eighth grades. In reading, 40 percent of the middle-school students could not read passages at an intermediate level of difficulty. In science, only half of these students displayed an understanding of basic scientific information. Finally, while most middle-school students could write a report based on personal experience, only slightly more than half demonstrated that they could use writing in a minimal way to persuade others or analyze information.

Because the achievement of high-school students reflects in part the final product of our K-12 education system, the profile of what America's high-school students appear to know and are able to do is particularly disturbing. Sixty-one percent of the 17-year-old students could not read or understand relatively complicated material, such as that typically presented at the high-school level. Nearly one-half appear to have limited mathematics skills and abilities that go little beyond adding, subtracting, and multiplying with whole numbers. More than one-half could not evaluate the procedures or results of a scientific study, and few included enough information in their written pieces to communicate their ideas effectively. Additionally, assessment results in other curriculum areas indicate that high-school juniors have little sense of historical chronology, have not read much literature, and tend to be unfamiliar with the uses and potential applications of computers.

These cumulative findings provide us with a great deal of food for thought. For example, if so many students are unable to perform relatively difficult tasks in their academic subjects, why are they not doing equally poorly in their classes? One possible reason for the difference between NAEP performance and classroom grades may be that students regard the assessment as incidental to their lives, and therefore are less engaged in these tasks than is usual in everyday class or real world experiences.

Yet other possibilities for the discrepancies may be that evaluation criteria generally used in subject classrooms are based on learning objectives different from those of NAEP, that teachers are unsophisticated evaluators of performance, that school performance standards are low, or that institutional goals have tended to support and reinforce the teaching and learning of less difficult concepts and skills to the neglect of those that are more challenging. Recent reports have tended to support this last contention, and if this is so, the goals, materials, and methods of instruction may need to be reformulated.

Factors Related to Achievement

These data suggest a remarkable consistency across recent assessments of student achievement in various academic subjects. By and large, students are learning the basics, and Black and Hispanic students are closing the historical gap in performance with their White peers. Yet despite these signs of progress, it remains true that only some of the nation's students can perform moderately difficult tasks and woefully few can perform more difficult ones. . . . [M]ost of the gains in average proficiency represent improvements in basic skills and knowledge rather than higher-level applications. It appears that while students are acquiring basic information in core subject areas, they are not learning to use their knowledge effectively in thinking and reasoning. . . .

In one sense, schools across the country can be congratulated for having reversed the negative trends in academic achievement evident during the 1970s. But while schools have been working to right the ills of yesterday, the ground rules have been changing. Across grades and subject areas, learning basic facts and procedures is no longer considered sufficient. Rather, there are new expectations for successful academic learning at all ages; students are expected to be capable of using knowledge for purposes that require them to go beyond reciting facts and displaying the routines they have been taught. However, it is in these very areas that students show the least improvement across assessments and may even be losing ground. To fulfill these new expectations, students across the grades need to engage in activities that require them to apply, extend, and evaluate what they are learning and to relate new learning to what they already know.

Even at present, however, schools are not all alike and students are not taught the same things at the same times. There is a great deal of variation across schools in the emphasis on academic achievement and in patterns of course work, teaching practices, and materials—all of which are likely to have an impact on students' academic proficiency. Thus, in addition to studying achievement patterns, the NAEP assessments also have gathered information about the characteristics of differing learning environments and their associations with student achievement. The analyses do not reveal the underlying causes of these associations, which may be influenced by a number of different factors. Therefore, the results are most useful when they are considered in the context of other knowledge about the educational system, such as trends in instruction, changes in the school-age population, and societal demands and expectations.

Emphasizing Academic Achievement

Recent calls for educational reform have stressed the importance of providing students with an environment in which academic achievement is valued and supported. These proposed reforms have included calls for more homework, higher standards for performance, and more course work in traditional academic subjects. As part of its recent assessments, NAEP has asked students about the courses they have taken and about the amount of homework they do for each course. Across all subject areas assessed, there have been clear and consistent relationships between student reports about homework and coursework and their overall levels of subject-area proficiency.

... Approximately 15 percent of the high-school students reported that they were not assigned homework or did not do it, and these students had noticeably lower proficiency levels than did their classmates who reported regularly spending time on homework. The more homework eleventh-grade students reported, the higher their proficiency levels were likely to be. Results at lower grade levels also showed consistent relationships with proficiency, but the amount of homework associated with optimum performance varied somewhat. In elementary school, students who reported spending up to half an hour per day on homework tended to have the highest proficiency levels, while in middle school, students who reported spending one to two hours each day on homework tended to have the highest proficiency.

The amount of homework reported by students has increased during the past decade. In 1978, some 32 percent of 17-year-old students reported that they were not given homework assignments; in 1986, only 6 percent reported that homework was not assigned. Such shifts reflect a positive response on the part of our schools to calls for emphasis on academic work.

The assessment results also suggest that significant proportions of American students are avoiding advanced course work. In mathematics, a quarter of the eleventh graders were not taking a mathematics class in 1986, and of those who were taking classes, a quarter were taking lower-level courses such as General Mathematics, Pre-algebra, or Algebra I. Overall, 19 percent of the 17-year-olds reported that Pre-algebra was the highest-level course they had taken, and another 18 percent had ended their course work in Algebra I. Enrollment patterns have changed only slightly since 1978: In that year, 22 percent of the 17-year-olds stopped at Pre-algebra, compared with 19 percent in 1986. Similarly, 6 percent of the 17-year-olds had gone on to Pre-calculus in 1978, compared with 7 percent in 1986.

Enrollments in science classes have been even lower: Only 58 percent of the eleventh graders were taking a science class at the time of the 1986 assessment. Data from a follow-up transcript study indicated that by graduation, less than half (45 percent) of these high-school students had earned a year's credit in Chemistry, and only 20 percent a year's credit in Physics. Fortunately, trends in science course-taking appear to be on the rise; the mean number of full-year science courses taken by graduating seniors was 2.6 in 1987, compared to a mean of 2.2 in 1982.

Rethinking the Curriculum

Although many educators argue that increased course-taking is essential to strengthen students' academic proficiency, simply increasing the amount of course work is likely to be insufficient to bring proficiency up to expected levels. There are other aspects of the educational system that must also be addressed. For example, curricular reforms may be warranted. In science, curriculum in the United States has frequently been criticized as a "layer cake" in which students study different areas in isolation and then leave them behind for the rest of their school career. Even if they take science every year, American schoolchildren who pass through this layer-cake curriculum fare relatively poorly compared with their peers in other developed nations, where the work of each year builds upon and extends the work of the previous year. The argument against a layer-cake curriculum in science can also be applied to other subject areas. In many cases, the curriculum is treated as a collection of discrete content areas in which teachers move from one topic to another in lockstep fashion. As a result, lessons are often developed in isolation from one another and fail to help students relate their new learnings to what they already know. . . .

Providing Home Support

Closely related to high and consistent academic expectations at school is the extent to which expectations at home place a similar emphasis on academic success. NAEP assessments have asked students about levels of parental education, the availability of books and other reading materials at home, and the amount of attention the family gives to student homework. Responses to these questions have shown consistent relationships between home support and academic achievement: The more encouragement and resources provided at home, the more likely students are to do well in school. . . .

Conclusions

In general, this synthesis of students' achievement and the environments in which they learn suggests that we are at an educational crossroads, and a comprehensive change *en route* can have an extensive impact on the future of student learning. A number of implications that arise from the composite of reports discussed here can be particularly informative. When school and home variables support academic achievement, students are more likely to be academically successful. Simply emphasizing academic learning, however, may not be enough to ensure that students develop both subject-area knowledge and the ability to use that knowledge effectively. Most classrooms are relatively traditional in their approaches to instruction, relying heavily on teacher presentations, textbooks, and workbook- or teacher-prepared exercises. Such patterns of instruction appear to have been successful in helping large numbers of students attain basic levels of proficiency in each subject area, but they do not seem to have been successful in helping students to achieve higher levels of performance.

For these qualitatively different gains to occur, the goals of instruction need to be reconsidered. Teaching decisions were once guided by a hierarchy suggesting that students must first learn the facts and skills and later learn to apply them. Yet many educators now recognize the limitations of this stepping-stone view of education. Educational theory and research suggest a different pattern of generative teaching and learning, where learning content and procedures and how to use this learning for specific purposes occur interactively. Students learn information, rules, and routines while learning to think about how these operate in the context of particular goals and challenges in their own lives. When students engage in activities that require them to use new learning, both their knowledge of content and skills and their ability to use them develop productively together.

For more thoughtful learning to occur, teachers will need to orchestrate a broader range of instructional experiences than they presently use, providing students with opportunities to prepare for, review, and extend their new learning. Such activities might include, but not be limited to, the whole class discussions, workbooks, and dittos that prevail today. Discussion teams, cooperative work groups, individual learning logs, computer networking, and other activities that engage students as active learners will need to be added, and may even predominate. Using these new approaches will require teachers to move away from traditional authoritarian roles and, at the same time, require students to give up being passive recipients of learning. Instead, teachers will need to act more as guides, and students more as doers and thinkers. Some examples of this alternative mode of instruction can be found in current discussions of small group problem-solving experiences, collaborative learning, activity-based learning, and instructional scaffolding.

Since test and grades send messages to students about what is valued in their course work, the focus of tests also will need to shift. Instead of simply displaying their knowledge of facts and rules, students will need to show that they can think about and use their knowledge. A number of alternative assessment procedures have been suggested. For example, in course work, portfolios of selected work, simulations, problems, or cases can be used as the basis for assessing students' knowledge and abilities.

In short, extensive modifications in curriculum and instruction may be required to expand the range of learning experiences available to students at school. These modifications will undoubtedly be difficult, requiring changes in established procedures and traditions in the curriculum and in systems of evaluation; however, it is apparent that fundamental changes may be needed to help American schoolchildren develop both content knowledge and the ability to reason effectively about what they know—skills that are essential if they are to take an intelligent part in the worlds of life and work. Such changes will involve reshaping current notions of the goals of instruction, the roles of teachers and students, the language of instruction, the nature of instructional activities and materials, the signposts teachers use to know that they have been successful in their profession, and the evidence policymakers, administrators, parents, and the general public use to know that schools are doing their job and that students are learning.

Educators everywhere have the opportunity to use the NAEP results to great advantage—by reflecting upon the deeply entrenched beliefs, policies, and behaviors that impede the very changes we wish to make—and setting a charted course for change.

RUSHDIE'S DEATH SENTENCE
February 14, 1989

Iran's ruler, the Ayatollah Ruhollah Khomeini, provoked an international furor by calling upon Moslems everywhere to kill the author and publisher of the novel The Satanic Verses. *The eighty-eight-year-old religious leader's February 14 edict drove the author, Salman Rushdie, into hiding under police protection in Britain. Rushdie was born into a Moslem family in India in 1947 but had lived in England since 1968 and was a British subject.*

The death sentence outraged Western opinion, prompted Western governments to take diplomatic action against Iran, drew vehement protests from writers, thwarted Iranian factions pursuing rapprochement with the West, and exposed an abyss of cultural difference between Islamic and Western civilizations. While some Moslem leaders disapproved of Khomeini's death sentence, they were unanimous in condemning the novel.

Before the Iranian ruler called Rushdie's book "against Islam, the Prophet [Mohammed] and the Koran," riots in other countries had already expressed widespread Moslem anger at The Satanic Verses. *In Pakistan, six persons were killed and more than one hundred injured in a protest outside the American cultural center, and a crowd of Moslems in Bradford, England, burned copies of the book. It was banned in India, South Africa, and throughout the Moslem world.*

Rushdie denied that his fictional work was a blasphemy against Islam, and he complained that many of his attackers had not read the book. His initial reaction to their attacks was to say that he wished his book had been more critical, adding that "religious leaders who are able to behave like this, and then say this is a religion that must be above any kind of whisper of criticism: that doesn't add up."

Khomeini said that anyone who died trying to kill Rushdie would go straight to heaven, and his followers put a price on the author's head of more than $5 million. Asked if he took the threat seriously, Rushdie replied: "I think I have to take it very seriously indeed."

In a brief statement February 18 Rushdie said, "I profoundly regret the distress that publication has occasioned to sincere followers of Islam." Khomeini rejected Rushdie's apology and called upon Moslems to "send him to hell."

What Offended Moslems

In exploring the Moslem faith of his childhood in The Satanic Verses, *Rushdie recounts some legends of the prophet Mohammed. The passages of the book that most outraged Moslems appear in the dreams of one of the characters undergoing a protracted mental breakdown. In these dreams, a prophet named Mahound seems—at least to one of his followers—to be a fraud. In another dream sequence, prostitutes take on the names of the prophet's wives.*

William Graham, professor of the history of religion and Islamic studies at Harvard, tried to explain why these fantastic incidents upset Moslems. Noting that episodes from standard early Islamic works were interspersed with degrading images, he observed: "It's as if you took the Bible, and in the middle of the Sermon on the Mount, you showed Jesus fantasizing copulation with whores."

Public Reaction

While Moslems were outraged by the book, Westerners were outraged by the ayatollah's edict. Writers, in particular, protested the grim threat to freedom of expression. With petitions and public statements, many writers in Britain, the United States, and other countries publicly identified themselves with their threatened colleague.

A coalition of writers' organizations—Author's Guild, American PEN, and Article 19 (an international anticensorship organization)—sponsored a meeting in New York February 22 at which prominent authors issued statements and read passages from The Satanic Verses *and other Rushdie works.*

Writers were especially incensed by the decisions of some of America's largest bookstores chains to remove the books from their shelves. The Writer's Guild of America, which represents 3,200 writers for film, television, and radio, said that this action by the book chains "sets a dangerous precedent under which any type of literary material could be forced out of circulation if threats are made against the distributors, broadcasters, or exhibitors of that material."

An official of Viking Penguin, publisher of The Satanic Verses *in the United States, who asked that his name not be used for reasons of personal safety, observed that "unlike the major retailers, we have not pulled in our horns. We have never stopped publishing the book." The bookstore chains said their actions were in response to threats and were intended to protect their employees, but they subsequently resumed sales.*

Government Reactions

Britain, which had resumed diplomatic relations with Iran less than three months earlier, pulled its entire diplomatic staff out of Iran and ordered Iran to withdraw its diplomats from London. The twelve members of the European Community announced February 20 that they would recall their senior diplomats from Tehran and would freeze high-level visits and slow economic and political cooperation. Iran responded to the European action by withdrawing its own envoys from Western Europe and later broke relations with Britain.

More than a week elapsed before President George Bush—pressed by writers' organizations, newspapers, and civil liberties advocates who felt his administration was too slow and restrained in its response to the ayatollah's edict—issued a statement. "However offensive the book may be," the president said at a White House news conference February 22, "inciting murder and offering rewards for its perpetration are deeply offensive to the norms of civilized behavior. And our position on terrorism is well known. In the light of Iran's incitement, should any action be taken against American interests, the government of Iran can expect to be held accountable." Some observers felt that Bush's reaction was less outspoken than those of European leaders because of concern for U.S. hostages held by pro-Iranian factions in Lebanon.

Islamic scholar Bernard Lewis, writing in the Washington Post *February 24, saw the ayatollah's delayed reaction to the book, which had been published in England in September and reviewed in an Iranian magazine several months later, as an indication that the motives of his death decree were political rather than religious. Lewis detected "an obvious and striking parallel" with the seizure of the U.S. embassy and hostages a decade earlier, which reversed a movement in Iran to mend fences with the United States and left Iranian radicals in full control (Historic Documents of 1979, p. 867). "The Rushdie affair has stopped a similar move to restore relations with Europe," Lewis wrote, "and will probably have a similar effect on the internal balance of forces in Iran."*

Rushdie did not dare come out of hiding even after the aging Khomeini died June 3, twelve days after undergoing surgery in Tehran. Despite changes that occurred in Iran's ruling structure within the next few months, making Iran appear less intransigent than under Khomeini, the death threat apparently remained in effect.

Cultural Gulf

Whatever motivated the ayatollah, The Satanic Verses *affair revealed a profound gulf between Islamic and Western mentalities. In an effort to understand the Moslem reaction to the novel, some scholars made*

97

comparisons with Western laws against blasphemy and execution of heretics in past centuries. Other observers made comparisons with the anger among many Christians toward the recent film by Martin Scorsese, The Last Temptation of Christ.

In a March 5 article in the New York Times, *former president Jimmy Carter, while honoring the First Amendment right for showing this "fantasy," said the movie's "sacrilegious scenes were still distressing to me and many others who share my faith." Carter called Khomeini's death sentence "abhorrent," but he urged Western leaders to "make it clear that in protecting Rushdie's life and civil rights, there is no endorsement of an insult to the sacred beliefs of our Moslem friends."*

Only a few weeks before Khomeini's decree, his officially designated spiritual successor, the Ayatollah Hussein Ali Montazeri, had called his country's internal repression and radical international policies "grave errors that ruined the image of Iran and frightened the world by making it believe that our only objective is to kill." No such sentiments were heard in Iran after the decree, and Khomeini, in a February 22 speech to senior religious leaders, said that the Western reaction to The Satanic Verses *affair proved that moderate policies were pointless.*

> *Following is the death sentence issued by the Ayatollah Ruhollah Khomeini against Salman Rushdie, in English translation, as broadcast February 14, 1989, on Tehran Radio:*

I inform the Muslim people of the world that the author of the *Satanic Verses* book, which is against Islam, the Prophet, and the Koran, and all those involved in its publication who were aware of its content, are sentenced to death. I ask all the Moslems to execute them wherever they find them.

U.S. TRIBUTES AT HIROHITO'S FUNERAL
February 24 and 25, 1989

Emperor Hirohito, Japan's longest reigning monarch, died January 7 of cancer at age eighty-seven. His death recalled the turbulence of his sixty-two-year reign, testified to Japan's global influence, and raised questions about the nation's future. His funeral February 24 brought to Tokyo representatives from 180 nations and international organizations.

For the world community, the passing of the last of the World War II leaders revived memories of that conflict. For the Japanese, the death of the first emperor to have renounced divine status brought to the surface fundamental questions about their society and their nation. He was widely viewed as a link between prewar and present-day Japan.

Hirohito was succeeded on the Chrysanthemum Throne by his eldest son, Akihito, age fifty-five. Brought up in the postwar era, after the imperial family had been demystified, Akihito represents to the Japanese something quite different from his father. He married a commoner, raised his children himself, and ventured into the public and abroad, leaving the detached eminence that had shrouded his predecessors in mystery. Viewed by the Japanese as a modern man, he seemed suited for a democratic society whose prior aspirations to military glory have been replaced by the successful pursuit of material wealth.

The loss of divine authority in Japan was deep and sudden. Under the tutelage of the American military occupation, Hirohito disclaimed his divinity in 1946, and the separation of religion and state was written into the Japanese constitution. Although Americans found it useful to preserve a symbolic emperor as a stabilizing force as they pushed a democratic revolution in postwar Japan, they were eager to disrobe the emperor of the cloak of godliness in which he had been seen by the Japanese.

The experience of the war reinforced an American tendency to see democracies as peaceful and authoritarian regimes as aggressive. The religious basis of Japan's authoritarian government was, therefore, a primary target of American efforts to democratize and pacify the Japanese. The emperor remained a symbol of the state and unity of the people.

Bush's Reconciliation Journey

Japan's wartime population was indoctrinated in the Shinto belief that Japan, its people, and its emperor were divine and destined to rule. The resulting zeal of the Japanese soldier found its most dramatic expression near the war's end in the suicide missions of kamikaze pilots. American and other allied forces in the Pacific and Asia suffered the bitter experience of that military passion.

President George Bush, who represented the United States at Hirohito's funeral, had fought in the war against Japan. He survived the enemy fire that shot down the navy bomber he was flying. According to Secretary of State James A. Baker III, the tribute of this former wartime pilot symbolized the change. The wounds of war "have been healed, as far as the United States is concerned," Baker said.

British, Australian, and Canadian veterans groups opposed sending high-level representatives of their countries to the funeral. But sentiment in the United States was more concerned with current and future relations with Japan. Fear of economic competition with Japan, with which the United States in 1988 had a trade deficit of more than $54 billion, stirred Americans more than memories of military conflict.

Economic competition was one of the motives prompting the U.S. government to pressure Japan to assume a larger share of the burdens of military defense. The effort marked a reversal of U.S. policy after World War II, when strict limitations on the Japanese military forces were, at American insistence, written into the nation's constitution. Neither Japan's people nor its Asian neighbors were eager to see the country rearm.

Emperor's Wartime Role

A television "docudrama" produced by the British Broadcasting Corporation and distributed in the United States by the Public Broadcasting System portrayed Hirohito as contributing to Japanese militarism and personally involved in planning the attack on Pearl Harbor. Many scholars and other experts on Japan attacked that portrayal as wholly inaccurate. But after his death, Japanese praise of Hirohito as a man of peace provoked angry responses from some victims of Japanese aggression who remembered the young emperor astride his white horse symbolically leading his troops into battle.

Reacting to "unctious" eulogies, New Zealand Prime Minister Bob Tizzard said Hirohito "should have been shot or publicly chopped up at the end of the war." A leading South Korean newspaper, Dong-A Ilbo, in an editorial on January 9 said, "No matter how much Japan denies his responsibility, it won't be able to deny the fact that wars were declared in his name.... Japanese colonial role over many Asian countries was conducted in the name of the emperor."

Among historians, Hirohito's defenders say he was a symbolic monarch powerless to resist manipulation by Japan's military, while others consider him a willing accomplice who could have used his moral authority to oppose aggression.

Ceremonial Compromise

In Japan, only a tiny minority would agree with the view of Masahiro Tomura, a Japanese clergyman of the United Church of Christ, who warned that Shinto belief in a divine emperor destined to conquer other nations was only "dormant" and would reemerge in a time of crisis. For the ordinary Japanese, that belief had faded into the background of modern life and normally received little attention. But the emperor's death provoked a heated dispute over the propriety of religious rituals at the funeral.

In search of a compromise between the traditional funeral rites of the divine emperor and ceremonies appropriate to a secular chief of state, the government decreed that a curtain would partly block the religious events from foreign guests' view, and that Shinto symbols would be removed as soon as the religious proceedings were over. Traditionalists were unhappy with this compromise. Japan's Communist party boycotted the funeral, and leaders of the largest opposition group, the Japan Socialist party, arrived late to miss the Shinto ceremonies.

Deference if Not Reverence

Although the emperor may have lost the aura of divinity, in his passing he still evoked mass deference from his people. When he became gravely ill in September, government officials canceled trips abroad, popular singers postponed lavish weddings, and schools put off annual autumn festivals.

This deference provoked debate over what is fitting behavior toward a modern Japanese emperor. Raisuke Honda, political editor of Yomiuri Shimbun, *one of Japan's biggest dailies, wrote: "The present excessive mood of self-restraint stems from a 'follow your neighbor' psychology." The rival* Asahi Shimbun *observed: "When it comes to issues surrounding the Imperial Family, the mass orientation among the Japanese people builds up fast."*

Thousands lined the streets as the emperor's hearse and a thirty-car procession moved from the Imperial Palace in a cold rain to a shrine of white cypress, built for the occasion in a public park. The park had been closed for more than a month because leftist radicals had vowed to disrupt the funeral, and thirty-two thousand police patrolled quiet city streets from which traffic had been barred and watched from helicopters and a blimp overhead.

Attendants provided rice, sake, quail, pheasant, fish, seaweed, and bean-paste sweets for the emperor's journey to the spirit world. Then, while foreign representatives and ten thousand Japanese dignitaries paid tribute in the gloomy cold, Akihito, in a brief personal statement more colloquial than the traditional oration, delivered the funeral eulogy.

Following are excerpts from President Bush's remarks at news conferences at the U.S. ambassador's residence in Tokyo on February 24 and February 25, 1989, following the funeral of the Emperor Hirohito:

FEBRUARY 24 REMARKS

... This has been a very moving day in a lot of ways, and I simply want to thank our Japanese hosts, who managed this complicated logistics and put on a marvelous pageant in honor of the late Emperor, beautifully staged and beautifully carried off, on schedule, working against the elements, but nevertheless with a dignity and a ceremony that was appropriate. And I have great respect for what they did and the way in which they did it, and I am proud to have represented the United States of America here today.

FEBRUARY 25 REMARKS

Q. Mr. President, I'm just curious whether you, as a World War II veteran who was shot down not all that far from here, felt any sense of unease yesterday appearing before the coffin and bowing before the Emperor and the new Emperor?

The President. No, I didn't. And I can't say that in the quiet of the ceremony that my mind didn't go back to the wonder of it all, because I vividly remember my wartime experience. And I vividly remember the personal friends that were in our squadron that are no longer alive as a result of combat, a result of action. But my mind didn't dwell on that at all. And what I really thought, if there was any connection to that, is isn't it miraculous what's happened since the war. And I remember the stories, in reading as preparation for this visit—the visit of [Gen. Douglas] MacArthur and the former Emperor here. That was historic, and that set a whole new direction. And MacArthur's decision at that time proved to be correct in terms of Japan's move towards democracy. And so, I honestly can tell you that I did not dwell on that and didn't feel any sense other than my mind thinking of personal relationships and things of that nature, but nothing to do about whether it was right to be here. I was certain from the day that I committed to come here that this was correct for the United States, and perhaps having been in combat in World War II, maybe the decision was more correct; maybe it was more profound to be here. It leaves out my experience.

I'm representing the United States of America. And we're talking about a friend, and we're talking about an ally. We're talking about a nation with whom we have constructive relationships. Sure, we've got some problems, but that was all overriding—and respect for the Emperor. And remember back in World War II, if you'd have predicted that I would be here because of the hard feeling and the symbolic nature of the problem back then of the former Emperor's standing, I would have said, "No way." But here we are, and time moves on; and there is a very good lesson for civilized countries in all of this.

REJECTION OF TOWER
AS SECRETARY OF DEFENSE
February 28, 1989

After a bruising battle, the Senate handed President George Bush his first major defeat by rejecting the nomination of John Tower to be secretary of defense. The Senate Armed Services Committee's 11-9 vote February 23 to report the nomination as unfavorable forecast the eventual outcome. The vote was along strict party lines, with all committee Democrats, led by Chairman Sam Nunn, D-Ga., opposing and all Republicans supporting Tower's confirmation.

On February 28, the committee approved a majority report and also attached a minority report. Floor debate on the nomination began the week of February 27, and on March 9 the full Senate voted 47-53 to deny the president's selection. Only three Democrats (Lloyd Bentsen of Texas, Chistopher J. Dodd of Connecticut, and Howell Heflin of Alabama) supported the nomination; one Republican (Nancy Landon Kassebaum of Kansas) opposed it.

Speculation that Bush would choose Tower, a sixty-three-year-old fellow Texan and former chairman of the Armed Services Committee, to be his secretary of defense surfaced soon after the November 8 election. But it was not until December 16 that Bush announced Tower as his selection, saying he was "totally satisfied" with an extensive FBI investigation of the nominee's background.

The committee opened its hearings January 25, with two days of testimony by Tower. Calling himself "a realist," Tower offered assurances to the panel that he would run the Pentagon under the fiscal restraints he once vigorously opposed. As a senator for twenty-four years (1961-1984) and Armed Services Committee chairman for the last four of those years, Tower was a combative and influential supporter of defense spending.

At the beginning, there was almost no mention of Tower's alleged drinking and womanizing, which had been among the subjects covered in the FBI probe. But almost immediately, the question of Tower's ties with Pentagon contractors arose. Documents made public by the committee showed that from 1986 to 1988 Tower earned $763,777 from defense firms with whom he contracted as a political consultant after he left the Senate. Replying that he had terminated his consulting contracts and had no financial interest in his former clients, Tower said he would face no conflict of interest as defense secretary.

Tower's personal conduct became an issue later in the hearings. On January 31, conservative activist Paul M. Weyrich questioned the nominee's "moral character" and speculated that foreign governments might use damaging information about Tower to bring pressure on the U.S. government.

Confirmation Arguments

By the time the nomination reached the Senate floor, the debate turned on three issues: Tower's fitness to run the Department of Defense, the kind of information the Senate should use in judging a nominee, and how much freedom it should have to challenge a president's selection of his cabinet.

A central theme of the Republicans' case for confirming Tower was that the Democrats were departing radically from the Senate's traditional deference to a president's choice of his top advisers. Moreover, the Republicans contended, the Democrats were doing so on the basis of largely unsubstantiated allegations by unidentified sources contained in several FBI interviews that, in some instances, were contrary to the senators' personal knowledge. Supporters pointed to Tower's record of achievement in Congress and lauded his later performance as chairman of an investigation of the Iran-contra affair (Tower Commission Report, Historic Documents of 1987, p. 205) and as chief U.S. negotiator in strategic arms reduction talks (START) with the Soviet Union in 1985-1986.

Sen. John W. Warner of Virginia, the committee's ranking Republican, dismissed most of the charges against Tower as "a cobweb of fact, fiction and fantasy." Democrats insisted that the voluminous summaries of more than four hundred FBI interviews contained specific, damaging allegations against the nominee. But in the main, they argued that it was the cumulative weight of all the evidence against Tower that formed their judgment, rather than any one, decisive item. The senators were permitted to read the FBI report, but—as is customary—it was not made public.

Democrats insisted that the only issue was Tower himself. "This was a unique case," Nunn said shortly before the Senate voted. "I do not believe that we will have another nomination with this number of [negative] allegations and this degree of controversy in my lifetime."

First Rejection in Three Decades

The vote against Tower was only the ninth time in the Senate's two-hundred-year history that it had turned down a president's cabinet choice. Never before had it disapproved a cabinet nominee at the start of a president's first term in office. The rejection precedent was set in 1834, when the Senate blocked President Andrew Jackson's selection of Roger B. Taney to be secretary of the Treasury. Taney had incurred senatorial opposition for leading Jackson's attack on the Central Bank of the United States; his nomination was defeated by a vote of 18 to 28.

The last previous cabinet rejection occurred in 1959, when the Senate voted down (46-49) President Dwight D. Eisenhower's choice of Lewis L. Strauss to be secretary of commerce. Opponents argued that Strauss lacked candor and was uncooperative as chairman of the Atomic Energy Commission and during confirmation hearings.

After the Tower nomination was defeated, the Senate's Republican leader, Bob Dole of Kansas, called the rejection a naked grab for power by the Senate's Democratic majority. "This has been a pitched partisan battle, and has been for weeks," Dole said, adding that the Senate had become "a pipeline for gossip . . . a partisan hotbed of character assassination." The day after the vote, Vice President Dan Quayle charged that Tower's opponents had "degraded the Senate" in "a McCarthyite, mudslinging campaign."

Cheney's Confirmation

President Bush took a more conciliatory tone. He said that while he regretted that some members had opposed Tower on the basis of "perceptions based on groundless rumor," now "we owe it to the American people to come together and move forward." The next day, he named Rep. Dick Cheney, R-Wyo., to the defense post. One week later, the Senate approved the nomination on a 92-0 vote.

Cheney, beginning his sixth House term, had just been elected minority whip, his party's number-two position in that chamber. He had been the ranking House Republican on a select congressional committee that investigated the Iran-contra affair. As a member of the House Intelligence Committee, he acquired a reputation as a leading Republican expert on intelligence affairs and as a strong supporter of President Ronald Reagan's defense buildup.

In contrast to Tower, Cheney had little direct experience in defense issues. However, he could claim several years' experience working in the executive branch before entering Congress. This included serving President Gerald R. Ford as White House chief of staff. At age forty-eight, Cheney had spent most of his professional life in Washington. He thus joined a cabinet composed almost entirely of Washington "insiders."

107

Following are excerpts from the Senate Armed Services Committee's majority report recommending against the nomination of John Tower to be secretary of defense, and from its minority report supporting the nomination, both issued February 28, 1989:

Majority Report

[Signed by Sens. Sam Nunn (Ga.), Jim Exon (Neb.), Carl Levin (Mich.), Edward M. Kennedy (Mass.), Alan J. Dixon (Ill.), Jeff Bingaman (N.M.), John Glenn (Ohio), Al Gore (Tenn.), Tim Wirth (Colo.), Richard C. Shelby (Fla.), and Robert C. Byrd (W.Va.), all Democrats.]

Roles of the Secretary of Defense

The Secretary of Defense is the head of, and has authority, direction, and control over, the Department of Defense. He also is the principal assistant to the President in all matters relating to the Department of Defense. In these capacities, the Secretary has four principal roles: policy maker, manager, military commander, and leader.

The Secretary of Defense has a major policy-making role. He is a statutory member of the National Security Council. The Secretary of Defense advises the President on, and manages for him, the military aspects of national security strategy and policy. He plays the lead role in formulating military strategy and policy. Given the complexity of the international security environment, the breadth of U.S. global and regional security interests, and the widely varied missions of U.S. military forces, the policy-making role of the Secretary of Defense is a formidable one, and he must be skilled in both strategic and policy planning.

The Secretary of Defense, as the head of the largest and most complex organization in the Free World, has an important managerial role. The Department of Defense's annual budget of $300 billion is equal to the total sales of the four largest U.S. industrial corporations: General Motors, Exxon, Ford Motor, and IBM. The combination of the 2-million, active-duty, military personnel and 1-million civilian personnel in the Department of Defense are greater than the workforce of the 14 largest U.S. industrial corporations. The task of managing the Department of Defense is an enormous one without parallel in American business.

The Secretary of Defense is also in the chain of command for military operations, which runs from the President to the Secretary of Defense to the unified and specified combatant commanders in the field. The President and the Secretary of Defense constitute what is termed the "National Command Authorities" for U.S. military forces and nuclear weapons.

Subject to the direction of the President, the combatant commanders perform their duties under the authority, direction, and control of the Secretary of Defense. Despite his civilian status, the Secretary's powers and authority make him a military commander. The Secretary of Defense is, in essence, the Deputy Commander in Chief. Just like the President, the Secretary of Defense must be prepared to carry out his military command responsibilities 24 hours of each day.

Events of the last 20 years have indicated the unpredictable nature and timing of international crises. Because the United States has global security interests and military forces forward-deployed worldwide, crises involving U.S. interests and forces could occur at any time of the day, including "off duty" hours in Washington. In fact, because the United States is separated by vast oceans from the Eurasian land mass and Africa, crises there normally occur during "off duty" hours in Washington. . . .

Closely related to, but distinct from, the Secretary of Defense's roles as a manager and military commander is his role as a leader. In addition to managing and commanding, the Secretary of Defense must be able to inspire and to effectively influence the behavior of his subordinates. Effective leadership is critical in the Department of Defense. The leadership potential of the Secretary of Defense depends, in part, on the confidence and respect of his subordinates, which are largely determined, at least initially, by his reputation.

The leadership role of the Secretary of Defense also carries responsibility for setting the example for the entire U.S. military establishment. Because lives, careers, battles, if not the fate of the Nation, are at stake, we have consistently insisted on the highest standards of moral conduct and integrity for the professional military officer corps. The example that the Secretary of Defense sets will significantly influence whether these high standards are maintained.

Committee's Evaluation of the Qualifications of Senator Tower

Senator Tower has a substantial understanding of national security policy and international security affairs. His 20-year service as a Member of the Senate Armed Services Committee, including 4 years as Chairman, his service as Chief U.S. Negotiator in the Strategic Arms Reduction Talks (START), and his chairmanship of the Tower Board have provided Senator Tower with a solid background on national and international security issues. His expertise was evident during the Committee's hearings, during which Senator Tower was questioned on a wide range of national and international security policy issues.

Although Senator Tower has a number of strong qualifications for the position of Secretary of Defense, the Committee's overall assessment was unfavorable. The Committee's major concerns focused on Senator Tower's standards of personal conduct, discretion, and judgment. These concerns included: (1) excessive use of alcohol; (2) the provision of consulting services to defense contractors on the probable outcomes of ongoing, confidential, arms control negotiations shortly after serving as an arms control negotiator, which created the appearance of using public office for private gain; and (3) a number of incidents of indiscreet behavior toward women. In the aggregate, these concerns led the Committee to determine that Senator Tower's personal conduct, discretion, and judgment did not meet the demanding standards of the position of Secretary of Defense, especially in terms of his suitability to serve in the chain of command for military operations, a leadership example for the men and women in uniform and the civilian employees of the Department of Defense, and his ability to restore public confidence in the integrity of defense management.

The Committee examined a number of matters concerning Senator Tower's integrity, particularly regarding his personal conduct. Senator Tower has had a distinguished public career. Notwithstanding this fact, the record of Senator Tower's personal conduct, use of alcohol, and relationships with contractors could not be ignored. The Committee's concerns about these matters are discussed in subsequent sections of this report as well as in the Executive Annex to this report, which is filed and available for review by all Senators in the Office of Senate Security.

The Committee determined that Senator Tower's excessive use of alcohol is incompatible with the vast responsibilities of the Secretary of Defense, particularly as the second most senior member of the military chain of command. Moreover, there are examples of indiscreet conduct toward women which raise questions about Senator Tower's judgment and personal example for efforts in the Department of Defense to end discrimination toward, and sexual harassment of, women.

Senator Tower has the requisite experience and expertise for the traditional roles of the Secretary of Defense in policy making and handling external affairs. The Committee has serious concerns, however, about Senator Tower's suitability to serve in the chain of command for military operations. The committee believes that Senator Tower, if he were a military officer, would be precluded from serving in the most sensitive command positions. The Committee also doubts Senator Tower's ability to provide effective leadership, which will require commanding the confidence and respect of his subordinates and setting the moral standards for the entire U.S. military establishment.

Nearly all of Senator Tower's adult life has been committed to public service. Unfortunately, his service as an arms control negotiator was followed soon thereafter by establishment of a consulting service in which he provided some of the nation's largest defense contractors with advice about the probable outcomes of ongoing, confidential, arms control negotiations and the implications of such outcomes on future product development. Such activities reflect questionable judgment and weaken confidence in his commitment to the public interest. At this time of increasing public concerns about the integrity of defense management, particularly as it relates to the acquisition process, it is imperative that the Secretary of Defense be viewed as having the commitment, interest, and expertise to forcefully reform and manage the Department of Defense. The Committee is doubtful of Senator Tower's ability to restore public trust in defense management.

Alcohol Abuse

The Committee examined in detail the issue of Senator Tower's use of alcohol. There are serious allegations in the FBI report based on a number of firsthand, personal observations by named individuals with no known motive to lie. These include incidents in the recent past.

There is also evidence on the other side of this question. There is the record of Senator Tower's performance as the Chief U.S. Negotiator for the START talks in Geneva and on the Tower Board. By all accounts, Senator Tower performed well in these assignments. There are also a large number of testimonials by distinguished government officials and Members of the Senate.

But the record of alcohol abuse by the nominee cannot be ignored. The Committee had to determine whether Senator Tower has shown a pattern of excessive drinking in the past; if so, whether he has acknowledged and dealt with this problem; and whether this pattern continues into the recent past or even today.

The record of the FBI Report and the Committee's own review show a clear pattern of excessive drinking and alcohol abuse by Senator Tower during the 1970's. Senator Tower and his close associates and friends have conceded that Senator Tower had a drinking problem in the 1970's. Even the Administration has acknowledged that the nominee had a pattern of excessive drinking during this period. There is substantial evidence that this pattern continued in the 1980's.

The committee searched in vain for a point in time when the nominee himself acknowledged this problem and dealt with it decisively. The nominee made it very clear that he has never sought medical assistance for his drinking problem. There are significant inconsistencies in what Senator Tower told the FBI in the first report read by President Bush before his announcement, what Senator Tower told the FBI in subsequent reports, his executive session testimony to the Committee, and his public statements. These inconsistencies are addressed in the Executive Annex to this report.

Concerning "alcohol abuse," Department of Defense Directive 1010.4 states very clearly that it "is incompatible with the maintenance of high standards of performance, military discipline, and readiness." Military commanders state that the selection and assignment of military personnel to sensitive positions of command or those involving responsibility for nuclear weapons are so rigorously controlled that alcohol abuse would result in immediate disqualification or transfer.

For example, Department of Defense Directive 5210.42 (Nuclear Weapons Personnel Reliability Program) and implementing Service regulations provide for the screening of all personnel selected for or assigned in positions responsible for nuclear weapons. This includes personnel such as:

a) aircraft and missile crews assigned to systems that deliver nuclear weapons.

b) command and control personnel in the command or staff line who could direct the disposition and employment of nuclear weapons.

c) nuclear maintenance personnel.

d) nuclear storage and supply personnel.

e) security guards who control access to nuclear weapons facilities and systems.

f) communications security personnel who receive, maintain, and distribute authenticators and codes.

The DOD Directive sums up the Personnel Reliability Program screening and disposition policy with regard to alcohol abuse as follows:

"Disqualifying. Any of the following traits or conduct shall normally be considered disqualifying.

"a) Alcohol abuse."

Alcohol abuse is defined in the DOD Directive as: "Any irresponsible use of an alcoholic beverage causing misconduct or unacceptable social behavior, or impairing work performance, physical or mental health, financial responsibility, or personal relationships."

With regard to selection for, and assignment to, command positions, senior military commanders indicated there is no tolerance for alcohol abuse. Each of the military services views these assignments as special positions in the chain of command that must be filled by individuals who are not only professionally peerless but who are in control of their faculties at *all* times. They further indicated that command jobs at *all* levels are demanding in this respect; that all who aspire to command know this; and that rotations into and out of these positions recognize the demanding nature of these jobs.

Examples of these kinds of command positions include:

a) Company Commander of an Army rifle company assigned on patrol duty in the Demilitarized Zone (DMZ) in Korea.

b) Captain of an attack or Trident submarine on patrol.

c) Wing Commander, or even a Squadron Commander, of an Air Force F-111 Tactical Fighter Wing in England.

d) Brigade Commander of the Berlin Brigade.

e) Army M-1 Tank Commander, an E-5, in the 2nd Armored Cavalry Regiment (quick reaction team) on the border in Germany.

f) Commander in Chief, Strategic Air Command (CINCSAC).

The Committee determined that Senator Tower's excessive use of alcohol would disqualify him from being assigned to many sensitive positions in the Department of Defense. The committee determined that these disqualifying standards should be applied to the most sensitive position in the Department of Defense, that being the position of Secretary of Defense.

The alcohol abuse issue is discussed in greater detail in the Executive Annex to this report.

Senator Tower's Activities as a
Defense Industry Consultant

From mid-1986 until December 1988, Senator Tower provided consulting services to a number of defense and aerospace firms, including LTV

Aerospace & Defense Co.; Martin-Marietta Information Systems; Rockwell International Inc.; Textron Inc.; British Aerospace Inc.; Hicks & Associates; and Jeford-McManus International Inc. Senator Tower received a total of $1,028,777 (gross receipts) from these firms during the approximately two and one-half years he provided such services.

In the 13 months prior to his employment as a defense consultant, Senator Tower served as the Chief U.S. Negotiator for the Strategic Arms Reduction Talks (START) in Geneva. Shortly after leaving those ongoing talks, he became a consultant to companies, such as Martin-Marietta, Rockwell International, and Textron, that are engaged in programs that are related to or under discussions in START, including the MX missile, the Midgetman missile, the Titan II and Titan IV space boosters, the Advance Launch System, enhanced guidance and control for the Minuteman missile, research and development on advanced missiles and re-entry vehicle systems, support and follow-on activities for the B-1B bomber, and systems related to the Strategic Defense Initiative (SDI).

The State Department has issued guidance governing post-employment activities, which cautions against disclosure of "inside" information, as well as classified and administratively controlled information. Former employees are advised to take care not to communicate any confidential information to subsequent employers.

Although Senator Tower's consulting clients had an enormous stake in programs which could be directly affected by the outcome of the START talks, he did not take care to avoid discussing the probable results of the talks with them. According to his testimony before the Committee, he provided advice to his clients on the "implications of INF and other arms control negotiations on ... future product development." Senator Tower also testified that he advised his clients on the "probable outcomes" of the arms control talks.

Although Senator Tower told the Committee that his advice was based on "enlightened guesswork" and publicly available information, the rapid shift from status as a negotiator to status as a consultant—giving advice on the probable outcomes of ongoing negotiations—created the appearance of using inside information for private gain.

As a result of his involvement in START negotiations and access to the parallel INF and Space and Defensive Systems negotiations, Senator Tower possessed the most sensitive information that could be obtained on the impact of the negotiations on a contractor's "future product development." Senator Tower, as a key arms control envoy, would have been aware of U.S. negotiating strategies, real U.S. goals, fallback positions, and potential "quid pro quo" trade-off offers that were proposed and debated by the U.S. interagency process, whether or not the particular options were approved. He would thus have gained considerable insight into the likely future directions of the negotiations after his departure. This would include clear understandings regarding those U.S. START positions that were non-negotiable, and those positions from which we were or might be prepared to retreat, under some conditions.

Senator Tower's position gave him insight into the U.S. position on unresolved issues within the general START framework, including banning all mobile ICBMs, establishing "counting rules" for bombers, dealing with strategic defenses, and determining allowed numbers of non-deployed missiles. Furthermore, access to the interagency deliberations would have provided Senator Tower with insight into the views of the Office of the Secretary of Defense, Joint Chiefs of Staff, and the individual military Services on proposed budget levels for strategic systems or on new start decisions for individual weapons system proposals.

The Committee has long recognized the importance of a healthy interchange between the public and private sectors, particularly in terms of encouraging people from industry with technical and managerial skills to engage in public service. But Senator Tower's decision to provide consulting services on arms control matters so soon after serving as an arms control negotiator crossed a line with regard to the "revolving door" which is of great concern to the Committee.

Senator Tower showed poor judgment by placing himself in a situation in which there was such an obvious tension between the information he acquired as an arms control negotiator and his obligations to his consulting clients. The Committee has no evidence that Senator Tower provided his clients with classified information. In the Committee's judgment, however, this situation created the appearance of using public office for private gain and casts doubt on his ability to command public confidence in the integrity of the defense acquisition system. In his own testimony before the Committee, Senator Tower noted the importance of public confidence: "... if we are to maintain a strong defense establishment in this country, we must restore public confidence, not just in the Pentagon but in the national security process." Similarly, he testified: "... we do have to be concerned about public perceptions because I think the essence of what is required for democracy to succeed is public confidence in their institutions, popular confidence in public institutions, stated better."

Senator Tower's testimony before the Committee does not reflect a sensitivity to "revolving door" problems:

> The Chairman: "Would it be wrong to give advice, not giving the negotiating position to a client, but to give advice that really was based on that knowledge?"
>
> Senator Tower: "Now you are getting into some intangibles here. It is a pretty grey area and it is kind of difficult to come up with a conclusive answer on that. Let me say that I do not believe that I ever did anything or gave any advice that was improper."

* * *

> Senator Levin: "... In your situation, do you see that there is an appearance problem, when the chief negotiator, an ambassador to START talks, then leaves those talks and advises clients who have a very heavy stake in the outcome of those talks? In that situation,

without suggesting any impropriety in actuality, without suggesting in the slightest that you advised them of confidential or privileged information, just the fact that you are advising them, as you put it, on probable outcomes of those talks, do you see an appearance problem there? That is my question."

Senator Tower: "I do not see it, Senator, because the question has not been raised until now. Nobody has ever questioned me on that before now...."

As President Bush noted earlier this year, "government should be an opportunity for public service, not private gain." He noted as a "guiding principle" that government employees must "avoid even the appearance of what is wrong." Senator Tower possessed a wealth of "inside" information on the arms control negotiations. Because of his position, his advice to his clients on effect of the "probable outcomes" of these negotiations on their product development was valuable to the clients. In that circumstance, he created the appearance of using public office for private gain.

The Ill Wind investigation into DOD procurement fraud—coming less than two years after the Packard Commission described the acquisition system as "fundamentally ill"—has substantially undermined public confidence in the acquisition process. The public must develop confidence that acquisition decisions are based on competent, expert decisions, rather than calculations flowing through a revolving door.

It is critical that the new Secretary of Defense act vigorously to reform the defense acquisition process, which has been plagued by allegations of illegal and unethical practices, and restore public confidence in the integrity of defense management. Senator Tower's own activities would greatly complicate efforts to accomplish these tasks. His post-START consulting employment reflected insensitivity to the appearance that he has used inside information for private gain. His activities would weaken public confidence that defense acquisition decisions will be based solely on the public interest.

Behavior Toward Women

The Committee examined a number of allegations concerning the nominee's behavior toward women. The Committee's record on this issue demonstrates no finding of liaisons with female foreign nationals and, hence, no security violations that such activities would entail. Nor does the record support the allegation that the nominee exerted sexual pressure on employees and associates of the opposite sex. There are, however, a number of examples of personal conduct which the Committee found indiscreet and which call into question Senator Tower's judgment. These examples add to the cumulative body of concern the Committee has about this nomination.

The Committee is also concerned about the personal example that the Secretary of Defense must set for efforts in the Department of Defense to end discrimination toward, and sexual harassment of, women. The U.S. Armed Forces have been asked to fully integrate women into the force, treating them equally in all ways, except for combat eligibility. Serious problems still exist, however, with the status and treatment of women in the military. In this regard, the Secretary of Defense's conduct must be beyond reproach and must meet the highest moral standards. . . .

Minority Report

[Signed by Sens. John Warner (Va.), Strom Thurmond (S.C.), William S. Cohen (Maine), Pete Wilson (Calif.), John McCain (Ariz.), Malcolm Wallop (Wyo.), Slade Gordon (Wash.), Trent Lott (Miss.), and Daniel R. Coats (Ind.), all Republicans.]

We, the nine Republican Members of this Committee, with many years of combined personal knowledge and observation of and experience with the Honorable John Goodwin Tower, do hereby dissent and disassociate ourselves from the vote and recommendation of the eleven Democrat Members of the Committee that the Senate should not confirm John Tower to be Secretary of Defense. Rather, we as a group, and each of us individually, find that John Tower is highly qualified to serve as Secretary of Defense, and therefore do recommend to the Senate that it advise and consent to the President's nomination of John Tower.

We reject the recommendation of the Majority because it is *apparently* based upon a body of fact and allegation lacking the weight of corroboration required by Senate precedents of 200 years. Those precedents accord a President the right to select his advisers, and such precedents have been exercised in support of a President several hundred times for a Cabinet position and denied in but eight instances.

By electing to base their vote and recommendation on this information, the Majority of the Committee has chosen to reject, as unworthy of belief, the single most credible body of evidence available to the Senate: the personal knowledge and experience of the 70 Members of the Senate today who served with John Tower in the Senate, including that of 14 Members of this Committee. To our knowledge, not a single one of those 70 Members, whose combined period of service with John Tower exceeds 650 years, has brought to the Committee's attention personal knowledge of even a single incident calling into question John Tower's fitness to serve as Secretary of Defense. Rather, prior to the President's nomination of John Tower on January 20, 1989, 12 of those Members were asked for their opinion and gave their recommendation for John Tower to serve as Secretary of Defense. Among those giving such a favorable recommendation are six Democrat Members of this Committee.

Their dramatic change of position is apparently based on those Members' belief that credible evidence before the Committee raises four concerns, namely: (1) a concern that the nominee is perceived to have a conflict of interest; (2) a generalized concern about the nominee's attitude toward women; (3) a concern that the nominee has a "problem" with alcohol; and (4) a concern that the nominee would be unable effectively to perform his duties because of questions that have been raised publicly about the other three concerns, regardless of whether the evidence justifies those other concerns. In order to make clear our reasons for recommending that John Tower be confirmed, it is necessary that we set forth our views of each of these issues, and do so under the handicap of being unable to refer publicly to facts in the Committee record, including the FBI report. It is imperative that the confidentiality of this record be maintained.

First, the nominee has no legal or actual conflict between his personal financial interests and the public interests which he would be asked to represent as Secretary of Defense. He has no remaining financial interest in any firm or entity which does any business with the Department of Defense. Without such personal interests, there can be no conflict. There is no official act that the nominee could take or fail to take that would result in his financial status being altered in any way. The nominee has severed all previous connections with firms that contract with the Department of Defense and has agreed not to acquire any interest in such firms during his tenure as Secretary of Defense. The nominee has fully complied with the law applicable to Federal officials concerning conflict of interests, specifically, the Ethics in Government Act of 1978, with all Executive Branch regulations applicable to conflict of interests, and with all previously announced standards of this Committee. In short, the nominee meets all tests previously used by this Committee in evaluating whether a nominee is qualified to serve with respect to conflict of interests. Therefore, if the Majority view is to be justified, the Majority must now be applying some new standard to this nominee.

What is this new standard that the Majority now apparently seeks to apply to this nominee and, we must presume, all other nominees to positions in the Department of Defense? Apparently, that standard, as best as can be determined from the public statements of Majority Members, is that a nominee could be found unfit to serve, even when it is clear that no legal or actual conflict exists, if a "perceived" conflict arises about a nominee's interests. We reject such a standard as unfair to this nominee and to all of those who would aspire to public service in the future.

Not only has John Tower complied with all laws, regulations, and defined standards of this Committee regarding conflicts of interest, he has taken an extra step by announcing his pledge to recuse himself from any suspension or debarment issues which may arise in the Department of Defense involving any of his previous defense contractor consulting clients. This step was taken voluntarily by the nominee to remove even the appearance that he would have a conflict of interest.

We find that John Tower has no legal or actual conflict between his private interests and the public interests he is being asked to represent. We find that John Tower has taken all actions with respect to his personal financial affairs required by law, regulation, and recognized standards of this Committee and the Senate. We cannot and will not cast our votes so as to suggest that this or any other nominee must bear the burden of removing public misperceptions.

Second, a generalized concern has been expressed about the nominee's attitude toward women. We accept the Chairman's statement that the record "does not support the allegation that the nominee exerted sexual pressure on employees or associates of the opposite sex." We also find no evidence that the nominee ever denied an individual a fair and equal opportunity for employment or advancement based upon an individual's gender. Rather, while serving in the Senate and other public and private positions, the nominee has actively encouraged and supported the professional advancement of highly qualified female employees and associates. Furthermore, we specifically find no evidence worthy of belief that the nominee ever had any improper relationship with females while serving as a START negotiator in Geneva.

We must record our view that only a limited portion of a nominee's personal relationships with members of the opposite sex is properly subject to review and concern by this Committee in judging a nominee's fitness for office in the Department of Defense. This Committee clearly has a responsibility to ensure that a nominee for a position in the Department of Defense is not and has not been involved in any illegal or improper relationship with a member of the opposite sex which could, because of the illegality or impropriety, render the nominee subject to blackmail, pose a threat to the national security, or embarrass the United States. This Committee has closely examined this issue and has found no evidence to indicate that this nominee has ever been involved in such a situation.

Beyond the issue of work and professional relationships, which are clearly relevant to a nominee's fitness to serve as an official in the Department of Defense, we believe that a nominee's relationships with members of the opposite sex are properly treated as private and are not subject to this Committee's scrutiny.

Third, the Majority has concluded that John Tower should not be confirmed as Secretary of Defense because he has some undefined problem with alcohol use. Since the Majority has failed to define clearly the standard to which they seek to hold the nominee with respect to alcohol use during his tenure as Secretary of Defense, it is not possible for us to provide our analysis of whether the evidence concerning the nominee's use of alcohol fails to meet this moving target. Therefore, we opt to set forth clearly the standard which we believe should apply with respect to a Cabinet nominee.

We believe that this Committee, the Senate as a whole, and the American people have a right to expect and demand that the person occupying a Cabinet position will be at all times while serving in that position fully capable, mentally and physically, to carry out all responsibilities of that office, whether those responsibilities arise from law or from Presidential direction. We find no evidence, or even a corroborated allegation, that John Tower could not or would not fully meet this highest of standards during his tenure as Secretary of Defense.

John Tower has testified that he is not now nor has he ever been dependent on alcohol. We accept that testimony as truthful; we are not aware of any credible evidence to the contrary. John Tower has freely stated that, during the 1970's, he consumed substantial amounts. Likewise, we accept that testimony as truthful, as we are aware of no dispute with that position. However, at the same time we find no evidence that even during this period of time, while the nominee served in the United States Senate, he ever permitted his use of alcohol to interfere with any of the duties of that office. To the contrary, we believe the actual experiences of the Members of the Senate who served with him and the experiences of those who worked for him during that period constitute the best evidence—uncontrovertible evidence—of the nominee's ability to maintain control over his use of alcohol during that period. To our knowledge, there has not been a single piece of evidence brought to the Committee's attention by any Member or former Member that contradicts our findings in this regard.

The nominee has also represented that, in the late 1970's, he altered his tastes for alcohol, so that his use of liquor diminished and he enjoyed primarily wine. He has testified that, even more recently, he has limited his alcohol drinking to wine with meals. Once again, we find that testimony supported by the evidence. While there is some evidence that the nominee occasionally has a drink of liquor, we find that to be of little consequence. We are again struck by the total lack of any credible evidence even suggesting that the nominee has at any time been unable or neglected to perform each and every public duty and responsibility which was entrusted to him.

During the 1980's, these public duties included those of United States Senator, Chairman of this Committee, United States Ambassador and negotiator to START, and Chairman of the President's Special Review Board on the Iran-Contra Affair. Not one iota of credible evidence even suggests that the nominee ever failed to be both physically and mentally ready and able to perform every duty then entrusted to him, regardless of the time of day or night when he was called upon to perform those duties. If the Senate seeks support of our view in this regard, we especially recommend a review of the evidence concerning Senator Tower's use of alcoholic beverages, limited as it was, while serving as arms control negotiator in Geneva. We find it especially telling that the evidence about the nominee's alcohol use while negotiating with the Soviets indicates virtually no use except at formal or delegation functions. This body of evidence, or more precisely, this lack of evidence, strengthens our conviction that John Tower is in complete control of any use of alcohol and that he fully recognizes that the requirements of a particular public office require differing standards on the use of alcohol.

The ultimate question is whether there is any evidence that the nominee could not or would not, because of alcohol use, always be fully capable, both mentally and physically, to carry out the duties and responsibilities of the Office of Secretary of Defense. We agree completely with the nominee that this position is one that requires that capability 24 hours a day, 365 days a year. We believed John Tower when he told this Committee that he would never use alcohol while Secretary of Defense in any way that might ever compromise his ability to exercise those responsibilities.

John Tower has now taken the ultimate step—he has solemnly pledged that he will consume no alcoholic beverages during his tenure as Secretary of Defense. This extraordinary act, occurring *after* we had already reached our conclusion that John Tower is fully qualified to serve as Secretary of Defense, should assuage any concerns of Members about the nominee's use of alcohol.

Our review of the totality of the evidence concerning the nominee's alcohol use through the years supports our firm view that John Tower has never allowed alcohol to interfere with the performance of his duties, whatever those duties were at the time. We find no reason to believe, and cannot believe, that

119

this dedicated public servant would suddenly permit that to occur as he assumes the duties of the most important position he has ever been asked to hold.

Finally, it seems that some Members of the Majority may justify their votes, not upon any specific evidence concerning the nominee's performance or conduct, but rather by expressing doubts about his ability to be an effective Secretary of Defense because they perceive that he has been damaged by the rumor and innuendo of recent weeks. We reject that view as unfair not only to this nominee but to the Senate and the Nation. We have known John Tower, many of us for years. He is not and will not be weakened by gossip and rumor. Furthermore, we do not and will not concede that this or any other nominee's fitness can be judged by the number of allegations that can be recorded against him during the course of a confirmation process. To base a confirmation decision on such criteria is to convert the Constitutional advise and consent power into nothing more than a popularity contest. Permitting fears about the possible effect of rumor and innuendo to become the basis for decisions on a nominee's fitness to serve amounts to an admission that this Committee, and the Senate as a whole, cannot distinguish between fact and fiction. We do not believe that to be the case. The facts show that John Tower is fully and ably qualified to serve as the Secretary of Defense—the facts are not and cannot be altered by allegation, rumor, or innuendo. We choose to rely on the facts.

In summary, there is broad agreement that John Tower is highly qualified to serve as Secretary of Defense based upon his knowledge, experience, and proven public record of performance in many demanding assignments. His grasp of the national security issues facing this Nation is unquestioned. He is the President's choice to be his principal assistant on the role of the Department of Defense in our nation's overall national security. There is not that weight of evidence, as measured by the precedents of 200 years in the United States Senate, to vote to deny the President his steadfast choice for this Cabinet post. In fact, there is an affirmative duty for us to act in support of the President.

Therefore, we the nine Republican Members of this Committee on Armed Services, do record our disagreement with the vote of the Committee's Majority, and do recommend to the Senate that it give its consent to the President's nomination of the Honorable John Goodwin Tower to be the Secretary of Defense.

March

**Bicentennial Commemorations of
Congress and Inaugural** 123

Brady Plan for World Debt Relief 137

Gorbachev's New Farm Policy 145

Toxic Waste Treaty. 153

**Agreements on the Future
of the Contras** 161

**Remarks on Soviet Election and
Perestroika.** 173

Court Rulings on America's Cup Race 183

Pleas for Higher Judiciary Pay 195

BICENTENNIAL COMMEMORATIONS OF CONGRESS AND INAUGURAL

March 2 and April 30, 1989

The federal government marked two hundred years of existence in 1989 with events commemorating the First Congress and the first presidential inauguration. On March 2 in Washington, D.C., the House and Senate met together in the House chambers to hear lawmakers and invited guests appraise the significance of the First Congress and its imprint on two centuries of legislative government. Congress initially convened and George Washington became president in New York City, the temporary seat of the new government devised by the recently ratified U.S. Constitution. Accordingly, a bicentennial reenactment of the first inaugural was staged in New York on April 30.

Although all three branches of the federal government trace their origins to 1789, Congress organized first. It had to, in order to count the electoral votes and confirm Washington's election, and later to pass legislation organizing the executive and judicial branches. The First Congress intended to convene March 4, 1789, but lawmakers from only five states had arrived in New York. Twenty-nine days passed before there was a quorum and business could begin. In one of the lawmakers' first acts, they met in joint session April 6 and formally declared Washington president. It was an easy task; the eleven states that had then ratified the Constitution (all except North Carolina and Rhode Island) cast all their electoral votes for him.

Washington received the news a few days later at his Virginia plantation, and departed on April 16, confiding to his diary: "I bade adieu to Mount Vernon, to private life, and to domestic felicity, and with a mind more oppressed than I have words to express, I set out for New York. . . . "

His misgivings apparently were not shared by citizens along his journey. He was feted in Baltimore, Wilmington, Chester, Philadelphia, Trenton, New Brunswick, Elizabeth, and finally in New York itself. Masses of people lined the waterfront of lower Manhattan Island to cheer his arrival April 23, by barge from the New Jersey shore. Amid the roar of gunfire salutes from ships in the harbor, he was received ashore by a collection of state and local dignitaries, and thousands of other New Yorkers. They cheered him along a short parade route to his new official residence at 3 Cherry Street, where another round of receptions began. One week later, Washington took the oath of office in an elaborate ceremony at Federal Hall, at the corner of Wall and Broad streets, in the heart of the present-day financial district.

With touches of eighteenth-century pomp, the inauguration of two hundred years earlier was reenacted at Federal Hall. To a crowd assembled below a platform extending from the Greek Revival columns at the edifice's front entrance, a bewigged actor (William Somerfield) repeated the oath of office in the words that Washington and all succeeding presidents have used. He promised to faithfully execute the office of president of the United States, and to the best of his ability defend and protect the Constitution. Washington was sworn into office at the same site, but he stood on the front portico of an ornate building that was replaced by the present one in 1814. The building then became the U.S. government's Subtreasury—reflecting New York's rising status as the nation's financial center—and in this century was renamed Federal Hall and designated a national historic site, operated by the U.S. Park Service.

As the inaugural scene was described by Douglas Southall Freeman, Washington's preeminent biographer, the new president bent forward and kissed the Bible on which he had placed his hand during the oathtaking. Robert R. Livingston, the chancellor of New York, who administered the oath, turned to the crowd and shouted: "It is done! Long live George Washington, President of the United States!" The onlookers took up the congratulatory cry, adding to the din of ringing church bells and booming cannons.

Whereas Somerfield read Washington's inaugural address from the platform to the latter-day crowd, Washington himself made the speech inside the building, in the Senate's new chambers. It was heard only by the members of Congress—then eighty-four in all—and a small group of other ranking officials, including Vice President John Adams. The speech was brief, only 1,425 words, pared down from a draft of seventy-five pages—on the advice of James Madison, Washington's secretary.

About the only matter of substance in the speech was Washington's recommendation that Congress approve action to amend the Constitution to meet objections raised against it. The two holdout states objected to the absence of a Bill of Rights, and some other states had agreed to accept the new government only with the understanding that those rights would soon be spelled out in the Constitution. The First Congress promptly approved for state ratification what became the first ten amendments, the Bill of Rights.

Washington, characteristically, also said he would refuse a salary and accept only expenses. And he expressed hope that his countrymen would forgive the errors he was bound to make. To carry out his work, he asked the assistance of "the Almighty Being who rules over the universe." After he spoke, Washington led his audience on foot to St. Paul's Chapel, an Episcopal church that he attended in New York, for a "Service of Thanksgiving."

This service was repeated for President George Bush and his entourage at the conclusion of the bicentennial reenactment, at which the forty-first president spoke. "How unlikely it must have seemed then that we might become United States," Bush said in his speech. "How uncertain that a republic could be hewn out of the wilderness of competing interests. How awesome the prospect must have seemed."

> *Following are excerpts from speeches at the 101st Congress's joint session March 2, 1989, commemorating the bicentennial of the First Congress, as recorded in the* Congressional Record; *and excerpts from the White House text of President Bush's speech in New York April 30, at the reenactment of the nation's first presidential inauguration:*

COMMEMORATIVE REMARKS IN CONGRESS

The SPEAKER. The Chair recognizes the gentlewoman from Louisiana, the Honorable LINDY BOGGS, Chairman of the Commission on the Bicentenary of the House of Representatives.

Mrs. BOGGS. Mr. Speaker, Mr. Vice President, leaders of the House and Senate, Members of the House and Senate, distinguished guests, ladies and gentlemen, it is my great honor to welcome you to this joint meeting in commemoration of the 200th anniversary of Congress. This occasion is a very special part of the celebration of the Bicentennial of Congress, which will be marked by historical publications, ceremonies, exhibits, a special film, and other activities during 1989.

All three branches of the Federal Government trace their beginnings to 1789, but it was Congress which assembled first, and successfully launched the United States of America. So, it is fitting that the first branch assemble on this day in recognition of the noble work of our predecessors and in anticipation of the events yet to come that will celebrate the executive and judicial branches.

As today's ceremony began, officers of the House and Senate brought into the Chamber some special objects that are dear to Congress. The two Journals, one for the House and one for the Senate, contain the record of the beginning of Congress in 1789. Each legislative day for the past two centuries the House and Senate have recorded their actions and formally approved their Journals. They represent our beginnings as a legislature, and they are symbols of the unbroken record of two centuries of representative government under the U.S. Constitution.

These two particular copies of the Journals were George Washington's personal copies and they are kept at the National Archives.

The mace of the House of Representatives, a silver eagle atop a silver globe of the world, supported by 13 ebony rods, each representing one of the Original Thirteen States, is a symbol of authority of the House.

This particular mace has been used since 1841, and is always in the Chamber when the House is in session.

The ivory gavel is one of the great treasures of the Senate. According to tradition, John Adams, the Nation's first Vice President, used the gavel at the first session of the Senate in 1789. Thomas Jefferson may have used this same gavel to call the Senate to order when he was Vice President of the United States and President of the Senate from 1797 to 1801. Jefferson compiled his Manual of Parliamentary Practice to guide him as he presided over the Senate. Those rules are still consulted almost 200 years later.

Behind me on the Speaker's desk sits an old silver inkwell that has been in the House for at least 168 years. It appears in a portrait of Henry Clay of Kentucky painted in 1821. Clay was the first great Speaker of the House, and went on to a distinguished career as one of the greatest U.S. Senators in history.

We have gathered these volumes and these special artifacts to remind us of the past and to show the continuity of the traditions of Congress, traditions which are as strong today as they were in the past.

It is my great pleasure to introduce to you Senator ROBERT C. BYRD, the President pro tempore of the Senate and the Chairman of the Senate Bicentennial Commission. . . .

Senator BYRD. . . .

The ink had only barely dried on the new Constitution which two of the Original Thirteen States had not yet ratified. The newly elected President, George Washington, waited to be sworn into office; nor had the Vice President taken his oath. Neither of the two constitutional officers of Congress, the Speaker of the House and the President pro tempore of the Senate, had been elected. The Cabinet, the Supreme Court, and the entire Federal judiciary remained mere phrases in the Constitution, as yet unformed by legislation.

Members of the First Congress set about to mold the aspiration of the Constitutional Convention into the reality of a government that would unite the separate States into a Nation, a government that would forge the citizens of these States into one people, a government that would preserve domestic tranquility and defend against foreign aggression, a government that would divide power into three branches, with checks and balances among them to prevent any part of it from becoming tyrannical. Moreover, it was a government and a nation that could grow.

In 1791 Congress voted to admit Vermont as the first new State outside the original 13. Over the course of the next two centuries, the Nation expanded across the continent and to the Pacific and into the Pacific. Today a majority of us represent States that not only did not exist in 1789 but also whose areas at that time lay under foreign control. A map of 1789 would show my own State of West Virginia as simply the western region of Virginia, still 74 years and a bloody Civil War away from separate statehood.

Whether those of us in this 101st Congress represent one of the Original Thirteen States or one of the additional 37 States, the commonwealth of Puerto Rico, the District of Columbia, and American Samoa, Guam or the Virgin Islands, we share a commonality to our predecessors in the First Congress, and we are here today as a result of the work done by them and by succeeding generations of Senators and Representatives. We have inherited from them the responsibility for making the laws of this Nation, for determining the course today, and into the future centuries. We celebrate 200 years of history, a proud accomplishment of the democratic government and a representative national legislature. . . .

The PRESIDENT pro tempore (presiding). The Chair recognizes the Speaker of the U.S. House of Representatives, Mr. JIM WRIGHT.

Mr. WRIGHT. Two hundred years ago the First Congress came to New York to breathe life into the new Constitution and to make a reality of the dream and promise of representative self-government.

Members of the new Congress arriving in New York were greeted by flags, musical salutes, church bells, and the roar of cannons. They, as well as the crowds that greeted them, were keenly aware that they were plowing new ground. They were attempting to create something unique in history. Madison said, "We are in a wilderness without a single footprint to guide us."

There were 59 Representatives and 22 Senators representing those 11 States which had ratified the new government at that point. Eight of them had served as delegates to the Constitutional Convention. All but two of them had served at some point in public office.

After reviewing the roster of the New Congress, an optimistic George Washington proudly proclaimed that "it will not be inferior to any assembly on Earth." A somewhat less enthusiastic James Madison, on the other hand, seemed to discern in the very distinctions that adorned the names of the Members of the House a cause for concern because he said, "I see on the list of representatives a very scanty proportion who will share in the drudgery of business."

The new House did not exactly get off to a running start. Only five States were represented on that first day, March 4, 1789, and it took 25 false attempts over a period of 29 days just to establish a quorum, without which they were unable to elect a Speaker and get down to business.

But get down to business they finally did. Even before George Washington could be inaugurated the new House had taken up the tariff bill to provide the needed revenue to run the new government and to pay off some of the debts that they had accumulated during the Revolutionary War. Oh yes, they already had a national debt. It was so severe in relative terms that Spain, which then owned Florida, was offering to help bail out the new government with cash payments to buy the Carolinas.

That first Congress, to its credit and to our lasting benefit, accumulated a very impressive legislative record. It gave form to the executive branch of Government by creating the Departments of State, Treasury, War and the Office of the Attorney General. It gave substance to the judicial branch of government by establishing the Supreme Court, a system of lesser Federal courts, and establishing a criminal code for the United States.

It began to tie together the thin sprinkling of pioneer settlements scattered along this eastern seaboard into one cohesive nation by authorizing a system of roads and bridges, trails and navigable streams.

But surely its most celebrated and most enduring contribution to the future was the writing by the First Congress of that lasting testament to individual human liberty, the American Bill of Rights.

Now for 200 years Congress has been a mirror of the nation—a distillate of our national strengths and weaknesses. Hale Boggs described it as a collection of ordinary men and women grappling with extraordinary problems.

William Redfield said Congress was "a fair cross-section of the people, showing us very much as we are and throwing our faults and virtues into high relief." Samuel Johnson, speaking for the ratification of the Constitution before the North Carolina Convention, sought to describe the quality and character of those Representatives whose election had been mandated by the Constitution. He said, "They are to be bone of our bone, flesh of our flesh."

In all of this the U.S. Congress is probably the most fascinatingly human institution in the world. It is beyond question the most criticized legislative assembly on Earth, and still the most honored. It can rise to heights of sparkling statesmanship, and it can sink to levels of crass mediocrity. In both postures it is supremely interesting precisely because it is human. The story of Congress is the story of people.

We were visited in 1831 by a distinguished French aristocrat named Alexis de Tocqueville who later wrote about American democracy. De Tocqueville was greatly impressed by the intellectual caliber of people in the Senate who at that time were not directly elected by the public, but rather chosen by State legislatures. But he was negatively impressed by the quality that he discerned in the House. He spoke of our "vulgarity and poverty of talent." These characteristics, which he thought created a general worthlessness to the House of Representatives, de Tocqueville attributed to the fact that its Members were directly elected, democratically, by the people. That French nobleman boldly prophesied that, unless the method of choosing Representatives was changed, this American Republic stood under the doom of "perishing miserably among the shoals of democracy." Well, that was 158 years ago.

In 1925, the House Speaker, Nicholas Longworth, philosophically opined that "from the beginning of the Republic it has been the duty of every freeborn voter to look down upon us and the duty of every freeborn humorist to make jokes about us." Not to neglect that duty, Will Rogers commented in about that same period that America had no distinctive indigenous criminal class—"except, of course for the Congress."

Even so, the Congress—called by Thomas Jefferson "the great commanding theater of the Nation," by another historian, the grand repository of the democratic principle, the butt of cartoonists, crusaders, and comedians alike—has endured for 200 years as the fulcrum of our system of representative self-government.

In this tripartite system, Congress sometimes has been overshadowed by a charismatic executive. Yet the Congress has managed in all circumstances to muddle through, sometimes leading and sometimes lagging, sometimes leaping and sometimes limping.

Toward the end of his career Sam Rayburn once was asked, "How many Presidents have you served under?"

The crusty old Texan snorted and replied, "Huh, I haven't served under any. I've served with eight."

And that system of representative self-government, of which Congress is an integral and indispensable part, with all its faults, and flaws and mortal imperfections, still is—just as it was in Lincoln's time, and may it forever remain—the last best hope of the Earth. [Applause.]

The PRESIDENT pro tempore. The Chair recognizes the Senator from Maine, the Honorable GEORGE MITCHELL, the majority leader of the U.S. Senate.

Senator MITCHELL. . . .

In 1830, John Quincy Adams was elected to the House of Representatives. He had previously served as an ambassador, as Secretary of State, and as President, yet he wrote of his election to the House, "My election as President of the United States was not half so gratifying." His sentiments were understood by the people of his time, but they would not be understood by the people of our time.

In the 20th century, and especially in the age of television, many, if not most, Americans have come to view the executive as the primary branch of government. That was not intended by the Members who wrote the Constitution. The Constitution's first article, which describes the powers of Congress, is longer than the other seven articles combined, and that is why Congress is called the first branch of Government. I do not claim that Congress is the primary branch, but I do remind all that it is a coequal branch of Government.

Indeed an independent legislature is a distinguishing feature of democracy. All forms of government have executives. In totalitarian societies that is usually all there is. Where legislatures exist in those societies they are merely tokens, wholly subservient to the executive.

This 101st Congress is part of the most successful effort at self-government in all human history. The brilliant success of the Founding Fathers is evidenced in the fact that in our two centuries of history we have had 41 presidents and no kings. No institution has contributed more to that happy result than the Congress.

Together the two Houses of Congress enact all legislation. Together they can override Presidential vetoes. The House originates revenue bills. The Senate's advice and consent is necessary for the ratification of treaties. The Constitution entrusts Congress with the power to tax, to provide for the common defense and general welfare. The Congress has the authority to regulate commerce, to establish a judicial system, to declare war, to raise and support the Army and the Navy.

With that broad authority comes great responsibility. It is our responsibility to use the power with which we have been entrusted for the common good. . . .

The SPEAKER. The Chair recognizes the gentleman from Washington, The Honorable THOMAS S. FOLEY, majority leader of the U.S. House of Representatives.

Mr. FOLEY. . . . [W]hen the crowds cheered and cannons roared, as Speaker WRIGHT has said, on the First Congress' meeting in New York on March 4, 1789, the quarters which they were to inhabit were not yet finished, causing them to convene in makeshift circumstances. The first Members were planters and merchants and, as today, about a third of them were lawyers. There were . . . a few clergymen as Members as well. Despite a slow and rather disappointing start to their work, they obtained a brilliant conclusion, allowing Fisher Ames, a Member of the First Congress, to say of his colleagues that they were "on the whole, very good men, not shining, but honest and reasonably well informed."

Congressional terms overlap; individuals come and go—sometimes without much fanfare. Influences change, recede. I believe, however, I speak for the more than 10,000 of us who have served in the House of Representatives and over 11,000 who have served in the Congress, in saying that for most of us it has been the greatest pride and honor of our lives. . . .

John Quincy Adams returned to serve in the House of Representatives after being President of the United States, considering it a great honor to do so. According to the 63-year-old Mr. Adams, "No election or appointment conferred upon me ever gave me so much pleasure.". . .

With the great honor of being a Member of Congress has come throughout the years of our history close scrutiny and criticism, both individually and as an institution. That is appropriate, because the great pride of our service is that unlike great Cabinet officers or judges, we are here not by the appointment of the President, but by the election of the people.

The Congress has changed dramatically over the years with the coming of radio and television. It is perhaps the most closely followed branch of our government, clearly the most observed and commented upon. We are the only branch of Government that conducts its day-to-day business not only under the scrutiny of television, but in an almost verbatim RECORD. While the CONGRESSIONAL RECORD will perhaps never appear on the best-seller list, it does lay open to the American people, as does television coverage, the business that goes on here, their business.

We have perhaps the longest-standing continuous assembly in the world, along with that of Great Britain and its commonwealth. But it is perhaps only here that Members have an opportunity from the very first day of their service to participate directly in the affairs of the institution and to have the opportunity to actively serve the people of their State or their district in an immediate way.

We are, unfortunately, sometimes victims of the perception that the business of the Congress is somewhat disorderly and confused. This is because the business of making legislation is also the business of compromise and adjustment. That is not always understood. Although it is considered by some to be making a "deal" or trading away principles, it is, when done with principle, the most compelling and important of public business.

"The Congress," Woodrow Wilson said, "has been both extravagantly praised and unreasonably disparaged, according to the predisposition and temper of its various critics. The truth is," he said, "in this case as in so many others, something quite commonplace and practical. The Congress is just what the mode of its election and the conditions of public life in this country make it."

When the First Congress completed its work in 1789, it had, as the Speaker indicated, brilliant, almost unequalled results, to the point that journalists and other observers of the day in commenting on its achievements, decided that they had been truly phenomenal.

A friend wrote to Vice President Adams that "In no nation, by no legislature, was ever so much done in so short a period for the establishment of government, order and public credit and generally tranquillity.". . .

The SPEAKER. The Chair recognizes the Senator from Kansas, the Honorable BOB DOLE, minority leader of the U.S. Senate.

Senator DOLE. . . . During the last Congress I delivered a series of Bicentennial minutes offering vignettes on important or colorful or unusual events that happened in the Senate's history. White putting these together, I was repeatedly surprised to find Members of Congress wrestling with issues 100 and even 200 years ago that were as current as the headlines in today's newspapers. As the Speaker said, we were confronting Federal deficits. They were struggling with pay raises or helping a President get his nominees confirmed, and I find examples demonstrating that we have been doing it for 200 years.

Take today's joint gathering. In a sense it has been stated previously that this really commemorates today the first absence of the quorum because, although we officially began on March 4, 1789, they could not get a quorum, and we did not have the first real joint meeting until April 5, 1789. On that first occasion Members of the House walked up to the Senate Chamber in New York Federal Hall to count the electoral votes confirming George Washington's election as President.

The last joint session, prior to today's joint meeting, took place a month

131

ago when Members of the Senate walked through the Capitol of the House Chamber to hear President George Bush. During the two centuries in between joint meetings, we have heard Presidents, kings, prime ministers, admirals, and astronauts. In the past here stood Winston Churchill, Chester Nimitz, Carl Sandburg, Charles deGaulle, Neil Armstrong, Anwar Sadat, and Margaret Thatcher. Here Gen. Douglas MacArthur told a joint meeting in Congress that "old soldiers never die, they just fade away." Those were memorable moments in our history.

Beyond such out-of-the ordinary events as joint meetings, 1989 will mark the 200th anniversary of many of Congress' everyday routines. It was in 1789 that the House and Senate appointed their first committees, convened their first conference committees, elected their first officers, adopted their first rules, wrote and took their first oaths of office and enacted their first legislation, confirmed their first nomination, and established the first Cabinet officers, thereby beginning their first oversight of executive agencies.

Today, if you wonder why the clerks of the Senate and the House bow when they deliver bills and messages in each House, that was prescribed by the First Congress. If you ever wonder why we formally address our Chief Executive as the President of the United States of America, the First Congress decided that.

The first choice, by the way, of a special Senate Committee on Titles was: His Highness, President of the United States of America and Protector of the Rights of the Same. . . .

The House Chaplain who opened this session with a prayer and the Senate Chaplain who will close it are the successors of Chaplains chosen by the First Congress. So, too, are the Secretary of the Senate and the Clerk of the House who presented the Journals of Congress, Journals which are still being recorded by our clerks today.

About the only job you would not have found in that First Congress was mine, or GEORGE MITCHELL'S or BOB MICHEL'S or TOM FOLEY'S. There were no party leaders in the First Congress because there were no political parties. With parties and party offices coming later, it reminds us that we are constantly adding to the history of this institution. We build on foundations laid before us as others will build upon what we leave behind.

Perhaps the best that can come out of our celebrations of Congress' yesterdays is a greater awareness of how much the past has shaped us and how much we can help shape America's tomorrow.

Now I have the pleasure of introducing . . . a very special guest speaker, David McCullough. . . . He is a narrator of the forthcoming CBS documentary produced in honor of the congressional bicentennial. . . .

David McCULLOUGH. . . .

On a June afternoon in 1775, before there was a Congress of the United States, a small boy stood with his mother on a distant knoll, watching the battle of Bunker Hill. That was Adams, John Quincy Adams, diplomat, Senator, Secretary of State, and President, who in his lifetime had seen more, contributed more to the history of his time than almost anyone and who, as no former President ever had, returned here to the Hill to take a seat in the House of Representatives, in the 22d Congress, and thrilled at the prospect. And it was here that this extraordinary American had his finest hours.

Adams took his seat in the old House—in what is now Statuary Hall—in 1831. Small, fragile, fearing no one, he spoke his mind and his conscience. He championed mechanical "improvements" and scientific inquiry. To no one in Congress are we so indebted for the establishment of the Smithsonian Institution. With Congressman Lincoln of Illinois and Corwin of Ohio, he cried out against the Mexican War, and for 8 long years, almost alone, he battled the infamous gag rule imposed by southerners to prevent any discussion of petitions against slavery. Adams hated slavery, but was fighting, he said, more for the unlimited right of all citizens to have their petitions heard, whatever their cause. It was a gallant fight and he won. The gag rule was permanently removed.

Earlier this year, at the time of the inaugural ceremonies, I heard a television commentator broadcasting from Statuary Hall complain of the resonance and echoes in the room. What resonance. What echoes.

John Quincy Adams is a reminder that giants come in all shapes and sizes and that, at times, they have walked these halls, their voices have been heard, their spirit felt here. . . .

Many splendid books have been written about Congress. . . . But a book that does justice to the story of Adams' years in the House, one of the vivid chapters in our political history, is still waiting to be written, as are so many others.

Our knowledge, our appreciation, of the history of Congress and those who have made history here are curiously, regrettably deficient. The plain truth is historians and biographers have largely neglected the subject. Two hundred years after the creation of Congress, we have only begun to tell the story of Congress—which, of course, means the opportunity for those who write and who teach could not be greater. . . .

BUSH'S BICENTENNIAL SPEECH

. . . Two centuries ago, standing here, a man took an oath before a new nation and the eyes of God, an oath that I, like 40 before me, have since had the privilege to take. Everyone here today can still feel the pulse of history, the charge and power of that great moment in the genesis of this nation. Here the first Congress was in session, beginning a tradition of representative government that has endured for 200 years. Here the representatives of 13 colonies struggled to find balance, order, and unity between them. And here our first President issued a solemn address.

One who was there wrote: "This great man was agitated and embarrassed more than ever he was by the leveled cannon or pointed musket. He trembled and, several times, could scarce make out to read." Well, as

Representative Boggs pointed out, who wouldn't have felt some trepidation, undertaking a task which has never been tried in the world's history?

And on that day, Washington spoke of his conflict of emotions. He admitted his anxieties and deficiencies, as honest men will. But then, as his first official act, he turned to God, fervently, for strength, for he knew that the advancement of America, while it might rely on its Presidents, would surely depend on Providence.

How unlikely it must have seemed then that we might become United States. How uncertain that a republic could be hewn out of the wilderness of competing interests. How awesome the prospect must have seemed to the man charged with guiding the new Republic, made possible by his leadership in battle.

But George Washington defined and shaped this office. It was Washington's vision, his balance of power and restraint as he watched over the Constitutional Convention in 1787, that gave the delegates enough confidence to vest powers in a Chief Executive unparalleled in any freely elected government, before or since. It was Washington's vision, his balance, his integrity that made the Presidency possible. The Constitution was, and remains, a majestic document. But it was a blueprint, an outline for democratic government, in need of a master builder to ensure its foundations were strong. Based on that document, Washington created a living, functioning government. He brought together men of genius, a team of giants, with strong and competing views. He harnessed and directed their energies. And he established a precedent for 40 Presidents to follow.

For all of the turmoil and transformation of the last 200 years, there is a great constancy to this office and this Republic. So much of the vision of that first great President is reflected in the paths pursued by modern Presidents. Today we reaffirm ethics, honor, and strength in government. Two centuries ago, in his first Inaugural Address, Washington spoke of a government "exemplified by all the attributes which can win the affections of its citizens and command the respect of the world." Today, we say that leaders are not elected to quarrel but to govern. On that spring day in 1789, Washington pledged that "no party animosities will misdirect the comprehensive and equal eye which ought to watch over this great assemblance of communities and interests." Today, we seek a new engagement in the lives of others, believing that success is not measured by the sum of our possessions, our positions, or our professions, but by the good we do for others. Two hundred years ago today, Washington said there exists "in the economy and course of nature, an indissoluble union between virtue and happiness, between duty and advantage." And so, today we speak of values. At his inauguration, Washington said that "the foundations of our national policy will be laid in the pure and immutable principles of private morality." And over the last 200 years, we've moved from the revolution of democracy to the evolution of peace and prosperity.

But so much remains constant; so much endures; our faith in freedom—for individuals, freedom to choose, for nations, self-determination and democracy; our belief in fairness—equal standards, equal opportunity, the chance for each of us to achieve, on our own merits, to the very limit of our ambitions and potential; our enduring strength—abroad, a strength our allies can count on and our adversaries must respect, and at home, a sense of confidence, of purpose, in carrying forward our nation's work. . . .

George Washington, residing at Mount Vernon, felt himself summoned by this country to serve his country, not to reign, not to rule, but to serve. It was the noblest of impulses because democracy brought a new definition of nobility. And it means that a complete life, whether in the 18th or 20th century, must involve service to others. Today, just as Washington heard the voice of his country calling him to public service, a new generation must heed that summons. More must hear that call.

And today we stand; free Americans, citizens in an experiment of freedom that has brought sustained and unprecedented progress and blessings in abundance. As we dedicate a museum of American constitutional government, let us together rededicate ourselves to the principles to which Washington gave voice 200 years ago. Let our motivation derive from the strength and character of our forefathers, from the blood of those who have died for freedom, and from the promise of the future that posterity deserves. Let us commit ourselves to the renewal of strong, united, representative government in these United States of America.

God bless you, and may God forever bless this great nation of ours. Thank you all very, very much.

BRADY PLAN FOR
WORLD DEBT RELIEF
March 10, 1989

Treasury Secretary Nicholas F. Brady unveiled a new plan for world debt relief on March 10, marking the Bush administration's entry into an arena where previous efforts by the Reagan administration had come to naught. Brady signaled a change of approach to the problem in an address before a conference on Third World debt sponsored by the Brookings Institution and the Bretton Woods Committee. It was held in Washington, D.C.

Brady spoke of taking new measures to reduce—not just stretch out— the debt many poorer countries of the world said was crushing their ability to recover from the 1988 world recession. His term "debt reduction"—signifying an effort to use the financial resources of the industrialized nations to write down some of the loans to the Third World—was not in the Reagan administration's lexicon. Since 1985, U.S. policy had focused on promoting economic growth in developing countries, tied to large amounts of new lending. But that plan, articulated by James A. Baker III, who was then Treasury secretary, had not reduced the debt burden nor led to significant growth. (IMF-World Bank Conference, Historic Documents of 1985, p. 643)

Several leaders of debtor countries warned that the austerity required to meet repayment schedules was breeding social unrest, which in some places had turned into civil strife. Recent political turmoil in Venezuela, Argentina, Mexico, and Brazil contributed to a sense of urgency on the part of the Bush administration. Speaking at the debt conference, attended by large numbers of business executives, including bankers and many engaged in international trade, Brady conceded that the results of the Baker plan had been disappointing. For many countries, he said, progress remained "out of reach." Baker generally was unable to persuade the commercial banks to continue lending to the same countries that owed them huge sums of money.

The same day that Brady revealed his plan, Treasury Undersecretary David C. Mulfor testified before congressional committees that it would lead to a 20 percent debt reduction in the overall debts of thirty-nine heavily indebted countries. Officials in several of the affected countries said they expected much more relief than that. President Carlos Andres Perez of Venezuela, for instance, said he had been led to believe that the debts might be cut in half. However, Brady's plan was generally well received in Congress, and it was tacitly endorsed by the finance ministers of the so-called Big Seven countries—the United States, Japan, West Germany, France, Italy, Britain, and Canada—when their leaders met in Paris in July for an annual "economic summit." (Bush's Remarks in Europe and Economic Report, p. 411)

Elements of the Brady Plan

Brady's plan put more pressure on the commercial banks than Baker's did. Brady called on them to write off, or forgive, part of sums they were owed and to reduce the debt-service charges. In return, the remainder of the banks' trimmed-back loans would, in effect, be guaranteed—although the word was not used— but the International Monetary Fund (IMF) and the World Bank.

The IMF and World Bank—formally the International Bank for Reconstruction and Development—were devised at the Bretton Woods Conference in New Hampshire, where at the close of World War II the victorious Allies drew up a system to ensure stability in international financial dealings after the war. The IMF monitors exchange rates and steps in, when necessary, to correct imbalances; one method is to disburse loans to countries that agree to take certain steps—often austerity measures—to help themselves. The World Bank makes longer-term loans to foster Third World development. Each institution set aside $10 billion to back the remaining loans of commercial banks that would participate in the Brady plan.

Agreement with Mexico

Mexico on July 23 became the first country to reach an agreement under Brady guidelines for gaining debt relief from commercial banks in the United States and abroad. Once the Washington-negotiated pact was ratified by some five hundred creditor banks—which together held $54 billion of Mexico's medium-term and long-term foreign debt—each bank could (1) forgive 35 percent of its loans to Mexico, (2) reduce the interest rates by an equivalent amount, or (3) make new loans to Mexico. Under the first option, the bank would retain the prevailing interest rate on the remaining amount of the original loan. Under the second option, a bank would exchange its credits for new bonds carrying a fixed annual interest *rate of 6.25 percent, well below the prevailing rates of more than 10 percent. The new bonds would be backed by as much as $7 billion of U.S. Treasury securities and escrow accounts financed by the IMF, World Bank, and Japan. If a bank opted to make additional loans, they would have to equal 25 percent of the value of its existing Mexican loans. That money would be lent in roughly equal amounts annually over the next four years.*

"This is a great moment for Mexico," President Carlos Salinas de Gortari said of his country's agreement. Other reactions were more muted—largely over the uncertainty of whether the banks would choose debt reduction over new loans. But even if new loans became the norm, they would give the country some breathing room. The new loans could be used to pay installments on the old ones, and give its economy time to revive before the new loans started to come due.

Brady's Mexican agreement set a precedent for debt-reduction negotiations that were expected to follow with several other heavily indebted countries. "I think we have established a pattern for a realistic transaction that would work," he said. However, some bank analysts and other observers cautioned that it might be more difficult to work out deals with other countries. "Mexico is the easiest case among the deeply indebted nations," the Wall Street Journal *commented editorially on July 26, adding: "There is no reason to suppose a magic formula has been found for world debt."*

Following are excerpts from Treasury Secretary Nicholas F. Brady's address to a conference on Third World debt, sponsored by the Brookings Institution and the Bretton Woods Committee, in Washington, D.C., March 10, 1989:

More than 40 years ago, the representatives of 44 nations met at Bretton Woods, New Hampshire, to build a new international economic and financial system. The lessons learned from a devastating world depression and global conflict guided their efforts....

The enduring legacy provided by the Bretton Woods institutions is lasting testament to the success of their efforts. This community of purpose still resides in these institutions today. We must once again draw on this special sense of purpose as we renew our efforts to create and foster world growth.

These past 7 years, we have faced a major challenge in the international debt problem. This situation is, in fact, a complex accumulation of a myriad of interwoven problems. It contains economic, political, and social elements. Taken together, they represent a truly international problem, for which no one set of actions or circumstances is responsible, and for which no one nation can provide the solution. Ultimately resolution depends on a great cooperative effort by the international community. It requires the mobilization of the world's resources and the dedication of its goodwill.

Since 1982 the world community has endeavored to come to terms with international debt. In 1985 we paused and took stock of our progress in addressing the problem. As a result of that review, together we brought forth a new strategy, centered on economic growth. This still makes sense. However, it is appropriate that now, almost 4 years later, we again take stock. Thus in recent months, we have undertaken to look afresh at the international debt situation. The purpose was to discover what progress has been made; to see where we as a community of nations have succeeded and where we have not. And where our success has not met our expectations, to understand why we have not achieved our goals. . . .

Recent Progress

Our review confirmed that we have accomplished much, but much remains to be done. The experience of the past 4 years demonstrates that the fundamental principles of the current strategy remain sound.

- Growth is essential to the resolution of debt problems.
- Debtor nations will not achieve sufficient levels of growth without reform.
- Debtor nations have a continuing need for external resources.
- Solutions must be undertaken on a case-by-case basis.

In recent years, we have seen positive growth occur in many debtor nations. Last year six major debtor nations realized more than 4% positive growth. This is primarily due to the debtors' own efforts. The political leadership of many of these nations have demonstrated their commitment to implement vital macroeconomic and structural reforms. In many countries, this has been reflected in the privatization of nationalized industries. In some countries, there has also been a move toward opening their shores to greater foreign trade and investment. Current account deficits have been sharply reduced, and the portion of export earnings going to pay interest on external debt has declined. These are significant achievements. All the more so, since in parallel progress, a number of debtor nations have advanced toward more democratic regimes. This has required great courage and persistence. The people of these countries have made substantial sacrifices for which they have earned our admiration. We must work together to transform these sacrifices into tangible and lasting benefits.

In another positive development, we have avoided a major disruption to the global payments system. Commercial banks have strengthened their capital and built reserves, placing them in a stronger position to contribute to a more rapid resolution of debt problems. The "menu" approach of the current strategy has helped to sustain new financial support while also encouraging debt reduction efforts. The banks have provided loans in support of debtor country economic programs. The stock of debt in the major debtor countries has been reduced by some $24,000 million in the past 2 years through various voluntary debt-reduction techniques.

However, despite the accomplishments to date, we must acknowledge that serious problems and impediments to a successful resolution of the debt crisis remain. Clearly in many of the major debtor nations, growth has not been sufficient, nor has the level of economic policy reform been adequate. Capital flight has drained resources from debtor nations' economies. Meanwhile neither investment nor domestic savings has shown much improvement. In many cases, inflation has not been brought under control. Commercial bank lending has not always been timely. The force of these circumstances has overshadowed the progress achieved. Despite progress, prosperity remains, but for many, out of reach.

Other pressures also exist. The multilateral institutions and the Paris Club have made up a portion of the shortfall in finance. Commercial bank exposure of the major debtors since 1985 has declined slightly, while the exposure of the international institutions has increased sharply. If this trend was to continue, it could lead to a situation in which the debt problem would be transferred largely to the international institutions, weakening their financial position. . . .

In considering next steps, a few key points should be kept in mind.

First, obviously financial resources are scarce. Can they be used more effectively?

Second, we must recognize that reversing capital flight offers a major opportunity, since in many cases flight capital is larger than outstanding debt.

Third, there is no substitute for sound policies.

Fourth, we must maintain the important role of the international financial institutions and preserve their financial integrity.

Fifth, we should encourage debt and debt service reduction on a voluntary basis, while recognizing the importance of continued new lending. This should provide an important step back to the free markets, where funds abound and transactions are enacted in days, not months.

Finally, we must draw together these elements to provide debtor countries with greater hope for the future.

Strengthening the Current Strategy

Any new approach must continue to emphasize the importance of stronger growth in debtor nations, as well as the need for debtor reforms and adequate financial support to achieve that growth. We will have success only if our efforts are truly cooperative. And to succeed, we must have the commitment and involvement of all parties.

First and foremost, debtor nations must focus particular attention on the adoption of new policies which can better encourage new investment flows, strengthen domestic savings, and promote the return of flight capital. This requires sound growth policies which foster confidence in both domestic and foreign investors. These are essential ingredients for reducing the future stock of debt and sustaining strong growth. Specific policy measures in these areas should be part of any new International Monetary Fund (IMF) and World Bank programs. It is worth noting that total capital flight for most major debtors is roughly comparable to their total debt.

Second, the creditor community—the commercial banks, international financial institutions, and creditor governments—should provide more effective and timely financial support. A number of steps are needed in this area.

Commercial banks need to work with debtor nations to provide a broader range of alternatives for financial support, including greater efforts to achieve both debt and debt service reduction and to provide new lending. The approach to this problem must be realistic. The path toward greater creditworthiness and a return to the markets for many debtor countries needs to involve debt reduction. Diversified forms of financial support need to flourish, and constraints should be relaxed. To be specific, the sharing and negative-pledge clauses included in existing loan agreements are a substantial barrier to debt reduction. In addition, the banking community's interests have become more diverse in recent years. This needs to be recognized by both banks and debtors to take advantage of various preferences.

A key element of this approach, therefore, would be the negotiation of a general waiver of the sharing and negative-pledge clauses for each performing debtor to permit an orderly process whereby banks, which wish to do so, negotiate debt or debt service reduction transactions. Such waivers might have a 3-year life to stimulate activity within a short but measurable timeframe. We expect these waivers to accelerate sharply the pace of debt reduction and pass the benefits directly to the debtor nations. We would expect debtor nations also to maintain viable debt/equity swap programs for the duration of this endeavor and would encourage them to permit domestic nationals to engage in such transactions.

Of course, banks will remain interested in providing new money, especially if creditworthiness improves over the 3-year period. They should be encouraged to do so, for new financing will still be required. In this connection, consideration could be given in some cases to ways of differentiating new from old debt.

The international financial institutions will need to continue to play central roles. The heart of their efforts would be to promote sound policies in the debtor countries through advice and financial support. With steady performance under IMF and World Bank programs, these institutions can catalyze new financing. In addition, to support and encourage debtor and commercial bank efforts to reduce debt and debt service burdens, the IMF and World Bank could provide funding, as part of their policy-based lending programs, for debt or debt service reduction purposes. This financial support would be available to countries which elect to undertake a debt-reduction program. A portion of their policy-based loans could be used to finance specific debt-reduction plans. These funds could support collateralized debt for bond exchanges involving a significant discount on outstanding debt. They could also be used to replenish reserves following a cash buyback.

Moreover, both institutions could offer new, additional financial support to collateralize a portion of interest payments for debt or debt service reduction transactions. By offering direct financial support for debt and debt service operations, the IMF and the World Bank could provide new incentives, which would act simultaneously to strengthen prospects for greater creditworthiness and to restore voluntary private financing in the future. This could lead to considerable improvements in the cash flow positions of the debtor countries.

While the IMF and World Bank will want to set guidelines on how their funds are used, the negotiation of transactions will remain in the market place—encouraged and supported, but not managed, by the international institutions.

It will be important that the IMF and the World Bank both be in a strong financial position to fulfill effectively their roles in the strengthened strategy. The Bretton Woods Committee has provided an important public service in mobilizing capital resources for these institutions. The capital of the World Bank has recently been replenished with the implementation of the recent general capital increase providing approximately $75,000 million in new resources to the World Bank.

With respect to the IMF, the implementation of these new efforts to strengthen the debt strategy could help lay the basis for an increase in IMF quotas. There are, of course, other important issues that have to be addressed in the quota review, including the IMF arrears problem and a need for clear vision of the IMF's role in the 1990s. It is our hope that a consensus can be reached on the quota question before the end of the year.

Creditor governments should continue to reschedule or restructure their own exposure through the Paris Club and to maintain export credit cover for countries with sound reform programs. In addition, creditor countries which are in a position to provide additional financing in support of this effort may wish to consider doing so. This could contribute significantly to the overall success of this effort. We believe that creditor governments should also consider how to reduce regulatory, accounting, or tax impediments to debt reduction, where these exist.

The third key element of our thinking involves more timely and flexible financial support. The current manner in which "financial gaps" are estimated and filled is cumbersome and rigid. We should seek to change this mentality and make the process work better. At the same time, we must maintain the close association between economic performance and external financial support.

While we believe the IMF should continue to estimate debtor financing needs, we question whether the international financial institutions should delay their initial disbursements until firm, detailed commitments have been provided by all other creditors to fill the financing "gap." In many instances, this has served to provide a false sense of security rather than meaningful financial support. The banks will themselves need to provide diverse, active, and timely support in order to facilitate servicing of the commercial debt remaining after debt reduction. Debtor nations should set goals for both new investment and the repatriation of flight capital and to adopt policy measures designed to achieve those targets. Debtor nations and commercial banks should determine through negotiations the portion of financing needs to be met via concerted or voluntary lending and the contribution to be made by voluntary debt or debt service reductions.

Finally, sound policies and open, growing markets within the industrial nations will continue to be an essential foundation for efforts to make progress on the debt problem. We cannot reasonably expect the debtor nations to increase their exports and strengthen their economies without access to industrial-country markets. The Uruguay Round of trade negotiations provides an important opportunity to advance an open trading system. We must all strive to make this a success. . . .

If we work together, we can make important progress toward our key objectives:

- To assure that benefits are available to any debtor nation which demonstrates a commitment to sound policies;
- To minimize the cost or contingent shift in risk to creditor governments and taxpayers;
- To provide maximum opportunities for voluntary, market-based transactions rather than mandatory centralization of debt restructurings; and
- To better tap the potential for alternative sources of private capital.

In the final analysis, our objective is to rekindle the hope of the people and leaders of debtor nations that their sacrifices will lead to greater prosperity in the present and the prospect of the future unclouded by the burdens of debt.

GORBACHEV'S NEW FARM POLICY
March 15, 1989

Soviet leader Mikhail S. Gorbachev on March 15 called for "radical" political, economic, social, and cultural changes in rural development as he set forth an agricultural program designed to reverse sixty years of Soviet agrarian history. In place of centralized "command" policies, Gorbachev sought to "restore the farmer as the master" of the land.

Gorbachev's report to the Communist party's Central Committee extended to agriculture the economic policy of perestroika (restructuring) by which he hoped to revive a stagnant economy. Gross inefficiency in Soviet agriculture had produced a food crisis that jeopardized Gorbachev's other reforms, and he sought to revitalize food production by "granting farmers broad opportunities for displaying independence, enterprise and initiative."

While cloaked in Marxist rhetoric, both the philosophy and the specific proposals in the report challenged the foundations of Soviet economic and political thought. They also challenged deeply entrenched institutions and habits. The Soviet Union's 14 million "farm workers" include 4 million bureaucrats; the latter are loath to give up power, and many farmers have grown comfortable with an undemanding system.

The system's failure has made the Soviet Union a huge food importer, and its inefficiency is especially glaring when compared with the United States, whose 3 million farmers produce huge food exports. Gorbachev used the obvious and longstanding failure of Soviet agriculture to justify radical departure from Soviet orthodoxy. Western observers say that unless his reforms produce quick results, continuing food shortages may both undermine his popular support and embolden his enemies in the government. The fate of Gorbachev's political and economic reforms may hinge on the success of his efforts to produce what he called "a serious change in the mentality" of rural workers and managers.

Roots of the Problem

Even before the Bolshevik Revolution of 1917, agriculture in Russia lagged behind the rest of Europe. The medieval institution of serfdom, which tied the peasant to his local soil, was not abolished until 1861, centuries after comparable reforms in Western Europe. In a nation where the landed aristocracy measured their wealth by the number of "souls" they owned, the mentality of "independence, enterprise and initiative" that Gorbachev sought to nurture did not take deep root.

At the brink of the revolution, when 82 percent of Russia's 166 million people lived in rural areas, 40 percent of agricultural lands belonged to the state, church, or large landowners. Richer peasants (kulaks), whose farms were the most efficient, held only 23 percent of the land.

As the czarist regime collapsed during World War I, Lenin's slogan of "land to the peasants" had tremendous appeal in this rural nation. With the outbreak of civil strife, the peasants seized the estates of large landowners and divided up the land. The day after Vladimir Lenin seized power, in keeping with Marxist ideals of public ownership of the means of production, a decree was issued nationalizing all land. In practice, the decree was ignored.

During the ensuing civil war, agriculture, like the rest of the economy, collapsed. Peasants hid their harvests from Red Army "food battalions" requisitioning food for the cities and the soldiers. It has been estimated that 5 million people died of starvation in this period. The Communist government attempted to establish collective farms, but it almost totally failed to persuade the peasants to join them.

The need to appease the peasantry was a major reason for Lenin's introduction in 1921 of a New Economic Policy (NEP), which deviated from Marxist orthodoxy by encouraging some private enterprise. Peasants were allowed to keep the land they had seized, and to sell their own produce. This incentive quickly restored agricultural production, and by 1928 prewar levels of production were surpassed.

Such private enterprise was in direct conflict with Marxist ideals of public ownership. Under Joseph Stalin, who succeeded Lenin, collectivization of agriculture began in earnest with the end of the NEP in 1928 and grew steadily more coercive. By 1937, 93 percent of the peasant households and 99 percent of the agricultural land were absorbed in the collective system. The peasants resisted and suffered brutal treatment.

Kulaks by the millions were driven off the land or killed. The memory of this harsh treatment of farmers who had shown initiative under Lenin's NEP enterprise was highly relevant as Gorbachev sought to encourage enterprise among today's farmers.

In a historical analysis seeking to "uncover the roots" of today's agricultural problems, Gorbachev acknowledged that "millions of peasants together with their families were torn away from the land and their native areas; they suffered misfortunes, often dying in camps and exile." Gorbachev blamed this "human tragedy" on a simplistic view of socialism that relied on coercion for "a rapid remoulding of the entire peasantry along proletarian lines, the conversion of the small-scale peasant economy into a special system of big factory-like farms functioning on an industrial basis."

New Variety

While objecting to collectivization, Gorbachev avoided wholesale condemnation of collective farming or its goal of "socialist transformation" of the countryside. His reform called for a variety of forms of agricultural production, ranging from strengthening efficient collective farms to long-term leaseholds for individual farmers and groups of farmers. The need to avoid disruption of production, and the need to placate opponents of change, ruled out across-the-board reforms.

Allowing farmers to lease land and equipment for up to fifty years was perhaps the boldest departure from Soviet orthodoxy toward privatization. The idea evoked little enthusiasm outside the restive Baltic republics. Yegor Ligachev, a leading conservative who had been demoted by Gorbachev from ideological chief to minister of agriculture, when asked in February if inefficient collective farms should be turned over to leaseholders, said that "it was not for this that we established Soviet power."

Gorbachev proposed guarantees that this policy is "serious and long-term." He also acknowledged that leaseholding is "received with caution" by collective farmers who, accustomed to steady income regardless of productivity, have lost "the habit of working conscientiously." To "put an end to this," Gorbachev called for pegging their payment to results. He also sought effective guarantees that producers would have more freedom to sell their agricultural products where they chose.

He did not, however, advocate free-market prices. While recognizing a need for price reform, he said at the close of the meeting that "people would not understand" a lifting of controls on food prices. Indeed, an increase in food prices for the sake of perestroika in agriculture could turn the public against Gorbachev's whole program for economic restructuring. It could also jeopardize his political reforms (glasnost) that are aimed at making the Soviet Union a more open society.

> Following are excerpts from Mikhail S. Gorbachev's report to the Soviet Communist party's Central Committee, March 15, 1989, as translated by Novosti Press Agency Publishing House in Moscow and titled, "On the Agrarian Policy of the CPSU [Communist Party of the Soviet Union] in the Present Conditions":

147

I.

... Over the past two decades the agrarian sector received many resources, including capital investment, machinery and mineral fertilizers. A large-scale programme to improve the land has been carried out. But we failed to obtain either the returns on which we had counted or the increment which we had expected from the measures adopted.

So far we have been unable to find a radical solution to the food problem despite the fact that the country possesses great potential.

The state of affairs with the preservation and rational use of land, our main national wealth, is extremely unsatisfactory. In the past 25 years twenty-two million hectares [54.3 million acres] of farmland have been lost. . . .

The fertility of fields is declining in most regions. More than three million hectares of irrigated land—the "golden fund" of every state—have practically dropped out of cultivation due to mismanagement. It should be added that the country has lost more than ten million hectares of flood meadows and pastures during the past two decades due to ill-conceived hydropower generation projects.

The huge losses of agricultural produce are also disturbing. Mismanagement is responsible for the loss of up to 20 per cent of everything produced in the countryside. The figures for some products are even higher—30-40 per cent.

The countryside lags far behind urban areas in social and cultural development. Lack of good roads is a problem for all regions. It is a sheer disaster in the non-black-earth zone. . . .

I do not wish to whip up passions, but it ought to be said, nevertheless, that the situation is so grave in many regions that people are abandoning the land, moving out of villages. Migration of the rural population has reached a critical level in several regions of the country.

What is the matter? Why didn't our measures, including some very serious ones, yield the desired results, why didn't they bring about the necessary changes in the countryside? This is the main question that has to be answered. We must get to the bottom of it, uncover the roots of the current acute problem in our countryside, in the country's food supply. We must find ways of solving it. . . .

II.

... All in all, implementation of the New Economic Policy confirmed the correctness of Lenin's economic management principles and methods, his evaluation of the role of cooperatives and of trade exchange with the peasantry as the "economic foundation of socialism."

But in the second half of the 1920s the New Économic Policy encountered a number of difficulties and contradictions brought on by the complicated state of the national economy. Industry was weak and it could not provide the peasants with a sufficient number of necessary goods. As a result, the development of agriculture was increasingly curbed by the limited material and technical possibilities. . . . Meanwhile the large-scale work to implement industrialization plans required more and more material, labour and financial resources. The urban population increased by approximately four per cent a year. The money incomes of the working people and their effective demand grew rapidly. People in towns began to experience a shortage of bread and other foodstuffs. Rationing had to be introduced.

A crisis situation made itself felt in the country. . . . At that crucial stage of our history the country's leadership did not take the road of a search for economic methods to solve problems and contradictions, the elaboration of an economic policy suited to the new conditions and based on Leninist principles and on NEP experience. It took a different, diametrically opposite road—that of curtailing the NEP and commodity-money relations, belittling the role of material incentives to work, and applying administrative command methods to the solution of socio-economic tasks. . . .

The peasants' natural discontent brought on by all those actions was interpreted as a sort of sabotage. This was used as a justification for the need to apply repressive measures. . . .

The individual's aspiration to be master on his own land, the aspiration which had been legislatively recognized by the Decree on Land, was declared to be a left-over of the private-owner mentality. The entire diversity of land management techniques was practically reduced to one form. Any economic independence of collective and state farms was ruled out and their members were put in the position of day-labourers. . . . [A] ramified bureaucratic apparatus came to dominate collective and state farms and the peasantry.

As a result, tremendous damage was inflicted upon agriculture. The cattle population plummeted, the output of farm products sharply diminished, the provision of towns with food deteriorated, and consumption in villages decreased. In 1932-1933 famine broke out in a number of places. . . . Millions of peasants together with their families were torn away from the land and their native areas; they suffered misfortunes, often dying in camps and exile. . . .

In subsequent years our experience has more than once shown the need to eliminate the restraints resulting from the strict regulation of the economic activity of collective and state farms, to renounce command methods in the management of the agricultural sector, and to restore the Leninist principles of relations with the peasantry. But this was not done at the time.

The war [World War II] dealt a most severe blow to the country's agriculture. The productive forces in the countryside, which were at a low level as it was, were seriously undermined. . . .

For the sake of objectivity, it should be said that major steps were taken in the post-war years to restore agriculture in the war-ravaged regions of the Russian Federation, the Ukraine, Byelorussia and the Baltic area. But a new agrarian policy, which the countryside so needed, was never elaborated. . . .

The payment collective farmers received for their work was rather symbolical. They had to live mainly off their small-holdings; still worse, they had to pay exorbitant taxes on them.

Every peasant household had to pay taxes on land and to give to the state, often regardless of whether this was within its ability, a fixed quantity of meat, milk, eggs, wool and other products.

The situation often became absurd. One invention called for levying a tax on each fruit tree, no matter whether it yielded fruit or not.

The neglectful attitude of the collective farmers also manifested itself in the fact that they were not entitled to old-age pensions. They had no passports and could not leave their villages without permission.

After 1953 major economic, political and organizational measures were taken to strengthen agriculture.

In accordance with the decisions of the September 1953 Plenary Meeting of the CPSU Central Committee, more realistic purchase prices for farm produce were introduced, the principle of planning from the bottom up was declared and the tax policy was regulated.

Material incentives for rural workers increased, pensions were introduced and the restrictions of the passport system began to be lifted. The collective farms received the right to make changes in their statutes to reflect local conditions. A large-scale programme to reclaim 42 million hectares of virgin and long-fallow lands was implemented.

These measures began to bear fruit, and agriculture started to move forward at rather high rates.

On the whole the growth of agricultural production amounted to 34 per cent in the five years after 1953 as compared with the previous five-year period. Intensive factors came to have a greater impact on the results of management.

The process of restoring health to the economy of the collective farms was underway. Cash incomes per household increased by 130 per cent in 1957 as compared with 1952 and farmers were paid three times more for one day's work. . . .

But unjustified interference in the activities of collective and state farms, the foisting of all manner of directives on them by central authorities, and unwarranted reorganization drives resumed. . . .

The steadily growing cost of building materials and other capital goods needed in agriculture, and the selling of machinery to collective farms by machine and tractor stations at high prices had a negative effect on the economic position of cooperative and state-run farms, fettered the process of large-scale production and once again led to unbalanced exchange. . . .

Another attempt to develop an effective agrarian policy was launched at the Central Committee's Plenary Meeting in March 1965.

In keeping with its decisions, measures were taken to redistribute national income in favour of the farming sector, to tackle villages' social problems more fully, to employ economic methods in developing the farming sector, and to intensify production on collective and state farms. The purchase prices of farm produce were raised.

These measures were supported by farmers and boosted the country-side's economic activity. The 8th five-year-plan period, as you know, had fairly successful results.

But the decisions of the March 1965 Plenary Meeting also failed to be implemented, and the course charted by it was later seriously twisted. . . .

As a result, by 1980 both collective and state farms had ended up, on the whole, in the red, although in 1970 the overall profit rate of state farms amounted to 22 per cent, and that of collective farms, to 34 per cent.

In the late '60s and early '70s, an attempt was made to solve the problems of stepping up agricultural growth by widely promoting interfarm coopera-tion and creating agro-industrial enterprises and complexes.

But even these measures, right as they were in principle, were divorced from reality.

A considerable part of the money funnelled to the countryside was spent on costly construction projects and thus converted into "walls" rather than improved soil fertility, machines and better social amenities in villages.

In the final analysis, the expenses often brought heavy losses instead of the desired economic benefits.

Unregulated economic relations in the farming sector, continuing out-dated methods of economic management, and bad mistakes in the way labour was organized and paid for seriously lessened material incentives for rural workers.

In this situation even guaranteed pay for farmers' work—which in itself was an important social gain at the time—resulted in increased parasitic attitudes since it wasn't pegged to the end results of production. . . .

In a word, farming, the entire agricultural sector and all our economy in general had found themselves by the beginning of the '80s, in a state that cried out for emergency measures.

It was decided in this situation to work out a Food Programme which was then endorsed by the May 1982 Central Committee Plenary Meeting.

In this way it proved somehow possible to halt the growing crisis and even to improve the situation in agriculture. You know appropriate data. But then the decisions of the May 1982 Plenary Meeting bore the imprint of the time and were essentially compromise halfway-measures.

An in-depth analysis of the nation's economic development, which was made at the April 1985 and subsequent Plenary Meetings of the Central Committee, the 27th Congress and the 19th Party Conference, and a critical assessment of the state of affairs in the food sector make it imperative today to examine the entire package of agrarian problems once again. . . .

III.

Comrades, we should work out an agrarian policy that would enable us in the near-term future to blunt the edge of the food problem, and in the 13th five-year-plan period, to grow enough farm produce, in terms of both amount and choice, to stabilize food supplies.

Following the new agrarian policy, we should make major social and economic changes in the countryside and reach modern standards in agricultural production and in the transportation, storage and processing of farm produce, which will be an important factor for the harmonious development of the entire economy....

We should ensure scope for diverse forms of economic management—collective and state farms, agricultural firms and integrated complexes, farmers' households and small-holdings, agricultural facilities belonging to industrial, construction and other non-agricultural enterprises, auxiliary farming activities, and so on....

The most important thing is that the new mechanism of economic management, cooperation and leasing should fully bring out the immense potential inherent in collection and state farms and put into effect the original concept behind the transition to collective forms of work....

There is resistance to things new, and it will not disappear overnight. The experience of the past two-three years has shown that real obstacles in the way of the transition of collective and state farms and other enterprises to lease contract are reduced to two issues.

On the one hand, people want to have secure legal guarantees that would make them confident that our policy is serious and long-term....

Leasing is also received with caution by that part of collective farmers and workers who have lost, over many years, the habit of working conscientiously and got used to steady incomes irrespective of the end results of their work. We must put an end to this if we want to advance. We must make payment depend on the end result. This will put many things in order....

The documents circulated among you envisage the introduction of new purchase prices of farm produce as of January 1, 1990. These prices are to include the presently added increments. The number of pricing zones is to be reduced sharply. Production in regions with the most favourable conditions should be stimulated the most. It is also planned to make price formation more flexible. Pricing should not be the prerogative of central agencies alone and, therefore, there should be a reduction in the range of prices set in a centralized way. And, conversely, there should be greater room for contractual prices, particularly on early-ripening, seasonal and perishable products—potatoes, vegetables and fruits, the way it has been done of late in most socialist countries....

Perestroika presupposes a radical change in the system of managing the agrarian sector at all levels....

A new system should also fully meet the requirements of our political reform. What I mean is first of all a transition to the full power of the Soviets on the territory under their jurisdiction, a steep rise in the role of work collectives, and genuine democratisation of management at all levels....

TOXIC WASTE TREATY
March 22, 1989

Meeting in Basel, Switzerland, representatives from 117 nations on March 22 agreed to put forth a treaty restricting international trade in hazardous wastes. The treaty goes into effect after twenty nations ratify it—possibly by 1991. Nuclear wastes were excluded, largely at the insistence of the United States, which argued that regulation of those wastes should be subject to separate accords under the International Atomic Energy Agency.

Thirty-six nations immediately signed the pact for expected future ratification by their governments. Others, including the United States, said they wanted to study the document further. According to Andrew D. Sens, director of the State Department's Office of Environmental Protection, the agreement would have to go through interagency review before the Bush administration would sign it.

The treaty required government signatories to "take the appropriate measures" to reduce hazardous waste generation and export. Government approval would be required for international trade in such substances, and the exporting country's government would have to guarantee safety. Countries such as Switzerland, where a number of waste brokers maintain offices, would be obligated to prosecute the dealers if they exported recklessly. Governments of recipient countries, or of countries through which waste was shipped, would be notified of all toxic trade arrangements and could veto them.

According to estimates by the Organization of Economic Cooperation and Development (OECD), between 100,000 and 120,000 international shipments of toxic waste, amounting to 2.5 million metric tons, originated in Western Europe alone. Eighty percent was shipped to other West European countries, 15 percent to Eastern Europe, and 5 percent to developing countries. The U.S. Environmental Protection Agency calculated that hundreds of tons of toxic waste were smuggled out of the United States annually, leaving U.S. officials unable to determine where they were being sent and if the recipient countries could properly dispose of such wastes. According to Greenpeace, an environmental protection lobby, American companies had illegal export sales arrangements with at least forty-four countries. Many of those recipients, particularly in Africa, were not equipped to handle disposal of the wastes.

During the conference, a majority of African nations, supported by Greenpeace, argued for a total ban on all international toxic waste exports. Representatives of developing nations also expressed concern that they would be unable to enforce adherence to the pact. "We are unhappy because the treaty has been watered down," said Ahmed Mohammed Taylor-Kamara, Sierra Leone's minister of the environment.

"This treaty puts an international stamp of approval on a horrible business," said James Puckett, a toxic waste expert with Greenpeace. Spokesmen for the organization said the agreement had so many loopholes that widespread abuses could continue in the hazardous waste trade.

Assessing the treaty, Sens of the State Department said, "It's a convention [treaty] with many useful features in protecting human health and the environment." The agreement "has not halted the commerce in poison," said Mustafa K. Tolba, executive director of the United Nations Environment Programme. "But it has signaled the international resolve to eliminate the menace hazardous wastes pose to the welfare of our shared environment and to the health of all the world's people."

"The convention contains many strong statements, but the importance of the convention will lie in how it is applied," said Brice Lalonde, France's minister of the environment. Giorgio Ruffolo, Italy's minister of the environment, called the treaty "the first serious international effort to regulate hazardous waste. We think it should allow us to control this type of traffic."

Following are excerpts from "The Basel Convention on the Control of Transboundary Movements of Hazardous Wastes and Their Disposal," as presented March 22, 1989:

Preamble

The Parties to this Convention,

Aware of the risk of damage of human health and the environment caused by hazardous wastes and other wastes and the transboundary movement thereof,

Mindful of the growing threat to human health and the environment posed by the increased generation and complexity, and transboundary movement of hazardous wastes and other wastes,

Mindful also that the most effective way of protecting human health and the environment from the dangers posed by such wastes is the reduction of their generation to a minimum in terms of quantity and/or hazard potential,

Convinced that States should take necessary measures to ensure that the management of hazardous wastes and other wastes including their transboundary movement and disposal is consistent with the protection of human health and the environment whatever the place of their disposal,

Noting that States should ensure that the generator should carry out duties with regard to the transport and disposal of hazardous wastes and other wastes in a manner that is consistent with the protection of the environment, whatever the place of disposal,

Fully recognizing that any State has the sovereign right to ban the entry or disposal of foreign hazardous wastes and other wastes in its territory,

Recognizing also the increasing desire for the prohibition of transboundary movements of hazardous wastes and their disposal in other States, especially developing countries,

Convinced that hazardous wastes and other wastes should, as far as is compatible with environmentally sound and efficient management, be disposed of in the State where they were generated,

Aware also that transboundary movements of such wastes from the State of their generation to any other State should be permitted only when conducted under conditions which do not endanger human health and the environment, and under conditions in conformity with the provisions of this Convention,

Considering that enhanced control of transboundary movement of hazardous wastes and other wastes will act as an incentive for their environmentally sound management and for the reduction of the volume of such transboundary movement,

Convinced that States should take measures for the proper exchange of information on and control of the transboundary movement of hazardous wastes and other wastes from and to those States,

Noting that a number of international and regional agreements have addressed the issue of protection and preservation of the environment with regard to the transit of dangerous goods,

Taking into account the Declaration of the United Nations Conference on the Human Environment (Stockholm, 1972), the Cairo Guidelines and Principles for the Environmentally Sound Management of Hazardous Wastes adopted by the Governing Council of the United Nations Environment Programme (UNEP) by decision 14/30 of 17 June 1987, the Recommendations of the United Nations Committee of Experts on the Transport of Dangerous Goods (formulated in 1957 and updated biennially), relevant recommendations, declarations, instruments and regulations adopted within the United Nations system and the work and studies done within other international and regional organizations,

Mindful of the spirit, principles, aims and functions of the World Charter for Nature adopted by the General Assembly of the United Nations at its thirty-seventh session (1982) as the rule of ethics in respect of the protection of the human environment and the conservation of natural resources,

Affirming that States are responsible for the fulfillment of their international obligations concerning the protection of human health and protection and preservation of the environment, and are liable in accordance with international law,

Recognizing that in the case of a material breach of the provisions of this Convention or any protocol thereto the relevant international law of treaties shall apply,

Aware of the need to continue the development and implementation of environmentally sound low-waste technologies, recycling options, good house-keeping and management systems with a view to reducing to a minimum the generation of hazardous wastes and other wastes,

Aware also of the growing international concern about the need for stringent control of transboundary movement of hazardous wastes and other wastes, and of the need as far as possible to reduce such movement to a minimum,

Concerned about the problem of illegal transboundary traffic in hazardous wastes and other wastes,

Taking into account also the limited capabilities of the developing countries to manage hazardous wastes and other wastes,

Recognizing the need to promote the transfer of technology for the sound management of hazardous wastes and other wastes produced locally, particularly to the developing countries in accordance with the spirit of the Cairo Guidelines and decision 14/16 of the Governing Council of UNEP on Promotion of the transfer of environmental protection technology,

Recognizing also that hazardous wastes and other wastes should be transported in accordance with relevant international conventions and recommendations,

Convinced also that the transboundary movement of hazardous wastes and other wastes should be permitted only when the transport and the ultimate disposal of such wastes is environmentally sound, and,

Determined to protect, by strict control, human health and the environment against the adverse effects which may result from the generation and management of hazardous wastes and other wastes,

Have agreed as follows:

[Articles 1-5 omitted]

Article 6
Transboundary Movement Between Parties

1. The State of export shall notify, or shall require the generator or exporter to notify, in writing, through the channel of the competent authority of the State of export, the competent authority of the States concerned of any proposed transboundary movement of hazardous wastes or other wastes. Such notification shall contain the declarations and information specified in Annex VA, written in a language acceptable to the State of import. Only one notification needs to be sent to each State concerned.

2. The State of import shall respond to the notifier in writing consenting to the movement with or without conditions, denying permission for the movement, or requesting additional information. A copy of the final response of the State of import shall be sent to the competent authorities of the States concerned which are Parties.

3. The State of export shall not allow the generator or exporter to commence the transboundary movement until it has received written confirmation. . . .

[Articles 7-8 omitted]

Article 9
Illegal Traffic

1. For the purpose of this Convention, any transboundary movement of hazardous wastes or other wastes:

  (a) without notification pursuant to the provisions of this Convention to all States concerned; or
  (b) without the consent pursuant to the provisions of this Convention of a State concerned; or
  (c) with consent obtained from States concerned through falsification, misrepresentation or fraud; or
  (d) that does not conform in a material way with the documents; or
  (e) that results in deliberate disposal (e.g. dumping) of hazardous wastes or other wastes in contravention of this Convention and of general principles of international law,

shall be deemed to be illegal traffic.

2. In case of a transboundary movement of hazardous wastes or other wastes deemed to be illegal traffic as the result of conduct on the part of the exporter or generator, the State of export shall ensure that the wastes in question are:

  (a) taken back by the exporter or the generator or, if necessary, by itself into the State of export, or, if impracticable,
  (b) are otherwise disposed of in accordance with the provisions of this Convention,

within 30 days from the time the State of export has been informed about the illegal traffic or such other period of time as States concerned may agree. To this end the Parties concerned shall not oppose, hinder or prevent the return of those wastes to the State of export.

3. In the case of a transboundary movement of hazardous wastes or other wastes deemed to be illegal traffic as the result of conduct on the part of the importer or disposer, the State of import shall ensure that the wastes in question are disposed of in an environmentally sound manner by the importer or disposer or, if necessary, by itself within 30 days from the time the illegal traffic has come to the attention of the State of import or such other period of time as the States concerned may agree....

[Articles 10-13 omitted]

Article 14
Financial Aspects

1. The Parties agree that, according to the specific needs of different regions and subregions, regional or sub-regional centres for training and technology transfers regarding the management of hazardous wastes and other wastes and the minimization of their generation should be established. The Parties shall decide on the establishment of appropriate funding mechanisms of a voluntary nature.

2. The Parties shall consider the establishment of a revolving fund to assist on an interim basis in case of emergency situations to minimize damage from accidents arising from transboundary movements of hazardous wastes and other wastes or during the disposal of those wastes.

Article 15
Conference of the Parties

1. A Conference of the Parties is hereby established. The first meeting of the Conference of the Parties shall be convened by the Executive Director of UNEP not later than one year after the entry into force of this Convention. Thereafter, ordinary meetings of the Conference of the Parties shall be held at regular intervals to be determined by the Conference at its first meeting.

2. Extraordinary meetings of the Conference of the Parties shall be held at such other times as may be deemed necessary by the Conference, or at the written request of any Party, provided that, within six months of the request being communicated to them by the Secretariat, it is supported by at least one third of the Parties.

3. The Conference of the Parties shall by consensus agree upon and adopt rules of procedure for itself and for any subsidiary body it may establish, as well as financial rules to determine in particular the financial participation of the Parties under this Convention.

4. The Parties at their first meeting shall consider any additional measures needed to assist them in fulfilling their responsibilities with respect to the protection and the preservation of the marine environment in the context of this Convention.

5. The Conference of the Parties shall keep under continuous review and evaluation the effective implementation of this Convention. . . .

7. The Conference of the Parties shall undertake three years after the entry into force of this Convention, and at least every six years thereafter, an evaluation of its effectiveness and, if deemed necessary, to consider the adoption of a complete or partial ban of transboundary movements of hazardous wastes and other wastes in light of the latest scientific, environmental, technical and economic information. . . .

[Articles 16-18 omitted]

Article 19
Verification

Any Party which has reason to believe that another Party is acting or has acted in breach of its obligations under this Convention may inform the Secretariat thereof, and in such an event, shall simultaneously and immediately inform, directly or through the Secretariat, the Party against whom the allegations are made. All relevant information should be submitted by the Secretariat to the Parties.

Article 20
Settlement of Disputes

1. In case of a dispute between Parties as to the interpretation or application of, or compliance with, this Convention or any protocol thereto, they shall seek a settlement of the dispute through negotiation or any other peaceful means of their own choice.

2. If the Parties concerned cannot settle their dispute through the means mentioned in the preceding paragraph, the dispute, if the parties to the dispute agree, shall be submitted to the International Court of Justice or to arbitration under the conditions set out in Annex VI on Arbitration. However, failure to reach common agreement on submission of the dispute to the International Court of Justice or to arbitration shall not absolve the Parties from the responsibility of continuing to seek to resolve it by the means referred to in paragraph 1.

3. When ratifying, accepting, approving, formally confirming or acceding to this Convention, or at any time thereafter, a State or political and/or economic integration organization may declare that it recognizes as compulsory *ipso facto* and without special agreement, in relation to any Party accepting the same obligation:

(a) submission of the dispute to the International Court of Justice; and/or
(b) arbitration in accordance with the procedures set out in Annex VI.

Such declaration shall be notified in writing to the Secretariat which shall communicate it to the Parties.

Article 21
Signature

This Convention shall be open for signature by States, by Namibia, represented by the United Nations Council for Namibia, and by political and/or economic integration organizations, in Basel on 22 March 1989, at the Federal Department of Foreign Affairs of Switzerland in Berne from 23 March 1989 to 30 June 1989, and at United Nations Headquarters in New York from 1 July 1989 to 22 March 1990. . . .

[Articles 22-26 omitted]

Article 27
Withdrawal

1. At any time after three years from the date on which this Convention has entered into force for a Party, that Party may withdraw from the Convention by giving written notification to the Depositary.

2. Withdrawal shall be effective one year from receipt of notification by the Depositary, or on such later date as may be specified in the notification. . . .

AGREEMENTS ON THE FUTURE OF THE CONTRAS

March 24 and August 7, 1989

After nearly eight years of bitter domestic dissension over the Reagan administration's Central American policy, President George Bush and congressional leaders formally agreed on March 24 to a compromise permitting the United States to speak with one voice in that region. The agreement signed by Bush and congressional leaders denied further U.S. military aid to the Nicaraguan contra forces opposing Managua's Sandinista government but let them receive other assistance, at least until the government fulfilled its pledge to hold national elections in Nicaragua by February 25, 1990.

Some five months later Central American leaders asked that the guerrilla force be disbanded well before the election. The five Central American countries signed an accord August 7 that called for the "voluntary demobilization, repatriation or relocation" of the contras by December 5, 1989, despite objections from the Bush administration. Presidents of the five countries—Oscar Arias Sánchez of Costa Rica, Vinicio Cerezo Arevalo of Guatemala, José Azcona Hoyo of Honduras, Daniel Ortega Saavedra of Nicaragua, and Alfredo Cristiani of El Salvador—came to the agreement during two days of meetings at the Caribbean resort of Tela, Honduras. U.S. officials contended that the continued presence of the guerrillas would be needed to keep pressure on the Nicaraguan government to hold the elections. But having failed to block the agreement, the administration said it would support it as a way of forcing that government to become more democratic.

Several thousand contra fighters, and tens of thousands of their family members and supporters, were camped in rural bases in Honduras along the Nicaraguan border, and an uncertain number remained in Nicaragua. The contras and their Sandinista foes generally had respected a cease-fire agreement since March 1988, one month after Congress initially cut off military aid to the guerrillas (Central American Cease-Fire, Historic Documents of 1988, p. 241). As refugees, the contras would face an uncertain future. Most of them presumably would be unwilling to return to Nicaragua, and they were probably unwelcome in the United States or Central America. The White House-congressional accord envisioned that eventually they would be relocated with human rights guarantees in Nicaragua or other nearby countries.

In return for congressional endorsement of further nonmilitary aid to the contras, Bush pledged to support the efforts of Central American presidents to seek a lasting solution to the region's civil strife. Bush also yielded to congressional demands for interim, informal congressional veto power over the continuation of contra aid beyond November 30 if the administration appeared to be undermining the peace process. That process was outlined in the so-called Esquipulas II Agreement of August 1987 and Tesoro Beach accords of February 1989. Both documents adopted the names of the Central American localities where they were signed by the five presidents.

At the Tesoro Beach meeting, President Ortega pledged to hold the Nicaraguan elections in February. The pact called on all Nicaraguans to participate in the electoral process and stated that "international observers, especially delegates of the United Nations, will be invited to be present in all electoral districts." The agreement provided a four-month period for political parties to organize, followed by a six-month campaign leading to legislative, municipal, and presidential elections.

As part of the plan, the Nicaraguan government agreed to give all political parties full access to the media and to release most of the 3,300 contras and former national guardsmen held in prison. In partial fulfillment of that provision, 1,894 political prisoners, many incarcerated since the Sandinistas came to power ten years ago, were freed March 17.

Bush's New Strategy

On April 22, the Nicaraguan government approved a new electoral law for the coming campaign. Opposition leaders charged that provisions of the law fell short of guaranteeing full access to the media and a genuinely free election. Nonetheless, Bush's compromise with Congress halted the longstanding effort of President Ronald Reagan to topple Nicaragua's Marxist-oriented Sandinista government through military support of the contras, who formed a rebel army trained and equipped by the United States. Bush pledged to use a combination of diplomatic and economic pressures to force the Sandinistas to open their political system and to reintegrate the opposition into the Nicaraguan political process.

The new strategy also implicitly committed the United States to closer cooperation with Latin America, Europe, and even with the Soviet Union—until this point its principal antagonist in Central America. In the wake of the March 24 accord, the president invited three Central American leaders to the White House for consultation.

They were President Arias of Costa Rica, author of the Esquipulas II pact, for which he won the Nobel Peace Prize in 1987 (Arias Nobel Peace Prize Speech, Historic Documents of 1987, p. 1007); *President Carlos Andres Perez of Venezuela, a prominent figure in peace activities in Central America for more than five years; and Cristiani, the president-elect of El Salvador whose ultra-right ARENA party had been anathema to the United States because of its reputed links to Salvadoran death squads.*

President Bush also extended an olive branch to Soviet leader Mikhail Gorbachev, asking him to reduce Soviet support for the Sandinista regime and to urge Cuban president Fidel Castro to do the same. No response was forthcoming from Gorbachev or Castro during Gorbachev's visit to Cuba in April. But in mid-May Gorbachev sent Bush a letter saying that Moscow was prepared to end arms aid to Nicaragua in view of the shift in U.S. policy. The White House afterward complained that arms shipments were continuing. Bush raised the issue with Gorbachev in December when the two held shipboard meetings at Malta. (Bush-Gorbachev on Malta; Bush and Baker on NATO, p. 637)

The matter had come into sharper focus on November 25 when an aircraft identified as Nicaraguan crashed in El Salvador and was discovered to be transporting twenty-four advanced anti-aircraft missiles, presumably to rebel troops then engaged in heavy fighting with U.S.-aided government forces in El Salvador. Nicaragua's involvement threatened to wreck the peace process, which already had been damaged by the contras' refusal to disarm by the December 5 deadline. At Arias's urging, the five Central American presidents met again in Costa Rica on December 10-12. They hammered out an accord calling for all outside funds for the contras to be channeled through a joint United Nations-Organization of American States commission. It had been formed in August at the president's behest to oversee the dismantling of the contra fighting force. In this way, added pressure could be brought on the contras to disband. Ortega, in turn, had to agree to stop supplying the rebels in El Salvador.

Compromise Agreement

Bush's new secretary of state, James A. Baker III, was charged with forging a bipartisan consensus on a new U.S. approach to Central America. He engineered the compromise on Capitol Hill, attracting enough middle-of-the-road support so that when the contra aid package came to a vote in Congress on April 13, it passed the House of Representatives 309-110 and the Senate 70-28.

Several conservatives saw the compromise as a "sell out" of the contras, whom the United States had backed throughout most of the 1980s. Sen. Steve Symms, R-Idaho, for example, said the compromise was "a bad deal ... a disaster." Several liberals insisted on ending all contra support. But moderate voices prevailed. Rep. Mickey Edwards, R-Okla., a contra supporter, said the compromise met his goal of "keeping the contras alive." Rep. David Obey, D-Wis., on the other hand, said the compromise "ends the contra war." Politicians on both sides said the compromise gave the Bush administration flexibility in Central America.

Secretary Baker characterized the administration's actions as a "carrot and stick" approach, in which the United States could offer inducements to the Sandinistas to comply with Central American peace plans, while keeping open options in case the Sandinistas backslid on their commitments. He said the United States would consider lifting its trade embargo against Nicaragua, improving diplomatic relations between the two countries, curtailing U.S. military maneuvers in Honduras, and even renewing aid to Nicaragua, which was cut off in 1981.

If, on the other hand, the Sandinistas do not move toward democracy, Baker said the United States could tighten its trade embargo, further curtail diplomatic relations, and pressure its allies to cut economic ties to Nicaragua. Ultimately, he told a Senate appropriations subcommittee, the administration had the option of "coming back up to Capitol Hill and asking you for military assistance" for the contras.

While the policy shift created some controversy in Washington, it was generally welcomed in Central America. Genuine peace in that region, however, was still an elusive goal as the year drew to a close.

> *Following are the texts of the bipartisan accord on Central America, signed at the White House on March 24, 1989, by President Bush, House Speaker Jim Wright, D-Texas, Senate Majority Leader George J. Mitchell, D-Maine, Senate Minority Leader Bob Dole, R-Kan., House Majority Leader Thomas S. Foley, D-Wash., and House Minority Leader Robert H. Michel, R-Ill., and of the president's statement, issued the same day. These texts are followed by excerpts from the Tela Declaration, as translated from Spanish by the State Department. It was signed August 7, by the five Central American presidents:*

CENTRAL AMERICAN AGREEMENT

The Executive and the Congress are united today in support of democracy, peace and security in Central America. The United States supports the peace and democratization process and the goals of the Central American Presidents embodied in the Esquipulas Accord.

The United States is committed to working in good faith with the democratic leaders of Central America and Latin America to translate the bright promises of Esquipulas II into concrete realities on the ground.

With regard to Nicaragua, the United States is united in its goals: democratization; an end to subversion and destabilization of its neighbors;

an end to Soviet bloc military ties that threaten U.S. and regional security. Today the Executive and the Congress are united on a policy to achieve those goals.

To be successful the Central American peace process cannot be based on promises alone. It must be based on credible standards of compliance, strict timetables for enforcement, and effective ongoing means to verify both the democratic and security requirements of those agreements. We support the use of incentives and disincentives to achieve U.S. policy objectives.

We also endorse an open, consultative process with bipartisanship as the watchword for the development and success of a unified policy towards Central America. The Congress recognizes the need for consistency and continuity in policy and the responsibility of the Executive to administer and carry out that policy, the programs based upon it, and to conduct American diplomacy in the region. The Executive will consult regularly and report to the Congress on progress in meeting the goals of the peace and democratization process, including the use of assistance as outlined in the Accord.

Under Esquipulas II and the El Salvador Accord, insurgent forces are supposed to voluntarily reintegrate into their homeland under safe, democratic conditions. The United States shall encourage the government of Nicaragua and the Nicaraguan Resistance to continue the cessation of hostilities currently in effect.

To implement our purposes, the Executive will propose and the bipartisan leadership of the Congress will act promptly after the Easter Recess to extend humanitarian assistance at current levels to the Resistance through February 28, 1990, noting that the government of Nicaragua has agreed to hold new elections under international supervision just prior to that date. Those funds shall also be available to support voluntary reintegration or voluntary regional relocation by the Nicaraguan Resistance. Such voluntary reintegration or voluntary regional relocation assistance shall be provided in a manner supportive of the goals of the Central American nations, as expressed in the Esquipulas II agreement and the El Salvador Accord, including the goal of democratization within Nicaragua, and the reintegration plan to be developed pursuant to those accords.

We believe that democratization should continue throughout Central America in those nations in which it is not yet complete with progress towards strengthening of civilian leadership, the defense of human rights, the rule of law and functioning judicial systems, and consolidation of free, open, safe, political processes in which all groups and individuals can fairly compete for political leadership. We believe that democracy and peace in Central America can create the conditions for economic integration and development that can benefit all the people of the region and pledge ourselves to examine new ideas to further those worthy goals.

While the Soviet Union and Cuba both publicly endorsed the Esquipulas Agreement, their continued aid and support of violence and subversion in Central America is in direct violation of that regional agreement. The United States believes that President Gorbachev's impending visit to Cuba represents an important opportunity for both the Soviet Union and Cuba to end all aid that supports subversion and destabilization in Central America as President Arias has requested and as the Central American peace process demands.

The United States government retains ultimate responsibility to define its national interests and foreign policy, and nothing in this Accord shall be interpreted to infringe on that responsibility. The United States need not spell out in advance the nature or type of action that would be undertaken in response to threats to U.S. national security interests. Rather it should be sufficient to simply make clear that such threats will be met by any appropriate constitutional means. The spirit of trust, bipartisanship, and common purpose expressed in this Accord between the Executive and the Congress shall continue to be the foundation for its full implementation and the achievement of democracy, security, and peace in Central America.

PRESIDENT'S STATEMENT

The President of a Central American democracy was asked recently what is the most important step the United States can take. He said, "Speak with one voice." Today, for the first time in many years, the President and Congress, the Democratic and Republican leadership in the House and Senate, are speaking with one voice about Central America.

In my inaugural address I reached out my hand to the leadership of Congress in both parties asking them to join with me to rebuild a bipartisan foreign policy based on trust and common purpose. Today, I am gratified that the Speaker and the Majority and Minority Leaders of the Senate and House have extended their hands back to me.

We have signed today together a Bipartisan Accord on Central America. It sets out the broad outlines of U.S. policy towards that troubled region and commits both the Executive and Congress to work together to achieve it.

The goals we seek are the goals which the people of Central America yearn for: democracy, security, and peace. Those are the pledges made by the Central American Presidents in the Esquipulas II Accord. That agreement is an integrated whole: all of its provisions must move forward together if any of them are to be fulfilled. Our challenge now is to turn those promises into concrete realities on the ground.

The only way we can meet that challenge is if Latin democratic leaders and the United States work together, with the support of our European friends and allies, as true partners with candor and mutual respect. I believe Latin leaders are asking for that kind of relationship as we confront together the many challenges facing our hemisphere. As president, I pledge the United States is ready to respond.

Under this Central America agreement, insurgent forces have the right to re-integrate into their homeland under safe, democratic conditions with full civil and political rights. That is the desire of the Nicaraguan Resistance. It is what they are fighting for. We hope and believe it can be achieved through a concerted diplomatic effort to enforce this regional agreement.

To achieve these goals the bipartisan leadership of Congress has agreed to support my request for continued humanitarian assistance to the Nicaraguan Resistance through the elections scheduled in Nicaragua for Feb. 28, 1990.

There will be extensive consultations and review with respect to these funds effective Nov. 30, 1989, by the bipartisan leadership and relevant committees. However, I have been assured that the leadership in both Houses supports the extension of this assistance through the Nicaraguan elections barring unforeseen circumstances.

There is no shortcut to democracy; no quick fix. The next weeks and months will demand patience and perseverance by the democratic community and the hard, technical work of ensuring compliance with the Esquipulas Accord. The United States will work in good faith to support that kind of diplomatic effort, but we will not support a paper agreement that sells out the Nicaraguan people's right to be free.

We do not claim the right to order the politics of that country. That is for the people of Nicaragua to decide. We support what the Esquipulas Accord requires: free, open, political processes in which all groups can fairly and safely compete for political leadership. That means the playing field must be level; all, including the current government, must respect the majority's decision in the end, and the losers must also retain the political rights to operate as a legal opposition and contest again for political authority in the next recurring election contest.

The burden of proof is on the Sandinista government to do something it has steadfastly refused to do from 1979 to 1989: to keep its promises to the Nicaraguan people to permit real democracy; keep its promises to its neighbors not to support subversion in Central America; and keep its obligation to this hemisphere not to permit the establishment of Soviet bloc bases in Central America. If those promises are kept we have an opportunity to start a new day in Central America; but if those pledges continue to be violated, we hope and expect that other nations will find ways to join us to condemn those actions and reverse those processes.

The Soviet Union also has an obligation and an opportunity: to demonstrate that its proclaimed commitment to "new thinking" is more than a tactical response to temporary setbacks, but represents instead a new principled approach to foreign policy.

In other regional conflicts around the world the Soviet Union has adopted a welcome new approach that has helped resolve long-standing problems in constructive ways. In Central America what we have seen from the Soviet Union and Cuba can only be described as "old thinking."

In the last decade, the Soviet bloc has poured at least $50 billion in aid into Cuba and Nicaragua. Soviet and Cuban aid is building in Nicaragua a military machine larger than all the armies of the other Central American nations combined and continues to finance violence, revolution, and destruction against the democratically elected government of El Salvador. Indeed, Soviet bloc military support for the Marxist guerrillas has increased since the United States ended military support for the Nicaraguan Resistance and Soviet military aid to the government of Nicaragua continues at levels wholly uncalled for by any legitimate defensive needs. The continuation of these levels of Soviet bloc aid into Central America raises serious questions about Soviet attitudes and intentions towards the United States.

The Soviet Union has no legitimate security interest in Central America; and the United States has many. We reject any doctrine of equivalence of interest in this region as a basis for negotiations. Instead, the Soviet Union and Cuba have an obligation to the leaders of Central America to stop violating the provisions of the Esquipulas Accord which the Soviet Union and Cuba both pledged to uphold. The time to begin is now.

In signing the Esquipulas Accord, President Oscar Arias of Costa Rica said: "Without democracy, there can be no peace in Central America." He is right. But with democracy and peace in Central America can come new hope for economic development in which all of the people of the region can share. One can look at the terrible violence ravaging Central America and despair, but I have a different view of its future.

I can see a democratic Central America in which all of the nations of the region live in peace with each other; where the citizens of the region are safe from the violence of the state or from revolutionary guerrillas; where resources now devoted to military defense could be channeled to build hospitals, homes and schools. That is not a dream if all the people and nations of the Americas will it to be true. I hope the Esquipulas Accord and perhaps, also, the Bipartisan Accord, will someday be seen as the first step toward its fulfillment.

TELA DECLARATION

The presidents of Costa Rica, El Salvador, Guatemala, Honduras, and Nicaragua, honoring their historic commitment to achieve firm and lasting peace in Central America, recalling the Guatemala procedures adopted on 7 August 1987 and the Alajuela and Costa del Sol Declarations, in accordance with Resolution 637 unanimously adopted by the UN Security Council on 27 July 1989, in an attempt to advance toward achieving the goals of the Central American peace process, and as a firm example of their determination to fully respect international law, have agreed on this joint plan for the voluntary demobilization, repatriation, or relocation of the members of the Nicaraguan Resistance [RN] and their families as well as the assistance for the demobilization of all those persons involved in armed actions in the countries of the region when they voluntarily request it. . . .

[Chapter I]

In accordance with the Esquipulas procedures and the Costa del Sol declaration, the Nicaraguan Government has expressed its willingness to strengthen its national reconciliation and democratization processes, thus contributing to encouraging the RN to accept the voluntary repatriation. Therefore, the Nicaraguan Government has decided to sign this plan aimed at achieving the repatriation of a majority of the members of the RN, the only exception being those who choose to be relocated in third countries.

The five Central American governments have reiterated their commitment to prevent persons, organizations, or groups from using their territory to destabilize other states and to stop all types of aid to armed groups, with the exception of humanitarian aid that will be used for the purposes defined by the presidents in this plan.

1. The International Support and Verification Commission, as of today to be known as the CIAV, will be created to implement and fulfill the plan. The UN and OAS [Organization of American States] secretaries general will be invited to participate in the commission. . . .

2. The CIAV must be created within 30 days of the signing of this agreement. The five Central American presidents hereby urge the RN to state its acceptance of this plan within 90 days after the creation of the CIAV. During those 90 days the Nicaraguan Government and the CIAV will hold direct meetings with the RN to promote their return to Nicaragua and join the political process. After the plan has been fulfilled, the CIAV will issue a report to be presented to the Central American presidents.

3. The CIAV will be responsible for all activities that will make the voluntary demobilization, relocation, or repatriation possible. The CIAV will also be responsible for welcoming and settling those who repatriated. The commission will also ensure that the conditions are adequate for the repatriated persons to join civilian life and to carry out follow-up and control activities demanded by the process.

4. The CIAV will carry out its activities with the help of the Central American governments and will seek the support of specialized organizations with experience in the region and other organizations as they may deem necessary. Said organizations will be officially invited by the governments, and among their objectives will be to facilitate the implementation of the plan, ensure that the human rights of the repatriated are being respected, and that they are earning an adequate income.

5. Once the CIAV has been created it will immediately begin to:

A. Hold the necessary meetings with the Nicaraguan Government authorities, the other Central American governments, the RN, the humanitarian organizations in an attempt to facilitate the implementation of the plan.

B. Visit the RN and refugee camp to:

1. Explain the extent and benefits of the plan.

2. Learn of the existing human and material resources.
3. Organize distribution of humanitarian aid.
4. Assume responsibility, as much as possible, for the distribution of food, medical attention, clothes, and other basic needs at the RN camps—this will be done through the support organization—and carry out efforts for settling in third countries those who do not wish to be repatriated and offer them the necessary help.
5. (Number 5 not provided in original text.)
6. The CIAV will issue certificates to every Nicaraguan citizen who accepts the plan and will implement the voluntary repatriation plan for those who wish to return to Nicaragua. The departure and entry points will be through the border posts mutually agreed on by the governments. At these border posts the Nicaraguan Government, in the presence of CIAV representatives, will issue the necessary documents guaranteeing the rights of the person. At the same time, relocation in third countries for those who do not wish to be repatriated will begin. In these cases, the Niaraguan Government, with the help of the CIAV, will issue passports to all who may request them. The five presidents urge the international community to offer financial support for this demobilization plan.

Procedures:

7. As of its creation, and in fulfillment of the plan for the voluntary demobilization, repatriation, or relocation in Nicaragua and third countries, the CIAV will establish the procedures for the surrender of weapons, equipment, and war materiel by the members of the RN. This materiel will remain in the commission's custody while the five presidents decide on the what will be done with it.
8. The CIAV will verify the dismantling of camps left behind by the Nicaraguan Resistance and refugees.
9. Those repatriated—circumstances permitting—will be directly escorted by the CIAV to the site of their definitive resettlement that will be—as much as possible—their place of origin or a place chosen by consensus by the Nicaraguan Government and the CIAV.

   To implement this, temporary residence areas can be established in Nicaragua under CIAV control and supervision while a permanent site is chosen. Land will be distributed among, and economic and technical aid will be provided to, those repatriated who wish to become involved in agriculture. This will depend on the possibilities of the Nicaraguan Government, the experience of specialized international organizations, and the amount of funds obtained for this purpose.
10. The CIAV will establish—with the help of the Nicaraguan Government—reception centers that will be able to provide basic services, first aid, family counselling, economic aid, transportation

for the settlement areas, and other social services.

11. To ensure the necessary guarantees to those repatriated, the CIAV will establish—from the very beginning of the program—follow-up offices to allow people to voice—when they need to do so—complaints of possible failures to comply with guarantees originally offered for their repatriation. These offices will operate as long as the CIAV—in consultation with the Central American Governments—deem it necessary. Personnel from these offices will periodically visit those repatriated to verify fulfillment of the guarantees offered and draft reports on compliance with this plan. The CIAV will forward these reports to the five Central American presidents.

12. Situations not foreseen in this chapter will be resolved by the CIAV in consultation with the Central American governments and the institutions or person involved.

[Chapter II]

... The demobilization of these people must be implemented in keeping with procedures specified in Esquipulas II and the legislation and local organizations of the affected country. To guarantee this assistance, the. CIAV can be officially invited by Central American Governments to do so.

[Chapter III]

To contribute toward ending armed actions in the Republic of El Salvador, the Governments of Costa Rica, Guatemala, Honduras, and Nicaragua reaffirm their firm conviction on the need to immediately and effectively end hostilities in that fraternal country.

Therefore, they vehemently urge of FMLN [Farabundo Marti National Liberation Front] to hold a constructive dialogue to achieve a just and lasting peace. The governments mentioned here also urge the Salvadoran Government to implement—with full guarantees and in keeping with Point 2 of the Guatemala procedure—the incorporation of FMLN members to peaceful life.

The Salvadoran Government reaffirms its unrestricted respect of its commitments to achieve national reconciliation and continue strengthening the pluralist, participative, and representative democratization process that is already under way through which social justice and full respect for all human rights and the basic freedoms of the Salvadorans are promoted.

Once it is agreed that the FMLN will forsake the armed struggle and return to institutional and democratic life through dialogue, steps will be taken to demobilize the members of the FMLN using, to this effect, the procedure established in Chapter I of this plan insofar as it is applicable and with any modifications required in this case to facilitate its implementation.

The foregoing notwithstanding, any FMLN members who at any time voluntarily decide to lay down arms and to join El Salvador's political and civilian life may also enjoy the benefits of this plan.

Agreed to and signed at the port city of Tela, Republic of Honduras, on 7 August 1989.

[Signed] Oscar Arias Sánchez, president, Republic of Costa Rica; Alfredo Cristiani, president, Republic of El Salvador; Vinicio Cerezo Arevalo, president, Republic of Guatemala; José Azcona Hoyo, president, Republic of Honduras; Daniel Ortega Saavedra, president, Republic of Nicaragua.

REMARKS ON SOVIET ELECTION AND PERESTROIKA
March 26, April 27, and May 12, 1989

The Soviet Union held its freest election in more than seventy years on March 26, in which about half of the 2,250 seats for the new Congress of People's Deputies were contested. Voters were thus offered a choice of candidates in a nationwide election for the first time since 1917. On that occasion Vladimir Lenin's Bolsheviks were outpolled by the Socialist Revolutionaries. He retaliated by seizing control of the Russian government.

Permitting genuine electoral contests was another step in Soviet leader Mikhail S. Gorbachev's perestroika *campaign for a restructuring of Soviet society. This entailed introducing a limited amount of democracy into the heretofore monolithic Soviet system, as he had foretold in a speech to the* Communist party's Central Committee in January 1987. (Gorbachev on Democratic Reforms, Historic Documents of 1987, p. 79)

The election did not jeopardize the Communist party's dominance— almost 90 percent of the candidates were Communists—but it resulted in the defeat of several senior Communist officials and brought into office many candidates, Communists and non-Communists, who were outspokenly critical of the party. On election day in Moscow, Gorbachev cast his ballot and told news reporters that the new-style election campaign made "a big stride in democratizing society."

Among the losers were party chiefs in Moscow, Leningrad, Kiev, Minsk, and several other big cities. Boris Yeltsin, who had been expelled from the ruling Politburo and deposed as the Moscow party boss in 1988, gained a degree of revenge by winning 89 percent of the votes in the Soviet capital. His popularity was attributed to his strong attacks on party privileges.

The party's Old Guard probably suffered its biggest embarrassment in Leningrad, where regional boss Yuri Solovyev, an influential Politburo member, was soundly defeated. The party's distress was soon brought into full view April 27 when the newspaper Pravda *published transcripts of a Central Committee meeting, at which some of the election's disgruntled losers vented their feelings.*

For instance, Solovyev complained that "people who carry party membership cards openly speak against the the CPSU [Communist Party of the Soviet Union]." Party official Vladmir I. Melnikov was quoted as saying that "secretaries of city and district party committees are announcing that . . . they are not going to take part in . . . [future] elections because there is a 100 percent guarantee they will not be elected." His colleague, Ratmis S. Bobovikov, was incensed that the question "what kind of army must we have?" became a campaign issue, and furthermore, on Lenin's birthday, a candidate in Leningrad had suggested removing Lenin's body from public display in the Kremlin.

Electoral Changes

The new election law that brought all this about was adopted in December 1988 at Gorbachev's urging. He told the Supreme Soviet on November 29 that "the draft law on elections . . . put before you represents a truly radical updating of our electoral system." The most distinctive feature of the new law, he added, "envisages elections having more than one candidate run for each deputy's position. . . . But what's most important today is the question of how this will be used to create a full-fledged corps of deputies capable of running the country at the time of perestroika."

One-third of the 2,250 seats in the new legislature were set aside for the Communist party, trade unions, Communist youth league, and other officially sanctioned organizations. While some of those 750 seats were opened to lively contests within the various organizations, many of them were filled by Gorbachev and his followers. Even some of the 1,500 remaining seats, those decided in the March 26 balloting, were not contested. In all, 2,895 candidates sought the 1,500 seats, with some races attracting three or more competitors. Election officials estimated that about 80 percent of the Soviet Union's 184 million eligible voters went to the polls in this the first nationwide election in which voting was not compulsory.

New Congress Convenes

The newly elected congress met almost daily from May 25 until June 9 in the Kremlin's Hall of Palaces before television cameras that broadcast the often acrimonious proceedings to viewers throughout the Soviet Union. The delegates' first two tasks, as required by law, were choosing a president of the Soviet Union and electing from their own ranks a 542-member parliament, to be called the Supreme Soviet—replacing a larger, rubber-stamp body of the same name. As expected, they elected Gorbachev president, though with eighty-seven dissenting votes and only after hours of sometimes unfriendly questioning. At a later time, Leonid K. Sukhov, a chauffeur and delegate from Kharkov, denounced Gorbachev as a Napoleon surrounded by "sycophants," and compared the president's wife, Raisa, to the emperor's wife, Josephine.

Gorbachev gained power upon becoming the Communist party's general secretary in March 1985 at the death of Konstantin U. Chernenko. In October 1988 the old Supreme Soviet formally made Gorbachev head of state. His title, chairman of the Presidium, was the equivalent of president. The Presidium, or executive council, met between sessions of the Supreme Soviet. The new presidency to which Gorbachev was elected by the People's Congress had broader authority and more executive functions than it formerly had. He would preside, as before, over the Supreme Soviet and the Presidium. The latter was restructured as a coordinating body composed, in addition to him, of a senior vice president, and fifteen other vice presidents representing the various Soviet republics. For senior vice president, the delegates approved Gorbachev's former chief of staff, Anatoly I. Lukyanov.

The new Supreme Soviet, the national legislature, seemed destined to overshadow the congress. Whereas future congresses could expect to meet only a few days every year, the legislature was required to hold two four-month sessions annually. In the initial voting by the People's Congress for Supreme Soviet membership, the party's clout was evident. Only one of the twelve members chosen from Moscow, for instance, was a dissident. He was Roy A. Medvedev, the historian. Yeltsin was among those excluded—a fact that prompted angry phone calls to the Kremlin and a protest rally attended by several thousand persons in a Moscow park.

Gorbachev subsequently ruled that Yeltsin, often his harshest critic, could serve if one of the chosen members could not. As if on cue, a member resigned, yielding his seat to Yeltsin. The Supreme Soviet convened June 7 and promptly appointed fourteen standing committees to oversee all aspects of government, including the KGB, the secret police.

In the meantime, on May 30, in his inaugural address as president, Gorbachev revealed the size of the Soviet military budget ($128 billion at the official exchange rate) and said he was postponing until 1990 local elections that had been planned for the fall and were intended to bring about the decentralization of political power. His action—regarded as a concession to local Communist officials who feared defeat—was reversed two months later to meet a demand from striking coal miners. Gorbachev also made other concessions to persuade several hundred thousand miners to return to work in July.

American Reaction

Americans, no less than the people in the Soviet Union, sometimes appeared amazed at the turn of events. President George Bush, speaking at Texas A&M University on May 12, asked rhetorically: "Who would have thought that we would see the deliberations of the Central Committee on the front page of Pravda, *or dissident Andrei Sakharov seated near the councils of power?" But the president appeared unconvinced that permanent change had taken place in the Soviet Union. "These are hopeful—indeed, remarkable—signs. And let no one doubt our sincere desire to see* perestroika, *this reform, continue and succeed. But the national security of America and our allies is not based on hope. It must be based on deeds. And we look for enduring, ingrained economic and political change."*

Arthur Schlesinger, Jr., the historian long identified with Democratic politics, scolded Bush in a Wall Street Journal *guest column on May 17 for emphasizing "deeds"—"as if Mr. Gorbachev had not already done things that would have been regarded as unimaginable a decade ago"— and laying down new "tests" to be passed. In a similar vein, the* New York Times *contended editorially on April 27 that a purge of the Central Committee, which Gorbachev had carried out two days earlier, should dispel what it characterized as the Bush administration's doubts that the Soviet leader might hold sufficient power to carry out his reforms.*

Bush's words took on a more conciliatory tone at the annual summit meeting of the North Atlantic Treaty Organization (NATO) in Brussels, May 29-30. There the president proposed a sweeping reduction in American and Soviet conventional military arms and personnel in Europe. He suggested that the two countries could negotiate a treaty within a year to bring about such cuts. On that occasion, Bush told news reporters that while he could not predict what will happen in the Soviet Union, "I want him [Gorbachev] to succeed." Bush added: "He seems stronger now than he has been earlier on. But he faces enormous problems."

Gorbachev himself was quoted in a July 21 Pravda *account of a Central Committee meeting as telling his high-ranking party colleagues that there was no turning back from what had been set in motion by* perestroika.

Following are excerpts from translations of an election story published in Pravda *March 26, 1989; of remarks by Communist officials at a Moscow meeting of the Central Committee, as quoted in* Pravda *April 27; and excerpts from a White House transcript of a speech by President Bush at Texas A&M University, May 12:*

PRAVDA ELECTION STORY

Soviet leader Mikhail Gorbachev cast his ballots in the parliamentary elections ... in a polling station in Moscow's Oktyabrsky district.

Interviewed after voting by Soviet and foreign reporters, he described the new-style Soviet election campaign as "a big stride in democratizing society."

Gorbachev added that the new election code makes it possible to form a new state legislature that will be "capable of fulfilling the very difficult, uphill, innovative tasks of *perestroika*."

When asked about some issues raised at pre-election meetings, in particular political pluralism, he said world experience demonstrates that alternative parties by themselves are not a panacea for solving problems.

"The key to bringing out the potential of Soviet Socialist society lies in identifying the diverse interests of people and harmonizing them, it lies in democracy and public openness," he explained.

This is why, Gorbachev continued, "we intend to further the democratization process which will cover all spheres, economic, political and cultural."

"That is the important thing. Far from backpedaling in this respect, we shall, on the contrary, continue to open up possibilities of our system," the Soviet leader said.

Replying to a question about recent criticisms of Boris Yeltsin, Gorbachev recalled that criticisms during the election campaign were leveled not only at Yeltsin but also at the past and the present, including some of the things done in the course of *perestroika.*

"It is good that both the activities of the present leadership and the activities of state agencies are subject to criticism. That's how it should be," he declared.

Asked whether there is unity in the Soviet Communist Party leadership, Gorbachev said that there are discussions in the Politburo but it is unanimous in that it is vital to upgrade socialism, bring out its potential and extend democracy.

Reporters asked the Soviet leader to comment on the 12 votes cast against him during balloting at the last Central Committee plenum to elect the party's representatives to the state legislature.

"That wasn't many," he exclaimed. "I would have been disappointed if there hadn't been any criticism at all."

Gorbachev noted that, in his opinion, not everything has been going as one would like it to and at the desired pace.

"But the job, a hard, arduous job, is making progress. And we must not attempt anything foolish, try any great leaps forward or overreach ourselves because we should not put the fate of the people in jeopardy," he said.

CENTRAL COMMITTEE REMARKS

Yuri F. Solovyev, *first secretary of Leningrad region:*
For understandable reasons, it is not easy for me to speak today. As you

know, none of the six party and soviet leaders of Leningrad received sufficient votes. The situation was similar in a number of regions.

From our point of view the economic reform is idling. One gets the impression that we have never dealt with this before. Here one may add that there was haste and lack of proper thinking when a number of laws, like the struggle against alcoholism and on cooperatives, were adopted. Growth of illicit incomes, now uncontrolled, profiteering that has become practically legal, intensive flow of skilled workers from state-run enterprises cause intense displeasure in the population. We witness the previously unseen imbalance of the economy and money supply. A danger of group industrial selfishness has emerged and is becoming clearly seen. I mean such phenomena as price increases and the disappearance of cheap products. As life showed, electing industrial managers does not facilitate the economic reforms, and in fact sometimes hinders it.

On the other hand, an opinion has formed among some of our youth that the C.P.S.U. turned out to be the party of "mistakes and crimes before the people." Most workers' collectives strongly believe that the changes so far have brought benefits to the cooperators or to the people inclined toward profiteering.

I say all this not to shift some responsibility onto the center's shoulders, which, incidentally, is what our ideological opponents—let's call them by their true name—are striving for, trying to create distrust, conflict between the central and local bodies.

It's no secret that it has gone so far that people carrying party membership cards openly speak against the C.P.S.U., against its vanguard role in the society, and stand for turning the party of action into a party of discussion clubs.

Vladmir I. Melnikov, *first secretary, Komi Oblast party committee:*
... Comrades. More elections are ahead. Today secretaries of city and district party committees are announcing in such a situation they are not going to take part in these elections because there is a 100 percent guarantee that they will not be elected.

The impression is such that many difficulties are created almost intentionally. For instance the well-aimed salvo that the press and television fired at the first secretaries of regional party committees. Did this not influence the outcome of the elections? ...

Comrades, look at our movies and our journals. Where's the patriotism, the civic attitude? Where's the labor discipline? How are we going to educate our young? We are educating them in an entirely different mein. Can this really not worry the ideological staff of the Central Committee and Politburo?

Ratmir S. Bobovikov, *party chief of the Vladimir region:*
... The atmosphere of democratization and *glasnost,* freedom of expression of one's will, is used by some people to undermine from inside the positive processes that are going on in the country and to impose controversial points of view.

The mass media often lack a principled approach in this matter. Why do we need a discussion of what kind of army we must have? It would be better to treat our army with more care and strengthen its authority, the authority of its personnel and, officer corps, of those who fulfilled their internationalist duty. One cannot agree with those who offer to open up the borders, declassify all the military secrets. Even under *glasnost* there must and will remain plants and design bureaus hidden from too-curious eyes.

Sometimes we come across irresponsibility in the choice of topics to be discussed on TV.... It also caused me great indignation when, on the birthday of Lenin, Mark Aleksandrovich Zakharov suddenly talked about removing Lenin from the mausoleum and whether or not to inter him in the earth, as if this were a private enterprise and not a state-run television. Lingering over such issues is simply immoral. Literally in the morning people were phoning party committees and asking in bewilderment how it was possible to understand this? Whose opinion is this? They also asked us why, for example, are responsible officials, secretaries of the Central Committee, in particular comrades Yakovlev and Medvedev, who in the Politburo are responsible for ideology, do not personally participate in open discussions at rallies and don't rebuff our ideological foes? And they would not have to go far. Everyone knows that in Moscow, there's no shortage of rallies.

The elated tone of the articles in our press about how bourgeois leaders praise *perestroika* also causes natural questions in people. Because they remember well Lenin's testament: think carefully any time your class enemy praises you.

REMARKS BY PRESIDENT BUSH

... The Soviet Union says that it seeks to make peace with the world, and criticizes its own postwar policies. These are words that we can only applaud. But a new relationship cannot simply be declared by Moscow, or bestowed by others. It must be earned. It must be earned because promises are never enough. The Soviet Union has promised a more cooperative relationship before, only to reverse course and return to militarism. Soviet foreign policy has been almost seasonal—warmth before cold, thaw before freeze. We seek a friendship that knows no season of suspicion, no chill of distrust.

We hope *perestroika* is pointing the Soviet Union to a break with the cycles of the past—a definitive break. Who would have thought that we would see the deliberations of the Central Committee on the front page of *Pravda,* or dissident Andrei Sakharov seated near the councils of power? Who would have imagined a Soviet leader who canvasses the sidewalks of Moscow and also Washington, D.C.? These are hopeful—indeed, remarkable—signs. And let no one doubt our sincere desire to see *perestroika,* this reform, continue and succeed. But the national security of America and our allies is not predicated on hope. It must be based on deeds. And we look for enduring, ingrained economic and political change.

While we hope to move beyond containment, we are only at the beginning of our new path. Many dangers and uncertainties are ahead. We must not forget that the Soviet Union has acquired awesome military capabilities. That was a fact of life for my predecessors, and that's always been a fact of life for our allies. And that is a fact of life for me today as President of the United States.

As we seek peace, we must also remain strong. The purpose of our military might is not to pressure a weak Soviet economy, or to seek military superiority. It is to deter war. It is to defend ourselves and our allies, and to do something more—to convince the Soviet Union that there can be no reward in pursuing expansionism, to convince the Soviet Union that reward lies in the pursuit of peace.

Western policies must encourage the evolution of the Soviet Union toward an open society. This task will test our strength. It will tax our patience. And it will require a sweeping vision. Let me share with you my vision. I see a Western Hemisphere of democratic, prosperous nations, no longer threatened by a Cuba or a Nicaragua armed by Moscow. I see a Soviet Union as it pulls away from ties to terrorist nations like Libya, that threaten the legitimate security of their neighbors. I see a Soviet Union which respects China's integrity, and returns the Northern Territories to Japan; a prelude to the day when all the great nations of Asia will live in harmony.

But the fulfillment of this vision requires the Soviet Union to take positive steps, including:

First, reduce Soviet forces. Although some small steps have already been taken, the Warsaw Pact still possesses more than 30,000 tanks, more than twice as much artillery and hundreds of thousands more troops in Europe than NATO. They should cut their forces to less threatening levels, in proportion to their legitimate security needs.

Second, adhere to the Soviet obligation, promised in the final days of World War II, to support self-determination for all the nations of Eastern Europe and Central Europe. And this requires specific abandonment of the Brezhnev Doctrine. One day it should be possible to drive from Moscow to Munich without seeing a single guard tower or a strand of barbed wire. In short, tear down the Iron Curtain.

And third, work with the West in positive, practical—not merely rhetorical—steps toward diplomatic solution to these regional disputes around the world. I welcome the Soviet withdrawal from Afghanistan and the Angola agreement. But there is much more to be done around the world. We're ready. Let's roll up our sleeves and get to work.

And fourth, achieve a lasting political pluralism and respect for human rights. Dramatic events have already occurred in Moscow. We are impressed by limited, but freely contested elections. We are impressed by a greater toleration of dissent. We are impressed by a new frankness about the Stalin era. Mr. Gorbachev, don't stop now.

And fifth, join with us in addressing pressing global problems, including the international drug menace and dangers to the environment. We can build a better world for our children.

As the Soviet Union moves toward arms reduction and reform, it will find willing partners in the West. We seek verifiable, stabilizing arms control and arms reduction agreements with the Soviet Union and its allies. However, arms control is not an end in itself, but a means of contributing to the security of America, and the peace of the world. I directed Secretary Baker to propose to the Soviets that we resume negotiations on strategic forces in June. And as you know, the Soviet Union has agreed.

Our basic approach is clear. In the Strategic Arms Reductions Talks, we wish to reduce the risk of nuclear war. And in the companion defense and space talks, our objective will be to preserve our options to deploy advanced defenses when they're ready. In nuclear testing we will continue to seek the necessary verification improvements in existing treaties to permit them to be brought into force. And we're going to continue to seek a verifiable global ban on chemical weapons. We support NATO efforts to reduce the Soviet offensive threat in the negotiations on conventional forces in Europe. And, as I've said, fundamental to all of these objectives is simple openness. . . .

COURT RULINGS ON
AMERICA'S CUP RACE
March 28 and September 19, 1989

America's Cup, a trophy that long has been the symbol of supremacy in international yachting, became the object of two contradictory rulings in New York state courts in 1989. At issue was whether the San Diego Yacht Club had violated established racing rules and thereby ensured victory for its own boat over a challenger from New Zealand in America's Cup competition in September 1988.

On behalf of its boat New Zealand, *the Mercury Bay Boating Club had filed suit in New York, asking to be awarded the cup. The case rested in New York because the America's Cup races are conducted under terms of a charitable trust created in the nineteenth century under laws of that state. The cup was donated by six owners of the New York Yacht Club in July 1851 "as a perpetual challenge cup for friendly competition between foreign countries." A few months later the club's yacht* America *won the first competition, a race against several British vessels around the Isle of Wight off the southern English coast.*

American yachts turned back all challengers until 1983, when the New York club's Liberty *lost to* Australia II, *the entry of the Royal Perth Yacht Club of Western Australia. The Australian club was the cup's holder and trustee until the 1987 races, when the San Diego Yacht Club's* Stars & Stripes '87 *triumphed over the Australian entry,* Kookabura III, *returning the trophy to the United States. Soon afterward, the Mercury club led by New Zealand investment banker Michael Fay challenged the new champion to race with yachts about twice as long as the 12-Meter Class boats, whose basic dimensions have by gentlemen's agreement been the standard for all America's Cup contenders since World War II.*

Although three or four years usually elapse between America's Cup regattas, Fay insisted that races be held in 1988, closed to all challengers except him. Dennis Conner—whose American crew lost the cup in 1983 and won it back in 1987—refused on behalf of the San Diego Boat Club. Fay then sued and won a ruling from Justice Carmen Beauchamp Ciparick of the New York State Supreme Court, on November 25, 1987, that his challenge be accepted.

Conner responded by introducing a catamaran, Stars & Stripes, *a craft with twin hulls never before used in America's Cup racing. In many sailing conditions, catamarans are considered inherently faster than monohull boats. The New Zealand boat raced under protest and was decisively beaten in the 1988 races.*

Fay went back to Judge Ciparick's court, asking that the winner be disqualified and the cup awarded to New Zealand by forfeit. She ruled in his favor the following March 28, saying that by racing with a catamaran the San Diego Yacht Club had "clearly deviated from the intent of the [America's Cup] donor."

Her ruling caused consternation in American yachting circles and in the San Diego business community. A loss of the trophy to New Zealand would mean that that country, rather than the United States, would host the next challenge races in which as many as twenty-three countries might participate. The San Diego Chamber of Commerce estimated that the cup's transfer would deprive the city of $1.2 billion in income from tourism and related economic activity at the races, which then were expected to be held there in 1991. Some observers of the yachting scene contended that the America's Cup had become an international sports event drawing the kind of attention that the Olympic games or World Cup receive.

The San Diego club—joined by the Perth club—appealed the ruling to the New York State Supreme Court's Appellate Division. In the September 19 decision from the appeals court, a five-member panel of judges voted 4-1 to overturn Judge Ciparick's ruling. "San Diego's catamaran was an eligible yacht," Judge Joseph P. Sullivan wrote in the thirty-page majority opinion. "It was the winner of the two races held on September 7 and 9, 1988, for the America's Cup and as the winner is entitled to the America's Cup." In the sole dissenting opinion, Justice Bentley Kassal said: "I cannot accept that such a gross mismatch was permissible under the deed of the gift [of the America's Cup by its donors]."

Judge Israel Rubin, in a concurring opinion, observed that "true yachtsmen" should pursue victory "on the water and not in the courtroom." However, the decision did not necessarily remove the dispute from the courtroom. Fay promptly asked the state's highest court, the Court of Appeals, to accept the case on further appeal. His attorney, George Thompkins, estimated that if the appeals court agreed to hear the case, deliberations could last as long as nine months.

The legal proceedings already appeared to have delayed the next

America's Cup competition until 1992 or beyond. However, some progress had been reported in the planning for that event, whenever it is held. Hopeful competitors were reported to have agreed that it would be raced in boats with keel lengths of seventy-five feet, and agreed to a set of racing rules that would be enforced by an independent panel of experts.

Following are excerpts from the ruling by Judge Carmen Beauchamp Ciparick of the New York Supreme Court, issued March 28, 1989, disqualifying the San Diego Yacht Club's Stars & Stripes *as winner of the 1988 America's Cup and awarding the title to the* New Zealand, *the entry of the Mercury Bay Boating Club, and from the majority and dissenting opinions in the 4-1 reversal of her decision, issued September 19, by a panel of the court's Appellate Division:*

STATE SUPREME COURT RULING

JUDGE CARMEN BEAUCHAMP CIPARICK delivered the opinion of the Court:

In the wake of the September, 1988 San Diego Yacht Club ("San Diego") defense of the America's cup, both the challenger, the Mercury Bay Boating Club Inc. ("Mercury Bay") and the defender call upon this court to determine the lawful holder of the Cup.

The parties initially appeared before this court in a dispute over the validity of the underlying July, 1987 challenge by Mercury Bay to sail a match for the America's Cup with a yacht measuring ninety feet on the load water-line. The court found the challenge to be valid and declined to amend the Deed of Gift to bar such a challenge as sought by San Diego. The parties were then directed in the December 21, 1987 judgment of the court to sail a match for the America's cup in accordance with the terms of the Deed of Gift.

Thereafter, Mercury Bay sought to hold San Diego in civil contempt for threatening to defend the America's Cup in a catamaran. This court's decision of July 25, 1988 determined that there was, at that juncture, no basis for a finding of contempt nor for rendering an advisory opinion. The court further stated that "Nothing in this decision should be interpreted as indicating that multihulled boats are either permitted or barred under the America's Cup deed of gift." The parties were expressly advised therein of the risk of forfeiture under the Deed.

San Diego's subsequent September, 1988 defense of the America's Cup with a catamaran and victory in races held on September 7th and 9th is the genesis of the current motion by both parties to determine the lawful holder of the Cup.

The court notes that despite the urgings of the court and the global yachting community, San Diego and Mercury Bay were unable to reach an agreement as to acceptable terms of the race so as to conduct the competition under the "mutual consent" provisions of the Deed of Gift and to provide for multinational participation. Instead, the parties competed in all respects under the "challenge" provisions of the Deed of Gift for what is apparently the first time since the original conveyance of the America's Cup to the New York Yacht Club in July, 1857.

The Deed of Gift as amended in 1887 was uniquely designed to permit the holder of the Cup and a challenger to agree on virtually all of the terms of the race, including the type of vessel, with certain limitations. . . .

The nature of the issue facing this court is not in controversy. This court must determine whether, under the Deed of Gift, San Diego was permitted to defend the Mercury Bay challenge for the America's Cup with a multihulled vessel, specifically, a catamaran. The issue is unique as this is the first time in America's Cup history that resort to litigation has been necessary to determine the Cup victor. In addition, this is the first time in the over one hundred and thirty year history of the world's most prestigious yachting competition that a yacht club has chosen to compete with a multihulled vessel; to which the challenger has objected throughout.

To determine the disqualification question the court must look to the Deed of Gift which sets forth the race conditions and the basic specifications of the vessels. San Diego argues that, other than the following express limitations of the Deed requiring that the competing vessels be:

> "Propelled by sails only. . . "
>
> and
>
> "if of one mast, shall not be less than forty-four nor more than ninety-feet on the load water line. . . ."

the defending club may choose any type of vessel without regard to the nature of the challenging vessel or its specifications. Mercury Bay, on the other hand, contends that the Deed of Gift, read as a whole, limits the defender beyond the foregoing express terms of the Deed of Gift so as to require the defender to compete in a match on equal terms with "a like or similar vessel". . . .

The Deed of Gift is devoid of references to multihulled vessels. Nor does the Deed state in specific terms the type of vessel or restrictions as to specifications of the defending vessel. The Deed provides that the competing vessel, "if of one mast shall be not less than forty-four nor more than ninety feet on the load water-line." . . . It is only in the challenge provision that specifications are fixed. The relevant provision provides in pertinent part

> "The Challenging club shall give ten months' notice in writing, naming the days for the proposed races: . . . Accompanying the ten months' notice of challenge there must be sent the name of the owner and a certificate of the name, rig, and following dimensions of the challenging vessel, namely, length on load water-line: beam at load water-line and extreme beam: and draught of water: which dimensions shall not be exceeded:"

. . . When considering the Deed's basic specifications and the challenge notice requirements, the conclusion is inescapable that the donor contemplated the defending vessel to relate in some way to the specifications of the challenger. The requirement that the challenging vessel not exceed the dimensions given in the notice of challenge further supports the proposition that the Cup defender would rely on these specifications....

The use of the terms "centre-board or sliding keel" in the singular would tend to indicate that the donor did not contemplate multihulled vessels competing for the Cup. Catamarans were in existence in racing at the time of the Third Deed of Gift and the donor could have provided for their participation by utilization of the plural in reference to centre-board or by specifying dimensions permissible for catamarans....

Perhaps the most significant sentence of the Deed is the one setting forth the trust purpose. The pertinent provision states:

> "This Cup is donated upon the condition that it shall be preserved as a perpetual Challenge Cup for friendly competition between foreign countries."

The emphasis of the America's Cup is on competition and sportsmanship. The intention of the donor was to foster racing between yachts or vessels on somewhat competitive terms. The Deed of Gift, when read as a whole, expresses the intent of the donor that the defender of the America's Cup, operating within the limitations of the challenge provisions, select a vessel that is competitive with that of the challenger. While this may not rise to the level of a "like or similar" standard, the import is clear from the provisions of the Deed of Gift that although design variations are permitted, the vessels should be somewhat evenly matched.

The court finds that the intent of the donor, as expressed in the Deed of Gift, was to exclude a defense of the America's Cup in a multihulled vessel by a defender faced with a monohull challenge. The challenge provision would be rendered meaningless if the defender was provided with the specifications of the challenging vessel and then afforded ten months to produce a vessel with an insurmountable competitive advantage. To sail a multihulled vessel against a monohulled yacht over the type of course contemplated by the donor is, in the opinion of most boating authorities, to create a gross mismatch and, therefore, is violative of the donor's primary purpose of fostering friendly competition....

While a competitive standard such as the "like or similar vessels" standard offered by Mercury Bay may not always be easily implemented, there is no doubt that San Diego's defense of the America's Cup in a catamaran against Mercury Bay's monohull challenge clearly deviated from the intent of the donor.... Accordingly, San Diego shall be disqualified in the September 1988 competition....

The defender of the America's Cup is more than the current champion yacht club. The yacht club winning the America's Cup becomes the sole trustee under the Deed of Gift and has an obligation thereunder to insure a fair competition. The holder of the America's Cup is bound to a higher obligation than the victor of the Stanley Cup or the Superbowl. In organized sports such as hockey or football there is a central authority for the development and enforcement of competition rules. The defender of the America's Cup, as trustee, is charged with the responsibility of insuring that a subsequent defense is carried out in accordance with the letter and spirit of the Deed of Gift. San Diego clearly fell short of its obligations as trustee of the Deed of Gift....

The application by Mercury Bay for disqualification of San Diego Yacht Club is granted. The application by San Diego is denied.

APPELLATE DIVISION'S OPINIONS

JUDGE JOSEPH P. SULLIVAN, Jr., for the majority:

This appeal is from an order which, on the basis of a determination that the defense of the America's Cup in a catamaran violated the provisions of the Deed of Gift of the America's Cup, set aside the results of the 1988 America's Cup races between the yachts of the San Diego Yacht Club and Mercury Bay Boating Club, declared Mercury Bay's challenging yacht, *New Zealand,* to be the winner of those races, and ordered San Diego, a trustee of the America's Cup, to forfeit the Cup to Mercury Bay....

The Deed of Gift specifies the permissible length for the competing vessels and outlines the timing and supporting documents necessary for a valid challenge. The only constraints on boat design are set forth in the Deed, which states that a challenger is entitled to a match against any "yacht or vessel", "propelled by sails only", which, if single-masted, must measure between forty-four and ninety feet on the load water-line. The challenger may determine the dimensions of its boat within this specified size range, as well as the time of the race, on condition that it provide at least ten months' notice to the defender. Races must be conducted between May 1 and November 1 in the Northern Hemisphere, and between November 1 and May 1 in the Southern Hemisphere.

The Deed of Gift also provides that America's Cup races shall be sailed under the rules of the club holding the Cup. San Diego follows the rules of yacht racing promulgated by the International Yacht Racing Union (IYRU). Under the IYRU rules, an International Jury, whose decisions are final, referees the match and decides all protests.

The Deed of Gift leaves all other details for resolution by the competitors:

> The Club challenging for the Cup and the Club holding the same may, by mutual consent, make any arrangement satisfactory to both as to the dates, courses, number of trials, rules and sailing regulations, and any and all other conditions of the match, in which case also the ten months' notice provision may be waived.

By this "mutual consent" provision, the Deed envisions the competitors' agreement on the overwhelming number of issues not controlled by the literal terms of the trust instrument. Failing such agreement, however, the Deed of Gift provides explicitly that the defender shall set the venue and the courses for the race.

The Deed of Gift is silent as to the type of boat to be used by the defender, stating only that "[t]he challenged Club shall not be required to name its representative vessel until at a time agreed upon for the start, but the vessel when named must compete in all the races, and each of such races must be completed with seven hours." Although both monohulls and multihulls were in existence at the time of its final revision in 1887, the Deed of Gift does not explicitly bar the use of a multihulled vessel or require the trustee to defend in a vessel having the same number of hulls as a challenger. Nor is there any express mandate that the competing vessels be identical or even substantially similar.

Nevertheless, until 1988, monohulls have been utilized throughout the history of the America's Cup competition since all the races were conducted under the "mutual consent" provision of the Deed of Gift. Between 1857 and 1937, New York successfully defended the America's Cup sixteen times, twice against Canadian challengers in the 1870's, and on the other fourteen occasions against challengers from British yacht clubs. In each instance, only a single challenger competed.

In the twenty years after the 1973 race there was little interest in the America's Cup, and challenges were not forthcoming. The large ocean-going yachts, known as "J-boats," which were used in the competition prior to World War II, had become too expensive to maintain, and were no longer being built. At that time, the Deed of Gift permitted only the use of boats measuring between 65 and 90 feet on the load water-line. In 1956, in an attempt to revive interest in the competition, New York successfully petitioned the court and obtained an amendment of the Deed lowering the minimum water-line length from 65 to 44 feet, so that the competition could be conducted in yachts of the International 12-Meter Class, and deleting the requirement, which had put foreign challengers at a disadvantage, that the challenger said to the site of the match "on its own bottom"....

The first post-war match was sailed in 1958. With the exception of the 1988 match, every match since World War II had been conducted in 12-Meter yachts. As the event grew more successful and generated greater public awareness, an increasing number of challengers expressed interest in competing for the Cup.

The Deed of Gift provides that "when a challenge from a Club fulfilling all the conditions required by this instrument has been received, no other challenge can be considered until the pending event has been decided." Since this provision allows the first challenger to exclude all others, a mechanism which would accommodate multiple challengers was sought. On December 7, 1962, New York issued a memorandum stating that in the event it successfully defended the Cup in 1964, and, within thirty days, received more than one challenge for the next match, it would regard the challenges as "received simultaneously" and "after due consideration [would] determine which to accept", that it expected to defend the Cup in 12-Meter yachts (and would give two years' notice of a change in class); and that it believed that "it would be in the best interest of the sport and of the competition for the America's Cup if such matches were not held more frequently than once every three years." New York issued a similar memorandum shortly before each subsequent defense....

Even before the culmination of its 1987 America's Cup campaign, San Diego had intended, if successful, to conduct its first defense of the Cup in 1990 or 1991 in 12-Meter yachts, and in the familiar and traditional multiple-challenger format. Yacht clubs all around the world began preparations to compete in that event. In the midst of these preparations, Mercury Bay, by letter dated July 15, 1987, issued a notice of challenge to San Diego demanding a match less than a year later, and disclosing the dimensions of a challenging yacht of a size, 90 feet on the load water-line, that had not been built in fifty years. As noted previously, this length was the largest permitted under the Deed of Gift. Most foreign yacht clubs would be unable to compete on the terms demanded by Mercury Bay inasmuch as they were already preparing for a match in 12-Meter yachts. San Diego announced that the terms of challenge were unacceptable.

On September 2, 1987, Mercury Bay filed suit, seeking a declaration of the validity of its challenge, and for a preliminary injunction prohibiting San Diego from considering any other challenges before its own. Several days later, San Diego, as trustee of the America's Cup, commenced a second action, seeking an interpretation or amendment of the Deed of Gift to authorize a continuation of the uniform practices of the only two prior trustees. Specifically, San Diego urged the court to permit an elimination series so as to further, to the greatest extent possible, the donor's stated purpose of fostering "friendly competition between foreign countries". It was alleged that Mercury Bay sought to exclude challengers from at least nine other countries, and "to return the competition to an age when it could only be enjoyed by that handful of individuals with sufficient means to journey to the site of the competition." In opposing San Diego's application, Mercury Bay insisted that the Deed of Gift was clear and unambiguous and should be enforced according to the plain meaning of its literal terms.

The Attorney General of the State of New York participated in both proceedings pursuant to EPTL 8-1.1(f), which provides that the Attorney General shall represent the beneficiaries of charitable trusts. He supports San Diego's position in both proceedings, which were heard together and decided without taking testimony. The court rejected San Diego's application to interpret or amend the Deed of Gift and granted the motion for a preliminary injunction, declaring that Mercury Bay's notice of challenge was valid, and holding that San Diego's options were to "accept the challenge, forfeit the cup, or negotiate agreeable terms with the challenger."

Both parties thereafter made various proposals under the mutual consent clause of the Deed, but to no avail, and San Diego proceeded with its preparations for a defense of the Cup. Although not required to name its boat until the start of the first race, in late January 1988 San Diego announced its decision to race in a multihull yacht, the dimensions of which would fall within the parameters permitted by the Deed of Gift, although it would be smaller than Mercury Bay's crew-ballasted, fin-keel monohull.

Mercury Bay sought to hold San Diego in contempt, arguing that its announced intention to meet Mercury Bay's challenge in a catamaran would deny Mercury Bay the "match" to which it was entitled under the Deed of Gift and therefore violate the court's earlier order. Mercury Bay claimed that the Deed's use of the word "match" required the defending vessel to be "like or similar" to the challenging vessel. San Diego responded that the court's prior decision had construed the Deed literally, that nothing in the Deed required similarity of vessels, and that the degree of similarity demanded by Mercury Bay was available only by consent.

By decision dated July 25, 1988, the court denied Mercury Bay's motion. . . . It directed the parties "to proceed with the races and to reserve their protests, if any, until after the completion of the America's Cup races." San Diego and Mercury Bay thereafter sailed a match for the America's Cup in early September 1988. San Diego's defending catamaran *Stars & Stripes* defeated Mercury Bay's monohull *New Zealand* two races to none.

Mercury Bay, arguing that San Diego's defense of the America's Cup in a multihull yacht violated the Deed of Gift and the court's prior order, moved to set aside the results of the races, and have Mercury Bay declared the winner, and for an order directing that the Cup be turned over to it. San Diego cross-moved for a declaration that its defense complied with the Deed and the court's order. Both motions addressed whether, in the absence of mutual consent, the Deed of Gift requires the trustee to defend the America's Cup in a vessel "like or similar" to the challenging vessel. Finding that San Diego had attempted "to retain the Cup at all costs so that it could host a competition on its own terms", thereby violating "the spirit of the Deed", the court held that "San Diego's defense of the America's Cup in a catamaran against Mercury Bay's monohull challenge clearly deviated from the intent of the donor" that the competing vessels be "somewhat evenly matched." San Diego's yacht was disqualified, Mercury Bay's challenger declared to be the winner of the two races, and San Diego directed to assign and transfer the America's Cup, and thus the trusteeship, to Mercury Bay. San Diego and the Attorney General appeal. We reverse. . . .

In finding that the vessels must be "somewhat evenly matched", the court promulgated a rule that is neither expressed in, nor inferable from, the language of the Deed of Gift, which expressly and specifically addresses both the type of vessel eligible to compete and the required degree of similarity between the competing vessels. . . .

The [lower] court relied upon the clause, described by it as "the most significant sentence of the Deed", which sets forth the condition of the gift, namely, that the America's Cup was established to foster "friendly competition between foreign countries". This language is precatory only and imposes no affirmative obligation on the trustee to use any particular type of vessel in its defense of the Cup.

As a second ground, the court found that because the challenger must notify the defender of four specified dimensions of the challenging vessel, the defender is required to conform its boat to the challenger's. We cannot find such an intent, especially since the author of the Deed could have stated the rule in a few words, had he so desired. For example, in providing that the defender shall race in "any one yacht or vessel", he could have added the phrase "of the same dimensions" or "somewhat evenly matched to that of the challenger". But no such phrase appears....

As already noted, other than a water-line length limitation, the Deed does not contain any design restraints. It states that the defender may race "any one yacht or vessel constructed in the country of the Club holding the Cup," and, while "any yacht" might seem sufficient to assure the broadest range of eligibility, the Deed language goes even further in extending eligibility to "any vessel", perhaps the most expansive term conceivable for any water-borne vehicle. In the face of language of such breadth—"any one yacht or vessel"—the burden was on Mercury Bay to point to some term of the Deed excluding multihulls, or to an intent, clearly expressed therein, to accomplish such a result. It failed to make such a showing....

... [T]he difficulty with reading into the Deed of Gift a "somewhat evenly matched" requirement is that is establishes a completely unworkable standard. In any yachting competition, whether match (one-on-one) or fleet racing (many competitors over the same course), the degree of similarity of the yachts eligible to compete in the event is dictated by objective, measurable standards expressly set forth in the rules governing the event....

Thus, given its obvious deficiency as a measurable standard, a "somewhat evenly matched" requirement has the potential, in the absence of mutual consent, to foster judicial involvement in the question of boat eligibility, a matter which, in our view, is best left to those charged with the responsibility for judging the match. It should be noted that under the IYRU rules, compliance by a yacht with the applicable class or rating rule is determined by a measurement committee which physically measures the yacht and its sails, and certifies that the yacht complies with the rule, or refuses so to certify. Any competitor dissatisfied with the conclusion of the measurement committee may protest its decision to the International Jury, which has the authority to hear and determine a charge that a yacht has violated a rule, including those governing eligibility to compete in the event.

Finally, we believe that, even if the Deed of Gift were to be construed so as to bar the use of a catamaran in defense of the Cup against a monohull, the drastic remedy of forfeiture was unwarranted....

Since the [lower] court improperly relied on extrinsic evidence to construe an unambiguous instrument, thereby creating a totally new and unworkable eligibility rule, which it belatedly used to reverse the result of a match and to justify the extreme penalty of forfeiture, its order cannot stand.

Accordingly, the order of the Supreme Court, New York County should be reversed, on the law, without costs or disbursements, and a declaration made that San Diego's catamaran was an eligible yacht, that it was the winner of the two races held on September 7 and 9, 1988 for the America's Cup and that San Diego, as the winner of the two races, is entitled to the America's Cup. . . .

JUDGE BENTLEY KASSAL, dissenting:

. . . I cannot accept that such a gross mismatch was permissible under the Deed of Gift, which states that the Cup "shall be preserved as a perpetual Challenge Cup for friendly competition between foreign countries," and must therefore part company with the majority, which has dismissed this critical clause as mere "precatory" language.

The goal of fostering friendly competition is the condition upon which the Cup was donated. As such, it expresses an intent of the donor which must not be lost in the quest for victory, and which may not be measured solely through reference to physical dimensions.

. . . [I]t is clear that San Diego was aware that the eligibility of its catamaran defender had not been determined in the earlier proceeding. Indeed, counsel for San Diego acknowledged the risk of disqualification— as well as the risk of forfeiture—when he stated, during the contempt motion hearing, "[I]f it appears . . . San Diego has not defended the cup in accordance with the deed that it would be appropriate for Mercury Bay to come into court and ask the Court to order a forfeiture of the cup." It so appears.

The 1988 America's Cup races were manifestly unfair in every sense. True sportsmanship and the integrity of this great sport demand far more, as does the very Deed of Gift by which this competition has been sponsored for over a century. . . .

PLEAS FOR HIGHER
JUDICIARY PAY
March 29 and May 3, 1989

In a rare lobbying effort by a chief justice of the United States, William H. Rehnquist appeared before the House Post Office and Civil Service Committee on May 3 to appeal for higher pay for all federal judges. He was the first sitting chief justice to testify before a committee of Congress since Charles Evans Hughes spoke in 1935 against President Franklin D. Roosevelt's attempt to enlarge—"pack"—the Supreme Court.

"I believe the inadequacy of the current judicial salaries is the single greatest problem facing the judicial branch today," Rehnquist told the committee. Rehnquist and others depicted a federal judiciary whose morale had been weakened by a burdensome workload and salaries that were steadily eroded by inflation.

Rehnquist's appearance "indicates the gravity of the issue before us," said Rep. William D. Ford, D-Mich., the committee's chairman. The chief justice argued that if the judges did not receive a pay raise, "we are going to begin to see more resignations from the bench, more damage to the morale of the judges who remain, and more difficulty in recruiting new judges."

Rehnquist stressed that resignations were already at an all-time high. Only six federal judges resigned from 1959 to 1973, he said, but in 1984 and again in 1987 seven resigned.

Earlier Pay Raise Denied

The chief justice is also the presiding judge of the Judicial Conference of the United States, the governing body of the nation's federal judges. He said he came before Congress on behalf of the Judicial Conference, which in March had recommended a 30 percent pay increase for federal judges.

Because their salaries were linked to the lawmakers' pay, the federal judges were denied a proposed boost of 51 percent in February. At that time, Congress bowed to public outrage and voted to reject the raise for all high government officials just hours before it was due to go into effect automatically.

President George Bush later sent legislation to Congress to raise the salaries of judges and an additional 7,200 key executive branch officials by 25 percent. The National Commission on the Public Service, in a report issued March 29, recommended a 25 percent increase immediately for all top-level government officials, including judges and members of Congress, and more later to bring their purchasing power up to the level it was twenty years earlier. In that time, the average number of cases filed annually in federal district courts had increased from 339 per judge to 520.

Commission's Recommendations

The May 3 hearing was one of several held by the committee on the commission's report, "Leadership for America: Rebuilding the Public Service." Looking at a "quiet crisis" at all levels of government, the commission made a spate of recommendations for improving the quality and performance of senior administrative and professional levels of the federal government.

The twenty-six members of the National Commission on the Public Service were prominent persons with wide experience in the high levels of government, business, and academia. It was organized in 1987 largely through the efforts of its chairman, Paul A. Volcker, who formerly was chairman of the Federal Reserve Board, and it came to be known as the Volcker commission.

"Political appointees, judges and members of Congress have never been paid as much as those in the private sector with comparable responsibilities, and must accept financial sacrifice as part of their public responsibility," the report said. "Yet, even starting from these relatively lower levels, the senior positions in government continue to lose ground to inflation. Between 1969 and 1989, when a special effort was made to bring top government salaries into a reasonable relationship with the public sector, the purchasing power of executive, judicial and legislative salaries fell by 35 percent."

"Simply stated," Rehnquist testified on May 3, "judicial salaries . . . have over time been allowed to decline in real value to the point that federal judges are among the lowest paid of all attorneys of similar age and experience in the legal profession."

Salaries for federal judges ranged from nearly $82,000 a year for magistrates, to $89,500 for U.S. District Court judges, to $115,000 for the chief justice.

Judge Joseph F. Weis, Jr., on the Third U.S. Circuit Court of Appeals at Pittsburgh, who was appointed by Congress to head a federal courts' study committee, referred almost immediately to pay when asked about the health of the federal judiciary. He conceded, however, that public opinion was an obstacle to a pay raise for judges—just as it was for members of Congress.

"The public says, 'Why don't they struggle like the rest of us?' And that's pretty hard to answer," Weis said. "But members of the judiciary don't come from a specific group that the public comes from. The lawyers, they earn more than the average person."

Obstacles in Congress

Rep. Don Edwards, D-Calif., a member of the House Judiciary Committee, said $89,500—the yearly earnings of a federal appellate judge—was plenty of money for most lawyers. "They complain too much," he said of the judges. As for warnings that unless pay is raised and the caseload cut, there will be an exodus from the bench, Edwards said, "Every lawyer in the country wants to be a federal judge. They are great whiners."

Many lawmakers said it was unlikely that Congress would agree to a separate boost for judicial pay. They seemed to fear that giving the judges a separate pay raise would harm their own prospects for higher salaries.

President Ronald Reagan proposed an across-the-board salary increase of 51 percent for federal judges, members of Congress, and top executive branch officials shortly before he left the White House. Reagan based his proposal on a report by the Quadrennial Commission, whose job is to make pay recommendations every four years.

Congress, politically sensitive to giving itself pay raises, set up the commission as a way to distance itself from the process. As provided by law, pay raises recommended by the commission and endorsed by the president go into effect automatically unless Congress specifically votes them down. When the 1989 pay raise proposal was in the offing, members of Congress heard so many protests that they unexpectedly rejected it.

Following are excerpts from the report of the National Commission on the Public Service, "Leadership for America: Rebuilding the Public Service," issued March 29, 1989, and from a transcript of Chief Justice William H. Rehnquist's testimony May 3, before the House Post Office and Civil Service Committee:

COMMISSION REPORT
Summary and Main Conclusions

The central message of this report of the Commission on the Public Service is both simple and profound, both urgent and timeless.

In essence, we call for a renewed sense of commitment by all Americans to the highest traditions of the public service—to a public service responsive to the political will of the people and also protective of our constitutional values; to a public service able to cope with complexity and conflict and also able to maintain the highest ethical standards; to a public service attractive to the young and talented from all parts of our society and also capable of earning the respect of all our citizens.

A great nation must demand no less. The multiple challenges thrust upon the Government of the United States as we approach the 21st Century can only reinforce the point. Yet, there is evidence on all sides of an erosion of performance and morale across government in America. Too many of our most talented public servants—those with the skills and dedication that are the hallmarks of an effective career service—are ready to leave. Too few of our brightest young people—those with the imagination and energy that are essential for the future—are willing to join.

Meanwhile, the need for a strong public service is growing, not lessening. Americans have always expected their national government to guarantee their basic freedoms and provide for the common defense. We continue to expect our government to keep the peace with other nations, resolve differences among our own people, pay the bills for needed services, and honor the people's trust by providing the highest levels of integrity and performance.

At the same time, Americans now live in a stronger, more populous nation, a nation with unprecedented opportunity. But they also live in a world of enormous complexity and awesome risks. Our economy is infinitely more open to international competition, our currency floats in a worldwide market, and we live with complex technologies beyond the understanding of any single human mind. Our diplomacy is much more complicated, and the wise use of our unparalleled military power more difficult. And for all our scientific achievements, we are assaulted daily by new social, environmental, and health issues almost incomprehensible in scope and impact—issues like drugs, AIDS, and global warming.

Faced with these challenges, the simple idea that Americans must draw upon talented and dedicated individuals to serve us in government is uncontestable. America must have a public service that can both value the lessons of experience and appreciate the requirements for change; a public service that both responds to political leadership and respects the law; a public service with the professional skills and the ethical sensitivity America deserves.

Surely, there can be no doubt that moral challenge and personal excitement are inherent in the great enterprise of democratic government. There is work to be done of enormous importance. Individuals can make a difference.

But unfortunately there is growing evidence that these basic truths have been clouded by a sense of frustration inside government and a lack of public trust outside. The resulting erosion in the quality of America's public service is difficult to measure; there are still many examples of excellence among those who carry out the nation's business at home and abroad. Nevertheless, it is evident that public service is neither as attractive as it once was nor as effective in meeting perceived needs. No doubt, opposition to specific policies of government has contributed to a lack of respect for the public servants who struggle to make the policies work. This drives away much of our best talent which can only make the situation worse.

One need not search far to see grounds for concern. Crippled nuclear weapons plants, defense procurement scandals, leaking hazardous waste dumps, near-misses in air traffic control, and the costly collapse of so many savings and loans have multiple causes. But each such story carries some similar refrains about government's inability to recruit and retain a talented work force: the Department of Defense is losing its top procurement specialists to contractors who can pay much more; the Federal Aviation Administration is unable to hold skilled traffic controllers because of stress and working conditions; the Environmental Protection Agency is unable to fill key engineering jobs because the brightest students simply are not interested; the Federal Savings and Loan Insurance Corporation (FSLIC) simply cannot hire and pay able executives.

This erosion has been gradual, almost imperceptible, year by year. But it has occurred nonetheless. Consider the following evidence compiled by the Commission's five task forces on the growing recruitment problem:

- Only 13 percent of the senior executives recently interviewed by the General Accounting Office would recommend that young people start their careers in government, while several recent surveys show that less than half the senior career civil servants would recommend a job in government to their own children.
- Of the 610 engineering students who received bachelors, masters, and doctoral degrees at the Massachusetts Institute of Technology and Stanford University in 1986, and the 600 who graduated from Rensselaer Polytechnic Institute in 1987, only 29 took jobs in government at any level.
- Half the respondents to a recent survey of federal personnel officers said recruitment of quality personnel had become more difficult over the past five years.
- Three-quarters of the respondents to the Commission's survey of recent Presidential Management Interns—a prestigious program for recruiting the top graduates of America's schools of public affairs—said they would leave government within 10 years.

If these trends continue, America will soon be left with a government of the mediocre, locked into careers of last resort or waiting for a chance to move on to other jobs.

But this need not and should not be. By the choices we make today, we can enter the 21st century with a public service fully equipped to meet the challenges of intense competition abroad and growing complexity at home. The strongest wish of the Commission is that this report can be a step in that process, pointing toward necessary changes, while serving as a catalyst for national debate and further efforts at all levels of government.

America should and can act now to restore the leadership, talent, and performance essential to the strong public service the future demands. . . .

To further these basic goals, the Commission makes a series of specific recommendations throughout the report. . . .

First, Presidents, their chief lieutenants, and Congress must articulate early and often the necessary and honorable role that public servants play in the democratic process, at the same time making clear they will demand the highest standards of ethics and performance possible from those who hold the public trust. Members of Congress and their staffs should be covered by similar standards. Codes of conduct to convey such standards should be simple and straightforward, and should focus on the affirmative values that must guide public servants in the exercise of their responsibilities.

Second, within program guidelines from the President, cabinet officers and agency heads should be given greater flexibility to administer their organizations, including greater freedom to hire and fire personnel, provided there are appropriate review procedures within the Administration and oversight from Congress.

Third, the President should highlight the important role of the Office of Personnel Management (OPM) by establishing and maintaining contact with its Director and by ensuring participation by the Director in cabinet level discussions on human resource management issues. The Commission further recommends decentralization of a portion of OPM's operating responsibilities to maximize its role of personnel policy guidance to federal departments and agencies.

Fourth, the growth in recent years in the number of presidential appointees, whether those subject to Senate confirmation, noncareer senior executives, or personal and confidential assistants, should be curtailed. Although a reduction in the total number of presidential appointees must be based on a position-by-position assessment, the Commission is confident that a substantial cut is possible, and believes a cut from the current 3,000 to no more than 2,000 is a reasonable target. Every President must have politically and philosophically compatible officials to implement his Administration's program. At the same time, however, experience suggests that excessive numbers of political appointees serving relatively brief periods may undermine the President's ability to govern, insulating the Administration from needed dispassionate advice and institutional memory. The mere size of the political turnover almost guarantees management gaps and discontinuities, while the best of the career professionals will leave government if they do not have challenging opportunities at the sub-cabinet level.

Fifth, the President and Congress must ensure that federal managers receive the added training they will need to perform effectively. The education of public servants must not end upon appointment to the civil service. Government must invest more in its executive development programs and develop stronger partnerships with America's colleges and universities.

Sixth, the nation should recognize the importance of civic education as a part of social studies and history in the nation's primary and secondary school curricula. Starting with a comprehensive review of current programs, the nation's educators and parents should work toward new curricula and livelier textbooks designed to enhance student understanding of America's civic institutions, relate formal learning about those institutions to the problems students care about, and link classroom learning to extracurricular practice.

Seventh, America should take advantage of the natural idealism of its youth by expanding and encouraging national volunteer service, whether through existing programs like ACTION, the Peace Corps, and VISTA, or experiments with initiatives like President Bush's Youth Engaged in Service (YES), and some of the ideas contained in the Democratic Leadership Council's citizen corps proposal.

Eighth, the President and Congress should establish a Presidential Public Service Scholarship Program targeted to 1,000 college or college-bound students each year, with careful attention to the recruitment of minority students. Admission to the program might be modeled on appointment to the military service academies—that is, through nomination by members of Congress—and should include tuition and other costs, in return for a commitment to a determined number of years of government service.

Ninth, the President should work with Congress to give high priority to restoring the depleted purchasing power of executive, judicial, and legislative salaries by the beginning of a new Congress in 1991, starting with an immediate increase of 25 percent. At the same time, the Commission recommends that Congress enact legislation eliminating speaking honoraria and other income related to their public responsibilities.

Tenth, if Congress is unable to act on its own salaries, the Commission recommends that the President make separate recommendations for judges and top level executives and that the Congress promptly act upon them. Needed pay raises for presidential appointees, senior career executives, and judges should no longer be dependent on the ability of Congress to raise its own pay.

Eleventh, the President and Congress should give a higher budget priority to civil service pay in the General Schedule pay system. In determining the appropriate increase, the Commission concludes that the current goal of national comparability between public and private pay is simplistic and unworkable, and is neither fair to the civil service nor to the public it serves. The Commission therefore recommends a new civil service pay-setting process that recognizes the objective fact that pay differs by occupation and by localities characterized by widely different living costs and labor market pressures.

Twelfth, the President and Congress should establish a permanent independent advisory council, composed of members from the public and private sectors, both to monitor the ongoing state of the public service and to make such recommendations for improvements as they think desirable. The Commission applauds President Bush's pledge of leadership of the public service. Indeed, his recent statements reflect the spirit and concerns that led to the creation of the Commission. However, the problems that make up this "quiet crisis" are many and complex, and have been long in the making. Corrective action will not only require presidential leadership and congressional support, but must be part of a coherent and sustained long term strategy. The proposed independent advisory council is designed to ensure that the state of the public service remains high on the national agenda.

This report speaks directly to a number of audiences: to the *American people* about the importance to their civic institutions of talented men and women; to *young people* about the challenges and satisfactions they can find in serving their government; to *candidates for elective office* about the long-term costs of "bureaucrat bashing"; to the *media* about the need not only to hold public servants to high standards but also to recognize those who serve successfully; to *university schools of public affairs* about developing curricula for the training of a new generation of government managers; and to *business leaders* about the importance of quality government support to the private sector.

Finally, the report speaks to the *civil service* about its obligations to the highest standards of performance. The Commission fully supports the need for better pay and working conditions in much of government. But the Commission also recognizes that public support for those improvements is dependent on a commitment by the civil servants themselves to efficiency, responsiveness, and integrity.

REHNQUIST TESTIMONY

Mr. Chairman and Members of the Committee,

I appreciate the opportunity to appear today and offer my views on a matter of great importance: that is, the pressing need for salary reform in the federal judiciary.

I believe that the inadequacy of current judicial salaries is the single greatest problem facing the Judicial Branch today. In my view, the failure adequately to address this problem poses the most serious threat to the future of the judiciary, and its continued operations, that I have observed in my seventeen years of judicial service. These hearings, and the attention accorded to this issue by your Committee, give me reason to hope that this problem may be at least alleviated, if not completely solved in the near future.

I appear before you as presiding officer of the Judicial Conference of the United States, the governing body of the nation's federal judges. I assure you that the urgency with which I view this matter is shared by every member of the Judicial Conference. My views also reflect the concerns, expressed with increasing frequency and conviction, of the men and women serving in every circuit and district court across the land. We believe that something must be done to address this nagging problem of inadequate judicial pay, not only for the present, but for the long term as well.

On behalf of the Judicial Conference and the nation's federal judges, I urge this Committee to take appropriate action now. Specifically, I urge this Committee to support and the Congress to enact legislation that will immediately increase the pay of federal judges and provide a regular mechanism to evaluate and adjust their salaries in the future. At its last semiannual meeting, in March, the Judicial Conference considered what course of action to recommend. The Conference unanimously adopted a resolution calling for an immediate thirty percent increase in judicial salaries, coupled with provisions assuring that judicial officers receive regular periodic cost-of-living adjustments (COLAs) similar to those received by almost all other governmental personnel. We believe these steps would go a long way toward solving the current pay crisis and would provide a sorely-needed replacement for the currently unworkable, and unduly controversial quadrennial pay adjustment mechanism.

The Judicial Conference did not come lightly to this recommendation, nor did we ignore the recent unhappy history of salary increase proposals. We recognize that there was widespread public opposition to President Reagan's recommendations for an across-the-board raise for senior federal officials in the range of fifty percent. We believe, however, that a smaller increase of thirty percent for federal judges is both publicly acceptable and fully justified. We further recognize that there were institutional objections to the fifty percent pay increase proposal, which would have resulted in Congress' increasing its own pay by that substantial amount. Certainly the arguments favoring salary increases for members of Congress and high-ranking Executive Branch officials can be persuasively made. The Judicial Conference continues to support an increase in pay for senior officials in all three branches of government. Nevertheless, we defer to the Congress' determination of how best to provide fair salary adjustments for Executive and Legislative Branch officials, while asking the Committee for priority consideration of our urgent recommendations on behalf of the federal judiciary. . . .

As a result of this proposal, the current salary of Associate Justices of the Supreme Court would rise from $110,000 to $143,000; the salary of circuit judges would rise from $95,000 to $123,500, and the salary of district judges would rise from $89,500 to $116,350. The proposed adjustment would also have the effect of increasing salaries for United States Claims Court judges, United States bankruptcy judges, and full-time United States magistrates, all of whose salaries are linked by statute to the salary of a United States district judge. The revised salary levels for these other judicial officers are set forth in the section-by-section analysis attached to the proposed legislation.

The second key feature of the Judicial Conference's recommended legislation is the proposed adoption of a routine cost-of-living adjustment mechanism. We firmly believe that federal judges should receive the same sorts of periodic cost-of-living increases granted by statute to most other government employees, including government retirees. Moreover, we believe that providing for regular cost-of-living adjustments to judicial salaries could well obviate the need for the sort of sizable "catch-up" increases proposed by past quadrennial salary commissions, which have proved unacceptably controversial. Had federal judicial salaries been adjusted over the last twenty years to match the rate of increase in other government pay, they would be in the same range as the current proposal seeks to accomplish in one major adjustment. Protecting judicial salaries from the steady erosion of inflation is both a fair and practical alternative.

At present federal judges may receive periodic salary adjustments equivalent to those afforded to General Schedule (GS) federal employees only if Congress acts affirmatively to allow them. Congress' historical reluctance to increase its own pay levels has often meant that cost-of-living increases for other senior government officials have also been denied. Even when annual increases have been authorized, they generally have been inadequate to maintain the real value of judicial salaries. This is because the cost-of-living increases allowed to GS employees generally have been below the actual level of inflation measured by Consumer Price Index data.

The current system of protecting judicial salaries from the effects of inflation is fine in principle but severely flawed in practice. We recommend that this system be replaced with one that ties federal judicial cost-of-living increases to those received by civil service retirees and that allows the increases to take effect automatically, once their size is determined, without the need for a separate enactment. Once judicial salaries are increased sufficiently to compensate for the past years of effective decline, periodic cost-of-living adjustments equivalent to those afforded to civil service annuitants should keep judicial salaries current and maintain judges' purchasing power.

Before closing, I want to touch on what I believe to be the compelling arguments behind our recommendation. These arguments have not lost their force by virtue of being oft-repeated and easily understood. Stated simply, judicial salaries, which are constitutionally protected against diminution in amount, have over time been allowed to decline in real value to the point that federal judges are now among the lowest paid of all attorneys of similar age and experience in the legal profession. . . .

Having lived the last two decades in Washington, D.C., I am well aware of the traditional Washington response to statements like mine: everyone wants to see evidence of the cataclysmic disaster that surely must be in the making. I will concede that the problem facing the federal courts does not have the graphic impact of an Alaskan oil spill or the high visibility of potentially poisoned fruit at the corner grocery store. For just this reason, this issue has aptly been termed a "quiet crisis.". . .

April

Kennan Observes End of Cold War 207

Report on Black College Athletes 213

Congressional Hearing on
   Alaskan Oil Spill 225

Ethics Committee Reports,
   Wright's Resignation Speech 239

KENNAN OBSERVES
END OF COLD WAR
April 4, 1989

George F. Kennan, the architect of America's postwar policy of "containment" of the Soviet Union, told the Senate Foreign Relations Committee on April 4 that the world was witnessing in Russia "the break-up of much, if not all, of the system of power by which that country has been held together and governed since 1917." Committee members praised the insights of this eighty-five-year-old scholar and former diplomat and, joined by staff members and the hearing audience, accorded him a spontaneous and lengthy standing ovation.

Committee chairman Claiborne Pell, D-R.I., and other Senate veterans said that they could not remember any similar tribute to a witness before a Senate committee. The tribute reflected both reverence for Kennan's long career of interpreting international relations and gratitude for confirmation by a prestigious analyst of Soviet affairs of the growing American hope that the Cold War was over. It was particularly reassuring to hear from a statesman credited with rallying America to face the threat of Soviet expansionism that "whatever reasons there may once have been for regarding the Soviet Union primarily as a possible, if not probable, military opponent, the time for that sort of thing has clearly passed."

Kennan's Diplomatic Career

Soon after graduating from Princeton in 1925, Kennan began a distinguished diplomatic career that brought him in contact with some of the greatest tragedies of his era. He soon joined a select group of young Foreign Service officers being groomed for the day that U.S. relations

*with the Soviet Union—severed in 1917—would be resumed. Kennan was
posted to the Baltic nations of Estonia, Latvia, and Lithuania, which had
gained independence from the Russian empire at the time of the 1917
Bolshevik Revolution and were regarded as "listening posts" for the
Soviet Union. From 1929 to 1931 he was assigned to Berlin for special
training in Russian language, history, culture, and political theory. After
Washington and Moscow resumed relations in 1933, Kennan helped to
reopen the U.S. embassy in the Soviet capital and served there through
the time of Stalin's purges. He then served in Czechoslovakia during its
dismemberment by the Nazis in 1938, and in Berlin from the outbreak of
World War II in 1939 until the United States entered the war in
December 1941.*

*Thrust into the midst of national disasters, Kennan never lost a sense
of the human heartbreak he witnessed. This sensitivity was to find
literary expression in his published memoirs and to flavor his later
historical scholarship.*

Kennan's Writings

*Kennan's direct influence on U.S. foreign policy was brief but seminal.
In a period of slightly more than a year he produced three documents
that set the stage for the American policy makers of the next four
decades. In his "Long Telegram," sent from Moscow February 22, 1946,
Kennan sounded an alarm that is credited with awakening Washington
to Soviet expansionism.*

*In a May 25, 1947, report entitled, "Certain Aspects of the European
Recovery Program from the United States' Standpoint," Kennan unified
State Department thinking on the emerging Marshall Plan of economic
aid to war-torn Europe.*

*His most famous contribution to American policy was an article
published in the July 1947 issue of* Foreign Affairs *magazine signed by
"X." This article on "The Sources of Soviet Conduct," recognized within
weeks as Kennan's work, spelled out the "containment" policy that would
later be associated with his name.*

*Kennan's famous prescription called for "long-term, patient, but firm
and vigilant containment of Russian expansionist tendencies ... by the
adroit and vigilant application of counterforce at a series of constantly
shifting geographical and political points, corresponding to the shifts and
maneuvers of Soviet policy." An heir to this perspective, Henry Kissinger
was later to observe that "Kennan came as close to authoring the
diplomatic doctrine of his era as any diplomat in our history."*

*At the time, the commentator Walter Lippmann attacked containment
as a "strategic monstrosity," reactive, almost pathologically indiscriminate, and unduly militarized. Kennan himself was sympathetic to Lippmann's criticisms and dismayed by what he saw as a distortion of
containment into a rationale for American expansionism.*

*Kennan left the Foreign Service in 1953 to pursue historical scholar-
ship at the Institute for Advanced Study in Princeton, New Jersey. His*

ensuing books and articles cast this century's international relations, in particular relations between Russia and the West, in a perspective consistent with his diplomatic philosophy.

Kennan's Values

Kennan distrusted American tendencies to exaggerate Soviet power, to perceive the Kremlin as demonic, and to pursue diplomacy as a moral crusade. He was also distrustful of internationalist viewpoints that he considered naive. Kennan warned repeatedly against excessive reliance on nuclear deterrence, and in 1981 he called upon the two superpowers to halve their strategic nuclear arsenals.

But Kennan did not envision any fundamental transformation in international politics in response to the new threat of nuclear annihilation. On the contrary, he championed a return to the traditional diplomacy—to an era when aristocratic elites, untroubled by the passionate ideologies of the twentieth century or by social earthquakes in non-Western civilizations, could, as he put it in his Senate testimony, adjust differences "by the normal means of compromise and accommodation."

Calling himself an "expatriate in time," Kennan often expressed nostalgia for predemocratic societies and hostility toward contemporary trends in the civilization he worked to defend.

While generally classed among "realists" in foreign policy, Kennan attached less importance to military options and more importance to internal trends than other balance-of-power strategists. His earliest reports on the Soviet Union saw an internal weakness that would lead, as he put it in the "Mr. X" article, to "either the breakup or gradual mellowing of Soviet power." He urged that America exert international influence by dealing with its own domestic problems, thereby setting an example that would attract other nations rather than pressuring them with rewards and punishments.

As the 1980s drew to a close, a spate of books and articles honored Kennan as a prophet in his own time. Many writers focused on "contradictions" or "paradoxes" in Kennan's life and thought and tried to identify an underlying unity. These books included George Kennan and the Dilemmas of U.S. Foreign Policy, *by David Mayers;* Kennan and the Art of Foreign Policy, *by Anders Stephanson;* Cold War Iconoclast *by Walter L. Hixon; and Kennan's own* Sketches from a Life. *His appearance before the Senate Foreign Relations Committee was part of that same impulse to honor an elder statesman who had been proved prophetic by the turn of world events he had lived long enough to witness.*

Following is the text of George F. Kennan's statement to the Senate Foreign Relations Committee, April 4, 1989:

The following comments are addressed to the question of the future of Soviet-American relations.

What we are witnessing today in Russia is the break-up of much, if not all, of the system of power by which that country has been held together and governed since 1917.

Fortunately, that break-up has been most pronounced in precisely those aspects of Soviet power that have been most troublesome from the standpoint of Soviet-American relations, namely:

(a) The world-revolutionary ideology, rhetoric, and political efforts of the early Soviet leadership.

(Fortunately, these are no longer a significant factor in Soviet behavior.)

(b) The morbid extremism of Stalinist political oppression.

(This factor began to be greatly moderated soon after Stalin's death in 1953. Further very extensive modifications of it have been proceeding under Gorbachev; the remnants of it are now being dismantled at a pace that renders it no longer a serious impediment to a normal Soviet-American relationship.)

There remain, however, three factors that do indeed trouble the relationship and have to be considered when one confronts the questions of its future. These are:

(a) What many in the West consider to be the inordinate size of the peacetime conventional armed force establishment.

(b) What remains of the Soviet political and military hegemony in eastern, and parts of central, Europe.

(c) The rivalry between the two powers in the cultivation and development of nuclear and conventional weaponry; and

(d) To these factors, as ones presenting problems in Soviet-American relations, might be added the unstable and in some respects dangerous internal-political situation that now prevails in the Soviet Union.

I would like to comment, briefly, on each of these factors.

(a) The maintenance of what appear to be numerically excessive ground forces in peacetime has been a constant feature of Russian/Soviet policy for most of the last two hundred years. The reasons have been partly domestic and partly defensive. It is significant that never, in all this time, have these forces been employed to initiate hostilities against a major military power. Under Gorbachev's leadership, the size of the establishment is now being somewhat reduced. Altogether, this should not be a serious complication of the Soviet-American relationship.

(b) Since roughly the time of the increased troop movements into Czechoslovakia in 1968 the Soviet political hegemony over the other Warsaw Pact countries has been slackening; and now, since Gorbachev's advent to power, there has been a marked advance in the effective independence of these satellite governments. In the shaping of their economies and of their relations with western countries, those regimes now have essentially a free hand, provided only (a) that they do not challenge their obligations of membership in the Warsaw Pact, and (b) that they do not depart from use of the term "socialist" as the official designation of their economies. So tenuous is today the Soviet hold over these countries that I personally doubt that military intervention in any of these countries, along the lines of the action in Hungary in 1956, would now be a realistic option of Soviet policy. Not only would it be in crass conflict with Gorbachev's public commitments, but the consequences in the remainder of the satellite area, and among non-Russian nationalities of the Soviet Union, would be unpredictable.

(c) I do not consider that our government has made the efforts it could and should have made to reach acceptable agreements with the Soviet side for the reduction of either nuclear or conventional weapons. While this question is too complex for detailed treatment in this statement, I would like to offer these general comments:

There have been, in recent months and years, several interesting and encouraging initiatives and suggestions from the Soviet side to which we have been essentially unresponsive. Obviously, these initiatives and suggestions could not be taken at face value; they all called for exploration, in discussions with the Soviet side, of their reality and practical significance. But this exploration has not been seriously undertaken. I think it should have been.

The problem of reductions in conventional armaments had been needlessly complicated and distorted by the egregious exaggeration of the existing Soviet superiority in such weapons that has marked the public statements, and apparently the official assumptions, of our government. This, obviously, should be corrected.

The arsenals of nuclear weapons now in the possession of the Soviet Union and the United States are plainly vastly redundant in relation to the purpose they are supposed to serve. Owing to their over-destructiveness and their suicidal implications, these weapons are essentially useless from the standpoint of actual commitment to military combat; and whatever "deterrent" function they might usefully serve could be effectively served by far smaller forces. The statements and policies of our government appear to reflect an assumption that the maintenance of these excessive arsenals presents no serious problem, and that there is no urgency about the need for their reduction. I cannot share this complacency. Not only is there the danger that these weapons might come into use by accident, misunderstanding, or other inadvertence, but there seems to be a real and immediate danger that there will be further proliferation in the coming period. This danger calls urgently for a vigorous attack on the whole problem of proliferation; and a prerequisite for such an attack would be, as I see it, extensive reductions in the holdings of the two superpowers. It is unrealistic to suppose that the U.S. and the U.S.S.R. can continue indefinitely to cultivate these weapons in such excessive numbers and yet successfully deny to most of the world's governments the right to cultivate them at all.

(d) The domestic-political personal situation of Mr. Gorbachev is indeed in certain respects precarious, particularly in view of the meager results to date of his program of *perestroika* [restructuring]. But his position also has had important elements of strength, as does his program; and both have now been strengthened by the results of the recent election. His initiatives in foreign policy have not met with serious internal-political

211

resistance. There is therefore no reason to suppose that agreements entered into with his government under his leadership would not, if properly negotiated and formalized, be respected by his successors.

In summary, it appears to me that whatever reasons there may once have been for regarding the Soviet Union primarily as a possible, if not probable, military opponent, the time for that sort of thing has clearly passed. That country should now be regarded essentially as another great power like other great powers—one, that is, whose aspirations and policies are conditioned outstandingly by its own geographic situation, history, and tradition, and are therefore not identical with our own but are also not so seriously in conflict with ours as to justify any assumption that the outstanding differences could not be adjusted by the normal means of compromise and accommodation. It ought now to be our purpose, I consider, while not neglecting the needs of our general security, to eliminate as soon as possible, by amicable negotiation, the elements of abnormal military tension that have recently dominated Soviet-American relations, and to turn our attention, instead, to the development of the positive possibilities of this relationship, which are far from insignificant.

REPORT ON BLACK
COLLEGE ATHLETES
April 5, 1989

Anyone who watches sports is aware that a great number of college athletes are black. From an abundance of news stories and other observations, a viewer might conclude that these athletes generally come from impoverished backgrounds and often are ill-prepared for academic life. Nevertheless, they are admitted to college and, according to the same line of thinking, their athletic abilities are exploited until their playing eligibility expires. At that time, a few of the most athletically gifted enter professional sports and possibly earn enormous sums of money for awhile. Most of the rest drift away without their college degrees, unprepared for well-paying work.

Does that thinking have any basis in reality? A survey commissioned by the National Collegiate Athletic Association (NCAA) suggests that it does. The survey was conducted on forty-two campuses in March-July 1988 by the Center for the Study of Athletics, based in Palo Alto, California, an arm of the American Institutes of Research. On April 5 at its offices in Mission, Kansas, the NCAA issued the survey's findings in a report titled "The Experiences of Black Intercollegiate Athletes at NCAA Division I Institutions."

This report, the third in a series of NCAA reports prepared by the same groups, was prefaced, "Report No. 3." The first two reports, issued in November 1988, summarized the results and methodology of a national study of intercollegiate athletics in 1987-1988. All three reports resulted from an effort by the NCAA's Presidents' Commission to identify the effects of participation in intercollegiate athletics on student-athletes. The commission is composed of presidents from among the eight hundred member-institutions of the NCAA, whose rules govern the intercollegiate sports activities of those colleges and universities. The survey was confined to a selection of the NCAA's Division I schools; those accorded that status typically spend—and earn—far more on athletics than other institutions do. On all but three of the forty-two campuses where the survey was conducted, white students were predominant.

Academic and Discrimination Questions

The report on black athletes confirmed that large numbers of college football and basketball players were black, and far out of proportion to the overall number of black students on the campuses. Throughout Division I, blacks accounted for 37 percent of the football players, 56 percent of the men's basketball players, and 33 percent of the women's basketball players. In all other intercollegiate sports, the percentage was less but still double the percentage of blacks among all undergraduates on those campuses (8 versus 4 percent).

"Black football and basketball players on predominantly white campuses, as compared to those on predominantly black campuses, are more apt to feel ... racially isolated, and to feel racial discrimination," the report said. At the schools with the smallest numbers of black students, almost 70 percent of the black football and basketball players who took part in the survey said they had a sense of being different. More than half reported racial isolation and about a third reported racial discrimination. The survey results revealed that even more than other black students at the mostly white colleges, black athletes found it difficult to get to know a wide range of students. Being less well prepared for college-level study, black football and basketball players "are less likely than other black students to belong to student groups," the report said.

"College students who are black and who participate in either intercollegiate athletics or in other extracurricular activities differ in some rather striking ways from college students of other races," the report said. "They are less well prepared for college studies, as measured by their grade-point averages in high school and the Scholastic Aptitude Test (SAT) or American College Testing (ACT) Assessment Program, and their grade-point averages in college are lower. They are also from households with lower socioeconomic status."

Unrealistic Career Goals

Despite the differences in academic attainment, black athletes "are as likely as other student-athletes to be recruited actively and to be given athletic grants by Division I colleges and universities," the report added. Thus, it continued, "they are likely to face personal challenges in college that are beyond those faced by other student-athletes."

In season and out, the survey revealed, both black and nonblack college football and basketball players spent more time in athletics than in either preparing for or attending classes. On average, they missed two classes a week during the season, and one class a week at other times. The black athletes' grades were marginally below those of other black students. At predominantly white institutions, some 44 percent of the black football and basketball players reported having been put on academic probation.

The survey indicated that many black athletes in college nurtured unrealistic career aspirations. For example, nearly half of those in the mostly white colleges expected to become professional athletes although, statistically, the odds are stacked against them. And 35 percent of those who said they would "almost certainly" attend graduate school had grade point averages below 2.0, the point at which academic probation is invoked at the undergraduate level of Division I schools.

Criticism of the Colleges

The frequent failure of colleges and universities to educate their athletes, black and nonblack, came to public attention in many ways during 1989. Dexter Manley, a star pro football player with the Washington Redskins, testified at congressional hearings that he had great difficulty reading but was permitted to graduate from Oklahoma State University. Dr. John Campbell, the university's president, expressed embarrassment over Manley's disclosure but said that "there would be those who would argue that Dexter got exactly what he wanted out of OSU. He was able to develop his athletic skills and ability, he was noticed by the pros, he got a pro contract. He would not have had that opportunity had he not gone to Oklahoma State or some other university that had a decent, recognized athletic program. So maybe we did him a favor by letting him go through the system."

More typical, perhaps, are the athletes who never earn enough credits to graduate. Northeastern University in Boston, through its Center for the Study of Sports in Society, recently organized a consortium with thirty-nine other universities to give former athletes the opportunity to complete college courses, at no charge, toward a degree once their athletic eligibility expires.

Many of the coaches, educators, and sports administrators who met in June for a conference on ethics at the University of Rhode Island's Institute for International Sports agreed that the colleges and universities had placed a greater emphasis on obtaining money from sports entertainment than on educating the young men and women athletes who provided the entertainment. In the preceding months, Time magazine published a cover story about the failure of big universities with big sports programs to provide their players an education. A Sports Illustrated story called big-time college sports "an American disgrace."

Sixty-eight percent of the people who responded to a Media General/Associated Press poll released in April said they believed colleges placed too much emphasis on sports. A study conducted by the General Accounting Office, an agency of Congress, revealed that fewer than one-fifth of the men's varsity basketball players graduate at some of America's biggest universities. Those figures applied to thirty-five of

ninety-seven major collegiate basketball programs that the agency stud-
ied, according to a draft report made public in September.

Ninety-two college sports programs were cited in this decade for
NCAA rules violations. Seventy-six of them were in Division I. They
included forty-nine—nearly half—of the schools in the division's top
bracket, Division 1A, that traditionally field big-time football teams.
Punishment varied from mild reprimands to the so-called "death
penalty" in the case of Southern Methodist University in Dallas, Texas.
For repeated violations, SMU was forced to cancel its 1987 football
games; at the university's own volition, it decided to skip the 1988
season as well.

Some coaches and athletic directors have argued that such publicized
incidents distort the picture. For instance, Richard D. Shultz, the
NCAA's executive director and the former athletic director at the
University of Virginia, has insisted that what goes on in college sports is
"nine-nine percent positive." Mike Krzyzewski, basketball coach at Duke
University, saw matters from a different angle. "The letter of the NCAA
rules isn't violated as much as you might think," he was quoted as saying.
"But the intent is hammered to hell."

In Congress, the House Subcommittee on Postsecondary Education
held hearings in the spring of 1989 on the problems in big-time intercolle-
giate sports. At one hearing, Sen. Bill Bradley, D-N.J., a Rhodes scholar
who starred in college and professional basketball, appeared before the
subcommittee to push for legislation requiring colleges to disclose the
graduation rate for their student athletes. The NCAA, which itself
proposed to invoke a similar disclosure rule, also asked its member
institutions to consider a plan for reviewing, every five years, athletic
recruitment, admission standards, athletes' progress toward graduation,
graduation rates, and the behavior of coaches and players.

> *Following are excerpts from the report, "The Experiences of*
> *Black Intercollegiate Athletes at NCAA Division I Institu-*
> *tions," prepared by the Center for the Study of Athletics and*
> *the American Institutes of Research on behalf of the Presi-*
> *dents Commission of the National Collegiate Athletic Associ-*
> *ation, which publicly released the report April 5, 1989:*

1. Introduction

The data on Black student-athletes from the 1987-88 National Study of
Intercollegiate Athletes should inform and may disturb many persons in
higher education—from college administrators and teachers to athletics
directors and coaches. For prospective Black student-athletes, their families, and their communities, we hope these data will clarify many of the
demands associated with the roles of student and athlete on today's college
campuses.

In this chapter, we describe why the national study was conducted and
how we selected topics for this report. The final section of this chapter

describes the comparisons made in this report and how to interpret the figures and tables.

Impetus for the Study

On June 3, 1987, the Presidents Commission of the National Collegiate Athletic Association (NCAA) mailed to the NCAA members a policy paper titled *Agenda for Reform*. The paper provided the rationale for an 18-month national forum on the proper role of intercollegiate athletics within higher education. . . .

In the *Agenda for Reform,* the Presidents Commission listed eight broad sets of questions to be addressed during the national forum. The national study was designed to focus on the first four sets of these questions:

1. How do the experiences of college or university life of student-athletes compare with those of other students who devote a great deal of time to a particular extra-curricular activity?
2. How do the experiences of student-athletes differ depending upon whether one is a participant in big-time sports or in sports that are not given a heavy emphasis?
3. How do the experiences of student-athletes compare with those of other students in terms of courses taken, classes attended, time spent on or off campus, and tutoring received? How do student-athletes feel about and evaluate their experiences? Do they see themselves as beneficiaries of fine programs, or as exploited? How do they personally experience the balance between athletics and academics in their daily lives?
4. How are students-athletes recruited? How do recruitment activities differ depending upon the intensity of the athletic program? What are the differences in test scores and grade-point averages between athletes and other students? How do recruited students personally experience the process of choice of college and university and the role of athletic recruitment in that process? . . .

2. Background of Students and the Campus Environment

Overview

Although about 12% of the U.S. population is Black, the median enrollment of Black undergraduates in NCAA Division I colleges and universities is 4%. In Division I football and men's and women's basketball, Blacks are over-represented given their proportions in either the U.S. or undergraduate populations. Approximately 37% of the football players who participate at the Division I intercollegiate level are Black. Approximately 56% of the men's basketball players and 33% of the women's basketball players at Division I institutions are Black. College students who are Black and who participate in either intercollegiate athletics or in other extracurricular activities differ in some rather striking ways from college students of other races. They are less well prepared for college studies, as measured by their grade-point averages in high school and the Scholastic Aptitude Test (SAT) or the American College Testing (ACT) Assessment Program, and their grade-point averages in college are lower. They are also from households with lower socioeconomic status.

Despite the differences in their records of academic success in high school, Black student-athletes are as likely as other student-athletes to be recruited actively and to be given athletic grants by Division I colleges and universities. The campuses into which most enroll are predominately White. On those campuses, there is evidence that Black student-athletes perceive greater isolation and discrimination. Because of their backgrounds, their participation in athletics, and the small numbers of other Black students on predominately White campuses, Black student-athletes are likely to face personal challenges in college that are beyond those faced by other student-athletes. . . .

Academic and Socioeconomic Characteristics

Academic readiness and performance

The SAT and ACT are used by many colleges and universities as one component in evaluating applicants, but the tests have been criticized on the grounds that they are culturally biased instruments that discriminate against Black students. The developers of the test (the Educational Testing Service/The College Board and the American College Testing Assessment Program) point out that the instruments are developed and tested to eliminate any systematic racial or cultural bias and do predict success in college. Whether one thinks the tests are culturally biased or not, the fact is that the SAT and ACT are regarded by many in higher education as objective measures of ability to perform college-level work. Some administrators might assume that low scores are a measure of real deficit and act accordingly, either during the admissions process or in developing expectations of what a student might achieve. For these reasons alone, student scores on the college entrance tests cannot be ignored.

. . . About 58% of the Black football and basketball players score in the lowest quartile on the SAT and 57% score in the lowest quartile on the ACT. . . . The mean SAT score for Black football and basketball players is 740 and the mean ACT score is 14. The mean SAT score for NonBlack football and basketball players is 890 and the mean ACT is 19.

From the data . . . it is evident why some have raised concerns about Proposition 48 [formerly Bylaw 5-1-(j) and now Bylaw 14.3] and Proposition 42, which was passed at the 1989 NCAA Convention. Proposition 48 set academic standards for incoming college athletes, including minimum high school grade-point averages and minimum composite scores of 700 on the SAT or 15 on the ACT. It also specified that freshmen who meet the high school grade-point requirements but not the minimum test scores could participate as "partial qualifiers" and receive athletic aid but not practice and compete. Proposition 42 will eliminate the partial qualifier.... Proposition 48 went into effect the year the sophomores in this national study were entering college, and Proposition 42 is scheduled to go into effect in 1990.

... About 45% of the current Black football and basketball players in predominately White Division I institutions scored below 700 on the SAT, while 54% scored below 15 on the ACT. About 18% of the Black extracurricular students and 29% of the other Black students scored below 700 on the SAT, while 30% of the Black extracurricular students and 39% of the other Black students scored below 15 on the ACT.

... Black football and basketball players are twice as likely as NonBlack players to report high school grade-point averages in the lower quartile of the distribution obtained from the national study (i.e., B- and below). At the other end of the distribution, NonBlack football and basketball players are three times as likely to report high school grade-point averages in the upper quartile (i.e., A- and above). Differences like these in high school grade-point averages and test scores suggest that students have different experiences prior to college and are likely to be regarded differently by coaches, counselors, and instructors once they are enrolled....

Socioeconomic status

From the extensive research literature on learning and achievement, we know that socioeconomic status (SES) can have a strong effect on a student's success in college. We may also expect SES to have an effect on a student's frame of reference and to thereby affect how the student shapes priorities and goals for the future. SES is usually assessed by combining measures of parents; income, education, and work status. To develop the SES measure used in this study, we standardized and averaged the values of four variables: (1) annual family income, (2) father's education, (3) mother's education, and (4) father's occupation, or mother's occupation if father's occupation was not listed....

Finances and Financial Aid

Low SES poses problems for meeting the costs of a college education, both the obvious costs of tuition, room, board, and books, and the accompanying costs of traveling home, doing laundry, going out to campus events, or just eating outside of the dorm on an occasional basis. One way to pay the major costs of a college education is through athletic grants-in-aid.... Black football and basketball players are recruited by as many institutions as NonBlack football and basketball players. Because recruiting and athletic grants often go hand-in-hand, Black football and basketball players are as likely as their NonBlack teammates to receive athletic grants covering the full costs of tuition, books, and related education expenses.... Black football and basketball players and their families are as likely as their NonBlack teammates and their families to borrow money to cover the costs of their education, although the majority of each group do not borrow. Through athletic grants and some personal loans, Black football and basketball players, who come from lower SES backgrounds on the average, are able to meet the essential costs of going to college.

This leaves open the matter of the associated costs of college attendance, from relatively minor expenses such as a movie or a dinner out, to the more major costs of clothing or traveling home on a holiday to see one's family. . . . Almost two-thirds of the Black football and basketball players report they have $25 or less each month for personal expenses. Such an amount would hardly cover any of the associated minor costs of college attendance, let along such items as airline tickets home. . . .

Discrimination and Racial Isolation

. . . Black student-athletes may need the most to get off campus once in a while to visit with family and friends, but may find few opportunities to do so.

Black football and basketball players on predominately White campuses, as compared to those on predominately Black campuses, are more apt to feel different from other students, to feel that they lack control over their lives, to feel isolated from other students, to feel racially isolated, and to feel racial discrimination. (On predominately White campuses, NonBlack football and basketball players report similar feelings of lack of control and isolation, but are more apt to feel different from other students.) Almost 70% of the Black football and basketball players at the predominately White institutions with the fewest numbers of Black undergraduates report a sense of feeling different. Half of them report feeling they lack control over their lives. More than a quarter report feelings of isolation from other students. More than half report racial isolation, and about a third report racial discrimination. . . .

3. Significant Influences and Sources of Support

Overview

. . . Families are very important influences on the education and career plans of Black football and basketball players, as are their high school coaches and teachers who know well the reputations of the various Division I institutions. For some Black football and basketball players, college coaches and recruiting are key factors in their decision to attend a four-year college or university.

. . . The quality of their relationships with coaches and other students on the campuses can be very important in helping them do well in college. What do Black football and basketball players expect of their coaches? About half feel it is important for their coaches to encourage good performance in courses, to keep track of their course performance, and to listen to their problems outside of athletics. About 31% of the Black football and basketball players on predominately White campuses rate their coaches as doing an excellent job in these areas, while another 55% say their coaches are doing fairly well. Only 14% give their coaches a poor or terrible rating.

In their relationships with other students, Black football and basketball players at predominately White institutions find it harder to talk about their personal problems than do their counterparts at predominately Black institutions. On predominately White campuses, they also find it more difficult than Black extracurricular students to get to know other students and to be liked by others for just being themselves. After their families and friends, these Division I student-athletes name their teammates as their closest confidants.

. . . Some Black football and basketball players can use extra help, and at predominately White institutions they attend special classes on study skills and basic skills. For example, 54% of Black football and basketball players report having attended special college courses on note-taking and classroom listening skills. About 74% of Black football and basketball players at predominately White institutions say it is easier or much easier for them to get help from tutors because they are athletes. . . .

Relationships with Coaches

Given that recruitment is one factor in the educational decision making of Black football and basketball players, college coaches are likely to be key figures in this decisionmaking process. Because about two-thirds of the football and basketball players who are Black currently receive full athletic grants, it is likely that college coaches have considerable influence over them during their time as college students. . .

How well are their coaches doing? . . . Black football and basketball players and Black extracurricular students [were asked to] . . . rate their coaches or activity directors as doing an excellent job in helping with coursework and personal problems. . . . [A]pproximately equal percentages among the three groups . . . rate this performance "fair" (about 55% of the Black football and basketball players in predominately White institutions), "poor" (about 13% of the Black football and basketball players in predominately White institutions), and "terrible" (about 2% of the Black football and basketball players in predominately White institutions). . . .

. . . Compared to Black extracurricular students, we find that Black football and basketball players at predominately White institutions report greater difficulty in getting to know other students and in being liked by others for just being themselves. These Black football and basketball players also differ from their counterparts at predominately Black institutions in reporting greater difficulty in talking with others about personal problems. At predominately White institutions, Black football and basketball players differ from their NonBlack teammates on two dimensions. Fewer Black than NonBlack football and basketball players say it is harder for them as student-athletes to get to know students; more Black than NonBlack players find it harder to talk about their personal problems. . . .

Use and Availability of Educational Aids

. . . Compared to other Black students, Black football and basketball players receive the most help in managing their time. [They] . . . are more than twice as likely as other Black students to receive help in managing their time. . . .

Academic resources

In addition to special classes, colleges and universities provide educational assistance to students through the efforts of their faculty, tutors, and teaching assistants. Most institutions also provide students with academic counseling, to assist them in planning and carrying out programs of study. . . . Black football and basketball players perceive easier access to various forms of educational assistance than do other Black students—from getting help from professors to talking to academic counselors. . . .

[Chapter 4 omitted]

5. Progress Toward Goals

Personal Goals

Education and career goals

Considering the data on educational and career goals available from the national study, we conclude that Black football and basketball players set demanding goals for themselves. More than 80% of Black football and basketball players say that earning a college degree is of the greatest importance. . . . Black football and basketball players are more likely to regard earning a degree as of the greatest importance than are Black extracurricular students on the same campuses. For reference, Black football and basketball players in predominately White institutions are no different than their NonBlack teammates in rating the importance of getting a degree.

. . . [A] major in business [education] is most popular for both Black football and basketball players and Black extracurricular students. At predominately Black institutions, almost 45% of Black football and basketball players say they expect their degrees in business. At predominately White and predominately Black institutions, the top three choices of major for Black football and basketball players are identical—business, professional occupations, and communications. (Professional occupations include architecture, health sciences, home economics, library science, nursing, pharmacy, protective services, and public affairs.) About 7% of the Black football and basketball players on predominately White campuses and 9% of their counterparts on predominately Black campuses expect to get their degrees in physical education. About 32% of the NonBlack football and basketball players on predominately White campuses also pick business as their intended degree—the top choice for them, while 5% pick physical education.

Approximately 23% of the Black football and basketball players on predominately White campuses say they "almost certainly" will go on to graduate school. They are no different than their NonBlack teammates in this regard. . . .

Professional athletic careers

. . . [We] see that 44% of Black football and basketball players in predominately White institutions say, at the time of the survey, they expect to become professional athletes. In predominately Black institutions, 36% of the football and basketball players say they expect professional sports careers—44% versus 20%. . . .

Are the educational and career aspirations of Black football and basketball players, including expectations of professional athletic careers, consonant with their abilities? For getting a degree or attending graduate school, we can consider college GPAs [grade point averages] in making a preliminary assessment of how attainable the goals might be. In evaluating at this time whether expectations of careers in professional athletics might be fulfilled, we can only look at the team standing of the student-athletes. No data as to the athletic abilities of student-athletes were collected during the national study from coaches or other observers. . . .

. . . GPAs of 1.99 and below are cause for academic probation at many Division I institutions. . . . About 35% of all Black football and basketball players at predominately White and 22% at predominately Black institutions who say they will almost certainly attend graduate or professional school have GPAs of 1.99 or below. . . . For a comparison at predominately White institutions, 11% of the NonBlack football and basketball players who say they are almost certain of attending graduate or professional school have a GPA of 1.99 or below. . . .

To the extent that college GPA accurately indicates academic performance for Black football and basketball players, it seems as if some of them set goals and expectations for themselves that are not well matched to their performance levels. . . .

We examined whether any of the potential mismatches in ability levels and aspirations among Black football and basketball players at predominately White Division I institutions seem to be related to psychological measures of depression, anxiety, or self esteem. From the data currently available from the national study, we find no indications of such a relation for the importance of getting a degree, intention to attend graduate or professional school, aspiration for a high-status job at age 40, or aspiration for a professional athletic career. These very preliminary findings will have to be explored further by collecting additional data on the student-athletes in the national study. The consequences of mismatches in goals and abilities may not begin to become apparent until it is clear that a goal will not be met and a different one must be set. . . .

CONGRESSIONAL HEARING ON ALASKAN OIL SPILL

April 6, 1989

The nation's worst oil spill occurred March 24 in Alaska's Prince William Sound. The tanker Exxon Valdez hit a reef and ruptured, emptying more than 10 million gallons of crude oil into the icy waters. The oil created a slick covering more than one hundred square miles, coating vast stretches of shoreline, and fouling some of North America's prime fishing grounds.

Congress lost no time inquiring into the accident's causes and effects. The Senate Committee on Commerce, Science, and Transportation opened hearings April 6 by calling an array of federal officials and L. W. Rawl, board chairman and chief executive officer of the Exxon Corporation, to testify. The committee addressed a number of questions. Among them were: the fitness of the ship's captain in light of his history of alcohol abuse; whether oil companies were prepared to respond adequately to oil-spill disasters; the proper role of federal agencies in overseeing oil-tanker safety and oil cleanup; the extent of a company's liability; and whether additional laws were needed to protect the environment from offshore oil-drilling operations.

Events Leading to the Disaster

Investigations by state and federal authorities pointed to several troubling factors in the accident, aside from the matter of the captain's fitness and sobriety. One was that the tanker's crew had been reduced in size and was exhausted (they had worked an average of 140 hours a month of overtime). Others were the presence of unqualified pilots on the tanker's bridge, possibly inadequate monitoring of the vessel's operations *by the Coast Guard, and lack of preparation for oil spills.*

The Exxon Valdez *sailed out of the Prince William Sound narrows under the command of a harbor pilot. Alaskan state law required that a pilot—a skilled mariner with knowledge of local waters—be on board when tankers enter and leave the port of Valdez. His job done, the pilot left the ship about twenty minutes later and returned to shore. The ship's captain, Joseph J. Hazelwood, shortly thereafter radioed the Coast Guard that he was taking the ship on a southern course to avoid ice.*

Hazelwood then ordered another change of course, which took the ship out of the regular shipping lanes. The Coast Guard was not notified of the rerouting and lost radar tracking. Radio contact also was lost for twenty-five minutes before the disaster. Hazelwood put the ship on autopilot—which Coast Guard and Exxon officials later said regulations permit only in open sea—and went below to his cabin. Less than half an hour later, the ship ran aground on Bligh Reef. The ship's third mate, who was on the bridge but not licensed to navigate the tanker in Prince William Sound, said he was unable to avoid the crash.

The harbor pilot said he smelled alcohol on Hazelwood's breath. However, the captain's crew mates said he was not drunk. A test given him about ten hours after the accident found a blood-alcohol level lower than a drunk-driving limit set by Alaska for motorists but higher than the Coast Guard set for a seaman operating a moving ship. He had previously been treated for alcoholism. He pleaded not guilty in Anchorage May 3 to a state charge of operating the ship while intoxicated. His trial on that and five additional charges was to be held in Anchorage in January 1990.

Insufficient but Costly Cleanup Efforts

Once the oil spill occurred, the spotlight turned on the massive cleanup job. It quickly became apparent that neither Exxon nor the federal agencies with oversight responsibility had adequately prepared for the job. The 1972 Clean Water Act gave the Coast Guard responsibility for developing and monitoring plans for containing a spill, but the Coast Guard ceded authority to the Alyeska Pipeline Service Company, the consortium of oil companies (including Exxon) that operates the Trans-Alaska pipeline. The pipeline brings oil from fields on Alaska's North Slope across hundreds of miles of wilderness to the port at Valdez. After agreeing to establish a twenty-man round-the-clock oil-spill response team in Prince William Sound, Alyeska disbanded it in 1981, over the protests of the Alaska Department of Environmental Conservation.

After the ship hit the reef, fourteen hours elapsed before the first cleanup equipment reached the site. Once the cleanup effort began, high winds and strong currents impeded it. By then, oil had spread miles from the ship. The company then turned to using chemical dispersants to dissolve the massive slick, but with less-than-satisfactory results. Meanwhile, Exxon began assembling 10,000 workers and large amounts of equipment to try to protect and clean hundreds of miles of beaches.

Exxon and the Bush administration both were accused of responding too slowly. It was not until March 28—four days after the accident—that the president dispatched a high-level administration investigative team to Prince William Sound. Alaskan officials had meanwhile taken over coordination of the cleanup effort.

Exxon later estimated that the cleanup costs would total at least $1.28 billion, making it one of the most expensive industrial accidents in history. And that figure did "not include the potential effects of litigation, which cannot reasonably be assessed at this time," according to the same statement on July 24. Exxon faced dozens of lawsuits instigated by fishermen and wildlife groups. The state of Alaska sued the Exxon Shipping Company, owner of the tanker, and the parent Exxon Corporation—together with Alyeska, for damages. Exxon Corporation, in turn, sued the state. The company contended that the state hindered the cleanup efforts by disallowing the use of oil-dispersing chemicals and thereby drove up Exxon's cleanup costs.

Impact on Area's Economy, Wildlife

Prince William Sound was one of the worst imaginable sites for an oil spill. It was the crossroads for huge migrations of wildlife, including more than 200 species of birds, 111 of them water-related, and was home to one-fourth of the sea otters in American waters. The area had supported a fishing industry capable of earning $100 million a year. Despite rescue efforts by volunteers, thousands of oil-soaked birds and hundreds of otters died. Environmentalists reported widespread reproductive failure among the area's nesting bald eagles. The Sound's herring industry was closed, and many of the salmon hatchery grounds were put off-limits.

Aftermath: Long-Lasting Effects

Exxon temporarily ended its cleanup efforts September 15, demobilizing its work crews and pronouncing 1,100 miles of oil-soaked shoreline "environmentally stable." Other officials disputed that contention. Alaska's governor, Steve Cowper, said the state would spend $21 million during the winter to continue cleanup efforts and help Alaskans deal with the economic and psychological impact of the spill.

Oil companies announced the creation of a new organization, the Petroleum Industry Response Organization, to provide equipment and workers at strategic locations along the nation's coasts to respond quickly to catastrophic tanker spills. And Congress moved to clear legislation to set up a national fund to pay for cleanup and damage compensation—beyond the amounts for which the spiller is liable. The Alaskan spill, together with smaller ones elsewhere in American waters on a single weekend, June 23-24, created strong pressure for the legislation.

Following are excerpts from the Senate Committee on Commerce, Science, and Transportation hearing April 6, 1989, on the Exxon Valdez *oil spill:*

Opening Statement by Committee Chairman,
Ernest F. Hollings

... Good morning. We have convened this hearing to assess the impact and implications of the recent oil spill by an Exxon tanker in Prince William Sound near Valdez, Alaska. Daily, we are reminded that this is the largest oil spill in United States history. It is our responsibility as Members of the Commerce Committee to examine thoroughly the causes of the accident; to determine its short- and long-term effects on the environment as well as on the local economy; to assess the clean-up efforts by Exxon; and to determine what governmental action is required to prevent or minimize similar disasters in the future, whether in Alaska or elsewhere.

On March 24—13 days ago—the tanker, *Exxon Valdez,* struck a reef about 25 miles out of the port in Valdez, Alaska, spilling nearly 11 million gallons of oil into the pristine waters of Prince William Sound. There was a belated attempt to contain the oil, but it proved unsuccessful. Since that time, the oil has spread over more than 1,000 square miles in the Sound, blackening island beaches, covering plant and marine life, and endangering the $100 million local fishing industry. Already, Alaska fish and game officials have cancelled the herring season in the Sound—a loss of approximately $10 million.

However, the greatest losses have yet to be felt. The tanker ran aground in what is described as one of the richest concentrations of wildlife in North America. Prince William Sound is home to about 15,000 sea otters, 10 percent of the Alaskan sea otter population. Also, the Sound has a particularly diverse population of birds, fish, and other animals—the result of a subarctic habitat which includes fresh water from melting glaciers and saltwater from the sea, a mountainous coastline overlooking sandy beaches, and pine forests sheltering productive marshlands. At least 1,000 birds are already dead or dying. Among that number are two rare species, the yellow-billed loon and the merlet. Fishermen are especially concerned about their commercial salmon harvest, as well as king crabs and shrimp. Of course, this assessment is just the tip of the iceberg.

Moreover, scientists studying the disaster are not sure of the extent of the devastation to the wildlife there. Although larger spills have occurred, this disaster is unique because it is in a body of water ringed by islands and relatively isolated from the open sea. The island enclosure in Prince William Sound has delayed dissipation of the spill, exposing animals to the oil for an extended time and allowing the oil to soak into the beaches and sediments.

The entire sequence of events over the past two weeks has raised a number of questions about the way we do business in Alaska: why was Captain Hazelwood permitted to operate a supertanker when he had prior convictions for drunk driving? Why were Exxon officials so slow to respond to the accident, and why was the Alaska Pipeline Service so poorly prepared to respond to the emergency? Why did the U.S. Coast Guard fail to perform an immediate drug test on Hazelwood? Finally, the most important question—how can we prevent such a tragedy from happening again?

The obvious conclusion we must draw from this episode is that we are grossly unprepared for disasters of this scale. I quote the Chief of the Coast Guard Marine Safety division who acknowledged that "federal and state contingency plans were inadequate to contain the oil spill from the *Exxon Valdez.*" This is an obvious case of the ancient maxim that those who do not learn from the mistakes of the past are condemned to repeat them.

Bear in mind that this is far from the first oil spill to impact our coastlines. Previously, one of the largest oil spills in our waters was the *Argo Merchant,* a Liberian tanker which ran onto a shoal 30 miles off Nantucket Island in Massachusetts on December 15, 1976. The tanker leaked oil until it broke apart nine days later and lost the rest of its cargo, a total spill of 7.6 million gallons. Four years later, a federal court ruled that the *Argo Merchant* had been an unsafe ship, citing general misman-agement and neglect.

In a spill just last December 22, a barge with about 231,000 gallons of heavy bunker oil spilled off the southwest coast of Washington state. Unfortunately, a heavy storm pushed the oil toward land. Hundreds of miles of beaches, including pristine wilderness in Olympic National Park and Canada's Pacific Rim National Park, were covered in oil, and as many as 10,000 birds died. In that incident, the tug towing the barge had struck it while maneuvering to secure a line. Experts expect the effects of pollution from the spill to linger for years.

Outside the United States, there have been larger spills recorded. In June of 1979, the blowout of a well in the gulf of Mexico north of the Yucatan Peninsula resulted in the spill of 155 million gallons—the largest in history.

And the largest oil spill to occur in a coastal area took place on March 16, 1978. The *Amoco Cadiz,* owned by a subsidiary of Standard Oil of Indiana, ran aground two miles off the coast of France spilling 68 million gallons. Along the Brittany coastline an oil slick formed 18 miles wide and 80 miles long. The French government paid about $100 million in cleanup costs and compensation. Last month, a judge recommended a $115.2 million judgment against Amoco Corporation, with the French government to receive $44.4 million and affected jurisdictions about $7.5 million each.

We must realize that the damage from an oil spill to the marine ecosystem is both immediate and devastating. Many birds, fish, and marine mammals are killed by the toxic aftermath of an oil spill, and all are at risk of death by starvation, dehydration, or cold due to the inability of oil-stained fur and feathers to protect against freezing temperatures.

It is my understanding that the toll on marine life from the recent disaster is expected to be so immense that the Alaska Department of Environmental Conservation has transported refrigerated tractor-trailers to Valdez to store dead birds and animals; they will be collected by scientists as evidence in anticipated lawsuits.

All of this leads us to some very important issues which must be resolved. First, at a time when this country's future share in the oil market remains in question, we must closely examine whether the Arctic National Wildlife Refuge should be explored for future oil supplies. In light of the *Valdez* spill, it is all the more urgent and important to thoroughly investigate the damage done to the fragile marine ecosystem when a calamity such as this occurs. We must have a better understanding of the short- and long-term effects on various species of plants and animals. Secondly, the question of liability coverage must be reviewed. The question[s] are, "Who pays the bill?" "Which industries are adversely affected and how long?" "Who determines the limits on monetary compensation?" Thirdly, it is obvious that our laws are not an adequate deterrent to such disasters, or to the hundreds of accidents daily, which are the direct or indirect result of substance abuse. Why should the citizens of this country continue to be subject to the tyranny of small minds who abuse alcohol and drugs? Finally, what additional role should the federal government play in the regulation of the oil industry to prevent such events from occurring and to manage them when they do. If contingency plans are required, why are they not operational and who should approve them? . . .

Statement by Transportation Secretary
Samuel K. Skinner

. . . [A]t President Bush's request, EPA Administrator [William K.] Reilly, Admiral [Paul H.] Yost and I went to Prince William Sound to oversee the Federal effort and to assure that Exxon, as the vessel owner, was doing everything possible to minimize environmental damage. He wanted us to make sure that there was a concentrated effort. . . .

It is too early to have a complete factual analysis of this situation, but I think it is fair to say that Exxon has the primary responsibility for this accident. They have acknowledged it and they have been also primarily responsible for supporting the clean-up effort. . . .

Second, while I am confident human error will be dealt with appropriately we would miss the larger point if we were to leave it at that. My mind is not closed on this, but my impression is that a somewhat over-optimistic attitude crept into our readiness and ability to deal with a spill of this magnitude, or even that an accident of this size would occur.

The industry-government contingency planning was based on an assumed spill level that was quickly exceeded. The industry did not have enough equipment on hand. This was compounded by the remote location of the spill. But it goes without saying that every step of the planning for moving Alaskan oil by water had to assume a spill in just this locale.

Admiral Yost and I have overseen the Coast Guard response and I am satisfied with it, particularly the ability of the Coast Guard personnel to shift from patrol and other duties to supervising clean-up efforts.

However, I think any situation such as this calls on us to assess our contingency plans, as well as those of the industry and the states, and ensure that they are updated accordingly. That process is already under-way. . . .

Third, my instinct in a situation of this nature is not to throw up our hands and concede that we cannot do a better job with the ocean transportation of petroleum and that the only advisable course is to minimize reliance on ocean shipments. Our demand for sources of independent energy is too important for that. . . .

. . . [I]t is also time to reassess the need for comprehensive oil spill liability and compensation legislation. Legislation has passed the House twice, but it has floundered in the Senate. This Administration would be pleased to work with the Environment and Public Works Committee and other interested parties to restart the process. . . .

The Bush Administration has committed its resources to working with the Congress on responsible legislation. It is important to recognize that the Valdez spill illustrates dramatically the vulnerabiliy of our coasts and rivers to the continuing threat of oil pollution.

In the case of the spiller, Exxon, it has stated that it takes responsibility for clean-up and damages and they have the financial resources to do the job, but if the spill were from a foreign flag carrier, not carrying Alaskan oil, and whose owner had few other resources, there would be no means under current law to assure that damages are met. Clearly, an alternative is needed. . . .

Statement of EPA Administrator William K. Reilly

. . . I think that . . . the Nation may need to reconsider the decisions it has made, the sense of complacency, perhaps, that has characterized our attitude toward oil spills.

It strikes me that, from an environmental point of view, over the last several years we have become very absorbed, very focused on toxic spills, hazardous waste, some of the more exotic problems of medical waste on beaches, and things of that sort, all very serious, difficult problems urgently in need of attention.

But, at the same time, we have perhaps become less attentive to the need for maintaining our readiness to address the more conventional and more familiar problems, partly because they declined. Oil spills over the years have diminished, both around the world and in the United States.

We need to look at the adequacy of our response capability and, I think probably also, at some of the technology that is available to deal with problems of this sort. Because one certainly has to acknowledge that in this situation it was far from enough. . . .

Senator KERRY. . . . [H]ow do you rate the response, the federal response in this, and what lessons do you draw at this point in time? . . .

Mr. REILLY. The response, I think, focused on the proper priorities. By the time that the spill had been understood, reported, obviously all of that got off to a quite slow start on the part of the company. . . .

There are, no doubt, a great many lessons to be learned here, and there is no shortage of groups that are now investigating—formal and informal—

public and private, the adequacy of the response, the civil and criminal liabilities, and the changes that may need to be made in contingency planning there as in other places. I think all of that is going to go on. I am not prepared at this time to say who struck John or to try to do anything more than focus right now on the cleanup. . . .

Senator BRYAN. . . . I am not sure—gentlemen, with all due respect I am not sure that I have gotten a satisfactory answer to the question that Senator Stevens has propounded and the Chairman has followed up. I am not sure who is in charge here.

Your response, Mr. Reilly, sounded to me as a lawyer like a qualified response. You said the Coast Guard is with respect to the federal perspective. What I would like to know is if Exxon and the Coast Guard have a difference of opinion as to how one ought to proceed. Who is the lead dog in this operation?

Mr. REILLY. The question of federalization was one that we faced with the President right from the beginning, and he made it very clear that if that was something that needed to be done, he was prepared to do it.

In the conversations we had in Alaska, that was not requested of us. The governor did not see anything to be served by it. One had to ask the question what difference would it make if one were to federalize this effort, would we undertake activities that the governor and others wanted to see undertaken that were not at that time already being addressed. So, that was the reaction in Alaska, that was what we reported back, and it was on that basis, I think, that the President made the decision he did.

Senator BRYAN. Mr. Reilly, I am not trying to be critical of you or the president. I am just trying to find out in the vernacular of the street who the hell is calling the shots.

Secretary SKINNER. Let me see if I can take another shot at it. The United States Coast Guard is in charge. The District Commander is up in Alaska and has been there almost from day one. He—Exxon is putting considerable resources, as I indicated to you a minute ago. Those resources are directed by the United States Coast Guard. . . .

Senator BREAUX. What is wrong with the system, from an early preliminary view, that allowed this to happen? I mean, here is the largest U.S. tanker in the fleet being operated by a person who has been convicted of DWI, who cannot drive that station wagon but is allowed to drive and to captain the largest super tanker in the fleet?

Secretary SKINNER. Well, although he was required to do so, he did not disclose his DWI and so there is a failure. It is like somebody that goes in to buy a firearm and does not disclose he is a prior felon.

Senator BREAUX. Okay, well, the guy could be a terrorist and get a license to operate a super tanker under our system. Is that right? If he just says, I have never been a terrorist, I have never been a drunk, I do not use drugs and here is my license. I mean, that is the system we have, is what you are telling us.

Secretary SKINNER. I think the main backup that we rely on is the company's background investigation of its employees. We do not have—to answer your question directly, senator, we do not have a system where we do background investigations on every pilot, on every vessel that is hauling commodities in this country.

Senator BREAUX. I would suggest that a captain of a shrimp boat that is 60 feet long, we can buy that, but a super tanker loaded with volatile material—well, that is another question. . . .

Secretary SKINNER. There is no excuse for the fact that a man who was licensed and, if sober, properly qualified to make this trip was not at the bridge. That is a human error of major magnitude. He should have been there. It is like having the captain of the airplane sit in the back sleeping and having a flight attendant, or the flight engineer, up in the left seat. . . .

Senator BREAUX. I will tell you that we did not do so in this case. We did not check to see whether that captain was qualified to get a Coast Guard license..He was able to operate a ship with a valid captain's license, that was stamped with approval by the Coast Guard, with that kind of a record is unacceptable. . . .

The CHAIRMAN. We are going to move on to the chairman of Exxon, who has obliged us by attending, and he [is] waiting now to tell his story. But let us first hear from Senator Exon.

Senator EXON. Mr. Chairman, you have made that pronunciation of my name incorrect for ten years now. I have not objected to it previously.

But I would state for the record that the name is "Exun." It is E-x-o-n with one x. I have often said the other people are the double cross boys.

And they are now brought further disrepute on the once honorable name of Exxon. . . .

The CHAIRMAN. . . . Mr. Rawl, we would appreciate hearing from you now, sir. Mr. Rawl, we have your statement. It will be included in the record in its entirety, and under the circumstances, you can deliver it in its entirety, if you wish, or summarize, either way.

Statement by L. G. Rawl, Board Chairman and Chief Executive Officer, Exxon Corp.

I will summarize my statement.

I am here to provide a frank response to questions regarding the *Exxon Valdez* oil spill and to describe our continuing efforts to deal with its consequences.

Before I do this, however, I want to express my sincere regret as to what happened on behalf of all the employees of Exxon and certainly on behalf of myself. I really cannot tell you how sorry we are this disaster occurred, and we are particularly sympathetic to the impacts on the residents of Alaska and particularly those in the Prince William Sound area. That is where the spill is creating a great deal of problems.

As has been said many times this morning and by us earlier we take full responsibility. As we have done from the beginning. We will continue doing all we can to clean up and mitigate the spill's effects and all necessary resources are being fully employed.

It has already been mentioned by Secretary Skinner that the environment in this area, its remoteness, the high tides and the associated physical problems make it a particularly difficult problem.

A few comments about the spill, just to put it into perspective. As mentioned before the spill is estimated at 240,000 barrels which occurred early on March 24.

We have other factual information. The weather was clear. The ship had no known mechanical difficulties. A course change was requested and authorized because of ice in the outgoing channel.

The captain subsequently left the bridge and tests made sometime after the grounding showed the captain's alcohol level was above the limits established by the Coast Guard. That is clear.

There are still many unanswered questions as to what occurred during this period. We are conducting, of course, not one but many investigations within the company as are the National Transportation Safety Board and the Coast Guard. There are other federal and state investigations underway, and we are participating in all of these.

The oil spill contingency plan was activated immediately. It called for a two-phased response. The first phase was the responsibility of Alyeska. The second phase was our responsibility as the shipper, and our response was immediate.

We immediately established the priorities. The first priority was to prevent additional spills from the damaged tanker which had approximately one million barrels of North Slope crude on it, and certainly to try to immediately mitigate the impact of the spill on the environment and the people of Alaska.

A major mobilization began immediately and by now involves, as the Secretary said, many hundreds of people or thousands of people, a lot of boats, planes, helicopters, etc. I will not go into all those details.

Currently we are receiving support from a large number of organizations. We have a large number of experts, academics and so forth under contract, and we have 200 Exxon experts and other consultants that are managing ... our part of effort. We are mobilized to mitigate the economic impact on the communities of Prince William Sound. . . .

We cannot judge how long recovery will take in Prince William Sound, but I can assure you that since March 24th the accident has been receiving our full attention and will continue to do until the job is done.

We are continuing to cooperate fully to establish the facts as to what happened. More importantly, however, we want to help in any way we can determine what might be done to reduce the chances of such an incident happening again. I can assure you actions are already underway within Exxon to revise policies and procedures in the light of this accident and to preclude what happened from happening again.

The CHAIRMAN. Exactly on that point has Exxon learned, Mr. Rawl, not to risk such a valuable cargo and such an immense vessel the length of three football fields which takes a couple of miles or so to even turn course, to risk that to just one pilot and not have a copilot?

I mean is that—right now if I went out on, let us say, three or four other Exxon supertankers this morning, would I find only one pilot, master pilot, licensed and capable?

Mr. RAWL. No, sir. The Prince William Sound area is unusual. Most of the three mates plus the captain are licensed to pilot the ship in many areas and on the open ocean. In Prince William Sound, as has been said many times this morning, the state pilot takes it to a certain point. . . . But in this case the pilot was also the captain. Obviously we had no knowledge that he was impaired.

I think it is possible, however, as I understand the law there, to have two mates on the bridge at the same time in a case like this. . . . There were actually four people on the bridge when the skipper was on the bridge. There was a lookout on one of the wings. There was the person in charge which then was the captain. There was a third mate. It was his shift, and there was also the man steering the vessel or the helmsman. So that was the situation.

If the captain had sent for another mate before he went below, as I understood it, that would have been legally responsive regarding whether or not the ship would have hit the reef, I would expect it would have had a much better chance of getting through there. I have had a lot of difficulty understanding this accident myself, I can assure you.

The CHAIRMAN. Well, I think that is the first lesson we have learned this morning about the copilot. It is thoroughly equipped because the person—the second mate wasn't a qualified master as is required in those waters.

Now, you said, of course, you did not have any knowledge, and yet they will say in the law that—does the record show that this particular master of the vessel had three convictions of driving under the influence of alcohol? In other words, he had an alcohol problem?

Mr. RAWL. Yes, sir, it shows that.

The CHAIRMAN: That would scare me to death in a board room if I were there on Exxon's board if you told me that the fellow had three convictions running with that expensive cargo. . . . I mean, you have got no explanation for that.

Mr. RAWL. No, sir. . . .

The CHAIRMAN. On the response you said that the first phase response, the first was for Alyeska, and the second in line was for you, Exxon, and you responded immediately inferring that perhaps it was not a prompt or an immediate response by Alyeska. What is your position on that?

Mr. RAWL. Well, I am sure you have heard this before, but there are a number of oil spill contingency plans that are involved in this situation. One of them was the Alyeska oil spill contingency plan which, by the way, had to be in place before the pipeline started up. It was in 1977 or 1976 that this plan was first in place. It has been revised several times since then.

Subsequently, the shippers were separated from the pipeline plan, and had to have their own oil spill contingency plans. I think that was in early 1982.

When I said the first phase was Alyeska's responsibility—the spill envisioned for Alyeska in phase one is a relatively small spill. I think the numbers were mentioned this morning. It was always been recognized that a large tanker spill was possible in Prince William Sound, however, nobody ever thought it was probable that a spill would be this large. . . .

Now, an important part of the contingency's plan for a spill that large required approval by the federal agencies, the EPA, and the State of Alaska. . . .

Senator STEVENS. Let me tell the committee that Bill Stevens is a friend of mine. In fact, I think distantly we are related. We talked about that one night.

He is the president of your tanker company. He came to Alaska and made a statement saying that Exxon would accept total responsibility for this. You have made a similar statement here now. But after Mr. Stevens left Alaska, your legal department indicated that as far as the liability to the customers, in terms of failure of delivery, that Exxon was going to rely upon an act of God theory.

Is that correct?

Mr. RAWL. When Mr. Stevens made his statement, and by the way, Senator, as you probably know, he is the President of Exxon U.S.A., which is our principal operating affiliate in this country, he was talking about the impact of this spill in Alaska. When you start getting into something downstream of that, in terms of—and I assume you are talking about customers and items of that nature—then it can roll on around the world, and there is just no end to it.

Senator STEVENS. I just want you to know it was interpreted in Alaska as being a second thought of Exxon, and it left a significant doubt in the mind of Alaskans as to the extent that the Exxon major international company was going to accept the statement of liability that Mr. Stevens had made.

And many of us are lawyers, but your lawyers are liable to go to court and say, after all, that was not a legal obligation, it was a statement of policy, and we are now defending against these suits.

What is the policy of Exxon with regard to any expense that develops as a result of this spill?

Mr. RAWL. Well, obviously, I have said again here this morning, it is our intention to stay after this spill, clean it up to the best of scientific ability—or to the best that we can do. And also to pay those people in your state that have been damaged by this spill. And there are a variety of kinds of damages.

Now when you talk about suits, we have got suits, as I am sure you are aware of. A lot of you are lawyers, I am not a lawyer, but the fact is, there is a lot of these suits that are legitimate suits, and hopefully none of the people in Alaska who are damaged will have to go to court. . . .

Senator GORTON. Can you give me the chain of command that would go from you, as chairman of the parent corporation, down through that subsidiary corporation, to this captain? Or maybe work it back up, who is the captain's supervisor, and who is his supervisor, and so on, up to you?

Mr. RAWL. Well, when it gets to the lower levels, I lose the track. But the captain has a supervisor. And then that supervisor and there may be another supervisor in between, reports to a manager on the West Coast of the U.S.

There are also other people who tell this captain what to do in terms of scheduling. As you know these captains work a few weeks on and a few weeks off. I am not precise on the time.

But then that individual on the West Coast who is in Benicia, California in the San Francisco area, would report in to Houston where we have someone we might call an operations manager.

And then there is a president of the Exxon Shipping Company who reports to a senior vice president of Exxon U.S.A., who reports to the president of that company.

We have management committees at the level of Exxon U.S.A. We have management committees in New York, and then the president of that company would report to me.

Now I do not know how many levels that is.

Senator GORTON. Well, I want very earnestly to make a suggestion to you, Mr. Rawl. Whatever the success of Exxon in the past, it now has the dubious distinction of having caused one of the most severe and perhaps the most severe man-made disaster, environmental disaster in our history.

We are constantly comparing ourselves in this country, sometimes unfavorably, sometimes I may say unfairly, with the Japanese. But as I understand their corporate structure, you know, when something like this happens, everyone takes responsibility, from the individual who was directly in charge of it, up to the CEO. And everyone offers his resignation at that point so that a new team can take over and restore the credibility of the corporation.

I suggest the disaster that your company has caused calls for that kind of response. I would be perfectly happy to hear your comment on it, but that expresses my opinion on this disaster.

Mr. RAWL. I appreciate that expresses your opinion. I doubt if I have to comment on it except that a lot of the Japanese kill themselves also, and I refuse to do that.

Senator GORTON. I am not asking for that, but the resignations I think are in order.

Mr. RAWL. I do not think so. . . .

ETHICS COMMITTEE REPORTS, WRIGHT'S RESIGNATION SPEECH

April 13, April 17, and May 31, 1989

In an emotional, hour-long defense of his reputation, Rep. Jim Wright, D-Texas, told the House of Representatives May 31 that he would resign as Speaker of the House. He subsequently resigned also as a member of Congress, effective June 30, vacating a seat he had held thirty-four years. He was the first Speaker ever forced from office by scandal. His dramatic farewell speech was televised nationally.

Wright's resignation came six weeks after the bipartisan House ethics committee reported it had "reason to believe" that he had violated House rules on gifts and income in sixty-nine instances. At the same time, April 17, the committee released a lengthy statement—dated April 13—of the allegations against him. Chicago attorney Richard J. Phelan, whom the committee hired to conduct the investigation, released a more detailed— and damning—report of 279 pages.

The weight of the findings overwhelmed Wright's months-long defense of his conduct and swept him from office.

Only three other Speakers had previously resigned from office. Henry Clay left in 1814 to serve on a peace commission negotiating the end of the War of 1812. He became Speaker again, resigning a second time, in 1820, for financial reasons. Andrew Stevenson of Virginia left in 1834 to become ambassador to Great Britain, and Schuyler Colfax of Indiana resigned in 1869 to become vice president. Several other Speakers faced accusations of improprieties and ethical violations, but none was forced from office.

Formally known as the Committee on Standards of Official Conduct, the House ethics committee opened the investigation of Wright on June

9, 1988. Rep. Newt Gingrich, R-Ga., had filed a complaint against the Speaker. Common Cause, a nonprofit "citizens lobbying group," also urged the committee to investigate Wright.

The ethics committee, in its report, said that twice Wright had created mechanisms the committee believed were actually ways of camouflaging money he was not allowed to receive under House rules. One "mechanism" was described as an investment company, Mallightco. Phelan said in his separate report that the company "was designed and used to give cash to the Wrights [Wright and his wife, Betty], and not as a legitimate business venture...." The company's biggest expense in 1981-1984 was the $18,000-a-year salary paid to Wright's wife.

There was no evidence either "supporting or establishing that the money paid to Mrs. Wright was in return for identifiable service or work products," the committee said. The company was formed by the Wrights with George Mallick and his wife, Marlene. Mallick, a Texas businessman, had a direct interest in legislation before Congress, the committee said.

Its report said that Wright had the free use of condominiums in Fort Worth, his home city, and that his wife had the use of a car. The committee said Wright should have disclosed the $18,000 salary, and car and condo use, as gifts. He did not report them at all. Members of the House were prohibited from taking gifts of more than $100 from a person with a direct interest in legislation.

The other mechanism, the committee said, was a publishing deal involving Wright's book, Reflections of a Public Man. *In seven cases, the report said, the committee found clear reason to believe that bulk sales of the book were substituted for the payment of a speaking fee. Wright received an unusually high 55 percent royalty on his book.*

The ethics committee, composed of six Democrats and six Republicans, operated under the chairmanship of Rep. Julian C. Dixon, D-Calif. While the committee adopted the report unanimously, not all the votes on all the counts proposed were unanimous.

Ethics Climate

Only days before Wright resigned, Rep. Tony Coelho, D-Calif., the House majority whip, stunned his colleagues by announcing that he would resign from Congress. Coelho had become the object of an investigation centering on his purchase of $100,000 in "junk" bonds. He resigned, Coelho said, rather than put his family, the House, and his party through a long probe of his finances.

In the midst of considerable turmoil in the House, Rep. Thomas S. Foley, D-Wash., the majority leader, was elected Speaker June 6 to succeed Wright. A few days later, Rep. Richard A. Gephardt, D-Mo., was chosen majority leader, replacing Foley, and Rep. William H. Gray III, D-Pa., was elected majority whip, the number three position, succeeding Coelho. Upon becoming Speaker, Foley pledged "a spirit of cooperation and increased consultation," and he asked for debate "with reason and without rancor." Wright vacated his House seat June 30 and returned to his home in Texas.

Wright found himself fighting to save his Speakership at a time when the public seemed intent on spotlighting misconduct by its elected representatives. In former days, the twenty-one-year-old House ethics committee had a reputation for using its powers sparingly. In a number of cases, it considered that making public the details of a representative's misconduct was punishment enough. "The difference seems to be that the nation is in the grip of an ethics fever," Victor Kramer, a law professor and former special counsel to the Senate ethics committee, told Congressional Quarterly.

Some reform-minded members of Congress and other reformers hoped that the Wright resignation would be a catalyst leading to the clarification and strengthening of congressional rules that govern the relationship between private money and the public interest.

Wright's Record

Wright became Speaker at the opening of the 100th Congress in January 1987 upon the retirement of Rep. Thomas P. O'Neill, Jr., D-Mass. The performance of the House under Wright's leadership in the 100th Congress won considerable praise. It passed landmark legislation on foreign trade, catastrophic health insurance, welfare reform, and aid for the homeless.

The New York Times observed editorially at the close of the 1988 session that Wright's "personal conduct attracted wide, sometimes harsh, attention. But his boldness as a leader prompted more useful legislation than anyone expected."

Throughout the 100th Congress, Wright vigorously opposed policies of the Reagan administration aimed at supporting the contras in Nicaragua. He went so far as to conduct "private diplomacy." In November 1987 he met with Nicaraguan president Daniel Ortega and three contra leaders in an attempt to promote the Central American peace plan.

Repeatedly, the Reagan administration accused him of meddling in foreign affairs. The dispute came to a head in September 1988 when Wright reported that the Central Intelligence Agency had attempted to bring about disturbances in Nicaragua to undermine the peace plan. Reagan and Republican leaders charged that Wright had breached security standards when he said that he based his statement on "clear testimony from CIA people." Wright countered that everything had already been publicly revealed. Wright contended that from that time forward, "There was a determination on the part of certain people in the other [Republican] party to see that I was removed."

While he was fighting for his survival as Speaker, Wright was hit by an unexpected blow. The Washington Post recalled in a front-page story that Wright's top aide, John P. Mack, had brutally attacked and almost *killed a woman sixteen years earlier. Mack, convicted and imprisoned, had joined Wright's staff upon being released from prison and had worked his way to the top position. After the story's disclosure, Mack resigned from his post on May 12.*

Farewell Speech

In his farewell speech, Wright pictured himself the victim of an obsession with ethics enforced by "self-appointed vigilantes." He said, "All of us, in both political parties, must resolve to bring this period of mindless cannibalism to an end." Near the end of the speech Wright said, "Let me give you back this job you gave me as a propitiation for all of this season of bad will that has grown up among us; give it back to you."

> *Following are the House ethics committee's statement of April 13, 1989, listing alleged violations of House rules by Speaker Jim Wright, and Wright's farewell speech, May 31, 1989.* (The bracketed headings have been added by Congressional Quarterly to highlight the organization of the text.):

COMMITTEE'S LIST OF ALLEGATIONS

Relevant Standard of Conduct

At all times relevant to the violations hereafter alleged, the pertinent provisions of 2 U.S.C. 441i, House Rule XLIII, clause 4, House Rule XLIV, and House Rule XLVII stated as follows:

2 U.S.C. §441i

(a) No person while an elected or appointed officer or employee of any branch of the Federal Government shall accept any honorarium of more than $2,000 (excluding amounts accepted for actual travel and subsistence expenses for such person and his spouse or an aide to such person, and excluding amounts paid or incurred for any agents' fees or commission) for any appearance, speech, or article.

(b) Any honorarium, or any part thereof, paid by or on behalf of an elected or appointed officer or employee of any branch of the Federal Government to a charitable organization shall be deemed not to be accepted for the purposes of this section.

(c) For purposes of determining the aggregate amount of honorariums received by a person during any calendar year, amounts returned to the person paying an honorarium before the close of the calendar year in which it was received shall be disregarded.

(d) For purposes of paragraph (2) of subsection (a) of this section, an honorarium shall be treated as accepted only in the year in which that honorarium is received.

[As amended Pub. L. 98-63, section 908 (g), July 30, 1983, 97 Stat. 338].

House Rule XLIII

A Member, officer, or employee of the House of Representatives shall not accept gifts (other than personal hospitality of an individual or with a fair market value of $50* or less) in any calendar year aggregating $100 or more in value, directly or indirectly, from any person (other than from a relative of his) having a direct interest in legislation before the Congress or who is a foreign national (or agent of a foreign national). Any person registered under the federal Regulation of Lobbying Act of 1946 (or any successor statute), any officer or director of such registered person, and any person retained by such registered person for the purpose of influencing legislation before the Congress shall be deemed to have a direct interest in legislation before the Congress.

* This threshold for aggregating was $35 until the 100th Congress, 1st Session, with the adoption of H. Res. 5 on January 6, 1987.

House Rule XLIV

1. A copy of each report filed with the Clerk under title I of the Ethics in Government Act of 1978 shall be sent by the Clerk within the seven-day period beginning the date on which the report is filed to the Committee on Standards of Official Conduct. By July 1 of each year, the Clerk shall compile all such reports sent to him by Members within the period beginning on January 1 and ending on May 15 of each year and have them printed as a House document, which document shall be made available to the public.

2. For the purposes of this rule, the provisions of title I of the Ethics in Government Act of 1978 shall be deemed to be a rule of the House as it pertains to Member, officers, and employees of the House of Representatives.

House Rule XLVII

1.(a) Except as provided by paragraph (b), no Member may, in any calendar year beginning after December 31, 1978, have outside earned income attributable to such calendar year which is in excess of 30 per centum of the aggregate salary as a Member paid to the Member during such calendar year.

(b) In the case of any individual who becomes a Member during any calendar year beginning after December 31, 1978, such Member may not have outside earned income attributable to the portion of that calendar year which occurs after such individual becomes a Member which is in excess of 30 per centum of the aggregate salary as a Member paid to the Member during such calendar year.

2. For purposes of clause 1, honoraria shall be attributable to the calendar year in which payment is received.

3. For the purposes of this rule—

(a) The term "Member" means any Member of the House of Representatives, a Delegate to the House of Representatives, or the Resident

Commissioner in the House of Representatives. (b) The term "honorarium" means a payment of money or any thing of value to a Member for an appearance, speech, or article, by the Member; but there shall not be taken into account for purposes of this paragraph any actual and necessary travel expenses incurred by the Member to the extent that such travel expenses are paid or reimbursed by any other person, and the amount otherwise determined shall be reduced by the amount of any such expenses to the extent that they are not paid or reimbursed.

(c) The term "travel expenses" means, with respect to a Member, the cost of transportation, and the cost of lodging and means while away from his residence or the greater Washington, District of Columbia, metropolitan area.

(d) The term "outside earned income" means, with respect to a Member, wages, salaries, professional fees, honorariums, and other amounts (other than copyright royalties) received or to be received as compensation for personal services actually rendered but does not include—

(1) the salary of such Member as a Member;

(2) any compensation derived by such Member for personal services actually rendered prior to the effective date of this rule or becoming such a Member, whichever occurs later;

(3) any amount paid by, or on behalf of, a Member to a tax-qualified pension, profit-sharing, or stock bonus plan and received by such Member for such a plan; and

(4) in the case of a Member engaged in a trade or business in which the Member or his family holds a controlling interest and in which both personal services and capital are income-producing factors, any amount received by such Member so long as the personal services actually rendered by the Member in the trade or business do not generate a significant amount of income.

Outside earned income shall be determined without regard to any community property law.

Statement of Alleged Violation—Count One

The Committee has reason to believe that, during calendar years 1984-1987, Representative Wright violated House Rules XLIII, XLIV, and XLVII, as well as 2 U.S.C. 441i, in connection with the marketing and sale of his book, *Reflections of a Public Man*. The record indicates that in each of seven instances, Representative Wright received income denominated as royalty (based on a royalty of 55% of book price) from the sales of books, such sales having been arranged in lieu of traditional honoraria compensation for speeches. The Committee has reason to believe that the subject book sales were intended to avoid the limitations of law and House Rules on the reporting and receipt of outside earned income, honoraria, and gifts. Accordingly, the Committee believes that, notwithstanding that the congressman's income was nominally a royalty derived from the sale of books, because each "sale" was arranged as compensation for a speech, the result is that the income was, in fact, the honorarium for the speech. The seven instances, amount of income, and resultant alleged violations are described below. An eighth instance alleging an undisclosed gift is also described.

A. Calendar Year 1984

1. October 16, 1984, speech at Southwest Texas State University

The record indicates that Representative Wright gave a speech for which he received a $3,000 honorarium check. Subsequent to receipt of the honorarium, university officials were asked whether they wished to receive books from Representative Wright, who had reached the 30% annual limit on outside earned income imposed by House Rule XLVII. Arrangements were made for the school to receive $3,000 worth of the book, *Reflections of a Public Man*. Representative Wright received the check dated October 12, 1984, and endorsed it to Madison Publishing, which, in turn, deposited the check on November 28, 1984. By so doing, Wright received $1,650 (the 55-percent royalty proceeds) as royalty income in lieu of the $3,000 honorarium.

The Committee has reason to believe that, by accepting the honorarium (endorsing the check from the University), Representative Wright accepted an honorarium in excess of the $2,000 limit in violation of 2 U.S.C. 441i. Consequently, the Committee also has reason to believe that Representative Wright failed to disclose the proceeds as an honorarium on his Financial Disclosure Statement in violation of House Rule XLIV and exceeded the outside earned income limit imposed by House Rule XLVII.

B. Calendar Year 1985

1. April 1985 speech to National Association of Realtors (NAR)

The record indicates that Representative Wright spoke at NAR's April 1985 legislative meeting. The original $2,000 check from NAR to Representative Wright noted the payment was for the congressman's honorarium. This check was voided and a second $2,000 check was issued for the purpose of buying multiple copies of the congressman's book, *Reflections of a Public Man*.

Therefore, the Committee concludes there is reason to believe that the $1,100 Representative Wright received as royalty income from this sale of the books was, in fact, the honorarium for his speech to NAR and constituted unreported outside earned income in violation of the limitation of House Rule XLVII and House Rule XLIV regarding financial disclosure.

2. July 29, 1985, speech to Hamel & Park

The record indicates that Representative Wright made a speech at the request of the law firm of Hamel & Park for which Representative Wright was offered an honorarium. It was suggested that, in lieu of the honorarium which the firm indicated it was willing to pay, the firm should, instead, purchase $2,000 worth of Representative Wright's book, *Reflections of a Public Man*. The firm made the book purchase as suggested.

The Committee has reason to believe that the $1,100 Representative Wright received as royalty income from this sale of the books was, in fact, the honorarium for his speech to Hamel & Park and constituted unreported outside earned income in violation of the limitation of House Rule XLVII and House Rule XLIV regarding financial disclosure.

3. September 1985 speech to Van Liew Capital

The record indicates that Representative Wright gave a speech to Van Liew Capital clients in September, 1985. Correspondence arranging the congressman's appearance specified a $2,000 honorarium for his doing so.

The record further indicates that prior to Representative Wright's appearance, Van Liew Capital was informed that it could not pay Representative Wright directly for his speech due to limitations on outside earned income (House Rule XLVII). Instead, purchase of the congressman's book, *Reflections of a Public Man,* was suggested. Thereafter, Van Liew Capital issuéd a check to purchase $2,000 worth of the book.

The Committee concludes there is reason to believe that the $1,100 royalty which Representative Wright received from Van Liew Capital from this sale of the books was, in fact, the honorarium for his speech to the organization and constituted unreported outside earned income in violation of the limitation of House Rule XLVII and House Rule XLIV regarding financial disclosure.

4. Late Fall 1985 speech to Ocean Spray Massachusetts Growers (Ocean Spray)

The record indicates that although Ocean Spray offered Representative Wright a $2,000 honorarium for his speech, it was suggested that, instead, Ocean Spray buy copies of the congressman's book, *Reflections of a Public Man.*

Since the honorarium check had already been issued, a second check was prepared to effect the book purchase. In addition it was agreed that Ocean Spray would not receive any books, but, rather, Representative Wright would distribute them.

The Committee concludes there is reason to believe that the $1,100 Representative Wright received as royalty income from this sale of books was, in fact, the honorarium for his speech to Ocean Spray and constituted unreported outside earned income in violation of the limitation of House Rule XLVII and House Rule XLIV regarding financial disclosure.

The Committee has further reason to believe that since Ocean Spray did not receive any books, the books were a gift to the congressman in violation of House Rule XLIII, clause 4, and House Rule XLIV regarding disclosure of gifts.

C. Calendar Year 1986

1. March 11, 1986, speech to the Fertilizer Institute

The record indicates that in conjunction with Representative Wright's speech, the Institute had expressed its desire "to do something" for him, such as present the congressman with a suitable memento, "such as a plaque, or small gift, et cetera." It was suggested that the Institute purchase copies of the congressman's book, *Reflections of a Public Man.* Accordingly, prior to Representative Wright's appearance, the Fertilizer Institute purchased $2,023 worth of the book.

The Committee has reason to believe that the $1,112.65 Representative Wright received as royalty income from this sale of books was, in fact, the honorarium for his speech to the Fertilizer Institute and constituted unreported outside earned income in violation of the limitation of House Rule XLVII and House Rule XLIV regarding financial disclosure.

2. March 1986 speech to Mid-Continent Oil & Gas Association (Mid-Continent)

In conjunction with Representative Wright's speech to Mid-Continent's 1986 annual meeting, the record indicates that it was suggested that Mid-Continent purchase $1,000 worth of his book, *Reflections of a Public Man*, in lieu of paying an honorarium. Mid-Continent did not receive all the books it purchased but, rather, left distribution of most of the copies up to the congressman.

The Committee has reason to believe that the $550 Representative Wright received as royalty income from this sale of books was, in fact, the honorarium for his speech to Mid-Continent and constituted unreported outside earned income in violation of the limitation of House Rule XLVII and House Rule XLIV regarding financial disclosure.

Moreover, since Mid-Continent did not receive all the books it purchased, the Committee has further reason to believe that the books constructively given to Representative Wright for his distribution constituted a gift to the congressman in violation of House Rule XLIII, clause 4, and House Rule XLIV regarding disclosure of gifts.

D. Calendar Year 1987

The record indicates that Mr. S. Gene Payte, a Fort Worth, Texas, real estate developer, desired to give Representative Wright a $5,000 gift and, to that end, gave a check in that amount to Mrs. Wright. Representative Wright informed Mr. Payte he could not accept the gift and returned the check.

The record further indicates that later, on March 9, 1987, Mr. Payte decided to contribute $5,000 for revision and distribution of Representative Wright's book, *Reflections of a Public Man.*

Mr. Payte wrote an additional $1,000 check on August 7, 1987. Mr. Payte only received 300-500 copies of the books which were never revised as he wished.

Since Mr. Payte did not receive all of the books, the Committee has reason to believe that the books not delivered (500-700 copies) were a gift to the congressman but not reported in violation of House Rule XLIV regarding disclosure of gifts.

Statement of Alleged Violation—Count Two
Receipt of Gifts of Free Housing

The alleged violations described below arise as a result of Representative and Mrs. Wright's relationship with Mr. and Mrs. George Mallick, the two couples' joint ownership of an investment corporation known as Mallightco, Inc., and Mrs. Wright's purported employment association with the corporation.

The record indicates that during the period 1979 through 1984, Representative and Mrs. Wright were provided free housing in two apartments located in Fort Worth, Texas. Particularly with respect to the Wrights' free use of an apartment during 1980 through 1984, such free use was arranged by Mr. George Mallick but not as part of Mrs. Wright's compensation from Mallightco, Inc. The Committee has reason to believe that Mr. Mallick is an individual with a direct interest in legislation.

While the alleged gifts of free housing involved were assertedly provided to Mrs. Wright, the benefits derived therefrom are imputed to the congressman because of the circumstance indicating that the free housing was not provided to Mrs. Wright wholly independent of her spousal relationship. Notably, Representative Wright and Mr. Mallick maintained a close social relationship for a period of years prior to the time Mr. Mallick arranged the free housing. Finally, Representative Wright shared the benefits of Mr. Mallick's gift of free housing to the same extent as did his wife.

A. Calendar Year 1979

The record indicates that in calendar year 1979, Representative Wright received a gift of free housing valued at $2,151 arising out of his free use of an apartment located at 4212-C Hulen Place, Fort Worth, Texas, and controlled by George Mallick, an individual the Committee has reason to believe had a direct interest in legislation.

Because this gift to Representative Wright was not reported on his Financial Disclosure Statement for calendar year 1979 as required by House Rule XLIV, the committee has reason to believe that Representative Wright violated House Rule XLIV and House Rule XLIII, clause 4, the latter of which imposes a limit of $100 on gifts received from persons with a direct interest in legislation.

B. Calendar Year 1980

The record indicates that in calendar year 1980, Representative Wright received a gift of free housing valued at $2,868 arising out of his free use of an apartment located at 4212-C Hulen Place, Fort Worth, Texas, and controlled by George Mallick, an individual the Committee has reason to believe had a direct interest in legislation.

Because this gift to Representative Wright was not reported on his Financial Disclosure Statement for calendar year 1980 as required by House Rule XLIV, the Committee has reason to believe that Representative Wright violated House Rule XLIV and House Rule XLIII, clause 4, the later of which imposes a limit of $100 on gifts received from persons with a direct interest in legislation.

C. Calendar Year 1981

The record indicates that in calendar year 1981, Representative Wright received a gift of free housing valued at $3,279 arising out of his free use of apartments located at 4212-C Hulen Place, Fort Worth, Texas, and 1067 Roaring Springs Road, Fort Worth, Texas, and each controlled by George Mallick, an individual the Committee has reason to believe had a direct interest in legislation.

Because this gift to Representative Wright was not reported on his Financial Disclosure Statement for calendar year 1981 as required by House Rule XLIV, the Committee has reason to believe that Representative Wright violated House Rule XLIV and House Rule XLIII, clause 4, the latter of which imposes a limit of $100 on gifts received from persons with a direct interest in legislation.

D. Calendar Year 1982

The record indicates that in calendar year 1982, Representative Wright received a gift of free housing valued at $7,800 arising out of his free use of an apartment located at 1067 Roaring Springs Road, Fort Worth, Texas, and controlled by George Mallick, an individual the Committee has reason to believe had a direct interest in legislation.

Because this gift to Representative Wright was not reported on his Financial Disclosure Statement for calendar year 1979 as required by House Rule XLIV, the committee has reason to believe that Representative Wright violated House Rule XLIV and House Rule XLIII, clause 4, the latter of which imposes a limit of $100 on gifts received from persons with a direct interest in legislation.

E. Calendar Year 1983

The record indicates that in calendar year 1983, Representative Wright received a gift of free housing valued at $7,800 arising out of his free use of an apartment located at 1067 Roaring Springs Road, Fort Worth, Texas, and controlled by George Mallick, an individual the Committee has reason to believe had a direct interest in legislation.

Because this gift to Representative Wright was not reported on his Financial Disclosure Statement for calendar year 1982 as required by House Rule XLIV, the Committee has reason to believe that Representative Wright violated House Rule XLIV and House Rule XLIII, clause 4, the latter of which imposes a limit of $100 on gifts received from persons with a direct interest in legislation.

F. Calendar Year 1984

The record indicates that in calendar year 1984, Representative Wright received a gift of free housing valued at $7,800 arising out of his free use of an apartment located at 1067 Roaring Springs Road, Fort Worth, Texas, and controlled by George Mallick, an individual the Committee has reason to believe had a direct interest in legislation.

Because this gift to Representative Wright was not reported on his Financial Disclosure Statement for calendar year 1984 as required by House Rule XLIV, the Committee has reason to believe that Representative Wright violated House Rule XLIV and House Rule XLIII, clause 4, the latter of which imposes a limit of $100 on gifts received from persons with a direct interest in legislation.

Statement of Alleged Violation—Count Three
Receipt of Gifts of Reduced Housing Costs

The alleged violations described below arise as a result of Representative and Mrs. Wright's relationship with Mr. and Mrs. George Mallick. The record indicates that during the period 1985 through 1988, Representative and Mrs. Wright were provided reduced-rate housing in an apartment/ townhouse located in Fort Worth, Texas. During this period and notwithstanding the fact that Representative and Mrs. Wright had exclusive use and control of the apartment/townhouse which included the placement of their personal belongings and furnishings, payment for their use was based upon a per diem rate reflecting only those days for which the congressman and/or his wife were physically present in the apartment/townhouse.

Accordingly, the Committee has reason to believe that the per diem arrangement represented a gift to Representative Wright and his wife because it did not take into account the fact that the Wrights had totally relocated their personal effects in the apartment/townhouse in conjunction with their exclusive use of the facility. The Committee also has reason to believe that Mr. Mallick is an individual with a direct interest in legislation.

A. Calendar Year 1985

The record indicates that in calendar year 1985, Representative Wright received a gift of reduced housing cost valued at $6,918 arising out of his use of an apartment/townhouse located at 1067 Roaring Springs Road, Fort Worth, Texas, and controlled by George Mallick, an individual the Committee has reason to believe had a direct interest in legislation.

Because this gift to Representative Wright was not reported on his Financial Disclosure Statement for calendar year 1985 as required by House Rule XLIV, the committee has reason to believe that Representative Wright violated House Rule XLIV and House Rule XLIII, clause 4, the latter of which imposes a limit of $100 on gifts received from persons with a direct interest in legislation.

B. Calendar Year 1986

The record indicates that in calendar year 1986, Representative Wright received a gift of reduced housing cost valued at $6,088 arising out of his use of an apartment/townhouse located at 1067 Roaring Springs Road, Fort Worth, Texas, and controlled by George Mallick, an individual the Committee has reason to believe had a direct interest in legislation.

Because this gift to Representative Wright was not reported on his Financial Disclosure Statement for calendar year 1986 as required by House Rule XLIV, the committee has reason to believe that Representative Wright violated House Rule XLIV and House Rule XLIII, clause 4, the latter of which imposes a limit of $100 on gifts received from persons with a direct interest in legislation.

C. Calendar Year 1987

The record indicates that in calendar year 1987, Representative Wright received a gift of reduced housing cost valued at $7,044 arising out of his use of an apartment/townhouse located at 1067 Roaring Springs Road, Fort Worth, Texas, and controlled by George Mallick, an individual the Committee has reason to believe had a direct interest in legislation.

Because this gift to Representative Wright was not reported on his Financial Disclosure Statement for calendar year 1987 as required by House Rule XLIV, the committee has reason to believe that Representative Wright violated House Rule XLIV and House Rule XLIII, clause 4, the latter of which imposes a limit of $100 on gifts received from persons with a direct interest in legislation.

D. Calendar Year 1988

The record indicates that in calendar year 1988, Representative Wright received a gift of reduced housing cost valued at $1,704 arising out of his use of an apartment/townhouse located at 1067 Roaring Springs Road, Fort Worth, Texas, and controlled by George Mallick, an individual the Committee has reason to believe had a direct interest in legislation.

Because this gift to Representative Wright was not reported on his Financial Disclosure Statement for calendar year 1988 as required by House Rule XLIV, the committee has reason to believe that Representative Wright violated House Rule XLIV and House Rule XLIII, clause 4, the latter of which imposes a limit of $100 on gifts received from persons with a direct interest in legislation.

Statement of Alleged Violation—Count Four
Gift of Salary

The alleged violations described below arise as a result of Representative and Mrs. Wright's relationship with Mr. and Mrs. George Mallick, the two couples' joint ownership of an investment corporation known as Mallightco, Inc., and Mrs. Wright's purported employment association with the corporation. The record indicates that during the period 1981 through 1984, Mrs. Wright received a total of $72,000 ($18,000 a year) in compensation as an employee of Mallightco, Inc. During this four-year period, there was no evidence either supporting or establishing that the money paid to Mrs. Wright was in return for identifiable services or work products that she provided to Mallightco, Inc. Accordingly, the Committee has reason to believe that the compensation paid to Mrs. Wright was a gift from Mr. George Mallick who was in charge of the corporation's activities including those of its employees. The Committee also has reason to believe that Mr. Mallick is an individual with a direct interest in legislation.

While the alleged gifts of salary involved were assertedly provided to Mrs. Wright, the benefits derived therefrom are imputed to the congressman because of the circumstance indicating that such gifts were not provided to Mrs. Wright wholly independent of her spousal relationship. Notably, Representative Wright and Mr. Mallick maintained a close social relationship for a period of years prior to the time Mrs. Wright was placed on Mallightco, Inc.'s payroll.

A. Calendar Year 1981

The record indicates that in calendar year 1981, Mrs. Wright received compensation in the amount of $18,000 from Mallightco, Inc. Because there is no evidence supporting or establishing that the money paid to Mrs. Wright was in return for identifiable services or work products that she provided to Mallightco, Inc., the $18,000 paid to her was, therefore, an apparent gift.

Moreover, because this gift was not reported on Representative Wright's Financial Disclosure Statement for calendar year 1981 as required by House Rule XLIV, the Committee has reason to believe that Representative Wright violated House Rule XLIV and House Rule XLIII, clause 4, the latter of which imposes a limit of $100 on gifts received from persons having a direct interest in legislation.

B. Calendar Year 1982

The record indicates that in calendar year 1982, Mrs. Wright received compensation in the amount of $18,000 from Mallightco, Inc. Because there is no evidence supporting or establishing that the money paid to Mrs. Wright was in return for identifiable services or work products that she provided to Mallightco, Inc., the $18,000 paid to her was, therefore, an apparent gift.

Moreover, because this gift was not reported on Representative Wright's Financial Disclosure Statement for calendar year 1982 as required by House Rule XLIV, the Committee has reason to believe that Representative Wright violated House Rule XLIV and House Rule XLIII, clause 4, the latter of which imposes a limit of $100 on gifts received from persons having a direct interest in legislation.

C. Calendar Year 1983

The record indicates that in calendar year 1983, Mrs. Wright received compensation in the amount of $18,000 from Mallightco, Inc. Because there is no evidence supporting or establishing that the money paid to Mrs. Wright was in return for identifiable services or work products that she provided to Mallightco, Inc., the $18,000 paid to her was, therefore, an apparent gift.

Moreover, because this gift was not reported on Representative Wright's Financial Disclosure Statement for calendar year 1983 as required by House Rule XLIV, the Committee has reason to believe that Representative Wright violated House Rule XLIV and House Rule XLIII, clause 4, the latter of which imposes a limit of $100 on gifts received from persons having a direct interest in legislation.

D. Calendar Year 1984

The record indicates that in calendar year 1984, Mrs. Wright received compensation in the amount of $18,000 from Mallightco, Inc. Because there is no evidence supporting or establishing that the money paid to Mrs. Wright was in return for identifiable services or work products that she provided to Mallightco, Inc., the $18,000 paid to her was, therefore, an apparent gift.

Moreover, because this gift was not reported on Representative Wright's Financial Disclosure Statement for calendar year 1984 as required by House Rule XLIV, the Committee has reason to believe that Representative Wright violated House Rule XLIV and House Rule XLIII, clause 4, the latter of which imposes a limit of $100 on gifts received from persons having a direct interest in legislation.

Statement of Alleged Violation—Count Five
Gifts of Use of an Automobile
and Automobile Maintenance and Operation

The alleged violations described below arise as a result of Representative and Mrs. Wright's relationship with Mr. and Mrs. George Mallick, the two couples' joint ownership of an investment corporation known as Mallightco, Inc., and Mrs. Wright's purported employment association with the corporation. The record indicates that during the period 1983 through 1988, Mrs. Wright was provided the free use of a 1979 Cadillac Seville, including maintenance and operation costs (e.g., insurance, registration and repair) of the vehicle, assertedly by virtue of her employment association with Mallightco, Inc. The record further indicates that Mrs. Wright's employment association with Mallightco, Inc. terminated on December 31, 1984, and that her use of the vehicle subsequent to 1984 could not be predicated upon an employment association with the corporation.

Finally, the record indicates that the automobile was located in Washington beginning in 1983 and that the records of Mallightco, Inc., began referring to the Cadillac as Mrs. Wright's car. There is no evidence indicating that Mrs. Wright's use of the vehicle in Washington, D.C., was necessary since the corporation's business headquarters were located in

Fort Worth, Texas, and there is no record supporting or establishing that she performed any duties for Mallightco in the District of Columbia. Mrs. Wright's use of the vehicle was arranged by Mr. Mallick, an individual who the Committee believes has a direct interest in legislation.

While the alleged gifts of the free use of an automobile and associated operation and maintenance costs were assertedly provided to Mrs. Wright, the benefits derived therefrom are imputed to the congressman because of the circumstances indicating that such gifts were not provided to Mrs. Wright wholly independent of her spousal relationship. Notably, Representative Wright and Mr. Mallick maintained a close social relationship for a period of years prior to the time Mr. Mallick arranged the free use of the automobile and associated maintenance and operation costs.

A. Calendar Year 1983

The record indicates that in calendar year 1983, Mrs. Wright was provided free use of a 1979 Cadillac Seville which was an asset of Mallightco, Inc., and under the control of George Mallick, an individual the Committee has reason to believe had a direct interest in legislation. Because there is no evidence that Mrs. Wright required the use of this automobile during her employment association with Mallightco, Inc., the free use of the automobile was a gift to Representative Wright and his wife valued at $1,416.

Since the gift of automobile usage was not reported on Representative Wright's Financial Disclosure Statement for calendar year 1983 as required by House Rule XLIV, the Committee has reason to believe that Representative Wright violated House Rule XLIV and House Rule XLIII, clause 4, the latter of which imposes a limit of $100 on gifts received from persons having a direct interest in legislation.

In addition to the foregoing, the record indicates that in calendar year 1983, Representative Wright and his wife received a gift of $1,803.45 representing the costs to maintain and insure the 1979 Cadillac Seville provided by George Mallick, as described above.

Because this gift of the costs of automobile maintenance and operation was not reported on Representative Wright's Financial Disclosure Statement for calendar year 1983 as required by House Rule XLIV, the Committee has reason to believe that Representative Wright violated House Rule XLIV and House Rule XLIII, clause 4, the latter of which imposes a limit of $100 on gifts received from persons having a direct interest in legislation.

B. Calendar Year 1984

The record indicates that in calendar year 1984, Mrs. Wright was provided free use of a 1979 Cadillac Seville which was an asset of Mallightco, Inc., and under the control of George Mallick, an individual the Committee has reason to believe had a direct interest in legislation. Because there is no evidence that Mrs. Wright required the use of this automobile during her employment association with Mallightco, Inc., the free use of the automobile was a gift to Representative Wright and his wife valued at $1,416.

Since the gift of automobile usage was not reported on Representative Wright's Financial Disclosure Statement for calendar year 1984 as required by House Rule XLIV, the Committee has reason to believe that Representative Wright violated House Rule XLIV and House Rule XLIII, clause 4, the latter of which imposes a limit of $100 on gifts received from persons having a direct interest in legislation.

In addition to the foregoing, the record indicates that in calendar year 1984, Representative Wright and his wife received a gift of $1,648.58 representing the costs to maintain and insure the 1979 Cadillac Seville provided by George Mallick, as described above.

Because this gift of the costs of automobile maintenance and operation was not reported on Representative Wright's Financial Disclosure Statement for calendar year 1984 as required by House Rule XLIV, the Committee has reason to believe that Representative Wright violated House Rule XLIV and House Rule XLIII, clause 4, the latter of which imposes a limit of $100 on gifts received from persons having a direct interest in legislation.

C. Calendar Year 1985

The record indicates that in calendar year 1985, Mrs. Wright was provided free use of a 1979 Cadillac Seville which was an asset of Mallightco, Inc., and under the control of George Mallick, an individual the Committee has reason to believe had a direct interest in legislation. Because there is no evidence that Mrs. Wright required the use of this automobile during her employment association with Mallightco, Inc., the free use of the automobile was a gift to Representative Wright and his wife valued at $1,416.

Since the gift of automobile usage was not reported on Representative Wright's Financial Disclosure Statement for calendar year 1985 as required by House Rule XLIV, the Committee has reason to believe that Representative Wright violated House Rule XLIV and House Rule XLIII, clause 4, the latter of which imposes a limit of $100 on gifts received from persons having a direct interest in legislation. In addition to the foregoing, the record indicates that in calendar year 1985, Representative Wright and his wife received a gift of $1,477.80 representing the costs to maintain and insure the 1979 Cadillac Seville provided by George Mallick, as described above.

Because this gift of the costs of automobile maintenance and operation was not reported on Representative Wright's Financial Disclosure Statement for calendar year 1985 as required by House Rule XLIV, the Committee has reason to believe that Representative Wright violated House Rule XLIV and House Rule XLIII, clause 4, the latter of which imposes a limit of $100 on gifts received from persons having a direct interest in legislation.

D. Calendar Year 1986

The record indicates that in calendar year 1986, Mrs. Wright was provided free use of a 1979 Cadillac Seville which was an asset of Mallightco, Inc., and under the control of George Mallick, an individual the Committee has reason to believe had a direct interest in legislation. Because there is no evidence that Mrs. Wright required the use of this automobile during her employment association with Mallightco, Inc., the free use of the automobile was a gift to Representative Wright and his wife valued at $1,416.

Since the gift of automobile usage was not reported on Representative Wright's Financial Disclosure Statement for calendar year 1986 as required by House Rule XLIV, the Committee has reason to believe that Representative Wright violated House Rule XLIV and House Rule XLIII, clause 4, the latter of which imposes a limit of $100 on gifts received from persons having a direct interest in legislation.

In addition to the foregoing, the record indicates that in calendar year 1986, Representative Wright and his wife received a gift of $1,510 representing the costs to maintain and insure the 1979 Cadillac Seville provided by George Mallick, as described above.

Because this gift of the costs of automobile maintenance and operation was not reported on Representative Wright's Financial Disclosure Statement for calendar year 1986 as required by House Rule XLIV, the Committee has reason to believe that Representative Wright violated House Rule XLIV and House Rule XLIII, clause 4, the latter of which imposes a limit of $100 on gifts received from persons having a direct interest in legislation.

E. Calendar Year 1987

The record indicates that in calendar year 1987, Mrs. Wright was provided free use of a 1979 Cadillac Seville which was an asset of Mallightco, Inc., and under the control of George Mallick, an individual the Committee has reason to believe had a direct interest in legislation. Because there is no evidence that Mrs. Wright required the use of this automobile during her employment association with Mallightco, Inc., the free use of the automobile was a gift to Representative Wright and his wife valued at $1,416.

Since the gift of automobile usage was not reported on Representative Wright's Financial Disclosure Statement for calendar year 1987 as required by House Rule XLIV, the Committee has reason to believe that Representative Wright violated House Rule XLIV and House Rule XLIII, clause 4, the latter of which imposes a limit of $100 on gifts received from persons having a direct interest in legislation.

In addition to the foregoing, the record indicates that in calendar year 1987, Representative Wright and his wife received a gift of $2,849.02 representing the costs to maintain and insure the 1979 Cadillac Seville provided by George Mallick, as described above.

Because this gift of the costs of automobile maintenance and operation was not reported on Representative Wright's Financial Disclosure Statement for calendar year 1987 as required by House Rule XLIV, the Committee has reason to believe that Representative Wright violated House Rule XLIV and House Rule XLIII, clause 4, the latter of which imposes a limit of $100 on gifts received from persons having a direct interest in legislation.

F. Calendar Year 1988

The record indicates that in calendar year 1988, Mrs. Wright was provided free use of a 1979 Cadillac Seville which was an asset of Mallightco, Inc., and under the control of George Mallick, an individual the Committee has reason to believe had a direct interest in legislation. Because there is no evidence that Mrs. Wright required the use of this automobile during her employment association with Mallightco, Inc., the free use of the automobile was a gift to Representative Wright and his wife valued at $1,416.

Since the gift of automobile usage was not reported on Representative Wright's Financial Disclosure Statement for calendar year 1988 as required by House Rule XLIV, the Committee has reason to believe that Representative Wright violated House Rule XLIV and House Rule XLIII, clause 4, the latter of which imposes a limit of $100 on gifts received from persons having a direct interest in legislation.

In addition to the foregoing, the record indicates that in calendar year 1988, Representative Wright and his wife received a gift of $1,606.80 representing the costs to maintain and insure the 1979 Cadillac Seville provided by George Mallick, as described above.

Because this gift of the costs of automobile maintenance and operation was not reported on Representative Wright's Financial Disclosure Statement for calendar year 1988 as required by House Rule XLIV, the Committee has reason to believe that Representative Wright violated House Rule XLIV and House Rule XLIII, clause 4, the latter of which imposes a limit of $100 on gifts received from persons having a direct interest in legislation.

WRIGHT'S FAREWELL SPEECH

Mr. Speaker, for 34 years I have had the great privilege to be a member of this institution, the people's house, and I shall forever be grateful for that wondrous privilege.

I never cease to be thankful to the people of the 12th District of Texas for their friendship and their understanding and their partiality toward me. Eighteen times they have voted to permit me the grand privilege of representing them here in this depository of the democratic principle.

Only a few days ago, even in face of harsh news accounts and bitter criticisms, they indicated in a poll taken by the leading newspaper in the district that 78 percent of them approved of my services and that includes 73 percent of the Republicans in my district and I am very proud of that.

And you, my colleagues, Democrats and Republicans, I owe a great deal to you. You have given me the greatest gift within your power to give. To be the Speaker of the United States House of Representatives is the grandest opportunity that can come to any lawmaker anywhere in the Western world. And I would be deeply remiss if I didn't express my sincere appreciation to you for that opportunity.

I hope that I have reflected credit upon the people of my district who know me best, perhaps, and upon the people of this House who, next to them, who know me best.

[Proud of Congress]

I am proud of a number of the things that we have done together while you have let me be your Speaker. I am proud of the record of the 100th Congress. Many people feel that it is the most responsive and most productive Congress in perhaps 25 years. All of you who were here in that Congress had a part in that.

Many of the things we did were truly bipartisan in character. Together, we made it possible for great leaps forward to be made in such things as our competitiveness in the world. Together, we fashioned the beginnings of a truly effective war on drugs to stamp out that menace to the streets and schools and homes of our nation.

We began the effort to help the homeless. We still have work to do to make housing affordable to low-income Americans so that there won't be any homeless in this country. We did things to help abate catastrophic illness, provide welfare-reform legislation, clean-water legislation and a great many other things that I shall not detail.

For your help, your great work, and for permitting me to be a part of this institution while that was happening, I thank you. And I shall forever be grateful for your cooperation. And I love this institution.

And I want to assure each of you that under no circumstances, having spent more than half of my life here, this House being my home, would I ever knowingly or intentionally do or say anything to violate its rules or detract from its standards.

Now all of us are prone to human error. The Speaker of the House is in fact the chief enforcer of the rules of the House. It's really a wonderful thing that any member of the House may, at his will, bring question against any other member, and under our rules that has to be looked into. And I have no quarrel with that, nor any criticism of people who have served on the committee on standards. It's a thankless job and you have to have such things.

For over a year, well, just about a year, I have ached to tell my side of the story. That to which I have to respond keeps changing. But today, silence is no longer tolerable; nor for the good of the House is it even desirable.

[Not Bitter]

So without any rancor and without any bitterness or any hard feelings toward anybody, I thank you for indulging me as I answer to you and to the American people for my honor, my reputation and all the things I've tried to stand for all these years.

The past year, while the committee on standards has had these matters under advisement, I have ached for the opportunity to speak. Almost daily I besought them to let me come and answer whatever questions they had on their mind. Finally, on the 14th of September, they gave me one day in which to do that.

I gratefully went and spent the whole morning and the whole afternoon answering as candidly and freely as possibly I could any questions that anyone would ask and I believe when I left everyone was reasonably well satisfied.

Suffice to say that the five original charges that had been lodged were dropped, dismissed. In their place, however, came three additional charges. Some said 69. The 69 are merely a matter of multiple counting of the three.

In April, the committee said, well, they thought there was some reason to believe that rules may have been violated in these three basic areas. I owe it to you and to the American people to give a straightforward answer on those three areas.

[Not Infallible]

I'm convinced that I'm right; maybe I'm wrong. I know that each of us, as Benjamin Franklin suggested, should be careful to doubt a little his own infallibility. But before those charges were issued, as press leaks filtered out almost daily, tarnishing my reputation, and, by inference, spilling over onto the reputation of this institution, I pleaded for the privilege to come and answer those questions before charges were made. Under the rules, that was not permitted to me, and they were formally made.

And so let's look at it, one by one, dispassionately. The committee has raised these three basic questions. Doesn't say that there's clear and convincing proof that I violated the rules, doesn't say that they know that I violated the rules. It said they have some reason to believe I may have. And for these last few weeks I've been trying to refine that and get an opportunity to address it.

Now's the day. I'm going to do it now. The three questions are these. Did my wife Betty's employment, at $18,000 a year for some four years, by a small investment corporation which she and I formed with friends of ours, George and Marlene Mallick, and the attendant benefits of that employment—use of an apartment when she was in Fort Worth on company business and the use of a company-owned car—constitute merely a sham and a subterfuge and a gift from our friend Mr. Mallick? Was Betty's employment and those things related to it a gift?

You've read in papers the suggestion made by committee counsel that I may have received up to $145,000 in gifts from my friend Mr. Mallick. Half of it, $72,000, was Betty's income, Betty's salary. The other half involved the use of a car and the use of an apartment on a per diem basis.

[Defending Betty Wright]

Whether it's right or wrong, let's look at it. Betty's employment. Was that a gift? First question I should like to, I suppose you might be asking, why was Betty working for the corporation? Why did we put her to work at $18,000 a year? The answer is really very simple.

She was the only one of the four of us who had the time and the inclination to handle the job—to look into the investment opportunities that our investment corporation was created to explore. George Mallick was too busy looking after his own interests. He has business interests of his own. Marlene Mallick was raising a family. I was busy being a member of Congress and majority leader. I did not have any time to spend on it. Betty alone, among all of us, had the time, the opportunity, the experience, and the desire to give effort and energy to exploring and promoting investment opportunities.

She did, indeed, perform work. It paid off for the little corporation. She did it well. She studied and followed the stock market on regional stocks. I had brought into the corporation some that I had owned personally, in my personal estate. Betty advised us as to the best time to sell, the best time to buy, and the corporation made some money on those regional stocks. Not a lot of money by some people's standards, but we made some money. Betty's work paid for her salary, several times over.

She made very frequent contacts with a drilling company that was working on a series of exploratory west Texas gas wells, in which each of the partners had an interest, having all borrowed money from the corporation in order to invest. She visited the site of drilling and maintained contact with the company for us.

She went to New York and studied the gemstone business and the corporation made an investment in gemstones. We made some money on that. Betty also looked into the possibility of the corporation, Mallightco, building an apartment complex for young people, but she concluded that the interest rates were unfavorable. Betty also spent a considerable amount of time studying the wine-culture industry which was just getting started in Texas. She made an economic study that concluded it was too speculative for a little corporation of our type.

She looked into other prospective investments such as a small and limited partnership in the movie *Annie,* and a prospective venture in sulfur extraction, but advised against both of those investments. It was lucky for us that she did because people investing in them lost money.

I want to include for printing in the *Record* affidavits from several business people who know from their personal experience and attest to the work that Betty did in this regard. And it will appear in the *Record* at this point—an affidavit by Pamela L. Smith, one by Kay F. Snyder, one by John Freeman, one by Louis A. Farris, Jr. and one by J. B. Williams—all attesting to their personal knowledge of these things that Betty did in working for the corporation for $18,000 a year.

The outside counsel employed by the committee has suggested that Mrs. Wright's employment somehow amounted to a gift. I don't know why, but he assumed that the services she rendered could not have been worth $18,000 a year. How he concludes that she didn't perform duties is to me a mystery.

On page 20 of the statement of alleged violations I find a very strange suggestion based on a statement that, quote, "there was no evidence either supporting or establishing that the money paid to Mrs. Wright was in return for identifiable services or work products."

Frankly I don't know exactly what Mr. Phelan means by "work products." Does he want so many pages of canceled shorthand notes? So many pages of typed manuscript? She wasn't a carpenter. Is a woman's mental study and her time and her advice not to be counted as a work product? How the committee could conclude that there was no evidence that Betty performed duties is very puzzling to me. They don't offer any evidence that she did not.

When I was before the committee that wasn't one of the things that was being considered. They didn't ask me to go into any elaborate detail as I have just done, telling the things that she did. They assumed, assumed that there was no evidence. Ah, but there was evidence! The two people of whom questions were asked aside from myself, Mr. Mallick himself and Pamela Smith, both testified that she did work.

Mr. Phelan's report says that they couldn't identify but maybe 12 days in the whole four-year period in which she worked. Well, that's an inaccurate representation of what they said. Pamela Smith both in this affidavit and in her testimony before the committee clearly said she saw Betty there from five to seven days every month, and on weekends. And she spoke of her knowledge of her doing work in Washington and New York and elsewhere. So there's evidence.

Well, does one conclude that my wife's services to that little corporation were worth less than $18,000 a year? For most of her adult life, Mrs. Wright has been a business person, been an officer in a large hotel, an officer in a successful real estate and construction firm, a professional staff person on a congressional committee. She was making more than $18,000 when she worked at the congressional committee.

And here's the irony. The supreme irony. In 1976, when I was elected majority leader, Betty voluntarily left her job as a professional staff person on the committee so as to avoid any criticism of this institution or of her husband on the ground that we were both on the public payroll.

How many colleagues in the House and the Senate do you know whose wives are on the public payroll doing good work? And yet Betty didn't want to be the cause for even unfounded criticism. She was legally entitled to continue, she having occupied that job before our marriage. But she chose to leave and save the institution and her husband from unwarranted criticism. That's the kind of person she is.

Now it just seems to me there isn't any justification at all for anybody's even raising questions about whether she earned her $18,000 a year. Should a member of Congress have to prove that his wife earned that much money? Bear in mind, this money was not paid by Mr. Mallick. The money was paid by the corporation of which Betty and I were half-owners.

[Gifts from Mallick]

In addition to her salary as a gift, outside counsel contends in summing up $145,000 in gifts that Betty had the use of a company car. That is true, she did. For the first three years, it was used largely by Mr. and Mrs. Mallick.

It wasn't Mr. Mallick's car. It was the company car. The company bought and paid for it. We owned half of it. The next four years Betty had most of the use of it.

Now I've done what I can to resolve any doubt. I want to do the right thing, the honorable thing. I bought and paid for that car out of my personal funds. The trustee of my bank trust, at my instruction, paid the corporation full book value for the car on the day Betty first started driving it on company business, through the whole time she had it in her possession, plus interest. The interest amounted to about $9,000. What more can I do. Does that make it right?

Now concerning the apartment, Betty and I have been more than anxious to do what's right and honorable about that. We didn't think there was anything wrong with paying a per diem rate. The apartment was not held out for rent to anybody else. It wasn't owned for rental purposes. Mallick found he didn't want anybody else in the apartment. They owned about five apartments in this apartment unit complex area and held them out for their employees and their family. There wouldn't have been anybody in the apartment paying any amount of money at all if they hadn't permitted us, when we were in town and Betty was doing company business, to occupy the apartment. We paid on a daily basis for our use of that apartment.

Meanwhile, in an effort to resolve any doubt, last year I told Mr. Mallick that I didn't like the situation being criticized. He said, well, Ralph Lotkin, the committee counsel, said that it was all right. It was in the paper. Printed in the paper four years ago, the Fort Worth newspaper. A statement quoting the chief counsel of the committee on standards, Mr. Lotkin, saying he didn't see anything improper with it. I relied on that.

Nevertheless, last year I said to George Mallick, I said, I want to buy the apartment, George, I'll pay you for it. I did. I paid the amount suggested and appraised by two real estate persons in Fort Worth, $58,000. Now if anybody thinks that's too low a price I'll sell it to you today for $58,000.

Well, I just wanted to clear the air and remove doubts and say if we've made a mistake we've done what we can to set things right. I don't think we've violated any rules. I think you're entitled to know that. My respect for you leads me to want to tell you that.

[Mallick and Lobbying]

The second alleged violation continues on the assumption that Betty's employment and these little benefits that she had were gifts. And then it further assumes that George Mallick, our friend and business partner, had a direct interest in influencing legislation, which would make it illegal for us to accept gifts from him.

Now how do they arrive at that suggestion? I've known this man for more than 25 years. He's been my friend, good, decent, hard-working man of Lebanese extraction. His father had a wholesale grocery store there. His grandfather came with a wagon and a cart to Georgia. He's been successful, moderately so.

Never once in all the years that I've known this man has he ever asked me to vote for or against any piece of legislation. Not once. That's not the basis of our friendship. That's not the way our relationship goes. You have friends like that. They never ask for anything. All they want is to be friends. Not one time has he ever asked me to intercede with any administrative agency of government on behalf of him or of any institution in which he has an interest. Not once. Not once.

So how do they say that he had a direct interest in influencing legislation? On page 58 of the committee report, it is suggested that simply because he was in the real estate business, that he had some oil and gas investments, the committee might infer, that's the word, the committee might infer that he could be deemed a person with an interest of a direct nature in legislation.

The committee suggests he might have an interest in the tax code. Well, who doesn't? Every taxpayer's got an interest in the tax code. Everybody who ever expects to receive Social Security has an interest in the Social Security code. All people have an interest of some kind in the results of legislation, don't they?

That's not what we're talking about. We're talking about whether or not they have a direct interest in trying to influence the course of legislation.

Now, where would you go to find out what that means, if somebody wanted to associate with you in some way and be in business with you some way back home in a perfectly legal way, whether he had an interest in legislation or not? Whom would you consult if you were in doubt about it? I wasn't in doubt. But suppose you were? Wouldn't you think you'd consult the publications of the committee, consult the people who wrote the rules?

Well, the people who wrote the rules don't think George Mallick had an interest in the legislation. David Obey was the chairman of the committee that drafted those rules. He asserts clearly, unequivocally, emphatically, unambiguously, both in an affidavit that he wrote and the report he wrote for the *Washington Post* that doesn't fit George Mallick's case. He doesn't have an interest in legislation as defined under the rules, the rules that David and his committee wrote.

Harold Sawyer, former Republican member from Michigan, who served on that committee with David Obey, says the same thing. I have here an affidavit from Mr. Sawyer in which he states exactly that same conclusion.

And there's an affidavit of Donald F. Terry, who was currently—is employed now by the Committee on Small Business, but was a staff member on the Commission on Administrative Review, which was charged in 1976 with the responsibility of drafting new rules of official conduct for the House. Most of what he refers to has to do with the question of book royalties. I shall come to that next.

But in these matters, these three people who had a great deal to do with writing the rules say that's not what they intended when they wrote the rules. I offer these for printing in the *Record*.

Where else might you turn if you were in doubt? Might you not possibly go to the committee itself to see what advisory opinions it has given? Here is the publication that the committee sends to all of us to tell us what is and is not legal. Each year we receive this as instructions for filling out our financial disclosure statement.

Appendix E is an advisory opinion, No. 10, which defines who has a direct interest in legislation under the law. It says that if the member does not believe that the donor of the gift has a distinct or special interest in the congressional legislative process which sets him clearly apart from the general public, then the member should feel free to accept such gifts. That's the official advice from the committee—given to every member.

Then it defines in summary who has an interest in legislation as prohibited under the rule. Four classes, that's all: registered lobbyists, George Mallick's not a registered lobbyist; somebody that employs a registered lobbyist, George Mallick never did that; somebody who directs or operates a political action committee, George Mallick has never done that; or finally any other individual which the member knows, not should know or ought to suspect or ought to infer, but which the member knows has a distinct and special interest in influencing or affecting the legislative process. Not just somebody who's got an interest financially in the outcome of legislation, not at all! Somebody that you know who has a direct or special interest in influencing or affecting the legislative process which sets that individual apart from the general public.

That was just simply not the case. So he had no direct interest in the legislation, of any type that anybody could define. Now we have motions before the committee to set that aside, set aside that presumption of a man's having direct interest in legislation if they haven't got a reason to believe he has.

The only thing they have suggested is that in 1986 his son borrowed money from a savings and loan to build a little shopping center of his own—wholly apart and foreign to any investments Betty and I had, nothing to do with it at all; his son. And that in 1987 the lending institution had to foreclose.

Yeah, but the period when Betty was employed, presumably as a gift, was 1981 to 1984. He couldn't have known in '81 and '84 that his son was going to borrow money in '86 and that the thing would go bad in '87 and the economic decline would make it impossible to pay off his note on time; he couldn't have known that.

And anyway, would you stretch the thing to the point of saying that just anybody who has a member of his family that owes money to a bank or a savings and a loan is forbidden? Of course you wouldn't. That'd cover more than half the citizens of the country.

The people who wrote the rules don't believe that he's covered. The people who've been interpreting the rules don't believe he's covered. And so I think under all reasonable circumstances, that motion ought to be agreed to, it ought to be agreed to, if rules mean anything, if we're not just going to turn the whole thing on its head and change rules by whim every time we turn around.

[Wright's Book Deal]

Now the only other basic question, it's just one that remains, in the statement of alleged violations, concerns the sale of a book, a little book now you'll recall *Reflections of a Public Man,* which I wrote and which was sold sometimes in bulk quantities. People who took it and gave it away to other people—students, newspapers, public officials and members of their organizations.

And I wanted them to. I wanted to get the widest possible distribution of the book. A book that you write is kinda part of you. You think of it a child almost. It's probably not great literature, but I like it.

Marty Tolchin of the *New York Times;* John Silber, president of Boston University; Jim Lehrer of MacNeil/Lehrer Report, and Dr. Tucker, chancellor of TCU, all said nice things about it and I appreciate that.

Now, the contention of the committee as I understand it is that this book project to publish that book on which I got $3.25 for every book that sold was a kind of a sham and a subterfuge itself and an overall scheme for me to exceed and violate the outside earnings limitation of a member of Congress. I mean, do you think I'd do something like that?

Perhaps the book—$3.25 is what I got out of it, and I didn't get any advance. The purpose of the book was to publish something at a small cost and get wide distribution. If monetary gain had been my primary interest, don't you think I would have gone to one of the big Madison Avenue publications, the houses there that give you a big advance? I know people who received advances before a single book sells from those big companies, twice and three times as much as I got in the total sales of all those books. If it had been a scheme to get around outside earning limits, that's what I might have done.

I hear that a woman author of a book called *Mayflower Madam* got $750,000 in advance royalties. I don't know that to be true. A former

Speaker, Mr. O'Neill, is said to have received a million dollars for his excellent and readable book in advance before any of them were sold. I have read that a woman named Kitty Kelly has received as much as $2 million in advance royalties for a book she's written on Nancy Reagan, which as I understand it is not even an authorized biography. Well, so much for that.

It is true I think that people on my staff were eager to sell these books. They knew I wanted them sold. I've got to accept some responsibility for that if it was wrong, but the rule doesn't say it was wrong.

It couldn't have been an overall scheme to avoid outside earning limits because the rules are clear. They're not equivocal. The rules expressly exempt royalty income. And that, too, is attested to by David Obey. It's attested to by Donald Terry, who gives the rationale and the expression. There wasn't any exception. Book royalties were exempted.

Now maybe they shouldn't have been. Now maybe somebody got the impression that buying a book was the price of getting me to make a speech. I never intended that impression. I never suggested that. I hope that friends of mine did not. Of all the books that were sold, the outside counsel suggests that seven cases involve instances where individuals associated with organizations to which I made speeches bought multiple copies of the books and distributed them among members of the organization or others.

Now I have not been permitted to see the copy of their testimony, so I don't know exactly what they said. I've asked people on my staff, did you tell these folks that they had to buy these books or I wouldn't make a speech? They said no, they didn't.

The total amount as I figure from all of those sales that are involved is about $7,700, what I received. And I'd do whatever was necessary, whatever was right. If those people were under the impression that I wasn't going to make a speech to them unless they bought a bunch of books, if they wanted their money, I'd give them that money, I don't want the money. That's not important. What's important is a person's honor and his integrity.

During that three-year period when the counsel says there are seven instances where I made speeches to groups and they bought copies of these books, seven groups, seven instances, I made at least 700 speeches, for which I didn't get any honorarium, didn't offer to sell anybody a book. Nobody had the chance to buy a book. Do you suppose if there had been an overall scheme there wouldn't have been a wider kind of an experience than that?

I don't know. I'm just saying to you that I didn't intend to try to violate the outside earning limitations and I don't believe legally that I did.

Some of the rest of you make a lot of speeches. How many speeches do you suppose you make that you don't get anything for? Most of us do. Well, what can I do?

One other thing about the books that I suppose needs elaboration. It involves the allegation in the statement of alleged violations that a man named S. Gene Payte, a reputable businessman in Fort Worth, paid for more books than he got from the publisher, that they didn't deliver enough books to him. Now that's what was said in the report of the outside counsel.

[Conflicting Testimony]

S. Gene Payte, upon reading that report, issued an affidavit that is not ambiguous at all. Here's what Mr. Payte says. I'll read in part this affidavit and put the whole thing in the *Record*. He says: "I have read the report of special outside counsel Richard J. Phelan on the preliminary inquiry conducted pursuant to the committee's June 9 resolution as it relates to my testimony. I also have reviewed the transcript of my deposition testimony. The report, and also the conclusions reached by the special counsel, ignored much of the most pertinent testimony in the transcript, takes certain statements out of context, distorts clear statements of fact and in general fails fairly and accurately to summarize the matters as to which I testified."

But the conclusion reached by the special counsel that, quote, I quote from the outside counsel report, Wright violated rule so-and-so, clause four, was based on his [Mr. Phelan's] categorical assertion that, quote, "Gene Payte did not receive the books."

The special counsel asserts, Payte testified, and I am quoting, that he only received between 300 and 500 copies of the book, for $6,000, and makes the flat statement, quote, "Gene Payte did not receive the books," citing as authority Payte's transcript.

Now here is what Payte says: "On the contrary, I did not so testify. I stated not once, but three times that I believe that 1,000 books were delivered to me." Transcript 27, 40, 41.

Mr. Payte goes on: "The special counsel ignores this testimony. Instead, he cites transcript 77. And that citation does not support the special counsel's assertion. Transcript 77 shows that Congressman Myers, not I, made the comment, 'I believe you said you received three to 500 books?' I did not confirm that recollection, my reply being, 'I would like to have all the books.' In fact, I never so testified."

So this is a copy of that affidavit which I should like to submit for the *Record*, together with a copy of a letter that was sent by the committee to Mr. Payte after he issued this affidavit, telling him he ought not to comment.

What do you think of that? A private citizen, a reputable citizen of my community, misquoted in a document published at public expense, sent widely to newspapers throughout the country, widely cited as authority, uncritically, assumed to be accurate. The citizen being misquoted, issues an affidavit to straighten it out and so not be misquoted in the public record. And then he is warned by the committee that he may be held in violation and contempt of Congress if he doesn't shut up.

First Amendment rights supersede any rules of any committee. And any citizen of the United States ought to have the right to have his own testimony correctly characterized, and not be threatened, silenced, by a House committee. Any House committee owes to a citizen of the United States that right, that privilege.

Well, those are basically the matters that pend before the committee in our motion to dismiss. Those motions could clear the air.

Rules are important, just like the constancy of what a law means is important to a citizen. If they can resolve these particular legal issues, as to what constitutes direct interest in legislation, and whether or not book royalties are exempt as the rules say they are. I think it is important for the motions to be ruled upon, and I earnestly hope that the committee will look at it from that standpoint, and grant our motions.

Members are entitled to know what the rules mean, and if they still mean what they meant when they were written and promulgated. Now, maybe the rules need to be changed. If so, let's change them in the legal, orderly way, let's vote on them. Let's vote to change them.

["Mindless Cannibalism"]

Maybe the whole process needs some change and clarification. You know, we may want to consider, the House may want to consider establishing a House counsel to whom members can look for official advice and then rely on that advice.

The rules of the committee itself might need some reconsideration. Having gone through this agonizing experience for about a year now, I mean almost every day there is a new story in the newspaper, leaked, without any chance of me to know what is coming next and no chance of me to go to the committee and answer it and say, "Hey, wait a minute, that is not correct, that is not right."

Maybe the committee that is currently required to sit as a kind of grand jury and petit jury both, ought to have a different composition. Rather than those who issue the statement of alleged violation being the same people who have to judge them, I think it clearly is difficult to expect members who have publicly announced reason to believe there is a violation to reverse their position at a hearing stage and dismiss charges against a member. Maybe once a report of alleged violations is issued, the committee rules ought to allow the member to respond expeditiously.

You know, to deny a member the opportunity to reply quickly can cause serious political injury. It is unfair. Once alleged violations are announced, the committee ought to just immediately release to the member all the evidence that it could have to indicate that that's happened.

In my case, for example, the committee has yet to release any witness testimony or documents that it obtained during the investigation. Why hide the evidence? What is there to hide? This ought not to be the kind of proceedings in which strategic maneuvering be allowed to override fundamental relations of fair play.

I urge the abolition of the gag order, too, which the committee said it forbids any witness who comes and makes a deposition from discussing publicly or telling his side of the thing.

And, I just suppose the charges which the committee concludes are unfounded should not be published and widely disseminated as though they were true and bore the imprimatur of the committee's approval.

There are other things you want to consider. I am not trying to give you an exhaustive list of what might happen. I know there are others who have views that are equally relevant. Perhaps we want to consider outright abolition of all honoraria, speaking fees, altogether. Maybe we want to do that. I don't know. It's up to the House. In exchange for a straightforward, honest increase in the salary for members of all three branches of the government.

It is intolerably hurtful to our government that qualified members of the executive and legislative branches are resigning because of ambiguities and confusion surrounding the ethics laws, and because of their own consequent vulnerability to personal attack. That's a shame. It's happening. And it is grievously hurtful to our society.

When vilification becomes an accepted form of political debate, when negative campaigning becomes a full-time occupation, when members of each party become self-appointed vigilantes carrying out personal vendettas against members of the other party, in God's name that is not what this institution is supposed to be all about.

When vengeance becomes more desirable than vindication, harsh personal attacks upon one another's motives and one another's character drown out the quiet logic of serious debate on important issues, things that we ought to be involved ourselves in, surely that is unworthy of our institution, unworthy of our American political process.

All of us, in both political parties, must resolve to bring this period of mindless cannibalism to an end. There has been enough of it. I pray to God that we will do that and restore the spirit that always existed in this House.

When I first came here all those years ago in 1955 this was a place where a man's word was his bond and his honor and the truth of what he said to you were assumed. You didn't have to prove it.

I remember one time Cleve Bailey, West Virginia, in a moment of impassioned concern over a tariff bill, jumped up and made an objection to the fact that Chet Holifield had voted—in those days we shouted our answers to the votes, and Holifield was back there in the back.

And Bailey said, "I object to the gentleman's from California vote being counted. He came down and voted late." He said, "He was not in the chamber when his name was called and therefore he's not entitled to vote." It was a close vote. Speaker Rayburn grew red as a tomato and I thought he was going to break the gavel when he hammered. He said, "The chair always takes the word of a member."

And then because I was sitting over here behind Cleve Bailey, I heard other members come and say, "Cleve, you're wrong. Chet was back there behind the rail and I was standing by him when he answered. His answer just wasn't heard." Others said, "You shouldn't have said that."

And Cleve Bailey, crusty old West Virginian, came down here and abjectly, literally with tears in his eyes, apologized for having questioned the word of a member. Now, we need that.

Have I made mistakes? Oh, boy, how many! I made a lot of mistakes. Mistakes in judgment, oh, yeah. A lot of them. I'll make some more.

[On John Mack]

Recently, let me just comment on this briefly because it's such a sensational thing, and the injury's been done to me in this particular moment because of it. John Mack. Many of you remember him, know him. I think a lot of you like him and respect him. I helped John one time in his life when he was about 19 years old, 20. I didn't know him, never had met him. I didn't know the nature of a crime that he had been convicted of. I knew only that John Mack was a young man whom my daughter had known in high school. My daughter was married to his brother, incidentally. That's how she knew about John. And she mentioned it to me. All I knew was that he'd been convicted of assault and that he'd served 27 months in a Fairfax County jail.

Contrary to what's been published, I did not interfere with the court. I didn't suggest anything to the court. I didn't have anything to do with his sentencing. I really didn't know and didn't inquire—maybe that's bad judgment—I didn't inquire as to the exact nature of the crime. The sheriff's office in Fairfax County called and asked me if I would know of any job that I could help this young man get. They wanted to parole him. They said he'd been a model rehabilitated prisoner.

And I gave him a job as a file clerk, you know, $9,000 a year. After that he really blossomed and grew and developed and those of you who know him can't conceive as I never could conceive when finally just two years ago I read in the newspaper the precise nature of that crime. It just didn't fit his character. He married, had two beautiful children. Wonderfully responsible, and I think had become a very fine person.

Now, was that bad judgment? You know, maybe so. It doesn't have anything to do with the rules, but it's got all mixed up with it and I don't think that it's bad judgment to try to give a young man a second chance. Maybe I should have known more about it. . . .

And I don't believe that America really stands for the idea that a person should forever be condemned, but I think maybe ought to have a second chance. And that's what I thought in the case of John Mack. Good judgment or bad, I mean that's it. I believe in giving somebody a second chance.

[Resignation]

Have I contributed unwittingly to this manic idea of a frenzy of feeding on other people's reputations? Have I at all caused a lot of this? So maybe

I have. God, I hope I haven't, but maybe I have. Have I been too partisan? Too insistent? Too abrasive? Too determined to have my way? Perhaps. Maybe so.

If I have offended anybody in the other party, I'm sorry. I never meant to, would not have done so intentionally. I always tried to treat all of our colleagues, Democrats and Republicans, with respect.

Are there things I would do differently if I had them to do over again? Oh, boy, how many may I name for you? Well, I tell you what: I'm going to make you a proposition. Let me give you back this job you gave me as a propitiation for all of this season of bad will that has grown up among us; give it back to you. I will resign as Speaker of the House effective upon the election of my successor and I'll ask that we call a caucus on the Democratic side for next Tuesday to choose a successor. I don't want to be a party to tearing up the institution. I love it.

To tell you the truth, this year, it has been very difficult for me to offer the kind of moral leadership that the organization needs because every time I have tried to talk about the needs of the country, about the needs for affordable homes, Jack Kemp's idea or an idea that we are developing here, every time I have tried to talk about the need for minimum wage, tried to talk about the need for day-care centers, embracing ideas on both sides of the aisle, the media have not been interested in that. They wanted to ask me about petty personal finances. You need somebody else. So I want to give you that back.

We'll have a caucus on Tuesday. And then, I will offer to resign from the House sometime before the end of June. Let that be a total payment for the anger and hostility that we feel for each other.

Let's not try to get even with each other. Republicans, please don't get in your heads you need to get somebody else because of John Tower. Democrats, please don't feel you need to get somebody on the other side because of me. We ought to be more mature than that.

Let's restore to this institution the rightful priorities of what is good for this country. Let's all work together to try to achieve them. The nation has important business and it can't afford these distractions, and that is why I offer to resign.

I have enjoyed these years in Congress. I am grateful to all of you who have taught me things and been patient with me. Horace Greeley had a quote that Harry Truman used to like. "Fame is a vapor. Popularity an accident. Riches take wings. Those who cheer today may curse tomorrow. Only one thing endures. Character."

I am not a bitter man. I am not going to be. I am a lucky man. God has given me the privilege of serving in this, the greatest institution on Earth, for a great many years, and I am grateful to the people of my district in Texas, I am grateful to my colleagues, all of you.

God bless this institution. God bless the United States.

May

Statements on China's Protest
and Repression 275

Secretary Baker's Policy Address on
the Middle East..................... 289

President Bush's Proposal for
Conventional Arms Cuts 297

San Francisco Recognizes "Domestic
Partnerships"....................... 305

STATEMENTS ON CHINA'S PROTEST AND REPRESSION

May 15, June 5 and 6, 1989

In April and May the world was amazed when huge crowds demonstrated for democracy in China, and it was appalled when the Communist government brutally repressed the reform movement. The democratic movement had been fostered by a decade of economic reform in China and encouraged by political reforms in the Soviet bloc. The repression recalled both ancient Chinese traditions of authoritarian rule and the totalitarian system installed by China's Communist revolution.

While Western nations expressed outrage, experts on Chinese history and culture urged a restrained response. Although the government was firmly in control of the country, the immensity of public hostility to the regime had been revealed. Many felt that the aging rulers had lost the moral authority to govern China—what Confucian tradition calls "the mandate of heaven."

Americans saw on television student-led demonstrations in Beijing's expansive Tiananmen Square, where up to a million Chinese gathered to demand free speech, a free press, freedom of association, and an end to corruption. Then on June 4 TV audiences saw—before the Beijing government halted satellite transmission—the Chinese army killing unarmed demonstrators.

Congress responded to public outrage by pressing President George Bush to impose strict sanctions against the Chinese government. The president condemned the attack on unarmed civilians, expressed firm support for the democratic movement, halted arms sales, and restricted other U.S.-Chinese interaction, but he sought to avoid a complete break with the government led by eighty-four-year-old Deng Xiaoping.

The Demonstrations

The protests began April 18 when several thousand students marched through Beijing streets chanting democratic slogans, singing revolutionary songs, and mourning the April 15 death of ousted Communist party leader Hu Yoabang, who had pushed for political and economic reforms. During the rest of April and throughout May the size of the demonstrations grew steadily, reaching a peak of more than one million by May 17. Students traveled to the capital from throughout the country to participate in the protests. Nearly three thousand of the students engaged in a hunger strike from May 13 until May 20, the day after the government declared martial law, when they said they would need their strength for the struggle ahead.

In several cities in China, large crowds of protesters expressed support for the Beijing demonstrations. What began as a student movement rapidly won general support. Groups of factory workers, office workers, taxi drivers, journalists, government workers—even groups from the police, the army, and the cadre school of the Communist Party Central Committee—joined in the demonstrations in Tiananmen Square. Bands of students roamed the city asking for donations: merchants brought the protesters food, drink, clothing, sun hats, rain gear, medicine, or whatever they could offer; and taxi and pedicab drivers gave them free rides.

An American journalist, Orville Schell, observed in the June 29 New York Review that Western reporters "were often startled and even sometimes touched by the sense of self-sacrifice, and by the sweet and almost naive moderation they found among these Chinese students, many of whom had earnestly made out their wills in case the government reacted violently." Perry Link, writing in the same publication, said: "For the first time in years, strangers on the streets were polite to one another; people had rebounded from what had seemed an incurable cynicism. There was great camaraderie in the notion of all-of-us against them."

Gorbachev's Visit

The protesters took advantage of a visit to Beijing, May 15-18, by Soviet leader Mikhail S. Gorbachev. The world press was on hand for the first meeting in thirty years between leaders of the two biggest Communist countries. Their relations had been severely strained since the 1960s. The demonstrations not only forced Gorbachev to alter his itinerary, but also upstaged his historic visit. Protesters counted on restraint from the government during the visit and extolled the Soviet leader for the political reforms he was introducing in his country.

Gorbachev kept his distance from the demonstrators as the two nations announced the formal "normalization" of relations. The Soviet leader was quoted as telling Zhao Ziyang, head of the Chinese Communist party, that he had little sympathy for "hotheads" who demand change "in one night." But Zhao, while calling on the students to end their hunger strike, declared May 16 that the highest levels of the government and party "affirmed the students' patriotic spirit in calling for democracy and law, opposing corruption and striving to further reform." Prime Minister Li Peng, a target of demonstrators because of a record of opposing reforms, surprised observers by telling Gorbachev that "people in socialist countries should also enjoy freedom, democracy and human rights. China is prepared to improve these aspects of its political reform."

As the crowds in Tiananmen Square grew larger and larger, Li acceded to student demands for a meeting. But he became intransigent in a nationally televised "dialogue" with student leaders on May 18. The next day army units entered Beijing and some areas of the capital came under martial law.

Tens of thousands of Chinese blocked the first troop movements, defied martial law, and controlled large parts of the city. Some protesters were injured in clashes with riot police, but there were many incidents of soldiers showing sympathy for the protesters.

In the ensuing week, Zhao was stripped of power as Li summoned troops from outside the city. On June 4, troops and tanks fired on the crowds. While initial casualty estimates varied widely, subsequent analyses suggested that the number of dead was between 400 and 800.

Deng, who had been rumored dead or gravely ill, appeared on television June 8, surrounded by hard-line leaders. Removing doubts that he remained China's paramount leader, Deng said: "A very small number of people created turmoil, and this eventually developed into a counter-revolutionary rebellion. They are trying to overthrow the Communist Party, topple the socialist system and subvert the People's Republic of China so as to establish a capitalist republic."

U.S. Response

The West was horrified by the slaughter of unarmed civilians, and the arrest and execution of leading dissenters. Both houses of Congress on June 6 unanimously adopted resolutions condemning the repression and supporting President Bush's initial response. As the repression continued, Congress pressed the president to take tougher action against the Chinese government.

But Bush resisted public and congressional pressure to go beyond a freezing of relations. At a news conference, June 5, the president, who had been the official U.S. representative to China in 1974-1975, took note of China's "Middle Kingdom syndrome"—its ancient disdain and distrust for foreigners. He observed that the recent "building of democracy" owed much to "the relationship we have developed since 1972," the year when Richard M. Nixon's presidential visit to China ended America's refusal to recognize the Communist government. "The process of democratization of Communist societies will not be a smooth one," Bush said, "and we must react to setbacks in a way which stimulates rather than stifles progress toward open and representative systems."

In addition to halting arms sales and visits between U.S. and Chinese military leaders, Bush ordered the Immigration and Naturalization

Service to give "sympathetic review" to requests by Chinese students to stay in the United States longer than initially permitted. Chinese students in the United States and Europe staged protests against their government. But the largest demonstrations were in Hong Kong, a British crown colony scheduled to be returned to China in 1997.

Henry A. Kissinger, the former secretary of state, wrote in the June 11 Washington Post *that the reforms Deng initiated in 1979 had sent tens of thousands of Chinese students to Western countries "where they were exposed to values on which they are now insisting." Deng, who had been imprisoned as a "capitalist roader" when he struggled against Mao Zedong, was credited with opening China to market-oriented economic reforms. Thus China's own leaders launched the forces they later sought to suppress.*

The introduction of free-market incentives had stirred anxiety among the aging revolutionaries who had sacrificed greatly to end the appalling extremes of poverty and wealth in pre-Communist China. The protest challenged not only the Chinese Revolution, but Chinese tradition, in which emperors retained all power and resolved problems by force.

The state quickly regained control of China, but the impact of the protests and their repression had yet to be seen.

> *Following are the text of a statement in support of the student prodemocracy movement, signed by 500 faculty members of Beijing University on May 16, as translated into English for* The Chronicle of Higher Education; *President Bush's remarks and China-related questions at a White House news conference June 5, from an official transcript; and excerpts from a speech by Chairman Deng Xiaoping in Beijing June 9 to commanders of law-enforcement troops. (The bracketed headings have been added by Congressional Quarterly to highlight the organization of the text.):*

CHINESE INTELLECTUALS' STATEMENT

The "May 16 Circular" issued in 1966 is, in the minds of the Chinese people, nothing but a symbol of tyranny and darkness. Twenty-three years have passed, and today we are feeling the strong appeal of democracy and light. History has eventually come to a turning point.

Currently, a nationwide patriotic, democratic movement pioneered by young students is gaining momentum. In less than one month, large-scale mass demonstrations rose one after another in Beijing and other parts of the country, surging forward with great force. Several hundred thousand students took to the streets, protesting against corruption, calling for democracy and the rule of law, expressing the common opinions of workers, peasants, army men, cadres, intellectuals, and all other people in the working class.

This is the great awakening of the whole nation, which inherited and surpassed the "May 4th Movement" tradition [that originated in 1919 with demonstrations for democracy and science]. This is an important juncture in history that will decide China's destiny.

Since the Third Plenary Session of the Eleventh Party Congress of the [Chinese Communist Party] Central Committee held in December 1978, China has engaged in a modernization that promises national rejuvenation. Unfortunately, due to the slack development of political-system reform, the economic reform that has won its initial successes is suffering a serious setback, corruption becomes daily rampant, social conflicts have been sharply intensified, and the cause of reform is confronted with great crisis.

China is at a critical moment in history. At a time when the fate of the people, the country, and the party in power is to be decided, today, May 16, 1989, we—Chinese intellectuals at home and overseas who jointly signed this statement—solemnly declare in public our principled stand:

1. We hold that the Chinese Communist Party and the government have not adopted a wise attitude toward the current student movement, and signs show that not long ago they even intended to handle the student movement with high pressure and violence.

Lessons should be drawn from history: Such autocratic regimes as the Beijing government of 1919, the Kuomintang government in the 1930's and 40's, and the "Gang of Four" in the late 1970's all suppressed the student movements with violence, yet, without exception, they all ended up with humiliating failure.

History has proved that those who try to repress the student movement are destined to come to a disgraceful end. Recently, the Chinese Communist Party and the government began to take a praiseworthy, sensible stand, which has somewhat eased the tension. If they follow the laws of modern democratic politics, defer to the will of the people, [and] go along with world trends, then there will appear a democratic and stable China. Otherwise, a China with bright prospects will very possibly be led to the real abyss of turmoil.

2. To handle the present political crisis, the unavoidable prerequisite will be to recognize the legality of the autonomous student organization formed by democratic procedures. Denial of this prerequisite will contravene the freedom of association stipulated in China's constitution. The autonomous student organization was once labeled "illegal," which resulted in nothing but the aggravation of conflicts and the intensification of crisis.

3. It is government officials' corruption, strongly opposed by young students in the patriotic movement, that directly caused the current political crisis. The most serious error in the past 10 years' reform was not made in education but in the negligence of political-system reform.

The privileged bureaucratic system and feudalist prerogatives that remain basically intact in the reform have entered the economic situation. This is the genuine cause for pernicious corruption, which has not only devoured the fruits of economic reform, but also shaken the people's confidence in the Chinese Communist Party and the government. The Party and government should learn a profound lesson from this, [and] satisfy the people's demands in earnest by continuously carrying out the reform of the political system, abolishing prerogatives, eliminating "official profiteering," and clearing up corruption.

4. While the student movement was going on, news agencies such as the *People's Daily* and Xinhua News Agency withheld the true facts and deprived the citizens of their right to know.

The Communist Party Committee of Shanghai City suspended Mr. Qin Benli, chief editor of the newspaper *World Economic News,* from his duties. The completely erroneous course of action mentioned above reflects an attitude of brazen neglect of the constitution.

Freedom of the press is an effective means to combat corruption, maintain national stability, and promote social development. Absolute power without any supervision or restriction will definitely lead to absolute corruption. If press freedom is not actually practiced, if any non-official newspaper is not allowed to exist, then all the aspirations and promises for reform and opening to the outside world will be nothing but hollow words.

5. It is wrong to define the student movement as anti-party, anti-socialist political turmoil. The basic meaning of freedom of speech is the recognition and protection of the citizens' right to voice their political dissidence. Every single political movement since the liberation of China in 1949 was waged to suppress disagreeing political opinions. A society with only one voice is by no means a stable society.

It is necessary for the Chinese Communist Party and the government to remind themselves of the historical lesson drawn from the bitter experience of the "Eliminating the Hu Feng Counterrevolutionary Clique" movement, the "Anti-Rightist Movement," the Great Cultural Revolution, the "Campaign to Clear Up Spiritual Contamination," and the "Anti-Bourgeois-Liberalization" movement; to encourage the free airing of different views; to allow young students, intellectuals, and the whole people to discuss important state affairs. Only by doing so can true political stability and unity be realized.

6. It is wrong to propagate the "exposure and punishment" of the so-called "handful" of "bearded backstage manipulators behind the student movement." All citizens of the People's Republic of China, whether old or young, are politically equal in status, and have equal rights to participate in and comment on political affairs.

Liberty, democracy, and legality are never condescendingly bestowed gifts. All those who seek after truth and love freedom should make unremitting efforts to actually gain the rights our constitution promised to every citizen—namely, freedom of thought, freedom of speech, freedom of the press, freedom of publication, freedom of association, freedom of assembly, and freedom of demonstration.

We have come to a critical turning point in history.

The disaster-ridden Chinese nation should not miss its last opportunity, and there is no other way out.

Chinese intellectuals, who inherited the patriotic tradition and are constantly concerned about their country and people, should be aware of their unshirkable historical responsibility, step forward bravely to push forward the advance of democracy, and strive for the building of a politically democratic and economically developed modern China!

Long live the people!

Long live the free and democratic socialist motherland!

PRESIDENT BUSH'S NEWS CONFERENCE

The President. During the past few days, elements of the Chinese Army have been brutally suppressing popular and peaceful demonstrations in China. There has been widespread and continuing violence, many casualties, and many deaths. And we deplore the decision to use force, and I now call on the Chinese leadership publicly, as I have in private channels, to avoid violence and to return to their previous policy of restraint.

The demonstrators in Tiananmen Square were advocating basic human rights, including the freedom of expression, freedom of the press, freedom of association. These are goals we support around the world. These are freedoms that are enshrined in both the U.S. Constitution and the Chinese Constitution. Throughout the world we stand with those who seek greater freedom and democracy. This is the strongly felt view of my administration, of our Congress, and most important, of the American people.

In recent weeks, we've urged mutual restraint, nonviolence, and dialog. Instead, there has been a violent and bloody attack on the demonstrators. The United States cannot condone the violent attacks and cannot ignore the consequences for our relationship with China, which has been built on a foundation of broad support by the American people. This is not the time for an emotional response, but for a reasoned, careful action that takes into account both our long-term interests and recognition of a complex internal situation in China.

There clearly is turmoil within the ranks of the political leadership, as well as the People's Liberation Army. And now is the time to look beyond the moment to important and enduring aspects of this vital relationship for the United States. Indeed, the budding of democracy which we have seen in recent weeks owes much to the relationship we have developed since 1972. And it's important at this time to act in a way that will encourage the further development and deepening of the positive elements of that relationship and the process of democratization. It would be a tragedy for all if China were to pull back to its pre-1972 era of isolation and repression.

Mindful of these complexities, and yet of the necessity to strongly and clearly express our condemnation of the events of recent days, I am ordering the following actions: Suspension of all government-to-government sales and commercial exports of weapons, suspension of visits between U.S. and Chinese military leaders, sympathetic review of request by Chinese students in the United States to extend their stay, and the offer of humanitarian and medical assistance through the Red Cross to those injured during the assault, and review of other aspects of our bilateral relationship as events in China continue to unfold.

The process of democratization of Communist societies will not be a smooth one, and we must react to setbacks in a way which stimulates rather than stifles progress toward open and representative systems.

And I'd be glad to take a few questions before our Cabinet meeting, which starts in a few minutes.

[U.S. Action]

Q. Yes, Mr. President. You have said the genie of democracy cannot be put back in the bottle in China. You said that, however, before the actions of the past weekend. Do you still believe that? And are there further steps that the United States could take, such as economic sanctions, to further democracy in China?

The President. Yes, I still believe that. I believe the forces of democracy are so powerful, and when you see them as recently as this morning—a single student standing in front of a tank, and, I might add, seeing the tank driver exercise restraint—I am convinced that the forces of democracy are going to overcome these unfortunate events in Tiananmen Square.

On the commercial side, I don't want to hurt the Chinese people. I happen to believe that the commercial contacts have led, in essence, to this quest for more freedom. I think as people have commercial incentive, whether it's in China or in other totalitarian systems, the move to democracy becomes more inexorable. So what we've done is suspended certain things on the military side, and my concern is with those in the military who are using force. And yet when I see some exercising restraint and see the big divisions that exist inside the PLA [People's Liberation Army], I think we need to move along the lines I've outlined here. I think that it's important to keep saying to those elements in the Chinese military, "Restraint: Continue to show the restraint that many of you have shown." And I understand there are deep divisions inside the army. So this is, we're putting the emphasis on that side of it.

Q. Have you had any personal contact with the Chinese leadership? Why do you think they moved in the way they did? And why did you wait so long?

The President. Well, I don't think we've waited so long, Helen [Helen Thomas, United Press International]. We've been—I made very clear, in a personal communication to Deng Xiaoping [Chairman of China's Central Military Commission], my views on this. I talked to the Ambassador last night, Jim Lilley. He's been in touch constantly with the Chinese officials, and so, I don't feel that we've waited long, when you have a force of this nature and you have events of this nature unfolding. We are the United States and they are China, and what I want to do is continue to urge freedom, democracy, respect, nonviolence, and with great admiration in my heart for the students. So, I don't think we've waited long.

What was the other part of your question?

Q. What impelled the Chinese Government? They did wait a long time, more than we expected, really, and——

The President. Yes, they did.

Q. ——then they finally moved in. What do you think is the impetus?

The President. I'm glad you raised that point. We were, and have been, and will continue to urge restraint, and they did. The army did show restraint. When Wan Li was here, he told me—and this is very Chinese, the way he expressed it—the army loves the Chinese people. And they showed restraint for a long time, and I can't begin to fathom for you exactly what led to the order to use force, because even as recently as a couple of days ago, there was evidence that the military were under orders not to use force. So I think we have to wait now until that unfolds.

Q. Mr. President, could you give us your current, best assessment of the political situation there, which leaders are up, which are down, who apparently has prevailed there, and who apparently has lost?

The President. It's too obscure, it's too beclouded to say. And I would remind you of the history. In the Cultural Revolution days, Deng Xiaoping at Mao Zedong's right hand, was put out. He came back in 1976. He was put out again in the last days of Mao Zedong and the days of the Gang of Four. Then he came back in, and to his credit, he moved China towards openness, towards democracy, towards reform. And I don't think there's anybody in this country that can answer your question with authority at this point. It doesn't work that way in dealing with China.

Q. But Mr. President, there have been reports that Deng was behind the move to order the troops, and other reports that he's ailing and in a hospital. What do you know about that, sir?

The President. Don't know for sure on either, and I've talked to our Ambassador on that, as I say, last night, and we just can't confirm one way or another.

Q. Mr. President, you spoke of the need for the U.S. to maintain relations with China. But given the brutality of the attacks over the last couple of days, can the U.S. ever return to business as usual with the current regime?

The President. I don't want to see a total break in this relationship, and I will not encourage a total break in the relationship. This relationship is, when you see these kids struggling for democracy and freedom, this would be a bad time for the United States to withdraw and pull back and leave them to the devices of a leadership that might decide to crack down further. Some have suggested I take the Ambassador out. In my view, that would be 180 degrees wrong. Our Ambassador provides one of the best listening posts we have in China. He is thoroughly experienced. And so let others make proposals that in my view don't make much sense. I want to see us stay involved and continue to work for restraint and for human rights and for democracy. And then down the road, we have enormous commonality of interests with China, but it will not be the same under a brutal and repressive regime.

So I stop short of suggesting that what we ought to do is break relations with China, and I would like to encourage them to continue their change.

Q. Mr. Bush, you're sending a message to the military and to the Government. A couple of weeks ago, you told the students to continue to stand by their beliefs. What message do you want the students to hear from what you're saying right now?

The President. That we support their quest for democracy, for reform, and for freedom. And there should be no doubt about that. And then, in sending this message to the military, I would encourage them to go back to the posture of a few days ago that did show restraint, and that did recognize the rights for the people, and that did epitomize what that Chinese leader told me, that the army loves the people. There are still vivid examples of that.

Q. Should the students go home? Should the students stop trying to fight the army?

The President. I can't dictate to the students what they should do from halfway around the world. But we support the quest for democracy and reform, and I'd just have to repeat that. . . .

[Suppression of Student Demonstrations]

Q. Would you elaborate, Mr. President, on the question of economic sanctions—back to China. Did you consider economic sanctions for this morning's announcement, and what will you do if the violence escalates?

The President. I reserve the right to take a whole new look at things if the violence escalates, but I've indicated to you why I think the suspension of certain military relationships is better than moving against—on the economic side.

Q. Mr. President, do you feel that the Chinese leadership cares what the United States does or thinks right now?

The President. I think they are in the sense of contradiction themselves right now. China has historically been less than totally interested in what other countries think of their performance. You have to just look back to the Middle Kingdom syndrome. And you look back in history when outsiders, including the United States, were viewed as "barbarians." So historically China, with its immense pride and its cultural background and its enormous history of conflict, internal and external, has been fairly independent in setting its course.

I have had the feeling that China wants to be a more acceptable— acceptable in the family of nations. And I think any observer would agree that indeed, until very recent events, they've moved in that direction. So what I would like to do is encourage them to move further in that direction by recognizing the rights of these young people and by rebuking any use of force.

Q. Mr. President, more than most Americans, you understand the Chinese. How do you account for the excessive violence of this response?

Once the army decided to act, that they would drive armored personnel carriers into walls of people, how can you explain that?

The President. I really can't. It is very hard to explain, because there was that restraint that was properly being showed for awhile on the part of the military, challenged to come in and restore, what I'm sure they'd been told, order to a situation, which I expect they had been told was anarchic. And so I can't explain it. I can't explain it, unless they were under orders, and then you get into the argument about, well, what orders do you follow? And so I condemn it. I don't try to explain it.

Let me take these next two rows, and then I'll go peacefully. Sorry about you guys back there.

[Tougher Sanctions?]

Q. Will you, Mr. President, be able to accommodate the calls from Congress for tougher sanctions? Many lawmakers felt you were slow to condemn or criticize the violence in China before now, and many are pushing for much tougher action on the part of this country.

The President. I've told you what I'm going to do. I'm the President. I set the foreign policy objectives and actions taken by the executive branch. I think they know, most of them in Congress, that I have not only a keen personal interest in China, but that I understand it reasonably well. I will just reiterate to the leaders this afternoon my conviction that this is not a time for anything other than a prudent, reasoned response. And it is a time to assert over and over again our commitment to democracy, emphasize the strength that we give to democracy in situations of this nature. And I come back to the frontline question here: I do think this change is inexorable. It may go a couple of steps forward and then take a step back, but it is on the move. The genie will not be put back in the bottle. And so I am trying to take steps that will encourage a peaceful change, and yet recognize the fact that China does have great pride in its own history. And my recommendations are based on my knowledge of Chinese history.

So, I would argue with those who want to do something more flamboyant, because I happen to feel that this relationship is vital to the United States of America, and so is our adherence to democracy and our encouragement for those who are willing to hold high the banner of democracy. So we found, I think, a prudent path here.

Q. Do you think that the events in China can have a chilling effect on democratic reforms occurring in other Communist countries, particularly in the Soviet Union and Eastern Europe, when they look at the kind of uprising that was sparked in China?

The President. No. I think the moves that we're seeing in Eastern Europe today, and indeed, in the Soviet Union are going to go forward. And I think people are watching more with horror, and saying: How, given this movement towards democracy, can the Chinese leadership act in the way they have? And so I think this may be a sign to others around the world that people are heroic when it comes to their commitment to democratic change. And I would just urge the Chinese leaders to recognize that.

Q. Mr. President, there are reports that the Chinese military is badly divided and that, with this crackdown, the authorities brought in some troops from the Tibet conflict. If that's the case, how does suspending these military relationships encourage any kind of change? I mean, could you explain what the point of doing that is——

The President. I already did, David [David Hoffman, Washington Post]. You missed it. I explained it because I want to keep it on the military side. I've expressed here rhetorically the indignation we feel. I've recognized the history of China moving into its own Middle Kingdom syndrome, as it's done in various times in its past, and I want to encourage the things that have helped the Chinese people. And I think now the suspension is going to see a strong signal. I'm not saying it's going to cure the short-range problem in China. I'm not sure any outside country can cure the short range, the today in Tiananmen Square problem. But I think it is very important the Chinese leaders know it's not going to be business as usual, and I think it's important that the army know that we want to see restraint. And this is the best way to signal that.

Q. Would you fear conflict? You talked about the divisions within the Chinese Army. Do you or your advisors fear that there could actually be a civil conflict between army commanders?

The President. Well, I don't want to speculate on that, but there are differences, clearly, within the army in terms of use of force. Otherwise, they wouldn't be doing what David Hoffman properly pointed out is happening: units coming in from outside.

And it is not, incidentally, just in Tiananmen Square that the Chinese— that this problem exists. It is in Shanghai, it's in Chengdu today, it's in Guangzhou, I'm told, in a much smaller scale. But they brought the troops in from outside because the Beijing troops apparently demonstrated a great sensitivity to the cause of the young people and were—disciplined though they were, they opted for the side of democracy and change in the young people. So those others came in. But I certainly don't want to speculate on something that I don't have—I can't reach that conclusion, put it that way.

Q. There were some news reports that some of the soldiers' units had burned their own trucks in—have you received the same type of intelligence reports?

The President. I just saw speculation. I haven't got it on any—I don't believe the intelligence said that. But there are reports that it is very difficult for some of the military, who are much more sympathetic to the openness, to the demonstrators. And I, again, go back to the original question here that Tom asked. I think, with the change that's taken place so far, we're beyond kind of a Cultural Revolution response. I think the depth of the feeling towards democracy is so great that you can't put the genie back in the bottle and return to total repression. And I think what we're seeing is a manifestation of that in the divisions within the PLA. But I certainly want to stop short of predicting a civil war between units of the People's Liberation Army. . . .

CHAIRMAN DENG'S SPEECH

... The April 26 editorial of the "People's Daily" classified the problem as turmoil. The word was appropriate, but some people objected to the word and tried to amend it. But what has happened shows that this verdict was right. It was also inevitable that the turmoil would develop into a counter-revolutionary rebellion. We still have a group of senior comrades who are alive, we still have the army, and we also have a group of core cadres who took part in the revolution at various times. That is why it was relatively easy for us to handle the present matter. The main difficulty in handling this matter lay in that we had never experienced such a situation before, in which a small minority of bad people mixed with so many young students and onlookers. ...

The nature of the matter became clear soon after it erupted. They had two main slogans: to overthrow the Communist Party and topple the socialist system. Their goal was to establish a bourgeois republic entirely dependent on the West. Of course we accept people's demands for combating corruption. We are even ready to listen to some people with ulterior motives when they raise the slogan about fighting corruption. However such slogans were just a front. Their real aim was to overthrow the Communist Party and topple the socialist system. ...

In a word, this was a test, and we passed. Even though there are not so many veteran comrades in the army and the soldiers are mostly little more than 18, 19 or 20 years of age, they are still true soldiers of the people. Facing danger, they did not forget the people, the teachings of the Party and the interests of the country. They kept a resolute stand in the face of death. They fully deserve the saying that they met death and sacrificed themselves with generosity and without fear.

When I talked about passing muster, I was referring to the fact that the army is still the people's army. This army retains the traditions of the old Red Army.... [T]his army of ours is forever an army under the leadership of the Party, forever the defender of the country, forever the defender of socialism, forever the defender of the public interest, and they are the most beloved of the people.

At the same time, we should never forget how cruel our enemies are. For them we should not have an iota of forgiveness.

Rebellion

The outbreak of the rebellion is worth thinking about. It prompts us to calmly think about the past and consider the future. Perhaps this bad thing will enable us to go ahead with reform and the open-door policy at a more steady, better, even a faster pace. Also it will enable us to more speedily correct our mistakes and better develop our strong points. I cannot elaborate on this today. I just want to raise the subject here.

The first question is: Are the line, goals and policies laid down by the Third Plenum of the 11th Central Committee, including our "three-step" development strategy, correct? ...

We have already accomplished our first goal of doubling the gross national product. We plan to use 12 years to attain our second goal of doubling the GNP. In the 50 years after that, we hope to reach the level of a moderately developed country. A two-percent annual growth rate is sufficient. This is our strategic goal. ...

China is capable of realizing this goal. It cannot be said that our strategic goal is wrong because of the occurrence of this event.

The second question is this: Is the general conclusion of the 13th Party Congress of "One Centre, Two Basic Points" correct? Are the two basic points—upholding the four cardinal principles and persisting in the open policy and reforms—wrong?

... No, we haven't been wrong. ... If there is anything amiss, it's that these principles haven't been thoroughly implemented; they haven't been used as the basic concept to educate the people, educate the students and educate all the cadres and Party members.

Liberalization

... After the People's Republic was founded we promoted plain living. Later on, when life became a little better, we promoted spending more, leading to wastage everywhere. This, in addition to lapses in theoretical work and an incomplete legal system, resulted in backsliding.

I once told foreigner [sic] that our worst omission of the past 10 years was in education. What I meant was political education, and this doesn't apply to schools and students alone, but to the masses as a whole. ...

Policy

What is important is that we should never change China back into a closed country. Such a policy would be most detrimental. We don't even have a good flow of information. Nowadays, are we not talking about the importance of information? Certainly, it is important. If one who is involved in management doesn't possess information, he is no better than a man whose nose is blocked and whose ears and eyes are shut. Again, we should never go back to the old days of trampling the economy to death. ...

In political reforms we can affirm one point: We have to insist on implementing the system of the National People's Congress and not the American system of the separation of three powers. The US berates us for supressing students. But when they handled domestic student unrest and turmoil, didn't they send out police and troops, arrest people and shed blood? They were supressing students and the people, but we are putting down counter-revolutionary rebellion. What qualifications do they have to criticise us? From now on, however, we should pay attention to such problems. We should never allow them to spread. ...

SECRETARY BAKER'S POLICY ADDRESS ON THE MIDDLE EAST
May 22, 1989

In the Bush administration's first comprehensive statement on Middle East policy, Secretary of State James A. Baker III on May 22 called on Israel and its Arab foes to make compromises to restart the peace process. Using unusually blunt language, Baker insisted that Israeli leaders would have to give up "the unrealistic vision of a greater Israel" if they hoped to achieve peace. Greater Israel is a term generally used to describe an Israel that extends beyond its pre-1967 boundaries to include the West Bank and Gaza Strip, territories that it captured in the 1967 Arab-Israeli war.

Baker said Israel must accept the "land for peace" formula set forth in 1967 in the United Nations Security Council's Resolution 242. Moreover, he said, Israel should "forswear annexation" of its occupied territories; stop settlement activity; allow Palestinian schools to reopen; and "reach out to the Palestinians as neighbors who deserve political rights." Israel annexed the eastern section of Jerusalem, which was part of the West Bank—an area on the western side of the Jordan River formerly under Jordan's control. In recent years, Israeli governments have promoted Jewish settlements on the West Bank.

Baker also made demands on the Arab nations: to end their economic boycott of Israel, stop their challenges to Israel's standing in the United Nations and other international organizations, and "repudiate the odious line that Zionism is racism." Palestinians, he said, must "speak with one voice for peace" and transform the intifada—uprising—*into a "dialogue of politics and diplomacy" with Israel. The uprising, typically marked by Palestinian youths throwing stones at Israeli soldiers in the*

289

West Bank and Gaza Strip, started in December 1987 and showed no signs of abating. It had already resulted in hundreds of casualties, mostly Palestinians who were fired on by Israeli troops, or captured and beaten.

The secretary of state called on the Palestinians to "translate the dialogue of violence ... into a dialogue of politics and diplomacy." He said they must "understand that no one is going to 'deliver' Israel to you." He urged the Palestinians to "reach out to Israelis and convince them of your peaceful intentions."

Many Listeners Dismayed

Baker spoke to the annual Washington policy conference of the American Israel Public Affairs Committee (AIPAC), the powerful pro-Israel lobby. The predominantly Jewish audience of about 1,200 listened in silence as he recited his demands of Israel, but applauded enthusiastically as he listed steps that Arabs must take. Thomas A. Dine, the organization's executive director, said he thought "it was a fair speech" but many other listeners appeared dismayed that the tone seemed less laudatory toward Israel than was customary in speeches by Reagan administration officials.

Yitzhak Rabin, Israel's defense minister, who met with Baker immediately after the speech, told news reporters: "I didn't write the speech. Had I been the one, I would have written it in a totally different way. I would have directed the calls more toward the Palestinians and less toward Israel." Editorial opinion in the American press was generally favorable to the speech, which characteristically was called "even-handed" in its approach to both Israelis and Arabs. Unidentified officials at the State Department were quoted as saying that, if the speech veered in either direction, it was pro-Israel because Baker endorsed Israeli prime minister Yitzhak Shamir's plan for permitting Palestinians to hold elections in the territories as a prelude to peace negotiations.

Shamir's Election Proposal

"When Prime Minister Shamir visited Washington [in April], he indicated that he shared our view that the status quo was unacceptable," Baker said. "He brought an idea for elections to—in his words—'launch a political negotiating process' which would involve transitional arrangements and final status. The prime minister made clear that all sides would be free to bring their preferred positions to the table and that the negotiated outcome must be acceptable to all."

Israel put forth a more detailed version of the election proposal a few days before Baker spoke. It gave "us something to work with," the secretary said, and "deserves a constructive Palestinian and broader Arab response." The initial reaction of some Palestinian community leaders in the territories, and of the Palestinian Liberation Organization (PLO) at its headquarters in Tunis, was that free elections could not be held so long as the territories were occupied, and any negotiations must have as their goal an independent Palestine state.

Palestine Statehood Demand

In November 1988, the Palestine National Council—the PLO's parliamentary body—had met in Algiers and declared the existence of a Palestine state, though without defining its boundaries. Actual statehood, not just an abstraction, became the PLO's goal. Israeli spokesmen ridiculed the idea, and the Israeli government remained opposed to negotiating directly with the PLO, which it viewed as a terrorist organization. (Palestinian Declaration of Independence, Historic Documents of 1988, p. 905)

However, at the same meeting that the PLO council declared Palestine statehood, it struck a more conciliatory tone toward Israel. The council adopted a political platform recognizing UN Resolution 242 as the main basis for a Middle East peace conference. By doing so, the organization for the first time implicitly recognized Israel's right to exist. Soon afterward, PLO leader Yasir Arafat went further, explicitly renouncing terrorism, accepting Resolution 242, and recognizing Israel's sovereignty—as was demanded by the United States as a precondition for Washington to conduct talks directly and officially with the PLO. The first of these talks began in December 1988, over Israel's opposition.

Despite the new developments, the peace process showed little progress. In July, President Hosni Mubarak of Egypt sent through diplomatic channels a ten-point "working paper" suggesting conditions that might be acceptable to all sides. It sidestepped many of the existing obstacles to negotiations. The paper said nothing about a Palestine state but would require Israel to begin talks on a final settlement by a date to be specified, and to accept the principle of trading peace for land. In Israel's coalition government, the Likhud faction of Prime Minister Shamir oppose Mubarak's plan while the Labor faction accepted it. This stalemate led Baker to make a new appeal in October to the Egyptian and Israeli governments to try again to agree on a framework for Palestine negotiations. But the prospects appeared dim.

> *Following are excerpts from the State Department's transcript of Secretary of State James A. Baker III's speech May 22 to the American Israel Public Affairs Committee in Washington.* (The bracketed headings have been added by Congressional Quarterly to highlight the organization of the text.):

... There have been many, many analyses of the U.S.-Israeli relationship over the years, and most of them begin with the fact that we share common values of freedom and of democracy. This is the golden thread in the tapestry of United States-Israeli ties; and there are, if I might suggest it, other strands as well.

Ed [Levy of AIPAC] has mentioned some of what I did in the Reagan Administration, but let me tell you that I was proud to work in that

Administration, an Administration that recognized the importance of United States-Israeli strategic cooperation and an Administration that I think gave fiber and sinew to our strategic partnership.

I'm also proud to have had a small part to play in the historic free trade agreement which may well become a model for other nations. I really think we probably would not have gotten home on the Canadian-U.S. free trade agreement had we not had a U.S.-Israel free trade agreement. The President believes—President Bush believes—and I believe that on these issues there can only be one policy and that is a policy of continuity. American support for Israel is the foundation of our approach to the problems—the very, very difficult problems—of the Middle East. . . .

Not so long ago, we marked a decade of the Camp David Peace Accords. That occasion reminded us not only of how far we have come but of how much further we have to go. I would like to report to you that we and Israel have taken some important steps forward.

Before Prime Minister Shamir visited Washington, we had called for some Israeli ideas on how to restart the peace process. We did so based on our conviction that a key condition for progress was a productive United States-Israeli partnership. And I believe that the best way to be productive is through consultation rather than confrontation.

Let me assure you that we were not disappointed. The Prime Minister will, I'm sure, forgive me if I divulge to you a conversation at our very first meeting. The Prime Minister said, in preparing for his visit, he had studied President Bush and me, just as he suspected that perhaps we had studied him. I had been described by the media as an ever-flexible pragmatist. The Prime Minister, he said, had been described as an inflexible man of ideological principle. Then the Prime Minister volunteered that in his view the journalists were wrong, and they were wrong in both cases. "Yes," he said, "I am a man of principle, but I am also a pragmatist who knows what political compromise means." And he said that it was clear that I, although a pragmatist, was also a man of principle and that principle would guide my foreign policy approach. Needless to say, I didn't disagree with the Prime Minister.

If ever an opening statement achieved its goal of establishing a strong working relationship, this was it. I think it's fair to say that we understood each other to be pragmatists, but pragmatists guided by principle.

As we approach the peace process, together, we understand Israel's caution especially when assessing Arab attitudes about peace. I don't blame Israel for exercising this caution. Its history and, indeed, its geopolitical situation require it.

At the same time, I think that caution must never become paralysis. Ten years after Camp David, Egypt remains firmly committed to peace, and Arab attitudes are changing. Egypt's re-admission into the Arab League on its own terms and with the peace treaty intact, I think, is one sign of change. Evolving Palestinian attitudes are another. Much more needs to be done—to be demonstrated—that such change is real. But I don't think that change can be ignored even now. This is surely a time when ... the right mix of principles and pragmatism is required. ...

[U.S. Position]

First, the U.S. believes that the objective of the peace process is a comprehensive settlement achieved through negotiations based on United Nations Security Council Resolutions 242 and 338. In our view, these negotiations must involve territory for peace, security and recognition for Israel and all of the states of the region, and Palestinian political rights.

Second, for negotiations to succeed they must allow the parties to deal directly with each other, face-to-face. A properly structured international conference could be useful at an appropriate time, but only if it did not interfere with or in any way replace or be a substitute for direct talks between the parties.

Third, the issues involved in the negotiations are far too complex, and the emotions are far too deep, to move directly to a final settlement. Accordingly, some transitional period is needed, associated in time and sequence with negotiations on final status. Such a transition will allow the parties to take the measure of each other's performance, to encourage attitudes to change, and to demonstrate that peace and coexistence is desired.

Fourth, in advance of direct negotiations, neither the United States nor another party, inside or outside, can or will dictate an outcome. That is why the United States does not support annexation or permanent Israeli control of the West bank and Gaza, nor do we support the creation of an independent Palestinian state.

I would add here that we do have an idea about the reasonable middle ground to which a settlement should be directed. That is, self-government for Palestinians in the West Bank and Gaza in a manner acceptable to Palestinians, Israel and Jordan. Such a formula provides ample scope for Palestinians to achieve their full political rights. It also provides ample protection for Israel's security as well.

Following these principles, we face a pragmatic issue, the issue of how do we get negotiations underway. Unfortunately the gap between the parties on key issues such as Palestinian representation and the shape of a final settlement remains very, very wide. Violence has soured the atmosphere, and so a quick move to negotiations is quite unlikely. And in the absence of either a minimum of good will or any movement to close the gap, a high-visibility American initiative, we think, has little basis on which to stand.

If we were to stop here, the situation would, I think, be gloomy indeed. But we are not going to stop with the status quo. We are engaged, as I mentioned a moment ago; we will remain engaged; and we will work to help create an environment to launch and sustain negotiations. This will require tough but necessary decisions for peace by all of the parties. It will also require a commitment to a process of negotiations clearly tied to the search for a permanent settlement of the conflict.

[Israel's Election Proposal]

When Prime Minister Shamir visited Washington, he indicated that he shared our view that the status quo was unacceptable. He brought an idea for elections to—in his words—"launch a political negotiating process" which would involve transitional arrangements and final status. The Prime Minister made clear that all sides would be free to bring their preferred positions to the table and that the negotiated outcome must be acceptable to all. The United States welcomed these Israeli ideas and undertook to see whether it could help in creating an atmosphere which could sustain such a process.

Just last week the Israeli Cabinet approved a more detailed version of the Prime Minister's proposal, indicating Israeli Government positions on some, but not all, of the issues which are involved. The Israeli proposal is an important and very positive start down the road toward constructing workable negotiations.

The Israeli Government *has* offered an initiative, and it *has* [text emphases] given us something to work with. It has taken a stand on some important issues, and this deserves a constructive Palestinian and broader Arab response.

Much work needs to be done—to elicit Palestinian and Arab thinking on the key elements in the process, to flesh out some of the details of the Israeli proposals, and to bridge areas where viewpoints differ. Both sides, of course, are going to have to build political constituencies for peace. Each idea, proposal, or detail should be developed, if I may say so, as a deal-maker, not as a deal-breaker.

It may be possible to reach agreement, for example, on the standards of a workable elections process. Such elections should be free and fair, of course; and they should be free of interference from any quarter.

Through open access to media and outside observers, the integrity of the electoral process can be affirmed. And participation in the elections should be as open as possible.

Is is therefore high time for serious political dialogue between Israeli officials and Palestinians in the territories to bring about a common understanding on these and other issues. Peace, and the peace process, must be built from the "ground up." Palestinians have it within their power to help define the shape of this initiative and to help define its essential elements. They shouldn't shy from a dialogue with Israel that can transform the current environment and determine the ground rules for getting to, for conducting, and indeed for moving beyond elections.

We should not hide from ourselves the difficulties that face even these steps here at the very beginning. For many Israelis it will not be easy to enter a negotiating process whose successful outcome will in all probability involve territorial withdrawal and the emergence of a new political reality. For Palestinians such an outcome will mean an end to the illusion of control over all of Palestine, and it will mean full recognition of Israel as a neighbor and partner in trade and in human contact.

Ladies and gentlemen, we do not think there is a real constructive alternative to the process which I have outlined. Continuation of the status quo will lead to increasing violence and worsening prospects for peace. We think now is the time to move toward a serious negotiating process, to create the atmosphere for a renewed peace process. Let the Arab world take concrete steps toward accommodation with Israel—not in place of the peace process, but as a catalyst for it.

And so we would say: end the economic boycott; stop the challenges to Israel's standing in international organizations; repudiate the odious line that Zionism is racism.

["Unrealistic Vision" of Greater Israel]

For Israel, now is the time to lay aside, once and for all, the unrealistic vision of a greater Israel.

Israeli interests in the West Bank and Gaza—security and otherwise—can be accommodated in a settlement based on Resolution 242. Forswear annexation. Stop settlement activity. Allow schools to reopen. Reach out to the Palestinians as neighbors who deserve political rights.

For Palestinians, now is the time to speak with one voice for peace. Renounce the policy of phases in all languages, not just those addressed to the West.

Practice constructive diplomacy, not attempts to distort international organizations, such as the World Health Organization.

Amend the covenant. Translate the dialogue of violence in the *intifada* into a dialogue of politics and diplomacy. Violence will not work. Reach out to Israelis and convince them of your peaceful intentions. You have the most to gain from doing so, and not one else can or *will* [text emphasis] do it for you. Finally, understand that no one is going to "deliver" Israel for you.

[Requests Soviet Involvement]

For outside parties—in particular, the Soviet Union—now is the time to make "new thinking" a reality as it applies to the Middle East. I must say that Chairman Gorbachev and Foreign Minister Shevardnadze told me in Moscow ten days ago that Soviet policy is changing. New laws regarding emigration will soon be discussed by the Supreme Soviet. Jewish life in the Soviet Union is also looking better, with students beginning to study their heritage freely.

Finally, the Soviet Union agreed with us last week that Prime Minister Shamir's election proposal was worthy of consideration.

These, of course, are all positive signs. But the Soviets must go further to demonstrate convincingly that they are serious about new thinking in the Arab-Israel conflict. Let Moscow restore diplomatic ties with Israel, for example.

The Soviets should also help promote a serious peace process, not just empty slogans. And it is time for the Soviet Union, we think, to behave responsibly when it comes to arms and stop the supply of sophisticated weapons to countries like Libya.

Ladies and gentlemen, I said at the beginning of these remarks that the Middle East had approached a turning point. I believe that this region, which is so full of potential, will not remain immune from the changes which are sweeping the rest of the world. These changes begin with the quest for democracy, for individual freedom and for choice. Long ago, of course, Israel chose this path. And long ago the American people decided to walk with Israel in her quest for peace and in her quest for security.

The policy I have described today reaffirms and renews that course. For our part, the United States will move ahead steadily and carefully, in a step-by-step approach designed to help the parties make the necessary decisions for peace. Perhaps Judge Learned Hand expressed it best when he said, "... we shall have to be content with short steps; ... but we shall have gone forward, if we bring to our task ... patience, understanding, sympathy, forbearance, generosity, fortitude and above all an inflexible determination."

Thank you all very, very much. . . .

PRESIDENT BUSH'S PROPOSAL
FOR CONVENTIONAL ARMS CUTS
May 29, 1989

President George Bush chose the fortieth anniversary summit meeting of the North Atlantic Treaty Organization (NATO) to propose deep cuts in American and Soviet troop strength, conventional combat aircraft, tanks, and artillery in Europe. His proposal, made May 29 in Brussels to leaders of the fifteen other member countries, stilled complaints at home and abroad that he was too cautious in seizing opportunities presented by sweeping political change in the Soviet Union.

Bush's plan was widely viewed as a response to a flurry of foreign policy and arms control initiatives advanced by President Mikhail S. Gorbachev of the Soviet Union. With some of Bush's force-reduction specifics going farther than Gorbachev's, the American president appeared to have recaptured the diplomatic initiative in arms control maneuvering. Moreover, Bush engineered a NATO compromise statement that deferred a potentially bruising struggle in the alliance over the future of short-range nuclear missiles in its arsenal.

Meeting with news reporters in Brussels on May 29, Bush indicated that his plan had NATO's enthusiastic support and, if approved by the Soviet Union, it would result in a "revolutionary" agreement on conventional, or nonnuclear, military forces. He said a treaty could be concluded in a year and the military cuts made by 1992. The existing imbalance in European conventional forces was "so great" in the Soviet Union's favor, he said, that it was "the most urgent problem" for arms control negotiators to resolve.

By seeking to obtain prompt approval and implementation of his proposal, Bush succeeded in allaying West German concerns over the pace of arms reduction. When the United States and the Soviet Union signed an agreement in 1987 that eliminated land-based intermediate-range nuclear weapons, NATO was left with only short-range nuclear missiles; their range is about seventy-five miles. (U.S.-Soviet INF Treaty, Historic Documents of 1987, p. 945)

The West Germans were acutely aware that if the missiles were ever fired they would land on German soil, East or West. In an article in the February 1989 World Press Review, *Robert Mauthner wrote that a "telling slogan" in West Germany had become, "The shorter the range of nuclear weapons, the deader the Germans."*

Chancellor Helmut Kohl and other West German leaders pushed for US.-Soviet negotiations for a reduction of the short-range nuclear missiles. President Bush made it clear in Brussels that talks on short-range weapons could not begin until an agreement had been reached with the Soviet Union on nonnuclear arms and its implementation begun. However, he predicted that the agreement could be reached within a year—quite soon by the standards of arms control negotiations.

The prospect of an accelerated timetable gave the West Germans reason to hope that talks on the short-range missiles would not be far in the future.

Implications for Soviet Relations

The implications of Bush's diplomacy went even further. Beyond the arms proposal itself, his words did not convey an undertone of skepticism about new Soviet aims that had been evident in speeches he made earlier in May. In those speeches, highlighted by a Soviet-policy address at Texas A & M University, May 12, he stressed that Gorbachev would have to pass certain tests to earn the West's trust. In Brussels, the president emphasized opportunities instead. (Remarks on Soviet Election and Perestroika, p. 173)

Influential Democrats in Congress who earlier criticized Bush's stance as too rigid generally praised his arms-reduction plan. Sen. Joseph R. Biden, Jr., D-Del., chairman of the Foreign Relations Subcommittee on European Affairs, called it "very substantive." Sam Nunn, D-Ga., chairman of the Senate Armed Services Committee, said the plan offers a "sound negotiating position." Les Aspin, D-Wis., chairman of the House Armed Services Committee, called it "a pretty good proposal." In contrast, a few conservative Republicans expressed concern that Bush had abandoned well-founded security policies under pressure.

In a similar vein, a Trilateral Commission report coauthored by former secretary of state Henry A. Kissinger cautioned that the West should keep its guard up against Gorbachev's foreign policy initiatives. A task force of the New York-based commission, a public-policy study group, issued the report in April, authored by Kissinger, former French president Valery D'Estaing, and former Japanese president Yasuhiro Nakasone. It said that Gorbachev's "style" was "to flood the Western decision-making process with a rapid series of unilateral moves, some of them involving genuine concessions, others relying largely on psychological warfare."

Bush's Arms Plan

Perhaps the most surprising aspect of President Bush's arms proposal was its inclusion of troops. Previously, personnel were omitted from arms proposals because of verification difficulties. He proposed that U.S. and Soviet troop strength in Europe be limited to 275,000 each. The reduction would be relatively small for the United States, but huge for the Soviet Union. With an estimated 600,000 troops stationed in Eastern Europe, the Soviet Union would have to cut its forces by half. For the United States, the reduction would be about 30,000.

The Bush plan would impose a ceiling on both NATO and Soviet-bloc military aircraft and helicopters operating between the Atlantic Ocean to the Ural mountains at 15 percent below current NATO levels. In the past, the United States rejected Soviet proposals to cut combat aircraft strength. It then insisted that cuts be limited to tanks, artillery, and armored troop carriers.

> *Following is a White House transcript of President Bush's news conference in Brussels, May 29, 1989:*

The President. I'll have a brief statement before taking some questions. This morning I met with the other NATO leaders and shared with them my views on the role of the North Atlantic alliance in a changing Europe. NATO, we all agree, is one of the great success stories, and it's guaranteed the peace in Europe, provided a shield for 40 years for freedom and prosperity. And now our alliance faces new challenges at a time of historic transition as we seek to overcome the division of Europe. I call it beyond containment.

And today I'm proposing a major initiative to help move us toward that momentous objective. If it were accepted, it would be a revolutionary conventional arms control agreement. I believe the alliance should act decisively now to take advantage of this extraordinary opportunity, and I urge that NATO adopt a 4-point proposal to bring the Vienna negotiations to a speedy conclusion.

First, lock in Eastern acceptance of the proposed Western ceilings on each side's holdings of tanks and armored troop carriers. Additionally, we would seek agreement on a similar ceiling for artillery, provided there's some definitional questions that have to be resolved there. But all of the equipment reduced would be destroyed.

We would then, number two, expand our current NATO proposal so that each side would reduce to 15 percent below current NATO levels in two additional categories: attack and assault, or transport helicopters and all land-based combat aircraft. All of the equipment reduced would be destroyed.

And third, propose a 20-percent cut in combat manpower in United States-stationed forces and a resulting ceiling in U.S. and Soviet ground and air forces stationed outside of national territory in the Atlantic-to-the-Urals zone at approximately 275,000 each. This manpower ceiling will require the Soviets to reduce their forces in Eastern Europe by about 325,000 people. Withdrawn soldiers and airmen on both sides would be demobilized.

And then, fourthly, accelerate the timetable for reaching a CFE [conventional arms forces in Europe] agreement along these lines and implementing the required reductions. I believe that it should be possible to reach such agreement in 6 months or maybe a year and to accomplish the reductions by 1992 or 1993.

Now, if the Soviet Union accepts this fair offer, the results would dramatically increase stability on the continent and transform the military map of Europe. We can and must begin now to set out a new vision for Europe at the end of this century. This is a noble mission that I believe the alliance should be ready to undertake. And I have no doubt that we are up to the task.

And incidentally, in addition to these arms control proposals I mentioned in there, that we are prepared to change our no-exceptions policy on trade. And I called again for a ban on chemical weapons. And I would reiterate my support for our open skies proposal, and in the meeting it was discussed by the Prime Minister of Canada.

Helen [Helen Thomas, United Press International]?

Q. Mr. President, does this revolutionary plan signal the end of the Cold War?

The President. Well, I don't know what it signals, except it signals a willingness on our part to really put Mr. Gorbachev to the test now. And, so, I don't like to dwell in antiquated history. But I do like to get the idea that we are out front as an alliance, because this has broad alliance support, in challenging Mr. Gorbachev to move forward now more quickly on the most destabilizing part of the military balance, and that is on conventional forces.

Q. Well, were you pressured by him and the allies?

The President. No, I think I said when I first came in we were going to take our time and we were going to study and we're going to think it out. And we did exactly that. And you know and I know that some voices were raised in Congress that we were going too slow. But we knew exactly what we were doing all along, and we've now said: "This is what we suggest, and this is the way we plan to lead—lead the alliance and lead the free world."

Q. Mr. President, why is it possible to make such drastic cuts in conventional weapons and not move on nuclear aircraft—nuclear ground-based short-range missiles, which seems to disturb the Germans and really a majority of the alliance?

The President. Because the conventional forces, the existing imbalance, is so great that that is the most urgent problem and the most destabilizing.

Q. Following up on that question: If the Soviets accept this proposal, would that enable us to talk about reducing or eliminating short-range forces?

The President. After agreement was reached and after there was some implementation, yes. We are not unwilling to negotiate on SNF.

Q. What was the reaction of the NATO leaders this morning when you told them? Did you consult with all the allies before you put it on the table?

The President. We had widespread—and I would think everyone was consulted. I know we had widespread consultation and—

Secretary [of State James A.] Baker. The answer is yes.

The President. The answer is yes to all NATO members. And it's been done over the last few days.

Q. What did they tell you about it? Why did they find it appealing?

The President. Well, I'll leave it to them to wax euphoric. But I'll tell you, I was very, very pleased with the response in the meeting just concluded.

Q. Mr. President, can you ever see a time when you might not have nuclear forces in Europe?

The President. No.

Q. Never.

Q. Mr. President, is there any indication—

The President. We need the concept of flexible response, and I can't in the foreseeable future see us getting away from that.

Q. Is there any indication that this disagreement with the West Germans over the SNF issue will be resolved here at the NATO summit?

The President. Well, I'm not really at liberty to go into too much on that, because right now we put together a working group to try to work out some resolution. But you see, this bold proposal, in terms of conventional forces, should give those who have had difficulty with our position on SNF a chance to regroup and rethink and give them a little leeway that they haven't had heretofore.

Q. Do you expect early negotiation by the Secretary of State [Baker] with Mr. Shevardnadze or Mr. Gorbachev on this proposal, Mr. President?

The President. The sooner the better.

Q. There's been some criticism in Congress, as you mentioned, about that you have been too cautious in approaching the Soviet Union. Was that sentiment expressed today by anyone, and how did they—was there any mention of how the West should respond to Gorbachev?

The President. No, it wasn't mentioned by anyone in there. And generally, when it was—your question about how to respond to Gorbachev—without putting words into the mouths of various participants, there was enthusiastic endorsement. Now, I can't speak for everybody, but for those who have intervened so far.

Q. Mr. Bush, have you costed out this proposal? And did the budgetary constraints play any part in your decision to try to—

The President. No, the budgetary constraints didn't, and I haven't seen a full cost analysis. Some of this would be quite expensive for us, short-run—the pulling people out. But we did check militarily. I did not want to propose something that was militarily unsound. And our top military people are for this. Our SACEUR Commander [Supreme Allied Commander, Europe—General John Galvin], who wears many hats, who represents many countries, obviously, is for this. And so, we checked it in that sense.

Q. Mr. President, in some of your early policy speeches, you expressed deep skepticism about what was going on in the Soviet Union. You said this new relationship cannot be bestowed; it must be earned. Your Secretary of Defense [Cheney] said he felt Gorbachev would fail. What prompted change in your thinking to make a proposal like this?

The President. This is to put it to the test. This is to say: Here we go. We're out there now with a proposal that the United States puts forward and that has widespread alliance support. Now test it. How serious are you? Are you—really want to reduce the imbalances that exist in all these categories, or do we want rhetoric? And so, what we're saying—we're not changing; I'm not changing my mind. I've said I want to see *perestroika* succeed. I said I want to see us move forward in arms reductions. Indeed, we've set a date for the resumption of the START [Strategic Arms Reduction Talks] talks—but eyes wide open. And here we go now, on the offense with a proposal that is bold and tests whether the Soviet Union will move towards balance, or whether they insist on retaining an unacceptable conventional force imbalance.

The President. I've got time for—is this a followup?

Q. This is a followup. On the subject of Mr. Gorbachev, do you believe he will fail?

The President. I want to see him succeed. And I've said that, and I'll repeat it here. I'm not making predictions as to what's going to happen inside the Soviet Union. Those are hard tea leaves to read. But I would like to see him succeed. He seems stronger now than he has been earlier on. But he faces enormous problems. And I hope he looks at this proposal as a way to help solve some of those enormous problems. It gets to the question of finance to maintain this number of troops outside of his country.

Q. Mr. President, does this 4-point proposal represent your conditions that the Soviets must accept before you will open talks on the short-range missiles?

The President. Well, as I said earlier, we've got to have a reduction in conventional forces and then some implementation of that proposal.

Q. Mr. President, you described this as a proposal to the other allies. Do you expect it's going to be adopted as a formal alliance position at the end of the meeting, and then will you put it on the table at CFE very soon?

The President. I can't answer procedurally. I'd like to see it adopted. But I don't know that the people have had enough time to really—do you know what's planned on that, Al? [Alton G. Keel, Jr., Ambassador to NATO]

Ambassador Keel. I think, clearly, the alliance will adopt it, Mr.

President, in terms of the concept, but then will assign it to the proper mechanism here at NATO to finish the details on it.

Q. Why actually destroy the equipment and demobilize the troops?

The President. Well, because then we get verified—we hope—verified reductions that last. You can't just juggle around the players on the chessboard.

Q. Mr. President, following Helen's earlier question, there's been a lot of talk at the White House recently about public relations gambits. Do you believe that this initiative by the United States puts Mr. Gorbachev on the defensive, and does it in any way put the United States back on the top of any public relations war that might be going on?

The President. Well, one, we've eschewed getting involved in a public relations battle. This is too serious a business. Alliance security is too serious. The safety and security of American forces, for which I have direct responsibility as Commander in Chief, is too serious to be jeopardized by feeling we always have to be out front on some public relations gambit. And I think we all know that in certain quarters in the United States, my administration has taken a little bit of a hammering for not engaging in the public relations battle.

But what we've been doing is formulating what I think is a very prudent plan, and now that plan is out there on the table. So, I really can't comment on the public relations aspect. What I'm interested in is the security aspect and the strength of the alliance and then the future—the ability of the alliance to move beyond containment.

Q. A long-term benefit of this proposal would obviously be a decrease in defense spending. Now, how much of this proposal was driven by budget considerations?

The President. Well, I thought I answered that, but let me try again to be clearer. None. What drove the proposal was the military and alliance considerations. And I would agree that if this proposal is fully implemented—longer-run, as you put it—it would result in less spending, particularly if these troops and weapons are demobilized, as we say.

I've got time for one more and then I've got to go to a luncheon.

Q. Mr. President, just to be clear on one point, what you're proposing is an agreement with the Warsaw Pact, not anything that you will do unilaterally, that you won't take any of these steps yourselves outside an overall agreement with the—

The President. This is a NATO proposal, and it would be negotiated with the Pact. But it means that—obviously, when you're dealing with the Pact, that the Soviet Union is going to have to be the key player. And this part of the proposal, as it relates to U.S. troops, clearly is one where both the Soviet General Secretary and I have to have agreement. But I want to keep the negotiations and the initiatives inside of the alliance. We came over here to say the alliance has worked. It's kept the peace for 40 years. And we want to continue to keep it strong. And that's one reason I am very pleased with the alliance response to our proposal. They don't see it as soloing off there, taking care of U.S. interest. They see it as in the interest of the alliance.

And again, I believe I speak—I believe—well, I know most of the people there feel that way, and I hope all of them.

This is the last one, and then I'm going in peace.

Q. A tick-tock question: When did you make the final decision to accept this idea? How did it evolve?

The President. Twelve days ago.

Q. One last one, sir. Do you have any interest in discussing this with Mr. Gorbachev at a summit meeting? Do you have any interest or intention of discussing this proposal or other arms proposals with Mr. Gorbachev at a summit meeting?

The President. When I have a summit meeting with Mr. Gorbachev, I expect we'll discuss a wide array of subjects.

Q. Do you anticipate that this year?

The President. When that happens, I will have wide, farflung discussions and no date has been set for that.

Q. Why 12 days ago?

Q. Is it likely to be speeded up, though, Mr. President, because of this proposal?

The President. Hadn't thought of it, Jack [Jack Nelson, *Los Angeles Times*], in this connection, but I would not rule that out. But we'll see how it's digested there in Moscow. I hope favorably.

Q. Isn't it time for a summit now, sir, now that you've laid this out?

The President. Baker's got some more work to do.

SAN FRANCISCO RECOGNIZES "DOMESTIC PARTNERSHIPS"

May 30, 1989

San Francisco granted legal recognition to the "domestic partnership" of homosexuals and unmarried heterosexuals in an ordinance passed May 30 by the city-county Board of Supervisors and signed by Mayor Art Agnos. It provided for public registration of these relationships in the same way that other couples file marriage licenses.

The law was short-lived. Petition drives organized by fundamentalist Christians forced the issue on the ballot in the city's November 7 election. The law was repealed by a margin of two thousand votes, representing about 1 percent of the total. Agnos vowed to "come back again and again" with similar ordinances.

This was the first law of its kind, so broad in application, enacted by a major American city, although three smaller California cities already had similar laws. Several other cities across the country, including Seattle, Denver, Minneapolis, New York, and Washington, also considered such measures. In 1988, Los Angeles took a step in that direction.

San Francisco extended to domestic partnerships the same hospital visitation rights accorded to married couples, and it granted to city employees in a domestic partnership the same bereavement leave policy granted to married workers. The ordinance also extended health insurance benefits to domestic partners of city workers. These health and bereavement provisions were especially important to San Francisco's large homosexual community, which suffered severely from an epidemic of AIDS (Acquired Immune Deficiency Syndrome). The death toll approached five thousand late in 1989.

The ordinance defined a domestic partnership as "two people who have

305

chosen to share one another's lives in an intimate and committed relationship of mutual caring." The pair must live together, though they may also have separate living quarters. They must complete and sign a form called "Declaration of Domestic Partnership," in which they agree to share "basic living expenses."

Many rights and obligations conferred on married couples by California law were not granted by the city ordinance to domestic partners. For example, the partners, unlike spouses, were not granted automatic inheritance, automatic right to jointly acquired property, or the right to seek spousal support after divorce.

Gay rights suffered setbacks in two other local elections in California November 7. In Concord, a San Francisco suburb, the voters repealed an ordinance that barred discrimination against people with AIDS. And in Irvine, in Orange County south of Los Angeles, voters approved a measure to exclude homosexuals from that city's human rights law. The Rev. Louis P. Sheldon, head of the Traditional Values Coalition, which spearheaded the drives to put all three measures on the ballot, told a postelection news conference in Anaheim that "the people are saying . . . 'enough is enough.' "

In 1982, the San Francisco Board of Supervisors voted to extend health insurance coverage to domestic partners, but Mayor Dianne Feinstein vetoed the measure. Two years later she rejected a similar proposal recommended by her Task Force on Equal Benefits. Feinstein explained her 1982 veto in a letter to supervisor Harry Britt, a leader of the gay community. She wrote: "That San Francisco should be called upon to voyage into the unknown in terms of setting precedent for the entire nation for partnerships that may be fleeting and totally vacant of any mutual sense of responsibility or caring is, I believe, putting too much strain on our social fabric."

Gay Rights Laws Elsewhere

Across San Francisco Bay in Berkeley, the city council in 1985 unanimously extended to city employees' domestic partners any benefits, including city-paid health benefits, available to spouses. Similar measures were adopted in Santa Cruz and West Hollywood. In 1988 Los Angeles allowed unmarried city employees to use sick and bereavement leave upon the illness of a domestic partner if the couple had lived together a year and registered that relationship with the city.

Mayor Agnos, Feinstein's successor, said during his 1988 election campaign that he would support domestic partnerships. When he signed the ordinance, passed by a 9-0 vote of the board with two members absent, his press release called it "a landmark ordinance granting official recognition to gay, lesbian and unmarried heterosexual couples."

In New York, a group of gay teachers had sued the city, charging that its refusal to let them enroll their partners on the health plan, as though they were spouses, had deprived them of some of their pay. San

Francisco's extension of health benefits to domestic partners will not increase costs to the city because most city employees pay the full cost of the insurance of their spouses or dependents. But some fear that insurance premiums could rise because of the high incidence of AIDS among the homosexual population.

The New York Court of Appeals, the state's highest court, expanded the legal definition of a family by ruling July 6 that a gay couple who had lived together for a decade should be considered a family under New York City's rent-control regulations.

Differing Views

As for the San Francisco ordinance, the Roman Catholic Archdiocese of San Francisco argued that it would undermine traditional marriage. A spokesman for the archdiocese contended that the law set up a "parallel track" and encouraged impermanent commitments. He added, "The Catholic Church has always presumed that marriage is between a man and a woman, and that children are somehow a part of that."

Matthew Coles, a San Francisco attorney for the American Civil Liberties Union who helped draft the ordinance, argued that "if the family is in such feeble shape that this is a threat to it, then it's beyond hope, and nothing we can do is going to do any serious damage." Cynthia Goldstein, a National Gay Rights Advocates attorney in San Francisco, said the ordinance would "give some real power to our relationships." She expressed a hope that this new category of relationship would be sufficiently confusing to show that it would be "more logical just to let gay and lesbian couples get married."

Following is the text of the San Francisco domestic-partners ordinance, passed by the city-county Board of Supervisors, May 30, 1989:

Be it ordained by the People of the City and County of San Francisco:

Section 1. The San Francisco Police Code is amended by adding Article 40, sections 4001 to 4010, to read:

SEC. 4001. DISCRIMINATION AGAINST DOMESTIC PARTNERS

The City and County shall not discriminate against Domestic Partners or Domestic Partnerships in any way. This includes (but is not limited to) using marital status as a factor in any decision, policy or practice unless it used Domestic Partnership as a factor in the same way.

SEC. 4002. DOMESTIC PARTNERSHIPS: DEFINITIONS AND INFORMATIONAL MATERIAL

(a) Domestic Partnership Defined. Domestic Partners are two people who have chosen to share one another's lives in an intimate and committed relationship of mutual caring, who live together and have signed a Declaration of Domestic Partnership in which they have agreed to be jointly responsible for basic living expenses incurred during the Domestic

Partnership, and have established their partnership under Section 4005 of this Article.

(b) Additional Qualification to Become Domestic Partners. To be Domestic Partners, neither person may be married, the two may not be related to each other in a way which would bar marriage in California, and both must be 18 or older. Any different Domestic Partnership of which either was previously a member must have ended more than six months before the new Declaration of Domestic Partnership was signed (but this requirement does not apply if the earlier Domestic Partnership ended because of the death of one of its members).

(c) "Live Together" Defined. "Live together" means that two people share the same living quarters. It is not necessary that the right to possess the quarters be in both names. Two people may live together even if one or both have additional separate living quarters. Domestic Partners do not cease to live together if one leaves the shared living quarters but intends to return.

(d) "Basic Living Expenses" Defined. "Basic living expenses" means the cost of basic food, shelter and any other expenses of a Domestic Partner which are paid at least in part by a program or benefit for which the partner qualified because of the Domestic Partnership. The individuals need not contribute equally or jointly to the cost of these expenses as long as they agree that both are responsible for the cost.

(e) "Declaration of Domestic Partnership" Defined. A Declaration of Domestic Partnership is a form, provided by the County Clerk, in which two people agree to be jointly responsible for basic living expenses incurred during the Domestic Partnership and that all the other qualifications for Domestic Partners are met when the Declaration is signed. The form shall be contained in a booklet or packet with the informational materials described in paragraph (f). The form will require each partner to provide his or her primary residence address. The form must be signed under penalty of perjury. Unless it is filed with the city, the form must be witnessed and notarized. The City Attorney shall prepare appropriate forms.

(f) Informational Material. The San Francisco Human Rights Commission shall prepare informational material which will describe ways individuals in committed relationships may give their relationships the legal effect they would like them to have. The informational material shall state that the city is not providing legal advice and assumes no responsibility for the accuracy of the information provided.

SEC. 4003. ENDING DOMESTIC PARTNERSHIPS

(a) Termination. A Domestic Partnership ends when:

(1) the partners no longer meet one or more of the qualifications for Domestic Partnership; or

(2) one partner sends the other a written notice that he or she has ended the partnership; or

(3) one of the partners dies.

(b) Notice of Termination.

(1) To Domestic Partners. When a Domestic Partnership ends, the partners must execute a Notice of Termination naming the partners and stating that the partnership has ended (hereafter "Notice of Termination"). The Notice of Termination must be dated and signed under penalty of perjury by at least one of the partners. If the Declaration of Domestic Partnership for the partnership was filed with the County Clerk, the Notice of Termination must be filed with the Clerk; in all other cases, the Notice of Termination must be notarized and a copy given to whomever witnessed the Declaration of Domestic Partnership.

(2) To Third Parties. A Domestic Partner who has given a copy of a Declaration of Domestic Partnership to any third party in order to qualify for any benefit or right must, whenever the Domestic Partnership ends, give that third party a copy of the Notice of Termination. If that partner has died, the surviving partner must give the notice of termination to those third parties whom she or he knows were given a copy of the Declaration by the deceased partner in order to qualify for a benefit or right. The Notice must be sent within 60 days of the termination of the Domestic Partnership.

(3) Failure to Give Notice. Failure to give notice as required by this subsection will neither prevent nor delay termination of the Domestic Partnership. Anyone who suffers any loss as a result of failure to send either of these notices may sue the partner who has failed to send the required notice.

SEC. 4004. LEGAL EFFECT OF DECLARATION OF DOMESTIC PARTNERSHIP

(a) Rights and Duties Created. Neither this Article nor the filing of a Statement of Domestic Partnership shall create any legal rights or duties from one of the parties to the other other than the legal rights and duties specifically created by this Chapter or other ordinances or resolutions of the San Francisco Board of Supervisors which specifically refer to Domestic Partnership.

(b) Duration of Rights and Duties. Once a Domestic Partnership ends, the partners will incur no further obligations to each other under this Article.

SEC. 4005. ESTABLISHING EXISTENCE OF DOMESTIC PARTNERSHIP

(a) Domestic partners may establish the existence of their domestic Partnership by either:

(1) Presenting an original Declaration of Domestic Partnership to the County Clerk, who will file it and give the partners a certificate showing that the Declaration was filed by the Clerk; or

(2) Having a Declaration of Domestic Partnership notarized and giving a copy to the person who witnessed the signing. (See Section 4002(e) of this Article.)

(b) The County Clerk shall only accept for filing Declarations of

Domestic Partnership submitted by Domestic Partners who have a residence in San Francisco, or where one of the partners works in San Francisco.

(c) Amendments to the Declaration. A Partner may amend a Declaration of Domestic Partnership filed with the County Clerk at any time to show a change in his or her primary residence address.

(d) New Declarations of Domestic Partnership. No person who has created a Domestic Partnership may create another until six months after a Statement of Termination has been signed and either (i) filed with the County Clerk if the Declaration creating the partnership was filed or (ii) notarized; provided, however, that if the Domestic Partnership ended because one of the partners died, a new Declaration may be filed anytime after the notice of Termination has been filed or notarized.

(e) Evidence of Domestic Partnership. Anyone who requires a person to provide evidence of the existence of a Domestic Partnership must accept (but may choose not to require) as complete proof a copy of a Declaration of Domestic Partnership.

SEC. 4006. RECORDS, COPIES, FILING FEES

(a) County Clerk's Records. The County Clerk shall keep a record of all Declarations of Domestic Partnership, Amendments to Declarations of Domestic Partnership and all Notices of Termination received by the Clerk. The records shall be maintained so that Amendments and Notices of Termination are filed with the Declaration of Domestic Partnership to which they pertain.

(b) Filing Fees. The County Clerk shall charge a fee of $35 for filing Declarations of Domestic Partnership and shall charge a fee of $7 for providing certified copies of Declarations, Amendments or Notices of Termination. There will be no charge for filing Amendments or Notices of Termination.

SEC. 4007. VISITATION IN HEALTH CARE FACILITIES

(a) Patient Designation. Where a health care facility restricts a patient's visitors, the health care facility shall allow every patient to name those individuals whom the patient wishes to allow to visit, unless:

(1) no visitors are allowed; or

(2) the facility determines that the presence of a particular visitor named by the patient would endanger the health or safety of a patient or patients, or would endanger the primary operations of the facility.

(b) Domestic Partners Who Do Not Make Designations. If a patient with whom visiting is restricted has not made the designation provided for in subsection (a), and if the patient has not indicated that she or he wishes no visitors, the facility must allow the patient's Domestic Partner, the children of the patient's Domestic Partner, or the Domestic Partner of the patient's parent or child to visit, unless:

(1) no visitors are allowed; or

(2) the facility determines that the presence of a particular visitor named by the patient would endanger the health or safety of a patient or

patients, or would endanger the primary operations of the facility.

(c) Health Care Facility Defined. A "Health Care Facility" is any clinic, health dispensary or health facility licensed under Division 2 of the California Health and Safety Code, any mental hospital, drug abuse clinic or detoxification center.

SEC. 4008. RETALIATION

No person who seeks the benefit of this Article shall be discriminated against in any way for seeking that benefit. No person who assists someone else in obtaining the benefit of this Article shall be discriminated against in any way for such assistance.

SEC. 4009. ENFORCEMENT

(a) Civil Service Commission and Human Rights Commission. This Article may be enforced by the Civil Service Commission insofar as the actions, decisions, policies and practices at issue pertain to employees of the City and County in their capacity as employees. In all other respects, this Article may be enforced by the San Francisco Human Rights Commission pursuant to Sections 12A.5 and 12A.9 of the Administrative Code.

(b) Civil Action. This Article may be enforced by a civil action. A complaint to the Human Rights Commission is not a prerequisite to enforcement in a civil action. The plaintiff in such an action shall be entitled to recover only compensatory damages and no punitive damages.

(c) Remedies. Any court that finds that this Article has been violated or will be violated may use all the powers which it has to remedy or prevent a violation.

(d) Statute of Limitations. Any action to enforce this Article must be commenced no later than two years after the claimed violation.

SEC. 4010. OTHER LAWS

Nothing in this ordinance shall be construed to interfere in or mandate the exercise of discretion regarding matters over which any board or commission of the City and County has exclusive charter authority; or to conflict with any rights or requirements established by charter, state or federal law, including, but not limited to, the rights and obligations attendant to marriage under state and federal laws. Nothing in this ordinance shall be deemed to alter or to require the alteration of eligibility requirements for social service, public health, and other entitlement programs provided or administered by the City and County. Nothing in this ordinance shall be deemed to alter any existing memorandum of understanding to which the City and County is a party.

June

Khomeini's Death, Hostages, and
    U.S.-Iran Relations 315

Supreme Court Rulings on Civil Rights
    Laws 321

James Watt on Influence Peddling 333

Hungary's Belated Eulogy for
    1956 Uprising Heroes. 339

Court Ruling on Flag Burning 343

Energy Secretary's Environmental Plan. . . . 355

KHOMEINI'S DEATH, HOSTAGES, AND U.S.-IRAN RELATIONS

June 4 and August 4, 1989

Ayatollah Ruhollah Khomeini, the aged ruler of Iran and leader of its revolution, died June 3 in Tehran, twelve days after undergoing surgery for a digestive disorder. For a decade, Khomeini exercised unchallenged control of Iran's government and society, inspired a militant revival of the Shi'ite branch of Islam, encouraged fundamentalist revolutionaries throughout the Moslem world, attacked Western values and influence, proved a nemesis to the U.S. government, and became a villain to the American public. (American Hostages in Iran, Historic Documents of 1979, p. 867)

Khomeini's death raised fundamental questions about the future of Iran, the politics of the Middle East, the direction of Islam, and relations between Islamic civilization and the West. His passing also complicated international maneuvers concerning a handful of American hostages held in Lebanon by pro-Iranian guerrilla groups.

A series of dramatic events focused world attention once again on hostages taken in Lebanon's civil war. Israeli forces July 28 kidnapped Sheik Abdul Karim Obeid, a leader of a Lebanese Shi'ite Moslem group, the Party of God. Three days later, a guerrilla cell announced that it had killed an American hostage and released a videotape showing a figure, identified as William R. Higgins, a Marine Corps lieutenant colonel, swinging from a rope around his neck. Another guerrilla cell linked to the Party of God threatened to kill another American hostage, Joseph James Cicippio, by nightfall the next day unless Israel freed Obeid.

The threat to Cicippio was suspended following diplomatic efforts directed primarily at Iran, but the incident left behind new tensions between the United States and Israel, friction between groups competing in Iran for Khomeini's mantle, a cruel dilemma for George Bush—the third American president to be challenged by Shi'ite hostage-takers, and, for an American public horrified by the televised film of the hanging, a deepened sense of helpless outrage.

The Hostages

At least eight groups had claimed responsibility for kidnapping foreigners in Lebanon. It was not known whether some of those groups were in fact the same organization using more than one name. Several groups used the name Islamic Holy War, which had been and perhaps still was connected with the Party of God. The group claiming to have killed Higgins called itself the Organization of the Oppressed on Earth, and was believed to be connected to the family of Mohammed Ail Hammadi, who had been convicted in West Germany for involvement in a 1985 hijacking of a TWA airliner in Beirut. The group that threatened to kill Cicippio, the Revolutionary Justice Organization, was thought to be a Shi'ite group loyal to Iran.

At the time of the announcement of Higgins's death, sixteen Western hostages, eight of them American, were still believed to be in captivity in Lebanon. Two other American hostages were known to have been killed: William Buckley, kidnapped while serving as CIA station chief at the Beirut embassy, and Peter Kilburn, a librarian at the American University of Beirut. Six other hostages of various nationalities were known to have been killed, and another was missing and presumed dead.

Higgins, forty-four, was head of a seventy-five-member observer group attached to the UN Interim Force in Lebanon when he was kidnapped February 17, 1988. Israeli officials said they believed Higgins had been killed before Obeid was kidnapped. The CIA shared that view. Cicippio, fifty-eight, acting comptroller of the American University of Beirut, was kidnapped September 12, 1986.

U.S.-Israeli Tensions

After the announcement of Higgins's death and the threat to Cicippio, the White House July 31 issued a statement calling on all parties holding hostages in the Middle East to release them. The statement was widely interpreted as being designed to obtain an Israeli release of Obeid to avert the killing of American hostages. Earlier in the day, Senate Minority Leader Bob Dole, R-Kan., usually supportive of Israel, said: "Perhaps a little more responsibility on the part of the Israelis one of these days would be refreshing." Dole added that President Bush should seek "some understanding with the Israelis about future conduct that would endanger the lives of Americans." Rep. Lee Hamilton, D-Ind., chairman of the House Foreign Affairs Middle East subcommittee, complained that Israel had not consulted with the United States before kidnapping the sheik. "If we are going to be in on the crash landing," Hamilton said, "we would like to be in on the takeoff as well."

Other members of Congress rejected criticisms of Israel. Moshe Arad, Israeli's ambassador to the United States, wrote in the August 7 New York Times *that advance approval by the United States would have required it to undertake a course of action it was not prepared to follow. Disapproval could have derailed action that Israel regarded as vital to its interest and security.*

Diplomatic, Military Operations

Israel offered to exchange Obeid and other captured Shi'ite Moslems for Israeli soldiers and Western hostages held in Lebanon. The Revolutionary Justice Organization said August 3 it had suspended its decision to kill Cicippio to allow more time for the sheik's release, and it issued new demands for Israel to release Lebanese guerrillas and also Palestinians arrested in the uprising in the Israeli-occupied West Bank. The group said the decision had been prompted by the intervention of "certain parties and countries," apparently alluding to American appeals to many nations to intercede.

The Bush administration disclosed in a story leaked to the New York Times *that it had prepared military operations while it was pursuing diplomatic solutions. Administration officials were quoted as saying that the United States had warned Iran through diplomatic channels that it would retaliate militarily if Cicippio were killed. President Bush reportedly was prepared to order air strikes against suspected terrorist strongholds in Lebanon, including Baalback, where Shi'ite militants shared a base with 2,000 Iranian revolutionary guards. As vice president, Bush had headed the Reagan administration's task force on terrorism. The group's 1986 report rejected retaliatory strikes that carry a high risk of killing innocent people.*

Hojatolislam Hashemi Rafsanjani, who was elected president of Iran on July 28, soon offered to help end the hostage impasse in Lebanon. During a weekly prayer sermon at Tehran University on August 4, Rafsanjani said: "I wish to say—I address this to the White House—that Lebanon has a solution; the freedom of the hostages is solvable." Although Rafsanjani also vehemently denounced the United States and Israel, U.S. officials viewed his remarks as a hopeful signal. They considered him more pragmatic than Khomeini but noted that the new president was not fully in control of the government. In response to Rafsanjani's speech, President Bush said: "I don't want to raise hopes beyond fulfillment, but there's reason to be somewhat encouraged.

Multiple Conflicts

Iran's notion of Islam being at war with Western values survived Khomeini's death. Rafsanjani accused the West of trying to create in Lebanon a state controlled by Maronite Christians comparable to the Jewish state created in Palestine. This goal is impossible, he said, now that the Moslem people have been "awakened by the Islamic Revolution of Iran."

317

The Moslem perspective often baffled Westerners, who usually viewed conflicts in a secular framework of territories, governments, economies, and military forces. In Iran, the struggle between religious and secular viewpoints dominated both domestic and foreign policy issues. Until Shah Mohammed Reza Pahlavi was forced into exile in January 1979, he imposed on Iran the secular goals and power promised by Western technology. The United States, valuing Iran for its oil and strategic location on the Soviet border, supported the shah. It was thus identified by most Iranians with the corruption and the police-state repression of the shah's regime as well as with the secular temptations of material "progress." The revolution led by Khomeini was a passionate reaction against Western secularism. With his death, the balance between religious and secular priorities was thrown into doubt.

The continuing religious fervor of Iranians was attested by an outpouring of grief at Khomeini's funeral in Tehran on June 6. Frenzied crowds of mourners surged forward and caused his body to be tipped from the coffin, forcing the army to airlift it to a "martyrs' cemetery." But the loss of more than a million "martyrs" in Iran's eight-year war with Iraq, and the devastation of Iran's economy by that war, left Iran with immense practical problems.

Following are the White House's terse statement on June 4, 1989 about Ayatollah Ruhollah Khomeini's death; excerpts from a sermon President Hashemi Rafsanjani preached in Tehran August 4, as translated by the Foreign Broadcast Information Service, a U.S. government agency, and remarks by President Bush to questions at a White House news conference August 4.

WHITE HOUSE STATEMENT ON KHOMEINI'S DEATH

The official Iranian news agency has confirmed the death of the Ayatollah Khomeini. With his passing, we hope Iran will now move toward assuming a responsible role in the international community.

RAFSANJANI STATEMENT

I would briefly like to mention the issue of Lebanon.... There is a country known as Israel, the root of which is usurper and aggressive, and which officially enters a small town by helicopter with military forces, and abducts the Friday imam of that small town and a couple of his bodyguards.... There are no international laws which endorse such an action....

They could have committed this action without confessing to it. Then the action, even though an atrocity, would not have been impudence. But Israel confessed. It made a public announcement. This makes ... a mockery of all international standards.

What happened then? A number of innocent people whose identity is not even known, a number of unknown people who were combating covertly, announced that they had killed an individual whom they claimed to have captured as a spy. They hanged him in revenge.

Their reasoning was that, "Israel is America's agent, and we will take revenge on an American who is a supporter of the Israeli atrocity, and who is captive in our hands, in return for Sheik Abdul Karim Obeid." Well, this was their way. In addition, they threatened that they would also kill the rest of them if Obeid was not freed.

What can the world do under such conditions?

Here there is one clear point and another point which is ambiguous. The clear point is that a government has officially committed aggression and has officially confessed, and by the admission of all it has committed a crime. The ambiguous point is that a group has gone and taken a person who might be innocent. We do not know him. We have no judgment to pass on the colonel. We do not know who he is and cannot judge. We do not know that group either—whether they are truthful people or not.

Rather than go after a recognized criminal, one who shouts and declares that he is a criminal, you order your naval units to sail toward victimized Lebanon. How stupid can you be?

They do not want a solution. They are not prepared to abandon the sovereignty of the Maronite in Lebanon. They all hope that one day they will create a Maronite Israel in Lebanon. A Jewish Israel in Palestine, a Maronite Israel in Lebanon. But they made a mistake. When Israel was created in Palestine, there was no Islamic Government in Iran. On that day the Muslim people had not yet been awakened by the Islamic revolution of Iran.

Lebanon has a solution, may God so wish. Anyway, I wish to say—I address the White House—that Lebanon has a solution; the freedom of the hostages is solvable. They have intelligent and manageable solutions. One cannot solve the issue with such bullying ways, with arrogant confrontations, and tyranny. Come along wisely; we then will help you to solve the problems there so that the people of the region may live in peace and tranquility.

BUSH'S REMARKS

Q. Mr. President, what do you make of Rafsanjani's offer to help resolve the hostage crisis?

A. We have engaged in a very—a very—an extraordinarily broad exercise of diplomacy here in the last couple of days. And let me say I am—I would be—I am pleased about that. I don't know what—what it means fully, but I think the world is familiar with our policy. But there will be nothing that will be done, ever, that will create a new incentive for taking somebody else hostage. . . .

Q. What do you think was the motivating factor for the freeze on the execution, and where do you go from here?

A. I'd like to think that a broad spread appeal to nations in every corner of the globe had something to do with it. And many—

Q. You don't know?

A. I don't know for sure. And the response that I have had on my personal calls and that the Secretary has had on his, has been heartwarming. It's come from all sectors, and I have been very, very encouraged by that. And where we go from here, though, we'll just keep on trying.

Q. Mr. President, what has Iran's role been in this? And do you see an opening in the structure here to allow you to work for the release of the hostages?

A. Well, as I just answered, I was pleased that the—certainly pleased that the brutal murder that had been threatened was set aside. I don't know the total role of any individual country in that area in all of this, but when you see a statement that offers hope for the return of our hostages, I want to explore it to the fullest.

Q. Have you made a decision to take military action if another American hostage is killed?

A. I have made—I wouldn't—if I had made such a decision, I expect this would be the last place I'd be talking about it.

Q. Surely you must see this as a golden opportunity now—you have the momentum, you have a diplomatic flurry going on in Damascus, International Red Cross, apparently. I mean, is there is a new impetus?

A. . . . There's reason to be somewhat encouraged. But I think of the brutality of the process. A man condemned to die at 11; and then it's moved to 3 in the afternoon. Put yourself in the position of these families. Think of the hurt that just that four hours of experience causes somebody.

And I would just appeal to the civilized world, or any country anywhere in the world, to lay aside this holding of people against their will as hostages, and do what is right and decent and honorable in terms of the release of those hostages that are still held. . . .

SUPREME COURT RULINGS
ON CIVIL RIGHTS LAWS
June 5 and 12, 1989

During its 1988-1989 term, which ended July 3, the Supreme Court sharply narrowed the scope of major civil rights laws designed to correct discriminatory practices. Four of those decisions were handed down in June. The rulings confirmed a new conservatism in the Court, which former president Ronald Reagan had vowed to achieve. Reagan's last appointee to the Court, Anthony M. Kennedy, cast the deciding vote in all four of the decisions. The vote on each was 5 to 4.

During the Court's previous term, Kennedy replaced Lewis F. Powell, Jr., who had frequently sided with minorities in civil rights cases. Two other Reagan appointees—Sandra Day O'Connor and Antonin Scalia—joined Chief Justice William H. Rehnquist (whom Reagan elevated from associate justice) and Byron R. White to form the majority in those decisions.

Wards Cove Packing Co. v. Atonio

The divided Court on June 5 broke with an eighteen-year-old precedent in the case of Wards Cove Packing Co. v. Atonio *and made job discrimination more difficult to prove. Since 1971, in* Griggs v. Duke Power Co., *the Court had held that Title VII of the Civil Rights Act of 1964, which prohibited discrimination in employment, could be violated if an employer's personnel practices had an adverse effect on minorities— even in the absence of proof that an employer intended to discriminate. Those rulings also implied that once the adverse effect was demonstrated, it was up to employers to prove a business necessity for continuing the practices.*

In Wards Cove, *the five-member majority not only shifted the burden of proof to the plaintiff, it also held that statistics showing racial imbalances in job categories were not sufficient to document discrimination. Instead, plaintiffs were called on to prove, instance by instance, that particular employment practices had a discriminatory effect.*

Writing for the majority, Justice White said, "The ultimate burden of proving that discrimination against a protected group has been caused by a specific employment practice remains with the plaintiff at all times." In dissent, Justice John Paul Stevens said he could not "join this latest sojourn into judicial activism." Accusing the majority of "turning a blind eye to the meaning and purpose" of Title VII, Stevens added, "This casual—almost summary—rejection of the statutory construction that developed in the wake of Griggs *is most disturbing."*

Justice Harry A. Blackmun, in a separate dissent joined by Justices William J. Brennan, Jr., and Thurgood Marshall, said, "One wonders whether the majority still believes that race discrimination—or more accurately, race discrimination against non-whites—is a problem in our society, or even remembers that it ever was."

Martin v. Wilks

One week later, on June 12, the Court ruled that white firefighters in Birmingham, Alabama, were entitled to challenge a hiring and promotion plan negotiation in 1981 among black firefighters, the city, and a county personnel board. The white workers were not a party to the case. At issue were court-approved consent decrees that included goals for hiring and promoting black firefighters. At a hearing before the decrees were made final, a federal district court overruled objections from a group of white firefighters who opposed the race-oriented relief.

Writing for the majority, Rehnquist said a consent decree could be binding only on groups or individuals who had been directly involved in the original lawsuit. He also said parties to a discrimination suit who were negotiating consent decrees were responsible for bringing in other individuals or other groups that could be affected.

In a dissenting opinion, Stevens termed the court's decision "counter-productive," saying that it would discourage voluntary settlements of discrimination complaints, including discrimination on the basis of sex. The decision would result in "never-ending litigation" and could discourage employers from entering voluntary affirmative-action agreements, he said. Joining Stevens in dissent were Blackmun, Brennan, and Marshall.

Patterson v. McLean Credit Union

On June 15, again by a 5-4 margin, the Court narrowed the use of a 1866 statute that gave "all persons within the jurisdiction of the United States" the same rights as "white citizens" to make and enforce contracts. Unlike other civil rights statutes, notably Title VII of the 1964 Civil Rights Act, the statute allowed a court to award monetary damages to those who prevailed in discrimination suits.

Patterson *was the most anxiously awaited civil rights case of the Court's term. The Court heard it argued in February 1988, but the following April the Court unexpectedly asked that it be reargued. A major question had been whether the Court would reverse its 1976 ruling in* Runyon v. McCrary, *which held that the 1866 law could be used by private individuals to sue other individuals for damages in race bias cases. Previously, the law was assumed to prohibit only discrimination by the government. Since* Runyon, *the law had been invoked frequently in civil rights lawsuits and cited in more than one hundred lower-court rulings. A bipartisan group of 60 senators and 119 House members filed an advisory brief urging that* Runyon *be upheld.*

Writing for the majority, Kennedy said there was "no special justification" for overruling Runyon. *But he narrowly defined the statute's scope. It provided relief only if an act of discrimination involved "the making and enforcement of contracts," Kennedy wrote. He added that "the right to make contracts does not extend ... to conduct by the employer after the contract relation has been established, including breach of the terms of the contract or imposition of discriminatory working conditions."*

Writing for the minority (which again included Blackmun, Marshall, and Stevens), Brennan denounced the Court's "pinched reading" of the 1866 law. "When it comes to deciding whether a civil-rights statute should be construed to further our nation's commitment to the eradication of racial discrimination, the Court adopts a formalistic method of interpretation antithetical to Congress' vision of a society in which contractual opportunities are equal," he said.

Jett v. Dallas Independent School District

For the second time in eight days, the Court narrowed the application of the 1866 law, ruling 5-4 on June 22 that state and local government officials could not be held liable for discrimination unless the violation was part of an official policy. The majority opinion was written by O'Connor, who said Congress intended that lawsuits charging state and local officials with violations of the contract rights guaranteed in the 1866 law were subject to a subsequent 1871 law.

In a sharp dissent—signed by Blackmun, Marshall, and Stevens— Brennan called the decision "astonishing." Not only was he unconvinced that the statute should be narrowed, Brennan said, but he could not understand why the majority believed that the 1866 statute should be governed by limitations on a statute passed five years later "and covering a far narrower range of conduct."

City of Richmond v. J. A. Croson Co.

The June rulings continued a pattern established early in the Court's term. On January 23, a 6-3 majority struck down a Richmond, Virginia, plan that set aside 30 percent of the city's construction projects for minorities. Stevens joined Rehnquist, O'Connor, Scalia, Kennedy, and White in the majority. In the Court's opinion, O'Connor said minority set-aside programs could be justified only if they served the "compelling state interest" of redressing "identified discrimination" committed either by the government or by private parties. The Richmond plan did not meet that standard. Measures similar to the one struck down in the Richmond *case were in effect in 36 states and nearly 200 localities.*

Mixed Reaction: Possible Congressional Legislation

After the Patterson *ruling, Benjamin L. Hooks and Ralph G. Neas, chairman and executive director of the Leadership Conference on Civil Rights, said: "This Supreme Court term has been a disaster for all those committed to equal employment opportunities. Sadly, the Supreme Court, the principal protector of individual rights and liberties for the past thirty-five years . . . has been abandoning that historic role."*

Wade Henderson, an American Civil Liberties Union spokesman , said: "If these decisions are left unaddressed by Congress, they will undo the substantial gains we've made as a nation in settling the divisive issues of equal justice under law." The decisions were "a serious threat to the thirty-five years of progress we have achieved toward a better and fairer society," said Sen. Edward M. Kennedy, D-Mass.

But former solicitor general Charles Fried, who during the Reagan administration had urged the Court to side with the white firefighters in the Martin *case, said that such comments were "alarmist and incorrect." Bruce Fein, a constitutional lawyer, said the pattern "means that we have a Reagan court on civil rights and social welfare. It means we won't have the rampant social engineering emanating from federal judges."*

Civil rights advocates appealed to Congress to enact legislation over-turning many decisions. In 1982 and 1988 Congress passed laws repudiat-ing separate Court rulings that circumscribed antidiscrimination laws.

> *Following are excerpts from the Supreme Court's majority and dissenting opinions in* Wards Cove Packing Co. v. Atonio, *June 5, 1989, that made job discrimination more difficult to prove; and* Martin v. Wilks, *June 12, enabling white firefighters to challenge a pay and promotion plan for black firefighters in Birmingham, Alabama:*

<u>No. 87-1387</u>

Wards Cove Packing Company, Inc. et al.
Petitioners
v.
Frank Atonio et al.

On writ of certiorari to the United States Court of Appeals for the Ninth Circuit

[June 5, 1989]

JUSTICE WHITE delivered the opinion of the Court.

Title VII of the Civil Rights Act of 1964 makes it an unfair employment practice for an employer to discriminate against any individual with respect to hiring or the terms and condition of employment because of such individual's race, color, religion, sex or national origin; or to limit, segregate or classify his employees in ways that would adversely affect any employee because of the employee's race, color, religion, sex or national origin. *Griggs* v. *Duke Power Co.* (1971) construed Title VII to proscribe "not only overt discrimination but also practices that are fair in form but discriminatory in practice." Under this basis for liability, which is known as the "disparate impact" theory and which is involved in this case, a facially neutral employment practice may be deemed violative of Title VII without evidence of the employer's subjective intent to discriminate that is required in a "disparate treatment" case.

I

The claims before us are disparate-impact claims, involving the employment practices of petitioners, two companies that operate salmon canneries in remote and widely separated areas of Alaska. The canneries operate only during the salmon runs in the summer months. They are inoperative and vacant for the rest of the year. In May or June of each year, a few weeks before the salmon runs begin, workers arrive and prepare the equipment and facilities for the canning operation. Most of these workers possess a variety of skills. When salmon runs are about to begin, the workers who will operate the cannery lines arrive, remain as long as there are fish to can, and then depart. The canneries are then closed down, winterized, and left vacant until the next spring. During the off season, the companies employ only a small number of individuals at their headquarters in Seattle and Astoria, Oregon, plus some employees at the winter shipyard in Seattle.

The length and size of salmon runs vary from year to year and hence the number of employees needed at each cannery also varies. Estimates are made as early in the winter as possible; the necessary employees are hired, and when the time comes, they are transported to the canneries. Salmon must be processed soon after they are caught, and the work during the canning season is therefore intense. For this reason, and because the canneries are located in remote regions, all workers are housed at the canneries and have their meals in company-owned mess halls.

Jobs at the canneries are of two general types: "cannery jobs" on the cannery line, which are unskilled positions; and "noncannery jobs," which fall into a variety of classifications. Most noncannery jobs are classified as skilled positions. Cannery jobs are filled predominantly by nonwhites, Filipinos and Alaska Natives. The Filipinos are hired through and dispatched by Local 37 of the International Longshoremen Workers Union pursuant to a hiring hall agreement with the Local. The Alaska Natives primarily reside in villages near the remote cannery locations. Noncannery jobs are filled with predominantly white workers, who are hired during the winter months from the companies' offices in Washington and Oregon. Virtually all of the noncannery jobs pay more than cannery positions. The predominantly white noncannery workers and the predominantly non-white cannery employees live in separate dormitories and eat in separate mess halls.

In 1974, respondents, a class of nonwhite cannery workers who were (or had been) employed at the canneries, brought the Title VII action against petitioners. Respondents alleged that a variety of petitioners' hiring/promotion practices—e.g., nepotism, a rehire preference, a lack of objective hiring criteria, separate hiring channels, a practice of not promoting from within—were responsible for the racial stratification of the work force, and had denied them and other nonwhites employment as noncannery workers on the basis of race. Respondents also complained of petitioners' racially segregated housing and dining facilities. All of respondents' claims were advanced under both the disparate-treatment and disparate-impact theories of Title VII liability.

The District Court held a bench trial, after which it entered 172 findings of fact. It then rejected all of respondents' disparate-treatment claims. It also rejected the disparate-impact challenges involving the subjective employment criteria used by petitioners to fill these noncannery positions, on the ground that those criteria were not subject to attack under a disparate-impact theory. Petitioner's "objective" employment practices (e.g., an English language requirement, alleged nepotism in hiring, failure to post noncannery openings, the rehire preference, etc.) were found to be subject to challenge under the disparate-impact theory, but these claims were rejected for failure of proof. Judgment was entered for petitioners.

On appeal, a panel of the Ninth Circuit [Court of Appeals] affirmed [the lower court ruling] but that decision was vacated when the Court of Appeals agreed to hear the case en banc [by all the appellate judges]. The en banc hearing was ordered to settle an intra-circuit conflict over the question whether subjective hiring practices could be analyzed under a disparate-impact model; the Court of Appeals held—as this Court subsequently ruled in *Watson* v. *Fort Worth Bank & Trust* (1988)—that disparate-impact analysis could be applied to subjective hiring practices. The Ninth Circuit also concluded that in such a case, "[o]nce the plaintiff class has shown disparate-impact caused by specific, identifiable employment practices or criteria, the burden shifts to the employer," to "prov[e the] business necessity" of the challenged practice. Because the en banc holding on subjective employment practices reversed the District Court's contrary ruling, the en banc Court of Appeals remanded the case to a panel for further proceedings.

On remand, the panel applied the en banc ruling to the facts of this case. It held that respondents had made out a prima facie case of disparate-impact in hiring for both skilled and unskilled noncannery positions. The panel remanded the case for further proceedings, instructing the District Court that it was the employer's burden to prove that any disparate impact caused by its hiring and employment practices was justified by business necessity. Neither the en banc court nor the panel disturbed the District Court's rejection of the disparate-treatment claims. . . .

II

In holding that respondents had made out a prima facie case of disparate impact, the Court of Appeals relied solely on respondents' statistics showing a high percentage of nonwhite workers in the cannery jobs and a low percentage of such workers in the noncannery positions. Although statistical proof can alone make out a prima facie case, the Court of Appeals' ruling here misapprehends our precedents and the purposes of Title VII, and we therefore reverse. . . .

It is clear to us that the Court of Appeals' acceptance of the comparison between the racial composition of the cannery work force and that of the noncannery work force, as probative of a prima facie case of disparate impact in the selection of the latter group of workers, was flawed for several reasons. Most obviously, with respect to the skilled noncannery jobs at issue here, the cannery work force in no way reflected "the pool of *qualified* job applicants" or the "*qualified* population in the labor force." . . . If the absence of minorities holding such skilled positions is due to a dearth of qualified nonwhite applicants (for reasons that are not petitioners' fault), petitioners' selection methods or employment practices cannot be said to have had a "disparate impact" on nonwhites. . . .

The Court of Appeals also erred with respect to the unskilled noncannery positions. Racial imbalance in one segment of an employer's work force does not, without more, establish a prima facie case of disparate impact with respect to the selection of workers for the employer's other positions, even where workers for the different positions may have somewhat fungible skills (as is arguably the case for cannery and unskilled noncannery workers). As long as there are no barriers or practices deterring qualified nonwhites from applying for noncannery positions, if the percentage of selected applicants who are nonwhite is not significantly less than the percentage of qualified applicants who are nonwhite, the employer's selection mechanism probably does not operate with a disparate impact on minorities. Where this is the case, the percentage of nonwhite workers found in other positions in the employer's labor force is irrelevant to the question of a prima facie statistical case of disparate impact. As noted above, a contrary ruling on this point would almost inexorably lead to the use of numerical quotas in the workplace, a result that Congress and this Court have rejected repeatedly in the past. . . .

Consequently, we reverse the Court of Appeals' ruling that a comparison between the percentage of cannery workers who are nonwhite and the percentage of noncannery workers who are nonwhite makes out a prima facie case of disparate impact. Of course, this leaves unresolved whether the record made in the District Court will support a conclusion that a prima facie case of disparate impact has been established on some basis other than the racial disparity between cannery and noncannery workers. . . .

It is so ordered.

JUSTICE STEVENS, with whom JUSTICE BRENNAN, JUSTICE MARSHALL, and JUSTICE BLACKMUN join, dissenting.

Fully 18 years ago, this Court unanimously held that Title VII of the Civil Rights Act of 1964 prohibits employment practices that have discriminatory effects as well as those that are intended to discriminate. Federal courts and agencies consistently have enforced that interpretation, thus promoting our national goal of eliminating barriers that define economic opportunity not by aptitude and ability but by race, color, national origin, and other traits that are easily identified but utterly irrelevant to one's qualification for a particular job. Regrettably, the Court retreats from these efforts in its review of an interlocutory judgment respecting the "peculiar facts" of this lawsuit. Turning a blind eye to the meaning and purpose of Title VII, the majority's opinion perfunctorily rejects a longstanding rule of law and underestimates the probative value of evidence of a racially stratified work force. I cannot join this latest sojourn into judicial activism.

I

I would have thought it superfluous to recount at this late date the development of our Title VII jurisprudence, but the majority's facile treatment of settled law necessitates such a primer. This Court initially considered the meaning of Title VII in *Griggs* v. *Duke Power Co.* (1971), in which a class of utility company employees challenged the conditioning of entry into higher paying jobs upon a high school education or passage of two written tests. Despite evidence that "these two requirements operated to render ineligible a markedly disproportionate number of Negroes," the Court of Appeals had held that because there was no showing of an intent of discriminate on account of race, there was no Title VII violation. Chief Justice [Warren] Burger's landmark opinion established that an employer may violate the statute even when acting in complete good faith without any invidious intent. . . .

The opinion in *Griggs* made it clear that a neutral practice that operates to exclude minorities is nevertheless lawful if it serves a valid business purpose. "The touchstone is business necessity," the Court stressed. Because "Congress directed the thrust of the Act to the *consequences* of employment practices, not simply the motivation[,] . . . Congress has placed on the employer the burden of showing that any given requirement must have a manifest relationship to the employment in question." (emphasis in original). Congress had declined to act—as the Court now sees fit—to limit the reach of this "disparate impact" theory. . . .

JUSTICE BLACKMUN, with whom JUSTICE BRENNAN and JUSTICE MARSHALL join, dissenting.

I fully concur in JUSTICE STEVENS' analysis of this case. Today a bare majority of the Court takes three major strides backwards in the battle against race discrimination. It reaches out to make last Term's plurality opinion in *Watson* v. *Fort Worth Bank & Trust* (1988), the law, thereby upsetting the longstanding distribution of burdens of proof in Title VII disparate-impact cases. It bars the use of internal workforce comparisons in the making of a prima facie case of discrimination, even where the structure of the industry in question renders any other statistical comparison meaningless. And it requires practice-by-practice statistical proof of causation, even where, as here, such proof would be impossible. . . .

Nos. 87-1614, 87-1639, and 87-1688

John W. Martin et al.,
Petitioners
v.
Robert K. Wilks et al.

On writs of certiorari to the United States court of Appeals for the Eleventh Circuit

Personnel Board of Jefferson County, Alabama, et al.,
Petitioners
v.
Robert K. Wilks et al.

Richard Arrington, Jr., et al.
Petitioners
v.
Robert K. Wilks et al.

[June 12, 1989]

CHIEF JUSTICE REHNQUIST delivered the opinion of the court.

A group of white firefighters sued the City of Birmingham, Alabama (City) and the Jefferson County Personnel Board (Board) alleging that they were being denied promotions in favor of less qualified black firefighters. They claimed that the City and the Board were making promotion decisions on the basis of race in reliance on certain consent decrees, and that these decisions constituted impermissible racial discrimination in violation of the Constitution and federal statute. The District Court held that the white firefighters were precluded from challenging employment decisions taken pursuant to the decrees, even though these firefighters had not been parties to the proceedings in which the decrees were entered. We think this holding contravenes the general rule that a person cannot be deprived of his legal rights in a proceeding to which he is not a party.

The litigation in which the consent decrees were entered began in 1974, when the Ensley Branch of the NAACP and seven black individuals filed separate class-action complaints against the City and the Board. They alleged that both had engaged in racially discriminatory hiring and promotion practices in various public service jobs in violation of Title VII of the Civil Rights Act of 1964, and other federal law. After a bench trial on some issues, but before judgment, the parties entered into two consent decrees, one between the black individuals and the City and the other between them and the Board. These proposed decrees set forth an extensive remedial scheme, including long-term and interim annual goals for the hiring of blacks as firefighters. The decrees also provided for goals for promotion of blacks within the department.

The District Court entered an order provisionally approving the decrees and directing publication of notice of the upcoming fairness hearings. Notice of the hearings, with a reference to the general nature of the decrees, was published in two local newspapers. At that hearing, the Birmingham Firefighters Association (BFA) appeared and filed objections as *amicus curiae* [friend of the court]. After the hearing, but before final approval of the decrees, the BFA and two of its members also moved to intervene on the ground that the decrees would adversely affect their rights. The District Court denied the motions as untimely and approved the decrees. Seven white firefighters, all members of the BFA, then filed a complaint against the City and the Board seeking injunctive relief against enforcement of the decrees. The seven argued that the decrees would operate to illegally discriminate against them; the District Court denied relief.

Both the denial of intervention and the denial of injunctive relief were affirmed on appeal. The District Court had not abused its discretion in refusing to let the BFA intervene, thought the Eleventh Circuit, in part because the firefighters could "institut[e] an independent Title VII suit, asserting specific violations of their rights." And, for the same reason, petitioners had not adequately shown the potential for irreparable harm from the operation of the decrees necessary to obtain injunctive relief.

A new group of white firefighters, the *Wilks* respondents, then brought suit against the City and the Board in district court. They too alleged that, because of their race, they were being denied promotions in favor of less qualified blacks in violation of federal law. The Board and the City admitted to making race conscious employment decisions, but argued the decisions were unassailable because they were made pursuant to the consent decrees. A group of black individuals, the *Martin* petitioners, were allowed to intervene in their individual capacities to defend the decrees.

The defendants moved to dismiss the reverse discrimination cases as impermissible collateral attacks on the consent decrees. The District Court denied the motions, ruling that the decrees would provide a defense to claims of discrimination for employment decisions "mandated" by the decrees, leaving the principal issue for trial whether the challenged promotions were indeed required by the decrees. After trial the District Court granted the motion to dismiss. The court concluded that "if in fact the City was required to [make promotions of blacks] by the consent decree, then they would not be guilty of [illegal] racial discrimination" and that the defendants had "establish[ed] that the promotions of the black individuals ... were in fact required by the terms of the consent decree."

On appeal, the Eleventh Circuit reversed. It held that "[b]ecause ... [the *Wilks* respondents] were neither parties nor privies to the consent decrees, ... their independent claims of unlawful discrimination are not precluded." The court explicitly rejected the doctrine of "impermissible collateral attack" espoused by other courts of appeals to immunize parties to a consent decree from charges of discrimination by nonparties for actions taken pursuant to the decree. Although it recognized a "strong public policy in favor of voluntary affirmative action plans," the panel acknowledged that this interest "must yield to the policy against requiring third parties to submit to bargains in which their interests were either ignored or sacrificed." The court remanded the case for trial of the discrimination claims, suggesting that the operative law for judging the consent decrees was that governing voluntary affirmative-action plans.

We granted certiorari, and now affirm the Eleventh Circuit's judgment. All agree that "[i]t is a principle of general application in Anglo-American jurisprudence that one is not bound by a judgment *in personam* in a litigation in which he is not designated as a party or to which he has not been made a party by service of process." This rule is part of our "deeprooted historic tradition that everyone should have his own day in court." A judgment or decree among parties to a lawsuit resolves issues as among them, but it does not conclude the rights of strangers to those proceedings....

Affirmed.

JUSTICE STEVENS, with whom JUSTICE BRENNAN, JUSTICE MARSHALL, and JUSTICE BLACKMUN join, dissenting.

... Assuming that the District Court's findings of fact were not clearly erroneous—which of course is a matter that is not before us—it seems perfectly clear that its judgment should have been affirmed. Any other conclusion would subject large employers who seek to comply with the law by remedying past discrimination to a never-ending stream of litigation and potential liability. It is unfathomable that either Title VII or the Equal Protection Clause demands such a counter-productive result.

IV

The predecessor to this litigation was brought to change a pattern of hiring and promotion practices that had discriminated against black citizens in Birmingham for decades. The white respondents in this case are not responsible for that history of discrimination, but they are nevertheless beneficiaries of the discriminatory practices that the litigation was designed to correct. Any remedy that seeks to create employment conditions that would have obtained if there had been no violations of law will necessarily have an adverse impact on whites, who must now share their job and promotion opportunities with blacks. Just as white employees in the past were innocent beneficiaries of illegal discriminatory practices, so is it inevitable that some of the same white employees will be innocent victims who must share some of the burdens resulting from the redress of the past wrongs.

There is nothing unusual about the fact that litigation between adverse parties may, as a practical matter, seriously impair the interests of third persons who elect to sit on the sidelines. Indeed, in complex litigation this Court has squarely held that a sideline-sitter may be bound as firmly as an actual party if he had adequate notice and a fair opportunity to intervene and if the judicial interest in finality is sufficiently strong. . . .

There is no need, however, to go that far in order to agree with the District Court's eminently sensible view that compliance with the terms of a valid decree remedying violations of Title VII cannot itself violate that statute or the Equal Protection Clause. The City of Birmingham, in entering into and complying with this decree, has made a substantial step toward the eradication of the long history of pervasive racial discrimination that has plagued its fire department. The District Court, after conducting a trial and carefully considering respondents' arguments, concluded that this effort is lawful and should go forward. Because respondents have thus already had their day in court and have failed to carry their burden, I would vacate the judgment of the Court of Appeals and remand for further proceedings consistent with this opinion.

JAMES WATT ON
INFLUENCE PEDDLING
June 9, 1989

Attempting to put the best possible face on his lobbying activities after leaving office as secretary of the Interior, James G. Watt told a congressional panel June 9 that his "credibility was used to get a result." But Watt, a Republican, acknowledged that if he were a Democrat he would say that "Jim Watt engaged in influence peddling."

In further testimony that day before the House Government Operations Subcommittee on Employment and Housing, Watt said he was paid more than $400,000 in consulting fees between 1984 and 1986—of which $300,000 was for making eight telephone calls to Housing and Urban Development (HUD) officials, including Samuel R. Pierce, Jr., and meeting with him for half an hour.

Pierce, who headed the department as HUD secretary, served with Watt in President Ronald Reagan's cabinet. Watt undertook his consulting activities after he left the government. At Interior, Watt stirred the opposition of environmentalists and was forced to resign in October 1983. Among all of Reagan's cabinet members, Pierce served a full eight years, until January 1989.

Although lacking previous experience in housing issues, Watt lobbied Pierce and other top HUD officials on behalf of developers of low-cost housing. Watt sought to obtain approval for a previously rejected housing project in Essex, Maryland.

A Scandal at HUD

High-priced influence peddling by private consultants was only one aspect of a wide-ranging investigation into HUD operations during the

Reagan administration. The subcommittee's inquiry included matters of mismanagement, political favoritism, and possibly fraud and embezzlement. Jack F. Kemp, who succeeded Pierce as secretary, said that twenty-eight of the department's forty-eight programs had "significant problems" attributable to the scandal.

The subcommittee's findings provoked outrage among many members of Congress. Sen. Paul Sarbanes, D-Md., charged that the high consulting fees "deprived people who need housing of the opportunity to get housing." If consultants and developers had not been "raking off" HUD funds, Sarbanes said, "we would have had more money to build more units."

HUD's commitments of housing assistance to additional poor households dropped from an average of 316,000 a year from 1977 to 1980, during the Carter presidency, to 82,000 a year from 1981 to 1988, according to a joint report released in April by the Center on Budget and Policy Priorities and the Low Income Housing Information Service.

Watt's Testimony

While Watt shied away from having his activities labeled as "influence peddling," he did say that "the system is flawed." He added, "I'm not here to defend the system." He called his fee for the Maryland project the "going rate." The project, he said, included 300 units and "the street knowledge is that if you can get these—and it used to be higher in the late 1970s—that the fee is $1,000 to $2,000 a unit." Watt conceded that he had never visited the project in Maryland or others he had promoted in Puerto Rico and New Jersey.

As a consultant, Watt had worked with Joseph Strauss, who had been a special assistant to Pierce from 1981 to 1983. Himself a witness before the subcommittee, Strauss told of receiving huge consulting fees for helping to obtain subsidies from HUD for various projects.

"I make no bones about the fact that the reason James Watt was hired ... was not because of his housing knowledge or legal skills.... The reason was because of his access and influence." He added, "We were up against what I consider very, very powerful people."

Commenting on testimony from Watt, Strauss, and a number of other witnesses, Rep. Christopher Shays, R-Conn., a member of the panel, said: "It really stinks.... I think we have documented beyond a shadow of a doubt how bad the situation is."

Widespread Influence Peddling

Watt was only one of at least eleven former HUD officials and well-known Republicans who reaped large fees as consultants to HUD contractors. Former senator Edward W. Brooke, R-Mass., earned fees estimated at $183,000. In testimony before the subcommittee, Brooke denied that he had used "inappropriate influence." Louis B. Nunn, a former governor of Kentucky, was paid $694,000 for legal and consulting *work on a number of rehabilitation projects.*

Officers of Black, Manafort, Stone & Kelly, a Washington, D.C., consulting firm, received $326,000 after they obtained $3.1 million in rent subsidies for a project in Seabrook, New Jersey. Paul Manafort had been a consultant in the Reagan and Bush presidential campaigns.

William M. Taylor, a Republican national committeeman from Florida, received fees of $130,000 for consulting on four rehabilitation projects. Taylor frequently wrote to HUD officials using Republican National Committee letterhead.

Carla A. Hills, President Bush's international trade representative and a former secretary of Housing and Urban Development in the Ford administration, appeared before the subcommittee and defended her role in lobbying on behalf of the DRG Funding Corporation of Washington, D.C. HUD had accused the firm of "serious breaches" of rules and placed it under severe restrictions. For her work with DRG she was paid $33,500, but Hills said, "We worked as lawyers and we were paid as lawyers." She added, "I argued my client's case strictly on the merits, and as far as I know, the decisions were made strictly on the merits."

For the most part, the high-priced private consultants who lobbied Pierce and other HUD officials were recruited by developers involved with the government's so-called Section 8 program. That program provided qualified developers with long-term subsidies if they renovated substandard housing for low-income families. The developers, many of whom were also prominent Republicans, received rent subsidies and other funds from the federal government.

The Washington Post *quoted Kemp as saying on June 23, "The mood of the Congress is to do something on Housing and Urban Development. They want to know, am I moving fairly to take Republican politics out of it? And I have pledged to do that. HUD is not going to be the Republican National Committee."*

> *Following are excerpts of James G. Watt's testimony before the House Government Operations Subcommittee on Employment and Housing, June 9, 1989, and questions by subcommittee members, as taken from a transcript of the "MacNeil/Lehrer NewsHour":*

JAMES G. WATT: Questions have been asked about the role I played in helping to provide 312 units of low income housing in the County of Baltimore, Maryland. I did receive a fee for providing counsel and assistance to our team of business associates. How much effort and time were committed to the project? Sufficient to meet the objective of those who paid me, the developers.

REP. TOM LANTOS, D-Calif.: You had a contract with a developer with respect to the Essex, Maryland project, for which you were to be paid $300,000. Is that correct?

WATT: I was to be paid $300,000 if the project were successfully completed.

LANTOS: That's correct. How was the figure of $300,000 arrived at?

WATT: It was the offered amount and kind of the going rate.

LANTOS: The going rate of what?

WATT: The street knowledge is that if you can get these—and it used to be higher in the late '70s, that there was a thousand to two thousand dollars a unit—and that's what they offered. They offered $300,000 and that was the way it was settled. It seemed like a lot of money to me.

LANTOS: Well, it certainly seems like a lot of money to the people who live in those subsidized public housing projects, because those people may be making $10,000 a year and in a lifetime they don't make this money.

WATT: They're very grateful to have a home. They're grateful that we were successful in bringing this project to fruition.

LANTOS: No. Mr. Watt, I already explained to you they are grateful to the people who prevented the program from being totally destroyed by Pierce and the people who agreed with Pierce, who is on the record saying that that's what he intended to do.

WATT: I'm not contesting anything you've said on that, Mr. Chairman.

LANTOS: So let's leave the attitude aspect out of it, because I don't think that deals with—

WATT: I understand why you say that, of course.

LANTOS: Of course, you do.

WATT: But it's hard not to focus on it when you see the facility and you see the people and you realize that project may not have come into existence.

LANTOS: That's right. A more worthy project may have come into existence. That's one of our concerns.

WATT: I don't know about that.

LANTOS: This project came into existence because of influence peddling by you. A much more worthy and desirable and necessary project, where they didn't have the good judgment to hire you because you knew Pierce, didn't come into being. So this thing does not appear in isolation. I think you understand this every bit as well as we do. So let's put the great pride aside. The fact with respect to the pride remains that there was an attempt to kill the program, and it couldn't be killed entirely. What was retained was being taken advantage of.

REP. BARNEY FRANK, D-Mass.: We don't claim that you did anything illegal to get these fees, but the fact that those fees were necessary inevitably detracts from our ability efficiently to provide programs. That's what we have to look at. And the second question I have is that I just want to get to what you did to earn the fees. Before you left the Interior Department, in your pre-Secretary of the Interior days, did you do much housing work?

WATT: No.

FRANK: So you had never represented anybody before to get low income housing?

WATT: No.

FRANK: So you had no prior expertise in housing?

WATT: None at all.

FRANK: Had you ever advised anyone to strike a tax deal for low income housing or moderate income housing?

WATT: Not for housing, no.

FRANK: Leaving aside the propriety of what you did or didn't do, you took advantage of legal situations. George Washington Plunkett said, "I seen my opportunities, and I took 'em," and you did. But the result was that $300,000 was paid out for something that should have not been necessary for one meeting and that's our problem.

WATT: I think you framed it fairly, Congressman, and that is the problem that the committee needs to focus on. The program and doesn't do any good to demagogue Jim Watt, although it's fun.

REP. TED WEISS, D-N.Y.: Mr. Watt, as much as you dislike the term, itself, since it is a part of American language, would you give us your definition of influence peddling?

WATT: I only see it used and have only used it in a partisan attack. It's when one of, the Republican Party or Democrat Party accuses someone else of using his credibility or whatever to gain an objective.

WEISS: And you believe that it exists, do you not, in our society?

WATT: Of course.

WEISS: And within the context of that definition, given how you described your work, wouldn't you say that your work, in fact, fits that definition?

WATT: My credibility was used to get a result.

WEISS: Right. Therefore you engaged in influence peddling.

WATT: If I were a Democrat, I would say that Jim Watt engaged in influence peddling.

WEISS: And if you were an objective Republican, would you also believe that that was true?

WATT: No, I would say there's a skilled, talented man who used his credibility to accomplish an objective.

WEISS: Morally. Morally and ethically.

WATT: That by definition is also there.

HUNGARY'S BELATED EULOGY FOR 1956 UPRISING HEROES
June 14, 1989

Exactly thirty-one years after he was hanged as a traitor for leading the 1956 Hungarian uprising in defiance of Moscow, Imre Nagy (pronounced im-reh nuhdge) received a hero's burial in an elaborate, state-assisted public ceremony in Budapest on June 16. The Communist government—undergoing perestroika-inspired reform—two days earlier had issued a declaration of respect to the memory of the former prime minister and "to all victims of the popular uprising and national tragedy." The prime minister, Miklos Nemeth, and three other high-ranking Communists were conspicuously present at the funeral in Hero's Square in an apparent effort to identify themselves with a popular national cause.

In a dramatic pose witnessed by tens of thousands who thronged the square, and by millions of Hungarians on television, the four leaders stood briefly beside the coffins bearing the remains of Nagy and four of his colleagues who were also being honored. Their bodies had been dumped into unmarked graves in a potter's field, which the government had refused to identify until recently. A sixth coffin was empty, symbolically reserved for 260 other victims of the uprising whose bodies remained in unidentified graves. As each name was read, a torchbearer stepped forward and said: "He lives in us; he is not gone." The ceremony stood in marked contrast to what occurred one year earlier, on the thirtieth anniversary of Nagy's death. Police violently broke up an attempt by some dissidents to stage a modest ceremony in the Hungarian capital.

The striking turnabout in the Hungarian government's attitude was seen as an outgrowth of Mikhail S. Gorbachev's perestroika campaign.

The Soviet leader's loosening of political restraints in the Soviet Union inevitably extended to the Soviet-controlled nations of Eastern Europe, especially to Hungary and Poland. (Remarks on Soviet Election and Perestroika, p. 173)

Some commentators theorized that the current group of Communist leaders in Hungary needed to "rehabilitate" Nagy in an effort to heal the bitterness that resulted from the 1956 uprising. Charles Fenyvesi, an American who was born in Hungary and took part in the revolt, wrote in the Washington Post *on the day Nagy was reburied:* "Just as the Bedouins hold a ceremonial feast called sulba to mark the end of a blood feud, the East Europeans' reburial is designed to facilitate the reconciliation of old enemies: the families and confreres of those executed march in the same crowd as those who gave the orders for the executions."

The 1956 Uprising

The uprising occurred in November 1956 and was quickly crushed by Soviet tanks and soldiers, but only after street fighting in Budapest yielded several thousand casualties. It had been preceded by a "thaw" in Soviet relations with its satellite states in Eastern Europe. In February that year, at the Twentieth Communist Party Congress in Moscow, Soviet leader Nikita Khrushchev denounced Joseph Stalin's tyrannical reign and signaled that a less repressive era was in the offing. "De-Stalinization" created expectations in Hungary that slow-developing economic reforms did not fulfill. As the people became more restive that autumn, Moscow returned Nagy to the premier's post from which he had been removed in 1955 for pushing reforms too vigorously. The day before he was put back in office, a wave of anti-Soviet demonstrations swept through Budapest. Near the city park, the protesters toppled a statue of Stalin and dragged it through the streets in a carnival atmosphere.

Nagy was a lifelong Communist, and had spent nearly a third of his life—he was then sixty-two years old—in the Soviet Union. But he also saw himself as a Hungarian patriot, and finally had to choose between the two roles. That occurred when he and his cabinet, rejecting Moscow's demands for a crackdown, made their own demand. It was that Soviet troops be removed from Hungary. The Soviet commanders feinted a withdrawal but returned to Budapest in force during the night of November 3. Early the next morning, Nagy went on the radio to tell his fellow Hungarians that they had been attacked and their army was resisting. But Russian troops and armor crushed the resistance within a few days. Nagy took refuge in the Yugoslav embassy but was soon tricked into leaving it by a Soviet ruse. He was seized by Soviet secret police and imprisoned.

The next official word on his fate came June 17, 1958, when the Hungarian government announced that he and two associates had been put to death the previous day. According to some accounts, his death was delayed until then because of a futile Soviet attempt to force him to recant. Nagy's two associates—his defense minister, Pal Maleter, and a *journalist friend, Miklos Gimes—were also accorded reburial honors. And so were Nagy's minister of state, Geza Losonczy, and cabinet secretary, Jozsef Szilagyi. Losonczy began a hunger strike in prison and was said to have choked to death while being force fed, December 21, 1957; Szilagyi was executed April 24, 1958, after a show trial in which he denounced the Soviet intervention and the puppet government it put in place.*

Years of Kadar Oppression

That puppet government was headed by Janos Kadar, a Hungarian Communist who presided over a harsh repression. In recent years, however, he began gradually to lose power to an emerging reformist wing of the Hungarian Communist party—formally, the Hungarian Socialist Workers party. He was removed as party chief in May 1988, and a year later from the ceremonial position of party president. He died three weeks after the June 16 ceremonies for Nagy, and on the same day the Hungarian Supreme Court announced Nagy's full legal rehabilitation. It marked the end of the post-1956 period—a period inextricably associated with the name Janos Kadar.

Hungary moved into a new era without breaking stride. On October 7, the ruling party formally abandoned Communism and symbolically dropped the word "Workers" from its name, in preparation for free national elections to be held some time in 1990 for a new parliament. On October 19, existing opposition parties received legal standing and together they negotiated constitutional changes to declare Hungary a democratic republic on October 23. Unlike in 1956, Moscow did not interfere.

Following is a declaration issued by the government of Hungary, June 14, 1989, as provided in English translation by the Hungarian Embassy in Washington:

The Council of Ministers of the Hungarian People's Republic pays a tribute of respect to the memory of Imre Nagy and his comrades in misfortune, to all victims of the popular uprising and national tragedy of 1956 and shares the grief of their relatives.

The lessons of 1956 are being drawn. The Government is guided by an endeavour to do national and historical justice. It will in this spirit present a bill to the National Assembly concerning the establishment of the innocence of those involved who were held criminally responsible for acts against the State.

The Government will do all it can to ensure that no one in Hungary will ever again be condemned without legal grounds, in the name of political concepts. It has therefore proposed the National Assembly to abolish the death penalty for political offences, has endorsed and will submit to the legislature a bill amending the Chapter of the Penal Code on Offences against the State.

In assessment of Imre Nagy's activity it states that Imre Nagy was a prominent statesman, who recognized the need to change an inviable course of policy alien to our traditions and to assert national specifics and lasting human values. The ideas of Imre Nagy and his followers, their democratic and humane endeavours bearing national characteristics are important components of the current Government policy.

The Government invites citizens and their communities to think and act with responsibility when they attend the last honours paid to Imre Nagy and his fellow martyrs, at the funeral ceremony and events of commemoration everywhere in the country, and to reject any eventual attempt impeding the effort to create the conditions for solidarity and national consensus so urgently needed in the current situation of our society.

It is in the interest of all Hungarians, of all citizens of our country that the funeral ceremony and the last honours should take place in a manner worthy of a European nation, under the hallmark of justice and consensus.

On the eve of the day of mourning and tribute the Government reaffirms its utmost endeavour to ensure that the nation's prosperity is enhanced by national reconciliation and social consensus. The only guarantee for this can be provided by a consistent and irreversible reform policy seeking renewal and based on national specifics.

The Government dissociates itself from the mistaken and sometimes wrongful political decisions of the past and from the post-1956 measures of retaliation, expresses its resolve to close an era full of sad trials, and calls on the nation to join forces. Let us concentrate our efforts and creative energies on building a new, democratic Hungary!

COURT RULING
ON FLAG BURNING
June 21, 1989

The Supreme Court held on June 21 that burning the U.S. flag as a political protest amounted to symbolic "free speech," protected by the First Amendment. The landmark ruling had the effect of voiding a federal flag-desecration law and similar laws in forty-eight states—in all but Alaska and Wyoming. It also ignited a movement in Congress, championed by President George Bush, for the adoption of a constitutional amendment to nullify the ruling.

The Court split 5-4 but not strictly along the liberal-conservative lines that became familiar in the 1988-1989 Court term. William J. Brennan, Jr., leader of the Court's liberal bloc, wrote the majority opinion. He drew backing not only from two customary allies, Thurgood Marshall and Harry A. Blackmun, but also from Antonin Scalia and Anthony M. Kennedy, both appointees of Ronald Reagan. John Paul Stevens, who often lined up with Brennan, this time joined with Chief Justice William Rehnquist, Byron R. White, and Sandra Day O'Connor in dissent. Kennedy and Stevens wrote separate opinions—emphasizing the importance they attached to the case.

The case, Texas v. Johnson, *grew out of a protest demonstration in Dallas during the 1984 Republican National Convention. A demonstrator, Gregory Johnson, burned an American flag in front of City Hall. He was arrested and convicted of violating a state law against flag desecration. The Texas Court of Criminal Appeals overturned the conviction, and the state appealed to the Supreme Court.*

Brennan dismissed the state's assertions that Johnson's arrest and conviction were necessary to preserve peace and national unity. He rejected the state's twin arguments that the peace was breached and that the flag was being protected as a symbol of nationhood. Brennan concluded that the state's law was aimed directly at a suppression of views that it found offensive. "If there is a bedrock principle underlying the First Amendment," he wrote, "it is that the Government may not prohibit the expression of an idea simply because society finds the idea itself offensive or disagreeable .... " The justice added: "We are tempted to say, in fact, that the flag's deservedly cherished place in our community will be strengthened, not weakened, by our holding today."

In a separate concurring opinion, Kennedy said he accepted Brennan's view "without reservation" but with a "keen sense that this case, like others before us from time to time, exacts a personal toll ... and illustrates better than most that judicial power is often difficult to exercise." He continued: "The hard fact is that sometimes we must make decisions we do not like. We make them because they are right, right in the sense that the law and the Constitution, as we see them, compel the result."

Rehnquist, disagreeing with both colleagues, contended that Johnson's flag burning "was no essential part of any exposition of ideas, and at the same time it had a tendency to incite a breach of the peace." He continued: "Johnson was free to make any verbal denunciation of the flag he wished .... He could publicly burn other symbols of the government or effigies of public leaders." The chief justice concluded that an "uncritical extension of constitutional protection to the burning of the flag risks the frustration of the very purpose for which organized governments are instituted."

Stevens, a decorated Navy veteran of World War II, said in his separate dissenting opinion that if the ideas represented by the flag "are worth fighting for—and our history demonstrates that they are—it cannot be true that the flag ... is not worthy of protection from unnecessary desecration."

Protests by Bush and in Congress

The Court ruling provoked strong protests nationwide, which President Bush soon joined with a demand for a constitutional amendment to override the decision. At first he asserted that although the decision was "dead wrong" he would respect it. Within a week—at his White House news conference June 27—he said the amendment was needed. "I uphold our precious right to dissent," he said. "But burning the flag goes too far, and I want to see the matter remedied."

By the following day, a total of 172 House members and 43 senators had signed thirty-nine separate resolutions for a constitutional amendment to outlaw desecration of the U.S. flag. The Democratic leaders in Congress opposed a constitutional amendment but were wary of appearing not to care for the flag as a symbol of patriotism. It was still fresh in the minds of Democrats that their 1988 presidential candidate, Michael S. Dukakis, was badly burned by a Republican-ignited campaign issue over the

Pledge of Allegiance. While campaigning, Bush visited a flag factory and blasted Dukakis for vetoing a state law to require public school teachers to lead a daily recitation of the pledge.

The same day that Bush called for a constitutional amendment, the House Democratic leadership introduced a carefully worded resolution that expressed "profound concern" about the decision and generally condemned flag burning. It was passed with only five "no" votes.

The congressional Democrats rallied behind the idea of changing an existing antidesecration law instead of changing the Constitution. On June 23, two days after the Court ruled, the Senate's Judiciary Committee chairman, Joseph R. Biden, Jr., D-Del., added to an unrelated bill ready for Senate passage new wording for a law to protect the flag— which he predicted would survive if challenged in the courts. It was promptly approved on a voice vote.

Dick Thornburgh said the only way to reverse the Court decision was to amend the Constitution. Some Republicans suggested that a reaction to the flag ruling might be a test of patriotism. House Minority Whip Newt Gingrich, R-Ga., said it would be "hard to explain" a vote against a constitutional amendment to ban flag burning. Bush was asked at his news conference whether he was using the issue for partisan purposes. "I think respect for the flag transcends political parties...."

Court's Defenders Speak Up

By the time Congress took its annual August recess, a number of voices were raised in defense of the Court's ruling. On August 9, delegates to the semi-annual American Bar Association's meeting in Honolulu adopted a report opposing both a constitutional amendment and legislation to ban flag desecration. The report had been prepared by a blue-ribbon panel that included Cyrus Vance, the former secretary of state, and Erwin Griswold, the former solicitor general. In adopting the report, the delegates inserted language saying that they "abhorred" such activity.

Ira Glasser, executive director of the American Civil Liberties Union, said it "would be ironic if Congress and the states were to mark the 200th anniversary of the Bill of Rights by making an unprecedented exception to the First Amendment." James J. Kilpatrick, the conservative columnist, declared: "President Bush is dead wrong in calling for a constitutional amendment to overturn the Supreme Court's ruling...."

When Congress returned in September, the House promptly passed legislation similar to Biden's on a vote of 380 to 38. It was a narrowly written bill that sought to punish an individual who defaced the flag without threatening First Amendment freedoms. The Senate passed the House version October 4 by a similarly one-sided vote, 91-9, but only after eight hours of political oratory. President Bush and most congressional Republicans insisted that a constitutional amendment was still needed, and the Senate's Democratic leadership agreed to permit a vote on the constitutional question later in the session. But because of the press of legislative business, Republican leaders in the Senate said they were willing to postpone action until 1990. The test case in court quickly followed the new law's enactment. A group of protesters burned a flag on the U.S. Capitol steps October 30 so that they could be arrested and challenge the law's validity. Their case, United States v. Eichman, *was filed in U.S. District Court for the District of Columbia.*

Bringing about a change in the U.S. Constitution is difficult. Amending the document requires a two-thirds vote in the House and Senate, and ratification by three-fourths of the states. Of the nine proposed amendments to come to a vote in either chamber of Congress in the past twenty-five years, only two have been adopted: the Twenty-Fifth Amendment on presidential disability, and the Twenty-Sixth Amendment guaranteeing eighteen-year-olds the right to vote.

> *Following are excerpts from the Supreme Court's June 21 majority, concurring, and dissenting opinions in the case of* Texas v. Johnson, *which tested the constitutionality of burning the American flag in a public political protest:*

No. 88-155

Texas, Petitioner	
v.	On writ of certiorari to the United
Gregory Lee Johnson	States Court of Appeals for the
On writ of certiorari to the Court	Ninth Circuit
of Criminal Appeals of Texas	

[June 21, 1989]

JUSTICE BRENNAN delivered the opinion of the Court.

After publicly burning an American flag as a means of political protest, Gregory Lee Johnson was convicted of desecrating a flag in violation of Texas law. This case presents the question whether his conviction is consistent with the First Amendment. We hold that it is not.

I

While the Republican National Convention was taking place in Dallas in 1984, respondent Johnson participated in a political demonstration dubbed the "Republican War Chest Tour." As explained in literature distributed by the demonstrators and in speeches made by them, the purpose of this event was to protest the policies of the Reagan administration and of certain Dallas-based corporations. The demonstrators marched through the Dallas streets, chanting political slogans and stopping at several corporate locations to stage "die-ins" intended to dramatize the consequences of nuclear war. On several occasions they spray-painted the walls of buildings and overturned potted plants, but Johnson himself took no part in such activities. He did, however, accept an American flag handed to him by a fellow protestor who had taken it from a flagpole outside one of the targeted buildings.

The demonstration ended in front of Dallas City Hall, where Johnson unfurled the American flag, doused it with kerosene and set it on fire. While the flag burned, the protesters chanted, "America, the red, white and blue, we spit on you." After the demonstrators dispersed, a witness to the flag burning collected the flag's remains and buried them in his backyard. No one was physically injured or threatened with injury, though several witnesses testified that they had been seriously offended by the flag burning.

Of the approximately 100 demonstrators, Johnson alone was charged with a crime. The only criminal offense with which he was charged was the desecration of a venerated object in violation of Texas Penal Code Ann. § 42.09 (a)(3) (1989). After a trial, he was convicted, sentenced to one year in prison, and fined $2,000. . . .

II

Johnson was convicted of flag desecration for burning the flag rather than for uttering insulting words. This fact somewhat complicates our consideration of his conviction under the First Amendment. We must first determine whether Johnson's burning of the flag constituted expressive conduct, permitting him to invoke the First Amendment in challenging his conviction. . . .

The First Amendment literally forbids the abridgement only of "speech," but we have long recognized that its protection does not end at the spoken or written word. . . .

In deciding whether particular conduct possesses sufficient communicative elements to bring the First Amendment into play, we have asked whether "[a]n intent to convey a particularized message was present, and [whether] the likelihood was great that the message would be understood by those who viewed it." . . . Hence, we have recognized the expressive nature of students' wearing of black armbands to protest American military involvement in Vietnam; . . . of a sit-in by blacks in a "whites only" area to protest segregation, . . . of the wearing of American military uniforms in a dramatic presentation criticizing American involvement in Vietnam, . . . and of picketing about a wide variety of causes. . . .

Especially pertinent to this case are our decisions recognizing the communicative nature of conduct relating to flags. Attaching a peace sign to the flag, . . . saluting the flag, and displaying a red flag, we have held, all may find shelter under the First Amendment. . . . That we have had little difficulty identifying an expressive element in conduct relating to flags should not be surprising. The very purpose of a national flag is to serve as a symbol of our country; it is, one might say, "the one visible manifestation of two hundred years of nationhood.". . . Pregnant with expressive content, the flag as readily signifies this Nation as does the combination of letters found in "America.". . .

III

... Texas claims that its interest in preventing breaches of the peace justifies Johnson's conviction for flag desecration. However, no disturbance of the peace actually occurred or threatened to occur because of Johnson's burning of the flag. . . .

The State's position, therefore, amounts to a claim that an audience that takes serious offense at particular expression is necessarily likely to disturb the peace and that the expression may be prohibited on this basis. Our precedents do not countenance such a presumption. On the contrary, they recognize that a principal "function of free speech under our system of government is to invite dispute. It may indeed best serve its high purpose when it induces a condition of unrest, creates dissatisfaction with conditions as they are, or even stirs people to anger.". . .

Nor does Johnson's expressive conduct fall within that small class of "fighting words" that are "likely to provoke the average person to retaliation, and thereby cause a breach of the peace." . . . No reasonable onlooker would have regarded Johnson's generalized expression of dissatisfaction with the policies of the Federal Government as a direct personal insult or an invitation to exchange fisticuffs. . . .

We thus conclude that the State's interest in maintaining order is not implicated on these facts. The State need not worry that our holding will disable it from preserving the peace. We do not suggest that the First Amendment forbids a State to prevent "imminent lawless action." . . . And, in fact, Texas already has a statute specifically prohibiting breaches of the peace, Texas Penal Code Ann. § 42.01 (1989), which tends to confirm that Texas need not punish this flag desecration in order to keep the peace. . . .

IV

It remains to consider whether the State's interest in preserving the flag as a symbol of nationhood and national unity justifies Johnson's conviction. . . .

Johnson's political expression was restricted because of the content of the message he conveyed. We must therefore subject the State's asserted interest in preserving the special symbolic character of the flag to "the most exacting scrutiny.". . .

Texas argues that its interest in preserving the flag as a symbol of nationhood and national unity survives this close analysis. Quoting extensively from the writings of this Court chronicling the flag's historic and symbolic role in our society, the State emphasizes the " 'special place' " reserved for the flag in our Nation. . . . According to Texas, if one physically treats the flag in a way that would tend to cast doubt on either the idea that nationhood and national unity are the flag's referents or that national unity actually exists, the message conveyed thereby is a harmful one and therefore may be prohibited.

If there is a bedrock principle underlying the First Amendment, it is that the Government may not prohibit the expression of an idea simply because society finds the idea itself offensive or disagreeable. . . .

We have not recognized an exception to this principle even where our flag has been involved. . . .

. . . If we were to hold that a State may forbid flag burning wherever it is likely to endanger the flag's symbolic role, but allow it wherever burning a flag promotes that role—as where, for example, a person ceremoniously burns a dirty flag—we would be saying that when it comes to impairing the flag's physical integrity, the flag itself may be used as a symbol—as a substitute for the written or spoken word or a "short cut from mind to mind"—only in one direction. We would be permitting a State to "pre-scribe what shall be orthodox" by saying that one may burn the flag to convey one's attitude toward it and its referents only if one does not endanger the flag's representation of nationhood and national unity.

We never before have held that the Government may ensure that a symbol be used to express only one view of that symbol or its referents. . . .

. . . To conclude that the Government may permit designated symbols to be used to communicate only a limited set of messages would be to enter territory having no discernible or defensible boundaries. Could the Government, on this theory, prohibit the burning of state flags? Of copies of the Presidential seal? Of the Constitution? In evaluating these choices under the First Amendment, how would we decide which symbols were sufficiently special to warrant this unique status? To do so, we would be forced to consult our own political preferences, and impose them on the citizenry, in the very way that the First Amendment forbids us to do. . . .

There is, moreover, no indication—either in the text of the Constitution or in our cases interpreting it—that a separate juridical category exists for the American flag alone. Indeed, we would not be surprised to learn that the persons who framed our Constitution and wrote the Amendment that we now construe were not known for their reverence for the Union Jack. The First Amendment does not guarantee that other concepts virtually sacred to our Nation as a whole—such as the principle that discrimination on the basis of race is odious and destructive—will go unquestioned in the marketplace of ideas. . . . We decline, therefore, to create for the flag an exception to the joust of principles protected by the First Amendment. . . .

We are fortified in today's conclusion by our conviction that forbidding criminal punishment for conduct such as Johnson's will not endanger the special role played by our flag or the feelings it inspires. To paraphrase Justice [Oliver Wendell] Holmes, we submit that nobody can suppose that this one gesture of an unknown man will change our Nation's attitude towards its flag. . . .

We are tempted to say, in fact, that the flag's deservedly cherished place in our community will be strengthened, not weakened, by our holding today. Our decision is a reaffirmation of the principles of freedom and inclusiveness that the flag best reflects, and of the conviction that our toleration of criticism such as Johnson's is a sign and source of our strength. Indeed, one of the proudest images of our flag, the one immortal-ized in our national anthem, is of the bombardment it survived at Fort

349

McHenry. It is the Nation's resilience, not its rigidity, that Texas sees reflected in the flag—and it is that resilience that we reassert today.

The way to preserve the flag's special role is not to punish those who feel differently about these matters. It is to persuade them that they are wrong. "To courageous, self-reliant men, with confidence in the power of free and fearless reasoning applied through the process of popular government, no danger flowing from speech can be deemed clear and present, unless the incidence of the evil apprehended is so imminent that it may befall before there is opportunity for full discussion. If there be time to expose through discussion the falsehood and fallacies, to avert the evil by the processes of education, the remedy to be applied is more speech, not enforced silence." ... And, precisely because it is our flag that is involved, one's response to the flag-burner may exploit the uniquely persuasive power of the flag itself. We can imagine no more appropriate response to burning a flag than waving one's own, no better way to counter a flag-burner's message than by saluting the flag that burns, no surer means of preserving the dignity even of the flag that burned than by—as one witness here did—according its remains a respectful burial. We do not consecrate the flag by punishing its desecration, for in doing so we dilute the freedom that this cherished emblem represents.

V

Johnson was convicted for engaging in expressive conduct. The State's interest in preventing breaches of the peace does not support his conviction because Johnson's conduct did not threaten to disturb the peace. Nor does the State's interest in preserving the flag as a symbol of nationhood and national unity justify his criminal conviction for engaging in political expression. The judgment of the Texas Court of Criminal Appeals is therefore

affirmed.

JUSTICE KENNEDY, concurring.

I write not to qualify the words JUSTICE BRENNAN chooses so well, for he says with power all that is necessary to explain our ruling. I join his opinion without reservation, but with a keen sense that this case, like others before us from time to time, exacts its personal toll. This prompts me to add to our pages these few remarks.

The case before us illustrates better than most that the judicial power is often difficult in its exercise. We cannot here ask another branch to share responsibility, as when the argument is made that a statute is flawed or incomplete. For we are presented with a clear and simple statute to be judged against a pure command of the Constitution. The outcome can be laid at no door but ours.

The hard fact is that sometimes we must make decisions we do not like. We make them because they are right, right in the sense that the law and the Constitution, as we see them, compel the result. And so great is our commitment to the process that, except in the rare case, we do not pause to express distaste for the result, perhaps for fear of undermining a valued principle that dictates the decision. This is one of those rare cases.

Our colleagues in dissent advance powerful arguments why respondent may be convicted for his expression, reminding us that among those who will be dismayed by our holding will be some who have had the singular honor of carrying the flag in battle. And I agree that the flag holds a lonely place of honor in an age when absolutes are distrusted and simple truths are burdened by unneeded apologetics.

With all respect to those views, I do not believe the Constitution gives us the right to rule as the dissenting members of the Court urge, however painful this judgment is to announce. Though symbols often are what we ourselves make of them, the flag is constant in expressing beliefs Americans share, beliefs in law and peace and that freedom which sustains the human spirit. The case here today forces recognition of the costs to which those beliefs commit us. It is poignant but fundamental that the flag protects those who hold it in contempt.

For all the record shows, this respondent was not a philosopher and perhaps did not even possess the ability to comprehend how repellent his statements must be to the Republic itself. But whether or not he could appreciate the enormity of the offense he gave, the fact remains that his acts were speech, in both the technical and the fundamental meaning of the Constitution. So I agree with the Court that he must go free.

CHIEF JUSTICE REHNQUIST, with whom JUSTICE WHITE and JUSTICE O'CONNOR join, dissenting.

In holding this Texas statute unconstitutional, the Court ignores Justice Holmes' familiar aphorism that "a page of history is worth a volume of logic." ... For more than 200 years, the American flag has occupied a unique position as the symbol of our Nation, a uniqueness that justifies a governmental prohibition against flag burning in the way respondent Johnson did here....

The flag symbolizes the Nation in peace as well as in war. It signifies our national presence on battleships, airplanes, military installations, and public buildings from the United States Capitol to the thousands of county courthouses and city halls throughout the country. Two flags are prominently placed in our courtroom. Countless flags are placed by the graves of loved ones each year on what was first called Decoration Day, and is now called Memorial Day. The flag is traditionally placed on the casket of deceased members of the armed forces, and it is later given to the deceased's family. ... Congress has provided that the flag be flown at half-staff upon the death of the President, Vice President, and other government officials "as a mark of respect to their memory." ... The flag identifies United States merchant ships and "[t]he laws of the Union protect our commerce wherever the flag of the country may float."...

No other American symbol has been as universally honored as the flag. In 1931, Congress declared "The Star Spangled Banner" to be our national anthem. In 1949, Congress declared June 14th to be Flag Day. In 1987,

John Philip Sousa's "The Stars and Stripes Forever" was designated as the national march. ... Congress has also established "The Pledge of Allegiance to the Flag" and the manner of its deliverance. ... The flag has appeared as the principal symbol on approximately 33 United States postal stamps and in the design of at least 43 more, more times than any other symbol. ...

Both Congress and the States have enacted numerous laws regulating misuse of the American flag. Until 1967, Congress left the regulation of misuse of the flag up to the States. Now, however, Title 18 U.S.C. § 700(a), provides that: "Whoever knowingly casts contempt upon any flag of the United States by publicly mutilating, defacing, defiling, burning, or trampling upon it shall be fined not more than $1,000 or imprisoned for not more than one year, or both.". ...

The American flag, then, throughout more than 200 years of our history, has come to be the visible symbol embodying our Nation. It does not represent the views of any particular political party, and it does not represent any particular political philosophy. The flag is not simply another "idea" or "point of view" competing for recognition in the marketplace of ideas. Millions and millions of Americans regard it with an almost mythical reverence regardless of what sort of social, political, or philosophical beliefs they may have. I cannot agree that the First Amendment invalidates the Act of Congress, and the laws of 48 of the 50 States, which make criminal the public burning of the flag.

... [T]he public burning of the American flag by Johnson was no essential part of any exposition of ideas, and at the same time it had a tendency to incite a breach of the peace. Johnson was free to make any verbal denunciation of the flag that he wished; indeed, he was free to burn the flag in private. He could publicly burn other symbols of the government or effigies of political leaders. He did lead a march through the streets of Dallas, and conducted a rally in front of the Dallas City Hall. He engaged in a "die-in" to protest nuclear weapons. He shouted out various slogans during the march, including: "Reagan, Mondale which will it be? Either one means World War III"; "Ronald Reagan, killer of the hour, Perfect example of U.S. power"; and "red, white and blue, we spit on you, you stand for plunder, you will go under." ... For none of these acts was he arrested or prosecuted; it was only when he proceeded to burn publicly an American flag stolen from its rightful owner that he violated the Texas statute.

... As with "fighting words," so with flag burning, for purposes of the First Amendment: It is "no essential part of any exposition of ideas, and [is] of such slight social value as a step to truth that any benefit that may be derived from [it] is clearly outweighed" by the public interest in avoiding a probable breach of the peace. The highest courts of several States have upheld state statutes prohibiting the public burning of the flag on the grounds that it is so inherently inflammatory that it may cause a breach of public order. ...

... The Texas statute deprived Johnson of only one rather inarticulate symbolic form of protest—a form of protest that was profoundly offensive to many—and left him with a full panoply of other symbols and every conceivable form of verbal expression to express his deep disapproval of national policy. Thus, in no way can it be said that Texas is punishing him because his hearers—or any other group of people—were profoundly opposed to the message that he sought to convey. Such opposition is no proper basis for restricting speech or expression under the First Amendment. It was Johnson's use of this particular symbol, and not the idea that he sought to convey by it . . . for which he was punished.

. . . The uniquely deep awe and respect for our flag felt by virtually all of us are bundled off under the rubric of "designated symbols," . . . that the First Amendment prohibits the government from "establishing." But the government has not "established" this feeling; 200 years of history have done that. The government is simply recognizing as a fact the profound regard for the American flag created by that history when it enacts statutes prohibiting the disrespectful public burning of the flag.

The Court concludes its opinion with a regrettably patronizing civics lecture, presumably addressed to the Members of both Houses of Congress, the members of the 48 state legislatures that enacted prohibitions against flag burning, and the troops fighting under that flag in Vietnam who objected to its being burned: "The way to preserve the flag's special role is not to punish those who feel differently about these matters. It is to persuade them that they are wrong." . . .

The court's role as the final expositor of the Constitution is well established, but its role as a platonic guardian admonishing those responsible to public opinion as if they were truant school children had no similar place in our system of government. The cry of "no taxation without representation" animated those who revolted against the English Crown to found our Nation—the idea that those who submitted to government should have some say as to what kind of laws would be passed. Surely one of the high purposes of a democratic society is to legislate against conduct that is regarded as evil and profoundly offensive to the majority of people—whether it be murder, embezzlement, pollution, or flag burning.

Our Constitution wisely places limits on powers of legislative majorities to act, but the declaration of such limits by this Court "is, at all times, a question of much delicacy, which ought seldom, if ever, to be decided in the affirmative, in a doubtful case." . . . Uncritical extension of constitutional protection to the burning of the flag risks the frustration of the very purpose for which organized governments are instituted. The Court decides that the American flag is just another symbol, about which not only must opinions pro and con be tolerated, but for which the most minimal public respect may not be enjoined. The government may conscript men into the Armed Forces where they must fight and perhaps die for the flag, but the government may not prohibit the public burning of the banner under which they fight. I would uphold the Texas statute as applied in this case.

JUSTICE STEVENS, dissenting.

As the Court analyzes this case, it presents the question whether the State of Texas, or indeed the Federal Government, has the power to prohibit the public desecration of the American flag. The question is unique. In my judgment, rules that apply to a host of other symbols, such as state flags, armbands, or various privately promoted emblems of political or commercial identity, are not necessarily controlling. Even if flag burning could be considered just another species of symbolic speech under the logical application of the rules that the Court has developed in its interpretation of the First Amendment in other contexts, this case has an intangible dimension that makes those rules inapplicable.

A country's flag is a symbol of more than "nationhood and national unity." . . . It also signifies the ideas that characterize the society that has chosen that emblem as well as the special history that has animated the growth and power of those ideas. The fleur-de-lis and the tricolor both symbolized "nationhood and national unity," but they had vastly different meanings. The message conveyed by some flags—the swastika, for example—may survive long after it has outlived its usefulness as a symbol of regimented unity in a particular nation.

So it is with the American flag. It is more than a proud symbol of the courage, the determination, and the gifts of nature that transformed 13 fledgling Colonies into a world power. It is a symbol of freedom, of equal opportunity, of religious tolerance, and of goodwill for other peoples who share our aspirations. The symbol carries its message to dissidents both at home and abroad who may have no interest at all in our national unity or survival.

The value of the flag as a symbol cannot be measured. . . .

The ideas of liberty and equality have been an irresistible force in motivating leaders like Patrick Henry, Susan B. Anthony, and Abraham Lincoln, schoolteachers like Nathan Hale and Booker T. Washington, the Philippine Scouts who fought at Bataan, and the soldiers who scaled the bluff at Omaha Beach. If those ideas are worth fighting for—and our history demonstrates that they are— it cannot be true that the flag that uniquely symbolizes their power is not itself worthy of protection from unnecessary desecration.

I respectfully dissent.

ENERGY SECRETARY'S
ENVIRONMENTAL PLAN
June 27, 1989

After five months in office, Secretary of Energy James D. Watkins publicly castigated his department's management of plants that produce nuclear weapons and fuel for nuclear-powered warships. He announced at a press conference held June 27 that many managers and supervisers in the Department of Energy (DOE) lacked the technical skills to run the nuclear weapons system, gave him unreliable information on problems at the plants, and often lacked the discipline to safely operate nuclear plants.

"I am certainly not proud or pleased with what I have seen over my first months in office," Watkins said as he announced a ten-point plan to improve the department's performance. He said the measures "are essential to demonstrate that DOE is committed to complying with the nation's environmental laws and is capable of discharging its many responsibilities which include protecting the public health and safety."

In naming Watkins to the cabinet position, President George Bush emphasized his extensive experience with nuclear materials during a long career in the U.S. Navy. Watkins retired as a rear admiral, and prior to his cabinet appointment served as chairman of President Ronald Reagan's commission on AIDS (Acquired Immune Deficiency Syndrome). Watkins was credited with bringing order and credibility to a commission that was beset by dissent. (Presidential Commission Report on AIDS, Historic Documents of 1988, p. 415)

"When the president [Bush] asked me to take this job in January, he indicated that the problems faced by the Department of Energy were very serious in nature," Watkins told the Washington press conference. "The

underlying operating philosophy and culture of DOE was that the adequate production of defense nuclear materials and a healthy, safe environment were not compatible objectives. I strongly disagree with this thinking."

The New York Times *commented editorially that Watkins had caused "culture shock" at the department. The newspaper observed that he was "a product of the nuclear Navy, which, for taut discipline and technical sophistication, has few equals" while "much of the middle level of the department is characterized by the arrogance, incompetence and secretiveness that is the sign of an entrenched bureaucracy gone sour."*

Nuclear Waste Problems

The nuclear industry poses special environmental problems because it both uses and disposes of highly toxic and long-lived materials. The partial meltdown at the Three Mile Island plant near Harrisburg, Pennsylvania, in 1979, and the explosion at Chernobyl in the Soviet Union in 1986 underscored the risk to human health from nuclear facilities.

New construction of commercial nuclear plants virtually ceased in the late 1980s because of safety concerns and cost overruns—overruns that often derived from safety requirements and public fears. Similar concerns arose over several of the seventeen plants that are operated by the Department of Energy for the Department of Defense. Unlike commercial reactors, most of the nuclear weapons facilities were old, some dating from the Manhattan Project, which produced the first atomic bomb in World War II.

The DOE's nuclear facilities received considerable and sharply critical attention in the news media and in Congress during 1988. The Rocky Flats nuclear weapons facility near Denver, Colorado, was closed October 8, 1988, after three persons there were exposed to plutonium. The reactors at the Savannah River plant in South Carolina had been closed since early in the year over safety concerns. Workers went out on strike at a plant in Fernald, Ohio, over reports of chronic leakage of radiation. On June 30, 1989, the DOE promised to pay $73 million to settle claims made by 24,000 neighbors of the facility, the Feed Materials Production Center at Fernald, near Cincinnati, who said it had allowed the nuclear fuel uranium to pollute their water and air. The settlement amounted to an acknowledgment by the government—for the first time—that a weapons-production plant may have contaminated a nearby area. The government did not concede that emissions from the plant made any of the neighbors ill. But it said the money was intended to pay for claims of emotional distress.

The health effects of low-level radiation over long periods of time are largely unknown, but acute exposure to radiation can have fatal consequences, causing—among other things—"radiation sickness," leukemia, and other forms of cancer. It also has been implicated in birth defects.

Watkins's Plan

Foremost in the plan Watkins announced was a "resetting of priorities to reflect environment, safety and health" rather than production. He said award fees paid to contractors who run the plants would be based primarily on environmental compliance. Moreover, he directed the department to begin negotiating with the states in which plants are located to give state authorities access to safety information. A new agreement with Colorado, in regard to Rocky Flats, would serve as a model for the others, Watkins added.

The temporary storage of plutonium-contaminated wastes must continue at Rocky Flats until at least next year due to a delay in opening the Waste Isolation Pilot Plant near Carlsbad, New Mexico, because the quality of work there has been questioned. Watkins said he was surprised to learn that the department had ignored recommendations made by the National Academy of Sciences from 1983 to 1987 regarding the pilot plant. Watkins made clear it would not be opened until he was satisfied that the questions were answered satisfactorily.

Plans for the storage of highly radioactive wastes from military and civilian reactors at Yucca Mountain near Las Vegas, Nevada, were sidetracked by what Watkins called shortcomings in the department's staff. "It has been a nightmare for me to unravel the background sufficient to make some decisions," he said. High on the secretary's list of measures was the formation of investigative "tiger teams" whose members would go to the weapons-production facilities over the course of the year to check on compliance with environmental rules. To carry out the measures he outlined, Watkins said he was establishing a new management team and placing it under the direction of Victor Stello, Jr., an official at the Nuclear Regulatory Commission, who would become DOE's assistant secretary for defense programs.

Budget Increases

Watkins said he had ordered a review to see if the department was complying with the National Environmental Policy Act, which requires environmental impact statements, and vowed to give his personal attention to each decision on whether to order an impact statement. However, he did not say whether he would order such a statement for the overall system of bomb production.

As the secretary spoke, the National Resources Defense Council and twenty other environmental groups filed a lawsuit against the department to compel it to prepare such a statement. The plaintiffs said fourteen of the seventeen plants appeared to be in violation of hazardous-waste laws.

A thorough overhaul—cleaning up nuclear waste and upgrading or replacing the facilities—might require decades and, according to some estimates, cost more than $100 billion. To begin the cleanup, the Bush administration requested that Congress add $300 million to its previous *request for $2.1 billion in fiscal year 1990. That amount was already $300 million higher than the amount President Reagan asked for in the budget he sent Congress shortly before leaving office. Watkins envisioned the cost reaching $4.1 billion in 1994 and then leveling off.*

> *Following are excerpts from the press conference conducted by Secretary of Energy James D. Watkins at the department's auditorium in Washington, June 27, 1989. (The bracketed headings have been added by Congressional Quarterly to highlight the organization of the text.):*

When the President [George Bush] asked me to take this job in January, he indicated that the problems faced by the Department of Energy were very serious in nature. The underlying operating philosophy and culture of DOE was that the adequate production of defense nuclear materials and a healthy, safe environment were not compatible objectives. I strongly disagree with this thinking. I have pointed out several times that I strongly disagree with this thinking.

I agreed to serve as Secretary of Energy knowing full well that one of my immediate tasks would be to create a new culture of accountability within the Department. Today, I am announcing a 10-point initiative that will chart a new course for the Department toward full accountability in the areas of environment, safety, and health. These measures are essential to demonstrate that DOE is committed to complying with the nation's environmental laws and is capable of discharging its many responsibilities which include protecting public health and safety

I have undertaken these extraordinary steps to help restore the public credibility in the Department's ability to safely operate its unique defense, research, and test facilities. Because of the serious nature of the many management problems facing me at DOE [Department of Energy], I have found that I must undertake my own assessment of all DOE operations in order to come up with an adequate baseline of information, one upon which I can then make informed judgments.

The steps I announce today are also intended to help find a new way of successfully integrating the Department's national security mission with its environmental restoration and compliance activities. . . .

[New Objectives]

Deputy Secretary Henson Moore introduced the first of these initiatives on June 16, 1989 when he announced that the environment, safety and health objectives now take precedence over production objectives. This served as the basis for a comprehensive agreement between the Department of Energy and the state of Colorado regarding environmental compliance at the Rocky Flats Plant near Denver. This agreement is unprecedented in scope and in the degree of cooperation that it portends between DOE and the state. It will be a model for new DOE cooperation with the states. . . .

My second initiative concerns a new direction for the Department's award fee program. This initiative has two parts.

First, I am modifying the criteria for award fees to our defense production contractors so that not less than 51 percent of the available award will be based on compliance with environmental, safety and health requirements, including requirements that derive from state environmental laws, regulations of the Environmental Protection Agency and the DOE, and actions set forth in tri-party federal facility compliance agreements. A much smaller percentage is now the norm, such as the 20 percent figure in the Rocky Flats contract.

Second, I am directing that a provision be included in Departmental contracts stipulating that all of the potential award fee that may be earned will be at risk if a contractor fails in any of these three or other important award fee categories.

The third initiative I am announcing today is the formation of environmental "tiger teams," similar to the 25-person DOE investigative team that I sent to Rocky Flats. This includes reviewing operations, documentation agreements, planning, and the facility's performance in meeting environmentally-regulated schedules.

Two such teams will visit two DOE facilities within the next two weeks to conduct environmental compliance assessment. They will follow the environmental assessment protocol presently being performed at Rocky Flats. Six additional facilities will be visited within the next six months, and then 10 more facilities will be assessed in the following six months, for a total of 18 in the next year.

I intend to have environmental teams visit the remaining 17 major DOE facilities, total 35, one year later. All other environmentally less demanding facilities, totaling about 100 more, will be scheduled to complete compliance assessments by December 1992. To assist these teams in their work, I have requested for a special hotline to be established within DOE headquarters to allow citizens to report specific facility concerns.

My fourth initiative addresses Departmental compliance with NEPA [National Environmental Protection Act]. I am directing that the Department revise its procedures and establish a uniform policy on a site-by-site basis for implementing NEPA so that the preliminary NEPA decisions involve the Secretary of Energy from the outset and are fully coordinated with the governors of the states that host our facilities. . . . In the future, if the Department has to err in its judgment as to the extent of NEPA review required of new prospects, it will err on the side of full disclosure and complete assessment of potential environmental impacts.

My fifth initiative is one of the most important. I am establishing an entirely new management team under a new Assistant Secretary for Defense Programs. To head that office, the President has indicated his intent to nominate a strong, technically competent federal manager, Mr. Victor Stello, Jr., who currently serves as Executive Director of Operations at the Nuclear Regulatory Commission. . . .

Mr. Stello led the NRC in preparing its first environmental impact statement requirements and will bring this type of direction to the Office of Defense Programs. This is the first time we have selected an individual who has safety and environmental training and understands that production is a mutually compatible objective with environment, safety and health.

Strengthening the technical capability of the line management in the environment, safety and health areas, such as we did by establishing a brand new support group at Rocky Flats, is my sixth initiative. It is a well-known fact that the very large majority of our work in the field is actually carried out by private contractors. This fact in no way relieves DOE field managers of their own responsibility and accountability to ensure that contract execution meets expected performance standards of excellence.

On my watch, senior DOE officials will also be expected to ensure that their contractors comply with the operational, environmental, safety, health and security standards established by law or regulation. But to do this, DOE officials need sufficient numbers of appropriately skilled DOE line supervisors to support them. This support is not there today.

Accordingly, I intend to establish permanent positions and put into place DOE people with the requisite skills to support line managers in both field and headquarters positions.

This is the necessary precursor to DOE line managers' acceptance of full responsibility and accountability for these vital functions. When in place, primary accountability and responsibility will have been clearly fixed in the DOE line management at all levels. Additionally, line management performance will continue to be subject to both independent internal, DOE, and independent external, non-DOE, oversight as required by law or regulation.

My seventh and eighth initiatives concern the Department's epidemiological data on DOE and contractor employees.

[Independent Health Panel]

The seventh initiative that I am announcing today is the appointment of an independent panel of professional experts in public health, occupational health and epidemiology to advise me as I restructure the DOE epidemiology program. This panel will conduct a detailed evaluation of the entire range of DOE's epidemiologic activities. They will be charged with examining such areas as the goals and objectives of the epidemiology program; the budget and full-time equivalent resources allocated to epidemiologic research; program management and reporting structure; as well as other areas that are germane to the proper operation of our epidemiologic research program. I am ready to provide the resources necessary to do the job better, but I want outside experts to help me structure the program properly.

I have also asked the National Academy of Sciences to establish a standing "Committee on Radiation Epidemiologic Research Programs" . . . to provide ongoing independent scientific counsel to the Department of Energy regarding its epidemiologic research activities, including the creation of a comprehensive epidemiologic data repository. This committee will assure that DOE receives objective scientific advice on its epidemiological programs and on a continuous basis.

My eighth initiative is the establishment of a Comprehensive Epidemiologic Data Repository, CEDR, for all epidemiologically relevant information on past and present DOE and contract workers. The data will be located in a single place and stored in a format that can be easily used by any qualified researcher. Such a repository will enable scientists who are not affiliated with DOE to have access to the DOE worker data so they can conduct independent epidemiologic studies on the DOE worker population. . . .

Today, researchers unaffiliated with the Department cannot gain access to epidemiologic data on DOE workers. Realizing that the establishment of such a repository could take several years to complete, I have asked the National Academy of Sciences to advise the Department on appropriate criteria for allowing independent researchers near-term access to raw DOE worker data. The system we will establish based on NAS's recommendations will assure that DOE data is utilized to conduct studies that are both accurate and complete.

My ninth initiative involves worker safety. Full compliance with the OSHA [Occupational Safety and Health Administration] standards will be a central element of the five-year defense facilities modernization plan currently in preparation. Although DOE has adopted OSHA standards along with other national safety and health standards as a matter of stated policy, it is my intention to ensure that we are in compliance with OSHA standards in execution of policy. I can assure you today that we are not, at Rocky Flats.

In this regard, I will be formally requesting that OSHA participate with DOE in a series of inspections of DOE's defense production facilities. . . .

My tenth initiative is the first action taken as a result of the Environmental Restoration and Waste Management Five-Year Plan which I announced in March of this year.

The Administration, working with Congress, has provided an additional $300 million in the FY 1990 budget to accelerate the cleanup of our facilities over and above the previous administration's funding request. The original FY 1990 budget was $1.8 billion. President Bush increased this to $2.1 billion.

In recognition of the need for acceleration, an additional $300 million will be added. This increase will raise the present FY 1990 budget for the Department's environmental restoration and waste management activities from approximately $2.1 billion to $2.4 billion.

This funding will continue to increase in future years and as is currently estimated in our five-year planning efforts at approximately $4.0 billion in FY 1993; $4.1 billion in FY 1994; $4.1 billion in FY 1995.

However, I must restate that these figures are only preliminary estimates and will be refined as we progress in our planning efforts. . . .

The goal of the 10 initiatives that I have announced today is to restore credibility to the Department of Energy, and to provide the kind of environmentally responsible direction that is critical to achieving the important national missions of the Department of Energy.

With that statement, I will open myself up to questions. . . .

[Working with Governors]

Question: Secretary Watkins, considering what you say about WIPP [Waste Isolation Pilot Plant in New Mexico] not getting any new waste this year, don't you feel any pressure at all to get that site opened? Considering Governor [Cecil D.] Andrus [of Idaho] has said that by September he is not accepting any more waste, and that at about the same time, Governor [Roy] Romer of Colorado has said that he is not going to store any waste that Idaho won't take, do you not feel any pressure to get that site opened by September?

Watkins: No. I will do it when I do it right. And the pressure will be on me if we don't do it right and we have a flawed plan.

I believe we have had a flawed plan. We need to rectify a lot of issues in there. There are 26 unanswered recommendations of the National Academy from those '83 to '87 studies I told you about. We have to address those. . . .

Question: Both of those governors have said they would shut down their facilities, not taking any more waste. Do you take them seriously?

Watkins: I take the governors very seriously. Those governors have done the most responsible job, in my opinion, of wandering through this set of land mines that we have been walking through at Rocky Flats and Idaho and WIPP, and so have the members on the Hill. I have found everybody interested in doing this job right in the interests of the nation's national security. They want to get on with it. I have not found any obstacles there.

The obstacles have been in our own house, not with the states, in my opinion. . . .

Question: You talked repeatedly about taking the reins yourself, about you approving every decision. It sounds like you don't trust your own agency. In the meantime, you have your own people up on the Hill who talk about WIPP with finite timetables and a lot of programs that you are very critical of. This is a very schizophrenic message we are getting from the agency.

Watkins: You broke the code. That is why you are here today.

It is difficult for me to live off past statements, past studies, past baseline, past statements, past schedules. I can't do it on selected areas anymore. It doesn't mean I distrust the agency. It means that a culture was built up in here over a period of years that is very difficult to turn around. I am trying to turn it around very aggressively here by doing things that this Department has not done before in terms of its attention to these other important areas. This is what it is all about. The Department will come along. . . .

July

Supreme Court's Decision in
    Webster Abortion Case 365

Sentencing of Oliver North 391

Gorbachev's Vision of a Common Europe.. 399

Bush's European Trip and
    Economic Summit 411

Soviet Marshal Testifies to the
    U.S. Congress...................... 439

National Research Council Report on
    Black Americans 445

SUPREME COURT'S DECISION IN WEBSTER ABORTION CASE

July 3, 1989

The U.S. Supreme Court on July 3 upheld a 1986 Missouri law that placed restrictions on abortion. It stopped short of overturning the 1973 Roe v. Wade *case that made abortion legal on a nationwide basis, but left open the prospect of doing so later.* (Supreme Court on Abortion, Historic Documents of 1973, p. 101)

During the intervening sixteen years, the Court had repeatedly struck down state laws attempting to restrict abortion rights. However, it had done so with successively weaker majorities, reflecting the Court's increasingly conservative bent. The abortion case before the Court, Webster v. Reproductive Health Services, *was long anticipated as a probable vehicle for the new conservative majority to strike down the 1973 law. The drama built week after week until, finally, the ruling came on the last day of the 1988-1989 term. It was announced in quiet tones by Chief Justice William H. Rehnquist before a hushed crowd of officials and spectators in the courtroom. Throngs of people who could not be seated waited intently outside the Supreme Court building, many with picket signs in hand, ready to cheer or jeer the ruling.*

Although disappointed that the Court did not explicitly declare abortion illegal, abortion opponents ("pro-life") nevertheless declared the ruling a victory. Abortion-rights backers ("pro-choice") accepted it as a defeat. The ruling quickly mobilized an action campaign whose political impact became evident in Congress. By giving the states more authority to impose restraints on abortion, the Webster *decision made the states the new battleground in the abortion fight. Many political analysts who considered abortion the most divisive national issue for the past sixteen years thought it would likely remain as such well into the 1990s.*

The Legal Issues

It was evident in Webster *that a majority of the justices no longer considered abortion to be a fundamental right, as was expressed in the* Roe *decision. But the Court was badly divided on how far it wanted to go in the new direction.*

The provisions of the Missouri law at issue were: a preamble declaring that human life begins at conception; a ban on public hospitals or other taxpayer-supported facilities being used to perform an abortion except to save the mother's life; a prohibition against public doctors, nurses, or other health-care providers performing or assisting with an abortion not necessary to save the mother's life; and a requirement that physicians perform tests to determine whether any fetus believed to be twenty weeks or older is viable—that is, whether it could live outside the womb.

Rehnquist declared for the 5-4 majority that the preamble did not actually regulate abortion and, consequently, the Court did not have to pass constitutional judgment on it. Rehnquist was then able to get the same four justices who joined him in that vote—Anthony M. Kennedy, Byron R. White, Antonin Scalia, and Sandra Day O'Connor—to support his ruling that the state's ban on the use of public facilities and public employees in the performance of abortions was consistent with the Court's earlier abortion decisions.

Rehnquist and White had cast the only dissenting votes in the 1973 case. For Scalia and Kennedy, appointees of President Ronald Reagan, Webster *was their first opportunity to vote against abortion. O'Connor, an earlier Reagan appointee, had previously voiced criticism of* Roe *in sharper tones than she used in* Webster. *In fact, her vote proved decisive in letting* Roe *stand. (Court on Abortion, Historic Documents of 1983, p. 543; Historic Documents of 1986, p. 559)*

Court's Splintered Response

Writing for a three-member plurality that included only himself, Kennedy, and White, Rehnquist upheld the provision requiring doctors to test for fetal viability. He said the Missouri law "creates what is essentially a presumption of viability" at twenty weeks, but allows that presumption to be rebutted by medical judgment and testing.

Rehnquist agreed with the lower courts that had heard the case that required tests for fetal age, weight, and lung maturity placed additional costs and burdens on abortions performed in the second trimester of pregnancy. But he said the problem was not with the law but with the "rigid" trimester framework of the 1973 decision.

In Roe, *the Court held that the constitutional right of privacy included a woman's right to terminate a pregnancy. It said that during the first trimester, her decision would be virtually free of state interference. After* that the state had a "compelling interest" in protecting the woman's health and could regulate abortion to protect that interest. But abortion was not explicitly forbidden until the time the fetus became viable, generally about the twenty-fourth week, roughly the end of the second trimester.

William Webster, the Missouri attorney general, said in a newspaper interview that the twenty-week standard was adopted to allow a four-week margin of error by women and their physicians in estimating when pregnancy began. The case bears Webster's name as the state official who was sued by a clinic and group of doctors seeking to overturn the law. Portions of the law were ruled unconstitutional in federal district and appellate courts. The case was brought to the Supreme Court on a final appeal.

O'Connor's Pivotal Position

Justice O'Connor filed a separate opinion, saying it was unnecessary to reexamine the trimester framework. In another separate opinion, Justice Scalia called the Court's refusal to reaffirm or repudiate Roe the "least responsible" of the options before it. He was especially critical of O'Connor's reasoning. She refused either to join Scalia, who urged a forthright reversal of Roe, or Rehnquist, White, and Kennedy, who chipped at its trimester framework. "There will be time enough to reexamine Roe," she wrote, "and do so carefully."

Justice Harry A. Blackmun, author of the Roe decision, was joined in dissent by William J. Brennan and Thurgood Marshall. Blackmun was incensed by the Court's reasoning in Webster. He wrote that he had never seen justices go about their business "in such a deceptive fashion," and added: "By refusing to explain or justify its proposed revolutionary revision in the law of abortion, and by refusing to abide not only by our precedents, but also by our canons for reconsidering those precedents, the plurality invites charges of cowardice and illegitimacy to our door. I cannot say that these would be undeserved."

New Political Climate

Attorney General Dick Thornburgh, who on behalf of the Bush administration had urged the Court to overturn Roe, said that although the Webster decision had not done so "expressly," it was "most welcome in that it recognizes an increased role for state legislatures in regulating abortion."

The Florida Legislature became the first to be tested with the abortion issue after the Court spoke. Gov. Bob Martinez, a Republican foe of abortion, called the legislature into special session in October to pass six restrictive measures. The legislature's record was generally antiabortion, but on this occasion it voted down all six of the governor's proposals.

Press commentators and many politicians attributed the defeat to an outpouring of support nationally for abortion rights. For years, opinion polls have indicated that while Americans generally are ambivalent about abortion, a majority has consistently opposed making abortion illegal—as it was in most states before 1973. Colorado, in 1967, became the first state to legalize abortion.

The Webster ruling galvanized previously complacent supporters of abortion rights. Pro-choice organizations increased their lobbying and promotion activities. During the summer and into the fall, they sponsored rallies that drew big crowds in city after city across the country—often matching or exceeding the protest demonstrations that antiabortion groups had been staging at intervals since the 1973 decision.

Abortion became a prominent issue in two gubernatorial elections—held in Virginia and New Jersey—and in the New York City mayoral election. In all three races, the Democratic candidates were outspoken in defense of abortion rights and triumphed on November 7 over Republican opponents with antiabortion records. In Virginia, L. Douglas Wilder made abortion the central theme of his campaign and achieved a narrow victory, thus becoming the nation's first elected black governor. New York City likewise elected its first black mayor, David N. Dinkins. In New Jersey, the gubernatorial winner was James J. Florio, who vacated a seat in Congress.

Antiabortionists could still claim some legislative victories. After the Florida Legislature moved in one direction, the Pennsylvania General Assembly met soon afterward and moved the other way. It approved new restrictions on abortion. However, the restrictions were promptly challenged in court.

And in Congress, a flurry of activity aimed at removing abortion restrictions in federal funding ultimately fell victim to President George Bush's vetoes. Before the 1989 session of Congress ended November 21, President Bush had twice vetoed bills to let the District of Columbia use some of its own revenues to pay for abortions sought by women who could not otherwise afford them. Similarly, Bush vetoed legislation to remove the so-called Hyde Amendment—named for Rep. Henry J. Hyde, R-Ill. Since 1981, that amendment had permitted federal funding of abortion only for indigent victims of rape or incest.

GOP's Position in Question

The National Right to Life Committee, a leading antiabortion organization, praised the president for "standing tall in defense of pre-born children." But his vetoes drew the ire of pro-choice legislators, including some Republicans who expressed fear that their party's antiabortion stance would become a liability at election time. Sen. Bob Packwood, R-Ore., said, "This hurts Republicans generally."

Polls taken in the months following the July 3 Court ruling indicated no significant shift in opinion as to whether abortion should be legal or illegal. But a New York Times/CBS survey in September indicated that there had been an increase in the number of people who were worried

*that women might lose the right to have an abortion. About two-thirds of
the people surveyed in the September poll said they expected more limits
to be placed on abortion as a consequence of the* Webster *case.*

Upcoming Abortion Cases

*The same day the Supreme Court ruled in that case, it accepted three
more abortion cases for consideration in the 1989-1990 term. Two of the
cases,* Ohio v. Akron Center for Reproductive Health *and* Hodgson v.
Minnesota, *involved state laws that required both parents to be notified
when a minor daughter sought an abortion. Both cases were argued before
the justices November 29.*

*The third case—the one considered likeliest to bring about a reexami-
nation of the* Roe *decision—was settled out of court November 22, two
weeks before it was due to be argued. At issue in that case,* Turnock v.
Ragsdale, *was an Illinois law that required abortion clinics to meet costly
standards similar to those set for hospital operating rooms. The law had
been ruled unconstitutional in a lower court but a reversal was expected
in the Supreme Court. The settlement thus was viewed as a victory for
the abortion rights movement.*

> *Following are excerpts from the Supreme Court's majority,
> concurring, and dissenting opinions issued July 3, 1989, in
> the case of* Webster v. Reproductive Health Services, *which
> gave the states more authority to impose restrictions on
> abortion:*

No. 88-605

William L. Webster
Attorney General of
Missouri, et al., Appellants

v.

Reproductive Health Services
et al.

On appeal from the United States
Court of Appeals for the Eighth
Circuit

[July 3, 1989]

[CHIEF JUSTICE REHNQUIST delivered the opinion of the Court.]
This appeal concerns the constitutionality of a Missouri statute regulating
the performance of abortions. The United States Court of Appeals for the
Eighth Circuit struck down several provisions of the statute on the ground
that they violated this Court's decision in *Roe* v. *Wade* (1973), and cases
following it. We noted probable jurisdiction ... and now reverse.

I

In June 1986, the Governor of Missouri signed into law Missouri Senate Committee Substitute for House Bill No. 1596 (hereinafter Act or statute), which amended existing state law concerning unborn children and abortions. The Act consisted of 20 provisions, 5 of which are now before the Court. The first provision, or preamble, contains "findings" by the state legislature that "[t]he life of each human being begins at conception," and that "unborn children have protectable interests in life, health, and well-being." The Act further requires that all Missouri laws be interpreted to provide unborn children with the same rights enjoyed by other persons, subject to the Federal Constitution and this Court's precedents. Among its other provisions, the Act requires that, prior to performing an abortion on any woman whom a physician has reason to believe is 20 or more weeks pregnant, the physician ascertain whether the fetus is viable by performing "such medical examinations and tests as are necessary to make a finding of the gestational age, weight, and lung maturity of the unborn child." The Act also prohibits the use of public employees and facilities to perform or assist abortions not necessary to save the mother's life, and it prohibits the use of public funds, employees, or facilities for the purpose of "encouraging or counseling" a woman to have an abortion not necessary to save her life.

In July 1986, five health professionals employed by the State and two nonprofit corporations brought this class action in the United States District Court for the Western District of Missouri to challenge the constitutionality of the Missouri statute. Plaintiffs, appellees in this Court, sought declaratory and injunctive relief on the ground that certain statutory provisions violated the First, Fourth, Ninth, and Fourteenth Amendments to the Federal Constitution. They asserted violations of various rights, including the "privacy rights of pregnant women seeking abortions"; the "woman's right to an abortion"; the "righ[t] to privacy in the physician-patient relationship"; the physician's "righ[t] to practice medicine"; the pregnant woman's "right to life due to inherent risks involved in childbirth"; and the woman's right to "receive . . . adequate medical advice and treatment" concerning abortions.

Plaintiffs filed this suit "on their own behalf and on behalf of the entire class consisting of facilities and Missouri licensed physicians or other health-care professionals offering abortion services or pregnancy counseling and on behalf of the entire class of pregnant females seeking abortion services or pregnancy counseling within the State of Missouri." The two nonprofit corporations are Reproductive Health Services, which offers family planning and gynecological services to the public, including abortion services up to 22 weeks "gestational age," and Planned Parenthood of Kansas City, which provides abortion services up to 14 weeks gestational age. The individual plaintiffs are three physicians, one nurse, and a social worker. All are "public employees" at "public facilities" in Missouri, and they are paid for their services with "public funds," as those terms are defined by Mo. Rev. Stat. § 188.200 (1986). The individual plaintiffs, within the scope of their public employment, encourage and counsel pregnant women to have nontherapeutic abortions. Two of the physicians perform abortions. . . .

II

Decision of this case requires us to address four sections of the Missouri Act: (a) the preamble; (b) the prohibition on the use of public facilities or employees to perform abortions; (c) the prohibition on public funding of abortion counseling; and (d) the requirement that physicians conduct viability tests prior to performing abortions. We address these *seriatim*.

A

. . . The State contends that the preamble itself is precatory and imposes no substantive restrictions on abortions, and that appellees therefore do not have standing to challenge it. Appellees, on the other hand, insist that the preamble is an operative part of the Act intended to guide the interpretation of other provisions of the Act. They maintain, for example, that the preamble's definition of life may prevent physicians in public hospitals from dispensing certain forms of contraceptives, such as the intrauterine device.

. . . It will be time enough for federal courts to address the meaning of the preamble should it be applied to restrict the activities of appellees in some concrete way. Until then, this Court "is not empowered to decide . . . abstract propositions, or to declare, for the government of future cases, principles or rules of law which cannot affect the result as to the thing in issue in the case before it.". . . We therefore need not pass on the constitutionality of the Act's preamble.

B

. . . [The Court of Appeals] reasoned that the ban on the use of public facilities "could prevent a woman's chosen doctor from performing an abortion because of his unprivileged status at other hospitals or because a private hospital adopted a similar anti-abortion stance." It also thought that "[s]uch a rule could increase the cost of obtaining an abortion and delay the timing of it as well."

We think that this analysis is much like that which we rejected in *Maher* [v. *Roe*, 1977], *Poelker* [v. *Doe*, 1977], and [*Harris* v.] *McRae* [1980]. As in those cases, the State's decision here to use public facilities and staff to encourage childbirth over abortion "places no governmental obstacle in the path of a woman who chooses to terminate her pregnancy" (*McRae*). Just as Congress' refusal to fund abortions in *McRae* left "an indigent woman with at least the same range of choice in deciding whether to obtain a medically necessary abortion as she would have had if Congress had chosen to subsidize no health-care costs at all," Missouri's refusal to allow public employees to perform abortions in public hospitals leaves a pregnant woman with the same choices as if the State had chosen not to operate any public hospitals at all. The challenged provisions only restrict a woman's ability to obtain an abortion to the extent that she chooses to use a physician affiliated with a public hospital. This circumstance is more easily remedied, and thus considerably less burdensome, than indigency, which "may make it difficult—and in some cases, perhaps, impossible—for some women to have abortions" without public funding (*Maher*). Having held that the State's refusal to fund abortions does not violate *Roe v. Wade*, it strains logic to reach a contrary result for the use of public facilities and employees. If the State may "make a value judgment favoring childbirth over abortion and ... implement that judgment by the allocation of public funds," surely it may do so through the allocation of other public resources, such as hospitals and medical staff....

Maher, Poelker, and *McRae* all support the view that the State need not commit any resources to facilitating abortions, even if it can turn a profit by doing so. In *Poelker,* the suit was filed by an indigent who could not afford to pay for an abortion, but the ban on the performance of nontherapeutic abortions in city-owned hospitals applied whether or not the pregnant woman could pay. The Court emphasized that the Mayor's decision to prohibit abortions in city hospitals was "subject to public debate and approval or disapproval at the polls," and that "the Constitution does not forbid a state or city, pursuant to democratic processes, from expressing a preference for normal childbirth as St. Louis has done." Thus we uphold the Act's restrictions on the use of public employees and facilities for the performance or assistance of nontherapeutic abortions.

[Section C omitted]

D

Section 188.029 of the Missouri Act provides:

> "Before a physician performs an abortion on a woman he has reason to believe is carrying an unborn child of twenty or more weeks gestational age, the physician shall first determine if the unborn child is viable by using and exercising that degree of care, skill, and proficiency commonly exercised by the ordinarily skillful, careful, and prudent physician engaged in similar practice under the same or similar conditions. In making this determination of viability, the physician shall perform or cause to be performed such medical examinations and tests as are necessary to make a finding of the gestational age, weight, and lung maturity of the unborn child and shall enter such findings and determination of viability in the medical record of the mother."

... The viability-testing provision of the Missouri Act is concerned with promoting the State's interest in potential human life rather than in maternal health. Section 188.029 creates what is essentially a presumption of viability at 20 weeks, which the physician must rebut with tests indicating that the fetus is not viable prior to performing an abortion. It also directs the physician's determination as to viability by specifying consideration, if feasible, of gestational age, fetal weight, and lung capacity. The District Court found that "the medical evidence is uncontradicted that a 20-week fetus is *not* viable," and that "23½ to 24 weeks gestation is the earliest point in pregnancy where a reasonable possibility of viability exists." But it also found that there may be a 4-week error in estimating gestational age, which supports testing at 20 weeks.

In *Roe v. Wade,* the Court recognized that the State has "important and legitimate" interests in protecting maternal health and in the potentiality of human life. During the second trimester, the State "may, if it chooses, regulate the abortion procedure in ways that are reasonably related to maternal health." After viability, when the State's interest in potential human life was held to become compelling, the State "may, if it chooses, regulate, and even proscribe, abortion except where it is necessary, in appropriate medical judgment, for the preservation of the life or health of the mother."

In *Colautti* v. *Franklin,* [1979], upon which appellees rely, the Court held that a Pennsylvania statute regulating the standard of care to be used by a physician performing an abortion of a possibly viable fetus was void for vagueness. But in the course of reaching that conclusion, the Court reaffirmed its earlier statement in *Planned Parenthood of Central Missouri* v. *Danforth* (1976), that " 'the determination of whether a particular fetus is viable is, and must be, a matter for the judgment of the responsible attending physician.' " The dissent ignores the statement in *Colautti* that "neither the legislature nor the courts may proclaim one of the elements entering into the ascertainment of viability—be it weeks of gestation or fetal weight or any other single factor—as the determinant of when the State has a compelling interest in the life or health of the fetus." To the extent that § 188.029 regulates the method for determining viability, it undoubtedly does superimpose state regulation on the medical determination of whether a particular fetus is viable. The Court of Appeals and the District Court thought it unconstitutional for this reason. To the extent that the viability tests increase the cost of what are in fact second trimester abortions, their validity may also be questioned under *Akron,* . . . where the Court held that a requirement that second trimester abortions must be performed in hospitals was invalid because it substantially increased the expense of those procedures.

We think that the doubt cast upon the Missouri statute by these cases is not so much a flaw in the statute as it is a reflection of the fact that the rigid trimester analysis of the course of a pregnancy enunciated in *Roe* has resulted in subsequent cases like *Colautti* and *Akron* making constitutional law in this area a virtual Procrustean bed. Statutes specifying elements of informed consent to be provided abortion patients, for example, were invalidated if they were thought to "structur[e] . . . the dialogue between the woman and her physician." *Thornburgh* v. *American College of Obstetricians and Gynecologists* (1986). As the dissenters in *Thornburgh* pointed out, such a statute would have been sustained . . . for any other surgical procedure except abortion.

Stare decisis is a cornerstone of our legal system, but it has less power in constitutional cases, where, save for constitutional amendments, this Court is the only body able to make needed changes. . . . We have not refrained from reconsideration of a prior construction of the Constitution that has proved "unsound in principle and unworkable in practice."... We think the *Roe* trimester framework falls into that category.

In the first place, the rigid *Roe* framework is hardly consistent with the notion of a Constitution cast in general terms, as ours is, and usually speaking in general principles, as ours does. The key elements of the *Roe* framework—trimesters and viability—are not found in the text of the Constitution or in any place else one would expect to find a constitutional principle. Since the bounds of the inquiry are essentially indeterminate, the result has been a web of legal rules that have become increasingly intricate, resembling a code of regulations rather than a body of constitutional doctrine. As JUSTICE WHITE has put it, the trimester framework has left this Court to serve as the country's "*ex officio* medical board with powers to approve or disapprove medical and operative practices and standards throughout the United States."...

In the second place, we do not see why the State's interest in protecting potential human life should come into existence only at the point of viability, and that there should therefore be a rigid line allowing state regulation after viability but prohibiting it before viability. The dissenters in *Thornburgh,* writing in the context of the *Roe* trimester analysis, would have recognized this fact by positing against the "fundamental right" recognized in *Roe* the State's "compelling interest" in protecting potential human life throughout pregnancy. "[T]he State's interest, if compelling after viability, is equally compelling before viability."...

The tests that § 188.029 requires the physician to perform are designed to determine viability. The State here has chosen viability as the point at which its interest in potential human life must be safeguarded. See Mo. Rev. Stat. § 188.030 (1986) ("No abortion of a viable unborn child shall be performed unless necessary to preserve the life or health of the woman"). It is true that the tests in question increase the expense of abortion, and regulate the discretion of the physician in determining the viability of the fetus. Since the test will undoubtedly show in many cases that the fetus is not viable, the tests will have been performed for what were in fact second-trimester abortions. But we are satisfied that the requirement of these tests permissibly furthers the State's interest in protecting potential human life, and we therefore believe § 188.029 to be constitutional.

The dissent takes us to task for our failure to join in a "great issues" debate as to whether the Constitution includes an "unenumerated" general right to privacy as recognized in cases such as *Griswold* v. *Connecticut* [1965] ... and *Roe.* But *Griswold* v. *Connecticut,* unlike *Roe,* did not purport to adopt a whole framework, complete with detailed rules and distinctions, to govern the cases in which the asserted liberty interest would apply. As such, it was far different from the opinion, if not the holding, of *Roe* v. *Wade,* which sought to establish a constitutional framework for judging state regulation of abortion during the entire term of pregnancy. That framework sought to deal with areas of medical practice traditionally subject to state regulation, and it sought to balance once and for all by reference only to the calendar the claims of the State to protect the fetus as a form of human life against the claims of a woman to decide for herself whether or not to abort a fetus she was carrying. The experience of the Court in applying *Roe* v. *Wade* in later cases, suggests to us that there is wisdom in not unnecessarily attempting to elaborate the abstract differences between a "fundamental right" to abortion, as the Court described it in *Akron*, a "limited fundamental constitutional right," which JUSTICE BLACKMUN's dissent today treats *Roe* as having established, or a liberty interest protected by the Due Process Clause, which we believe it to be. The Missouri testing requirement here is reasonably designed to ensure that abortions are not performed where the fetus is viable—an end which all concede is legitimate—and that is sufficient to sustain its constitutionality.

The dissent also accuses us, *inter alia,* of cowardice and illegitimacy in dealing with "the most politically divisive domestic legal issue of our time." There is no doubt that our holding today will allow some governmental regulation of abortion that would have been prohibited under the language of cases such as *Colautti* v. *Franklin*, and *Akron* v. *Akron Center for Reproductive Health, Inc.* [1983]. But the goal of constitutional adjudication is surely not to remove inexorably "politically divisive" issues from the ambit of the legislative process, whereby the people through their elected representatives deal with matters of concern to them. The goal of constitutional adjudication is to hold true the balance between that which the Constitution puts beyond the reach of the democratic process and that which it does not. We think we have done that today. The dissent's suggestion, that legislative bodies, in a Nation where more than half of our population is women, will treat our decision today as an invitation to enact abortion regulation reminiscent of the dark ages not only misreads our views but does scant justice to those who serve in such bodies and the people who elect them.

III

Both appellants and the United States as *Amicus Curiae* have urged that we overrule our decision in *Roe* v. *Wade.* The facts of the present case, however, differ from those at issue in *Roe.* Here, Missouri has determined that viability is the point at which its interest in potential human life must be safeguarded. In *Roe,* on the other hand, the Texas statute criminalized the performance of *all* abortions, except when the mother's life was at stake. .... This case therefore affords us no occasion to revisit the holding of *Roe,* which was that the Texas statute unconstitutionally infringed the right to an abortion derived from the Due Process Clause, and we leave it undisturbed. To the extent indicated in our opinion, we would modify and narrow *Roe* and succeeding cases.

Because none of the challenged provisions of the Missouri Act properly before us conflict with the Constitution, the judgment of the Court of Appeals is

Reversed.

I

JUSTICE O'CONNOR, concurring in part and concurring in the judgment.

... "[I]t seems to me to follow directly from our previous decisions concerning state or federal funding of abortions, *Harris* v. *McRae* (1980), *Maher* v. *Roe* (1977), and *Poelker* v. *Doe* (1977), that appellees' facial challenge to the constitutionality of Missouri's ban on the utilization of public facilities and the participation of public employees in the performance of abortions not necessary to save the life of the mother cannot succeed. Given Missouri's definition of "public facility" as "any public institution, public facility, public equipment, or any physical asset owned, leased, or controlled by this state or any agency or political subdivisions thereof," there may be conceivable applications of the ban on the use of public facilities that would be unconstitutional. Appellees and *amici* suggest that the State could try to enforce the ban against private hospitals using public water and sewage lines, or against private hospitals leasing state-owned equipment or state land. Whether some or all of these or other applications of § 188.215 would be constitutional need not be decided here. *Maher, Poelker,* and *McRae* stand for the proposition that some quite straightforward applications of the Missouri ban on the use of public facilities for performing abortions would be constitutional and that is enough to defeat appellees' assertion that the ban is facially unconstitutional. "A facial challenge to a legislative Act is, of course, the most difficult challenge to mount successfully, since the challenger must establish that no set of circumstances exists under which the Act would be valid. The fact that the [relevant statute] might operate unconstitutionally is insufficient to render it wholly invalid, since we have not recognized an 'overbreadth' doctrine outside the limited context of the First Amendment.". . .

II

In its interpretation of Missouri's "determination of viability" provision ... the plurality has proceeded in a manner unnecessary to deciding the question at hand. I agree with the plurality that it was plain error for the Court of Appeals to interpret the second sentence of Mo. Rev. Stat. § 188.029 as meaning that "doctors *must* perform tests to find gestational age, fetal weight and lung maturity.". . . When read together with the first sentence of § 188.029—which requires a physician to "determine if the unborn child is viable by using and exercising that degree of care, skill, and proficiency commonly exercised by the ordinary skillful, careful, and prudent physician engaged in similar practice under the same or similar conditions"—it would be contradictory nonsense to read the second sentence as requiring a physician to perform viability examinations and tests in situations where it would be careless and imprudent to do so. The plurality is quite correct: "the viability-testing provision makes sense only if the second sentence is read to require only those tests that are useful to making subsidiary findings as to viability," and, I would add, only those examinations and tests that it would not be imprudent or careless to perform in the particular medical situation before the physician.

Unlike the plurality, I do not understand these viability-testing requirements to conflict with any of the Court's past decisions concerning state regulation of abortion. Therefore, there is no necessity to accept the State's invitation to re-examine the constitutional validity of *Roe* v. *Wade*. Where there is no need to decide a constitutional question, it is a venerable principle of this Court's adjudicatory processes not to do so for "[t]he court will not 'anticipate a question of constitutional law in advance of the necessity of deciding it.' ".... The Court today has accepted the State's every interpretation of its abortion statute and has upheld, under our existing precedents, every provision of that statute which is properly before us. Precisely for this reason reconsideration of *Roe* falls not into any "good-cause exception" to this "fundamental rule of judicial restraint...."
... When the constitutional invalidity of a State's abortion statute actually turns on the constitutional validity of *Roe* v. *Wade,* there will be time enough to reexamine *Roe.* And to do so carefully....

It is clear to me that requiring the performance of examinations and tests useful to determining whether a fetus is viable, when viability is possible, and when it would not be medically imprudent to do so, does not impose an undue burden on a woman's abortion decision. On this ground alone I would reject the suggestion that § 188.029 as interpreted is unconstitutional. More to the point, however, just as I see no conflict between § 188.029 and *Colautti* or any decision of this Court concerning a State's ability to give effect to its interest in potential life, I see no conflict between § 188.029 and the Court's opinion in *Akron.* The second-trimester hospitalization requirement struck down in *Akron* imposed, in the majority's view, "a heavy, and unnecessary, burden," more than doubling the cost of "women's access to a relatively inexpensive, otherwise accessible, and safe abortion procedure." By contrast, the cost of examinations and tests that could usefully and prudently be performed when a woman is 20-24 weeks pregnant to determine whether the fetus is viable would only marginally, if at all, increase the cost of an abortion. See Brief for American Association of Prolife Obstetricians and Gynecologists et al. as *Amici Curiae* 3 ("At twenty weeks gestation, an ultrasound examination to determine gestational age is standard medical practice. It is routinely provided by the plaintiff clinics. An ultrasound examination can effectively provide all three designated findings of sec. 188.029")....

Moreover, the examinations and tests required by § 188.029 are to be performed when viability is possible. This feature of § 188.029 distinguishes it from the second-trimester hospitalization requirement struck down by the *Akron* majority. As the Court recognized in *Thornburgh,* the State's compelling interest in potential life postviability renders its interest in determining the critical point of viability equally compelling. Under the Court's precedents, the same cannot be said for the *Akron* second-trimester hospitalization requirement. As I understand the

Court's opinion in *Akron,* therefore, the plurality's suggestion today that *Akron* casts doubt on the validity of § 188.029, even as the Court has interpreted it, is without foundation and cannot provide a basis for reevaluating *Roe.* Accordingly, because the Court of Appeals misinterpreted Mo. Rev. Stat. § 188.029, and because, properly interpreted, § 188.029 is not inconsistent with any of this Court's prior precedents, I would reverse the decision of the Court of Appeals. . . .

JUSTICE SCALIA, concurring in part and concurring in the judgment.
. . . The outcome of today's case will doubtless be heralded as a triumph of judicial statesmanship. It is not that, unless it is statesmanlike needlessly to prolong this Court's self-awarded sovereignty over a field where it has little proper business since the answers to most of the cruel questions posed are political and not juridical—a sovereignty which therefore quite properly, but to the great damage of the Court, makes it the object of the sort of organized public pressure that political institutions in a democracy ought to receive.

Justice O'Connor's assertion, that a " 'fundamental rule of judicial restraint' " requires us to avoid reconsidering *Roe,* cannot be taken seriously. By finessing *Roe* we do not, as she suggests, adhere to the strict and venerable rule that we should avoid " 'decid[ing] questions of a constitutional nature.' " We have not disposed of this case on some statutory or procedural ground, but have decided, and could not avoid deciding, whether the Missouri statute meets the requirements of the United States Constitution. The only choice available is whether, in deciding that constitutional question, we should use *Roe* v. *Wade* as the benchmark, or something else. What is involved, therefore, is not the rule of avoiding constitutional issues where possible, but the quite separate principle that we will not " 'formulate a rule of constitutional law broader than is required by the precise facts to which it is to be applied.' " The latter is a sound general principle, but one often departed from when good reason exists. . . .

The real question, then, is whether there are valid reasons to go beyond the most stingy possible holding today. It seems to me there are not only valid but compelling ones. Ordinarily, speaking no more broadly than is absolutely required avoids throwing settled law into confusion; doing so today preserves a chaos that is evident to anyone who can read and count. Alone sufficient to justify a broad holding is the fact that our retaining control, through *Roe,* of what I believe to be, and many of our citizens recognize to be, a political issue, continuously distorts the public perception of the role of this Court. We can now look forward to at least another Term with carts full of mail from the public, and streets full of demonstrators, urging us—their unelected and life-tenured judges who have been awarded those extraordinary, undemocratic characteristics precisely in order that we might follow the law despite the popular will—to follow the popular will. Indeed, I expect we can look forward to even more of that than before, given our indecisive decision today. And if these reasons for taking the unexceptional course of reaching a broader holding are not enough, then consider the nature of the constitutional question we avoid: In most cases, we do no harm by not speaking more broadly than the decision requires. Anyone affected by the conduct that the avoided holding would have prohibited will be able to challenge it himself, and have his day in court to make the argument. Not so with respect to the harm that many States believed, pre-*Roe*, and many may continue to believe, is caused by largely unrestricted abortion. That will continue to occur if the States have the constitutional power to prohibit it, and would do so, but we skillfully avoid telling them so. Perhaps those abortions cannot constitutionally be proscribed. That is surely an arguable question, the question that reconsideration of *Roe* v. *Wade* entails. But what is not at all arguable, it seems to me, is that we should decide now and not insist that we be run into a corner before we grudgingly yield up our judgment. The only sound reason for the latter course is to prevent a change in the law—but to think that desirable begs the question to be decided.

It was an arguable question today whether § 188.029 of the Missouri law contravened this Court's understanding of *Roe* v. *Wade*, and I would have examined *Roe* rather than examining the contravention. Given the Court's newly contracted abstemiousness, what will it take, one must wonder, to permit us to reach that fundamental question? The result of our vote today is that we will not reconsider that prior opinion, even if most of the Justices think it is wrong, unless we have before us a statute that in fact contradicts it—and even then (under our newly discovered "no-broader-than-necessary" requirement) only minor problematical aspects of *Roe* will be reconsidered, unless one expects State legislatures to adopt provisions whose compliance with *Roe* cannot even be argued with a straight face. It thus appears that the mansion of constitutionalized abortion law, constructed overnight in *Roe* v. *Wade*, must be disassembled doorjamb by doorjamb, and never entirely brought down, no matter how wrong it may be.

Of the four courses we might have chosen today—to reaffirm *Roe*, to overrule it explicitly, to overrule it *sub silentio*, or to avoid the question—the last is the least responsible. On the question of the constitutionality of § 188.029, I concur in the judgment of the Court and strongly dissent from the manner in which it has been reached.

JUSTICE BLACKMUN, With whom JUSTICE BRENNAN and JUSTICE MARSHALL join, concurring in part and dissenting in part.

Today, *Roe* v. *Wade* (1983) and the fundamental constitutional right of women to decide whether to terminate a pregnancy, survive but are not secure. Although the Court extricates itself from this case without making a single, even incremental, change in the law of abortion, the plurality and Justice Scalia would overrule *Roe* (the first silently, the other explicitly) and would return to the States virtually unfettered authority to control the quintessentially intimate, personal, and life-directing decision whether to carry a fetus to term. Although today, no less than yesterday, the Constitution and the decision of this Court prohibit a State from enacting laws that inhibit women from the meaningful exercise of that right, a plurality of this Court implicitly invites every state legislature to enact more and more restrictive abortion regulations in order to provoke more and more test cases, in the hope that sometime down the line the Court will return the law of procreative freedom to the severe limitations that generally prevailed in this country before January 22, 1973. Never in my memory has a plurality announced a judgment of this Court that so foments disregard for the law and our standing decisions.

Nor in my memory has a plurality gone about its business in such a deceptive fashion. At every level of its review, from its effort to read the real meaning out of the Missouri statute, to its intended evisceration of precedents and its deafening silence about the constitutional protections that it would jettison, the plurality obscures the portent of its analysis. With feigned restraint, the plurality announces that its analysis leaves *Roe* "undisturbed," albeit "modif[ied] and narrow[ed]." But this disclaimer is totally meaningless. The plurality opinion is filled with winks, and nods, and knowing glances to those who would do away with *Roe* explicitly, but turns a stone face to anyone in search of what the plurality conceives as the scope of a woman's right under the Due Process Clause to terminate a pregnancy free from the coercive and brooding influence of the State. The simple truth is that *Roe* would not survive the plurality's analysis, and that the plurality provides no substitute for *Roe*'s protective umbrella.

I fear for the future. I fear for the liberty and equality of the millions of women who have lived and come of age in the 16 years since *Roe* was decided. I fear for the integrity of, and public esteem for, this Court.

I dissent.

I

... In the plurality's view, the viability-testing provision imposes a burden on second-trimester abortions as a way of furthering the State's interest in protecting the potential life of the fetus. Since under the *Roe* framework, the State may not fully regulate abortion in the interest of potential life (as opposed to maternal health) until the third trimester, the plurality finds it necessary, in order to save the Missouri testing provision, to throw out *Roe*'s trimester framework. In flat contradiction to *Roe,* the plurality concludes that the State's interest in potential life is compelling before viability, and upholds the testing provision because it "permissibly furthers" that state interest.

A

At the outset, I note that in its haste to limit abortion rights, the plurality compounds the errors of its analysis by needlessly reaching out to address constitutional questions that are not actually presented. The conflict between § 188.029 and *Roe*'s trimester framework, which purportedly drives the plurality to reconsider our past decisions, is a contrived conflict: the product of an aggressive misreading of the viability-testing requirement and a needlessly wooden application of the *Roe* framework. . . .

Had the plurality read the statute as written, it would have had no cause to reconsider the *Roe* framework. As properly construed, the viability-testing provision does not pass constitutional muster under even a rational-basis standard, the least restrictive level of review applied by this Court. . . . By mandating tests to determine fetal weight and lung maturity for every fetus thought to be more than 20 weeks gestational age, the statute requires physicians to undertake procedures, such as amniocentesis, that, in the situation presented, have no medical justification, impose significant additional health risks on both the pregnant woman and the fetus, and bear no rational relation to the State's interest in protecting fetal life. As written, § 188.029 is an arbitrary imposition of discomfort, risk, and expense, furthering no discernible interest except to make the procurement of an abortion as arduous and difficult as possible. Thus, were it not for the plurality's tortured effort to avoid the plain import of § 188.029, it could have struck down the testing provision as patently irrational irrespective of the *Roe* framework.

The plurality eschews this straightforward resolution, in the hope of precipitating a constitutional crisis. Far from avoiding constitutional difficulty, the plurality attempts to engineer a dramatic retrenchment in our jurisprudence by exaggerating the conflict between its untenable construction of § 188.029 and the *Roe* trimester framework.

No one contests that under the *Roe* framework the State, in order to promote its interest in potential human life, may regulate and even proscribe nontherapeutic abortions once the fetus becomes viable. . . . If, as the plurality appears to hold, the testing provision simply requires a physician to use appropriate and medically sound tests to determine whether the fetus is actually viable when the estimated gestational age is greater than 20 weeks (and therefore within what the District Court found to be the margin of error for viability), then I see little or no conflict with *Roe*. Nothing in *Roe*, or any of its progeny, holds that a State may not effectuate its compelling interest in the potential life of a viable fetus by seeking to ensure that no viable fetus is mistakenly aborted because of the inherent lack of precision in estimates of gestational age. A requirement that a physician make a finding of viability, one way or the other, for every fetus that falls within the range of possible viability does no more than preserve the State's recognized authority. Although, as the plurality correctly points out, such a testing requirement would have the effect of imposing additional costs on second-trimester abortions where the tests indicated that the fetus was not viable, these costs would be merely incidental to, and a necessary accommodation of, the State's unquestioned right to prohibit non-therapeutic abortions after the point of viability. In short, the testing provision, as construed by the plurality is consistent with the *Roe* framework and could be upheld effortlessly under current doctrine.

How ironic it is, then, and disingenuous, that the plurality scolds the

Court of Appeals for adopting a construction of the statute that fails to avoid constitutional difficulties. By distorting the statute, the plurality manages to avoid invalidating the testing provision on what should have been noncontroversial constitutional grounds; having done so, however, the plurality rushes headlong into a much deeper constitutional thicket, brushing past an obvious basis for upholding § 188.029 in search of a pretext for scuttling the trimester framework. Evidently, from the plurality's perspective, the real problem with the Court of Appeals' construction of § 188.029 is not that it raised a constitutional difficulty, but that it raised the wrong constitutional difficulty—one not implicating *Roe*. The plurality has remedied that, traditional canons of construction and judicial forbearance notwithstanding.

B

Having set up the conflict between § 188.029 and the *Roe* trimester framework, the plurality summarily discards *Roe*'s analytic core as " 'unsound in principle and unworkable in practice.' "... This is so, the plurality claims, because the key elements of the framework do not appear in the text of the Constitution, because the framework more closely resembles a regulatory code than a body of constitutional doctrine, and because under the framework the State's interest in potential human life is considered compelling only after viability, when, in fact, that interest is equally compelling throughout pregnancy. The plurality does not bother to explain these alleged flaws in *Roe*. Bald assertion masquerades as reasoning. The object, quite clearly, is not to persuade, but to prevail.

1

The plurality opinion is far more remarkable for the arguments that it does not advance than for those that it does. The plurality does not even mention, much less join, the true jurisprudential debate underlying this case: whether the Constitution includes an "unenumerated" general right to privacy as recognized in many of our decisions, most notably *Griswold* v. *Connecticut* (1965), and *Roe*, and, more specifically, whether and to what extent such a right to privacy extends to matters of childbearing and family life, including abortion.... These are questions of unsurpassed significance in this Court's interpretation of the Constitution, and mark the battleground upon which this case was fought, by the parties, by the Solicitor General as *amicus* on behalf of petitioners, and by an unprecedented number of *amici*. On these grounds, abandoned by the plurality, the Court should decide this case.

But rather than arguing that the text of the Constitution makes no mention of the right to privacy, the plurality complains that the critical elements of the *Roe* framework—trimesters and viability—do not appear in the Constitution and are, therefore, somehow inconsistent with a Constitution cast in general terms. Were this a true concern, we would have to abandon most of our constitutional jurisprudence. As the plurality well knows, or should know, the "critical elements" of countless constitutional doctrines nowhere appear in the Constitution's text. The Constitution makes no mention, for example, of the First Amendment's "actual malice" standard for proving certain libels, see *New York Times* v. *Sullivan* (1964), or of the standard for determining when speech is obscene. See *Miller* v. *California* (1973). Similarly, the Constitution makes no mention of the rational-basis test, or the specific verbal formulations of intermediate and strict scrutiny by which this Court evaluates claims under the Equal Protection Clause. The reason is simple. Like the *Roe* framework, these tests or standards are not, and do not purport to be, rights protected by the Constitution. Rather, they are judge-made methods for evaluating and measuring the strength and scope of constitutional rights or for balancing the constitutional rights of individuals against the competing interests of government.

With respect to the *Roe* framework, the general constitutional principle, indeed the fundamental constitutional right, for which it was developed is the right to privacy, a species of "liberty" protected by the Due Process Clause, which under our past decisions safeguards the right of women to exercise some control over their own role in procreation. As we recently reaffirmed in *Thornburgh* v. *American College of Obstetricians and Gynecologists,* few decisions are "more basic to individual dignity and autonomy" or more appropriate to that "certain private sphere of individual liberty" that the Constitution reserves from the intrusive reach of government than the right to make the uniquely personal, intimate, and self-defining decision whether to end a pregnancy. It is this general principle, the " 'moral fact that a person belongs to himself and not others nor to society as a whole,' " that is found in the Constitution. The trimester framework simply defines and limits that right to privacy in the abortion context to accommodate, not destroy, a State's legitimate interest in protecting the health of pregnant women and in preserving potential human life. Fashioning such accommodations between individual rights and the legitimate interests of government, establishing benchmarks and standards with which to evaluate the competing claims of individuals and government, lies at the very heart of constitutional adjudication. To the extent that the trimester framework is useful in this enterprise, it is not only consistent with constitutional interpretation, but necessary to the wise and just exercise of this Court's paramount authority to define the scope of constitutional rights.

2

The plurality next alleges that the result of the trimester framework has "been a web of legal rules that have become increasingly intricate, resembling a code of regulations rather than a body of constitutional doctrine." Again, if this were a true and genuine concern, we would have to abandon vast areas of our constitutional jurisprudence. . . .

That numerous constitutional doctrines result in narrow differentiations between similar circumstances does not mean that this Court has abandoned adjudication in favor of regulation. Rather, these careful distinctions reflect the process of constitutional adjudication itself, which is often highly fact-specific, requiring such determinations as whether state laws are "unduly burdensome" or "reasonable" or bear a "rational" or "necessary" relation to asserted state interests. . . .

. . . If, in delicate and complicated areas of constitutional law, our legal judgments "have become increasingly intricate," it is not, as the plurality contends, because we have overstepped our judicial role. Quite the opposite: the rules are intricate because we have remained conscientious in our duty to do justice carefully, especially when fundamental rights rise or fall with our decisions.

3

Finally, the plurality asserts that the trimester framework cannot stand because the State's interest in potential life is compelling throughout pregnancy, not merely after viability. The opinion contains not one word of rationale for its view of the State's interest. This "it-is-so-because-we-say-so" jurisprudence constitutes nothing other than an attempted exercise of brute force; reason, much less persuasion, has no place. . . .

For my own part, I remain convinced, as six other Members of this Court 16 years ago were convinced, that the *Roe* framework, and the viability standard in particular, fairly, sensibly, and effectively functions to safeguard the constitutional liberties of pregnant women while recognizing and accommodating the State's interest in potential human life. The viability line reflects the biological facts and truths of fetal development; it marks that threshold moment prior to which a fetus cannot survive separate from the woman and cannot reasonably and objectively be regarded as a subject of rights or interests distinct from, or paramount to, those of the pregnant woman. At the same time, the viability standard takes account of the undeniable fact that as the fetus evolves into its postnatal form, and as it loses its dependence on the uterine environment, the State's interest in the fetus' potential human life, and in fostering a regard for human life in general, becomes compelling. As a practical matter, because viability follows "quickening"—the point at which a woman feels movement in her womb—and because viability occurs no earlier than 23 weeks gestational age, it establishes an easily applicable standard for regulating abortion while providing a pregnant woman ample time to exercise her fundamental right with her responsible physician to terminate her pregnancy. Although I have stated previously for a majority of this Court that "[c]onstitutional rights do not always have easily ascertainable boundaries," to seek and establish those boundaries remains the special responsibility of this Court. In *Roe*, we discharged that responsibility as logic and science compelled. The plurality today advances not one reasonable argument as to why our judgment in that case was wrong and should be abandoned.

C

Having contrived an opportunity to reconsider the *Roe* framework, and then having discarded that framework, the plurality finds the testing provision unobjectionable because it "permissibly furthers the State's interest in protecting potential human life." This newly minted standard is circular and totally meaningless. Whether a challenged abortion regulation "permissibly furthers" a legitimate state interest is the *question* that courts must answer in abortion cases, not the standard for courts to apply. In keeping with the rest of its opinion, the plurality makes no attempt to explain or to justify its new standard, either in the abstract or as applied in this case. Nor could it. The "permissibly furthers" standard has no independent meaning, and consists of nothing other than what a majority of this Court may believe at any given moment in any given case. The plurality's novel test appears to be nothing more than a dressed-up version of rational-basis review, this Court's most lenient level of scrutiny. One thing is clear, however: were the plurality's "permissibly furthers" standard adopted by the Court, for all practical purposes, *Roe* would be overruled.

The "permissibly furthers" standard completely disregards the irreducible minimum of *Roe:* the Court's recognition that a woman has a limited fundamental constitutional right to decide whether to terminate a pregnancy. That right receives no meaningful recognition in the plurality's written opinion. Since, in the plurality's view, the State's interest in potential life is compelling as of the moment of conception, and is therefore served only if abortion is abolished, every hindrance to a woman's ability to obtain an abortion must be "permissible." Indeed, the more severe the hindrance, the more effectively (and permissibly) the State's interest would be furthered. A tax on abortions or a criminal prohibition would both satisfy the plurality's standard. So, for that matter, would a requirement that a pregnant woman memorize and recite today's plurality opinion before seeking an abortion.

The plurality pretends that *Roe* survives, explaining that the facts of this case differ from those in *Roe:* here, Missouri has chosen to assert its interest in potential life only at the point of viability, whereas, in *Roe,* Texas has asserted that interest from the point of conception, criminalizing all abortions, except where the life of the mother was at stake. This, of course, is a distinction without a difference. The plurality repudiates every principle for which *Roe* stands; in good conscience, it cannot possibly believe that *Roe* lies "undisturbed" merely because this case does not call upon the Court to reconsider the Texas statute, or one like it. If the Constitution permits a State to enact any statute that reasonably furthers its interest in potential life, and if that interest arises as of conception, why would the Texas statute fail to pass muster? One suspects that the plurality agrees. It is impossible to read the plurality opinion and especially its final paragraph, without recognizing its implicit invitation to every State to enact more and more restrictive abortion laws, and to assert their interest in potential life as of the moment of conception. All these laws will satisfy the plurality's non-scrutiny, until sometime, a new regime of old dissenters and new appointees will declare what the plurality intends: that *Roe* is no longer good law.

D

Thus, "not with a bang, but with a whimper," the plurality discards a landmark case of the last generation, and casts into darkness the hopes and visions of every woman in this country who had come to believe that the Constitution guaranteed her the right to exercise some control over her unique ability to bear children. The plurality does so either oblivious or insensitive to the fact that millions of women, and their families, have ordered their lives around the right to reproductive choice, and that this right has become vital to the full participation of women in the economic and political walks of American life. The plurality would clear the way once again for government to force upon women the physical labor and specific and direct medical and psychological harms that may accompany carrying a fetus to term. The plurality would clear the way again for the State to conscript a woman's body and force upon her a "distressful life and future."

The result, as we know from experience, . . . would be that every year hundreds of thousands of women, in desperation, would defy the law, and place their health and safety in the unclean and unsympathetic hands of back-alley abortionists, or they would attempt to perform abortions upon themselves, with disastrous results. Every year, many women, especially poor and minority women, would die or suffer debilitating physical trauma, all in the name of enforced morality or religious dictates or lack of compassion, as it may be.

Of the aspirations and settled understandings of American women, of the inevitable and brutal consequences of what it is doing, the tough-approach plurality utters not a word. This silence is callous. It is also profoundly destructive of this Court as an institution. To overturn a constitutional decision is a rare and grave undertaking. To overturn a constitutional decision that secured a fundamental personal liberty to millions of persons would be unprecedented in our 200 years of constitutional history. Although the doctrine of *stare decisis* applies with somewhat diminished force in constitutional cases generally, even in ordinary constitutional cases "any departure from *stare decisis* demands special justification.". . . This requirement of justification applies with unique force where, as here, the Court's abrogation of precedent would destroy people's firm belief, based on past decisions of this Court, that they possess an unabridgeable right to undertake certain conduct.

As discussed at perhaps too great length above, the plurality makes no serious attempt to carry "the heavy burden of persuading . . . that changes in society or in the law dictate" the abandonment of *Roe* and its numerous progeny, *Vasquez* [v. *Hillery*, 1986], much less the greater burden of explaining the abrogation of a fundamental personal freedom. Instead, the plurality pretends that it leaves *Roe* standing, and refuses even to discuss the real issue underlying this case: whether the Constitution includes an unenumerated right to privacy that encompasses a woman's right to decide whether to terminate a pregnancy. To the extent that the plurality does criticize the *Roe* framework, these criticisms are pure *ipse dixit*.

This comes at a cost. The doctrine of *stare decisis* "permits society to presume that bedrock principles are founded in the law rather than in the proclivities of individuals, and thereby contributes to the integrity of our constitutional system of government, both in appearance and in fact.".... Today's decision involves the most politically divisive domestic legal issue of our time. By refusing to explain or to justify its proposed revolutionary revision in the law of abortion, and by refusing to abide not only by our precedents, but also by our canons for reconsidering those precedents, the plurality invites charges of cowardice and illegitimacy to our door. I cannot say that these would be undeserved.

II

For today, at least, the law of abortion stands undisturbed. For today, the women of this Nation still retain the liberty to control their destinies. But the signs are evident and very ominous, and a chill wind blows.

I dissent.

JUSTICE STEVENS, concurring in part and dissenting in part.

I

It seems to me that in Part II-D of its opinion, the plurality strains to place a construction on § 188.029 that enables it to conclude, "[W]e would modify and narrow *Roe* and succeeding cases." That statement is ill-advised because there is no need to modify even slightly the holdings of prior cases in order to uphold § 188.029. For the most plausible nonliteral construction, as both JUSTICE BLACKMUN ... and JUSTICE O'CONNOR ... have demonstrated, is constitutional and entirely consistent with our precedents.

I am unable to accept JUSTICE O'CONNOR's construction of the second sentence in § 188.029, however, because I believe it is foreclosed by two controlling principles of statutory interpretation. First, it is our settled practice to accept "the interpretation of state law in which the District Court and the Court of Appeals have concurred even if an examination of the state-law issue without such guidance might have justified a different conclusion.".... Second, "[t]he fact that a particular application of the clear terms of a statute might be unconstitutional does not provide us with a justification for ignoring the plain meaning of the statute.".... In this case, I agree with the Court of Appeals, ... and the District Court, ... that the meaning of the second sentence of § 188.029 is too plain to be ignored. The sentence twice uses the mandatory term "shall," and contains no qualifying language. If it is implicitly limited to tests that are useful in determining viability, it adds nothing to the requirement imposed by the preceding sentence.

My interpretation of the plain language is supported by the structure of the statute as a whole, particularly the preamble, which "finds" that life "begins at conception" and further commands that state laws shall be construed to provide the maximum protection to "the unborn child at every stage of development." I agree with the District Court that "[o]bviously, the purpose of this law is to protect the potential life of the fetus, rather than to safeguard maternal health.". . . A literal reading of the statute tends to accomplish that goal. Thus it is not "incongruous" to assume that the Missouri Legislature was trying to protect the potential human life of nonviable fetuses by making the abortion decision more costly. On the contrary, I am satisfied that the Court of Appeals, as well as the District Court, correctly concluded that the Missouri Legislature meant exactly what it said in the second sentence of § 188.029. I am also satisfied, for the reasons stated by JUSTICE BLACKMUN, that the testing provision is manifestly unconstitutional. . . .

II

The Missouri statute defines "conception" as "the fertilization of the ovum of a female by a sperm of a male," even though standard medical texts equate "conception" with implantation in the uterus, occurring about six days after fertilization. Missouri's declaration therefore implies regulation not only of previability abortions, but also of common forms of contraception such as the IUD and the morning-after pill. Because the preamble, read in context, threatens serious encroachments upon the liberty of the pregnant woman and the health professional, I am persuaded that these plaintiffs, appellees before us, have standing to challenge its constitutionality.

To the extent that the Missouri statute interferes with contraceptive choices, I have no doubt that it is unconstitutional under the Court's holdings in *Griswold* v. *Connecticut* (1965). *Eisenstadt* v. *Baird* (1972), and *Carey* v. *Population Services International* (1977). . . .

One might argue that the *Griswold* holding applies to devices "preventing conception," . . . that is, fertilization—but not to those preventing implantation, and therefore, that *Griswold* does not protect a woman's choice to use an IUD or take a morning-after pill. There is unquestionably a theological basis for such an argument, just as there was unquestionably a theological basis for the Connecticut statute that the Court invalidated in *Griswold*. Our jurisprudence, however, has consistently required a secular basis for valid legislation. . . . Because I am not aware of any secular basis for differentiating between contraceptive procedures that are effective immediately before and those that are effective immediately after fertilization, I believe it inescapably follows that the preamble to the Missouri statute is invalid under *Griswold* and its progeny.

Indeed, I am persuaded that the absence of any secular purpose for the legislative declarations that life begins at conception and that conception occurs at fertilization makes the relevant portion of the preamble invalid under the Establishment Clause of the First Amendment to the Federal Constitution. This conclusion does not, and could not, rest on the fact that the statement happens to coincide with the tenets of certain religions, . . . or on the fact that the legislators who voted to enact it may have been motivated by religious considerations. . . . Rather, it rests on the fact that the preamble, an unequivocal endorsement of a religious tenet of some but by no means all Christian faiths, serves no identifiable secular purpose. That fact alone compels a conclusion that the statute violates the Establishment Clause....

... The preamble to the Missouri statute endorses the theological position that there is the same secular interest in preserving the life of a fetus during the first 40 or 80 days of pregnancy as there is after viability—indeed, after the time when the fetus has become a "person" with legal rights protected by the Constitution. To sustain that position as a matter of law, I believe Missouri has the burden of identifying the secular interests that differentiate the first 40 days of pregnancy from the period immediately before or after fertilization when, as *Griswold* and related cases establish, the Constitution allows the use of contraceptive procedures to prevent potential life from developing into full personhood. Focusing our attention on the first several weeks of pregnancy is especially appropriate because that is the period when the vast majority of abortions are actually performed.

As a secular matter, there is an obvious difference between the state interest in protecting the freshly fertilized egg and the state interest in protecting a 9-month-gestated, fully sentient fetus on the eve of birth. There can be no interest in protecting the newly fertilized egg from the physical pain or mental anguish, because the capacity for such suffering does not yet exist; respecting a developed fetus, however, that interest is valid. In fact, if one prescinds the theological concept of ensoulment—or one accepts St. Thomas Aquinas' view that ensoulment does not occur for at least 40 days, a State has no greater secular interest in protecting the potential life of an embryo that is still "seed" than in protecting the potential life of a sperm or an unfertilized ovum....

Bolstering my conclusion that the preamble violates the First Amendment is the fact that the intensely divisive character of much of the national debate over the abortion issue reflects the deeply held religious convictions of many participants in the debate. The Missouri Legislature may not inject its endorsement of a particular religious tradition into this debate, for "[t]he Establishment Clause does not allow public bodies to foment such disagreement."...

In my opinion the preamble to the Missouri statute is unconstitutional for two reasons. To the extent that it has substantive impact on the freedom to use contraceptive procedures, it is inconsistent with the central holding in *Griswold*. To the extent that it merely makes "legislative findings without operative effect," as the State argues, it violates the Establishment Clause of the First Amendment. Contrary to the theological "finding" of the Missouri Legislature, a woman's constitutionally protected liberty encompasses the right to act on her own belief that—to paraphrase St. Thomas Aquinas—until a seed has acquired the powers of sensation and movement, the life of a human being has not yet begun.

SENTENCING OF
OLIVER NORTH
July 5, 1989

Standing before Judge Gerhard A. Gesell in a hushed U.S. District Court on July 5, Oliver L. North learned that he would be spared imprisonment for his part in the Iran-contra scandal and instead be ordered to do community service work. In Gesell's courtroom on May 4, the ex-Marine Corps officer had heard a jury declare him guilty on three of twelve felony charges: that he had obstructed a congressional investigation, destroyed government documents, and taken an illegal gratuity. All the charges, including nine on which North was acquitted, arose from secret activities he undertook while assigned to the Reagan White House.

At the sentencing, Gesell imposed—then immediately suspended— prison terms of up to three years. The judge told North that "you still lack full understanding . . . of how the public service has been tarnished," and that "jail would only harden your misconceptions." Rather than send North to prison, the judge ordered him to spend twelve-hundred hours assisting a drug-control program in the District of Columbia during a two-year period of probation, and to pay $150,000 in fines. Additionally, North was barred from holding federal office.

For all its drama, this climax to a long trial did not bring the highly publicized case to a conclusion. Only a few days later, North's attorneys filed an appeal on his behalf—and the case was considered likely to reach the Supreme Court. More than two years had elapsed since North, a Marine Corps lieutenant colonel on the National Security Council staff, had been implicated in an attempt to cover up efforts by the Reagan administration to illegally aid Nicaraguan guerrilla fighters (contras) by using profits from secret arms sales to Iran. The sales were intended to bring about the release of Americans being held hostage by pro-Iranian Moslem factions in Lebanon.

After the arms shipments to Iran were reported in the press, President Ronald Reagan conceded on national television November 13, 1986, that this had been done, but he denied that the U.S. government's dealing with the Ayatollah Ruhollah Khomeini was for hostages. Reagan had long vowed never to bargain over hostages. One week later he asked Attorney General Edwin Meese III to investigate the matter. On November 25, Meese made the stunning disclosure that profits from the arms sale had been diverted to the contras at a time that Congress—over Reagan's strong protests—had prohibited direct or indirect aid to them. Meese also announced that North was being dismissed from the National Security Council staff, and he further said that North's boss, Rear Adm. John M. Poindexter, was resigning as the president's national security adviser. (Reagan Administration on Iran Arms Deal and Contra Funding, Historic Documents of 1986, p. 1013)

Question of Reagan's Involvement

In February 1987, the presidentially appointed Tower Commission— headed by John Tower, a former Texas senator—portrayed the Iran-contra matter as a policy disaster caused by Reagan's hands-off manage-ment style and compounded by the willingness of White House staffers to sidestep the institutional process of making and carrying out decisions. Investigations did not stop there, however. The following July, North spent six days testifying before investigating committees on Capitol Hill—after receiving partial immunity from prosecution.

North told Congress that William J. Casey, director of the Central Intelligence Agency, approved the diversion of funds to the contras, but that he had no idea whether Reagan knew about it. By then Casey had died, and Reagan disclaimed any knowledge of the diversion. The committees, characterizing North as the point man for a "cabal of zealots," said the president bore the ultimate responsibility for wrongdo-ing by his aides.

According to the polls, North became a hero to many of the millions of Americans who watched the proceedings on television. Millions more looked upon him as a misguided patriot led astray by anti-Communist zeal or personal ambition. North stayed in the public eye, drawing large and enthusiastic crowds at speeches he made to raise funds for his legal defense.

On March 16, 1988, a federal grand jury in Washington indicted North and Poindexter, along with Richard V. Secord, a retired air force major general, and Albert A. Hakim, an Iranian-American arms dealer, accus-ing them of conspiring to defraud the government by providing the Nicaraguan rebels with proceeds from the arms sales to Iran. Two days later, North resigned from the Marine Corps. Judge Gesell, who was assigned the case, ruled that the four should be tried separately. North was the first to stand trial. However, Robert C. McFarlane, who was

Poindexter's predecessor as national security adviser, had already pleaded guilty to a misdemeanor charge of withholding information from Congress in connection with the Iran-contra affair. On March 3, 1989, while North's trial was under way, McFarlane received his sentence; he was given a $20,000 fine and ordered to perform two hundred hours of community service during two years of probation.

Secord pleaded guilty November 8 to one count of lying to Congress after plea bargaining resulted in eleven other felony counts being dropped. Sentencing was deferred until later. Secord had organized a secret enterprise to transfer arms to Iran and use the proceeds to supply the contras. Poindexter's trial date was set for January 22, 1990; Hakim awaited a trial date. Criminal charges against Joseph Fernandez, ex-CIA station chief in Costa Rica, were dismissed November 24 after Attorney General Dick Thornburgh invoked government secrecy rules to keep the defense from obtaining information purporting to show that Fernandez's superiors condoned his Iran-contra activities. U.S. District Court Judge Claude Hilton said that without the information Fernandez could not be assured of a fair trial.

Neither the North nor McFarlane cases could go forward until after the Supreme Court, on June 29, 1988, upheld the constitutionality of a 1978 post-Watergate law that provided for the appointment of independent counsels, or special prosecutors, to investigate claims of wrongdoing by government officials. A special prosecutor, Lawrence E. Walsh, had conducted the judicial investigations of North and McFarlane. (Court on Independent Counsel, Historic Documents of 1988, p. 465)

Further questions remained as to what government documents could be introduced in the trial without jeopardizing national security. North's attorneys, mapping a defense that portrayed North as a subordinate merely taking orders from on high, subpoenaed Reagan and Vice President George Bush to give evidence. Gesell declared that he had authority to order a president to appear in court but said he would use that power "only as a last resort." (Later, during the trial, he refused to direct Reagan to testify.) Moreover, the judge ruled that whatever knowledge Bush had of North's activities was not relevant to North's defense. Bush, like Reagan, professed no knowledge of illegal activities.

The Trial and Outcome

Even after the trial formally began January 31, jury selection was delayed while the judge, the Justice Department, and the White House wrangled over guidelines for the court's handling of secret documents. The three parties reached a compromise understanding on February 14, and a jury consisting of three men and nine women was sworn in a week later. The judge sent the case to the jurors on April 20, and they needed sixty-four hours of deliberation over a two-week period to render a verdict. Ultimately, they found North guilty of: (1) aiding and abetting the obstruction of Congress in November 1986 by creating false and misleading chronologies about the Iran arms sales and altering, destroy-

*ing, concealing, and removing National Security Council documents; (2)
altering, destroying, and removing those documents from the National
Security Council; and (3) illegally receiving $13,500 from Secord to install
a security system in his home. The jury acquitted him on other charges of
obstructing Congress; of lying to Congress, a presidential inquiry, and the
Department of Justice; of conspiring to defraud the Internal Revenue
Service; and of converting arms-sales profits to his own use.*

*Neither side seemed entirely pleased by the outcome. John W. Keker,
the independent counsel's chief trial lawyer, tersely said: "The jury has
spoken after a long and difficult trial. The principle that no man is above
the law has been vindicated." North, who sat expressionless as Judge
Gesell read the verdict, afterward claimed "partial vindication" but could
not hold back a tinge of bitterness as he spoke with reporters. "After more
than two and a half years and over $40 million of our taxpayers' money
spent on investigations, congressional inquiries, and a special prosecutor
who has compared me to Adolf Hitler," North said, "we now face many
months, perhaps years, fighting these remaining charges." The Hitler
reference during Keker's summation to the jury particularly galled
North. Joseph E. DiGenova, a former U.S. attorney for the District of
Columbia, said a similar remark in another case overturned a conviction
in the same appellate court that would hear North's appeal.*

*Earl Williams, one of the jurors, told news reporters that he thought
North was a likeable man and added: "I just think he got a raw deal."
The verdict suggested that the jury may have been most impressed by the
tangible evidence of North's shredding, altering, and falsifying documents. The jury also appeared to look more askance at North's actions
during the final stages of the cover-up; all three guilty counts involved
acts committed in November and December 1986. Perhaps the most
significant factor was the jury's apparent disregard or misunderstanding
of Gesell's instruction that North could not exonerate himself by asserting that he was ordered to break the law. North argued that he was
simply implementing the directives of McFarlane, Poindexter, Casey,
and, implicitly, Reagan.*

New Documents on Bush's Role

*The trial set off a new round of wrangling between Congress and the
White House over whether investigating committees received key government documents in 1987 and whether President Bush played a greater
role in contra fundraising than he acknowledged. On the day of the
verdict, Bush vigorously denied that in 1985 he had helped to elicit contra
support from Honduras in exchange for U.S. aid, as was suggested in one
of the trial documents. When asked about the Iran-contra scandal in
general, Bush said: "I think it was set to rest in the last election."*

*But Reps. Lee H. Hamilton, D-Ind., and David R. Obey, R-Wis.,
continued to pressure the administration. On the day the jury rendered
its verdict, the House Select Committee on Intelligence, at Hamilton's
request, authorized a staff investigation into the handling of documents*

released during the trial that hinted at a deeper Bush role. "We will be learning about Iran-contra for a long time to come," Hamilton remarked. "We learn something new at every stage of the game."

As for North's sentencing, Hamilton described it as "good and wise." North's supporters in Congress greeted it with relief and surprise. Describing the sentence as "creative and thoughtful," Rep. Robert K. Dornan, R-Calif., said he would delay sending the president a letter that had been signed by fifty-eight members of Congress requesting a pardon for North. As prosecutor, Keker contended that North had not shown remorse and deserved a prison sentence; probation, he said, "would diminish the seriousness of the crimes."

At the outset of the hour-long proceeding on July 5, North told the judge: "I grieve over what happened. One should not confuse a smile or a wave toward the ever-present press cameras that seem to follow me around as a lack of sensitivity over what has happened or lack of care about the consequences." Gesell responded by saying: "You have shown great remorse for your family and understandably so. It is often the tragic part of what happens when mistakes are made." But Gesell followed with his observation that North still did not understand how the public service had been tarnished.

Following is the text of Judge Gerhard A. Gesell's statement at his sentencing of Oliver L. North in U.S. District Court, Washington, D.C., July 5, 1989:

As I explain my sentence to you now I think you will see that—I hope you'll see that I am taking into account many of the matters that your lawyer and you have brought to my attention today. I hope you will also see that perhaps I place a greater value because of the nature of my job upon some aspects of the situation that brings you here than you yet have had an opportunity in the midst of all this turmoil to fully appreciate.

I can assure you, Colonel North, that I'm going to take into full consideration the important fact that before you came to the White House you had served your country with distinction in the highest traditions of the Marine Corps. And the court is not going to overlook that there were major matters of military and quasi-military nature which you performed, again with the highest distinction at great personal risk to yourself after you came to the White House. But I'm sure you realize that this case has little to do with your military behavior, commitment or expertise.

The indictment involves your participation in particular covert events. I do not think that in this area you were a leader at all, but really a low ranking subordinate working to carry out initiatives of a few cynical superiors. You came to be the point man in a very complex power play developed by higher-ups. Whether it was because of the excitement and the challenge or because of conviction, you responded certainly willingly and sometimes even excessively to their requirements. And along the way you came to accept, it seems to me, the mistaken view that Congress couldn't be trusted and that the fate of the country was better left to a small inside group, not elected by the people, who were free to act as they chose while publicly professing to act differently. Thus you became and by a series of circumstances in fact and I believe in your mind part of a scheme that reflected a total distrust in some constitutional values.

Now, a trial is a very extraordinary thing. As you stand there now you're not the fall guy for this tragic breach of the public trust. The jury composed of everyday citizens your supporters mocked and mocked throughout the trial understood what was taking place. Observing that many others involved in the events were escaping without censure or with prosecutorial promises of leniency or immunities, they used their common sense. And they gave you the benefit of a reasonable doubt.

You're here now because of your own conduct when the truth was coming out. Apparently you could not face disclosure and decided to protect yourself and others. You destroyed evidence, altered and removed official documents, created false papers after the events to keep Congress and others from finding out what was happening.

Now, I believe that you knew this was morally wrong. It was against your bringing up. It was against your faith. It was against all of your training. Under the stress of the moment it was easier to choose the role of a martyr but that wasn't a heroic, patriotic act nor was it in the public interest.

You have had great remorse for your family and understandably so. It is often the tragic part of what happens when mistakes are made. I believe you still lack full understanding, however, of how the public service has been tarnished. Nonetheless, what you believe is your own business and jail would only harden your misconceptions. Given the many highly commendable aspects of your life your punishment will not include jail. Indeed, community service may in the end make you more conscious of certain values which at times you and your associates appear to have overlooked in the elite isolation of the White House.

Your notoriety has caused many difficulties but it has also made you a rich man. And where you go from here is up to you, as I see it. You can continue to flame the myth by which you have supported yourself during these recent difficult years or you can turn around now and do something useful.

I fashioned a sentence that punishes you. It is my duty to do that. But it leaves the future up to you.

This is the sentence of the court. On count six where you are found guilty of aiding and abetting, obstruction of Congress, I'm going to impose a sentence of three years and suspend the execution of the sentence, place you on probation for two years, fine you $100,000 and I have to impose a special assessment of $50.

Under count nine, altering, removing and destroying the permanent historical records of the National Security Council I impose a sentence of two years, suspend the execution of sentence, place you on probation for two years, fine you $35,000 and impose a special assessment of $50 and I am required by statute to impose another mandatory penalty. You are hereby disqualified from holding any office under the United States.

Under count ten, receiving an illegal gratuity, I'll impose a sentence of one year, suspend the execution of that sentence, place you on probation for two years, fine you $15,000 and impose a special assessment again of $50. These sentences and the probation are to run concurrently. The fines are to run consecutively.

Your probation shall consist in addition to the normal requirements of community service in a total amount of 1200 [hours], 800 the first year, and 400 the second year and you will remain under the supervision of the District of Columbia probation officer who is familiar with your situation and who has prepared the pre-sentence report.

I want to talk to you about the community service. I've spent a lot of time thinking about it. I want the community to get the benefit of your organizational and administrative skills which are very, very high. I believe, as your counsel has indicated, that you are a caring person. And this community service I'm putting before you like many aspects of this case is unique. There is a model program to be tested in the District of Columbia, fully financed and in the final formative stages at the present time. It involves a program of counseling, training and educating and, where necessary, providing after care for District of Columbia inner city youths, most of whom are living in public housing surrounded by the drug culture. The work will involve no fund raising, no public speaking but a very complex administrative task of coordinating various private and D.C. [District of Columbia] resources in a program targeted to see if we can't stop the scourge of drugs that hits the young people of this city. And I'm asking you and directing that you participate in that program and give it your administrative skills, your organizational skills and if it succeeds, as I believe and hope it will, people are already selecting the candidates for that service in the inner city itself, it gives you an opportunity, I think, a sense of fulfillment and a chance to start something good and wholesome for the future.

That sentence in simple terms, I've had to give it to you in complex form because of the nature of the way the law has developed, but what it comes down to is that you have a three year suspended sentence, you're on probation for a period of two years. You will have to devote 1,200 hours to the community service I've indicated. You have to pay $150 in special assessments. You're fined a total of $150,000 and you are disqualified from holding office under the United States.

That is the sentence of the court.

GORBACHEV'S VISION
OF A COMMON EUROPE
July 6, 1989

Soviet president Mikhail S. Gorbachev on July 6 outlined to an assembly of West European parliamentary leaders his vision of a "common European home" from "the Atlantic to the Urals." In an address to the Council of Europe's parliamentary assembly in Strasbourg, France, Gorbachev spelled out more fully than on previous occasions his concept of Europe-wide cooperation in economic, cultural, and environmental affairs. The Soviet leader first broached the "common home" notion on a trip to France in 1985, but until his Strasbourg speech the idea seemed more rhetorical than substantive.

Gorbachev's speech also drew attention for his rejection of a Soviet policy that became known in the West as the Brezhnev doctrine. Leonid Brezhnev, one of Gorbachev's predecessors, defended Moscow's armed intervention in Czechoslovakia in 1968 by saying that the Soviet Union had a right and a duty to "come to the assistance of any fraternal socialist [communist] country" where communism was under attack. The intervention occurred that spring—the so-called Prague Spring—when the Czech Communist party moved to end censorship and permit other political parties.

Gorbachev never mentioned Brezhnev or the 1968 Czech events in his speech, but his allusion to that time and place seemed obvious. "Social and political orders in one or another country changed in the past and may change in the future," Gorbachev said. "But this change is the exclusive affair of the people of the country and is their choice. Any interference in domestic affairs, and any attempts to restrict the sovereignty of states—friends, allies, or any others—is inadmissible."

Gorbachev's Nonintervention

Later in the year, on a visit to Finland, Gorbachev was more emphatic about nonintervention. In Helsinki on October 25 he extolled Finnish neutrality and was reported to have told Finnish president Mauno Koivisto that the Soviet Union had no moral or political right to interfere in the affairs of its East European neighbors. Gennadi I. Gerasimov, a spokesman for the Soviet leader, recounted Gorbachev's remarks to news correspondents at the scene, and added: "I think the Brezhnev doctrine is dead."

Other events that occurred throughout the summer and autumn indicated that Gorbachev meant what he said. The Polish Communist party, overwhelmingly defeated in the country's first free elections in fifty years, was left with a governing situation so unstable that it reluctantly shared power with a non-Communist coalition led by the Solidarity labor movement—reportedly at Gorbachev's urging.

*Similarly, the Soviet leader was reported to have put his blessing on Hungary's equally notable "first." On October 7 the ruling Hungarian Socialist Workers (Communist) party formally abandoned communism in preparing to submit itself to the will of the electorate some time in 1990; on October 23 the government formally proclaimed Hungary a democratic republic. (*Hungary's Belated Eulogy for 1956 Uprising Heroes, p. 339*) That same day in Moscow, Foreign Minister Eduard A. Shevardnadze told the Supreme Soviet, the parliament, in a speech televised throughout the nation that the Soviet Union's 1979 invasion of Afghanistan and subsequent nine-year occupation violated Soviet law and international norms of behavior. (*Soviet Invasion of Afghanistan, Historic Documents of 1979, p. 965, Agreement on Afghanistan, Historic Documents of 1988, p. 257*)*

In the same spirit, Warsaw Pact representatives of the Soviet Union and four East European allies (Poland, Hungary, East Germany, and Bulgaria) met in Moscow on December 4 and condemned their suppression of the 1968 Czechoslovakian experiment in political liberalization. Romania, also a participant in the invasion, refused to sign the Warsaw Pact's confession of error. The Warsaw Pact is the Communist bloc's counterpart to the North Atlantic Treaty Organization (NATO) in the West.

Plea for European Cooperation

In Strasbourg, after setting forth his view on nonintervention, Gorbachev then went on to speak about a "restructuring" in Europe that would "make it possible to replace the traditional balance of forces by a balance of interests." He said that the "ultimate objective" of arms reduction talks with the United States was the "complete elimination" of nuclear weapons and deep cutbacks in conventional arms. He further advocated that through "political dialogue" there could begin a dismantling of military blocs such as the Warsaw Treaty and NATO.

Once the threat or fear of military action had been stilled, Gorbachev added, Europe could start building its "common home." In the meantime, he suggested, the Soviet Union should join with the Council of Europe in sponsoring international treaties on ecology, education, and Europe-wide television broadcasting. He named several European projects—ranging from a trans-European train to the disposal of nuclear waste—in which his country could cooperate. "The next step in this process," Gorbachev said, "is perhaps a trade and economic agreement between our country and the EC [European Community]." He had acknowledged on other occasions that his overriding interest was to restructure a lagging Soviet economy.

> Following are excerpts from Soviet president Mikhail S. Gorbachev's address to the Council of Europe's parliamentary assembly in Strasbourg, France, July 6, 1989, as translated by Tass, the official Soviet news agency:

... The concept of the "decline of Europe" circulated widely in the 1920s. This subject is still in fashion in some quarters. We do not share the pessimism about the future of Europe.

Europe was the first to have felt the consequences of the internationalization of economic and then of all social life. The interdependence of countries, as a higher stage of the process of internationalization, had an effect here far sooner than in other parts of the world.

Europe has more than once experienced attempts to unite by force. It has also known the noble dreams about a voluntary democratic community of European peoples. Victor Hugo said: "A day will come when you, France; you, Russia; you, Italy; you, Britain; and you, Germany—all of you, all nations of the continent will merge tightly, without losing your identities and your remarkable originality, into some higher society and form a European fraternity.... A day will come when markets, open to trade, and minds, open to ideas, will become the sole battlefields."

It is not enough now merely to state the interdependence and joint destinies of the European states. The idea of European unity should be collectively rethought in the process of the concerted endeavor by all nations—large, medium, and small.

Is it realistic to raise this question? I know that many people in the West regard the existence of two social systems as the major difficulty. But the difficulty is rather in the very common conviction—or even a political directive—that overcoming the split of Europe implies the "overcoming of socialism." This is a course toward confrontation, if not worse. There will be no European unity along these lines.

European states belong to different social systems. That is a reality. Recognition of this historical fact and respect for the sovereign right of every nation freely to choose a social system constitute the major prerequisites for a normal European process.

Social and political orders in one or another country have changed in the past and may change in the future. But this change is the exclusive affair of the people of that country and is their choice. Any interference in domestic affairs and any attempts to restrict the sovereignty of states— friends, allies, or any others—are inadmissible.

Differences among states are not removable. They are, as I have already said on several occasions, even favorable—provided, of course, that the competition between the different types of society is directed toward creating better material and spiritual living conditions for all people.

As a result of its restructuring, the USSR will be able fully to take part in this honest, equitable, and constructive competition. Given all the existing shortcomings and lagging, we well know the intrinsic strengths of our social system. And we are sure that we will be able to put them to use for the benefit of ourselves and for the benefit of Europe....

In the course of centuries Europe has made an indispensable contribution to world politics, economy, and culture, and to the development of the entire civilization. Its world historical role is universally recognized and praised.

Let us not forget, however, that the curse of colonial slavery spread worldwide from Europe. Fascism was born here. The most devastating wars began here. Europe may take legitimate pride in its accomplishments, but it has far from paid all its debts to humankind. This is yet to be done. This is to be done by pressing for changes in international relations in the spirit of humanism, equality, and justice and by setting an example of democracy and social achievements in their own countries.

The Helsinki process [1975 Helsinki Accords on Security and Cooperation in Europe] initiated this immense effort of world significance. Vienna and Stockholm [arms negotiations] have led it to fundamentally new frontiers. The documents adopted there are the most complete expression to date of the political culture and moral tradition of the European peoples.

We all, participants in the European process, are yet to use as fully as possible the prerequisites created by our common effort. This aim is served by our idea of the common European home.

Our idea of the common European home was born of the comprehension of new realities and the understanding of the fact that the linear continuation of the movement along which intra-European relations developed up to the last quarter of the twentieth century no longer matches these realities.

The idea is connected with our domestic economic and political restructuring, which was in need of new relationships primarily in that part of the world to which we, the Soviet Union, belong and with which we had been connected most of all for centuries.

We also took into account that the tremendous burden of armaments and the atmosphere of confrontation not only hindered the normal development of Europe, but at the same time prevented our country from joining in the European process economically, politically, and psychologically, and deformed our development.

These were the motives from which we decided to revitalize our

European policy, which in itself, incidentally, had always been of importance to us.

Matters concerning both the architecture of a "common home" and methods for building it and even "furnishings" were touched upon during meetings with European leaders recently. Conversations with President François Mitterrand [of France] on this subject in Moscow and in Paris were also fruitful and rather wide-ranging.

I do not claim today that I have a ready-made blueprint for such a "home." Instead I shall speak of what, in my view, is the main point— namely, the need for a restructuring of the international order in Europe to bring to the fore all European values and make it possible to replace the traditional balance of forces by a balance of interests.

But what does this involve? Let us first take security issues.

Within the framework of new thinking, we began with a critical reassessment of our notions of military confrontation in Europe, the scope of outside threats, and the importance of the factor of strength in security-building. This was not easy to do, and at times the effort was painful. But the endeavor resulted in decisions that make it possible to take East-West relations out of the "action-counteraction" vicious circle.

The joint Soviet-U.S. efforts in the field of nuclear disarmament have undoubtedly played an initial and considerable role in this respect. The Europeans not only endorsed the Treaty on the Elimination of Intermediate and Shorter-Range Missiles, but many also promoted its conclusion.

The Vienna talks opened up a fundamentally new phase in the arms reduction process. The talks already involve 23 countries, and not just two powers. All 35 participants in the CSCE [Helsinki Accords] process continue to work out confidence-building measures in the military field.

And although the two negotiating processes take place at different locations, they are intimately connected with each other.

There are and can be no "strangers" in efforts to build European peace—all are equal partners here, and every country, including neutral and nonaligned countries, bears its share of responsibility to its people and to Europe.

The philosophy of the "common European home" concept rules out the probability of an armed clash and the very possibility of the use of force or the threat of force—alliance against alliance, inside the alliances, wherever. This philosophy suggests that a doctrine of restraint should take the place of the doctrine of deterrence. This is not just a play on words, but the logic of European development prompted by life itself.

Our goals at the Vienna talks are well known. We consider it quite possible—and the U.S. President also supports this—to secure a substantially lower level of armaments in Europe in the course of two to three years, with the elimination of all asymmetries and imbalances, of course. And I emphasize—all asymmetries and imbalances. No double standards are admissible here.

We are convinced that it is also time to begin talks on tactical nuclear systems between all countries concerned. The ultimate objective is to

HISTORIC DOCUMENTS OF 1989   JULY

remove completely the weapons that threaten only the Europeans, who by no means intend to wage war on one another. Who then needs them, and what for?

To eliminate nuclear arsenals or to keep them at all costs are the options. Does the strategy of nuclear deterrence strengthen or undermine stability? The positions of NATO and the Warsaw Treaty on these issues look diametrically opposed. We do not dramatize the divergences, however.

We are looking for and invite our partners to look for solutions. We regard the elimination of nuclear weapons as a stage-by-stage process. The Europeans, without abandoning their positions, can jointly cover part of the way separating us from the complete elimination of nuclear weapons— the USSR while remaining loyal to non-nuclear ideals, and the West while remaining committed to the concept of "minimum deterrence."

However, it is worthwhile to find out what is behind the "minimum" notion, and where is the limit beyond which the potential of nuclear deterrence turns into an attack capability? There is much ambiguity in this respect, while the lack of clarity is a source of mistrust.

Why don't the experts in the Soviet Union, the United States, Britain, and France, as well as the countries on whose territories nuclear weapons are stationed discuss these issues in depth? If they arrive at some common evaluations, the problem will become simpler at the political level as well.

If NATO [North Atlantic Treaty Organization] countries are seen to be ready to enter into negotiations with us on tactical nuclear weapons, we could, upon taking counsel with our allies, of course, make further unilateral cuts in our tactical nuclear missiles in Europe without delay.

The Soviet Union and other Warsaw Treaty [East European] countries, outside the framework of the Vienna talks, are already unilaterally reducing their armed forces and armaments in Europe. Their structure and fighting strength are changing in line with the defensive doctrine of reasonable sufficiency.

This doctrine—from the point of view both of quantities of arms and troops and of their deployment, training, and all military activities—rules out the physical possibility of launching an attack and large-scale offensive operations.

This year we began to slash military spending. As was stated in the USSR Supreme Soviet, we intend, circumstances permitting, to reduce sharply—by 33.4 to 50 per cent—the share of our defense allocations in the national income by the year 1995.

We have begun the conversion of the defense industry in earnest. All countries participating in the CSCE process will encounter this problem in this or that way. We are prepared to exchange opinions and experience.

In our view, UN [United Nations] resources can also be utilized and a joint working group can be set up within the framework of the Economic Commission for Europe to study the problems of conversion.

In the face of European parliamentarians and, thus, the whole of Europe, I would like to speak once again of our simple and clear-cut positions on disarmament issues. They are the result of new thinking and have been legislatively sealed on behalf of all our people in the resolution of the Congress of Peoples Deputies of the USSR:

- we are for a nuclear-weapon-free world and for the elimination of all nuclear weapons by the turn of the century;
- we are for the full elimination of chemical weapons at the earliest date and for the elimination forever of the production basis for the development of such weapons;
- we are for a radical cut in conventional arms and armed forces down to the level of reasonable defense sufficiency, ruling out the use of military force against other states for attack purposes;
- we are for complete withdrawal of all foreign troops from the territories of other countries;
- we are categorically against the development of any space weapons whatsoever;
- we are for the elimination of military blocs and the development of a political dialogue between them with this end in view without delay and for the establishment of an atmosphere of trust ruling out any surprises;
- we are for profound, consistent, and effective verification of compliance with all treaties and agreements that may be concluded on disarmament issues.

I am convinced: It is high time that the Europeans brought their policy and conduct into line with new logic—not to prepare for war, not to intimidate one another, not to compete in the development of weapons, and still less, in attempts to "make up" for cutbacks, but to learn to lay jointly the foundations for peace.

If security is the foundation of the common European home, multifarious cooperation is its superstructure.

An intensive interstate dialogue—bilateral and multilateral—has become a sign of the new situation in Europe and the world in recent years. The range of agreements, treaties, and other accords has been considerably extended. Official consultations on diverse issues have become a feature of life.

The first contacts have been formed between NATO and the Warsaw Treaty organization, the EC [European Community] and the CMEA [Council for Mutual Economic Assistance], not to mention many political and public organizations in both parts of Europe.

We were pleased with the decision by the parliamentary assembly of the Council of Europe to grant "special guest status" to the Soviet Union. We are ready to cooperate. But we think that we can go even farther.

We could join some international conventions of the Council of Europe, open to other states, on ecology, culture, education, and television broadcasting. We are prepared to cooperate with specialized institutions of the Council of Europe.

The parliamentary assembly of the Council of Europe and the European parliament are based in Strasbourg. If our ties develop and become regular, we, certainly, with the consent of the French Government, would move toward opening a general consulate there. . . .

The need for a second conference of the Helsinki type is becoming increasingly topical. It is time for the present generation of leaders of the European countries, the United States, and Canada, to discuss, apart from most pressing issues, how they visualize the subsequent stages in the movement toward the European community of the twenty-first century.

As concerns the economic content of the European home, we consider the prospect for forming a vast economic space from the Atlantic to the Urals with a high degree of interdependence between its Eastern and Western parts as real, although not immediate.

The Soviet Union's transition to a more open economy is of fundamental importance in this sense. And not only for ourselves—for enhancing the efficiency of the national economy and meeting consumer requirements. This will enhance interdependence of the economies of the East and West and, consequently, have a salutary effect on the entire complex of European relations.

Similar features in the operations of economic mechanisms, strengthening ties, and economic incentives, mutual adaptation, and training respective specialists are long-term factors of cooperation, a pledge of stability of the European and international process as a whole. . . .

Perhaps specialists and representatives of respective governments should get together and sort out all these encrustations generated by the cold war, put secrecy within reasonable frameworks that are really dictated by security, and give a green light to a normal flow of scientific knowledge and technical art?

Such projects as, for instance, a trans-European express railway; a European program for developing new technologies and equipment; plans for utilizing solar energy, processing and disposing of nuclear waste, and enhancing the safety of nuclear power stations; additional information transmission channels using light conduits; and a European satellite communication system are equally important to the East and the West.

Developing a television system of a high degree of sharpness is exceptionally interesting. This work is being conducted in several countries, and it has a great future also for equipping the European home. Naturally, the more perfect and low-cost variant will be preferable.

In Paris in 1985, President Mitterrand and I put forward the idea of developing an international thermonuclear experimental reactor. This would be an inexhaustible source of ecologically clean energy.

Under the auspices of the International Atomic Energy Agency (IAEA) this project, which is the result of the combining of the research potentials of the Soviet Union, West European countries, the United States, Japan, and other states, is entering a stage of practical research.

Scientists forecast that it will be possible to build such a reactor by the turn of the century. This would be the greatest achievement of scientific thought and engineering and would serve the future of Europe and the whole world. . . .

The next step in this process is perhaps a trade and economic agreement between our country and the EC. We also attach substantial importance to it from the viewpoint of all-European interests.

Naturally, we by no means counterpose our contacts with the EC to contacts with other associations or states. EFTA [European Free Trade Association] countries are our good and long-standing partners.

It would also be sensible perhaps to speak of the development of relations through CMEA and EFTA channels and to utilize this channel of multilateral cooperation in the building of a new Europe.

A common European home will need to be kept ecologically clean. Life has taught us bitter lessons. Ecological hazards in Europe have long transcended national boundaries.

To form a regional ecological security system is a matter of urgency. It is quite likely that the CSCE process will evolve most quickly in this really high-priority field.

The first step could be to elaborate a long-term continental ecological program. Our proposal to set up an urgent ecological aid center at the United Nations is well known. Such a center or an agency with a system of warning and monitoring is utterly essential for Europe.

Perhaps the founding of an all-European ecological research and expertise institute, and in due course the establishment of an authority with powers to make binding decisions, can also be contemplated.

We know about large-scale projects to combat the mounting global threat. The USSR Academy of Sciences has set up an international institute for earthquake forecasting and is inviting scientists from all over the world to participate in the establishment of a scientific basis to deal with the problems of ecological security of the largest cities, to forecast droughts and the magnitude of climatic disasters.

The Soviet Union is prepared to provide satellites, ocean-going ships, and new technologies for these purposes. It would be useful perhaps to draw the military services of various countries, and first of all medical and engineering services, into international rescue and clean-up operations.

The humanitarian content of the CSCE process is decisive.

A world in which military arsenals would be cut but in which human rights would be violated cannot feel secure. We, for our part, have arrived at this conclusion finally and irrevocably.

The decisions made at the Vienna meeting signify a genuine breakthrough in this sense. A whole program for joint action of European countries has been mapped out with provision for the most diverse measures. Mutual understanding was reached on many issues which until recently were a stumbling block in East-West relations.

We are convinced that a reliable legal foundation should be furnished for the CSCE process. We visualize a common European home as a legal community, and we, for our part, have begun moving in that direction.

The resolution of the Congress of People's Deputies of the USSR, says, in part: "Relying on international standards and principles, including those contained in the Universal Declaration of Human Rights, the Helsinki accords and understandings, bringing domestic legislation in line with them, the USSR will contribute toward creating a world community of states ruled by law."

Here, too, Europe could be an example. Naturally, its international legal integrity comprises national and social peculiarities of states. Each European country, the United States, and Canada has its own laws and traditions in the humanitarian sphere, although universally recognized standards and principles also exist.

It would be useful to draw a comparison between existing legislation on human rights, setting up to this end either a special working group or something of a European institute of comparative human rights. Most probably we will not achieve a full convergence of views, considering the difference of social systems. But Vienna and the recent London and Paris conferences showed that common views and common approaches do exist and can be multiplied.

This allows me to speak about the possibility of creating a European legal framework. At the Paris humanitarian forum the Soviet Union and France acted as cosponsors of the initiative. The Federal Republic of Germany, Austria, Hungary, Poland, and Czechoslovakia have joined it.

A considerable extension of cultural cooperation, a deeper interaction in the field of humanities, and a new level of information exchanges are needed. To put it briefly, the process of getting to know each other better should be intensified. Television could play a special role here, since it makes it possible to ensure contacts among hundreds of millions of people rather than hundreds of thousands.

There are some dangers here, too. They should be recognized. Theater stages, cinema and television screens, exhibition halls, and publishing houses are flooded with commercial pseudo-culture, which is alien to Europe. There appears to be a contempt for national languages. All this calls for our general attention and joint work in the spirit of respect for all genuine national values.

This involves sharing experience in preserving our cultural heritage, measures to acquaint European peoples with the diversity of each other's modern culture, and collective assistance in language studies. This work may likewise include cooperation in preserving monuments of history and culture, coproduction of movies, television, and videofilms popularizing the achievements of national cultures and the best models of artistic creativity in the past and the present.

Ladies and Gentlemen. Europeans can meet the challenges of the next century only by pooling their efforts.

We are convinced that they need one Europe—peaceful and democratic—a Europe that preserves all of its diversity and abides by common humane ideals, a prospering Europe that extends a hand to the rest of the world. A Europe that confidently marches into the future. We see our own future in this Europe.

Perestroika, which has as its goal the fundamental renewal of Soviet society, also predetermines our policy aimed at the development of Europe exactly in this direction. *Perestroika* is altering our country, leading it to new frontiers. This process will go farther, deepening and transforming Soviet society in all areas—economically, socially, politically, and culturally, in all internal affairs and human relations.

We have embarked on this path firmly and irreversibly. The resolution of the Congress of People's Deputies of the USSR "On the Guidelines of the Domestic and Foreign Policies of the USSR" is a document that has sealed with the name of the people this choice of ours, the path of *perestroika*.

I call your attention to this resolution. It is of revolutionary importance to the destiny of the country you call a superpower. Once it is implemented, you, your governments, parliaments, and peoples will soon deal with a totally different socialist state.

This will have salutary impact, an impact on the whole of the world process.

Thank you.

BUSH'S EUROPEAN TRIP AND ECONOMIC SUMMIT

July 11-17, 1989

President George Bush embarked July 9 on a "delicate" mission to Eastern Europe that was followed by his attendance at the economic summit meeting in Paris. This fifteenth annual meeting of the Big Seven economic powers (the United States, Japan, West Germany, France, Italy, Britain, and Canada) opened July 14—Bastille Day—coinciding with festivities marking the bicentennial of the French Revolution. In some ways, the unusually harmonious gathering was upstaged by bicentennial pomp, which was interspersed with work sessions.

Bush concluded his European tour with a twenty-four-hour visit to the Netherlands before returning to Washington July 18. This, his second presidential trip to Europe, marked the first visit by an American president to Hungary and the Netherlands. In the Dutch city of Leiden, where the Pilgrims spent their last years before departing for America, Mayor Cornelis Goekoop informed the president that two Bush ancestors were among the Pilgrims who sailed from that city aboard the Mayflower *in 1620. In the very church (Pieterskerk) where the Pilgrims worshipped, the president recalled Holland's long devotion to freedom and expressed hope that it could be extended to Eastern Europe. "Our hope is that the unnatural division of Europe will come to an end," he told his Dutch audience, "that the Europe behind the wall will join its neighbors to the West in freedom."*

"Delicate Mission" to Eastern Europe

While flying from Washington to Warsaw, where the European visit began, Bush discussed with news reporters the delicacy of his mission to

Poland and Hungary. The Gorbachev-era loosening of restraints in the Soviet Union extended somewhat uncertainly into Eastern Europe, but most strongly in Poland and Hungary.

In Poland, the Solidarity labor movement had reached an agreement with the Communist-controlled government for a degree of power sharing. In parliamentary elections that followed in June, 35 percent of the seats were freely contested for the first time. Solidarity won all but one, and thus was accorded some cabinet positions. Hungary, too, was experiencing a degree of political thought that was previously unthinkable, and moving perhaps farther than any other Soviet-bloc country in its experimentation with a free-market economy.

In setting forth his vision of a "new Europe," and attempting to respond positively to Polish and Hungarian pleas for economic aid, Bush insisted nevertheless that he was not trying to create divisions between Eastern Europe and the Soviet Union. He said that Soviet leaders had "nothing to lose or fear from peaceful change" and pointedly credited Mikhail S. Gorbachev with creating conditions that permitted reform.

"I don't want to overpromise, do too little or do too much," Bush was quoted as saying aboard Air Force One on its flight across the Atlantic. "There are times in diplomacy when a certain delicacy is called for," he added. In his speeches and remarks in the following days the president offered an unlimited supply of political support for reform movements under way in Poland and Hungary, but only a small amount of direct economic aid.

His promised steps to help those two countries were constrained both by budget realities back home and a recognition that Washington was only a supporting partner in their quest for broader measures of economic and political freedom. Bush told leaders in both countries that the long-term solution to their economic problems lay in the evolution toward democracy and capitalism—a process that he acknowledged would take time and involve sacrifice by people who had suffered much since World War II. Both countries have been under Soviet domination since the war.

"There can be no substitute for Poland's own efforts, but I want to stress to you today that Poland is not alone," the president told the Polish Parliament on July 10. Bush offered similar words of encouragement in Hungary two days later in a speech at Karl Marx University in Budapest, saying that there "is no mistaking that Hungary is at the threshold of great and historic change." The United States, he said, "will be your partner in promoting economic reform."

Warm Welcome in Poland and Hungary

Bush received a generally warm reception in both countries, especially on July 11 when he traveled to Gdansk, Poland, the birthplace of the Solidarity movement. With Solidarity leader Lech Walesa at his side, the president stood in front of a monument erected in memory of workers slain in a 1980 protest in the nearby Lenin Shipyards and spoke to about twenty-five thousand cheering Poles. His speech was interrupted several times by cries from the audience, "President Bush! President Bush!" and "Lech Walesa! Lech Walesa!"

Later the same day at Budapest airport, some ten thousand Hungarians waited in a drenching rain to give the president an enthusiastic welcome. The next day he met government leaders in Budapest and delivered an address to the students and faculty of Karl Marx University. In the speech he extolled Imre Nagy, the hero of the 1956 Hungarian uprising that was crushed by Soviet tanks. In the freer political atmosphere prevailing in Hungary, Nagy received a state funeral thirty-three years after he was slain. His body was recovered from an unmarked grave and reburied in a national place of honor. (Hungary's Belated Eulogy for 1956 Uprising Heroes p. 339)

Economic Aid Plans

Before the university audience and Hungarian political officials, Bush spelled out his plan of economic aid for Hungary—just as he had outlined Polish economic aid in his July 10 speech to Poland's Parliament. The Polish proposals went somewhat beyond the limited trade concessions he mentioned in a speech April 27 in Hamtramck, Michigan, but it fell far short of what Walesa had in mind. The Solidarity leader earlier had asked for a $10 billion aid program featuring Western investments. White House spokesman Marlin Fitzwater said that Walesa's request "is probably not unreasonable in terms of the size of the challenge that Poland faces." But the administration did not accept it, and Fitzwater said the more limited offer from Bush "is as much as we can do at this time."

In the July 10 speech, Bush said he would request $100 million from Congress in grants and loans to create a "Polish-American Enterprise Fund" to help "capitalize and invigorate the Polish private sector" and would appeal to the World Bank to speed up approval of $325 million in loans to Poland. He reaffirmed a shift in policy he announced April 17 to support "early and generous" rescheduling of Poland's $39 billion in foreign debts even before the country reached agreement with the International Monetary Fund on what economic reforms it would have to undertake.

Under pressure from Congress, Bush later increased the size of his requests for both Poland and Hungary. Congress approved still more— $533 million for fiscal year 1990 and $938 million for 1990-1992—with the lion's share going to Poland.

Bush's original program for Hungary mirrored his plan for Poland in some ways but was substantially smaller. Its main features were (1) a $25 million appropriation request for a Hungarian-American Enterprise Fund, (2) liberalized trade rules with Hungary as soon as its Parliament enacted a new law easing restrictions on emigration, and (3) plans for cooperative agreements in the sciences and cultural affairs.

Economic Summit Success

In Paris, Bush asked his fellow leaders at the economic summit to create funds for Poland similar to the Polish-American Enterprise Fund he announced in Warsaw. Secretary of State James A. Baker III told news reporters that he would like to see the other six countries represented at the summit contribute at least $100 million each. The president indicated to a news conference at the end of the summit that he had received the assurances he and Baker sought from the other countries. "I was not disappointed," Bush said. However, he explained, "I didn't go in there with a specific package ... with dollar figures on it."

"By rejecting the dramatic gesture of a Marshall Plan for Eastern Europe," political analyst David S. Broder wrote in the Washington Post *July 18, "Bush avoided a major budget battle with Congress." Instead, he "allowed summit partners such as West Germany's [Chancellor] Helmut Kohl to give their own imprint to the design [for concerted action to aid Poland and Hungary]." In November, Kohl visited Poland and announced a $2.2 billion package of West German economic aid and financial relief for Poland, the largest amount provided by any Western government.*

While covering a wide range of concerns, including illegal drugs as well as the customary matters of global trade and finance, the 1989 summit conference was the first to address environmental issues in its final communiqué. Nearly one-third of the twenty-five page document was devoted to a review of evidence of deterioration in the quality of air and water throughout the world.

Following are excerpts from White House transcripts of President Bush's remarks July 11, 1989 at the Solidarity Workers Monument in Gdansk, Poland; his speech to students and faculty at Karl Marx University in Budapest, July 12; a news conference with the president conducted July 13 aboard Air Force One en route from Budapest to Paris; the final communiqué of the Paris economic summit conference, issued July 16; a Bush news conference in Paris at the summit's conclusion July 16; and the president's speech July 17 at Pieterskerk (St. Peter's Church) in the Dutch city of Leiden. (The bracketed headings have been added by Congressional Quarterly to highlight the organization of the text.):

REMARKS IN GDANSK, POLAND

The President. Hello, Lech Walesa! Hello, *Solidarność!* Hello, *Polska!* And congratulations on what you've done since I last visited: the first free elections in modern *Polska.* Poland has a special place in the American heart and in my heart. And when you hurt, we feel pain. And when you dream, we feel hope. And when you succeed, we feel joy. It goes far beyond diplomatic relations; it's more like family relations. And coming to Poland is like coming home. This special kinship is the kinship of an ancient dream—a recurring dream—the dream of freedom. "They are accustomed to liberty," wrote a Byzantine historian about the Slavic people more than a thousand years ago. And the spirit of the Poles has been conveyed across the centuries and across the oceans, a dream that would not die.

That dream was severely tested here in Gdansk. Fifty years ago this summer, the predawn quiet of this peaceful Baltic harbor was shattered by the thunder from the 15-inch guns of Nazi warship Schleswig-Holstein. Within the hour, iron panzers rolled across the Polish frontier. And Europe was plunged into darkness that would engulf the world.

For Poland the choices were few: surrender to tyranny or resist against impossible odds. And in the brutal fighting that followed, you set a standard for courage that will never be forgotten. In World War II, Poland lost everything—except her honor, except her dreams.

Before Poland fell, you gave the Allies "Enigma," the Nazis' secret coding machine. Breaking the unbreakable Axis codes saved tens of thousands of Allied lives, of American lives; and for this, you have the enduring gratitude of the American people. And ultimately, "Enigma" and freedom fighters played a major role in winning the Second World War.

But for you, the war's end did not end the darkness. The Cold War brought a long and chilly night of sorrow and hardship. And the dream was again denied. And yet there were glimmers of the long-awaited dawn. In the summer of 1980, you occupied the shipyards where we stand. And a patriotic electrician clambered over these iron gates and emerged as one of the heroes of our times—Lech Walesa. And above your streets a graceful monument rose, in the tradition of our own Statue of Liberty, to become a symbol recognized around the world as a beacon of hope....

Hope and hard work were the foundation of Poland's resurrection as a state in 1918. Against enormous odds, confidence and determination made that dream a reality. And these same qualities have brought you to this new crossroads in history. Your time has come. It is Poland's time of possibilities, its time of responsibilities. It is Poland's time of destiny, a time when dreams can live again: Solidarity reborn, productive negotiations between the Government of Poland and the Polish people, and the first fruits of democracy—elections....

Today, to those who think that hopes can be forever suppressed, I say: Let them look at Poland. To those who think that freedom can be forever denied, I say: Let them look at Poland. And to those who think that dreams can be forever repressed, I say: Look at Poland. For here in Poland, the dream is alive.

Yes, today the brave workers of Gdansk stand beside this monument as a beacon of hope, a symbol of that dream. And the brave workers of Gdansk know Poland is not alone. America stands with you.

The Audience. President Bush! President Bush! President Bush!

The President. Because Americans are so free to dream, we feel a special kinship with those who dream of a better future. Here in Poland, the United States supports the roundtable accords and applauds the wisdom, tenacity, and patience of one of Poland's great leaders: Lech Walesa. And again—

The Audience. Lech Walesa! Lech Walesa! Lech Walesa!

The President. And we cheer a movement that has touched the imagination of the world. That movement is *Solidarność*. And we applaud those who have made this progress possible: the Polish people. We recognize, too, that the Polish Government has shown wisdom and creativity and courage in proceeding with these historic steps....

Speaking before the new Parliament and the Senate—your freely elected Senate—I outlined steps that America is prepared to take to assist Poland as you move forward on the path of reform. It will not be easy. Sacrifice and economic hardship have already been the lot of the Polish people. And hard times are not yet at an end. Economic reform requires hard work and restraint before the benefits are realized. And it requires patience and determination. But the Polish people are not strangers to hard work and have taught the world about determination.

So, I say follow your dream of a better life for you and for your children. You can see a new and prosperous Poland not overnight, not in a year, but, yes, a new and prosperous Poland in your lifetime. It has been done by Polish people before. Hopeful immigrants came to that magical place called America and built a new life for themselves in a single generation. And it can be done by Polish people again. But this time, it will be done in Poland.

Just before I left a few days ago, I was asked in my beautiful Oval Office in the White House by one of your journalists if I would leave Poland and go to America, were I a young Pole. And I answered that in this time of bright promise, of historic transition, of unique opportunity, I would want to stay in Poland and be a part of it....

... Poland is where World War II began. And Poland is where, and why, the Cold War got started. And it is here, in Poland, where we can work to end the division of Europe. It is in your power to help end the division of Europe....

Poland is not lost while Poles still live. I came here to assure you we will help Poland. Goodbye, God bless you, and God save this wonderful country of Poland.

REMARKS AT KARL MARX UNIVERSITY IN BUDAPEST

... [I]t is a great pleasure for Barbara and me to be back in Budapest. And I am very proud to be the first American President to visit Hungary. Some might find it ironic that I am speaking at a university named after

Karl Marx. [*Laughter*] If you don't find it ironic in Hungary, try it on for size in the United States. But the fact that I am here today is less a cause for surprise than proof that America welcomes the unfettered competition of ideas. And I understand that 50 or so of the faculty from this great university have been either students or teachers in the United States of America. And that is a very good thing for my country, and I'm glad you came our way.

The University's principal task is to promote a competition—an unfettered competition of ideas. And that is the spirit that brings us together: a spirit that guided a great teacher at Karl Marx University whose name was Imre Nagy. As his funeral proceeded in Heroes Square a few weeks ago, the rising voice of Hungary was heard reciting the "Szozat" [patriotic poem]. And in this simple, somber ceremony, the world saw something more than a dignified act, an act of reconciliation: We witnessed an act of truth. It is on this foundation of truth, more solid than stone, that Hungarians have begun to build a new future. A generation waited to honor Imre Nagy's courage; may a hundred generations remember it. . . .

And today Hungary is opening again to the West, becoming a beacon of light in European culture. And I see people in motion—color, creativity, experimentation. I see a new beginning for Hungary. The very atmosphere of this city, the very atmosphere of Budapest, is electric and alive with optimism.

Your people and your leaders—government and opposition alike—are not afraid to break with the past, to act in the spirit of truth. And what better example of this could there be than one simple fact: Karl Marx University has dropped "Das Kapital" from its required reading list. Some historians argue that Marxism arose out of a humane impulse. But Karl Marx traced only one thread of human existence and missed the rest of the tapestry—the colorful and varied tapestry of humanity. He regarded man as hapless, unable to shape his environment or destiny. But man is not driven by impersonal economic forces. He's not simply an object acted upon by mechanical laws of history. Rather, man is imaginative and inventive. He is artistic, with an innate need to create and enjoy beauty. He is a loving member of a family and a loyal patriot to his people. Man is dynamic, determined to shape his own future.

The creative genius of the Hungarian people, long suppressed, is again flourishing in your schools, your businesses, your churches. And this is more than a fleeting season of freedom. It is Hungary returning to its normal, traditional values. It is Hungary returning home. Voices long stilled are being heard again. An independent daily newspaper is now sold on the streets. Commercial radio and television stations will broadcast everything from the news to the music of Stevie Wonder. And Radio Free Europe is opening its first Eastern European Bureau right here in Budapest.

Along your border with Austria, the ugly symbol of Europe's division and Hungary's isolation is coming down, as the barbed wire fences are rolled and stacked into bales. For the first time, the Iron Curtain has begun to part. And Hungary, your great country, is leading the way.

417

The Soviet Union has withdrawn troops, which I also take as a step in overcoming Europe's division. And as those forces leave, let the Soviet leaders know they have everything to gain and nothing to lose or fear from peaceful change. We can—and I am determined that we will—work together to move beyond containment, beyond the Cold War....

No, there is no mistaking the fact that we are on the threshold of a new era....

But to succeed in reform, you'll need partners—partners to help promote lasting change in Hungary. And I am here today to offer Hungary the partnership of the United States of America. Three vital spheres stand out in our partnerships: economics, the environment, and democratic and cultural exchange.

The United States believes in the acceleration of productive change, not in its delay. So, this is our guiding principle: The United States will offer assistance not to prop up the status quo but to propel reform....

And it is in this spirit that I want to announce the following measures. First, as I said in Warsaw, I will propose at the Paris economic summit concerted Western action, for Poland and Hungary, to back your reforms with economic and technical assistance from the summit partners. Of course, our efforts for Hungary will be targeted to your needs.

And second, I will ask the United States Congress to authorize a $25 million fund as a source of new capital to invigorate the Hungarian private sector. I'll also encourage parallel efforts from the other nations of the economic summit.

And third, once your Parliament passes the new emigration legislation proposed by your Council of Ministers, I will inform our Congress that Hungary is in full compliance with the Jackson-Vanik amendments to our 1974 trade law. No country has yet been released form the restrictions of this amendment. So, I am pleased to tell you that Hungary will be the first. And this action will give Hungary the most liberal access to the American market for the longest terms possible under our laws.

Fourth, America is prepared to provide your country with access to our Generalized System of Preferences, which offers selective tariff relief. Simply put, these last two measures will allow you to take advantage of the largest single market in the entire world.

And fifth, we've concluded a draft agreement to authorize the Overseas Private Investment Corporation—OPIC we call it—to operate in Hungary. And once our Senate passes the enabling legislation, OPIC will be able to provide insurance to encourage American investment in private enterprises in Hungary. Through OPIC, American business executives will see firsthand the great opportunity of Hungary. Private investment is critical for Hungary. It means jobs, innovation, progress. But most of all, private investment means a brighter future for your children, a brighter future for Hungary.

And yet economic progress cannot be at the expense of the air we breathe and the water we drink. Six weeks ago, in Mainz, I proposed cooperation between East and West on environmental issues. And that is why I will ask the United States Congress to appropriate $5 million to establish an International Environmental Center for central and eastern Europe, to be based right here in Budapest, which will bring together private and government experts and organizations to address the ecological crisis. After all, our shared heritage is the Earth. And the fate of the Earth transcends borders; it isn't just an East-West issue. Hungary has led eastern and central Europe in addressing the concerns of your citizens for cleaner air and water. And now you can do even more, working with the West to build a bridge of technical and scientific cooperation.

Along these lines, I am also pleased to announce that the United States has proposed an agreement between our two countries to establish scientific and technical cooperation in the basic sciences and in specific areas, including the environment, medicine, and nuclear safety.

It is my hope that this visit will also lead to a wider exchange between East and West so our scientists, our artists, and our environmentalists can learn from one another; so that our soldiers and statesmen can discuss peace; and our students—God bless them—can discuss the future.

But to discuss anything requires a common language. The teaching of the English language is one of the most popular American exports. And as students, you know that English is the lingua franca of world business, the key to clinching deals from Hong Kong to Toronto. So, to open the global market to more Hungarians, I am pleased to announce that the Peace Corps will, for the first time, operate in a European country. And our Peace Corps instructors will come to Budapest and all 19 counties to teach English.

And in such exchanges, we want to help you in your quest for a new beginning as a democratic Hungary. So, the United States is also committing more than $6 million to cultural and educational opportunities in eastern Europe. We will make available funds for a series of major new U.S.-Hungarian exchange programs—among Congressmen and legislative experts; among labor and business leaders; among legal experts; among community leaders, educators, and young people. We are creating dozens of fellowships to enable Hungarians to study at American universities. And we will fund endowed chairs in American studies at your universities, and books—many thousands of them—to fill the shelves of your new International Management Center and the libraries of schools and universities across Hungary.

And the United States will also open ... an American House in the center of Budapest. Today the celebrated American architect Robert Stern is releasing his design for this center, which will be an open house of books, magazines, and video cassettes—an open house of ideas.

And so, in conclusion, in economic reform and democratic change, in cultural and environmental cooperation, there are great opportunities and great challenges. . . .

Your challenge is enormous and historic: to build a structure of political change and decentralized economic enterprise on the ruins of a failed Stalinist system. . . .

And I believe with all my heart that you are ready to meet the future. I see a country well on the way. I see a country rich in human resources—rich in the moral courage of its people. I see a nation transcending its past and reaching out to its destiny. I congratulate you for having come so far. . . .

Let us have history write of us that we were the generation that made Europe whole and free. . . .

NEWS CONFERENCE EN ROUTE TO PARIS

Q. ——a good mood?

The President. Good mood. This visit to Hungary—well, Poland also—but both of them were very, very moving. And I just come away with this real acute sense now of the change that's taking place in Eastern Europe and a determination to play a constructive role in that change. The meetings with these Hungarian leaders—the most recent visit—were very good, very frank.

I've been to, what, 77, 79 countries, or something, as Vice President. And these talks were more than just diplomatic. I mean, you didn't rely on the printed card, and they didn't. I mean, they spoke right from the heart. They said what they thought. They made clear the difficulties that they were facing. And I tried to do the same thing. There was something very special and warm and personal about the meetings in both Poland and Hungary.

Q. Do you think you made a difference?

Q. I realize it wouldn't have been diplomatic for any of those leaders to say so, but did you hear any complaints in either place about the sufficiency of the packages you brought?

The President. No, and I think you're right: There may be a reason that they wouldn't say so. But I heard none at all, not one. And in fact, [Solidarity leader Lech] Walesa, who had been reported to be asking for $10 billion, moved off of that and said that what they wanted were more banks to come in that would loan those kinds of money. . . .

I think they understand that we are restricted in what we can do in terms of aid, or dollars of support, for some very worthy project. The thing that's impressive is the determination on the part of all these leaders to move towards economic freedom and political freedom. . . .

We met with the leaders and, then again, the opposition. And then they were all together at a reception. It's—change is absolutely amazing that's taking place in Eastern Europe.

Q. Do you think that you've made a difference?

The President. Yes, I do.

Q. What do you think that was?

The President. Well, I think the very fact that they can sit and talk to an American President in a reasonable way and I could tell them what I thought we would be able to do, how much we shared their desire for change, I think was fruitful to them. And I think they saw the friendship and respect for the United States from their people—the crowds on the street and the—any time there was interaction with the people it was dramatic. And I'm sure that makes a difference to the leaders. I think it shores up their desire for change because I think it shows all of us the genuine affection for the United States that exists in these countries....

Polish Political and Economic Reforms

Q. Is Poland going to get a government soon?

The President. I don't know, Helen [Helen Thomas, United Press International], I don't know. I would say yes, but I can't predict who the President's going to be.

Q. Did Walesa seem concerned?

The President. We discussed that very openly, but it's just something I can't predict the outcome....

Q. Did Walesa express any concerns about calling upon workers to make the kind of sacrifices required? Because that's another problem area.

The President. He didn't express concern about that, but I had an opportunity to make clear in private that—and publicly—that reforms were essential. There's no point going there under false colors and to try to have everything sweetness and light....

Eastern-Bloc Reforms

Q. Do you think your opinions may have encouraged reform in some of the other countries, such as, maybe, Romania or Czechoslovakia or East Germany; or might there be a backlash—

The President. Well, you want to be careful not to conduct yourself in such a way as to encourage a backlash. But I would think that this visit in the neighborhood would be watched by countries where economics and political change are lagging behind Poland and lagging behind Hungary. That isn't true of the Soviet Union, and it isn't true of Yugoslavia. But there are other countries that are probably watching and wondering. I am firmly convinced that this wave of freedom, if you will, is the wave of the future. And I would expect that this visit has been watched by the people of other Eastern European countries and, hopefully, giving encouragement to those who want to go the path of reform—political change, economic change—that these other countries are now following.

Q. Do you think they'll feel that talk is cheap from the United States, and what about a little more aid to encourage their reform movement?

The President. I didn't sense that....

Q. Are you going to tell the summit leaders that communism is dead?

The President. No. I'm going to tell them that there is dynamic change taking place in Eastern Europe, and I expect each one of them will want to tell me about their experiences with that. But I want to be sure that they know of our commitment to foster this change in a prudent way.

421

Paris Economic Summit

Q. [*Inaudible*]

The President. I haven't set up any yardsticks for that, Brit [Brit Hume, ABC News]. I don't think that there is a way to measure success at an economic summit. I mean, this isn't a summit where there is one major problem to be solved. There are problems on the agenda, but I expect at the conclusion of the meeting you'll see seven countries in harmony, pulling together on matters like the environment and, you know, the economies of the various countries and trade. All these are contentious matters bilaterally, but I think we can reach common understanding. So, maybe that would be the yardstick.

Q. ——Gorbachev to what's going on in Eastern Europe—approach seems to be—development in Eastern Europe and that you are a partner, but a limited partner. Isn't it Gorbachev's revolutionary approach to the East-West relationship that has given these people license to move forward? Isn't he glad they're moving forward?

The President. . . . [W]e're very pleased to see the *perestroika*. And let me repeat for the umpteenth time: I want to see it succeed.

Q. When are you going to tell him that personally?

The President. I don't know.

Q. This year? Geneva?

The President. No plans for that right now.

Q. Do you think it would be useful?

The President. I don't think there is any misunderstanding on his part about the position of the United States in terms of his reforms. I think maybe if there was ever any doubt about it those doubts have been dispelled; and if there was any recent doubts about it, those doubts will be dispelled by his friends in Poland and in Hungary because I made very clear to them that, you know, we're not there to poke a stick in the eye of Mr. Gorbachev. Just the opposite: to encourage the very kind of reforms that he is championing and more reforms. . . .

Eastern-Bloc Reforms

Q. From your conversation, did you get any sense of what the bottom line is in Eastern Europe as far as political change? I mean, what are the two or three points that you can't cross?

The President. No, there doesn't seem to be a bottom line because when you go to open, free, fair elections, who knows what's going to happen? Take a look at Hungary—I mean, at Poland. Take a look at those Polish elections. So, the change is so rapid and so devastating to old ways that I don't think you can put a bottom line on the thing.

Q. Perhaps Gorbachev is also looking at the elections?

The President. Probably looking at the elections at home. And that is a good thing. I tell you, the excitement of all this, you just feel it in talking to the leaders and feel it from the people.

Q. ——specific with leaders—that further economic reform—for example, did you discuss with them the sale of state-owned business or getting private enterprise to the people in both Poland and Hungary?

The President. Yes, both, but in varying degrees of detail....

Q. ——any Communists or are they all, essentially—they're all democratic, pluralistic——

The President. I met people that are caught up in this wave of historic change.

Q. What about——

Q. Are they changing their whole philosophy? They are Communists, aren't they?

The President. You asked whether one of the leaders made a big distinction between a Communist and a Socialist. And one of them pointed out that European socialism could well be the model of the future as opposed to the socialism that we equate with communism.

Q. What about the austerity side of this? Did you get into—2 years ago, the Poles would not get the votes they needed, and then you talk about belt-tightening. But did they talk to you about what they would do? And do you have any qualms that this might backfire? That if these supports are removed, the Poles may not get the candy they need to keep supporting the system?

The President. I had some feeling after some of the talks that the reforms that would be required would be very difficult for them. That's not universal, but it did come up.

Soviet-U.S. Relations

Q. ——in any way communicate that to Gorbachev?

The President. No, except indirectly saying, Please tell Mr. Gorbachev this, that, or the other.

Q. Would you have any plans to contact him——

The President. Well, we have regularized contacts with the Soviet Union now, and we will continue on those. But there could be occasion to do that....

Eastern-Bloc Reforms

Q. Mr. President, you talked about the changes, and you used the word, "amazing." Were you surprised by the things you saw?

The President. Not textbook surprised, but surprised at the feeling: the feeling and the emotion of it all and the frankness with which the leaders—in Hungary particularly, well, and also Jaruzelski and Walesa—talked about the change. I mean it was with emotion, and it wasn't your traditional "I'll read my cards, and you read your cards" kind of diplomacy. It was very special in that regard. There's an intensity to it, a fervor to it that moved me very much.

Q. *[Inaudible]*

The President. You mean like in Eastern Europe? Well, I think without the change in the Soviet Union it would have been highly unlikely that Eastern Europe would be achieving the kinds of changes, aspiring to the kinds of changes that it is aspiring to. . . .

Q. ——keep this policy alive?

The President. I don't think it's the U.S. role to keep the change alive. I mean, I think this is something that's the business of the Poles and of the Hungarians. This is their business; this is their life, their country. I think it would be rather arrogant to suggest that it's the United States that has the sole responsibility. That's not your question. But it, to the degree we can encourage change without intervention in the internal affairs—why, I'm all for that. . . .

SUMMIT COMMUNIQUÉ

Economic Declaration

1. We, the Heads of State or government of seven major industrial nations and the President of the Commission of the European Communities, have met in Paris for the 15th annual Economic Summit. . . .

2. This year's world economic situation presents three main challenges:

- The choice and the implementation of measures needed to maintain balanced and sustained growth, counter inflation, create jobs and promote social justice. . . .
- The development and the further integration of developing countries into the world economy. . . .
- The urgent need to safeguard the environment for future generations. . . .

International Economic Situation

3. Growth has been sustained by focusing policies on improving the efficiency and flexibility of our economies and by strengthening our cooperative efforts and the coordination process. In the medium term, the current buoyant investment seen during this period should pave the way for an increased supply of goods and services and help reduce the dangers of inflation. The outlook is not, however, without risks.

4. Until now, the threat of inflation in many countries has been contained, thanks to the concerted efforts of governments and monetary authorities. But continued vigilance is required and inflation, where it has increased, will continue to receive a firm policy response so that it will be put on a downward path.

5. While some progress has been made in reducing external imbalances, the momentum of adjustment has recently weakened markedly. There needs to be further progress in adjusting external imbalances through cooperation.

6. In countries with fiscal and current account deficits, including the United States of America, Canada and Italy, further reductions in budget

deficits are needed. Action will be taken to bring them down. This may help reduce the saving-investment gap and external imbalances, contribute to countering inflation and encourage greater exchange-rate stability in a context of decreasing interest rates.

7. Countries with external surpluses, including Japan and Germany, should continue to pursue appropriate macroeconomic policies and structural reforms that will encourage non-inflationary growth of domestic demand and facilitate external adjustment. . . .

Trade Issues

17. World trade developed rapidly last year. Yet protectionism remains a real threat. . . .

18. The successful negotiation of the Trade Negotiations Committee of the Uruguay Round in Geneva last April, thereby completing the mid-term review, is a very important achievement. It gives a clear framework for future work in all sectors including the pursuit of agricultural reform in the short term as well as in the long term. It also gives the necessary framework for substantive negotiations in important sectors not yet fully included in GATT disciplines, such as services, trade-related investment measures and intellectual property.

Developing countries participated actively in these negotiations and contributed to this success. . . .

We express our full commitment to making further substantive progress in the Uruguay Round in order to complete it by the end of 1990. . . .

General Problems of Development

24. We note with satisfaction that there has been substantial progress in the multilateral aid initiative for the Philippines that was given special attention in the [1988] Toronto economic declaration.

25. Faced with the worrying economic situation of Yugoslavia, we encourage its government to implement a strong economic reform program that can command bilateral and multilateral support.

26. The enhancement of the International Monetary Fund Structural Adjustment Facility, the World Bank special program of assistance for the poorest and most indebted countries and the fifth replenishment of the African Development Fund are all important measures benefitting those countries having embarked upon an adjustment process. We stress the importance attached to a substantial replenishment of International Development Association resources.

27. As we urged last year in Toronto, the Paris Club reached a consensus in September 1988 on the conditions of implementation of significant reduction of debt service payments for the poorest countries. Thirteen countries have already benefitted by this decision.

28. We welcome the increasing grant element in the development assistance as well as the steps taken to convert loans into grants and we urge further steps to this end. Flexibility in development aid as much as in

debt rescheduling is required.

29. We attach great importance to the efficient and successful preparation of the next general conference of the United Nations on the least developed countries, which will take place in Paris in 1990.

Strengthened Debt Strategy for
The Heavily Indebted Countries

30. Our approach to the debt problems has produced significant results, but serious challenges remain: in many countries the ratio of debt service to exports remains high, financing for growth promoting investment is scarce, and capital flight is a key problem. . . .

31. To address these challenges, we are strongly committed to the strengthened debt strategy. This will rely, on a case-by-case basis, on the following actions:

- borrowing countries should implement, with the assistance of the Fund and the Bank, sound economic policies, particularly designed to mobilize savings, stimulate investment and reverse capital flight;
- banks should increasingly focus on voluntary, market-based debt and debt service reduction operations, as a complement to new lending;
- the International Monetary Fund and World Bank will support significant debt reduction by setting aside a portion of policy-based loans;
- limited interest support will be provided, through additional financing by the International Monetary Fund and the World Bank, for transactions involving significant debt and debt service reduction. For that purpose, the use of escrow accounts is agreed;
- continued Paris Club rescheduling and flexibility of export-credit agencies;
- strengthening of the international financial institutions capability for supporting medium-term macroeconomic and structural adjustment programs and for compensating the negative effects of export shortfalls and external shocks.

32. In the framework of this strategy:

- we welcome the recent decisions taken by the two institutions to encourage debt and debt service reduction which provide adequate resources for these purposes;
- we urge debtor countries to move ahead promptly to develop strong economic reform programs that may lead to debt and debt service reductions in accordance with the guidelines defined by the two Bretton Woods institutions;
- we urge banks to take realistic and constructive approaches in their negotiations with the debtor countries and to move promptly to conclude agreements on financial packages including debt reduction, debt service reduction and new money. We stress that official creditors should not substitute for private lenders. Our governments are pre-

pared to consider as appropriate tax, regulatory and accounting practices with a view to eliminating unnecessary obstacles to debt and debt service reductions.

Environment

33. There is growing awareness throughout the world of the necessity to preserve better the global ecological balance. This includes serious threats to the atmosphere, which could lead to future climate changes. We note with great concern the growing pollution of air, lakes, rivers, oceans and seas; acid rain, dangerous substances; and the rapid desertification and deforestation. Such environmental degradation endangers species and undermines the well-being of individuals and societies. . . .

34. We urge all countries to give further impetus to scientific research on environmental issues, to develop necessary technologies and to make clear evaluations of the economic costs and benefits of environmental policies.

The persisting uncertainty on some of these issues should not unduly delay our action.

In this connection, we ask all countries to combine their efforts in order to improve observation and monitoring on a global scale.

35. We believe that international cooperation also needs to be enhanced in the field of technology and technology transfer in order to reduce pollution or provide alternative solutions.

36. We believe that industry has a crucial role in preventing pollution at source, in waste minimization, in energy conservation, and in the design and marketing of cost-effective clean technologies. The agricultural sector must also contribute to tackling problems such as water pollution, soil erosion and desertification.

37. Environmental protection is integral to issues such as trade, development, energy, transport, agriculture and economic planning. Therefore, environmental considerations must be taken into account in economic decision-making. In fact, good economic policies and good environmental policies are mutually reinforcing.

Clear assessments of the costs, benefits and resource implications of environmental protection should help governments to take the necessary decisions on the mix of price signals (e.g. taxes or expenditures) and regulatory actions, reflecting where possible the full value of natural resources.

We encourage the World Bank and regional development banks to integrate environmental considerations into their activities. International organizations such as the OECD [Organization for Economic Cooperation and Development] and the United Nations and its affiliated organizations, will be asked to develop further techniques of analysis which would help governments assess appropriate economic measures to promote the quality of the environment. We ask the OECD, within the context of its work on integrating environment and economic decision-making, to examine how selected environmental indicators could be developed. We expect the 1992 UN Conference on Environment and Development to give additional momentum to the protection of the global environment.

38. To help developing countries deal with past damage and to encourage them to take environmentally desirable action, economic incentives may include the use of aid mechanisms and specific transfer of technology. . . .

39. The depletion of the stratospheric ozone layer is alarming and calls for prompt action.

We welcome the Helsinki conclusions related, among other issues, to the complete abandonment of the production and consumption of chlorofluorocarbons covered by the Montreal protocol as soon as possible and not later than the end of the century. Specific attention must also be given to those ozone-depleting substances not covered by the Montreal protocol. We shall promote the development and use of suitable substitute substances and technologies. More emphasis should be placed on projects that provide alternatives to chlorofluorocarbons.

40. We strongly advocate common efforts to limit emissions of carbon dioxide and other greenhouse gases, which threaten to induce climate change, endangering the environment and ultimately the economy. We strongly support the work undertaken by the Intergovernmental Panel on Climate Change, on this issue.

We need to strengthen the worldwide network of observatories for greenhouse gases and support the World Meteorological Organization initiative to establish a global climatological reference network to detect climate changes.

41. We agree that increasing energy efficiency could make a substantial contribution to these goals. We urge international measures to improve energy conservation and, more broadly, efficiency in the use of energy of all kinds and to promote relevant techniques and technologies.

We are committed to maintaining the highest safety standards for nuclear power plants and to strengthening international cooperation in safe operation of power plants and waste management, and we recognize that nuclear power also plays an important role in limiting output of greenhouse gases.

42. Deforestation also damages the atmosphere and must be reversed. We call for the adoption of sustainable forest management practices, with a view to preserving the scale of world forests. The relevant international organizations will be asked to complete reports on the state of the world's forests in 1990.

43. Preserving the tropical forests is an urgent need for the world as a whole. . . .

To this end, we give strong support to rapid implementation of the Tropical Forest Action Plan which was adopted in 1986 in the framework of the Food and Agricultural Organization. We appeal to both consumer and producer countries, which are united in the International Tropical

Timber Organization, to join their efforts to ensure better conservation of the forests. We express our readiness to assist the efforts of nations with tropical forests through financial and technical cooperation, and in international organizations.

44. Temperate forests, lakes and rivers must be protected against the effects of acid pollutants such as sulphur dioxide and nitrogen oxides....

45. The increasing complexity of the issues related to the protection of the atmosphere calls for innovative solutions. New instruments may be contemplated. We believe that the conclusion of a framework or umbrella convention on climate change to set out general principles or guidelines is urgently required to mobilize and rationalize the efforts made by the international community....

46. We condemn indiscriminate use of oceans as dumping grounds for polluting waste. There is a particular problem with the deterioration of coastal waters. To ensure the sustainable management of the marine environment, we recognize the importance of international cooperation in preserving it and conserving the living resources of the sea. We call for relevant bodies of the United Nations to prepare a report on the state of the world's oceans....

We ask all countries to adhere to and implement fully the international conventions for the prevention of oil pollution of the oceans. We also ask the International Maritime Organization to put forward proposals for further preventive action....

Drug Issues

52. The drug problem has reached devastating proportions. We stress the urgent need for decisive action, both on a national and an international basis. We urge all countries, especially those where drug production, trading and consumption are large, to reduce demand, and to carry forward the fight against drug trafficking itself and the laundering of its proceeds.

53. Accordingly, we resolve to take the following measures within relevant fora:

- Give greater emphasis on bilateral and United National programs for the conversion of illicit cultivation in the producer countries. The United Nations Fund for Drug Abuse Control (UNFDAC) and other United Nations and multilateral organizations should be supported, strengthened and made more effective. These efforts could include particular support for the implementation of effective developmental and technical assistance.
- Support the efforts of producing countries who ask for assistance to counter illegal production or trafficking.
- Strengthen the role of the United Nations in the war against drugs through an increase in its resources and through reinforced effectiveness of its operation.

- Intensify the exchange of information on the prevention of addiction, and rehabilitation of drug addicts.
- Support the international conference planned for 1990 on cocaine and drug demand reduction.
- Strengthen the efficiency of the cooperative and mutual assistance on these issues, the first steps being a prompt adhesion to ratification and implementation of the Vienna Convention on illicit traffic in narcotic drugs and psychotropic substances.
- Conclude further bilateral or multilateral agreements and support initiatives and cooperation, where appropriate, which include measures to facilitate the identification, tracing, freezing, seizure and forfeiture of drug crime proceeds.
- Convene a financial action task force from Summit Participants and other countries interested in these problems. Its mandate is to assess the results of cooperation already undertaken in order to prevent the utilization of the banking system and financial institutions for the purpose of money laundering, and to consider additional preventive efforts in this field, including the adaptation of the legal and regulatory systems so as to enhance multilateral judicial assistance. The first meeting of this task force will be called by France and its report will be completed by April 1990.

54. International cooperation against AIDS.

We take note of the creation of an International Ethics committee on AIDS which met in Paris in May 1989, as decided at the Summit of Venice (June 1987). It assembled the Summit Participants and the other members of the EC [European Community], together with the active participation of the World Health Organization. . . .

PARIS NEWS CONFERENCE

The President. Well, we've just concluded two and a half days of intensive and productive meetings with the summit counterparts on economic and political issues. And let me take this opportunity first of all to thank President [François] Mitterrand [of France] for his most gracious hospitality. The summit, in my view, was a clear success.

We met in a time of sustained economic growth, and agreed that the prospects are good for the continued expansion, without inflation, of that growth. It was against this backdrop that we conducted a wide-ranging discussion on critical global issues, from East-West relations to the growing environmental challenge that we face. We came to Paris at a truly remarkable moment. The winds of change are bringing hope to people all around the world. And who would have thought just a few short years ago that we would be witness to a freely elected senate in Poland, or political pluralism in Hungary?

I was really touched by what I saw and heard in those two countries—people determined to keep their dreams alive, people determined to see a Europe whole and free. And that's why America brought to this summit our determination to support the reform movement in Hungary and Poland. People yearning for freedom and democracy deserve our support, and it's because of the community of values shared by these summit countries that we were able to agree to meet soon to discuss concerted action that will help Poland and Hungary.

Democracy and economic growth go hand in hand, whether in Eastern Europe, the Summit 7, or the developing world. And therefore, much of our discussion here in Paris centered on economics. We reaffirmed our international economic cooperation and our whole policy coordination process. Our strengthened debt strategy was firmly supported. We reaffirmed our determination to maintain and improve the multilateral trading system, calling for the completion of the Uruguay Round by the end of 1990, and extending the GATT [General Agreement on Tariffs and Trade] to new areas including agriculture.

This summit marked a watershed in the environment, and we agreed that decisive action is urgently needed to preserve the Earth. We committed to work together as well as with the developing world to meet our responsibility of global stewardship. The measures we've agreed to in Paris are timely, and they lay the groundwork for further specific steps when we meet again next year in the United States.

And finally, I was especially pleased to find that my colleagues share our sense of urgency and sense of the importance of the worldwide fight against drugs. Among other steps, we agreed to establish a financial action task force to find new ways to track and prevent the laundering of drug money. I look forward to meeting my summit colleagues in the United States next year as we continue working on these and other priority issues, build on the progress that we made—genuine progress that I think was made here in Paris. And I might say that I was very pleased that this meeting coincided with the bicentennial here. It was a very moving experience for all of us.

Now, I will be glad to take questions. Helen?

[Gorbachev's Role]

Q. Mr. [Soviet leader Mikhail] Gorbachev wants to play a part in the world economic discussions. Would he be welcomed at the next economic summit table?

P. Well, I think that's a little premature, but it was very interesting, I found, that a leader of the Soviet Union would address a letter to the French president as head of this year's summit. We talked about that letter a great deal. There's an awful lot that has to transpire in the Soviet Union, it seems to me, before anything of that nature would be considered.

We're talking about free-market economies here and—but I thought—I found fascinating the very fact of the letter. But there was no—there's certainly I don't think any indication that the next—that he will be attending the next summit. He'll get a very courteous and very thoughtful reply from Mr. Mitterrand.

Q. How about the poor countries, Bangladesh? Would they ever be welcome?

P. Well, this is an economic summit of countries whose economies are drawn together by the free economies of the West and so I don't think there's a question at this point of expanding the summit. There is concern about the economies in the world that aren't doing so well. Bangladesh is a country that does need aid and indeed the communiqué addressed itself to trying to help Bangladesh.

Q. Mr. President, you consulted with the NATO allies for military matters in Brussels and then you had an economic summit here in Paris. What's left before you sit down with Mr. Gorbachev for a superpower summit?

P. A little more time, I think.

Q. But isn't there anything that you were—any—don't you have anything to discuss with him now that you've gotten all this groundwork laid?

P. Oh, sure. Let me explain to those who aren't familiar with the policy that Secretary [of State James A.] Baker has met a couple of times with Mr. [Soviet Foreign Minister Eduard A.] Shevardnadze. There will be another such meeting of that nature, and at an appropriate time I will have a meeting with Mr. Gorbachev. But I don't think anything at the summit influenced the bilateral—that bilateral meeting. Yes—and then back here.

[Environmental Action]

Q. Mr. President, the summit calls for decisive action on the environment but various environmental groups are saying that you did not take decisive action. Could you respond to that?

P. Well, I did see some—one or two groups. They didn't think I took decisive action when I sent—or took proper action—when I sent a very far-reaching clean-air proposal up to the Congress. And—so some have been critical. Many have been supportive on the broad—the very fact— I'll tell you where we got a lot of support is the very fact that the communiqué addressed itself with some specificity to various environmental goals.

The whole concept of cooperation on research, technology and transfer to the LDCs [less-developed countries], the prevention of pollution, the idea of setting up monitoring stations so we can better predict, and thus avoid, environmental disaster. . . .

[Poland and Hungary]

Q. Mr. President, you promised in Poland and Hungary that you would seek concerted action on the part of the countries meeting here to help those countries, and there seems to have been a pledge that there would be concerted consideration of action—no dollar figure attached, and no specified action promised, and a meeting apparently planned. Do you feel you got what you wanted, sir?

P. I think so.... I was not disappointed. I didn't go in there with a specific package of—with dollar figures on it. And I think an early meeting to do just that is good....

[Soviet Overtures]

Q. Can you tell us, since you said that you spent a lot of time last night talking about Mr. Gorbachev's letter, can you tell us a little bit about those discussions? And can you tell us what your view is? What is an appropriate response from the West to such an extraordinary request by Mr. Gorbachev to become part of the economy of the Western democracies?

P. We would welcome any movement by the Soviet Union towards market-oriented or Western economies. There is no question about that. And there's nothing begrudging about our saying ... that I don't expect Mr. Gorbachev to sit as a member of the—at next year's summit. But the discussion was started off by, "What do you think he means by this?" And a lot of discussion, "We'll get the experts to analyze it." And all of that took place, and people concluded that it was just one more manifestation of the changing world we're living in. And that, I think, was the main message.

And then where we go from here—his—some of that has been addressed in the [economic summit] communiqué, because we talked in there about help for the Third World. And some of his letter, as you know, was on that very subject. So it was—when it came in, Mr. Mitterrand read it off to the group there and then said, "Well, what will we do?" And my suggestion was, which he had intended to adopt anyway, that he, as the man to whom the letter was addressed, would reply to it. So that's the way it was.

And the fact that it's happening, taking place—the president of the United States can go to Eastern Europe and witness the very kind of change we're talking about. I'll tell you ... the most—almost the most dramatic for me was when Mr. [Károlyi] Nemeth, the prime minister of Hungary, handed me that piece of barbed wire, tearing down the Iron Curtain between Hungary and Austria. Now, who would have thought that possible? ...

[Soviets' European Role]

Q. Mr. President, you've talked about a whole and united Europe. And Mr. Gorbachev has talked about a common European home. Are they the same concept or what is the difference? Is—does there—the difference between the role of the U.S. in those two statements?

P. Europe whole and free is our concept. His common European home is fine—so long, as I said earlier, you can move from room to room. And that means a coming along further on human rights; that means much more openness; it means support him when you see them move towards *perestroika* and *glasnost*. But it means an evolution in the Soviet Union, and it means an evolution in Eastern Europe. And we've begun to see it....

Q. In the meeting of the G-7 [Group of Seven industrialized nations at the Paris economic summit], is there room, or does—did you sense the countries want U.S. leadership, or they want the U.S. to be a coequal partner?

P. You mean, with the Soviets? No, I sense that they—that those colleagues feel that we have disproportionate responsibility. I think there's a keen interest in how I will work with the Soviets—there's no question about that. I felt that very clearly.

[Gorbachev's PR Maneuver]

Q. At the risk of seeming fixated by Mr. Gorbachev, when you discussed his letter, was there a suggestion from anybody that it might have been a bit of mischief, or an attempt to get some publicity out of the Western summit?

P. I can't say that that never occurred, but I don't think that after people thought about it rationally, that anyone was prepared to say that alone was what motivated this letter. There is change taking place, and I think for some time people really wondered whether I was a little begrudging in recognizing that change and encouraging that change. But I think, now that has been laid to rest....

[Changes in Eastern Europe]

Q. Mr. President, going back to the other day in Poland. An elderly man said that, "When people who talk to you boast about change, just remember that the communists still have the bayonets." So my question to you is, do you believe that countries like Poland and Hungary are really going to have serious and permanent change, or is there a line that their leaders and that Moscow just won't go past?

P. Well, no. I think that you've already seen serious change. I think you see the political situation in Hungary, for example, is absolutely amazing compared to the way we used to view—view Hungary. And if the Soviet Union, instead of taking their troops out of Hungary, had tried to tighten down, I don't expect we'd see the kind of change in Hungary that we're seeing today. And so I'd say that we're a long way from what Gorbachev has spelled out as a common European home, but it's moving. So let's encourage the progress. I think maybe I missed the nuance of your question.

Q. That there ought to—that there is a course that's going to lead to a permanent change; or again the question is, are the Soviets going to step in and pull the rug out from under it—

P. Well, I would quote Mr. Gorbachev's words back to him on that.

What he told me in New York and what Jim Baker has heard from Shevardnadze and what everybody who interacts with the Soviets here, and that is that *perestroika* is for real. You cannot set the clock back. It is going to go forward, and so I would see that as what guides now. However, I have said as long as there are enormous imbalances in conventional forces and in certain categories of strategic forces, the West should keep its eyes wide open. . . .

Q. I wonder, as you put all of this together, what you said about Poland and Hungary, and Gorbachev asking to join the world economy, as a matter of policy do you see the Cold War over, and do you think the West has won it?

P. I don't like to use, quote, "Cold War," unquote. That—that has a connotation of worse days in terms of East-West relationship. I think things have moved forward so that the connotation that those two words conjure up is entirely different now. . . . We have some big differences still. But let's encourage the change. . . .

[Whole and Free Europe]

Q. In Eastern Europe, you talked about two big concept links. One, encouraging democracy and moves toward a market economy; and two, that you weren't there to try to raise tensions with the Soviet Union or challenge them in any way. But my question is, if what you want is carried out, moves to democracy and a market economy, aren't you really talking about the dissolution of the Soviet empire, and is that what you mean when you call for a Europe that is whole and free?

P. The Soviet empire, if you mean the imposition of a Marxist system, or socialism—in their definition—system on others, yes, I'd like to see Europe whole and free. And . . . with the Soviets moving towards market . . . towards more freedom, towards more openness, they themselves have recognized that their system doesn't work. So, you don't run the risks or have the same tension that we might have had 10 years ago talking about the very same themes I talked about in Poland, in Hungary. . . .

REMARKS AT LEIDEN

. . . The Netherlands is an old friend, an honored ally of the United States. And the friendship between our nations is older than the American Constitution, and the United Provinces were one of the models that our founders looked to in creating a nation from 13 sovereign States.

And it's a pleasure to visit Leiden, a city whose very name has symbolized for centuries Dutch determination and the struggle for freedom against the forces of occupation. And for Americans, too, Leiden is a special city, a place where we trace our origins. So many of the individuals who shaped the modern world walked the cobbled streets of Leiden. And it was there that Hugo de Groot, known to the world as Grotius, the father of modern international law, studied in the Nation that is today the home of the International Court of Justice. And it was here that Rembrandt lived and worked and created a world of beauty that moves us still today. And it was here to Leiden that the Pilgrims came to escape persecution—to live, work, and worship in peace. In the shadow of Pieterskerk, they found the freedom to witness God openly and without fear. And here, under the ancient stones of the Pieterskerk, the body of John Robinson, the Pilgrims' spiritual leader, was laid to rest.

And it was from this place the Pilgrims set their course for a new world. In their search for liberty, they took with them lessons learned here of freedom and tolerance. And the Pilgrims faced a dangerous passage. But carried on the winds of hope, they arrived. And on the rocky coast of New England, at the edge of a wild and unsettled continent, they planted the seeds of a new world, a world that became America.

And today, as when the Pilgrims left this city, a new world lies within our reach. Our time is a time of great hope and a time of enormous challenges. The new world we seek is shaped by an idea, an idea of universal appeal and undeniable force, and that idea is democracy. The power of the democratic idea is evident everywhere—in the halls of government, in the hearts of people around the world. In the words of Victor Hugo: "No army can withstand the strength of an idea whose time has come." And, ladies and gentlemen, freedom's time has come....

The new world we seek is a commonwealth of free nations working in concert, a world where more and more nations enter a widening circle of freedom. In the pulpit here at the Pieterskerk, 1 year after peace was restored in Europe, Winston Churchill spoke to the people of Leiden. The Allies had triumphed over tyranny. The occupation was over. After 6 years of war and devastation, Churchill said: "The great wheel has swung full circle." And Europe then stood at the threshold of a new era, an era whose hope Churchill expressed in a single, simple phrase: "Let freedom reign."

And we all know what followed. Half of Europe entered that new era, and half of Europe found its path blocked, walled off by barriers of brick and barbed wire. The half of Europe that was free dug out from the rubble, recovered from the war, and laid the foundations of free government and free enterprise that brought unparalleled prosperity and a life in peace and freedom. And the other Europe, the Europe behind the wall, endured four decades of privation and hardship and persecution and fear.

And today that other Europe is changing. The great wheel is moving once more. And our time, the exciting time in which we live, is a time of new hope: the hope that all of Europe can now know the freedom—that The Netherlands has known, that America has known, and that the West has known. Our hope is that the unnatural division of Europe will now come to an end, that the Europe behind the wall will join its neighbors to the West, prosperous and free.

Poland and Hungary are on the cutting edge; they're on the forefront of this reform. And they've traveled far these past 12 months, farther than any of us once would have thought possible. In Warsaw, I spoke to the new Polish Parliament that includes 100 new freely elected Senators, elected to office in Eastern Europe's first truly free election in the postwar era. And in Hungary, I addressed the students and faculty of Karl Marx University, a university where the lessons of the free market are replacing the old teachings of "Das Kapital." At the shipyards of Gdansk and at the statue of the great Hungarian hero Kossuth, tens of thousands of people— literally tens of thousands filled the streets—new voices, full of new hope. And theirs were the faces of pilgrims on a journey, fixed on the horizon, on the new world coming into view.

And they know, as we do, that ultimately, whatever the odds, freedom will succeed. It's a lesson the world has learned several times this century, a lesson that you know so well, that the Dutch know so well. The Netherlands will never—I was talking at this lunch today with your able Prime Minister [Ruud Lubbers]—The Netherlands will never forget the nightmare of occupation. Some of you here today suffered through those long years.

And even then freedom endured. Pieterskerk—behind these walls, above the rafters—resistance fighters, university students took refuge from the forces of occupation and found safe haven in this church. Daily acts of heroism—the church sexton who brought them food, the neighborhood grocer who collected extra ration stamps—kept them alive, kept the spirit of dignity and human decency alive throughout The Netherland's dark night.

And why? Why would people endanger themselves to save others? They did it for the simplest, most human of reasons. In the words of Jan Campert, poet of the Dutch resistance, they acted because "the heart could not do otherwise."

Freedom can never be extinguished—not then, not now. Even in the Europe behind the Wall, the dream of freedom for all Europe has never died. It's alive today in Warsaw and Gdansk, in Budapest and, yes, across the Soviet Union.

So, the challenge that we face is a very clear one. We must work together toward the day when all of Europe, East and West, is free of discord, free of division, a day when people in every city and every town across this continent know the freedoms that we enjoy. And here in Leiden, where the pilgrims dreamed their new world, let us pledge our effort to create a new world in Europe, whole and free, a new world now within our reach. . . .

SOVIET MARSHAL TESTIFIES
TO THE U.S. CONGRESS
July 21, 1989

"My presentation ... is the first address of a Soviet serviceman to the U.S. Congress," said Marshal Sergei F. Akhromeyev, former chief of the Soviet general staff and currently the top military adviser to President Mikhail S. Gorbachev. In those words, the old soldier in his Red Army uniform underscored both the novelty of his guest appearance before the House Armed Services Committee on July 21 and the extent to which U.S.-Soviet restraints have been relaxed in the Gorbachev era.

Before a hushed audience in a U.S. Capitol hearing room, the marshal opened his remarks by observing through an interpreter that only two or three years ago it would have been unthinkable for a Soviet military officer to be in such a setting, and discussing—at the committee's suggestion—"the Soviet stand in the field of national security in the 1990s." Akhromeyev concluded his lengthy statement by inviting the U.S. armed forces to send a representative to speak to the Supreme Soviet Committee on Defense—whose function in Moscow is roughly comparable to that of the defense committees of Congress.

Defensive Soviet Strategy

Members of the Armed Services Committee stood and applauded their guest when he insisted that defense had become the key element in Soviet military strategy. "The USSR is firmly determined to adhere to the defensive military doctrine and to maintain its armed forces at the minimum level," he said. By the end of 1990, he said, Soviet ground-troop strength would drop 300,000 below its January 1 level of 1,596,000. It was a reduction that Gorbachev had ordered, Akhromeyev reminded, regard-

less of whether the United States and other countries of the North Atlantic Treaty Organization (NATO) made comparable cuts. But he held out hope that arms control negotiations would lead to force reductions of one million personnel on each side in Europe.

"I am personally convinced that neither the U.S. nor its allies intend today to unleash a warfare against the USSR and its allies," Akhromeyev said. However, his country's position is that "the war danger has not gone away since the reasons that engender it have not been eliminated," the marshal hastened to add. "Let me tell you in all candor that as far [as] my country is concerned," he continued, "we see the reason for war danger in the position-of-strength policy pursued by the U.S. and NATO...."

Several times in his statement, the Soviet official emphasized Moscow's concern over U.S. naval strength. American "reluctance" to negotiate a reduction in naval forces with the Soviet Union might impede other arms control initiatives, he suggested. "We regard reaching agreement on starting the talks to reduce our naval forces and limit military activities at sea to be a major prerequisite for further improvements of Soviet-American relations and switching them onto really peaceful rail tracks," he said.

"Stealth" Bomber Vote

Akhromeyev concluded his American visit July 28 by calling on President George Bush at the White House and speaking at the National Press Club. In that speech, the marshal repeated some of the main points of his congressional testimony. He indicated that if the United States proceeded with plans to build B-2 ("Stealth") bombers, the Soviet Union would move to counteract them.

The air force requested funding for 132 of these complex warplanes at an ultimate estimated cost of $70 billion. However, the House of Representatives on July 27 slashed the requested $4.88 billion funding for the bomber in the fiscal 1990 defense authorization bill to $3.0 billion and further voted to halt production until the air force scaled back the program. After the House voted, Rowland Evans and Robert Novak recalled in their syndicated newspaper column that William Odom, a retired general who once headed the National Security Agency, had testified on the defense bill that Gorbachev's strategy "is not at all defensive." Akhromeyev, they added, "apparently made a stronger impression on the House Armed Services Committee than did the American general."

> *Following are excerpts from the testimony of Soviet Marshal Sergei F. Akhromeyev before the House Armed Services Committee, July 21, 1989, as provided in translation by the committee. (The bracketed headings have been added by Congressional Quarterly to highlight the organization of the text.):*

... I am personally convinced that neither the U.S. nor its allies intend today to unleash a warfare against the USSR and its allies. I openly make these kinds of statements in my country. We are telling our people that the tensions in the world and war danger have diminished. And this has been the result of positive changes in the relations between the USSR and U.S. that I already mentioned.

We are convinced that political means to achieve national security will predominate in the 90s, while the role of military means must decrease. The USSR intends to work to this end in the 90s. This course was approved by ... the Congress of People's deputies of the USSR.

However, the war danger has not gone away since the reasons that engender it have not been eliminated. Now I am stating the position of the USSR and most likely you would not agree to it. Let me tell you in all candor that as far [as] my country is concerned we see the reason for war danger in the position-of-strength policy pursued by the U.S. and NATO [North Atlantic Treaty Organization] with regard to the USSR and WTO [Warsaw Treaty Organization]. Certain officials of the U.S. Administration publicly associate themselves with such policy. We realize, of course, that there have been some changes in the U.S. policies over the last few months. We appreciate the statement by the U.S. President in the Polish parliament where he said that the time had come to transcend the concept of deterrence framework and reach for a better relationship with the USSR and socialist countries of Central Europe. However, some days later a decision is taken in Paris to confirm the same deterrence strategy based primarily on nuclear weapons. A contradictory situation develops.

Creating the national ABM [Anti-Ballistic Missile] system in the U.S. is a source of danger to peace in the world. ... It is our view in the USSR that if the U.S. ABM system, particularly its space strike echelon, is created which is actually sought by the U.S. negotiating team in Geneva, the signing of a treaty cutting strategic offensive arms by 50% would become inappropriate. The arms race in strategic weapons, including new types of weapons, would become inevitable with all the negative effects for the entire world.

[Naval Force Concern]

We in the USSR are greatly concerned over the reluctance of the U.S. administration to open negotiations with the USSR on bilateral reductions of our naval forces. We are regarding this as the U.S. desire first to reach agreement with us on cutting the ground forces in Europe (the U.S. is interested in such an agreement, and we work to this end) and then build up its naval forces without any constraints, especially its carrier battle groups, thus gaining military superiority in order to dictate its will to the USSR from the position of strength. ... We regard reaching agreement on starting the talks to reduce our naval forces and limit military activities at seas to be a major prerequisite for further improvement of Soviet-American relations and switching them onto really peaceful rail tracks.

We are concerned that over 40 years ago the U.S. surrounded the USSR with a network of military bases, deployed a grouping of over 500,000 servicemen, large contingents of air and naval forces, and today the U.S. is not prepared to reduce those bases. . . .

I am saying all this not to lay claims to the U.S. Being your guest I do not share this attitude. I am saying this because you need to know that such kind of actions on the part of the U.S. have a direct bearing on the Soviet stand in the field of national security for the 90s. Had the U.S. deemed it possible to accommodate the Soviet concerns (which are well grounded), the policy of the USSR in the field of national security would have been different. . . .

Restructuring is under way in my country: revolutionary changes are taking place in economic relations, in the political system, in the relations between nationalities. Restructuring also covers the national security issues: a new military doctrine and guidelines for defense sufficiency have been worked out. These processes are taking place in the atmosphere of openness and growing democracy, in the environment of problems, difficulties and sometimes crisis situations. Some American officials are foretelling failure to us, others believe in success of our renewal. You are free to appraise our renewal any way you want. But we are confident that we will overcome our hardships and resolve the problems we are facing. . . .

[Strategic Offensive Arms]

As is well known, the USSR is prepared to completely eliminate nuclear weapons by the year 2000. However, our negotiating partners are not ready for this move. . . .

All in all, the U.S. by the year 2000 could possess over 2,000 strategic carriers and over 10,000 warheads for them. . . . We realize that you have some options to cut these forces by 50%.

As of the middle of 1989 the USSR . . . possesses 2,484 strategic carriers with about 10,000 warheads deployed on them. . . .

Provided the USSR-U.S. ABM treaty is observed as it was signed in 1972, no new types of strategic carriers other than the ones possessed by the USSR today would be deployed in the 90s.

We in the USSR are working on the options to reduce the strategic nuclear arms by 50 percent in keeping with the framework agreed upon by M. S. Gorbachev and R. Reagan in Washington in December 1987. . . .

It is most likely that the ceilings we have already agreed upon and a future treaty reducing the strategic offensive arms by 50% will provide the foundation for developing the Soviet strategic nuclear forces in the 90s. . . .

[Strategic Defensive Arms]

We in the Soviet Union are convinced that the ABM treaty as it was signed in 1972 should be the basis in the field of strategic defensive arms for building the Soviet-American relationship in the 90s. That treaty established physical interconnection between strategic offensive arms and strategic defensive arms. We proceed from the fact that this treaty permits our countries to set up one ABM defense area for each side, conduct research, development and testing with a view to creating land-based ABM systems. . . .

We proceed from the 1972 ABM treaty which permits R&D work to perfect land-based ABM systems but prohibits the work to test and deploy strike systems in place. I believe this is where the main difference lies between the Soviet and American stands on the ABM issue at the Geneva talks.

In developing the strategic offensive and defensive forces . . . we are guided by the principle of military parity. These forces should not necessarily have similar force structure. But they should be comparable with respect to their capability and flexibility of control. Strategic offensive forces must be ready in any environment to launch a retaliatory strike to inflict unacceptable losses on the side which was the first to use its strategic offensive forces.

[General Purpose Forces]

. . . New Soviet military doctrine was developed in the mid-eighties and adopted in 1987. . . .

In accordance with it we are reducing our armed forces by the end of 1990 by 500,000 troops, we are making the posture of our motor rifle and tank divisions in Central Europe defensive and we are undertaking other measures. . . .

. . . [B]oth sides maintain in Europe excessively large military groupings. They should be cut back. The relevant proposals in Vienna have been submitted both by the Warsaw Treaty Organization and by the NATO bloc. We are ready for a radical reduction of the armed forces in Europe. As you know, we haven't got a common approach to the problem of reducing the tactical nuclear weapons in the European continent. . . .

The Soviet naval grouping is deployed in this region with due regard for the military presence of the U.S. and Japan.

In our estimate the forces of the U.S. and Japan in this region outnumber the corresponding forces of the Soviet Union by two times in manpower, by four times in major surface warships, and by two times in attack aircraft.

To reciprocate, the Soviet Union deployed here the forces consisting of 326,000 men, 870 combat aircraft, 4,500 tanks, 4,100 armored vehicles, 7,000 guns and mortars, 55 major surface warships, 48 nuclear powered attack submarines. Apart from that, a small amount of resources are deployed on the Soviet-Chinese border.

We are ready to negotiate on a cutback of the armed forces in that region. The relevant proposals were put forward by M. S. Gorbachev in 1986 and 1988.

. . . After our pullout from Afghanistan the elements of the ground forces have been disbanded, the air units have been partly disbanded and partly returned to their permanent basing areas.

At present this grouping is insignificant. It is aimed at protecting our country's southern borders.

The armed forces in ... [the northern Soviet Union] are designed to repel air strikes which can be delivered on our country via the North Pole. . . .

[Soviet Combat Strength]

As of Jan. 1, 1989 the strength of the ground forces was 1,596,000 men. By Jan. 1, 1991 it will have been unilaterally reduced by 300,000 men and will make 1,296,000 men.

As it is known, we propose that the armed forces of both military alliances in Europe be reduced by 1 million men on each side. This proposal is on the negotiating table in Vienna. . . . Out of this number about 500,000 men will be Soviet servicemen.

That means that the ground forces will be completely different in force structure and manpower capable of repulsing an aggression, but incapable of conducting large offensive operations. . . .

Evolution of the front-level aviation in the 90s will directly depend on the progress of the talks on armed forces reduction in Europe, as well as on the evolution of the corresponding aircraft of the U.S. and NATO. In Vienna we proposed to cut back the attack aviation by 60-65 percent and keep 1,500 aircraft of this category for each side. . . .

The USSR is firmly determined to adhere to the defensive military doctrine and to maintain the armed forces at the minimum level. . . .

We intend to keep our strategic nuclear forces approximately equal to the U.S. strategic offensive forces and we do not intend to gain superiority in this field. . . .

Contacts between the [U.S. and Soviet] military establishments acquire ever increasing importance. The meetings of the Defense Ministers of the USSR and U.S., of the Chief of General Staff of the Soviet Armed Forces and the Chairman of the JCS [U.S. Joint Chiefs of Staff] ... proved very useful. All this creates a very favourable atmosphere of trust and decreased military tension. . . .

Mr. Chairman! Members of the Armed Services Committee! Ladies and Gentlemen!

Allow me once again to express my appreciation for the opportunity to speak before you on one of the most important subjects which determines the level of Soviet-American relations. My presentation in the U.S. Congress is the first address of a Soviet serviceman to the U.S. Congress, and I do hope it's not the last one.

For our part, the USSR Supreme Soviet committee on defense is extending an invitation to a representative of the U.S. Armed Forces of your own choice to speak at one of its sessions.

Mr. Chairman! This is the end of my presentation.

Thank you for your attention.

NATIONAL RESEARCH COUNCIL
REPORT ON BLACK AMERICANS
July 27, 1989

Although black Americans have made considerable gains in the last few decades, their overall socioeconomic status still lags far behind that of whites. These and other findings on the status of black Americans were released July 27 in a 608-page report by the National Research Council (NRC), the principal operating agency of the National Academy of Sciences and Engineering.

"If all racial discrimination were abolished today, the life prospects facing many poor blacks would still constitute major challenges for public policy," the report said, noting that racial discrimination was only one of several barriers to the improvement of the status of the nation's thirty million black people.

"Barring unforeseen events or changes in present conditions—that is, no changes in educational policies and opportunities, no increased income and employment opportunities, and no major national programs to deal directly with the problems of economic dependency—our findings imply several negative developments for blacks in the near future, developments that in turn do not bode well for American society," the committee concluded.

The report attributed the lack of progress in large part to an economic slowdown since 1973. It affected both blacks and whites but particularly hurt blacks at the lower end of the economic spectrum. Although blacks made great economic strides between 1940 and 1970, "since the early 1970s, the economic status of blacks relative to whites has, on average, stagnated or deteriorated," said Gerald D. Jaynes, professor of economics and a scholar in the African and African-American studies department at Yale University, who directed the NRC study. At the same time, he noted, there also had been a widening of status differences among groups of blacks.

The study, entitled "A Common Destiny: Blacks and American Society," was launched in 1984 after three years of preliminary planning. It was financed by the Carnegie Corporation; the Pew Charitable Trusts; the Ford, Robert Wood Johnson, Andrew W. Mellon, Rockefeller, and Alfred P. Sloan foundations; and the National Research Council fund at a cost of $2.7 million. The chairman of the twenty-two-member commission—composed of economic, political, and social scholars—was Robin M. Williams, Jr., professor emeritus of social science at Cornell University. More than one hundred experts participated in the undertaking.

Williams said that the study was initiated because the NRC felt there had been no comprehensive study of blacks in society since Swedish economist Gunnar Myrdal in 1944 published his groundbreaking work, An American Dilemma, and the Advisory Commission on Civil Disorders (known as the Kerner Commission) in 1968 warned that the United States was becoming a racially divided nation. (Kerner Report Update, Historic Documents of 1988, p. 185)

Major Findings

The report focused on six areas: participation in the political process, economic status, schooling, health, crime and criminal justice, and the well-being of children in families. Among the report's findings were:

- The full assimilation of blacks in a "color blind" society is unlikely in the foreseeable future.
- Housing segregation remains strong. Blacks were more likely than whites to be excluded from renting or buying in certain residential areas. Residential separation in large metropolitan areas was nearly as high in the 1980s as in the 1960s.
- Although large majorities of whites and blacks endorsed the principles of equal racial opportunity and treatment, those principles were endorsed less when they would result in close, frequent, or prolonged social contact between the races.

Concerning education, the report stated that programs in early intervention and compensatory education, such as Head Start and Chapter 1, had produced "overall positive effects on blacks' educational performance." But it also noted that the pace of school desegregation has slowed, and racial separation in education is significant, "especially outside the south."

The study found that black students showed small but steady gains in academic achievement and experienced dramatic increases in high school completion rates. But still, the report added, "[T]he odds that a black student will enter college within a year of graduation from high school are less than one-half the odds that a white high school graduate will do so."

Concerning black family life, the report found that half of all black families with children in 1985 were headed by women and received only 25 percent of the total black family income. Eighty-six percent of black children were likely to spend some time in a single-parent household, as compared with 42 percent of white children.

Reaction, Other Studies

The study had "two major findings—one positive, the other negative," said Jaynes. "By any calibration other than that of an unrepentant segregationist, race relations and blacks' status are remarkably improved since the World War II era. However, the major fraction of this improvement was in place by 1970. Since then, material measures of status relative to whites have not improved and many have deteriorated." The report "underscores how much we still have to do," said Ralph Neas, executive director of the Leadership Conference on Civil Rights.

On the other hand, according to Mary Francis Berry, professor of history at the University of Pennsylvania and a member of the U.S. Civil Rights Commission, "The most important thing about this report is that it may help to eradicate the myth of the perpetual underclass and culture as a reason for the lack of black progress."

Some critics of the study had objected that only half of the council members were black, and that some were considered politically conservative. Meanwhile, a parallel study by black scholars was being undertaken under the auspices of the William Monroe Trotter Institute for the Study of Black Cultures at the University of Massachusetts. "The [NRC] study may have come out better than we thought," commented Wornie L. Reed, director of the Trotter Institute and executive director of its study.

A five-year study conducted by the Population Research Center at the University of Chicago found that racial segregation in ten of the nation's largest cities was more deeply entrenched than many researchers had previously thought. The study, published in the August 4 issue of Demography *magazine, was financed by the National Institutes of Health. "It's not news to anyone that blacks are segregated in this society," said Douglas S. Massey, director of the center and the study. "What's new is that it's worse than we imagined. Racial segregation in this country is deeper and more profound than previous attempts to study it had indicated."*

At its annual conference, the National Urban League on August 7 warned that disparities between blacks and whites in employment, income, education, and other areas were so wide that parity was not likely until after the year 2000. A study released October 1 by the House Select Committee on Children, Youth, and Families found that nearly half of all black children in America live in poverty.

> *Following are excerpts from the National Research Council's report, "A Common Destiny: Blacks and American Society," released July 27, 1989:*

Just five decades ago, most black Americans could not work, live, shop, eat, seek entertainment, or travel where they chose. Even a quarter century ago—100 years after the Emancipation Proclamation of 1863—most blacks were effectively denied the right to vote. A large majority of blacks lived in poverty, and very few black children had the opportunity to receive a basic education; indeed, black children were still forced to attend inferior and separate schools in jurisdictions that had not accepted the 1954 decision of the Supreme Court declaring segregated schools unconstitutional.

Today the situation is very different. In education, many blacks have received college degrees from universities that formerly excluded them. In the workplace, blacks frequently hold professional and managerial jobs in desegregated settings. In politics, most blacks now participate in elections, and blacks have been elected to all but the highest political offices. Overall, many blacks have achieved middle-class status.

Yet the great gulf that existed between black and white Americans in 1939 has only been narrowed; it has not closed. One of three blacks still live in households with incomes below the poverty line. Even more blacks live in areas where ineffective schools, high rates of dependence on public assistance, severe problems of crime and drug use, and low and declining employment prevail. Race relations, as they affect the lives of inhabitants of these areas, differ considerably from black-white relations involving middle-class blacks. Lower status blacks have less access to desegregated schools, neighborhoods, and other institutions and public facilities. Their interactions with whites frequently emphasize their subordinate status—as low-skilled employees, public agency clients, and marginally performing pupils.

The status of black Americans today can be characterized as a glass that is half full—if measured by progress since 1939 or as a glass that is half empty—if measured by the persisting disparities between black and white Americans since the early 1970s. Any assessment of the quality of life for blacks is also complicated by the contrast between blacks who have achieved middle-class status and those who have not.

The progress occurred because sustained struggles by blacks and their allies changed American law and politics, moving all governments and most private institutions from support of principles of racial inequality to support of principles of racial equality. Gradually, and often with much resistance, the behaviors and attitudes of individual whites moved in the same direction. Over the 50-year span covered by this study, the social status of American blacks has *on average* improved dramatically, both in absolute terms and relative to whites. The growth of the economy and public policies promoting racial equality led to an erosion of segregation and discrimination, making it possible for a substantial fraction of blacks to enter the mainstream of American life.

The reasons for the continuing distress of large numbers of black Americans are complex. Racial discrimination continues despite the victories of the civil rights movement. Yet, the problems faced today by blacks who are isolated from economic and social progress are less directly open to political amelioration than were the problems of legal segregation and the widely practiced overt discrimination of a few decades past. Slow overall growth of the economy during the 1970s and 1980s has been an important impediment to black progress; in the three previous decades economic prosperity and rapid growth had been a great help to most blacks. Educational institutions and government policies have not successfully responded to underlying changes in the society. Opportunities for upward mobility have been reduced for all lower status Americans, but especially for those who are black. If all racial discrimination were abolished today, the life prospects facing many poor blacks would still constitute major challenges for public policy.

Summary of Major Findings

... The new "American dilemma" that has emerged after the civil rights era of the 1960s results from two aspirations of black Americans: equal opportunity—the removal of barriers to employment, housing, education, and political activities— and the actual attainment of equality in participation in these sectors of life.

Central to the realization of these aspirations are national policies promoting equality of opportunity for the most disadvantaged blacks (especially in areas such as employment and education) and the preservation among black people of attitudes and behaviors toward self-help and individual sacrifice that have enabled them to benefit from such opportunities. Black-white relations are important in determining the degree to which equal opportunity exists for black Americans. Whites desire equality of treatment in social institutions and in governmental policy; however, many whites are less likely to espouse or practice equality of treatment for blacks in their personal behavior. Thus, at the core of black-white relations is a dynamic tension between many whites' expectations of American institutions and their expectations of themselves.... [T]he divergence between social principle and individual practice frequently leads to white avoidance of blacks in those institutions in which equal treatment is most needed. The result is that American institutions do not provide the full equality of opportunity that Americans desire.

Foremost among the reasons for the present state of black-white relations are two continuing consequences of the nation's long and recent history of racial inequality. One is the negative attitudes held toward blacks and the other is the actual disadvantaged conditions under which many black Americans live. These two consequences reinforce each other. Thus, a legacy of discrimination and segregation continues to affect black-white relations....

We can summarize our main findings on the status of blacks in America in the late 1980s succinctly:

- By almost all aggregate statistical measures—incomes and living standards; health and life expectancy; educational, occupational, and

449

residential opportunities; political and social participation—the well-being of both blacks and whites has advanced greatly over the past five decades.
- By almost all the same indicators, blacks remain substantially behind whites.

Beyond this brief picture lies a more complex set of changes that affect the *relative* status of black Americans:

- The greatest economic gains for blacks occurred in the 1940s and 1960s. Since the early 1970s, the economic status of blacks relative to whites has, on average, stagnated or deteriorated.
- The political, educational, health, and cultural statuses of blacks showed important gains from the 1940s through the 1970s. In addition, some important indicators continued to improve after the early 1970s.
- Among blacks, the experiences of various groups have differed, and status differences among those groups have increased. Some blacks have attained high-status occupations, income, education, and political positions, but a substantial minority remain in disadvantaged circumstances.

These patterns of change have been largely determined by three factors:

- Political and social activism among black Americans and their white allies led to changes in governmental policies; particularly important were sweeping improvements in the legal status of blacks.
- Resistance to social change in race relations continues in American society.
- Broad changes in overall economic conditions, especially the post-1973 slowdown in the nation's economic growth, have significantly affected social and economic opportunities for all Americans. . . .

Blacks and Whites in a Changing Society

Two general developments in the status of black Americans stand out; each is reflective of a near-identical development in the population at large. First, for the period 1940-1973, real earnings of Americans improved steadily, but they stagnated and declined after 1973. Similarly, over these same periods, there was a clear record of improving average material status of blacks relative to whites followed by stagnation and decline. Second, during the post-1973 period, inequality increased among Americans as the lowest income and least skilled people were hurt most by changes in the overall economy. Similarly, there were increasing differences in material well-being and opportunities among blacks, and they have been extremely pronounced. . . .

A major reason [for the differences] is the performance of the economy. . . . A generation ago, a low-skilled man had relatively abundant opportunity to obtain a blue-collar job with a wage adequate to support a family at a lower middle class level or better. Today the jobs available to such men—and women—are often below or just barely above the official poverty line for a family of four. . . . [A]mong men who did not complete high school, blacks and whites had lower real earnings in 1986 than in 1969. . . .

Perhaps the most important consequences of the stagnating U.S. economy have been the effects on the status of children. . . . During the 1970s, approximately 2 of every 3 black children could expect to live in poverty for a least 1 of the first 10 years of their childhood, while an astounding 1 of 3 could expect at least 7 of those 10 years to be lived in poverty. . . .

Determinants of Black Status

Barriers and disadvantages persist in blocking black advancement. Three such barriers to full opportunity for black Americans are residential segregation, continuance of diffuse and often indirect discrimination, and exclusion from social networks essential for full access to economic and educational opportunities. . . .

The past five decades have shown that purposeful actions and policies by governments and private institutions make a large difference in the opportunities and conditions of black Americans. Such purposeful actions and policies have been essential for past progress, and further progress is unlikely without them. Many blacks attained middle-class status because government and private programs enabled them to achieve better educations and jobs, through employment and education programs and government enforcement of equal employment opportunity. . . .

Black initiative and identity have increasingly played primary roles in bringing about changes in government and private institutions and improvements in blacks' economic, social, and political status. . . .

Many blacks who have not succeeded live in environments in which social conditions and individual behavioral patterns are often detrimental to self-improvement. Such behaviors may be natural responses to group conditions and social forces perceived as beyond personal control. One-half of black families with children must manage their affairs with only one parent—almost always a mother. These families are overwhelmingly poor (59 percent were below the poverty line in 1987), have high rates of dependence on family assistance benefits, and live in areas with a high percentage of families in similar circumstances. . . .

Why do such behaviors and conditions persist? There are no simple answers to this crucial question and no answers that can be validated as scientific findings. We can say, however, that the evidence does not support some popular hypotheses that purport to explain female-headed households, high birth rates to unmarried women, low labor force participation by males, or poor academic performance solely on the basis of government support programs or, more generally, on the existence of a "culture of poverty" among the black poor. Black-white cultural differences have narrowed since 1960, not widened. . . .

Our analysis of the problem does identify a number of important contributory factors. Discrimination plays an important role in the lives of many blacks, and even in the absence of discrimination the opportunities of many blacks are limited. Black youths in poor environments probably anticipate little payoff from working for academic achievement and may underestimate their opportunities. Those in poorly staffed, dilapidated schools populated with underachieving students can easily fall into the trap of perceiving the pursuit of academic excellence as a poor investment. . . .

Yet the status of blacks is determined by the presence of both racial stratification and class (position within the socioeconomic structure of society). Changes in black-white relations and social opportunities do not affect blacks of different status in similar ways. For example, because of higher geographic concentrations of poor households among blacks, segregated residential areas affect the quality of schools and medical care available to low-income blacks more than they affect the availability of these resources to higher income blacks or low-income whites. And we have already noted that changes in the national economy have had particularly negative effects on lower status Americans, white and black. But changes have been most detrimental to the fortunes of blacks, and opportunities were curtailed most for blacks of lowest status. . . .

A Record of the Status of Black Americans

Large majorities of blacks and whites accept the principles of equal access to public institutions and equal treatment in race relations. . . . Yet there remain important signs of continuing resistance to full equality of black Americans. Principles of equality are endorsed less when they would result in close, frequent, or prolonged social contact, and whites are much less prone to endorse policies meant to implement equal participation of blacks in important social institutions. In practice, many whites refuse or are reluctant to participate in social settings (e.g., neighborhoods and schools) in which significant numbers of blacks are present. . . .

Although large-scale desegregation of public schools occurred in the South during the late 1960s and early 1970s—and has been substantial in many small and medium-sized cities elsewhere—the pace of school desegregation has slowed, and racial separation in education is significant, especially outside the South. And residential separation of whites and blacks in large metropolitan areas remains nearly as high in the 1980s as it was in the 1960s.

These findings suggest that a considerable amount of remaining black-white inequality is due to continuing discriminatory treatment of blacks. The clearest evidence is in housing. Discrimination against blacks seeking housing has been conclusively demonstrated. . . .

The residential separation of blacks and whites is nearly twice the rate of white and Asian-Americans, and it is often much greater than residential separation between Hispanic Americans and whites in many cities. . . .

Many blacks believe that their relative position in society cannot be improved without government policies to intervene with social institutions on behalf of minorities and the disadvantaged. In contrast with whites, blacks have highly favorable views of the high activity years of government policy intervention of the 1960s.

As a consequence of their heightened group consciousness, their belief that racial discrimination remains a major deterrent to black progress, and their history of collective social expression, black Americans vote at the same or higher rates than whites of comparable socioeconomic status, support redistributive policies more often than do whites, and participate in a wider variety of political activity. . . .

. . . Changes in black social structure have resulted from the rising incomes, occupations, and educations of many blacks. The exit of higher status blacks from inner cities has accentuated problems of increasing social stratification among blacks. The service needs of poorer blacks have placed strains on many black institutions, including schools, churches, and voluntary service organizations. These strains have resulted in a proliferation of activities devoted to the material needs of poor blacks by black organizations. . . .

Political Participation

. . . Active participation by blacks in American political life has had a major impact on their role in the society. . . . The number of black elected officials has risen from a few dozen in 1940 to over 6,800 in 1988. However, blacks comprise only about 1.5 percent of all elected officials. The election of black officials does result in additional hiring and higher salaries for blacks in public-sector jobs and more senior positions for blacks in appointive public office. The black proportion of federal, state, and local public administrators rose from less than 1 percent in 1940 to 8 percent in 1980; even so, it was less than blacks' 13 percent proportion of the U.S. population. As measured by the proportion of delegates to the national party conventions, black participation in the political party organizations has increased dramatically among Democrats since 1940, while black participation in Republican party affairs, after declining during the 1960s and 1970s, has returned to be about the same level as in 1940. . . .

Economic Status

Changes in labor market conditions and social policies of governments have had many beneficial effects on the economic status of black Americans. Yet the current economic prospects are not good for many blacks. Adverse changes in labor market opportunities and family conditions— falling real wages and employment, increases in one-parent families with one or no working adults—have made conditions especially difficult for those blacks from the most disadvantaged backgrounds. However, among blacks, changes in family structure per se have not been a major cause of continuing high poverty rates since the early 1970s.

Black-white differences are large despite significant improvements in the absolute and relative positions of blacks over the past 50 years. After initial decades of rising relative black economic status, black gains stagnated on many measures after the early 1970s. Lack of progress in important indicators of economic status during the past two decades is largely a consequence of two conflicting trends: while blacks' weekly and hourly wages have risen relative to whites, blacks' relative employment rates have deteriorated significantly. . . .

In terms of per capita incomes, family incomes, and male workers' earnings, blacks gained relative to whites fairly steadily from 1939 to 1969; measures of relative status peaked in the early to mid-1970s, and since have remained stagnant or declined. Women earn much less than men, but the gap between black and white women decreased steadily throughout the period until, by 1984, black women had earnings very close to those of white women. Employment rates of adult black men and women have been falling relative to those of white men and women throughout the period; black unemployment rates remain approximately twice those of white rates. The proportion of working black men and women in white-collar occupations and in managerial and professional positions increased throughout the period, but these gains show signs of slowing in the 1980s.

Uneven change in the average economic position of blacks has been accompanied, especially during the past 25 years, by accentuated differences in status among blacks. An important aspect of the polarization in the incomes of black families has been the growth of female-headed black families since 1960. It is among such families that the incidence of poverty is highest. It is no exaggeration to say that the two most numerically important components of the black class structure have become a lower class dominated by female-headed families and a middle class largely composed of two-parent families. The percentage of both blacks and whites living in households with incomes below the poverty line declined during the 1939-1975 period. But poverty rates have risen in the past decade, and black poverty rates have been 2 to 3 times higher than white rates at all times.

The major developments accounting for black gains in earnings and occupation status from 1939 to 1969 were South-to-North migration and concurrent movement from agricultural to nonagricultural employment, job creation, and national economic growth. After 1965, major factors responsible for improvements in blacks' status have been government policies against discrimination, government incentives for the equal employment opportunity of minorities, general changes in race relations, and higher educational attainment.

Schooling

Substantial progress has been made toward the provision of educational resources to blacks. Yet black and white educational opportunities are not generally equal. Standards of academic performance for teachers and students are not equivalent in schools that serve predominantly black students and those that serve predominantly white students. Nor are equal encouragement and support provided for the educational achievement and attainment of black and white students. . . .

Measures of educational outcomes—attainment and achievement—reveal substantial gaps between blacks and whites. Blacks, on average, enter the schools with substantial disadvantages in socioeconomic backgrounds and tested achievement. American schools do not compensate for these disadvantages in background: on average, students leave the schools with black-white gaps not having been appreciably diminished.

There remain persistent and large gaps in the schooling quality and achievement outcomes of education for blacks and whites. At the pinnacle of the educational process, blacks' life opportunities relative to whites' are demonstrated by the fact that the odds that a black high school graduate will enter college within a year of graduation are less than one-half the odds that a white high school graduate will do so. College enrollment rates of high school graduates, after rising sharply since the late 1970s, declined in the mid-1970s; while white enrollment rates have recovered, black rates in the 1980s remain well below those of the 1970s. The proportion of advanced degrees awarded to blacks has also decreased. While we cannot conclude with certainty that the cause has been the decline in (real) financial aid grants to students, other reasonable hypotheses can explain only a negligible component of this change.

Segregation and differential treatment of blacks continue to be widespread in the elementary and secondary schools. We find that school desegregation does not substantially affect the academic performance of white students, but it does modestly improve black performance (in particular, reading). When several key conditions are met, intergroup attitudes and relations improve after schools are desegregated. And desegregation is most likely to reduce racial isolation as well as improve academic and social outcomes for blacks when it is part of a comprehensive and rapid desegregation plan.

Differences in the schooling experienced by black and white students contribute to black-white differences in achievement. The differences are closely tied to teacher behavior; school climate; and the content, quality, and organization of instruction. Early intervention compensatory education programs, such as Head Start, have had positive effects on blacks' educational performance. Among the most recent cohorts to complete their education—people born in the late 1950s and early 1960s—blacks have a median education close to that of whites, 12.6 years, compared with 12.9 years for whites. But a remaining substantial gap in overall educational attainment is noncompletion: high school dropout rates for blacks are double those for whites.

Changes in academic achievement test scores show that, while black students' average scores remain well below white students' average scores, black performance has improved faster, and black-white differences have become somewhat smaller.

Health

There have been substantial improvements in life expectancy and health status for Americans since 1940. However, overall gains have not been evenly shared. . . .

455

Persisting wide gaps in the mortality and morbidity of blacks compared to whites remain at all ages except among the oldest old (people 85 and older). . . .

Blacks are underrepresented in the health professions (as compared to their population percentage); this is important since access to care by minorities and the poor increases with the availability of minority providers. . . .

Significant improvement in the health status of blacks will also depend on reducing health-damaging personal behaviors such as substance abuse, injuries (accidental and nonaccidental), homicide, and sexual activities that can cause ill-timed pregnancy or risk infection with sexually transmitted diseases. Slowing the transmission rate of the acquired immune deficiency syndrome (AIDS) in the black community is critical. . . .

Crime and Criminal Justice

Among black Americans, distrust of the criminal justice system is widespread. Historically, discrimination against blacks in arrests and sentencing was ubiquitous. Prior the the 1980s, very few blacks were employed as law enforcement officials, but in the 1980s, the percentage of blacks to whites in police forces has increased to substantial levels. Black representation among attorneys and judges has also increased, although it is not as high as that in the police.

Blacks are arrested, convicted, and imprisoned for criminal offenses at rates much higher than are whites. Currently, blacks account for nearly one-half of all prison inmates in the United States. . . . Blacks also suffer disproportionately from injuries and economic losses due to criminal actions. . . .

The role of discrimination in criminal justice has apparently varied substantially from place to place and over time. Some part of the unexplained differences in black-white arrest rates may be due to racial bias and the resulting differential treatment. Current black-white differences in sentencing appear to be due less to overt racial bias than to socioeconomic differences between blacks and whites: people of lower socioeconomic status—regardless of race—receive more severe sentences than people of higher status. An important exception may be bias in sentencing that is related to the race of the victim: criminals whose victims are white are on average punished more severely than those whose victims are black.

As long as there are great disparities in the socioeconomic status of blacks and whites, blacks will continue to be overrepresented in the criminal justice system as victims and offenders. And because of these disparities, the precise degree to which the overrepresentation reflects racial bias cannot be determined.

Children and Families

Changes since the mid-1960s among both blacks and whites have brought higher rates of marital breakup, decreased rates of marriage, rapidly rising proportions of female-headed households, and increasing proportion of children being reared in single-parent families. The changes have been much greater among blacks than among whites. . . .

Birthrates for both the white and black populations have fallen since the baby boom of the 1950s, and fertility rates have declined for women of all ages. By the mid-1980s, the lifetime fertility rates were similar for black and white women. Contrary to popular myth, birthrates among black teenagers—although still an important problem—have declined significantly during the past two decades.

In 1970, about 18 percent of black families had incomes over $35,000 (1987 constant dollars); by 1986 this proportion had grown to 22 percent. The increase in well-to-do families was matched by an increase in low-income families. During the same 1970-1980 period, the proportion of black families with incomes of less than $10,000 grew from about 26 to 30 percent. After declining during earlier decades, the percentage of black and white children in poverty began to increase in the 1970s. In 1986, 43 percent of black children and 16 percent of white children under age 18 lived in households below the poverty line.

Black and white children are increasingly different with regard to their living arrangements. As we noted above, a majority of black children under age 18 live in families that include their mothers but not their fathers; in contrast, four of every five white children live with both parents. . . . In the course of their childhood, 86 percent of black children and 42 percent of white children are likely to spend some time in a single-parent household.

The greater inequality between family types among blacks has important consequences for the welfare of future generations. Black female-headed families were 50 percent of all black families with children in 1985, but had 25 percent of total black family income, while 70 percent of black family income was received by black husband-wife families.

The data and analyses we have examined throw doubt on the validity of the thesis that a culture of poverty is a major cause of long-term poverty. Although cultural factors are important in social behavior, arguments for the existence of unalterable behavior among the poor are not supported by empirical research. The behaviors that are detrimental to success are often responses to existing social barriers to opportunity. The primary correlates of poverty are macroeconomic conditions of prosperity or recession and changes in family composition. However, increases in female-headed families have had only negligible effects on increasing black poverty rates since the mid-1970s. Importantly, attitudes toward work and the desire to succeed are not very different among the poor and the nonpoor. . . .

The Future: Alternatives and Policy Implications

In assessing the status of black Americans, we have asked what roles blacks play in the nation today and what role they are likely to play in the near future. Our conclusion is largely positive, but it is mixed. The great majority of black Americans contribute to the political, economic, and social health of the nation. The typical black adult—like the typical white adult—is a full-time employee or homemaker who pays taxes, votes in public elections, and sends children to school. Blacks make important contributions to all forms of American life, from the sciences and health care, to politics and education, to arts and entertainment. . . .

Barring unforeseen events or changes in present conditions—that is, no changes in educational policies and opportunities, no increased income and employment opportunities, and no major national programs to deal directly with the problems of economic dependency—our findings imply several negative developments for blacks in the near future, developments that in turn do not bode well for American society:

- A substantial majority of black Americans will remain contributors to the nation, but improvements in their status relative to whites are likely to slow even more as the rate of increase of the black middle class is likely to decline.
- Approximately one-third of the black population will continue to be poor, and the relative employment and earnings status of black men is likely to deteriorate further.
- Drugs and crime, teenage parenthood, poor educational opportunities, and joblessness will maintain their grip on large numbers of poor and near-poor blacks.
- High rates of residential segregation between blacks and whites will continue.
- The United States is faced with the prospect of continued great inequality between whites and blacks and a continuing division of social status within the black population.
- A growing population of poor and undereducated citizens, disproportionately black and minority, will pose challenges to the nation's abilities to solve the emerging economic and social problems of the twenty-first century. . . .

Income and Poverty

Between 1940 and 1974, poverty as officially measured by cash income declined sharply. The percentage of blacks living in poor households fell from 92 percent in 1939 to 30 percent in 1974; among whites, the change was from 65 to 9 percent. If that trend had continued, the percentage of poor people in the year 2000 would be about 1 percent among whites and 9 percent among blacks. However, the trends toward lower poverty rates came to an end in the early 1970s; since 1974 rates have stagnated or even increased. If the post-1974 trend is extrapolated to the year 2000, the poverty rate among blacks will be about 32 percent and the rate among whites about 15 percent. These are approximately the rates of the late 1970s. Of course such predictions are tentative.

Policy Alternatives

. . . On the basis of the findings and analyses of this study, we have identified four areas of national life in which there are major options for constructive social policies to improve opportunities for disadvantaged Americans and especially to reduce impediments to black advancement:

- Provision of education, health care, and other services to enhance people's skills and productive capabilities;
- Facilitation of national economic growth and full employment;
- Reduction of discrimination and involuntary segregation; and
- Development and reform of income-maintenance and other family assistance social welfare programs to avoid long-term poverty.

Each type of policy contains many complex possibilities. Feasible alternatives necessary must be developed through the political processes by which collective decisions are made. Here we wish only to note some salient opinions.

Several specific policy interventions have been effective in promoting black advancement and greater opportunities for all Americans. Most successful have been employment and training programs such as the Job Corps; early intervention and other compensatory education programs such as Head Start; governmental financial aid for postsecondary education; increased access to health care, particularly for pre- and postnatal clinical service for low-income women; and greater health insurance coverage for all poor and near-poor people. These specific policy interventions have been shown to work and to be beneficial to the nation. Improvements in program design are surely possible and should be given the highest priority by policy makers and practitioners.

The one issue that stands out above all others in this study is that of bringing the black population into gainful full employment. This is a major task for public policy. Economic opportunity alone will not solve all problems, of course, but it is the essential ground for other constructive developments. All the evidence reviewed in this report points to the central importance of jobs for men and women at pay levels that permit families to live above the poverty line. . . .

August

President Bush's Remarks on Signing
    S&L Bailout Bill 463

Baltic Freedom Statements.............. 469

Statements on Banning Pete Rose
    from Baseball........................ 477

PRESIDENT BUSH'S REMARKS
ON SIGNING S&L BAILOUT BILL
August 9, 1989

President George Bush on August 9 signed into law a bill he had helped push through Congress to salvage the nation's troubled thrift industry and reestablish it as the premier source of home financing. The legislation committed the U.S. government to the biggest bailout of a troubled private enterprise that it had ever undertaken. The new law provided $50 billion to close down or sell off about 500 insolvent or nearly insolvent savings and loan institutions (S&Ls), or "thrifts." Some experts estimated that in time as many as one-third of the 3,000 S&Ls might disappear, and far greater amounts of government funding might be required. Those estimates ran as high as $300 billion over the course of three decades.

It was a problem that Bush inherited when he entered the presidency. Many of the savings institutions had been incurring losses for several years. And these deficits were growing. The Federal Home Loan Bank Board reported that losses among the nation's 3,000 federally insured S&Ls amounted to $7.8 billion in 1987 and $12.1 billion in 1988.

Typically, these institutions were receiving lower rates of interest on long-term home loans that they had made in past years than they were currently being forced to pay their depositors in order to attract new money. In an attempt to break even, some resorted to speculative investments, which once might have been forbidden but were unquestioned in the deregulatory mood of the 1980s. Many of those investments turned sour in the 1981-1982 national recession. The recession lingered on through much of the decade in the oil-producing states of Texas, Oklahoma, and Louisiana. A disproportionate number of S&L bankrupt-

cies occurred in those states. Nationwide, the government was forced to take over more than 200 bankrupt institutions in 1988, half of them during the last three months of the year.

Since neither the White House nor Congress had any desire to tackle the issue head-on in a presidential election year, the postponed S&L crisis immediately became a priority item for the new Bush administration. Even before Bush entered the Oval Office, Treasury Department officials were put to work on a bailout plan, which he unveiled in broad outline on February 6.

The Bush Plan

His plan—which became the basis for legislation that Congress cleared August 4—called for selling the remaining bankrupt savings institutions to investors during the next five years (reduced to three years by Congress) or simply closing them down and paying off the depositors from an insurance fund that would be set up through a complex set of long-term financial arrangements. The cost would be borne by both the taxpayers and the 2,000 or so still healthy institutions. The government had long been committed to insuring deposits in federally chartered S&Ls, up to $100,000 each. But the closures in 1988 had drained the existing fund, and a new one needed to be established.

In passing the new law, Congress did more than provide more money. It restructured the federal regulation of the industry by creating a new chartering and supervisory agency in the Treasury Department—the Office of Thrift Supervision (OTS)—replacing the independent Federal Home Loan Bank Board. And the new thrift insurance fund was created under the supervision of the Federal Deposit Insurance Corporation, which formerly insured only bank deposits. The bank insurance fund had remained solvent all this time.

"This legislation comes to grips with the problems facing our savings and loan industry," President Bush said at the bill-signing ceremony in the White House Rose Garden. "It'll safeguard and stabilize America's financial system and put in place permanent reforms so these problems will never happen again." But in the six months of congressional debate that preceded the bill's passage it was evident that few lawmakers looked on it as a comprehensive solution to a problem so immense that its full scope could not be measured with certainty.

Question of Ultimate Costs

The biggest question was whether there would be enough money when the newly created OTS got down to the hard work of closing the grossly insolvent thrifts, and possibly hundreds more that teetered at the brink of bankruptcy. To close an S&L requires paying off its deposits, and insolvent thrifts had $400 billion or more in deposits. However, some of the money could be recovered by selling the assets of the failed thrift, either to new owners or to investors who wanted to acquire half-finished apartment complexes, empty office buildings, and shopping centers

464

whose builders had defaulted on their loans to the institution. Some experts estimated that the process would replenish the bailout fund far less than the Treasury Department anticipated. Its assumption was a forty-cent return on every dollar the government spent in the rescue operation.

Congress authorized the OTS to issue government-guaranteed notes worth 85 percent of the market value of the assets from the failed thrifts. And it capped at $16 billion Treasury payments to a new Savings Association Insurance Fund (SAIF), which picks up where the OTS leaves off. The administration sought unlimited authority for notes and contributions, but Congress would not go along.

There was an additional question about the state of the national economy. The administration's cost projections counted on favorable growth and lower interest rates over the next several years. Nor did the forecast factor in the possibility of a recession, which would likely push more S&Ls into insolvency. Many members of Congress predicted that they would be asked within the next two years to raise more bailout money. Two years earlier, they had passed a bill that was intended to solve the industry's problems. It provided a $10.8 billion bailout fund that was supplied solely by the healthy S&Ls rather than by the government.

M. Danny Wall, chairman of the Federal Home Loan Bank Board, contended through most of that year that a federal bailout was not needed. When his agency was replaced by the OTS, Wall became its director despite objections in Congress that he had lost credibility. Pressure generated by congressional hearings led to his resignation December 4. The hearings were conducted by the House Banking Committee, whose chairman, Rep. Henry B. Gonzalez, D-Texas, was Wall's most outspoken critic. The committee investigated the failure of the Lincoln Savings and Loan Association of Irvine, California, whose collapse is expected to cost the government $2 billion. Lincoln's former owner, Charles H. Keating, Jr., was accused of looting it for personal gain. He refused to testify, citing his right not to. Wall, who testified November 21, denied allegations that Lincoln had been shielded from proper regulatory supervision. It was revealed that five senators had intervened with regulators in Lincoln's behalf in April 1987, and that Keating had raised $1.3 million in contributions for their campaigns and other political causes. The senators—Democrats Alan Cranston of California, Dennis De Concini of Arizona, John Glenn of Ohio, and Donald W. Riegle, Jr., of Michigan, and Republican John McCain of Arizona— denied any wrongdoing. The matter was placed before the Senate Ethics committee.

The Budget Debate

The bill's passage was further troubled by an argument over putting some of the bailout expenses "off-budget"—not counting them as part of the government's budget expenditures. When the president sent his plan to Congress in February it called for the creation of a quasi-governmental *agency to sell $50 billion in bonds to the public—at slightly higher interest rates than the Treasury would have to pay. Congressional Democrats, and a few Republicans, rejected off-budgeting. Several compromises were explored but none became acceptable until after the president on August 3 threatened to veto an on-budget bill. The House approved an on-budget plan, but the Senate rejected it, forcing a compromise.*

As finally resolved, the new quasi-governmental corporation would borrow $20 billion from the Treasury during 1989, thus placing it on-budget. The remaining $30 billion would be borrowed during 1990 and 1991 by selling tax-exempt bonds to the public. These bonds would not be backed by the government and would be off-budget. The $50 billion in principal would be repaid in thirty years by using deeply discounted bonds that would be purchased with funds made available by the healthy segment of the thrift industry. However, interest costs would be borne mostly by the taxpayer and counted as part of the federal budget.

> *Following are excerpts from remarks by President Bush at the signing of the Financial Institutions Reform, Recovery, and Enforcement Act of 1989—the bailout bill—August 9, 1989, at the White House Rose Garden in the presence of several congressional leaders, Treasury Secretary Nicholas F. Brady, Secretary of Housing and Urban Development Jack F. Kemp, and members of the Federal Reserve Board, Council of Economic Advisers, and White House staff:*

... This legislation comes to grips with the problems facing our savings and loan industry. It'll safeguard and stabilize America's financial system and put in place permanent reforms so these problems will never happen again. And moreover, it says to tens of millions of S&L depositors: You will not be the victim of others' mistakes. We will see—guarantee—that your insured deposits are secure.

And this, of course, was government's intent when, in 1933, it created the Federal Deposit Insurance. And yet as that system incurred massive loans over the past couple of decades, the fund designed to protect depositors itself became insolvent. And the crisis has been told and retold. The Federal insurance fund was unable to make good on its commitments to the public or to close insolvent institutions. And their losses mounting, hundreds of bankrupt institutions were allowed to continue operating.

On February 6, I announced a plan to change all that: to protect insured depositors and to responsibly finance the closing or other resolution of all insolvent institutions. And we sought to abolish lax regulations, to increase penalties for wrongdoing, and to reform the financial system. And above all, we sought to protect those who have relied on government to faithfully fulfill its obligations.

I take a special pleasure in the historic legislation that I will sign here this morning. For the Task Group on Regulation of Financial Services, which I was proud to chair, began the effort to strengthen our financial system. And its work, and that of many others, was debated and defined by the United States Congress. And you see it here, all 371 pages of it. And, no, the bill is not perfect, but it is a first step, a crucial step, toward restoring public confidence. H.R. 1278 is responsive and responsible, and for that I salute the Congress. This bill balances America's need for financial security, competitiveness, and equity.

In particular, I want to thank two committee chairmen, Senator Don Riegle and Representative Henry B. Gonzalez, here with us today for their superb leadership in an extraordinarily difficult proceedings. And they were aided by Senator Jake Garn and Representative Chalmers Wylie, who helped make these proposals a reality; and of course, Senator Phil Gramm who I mentioned earlier; and numerous other members of the banking and other committees, from both sides of the aisle, who took up the cause of the public's interest. And then there's my friend, the Treasury Secretary, Nick Brady, whose dedicated efforts have been vital and whose leadership has been truly outstanding. And so have those of Director Dick Darman, over here, the head of the OMB [Office of Management and Budget]. I'd also like to mention Richard Breeden of the White House. I'd be remiss not to salute hundreds of others on the staffs of the various regulatory agencies and congressional committees. They, too, deserve our thanks.

And because of them, of you here today, and so many others, this legislation will give us the tools to make our thrift institutions and our financial system as a whole strong and stable. With this bill's substantial funding, we will begin, here and now, to eliminate the ongoing losses of the insolvent firms and to ensure that not one dollar of insured funds will be lost by any depositor.

Toward that end, this legislation abolishes the agency once responsible for thrift supervision. And in its place a new agency will operate as part of the Treasury Department, ensuring the taxpayers' interests will always come first. And at the same time, a completely new insurance fund will protect deposits in thrift institutions. The obligations of the new fund, called Savings Association Insurance Fund, SAIF, will be fully guaranteed by the full faith and credit of the United States. The new seal displayed here symbolizes this new fund and our commitment to protecting depositors.

Good steps? I'd say vital steps. And this legislation goes still further. Beginning today, penalties for wrongdoing by officers and directors in insured institutions will be increased up to $1 million per day. And criminal penalties will be toughened from yesterday's slap on the wrist to the clang of a prison door. Those who try and loot the savings of their fellow citizens deserve, and will receive, swift and severe punishment. And also, starting today, tougher requirements for safe and sound operating practices will begin to take effect. Never again will America allow any insured institution to operate normally if owners lack sufficient tangible capital to protect depositors and taxpayers alike. And today, too, we begin using the new resources available to accelerate the resolution of failed institutions and to recover every possible dollar from their assets for the taxpayers. And at the same time, we will seek to minimize adverse impact on local markets.

These reforms will help our system right itself. For while the S&L crisis isn't behind us, we have met and passed our first critical test. More hard choices, more challenges lie ahead. But we will meet them as we have this challenge: consulting, cooperating between Congress and the executive branch. And as we do, we will keep the new Federal Deposit Insurance System solvent and help serve those millions of small savers who make America great: the local paperboy looking ahead to college or the young couple dreaming of their first home, the retired teacher whose savings are her entire lifetime. We have a commitment to protect the savings of these American and millions like them across this country, and we will honor that commitment. . . .

BALTIC FREEDOM
STATEMENTS
August 23 and 26, 1989

Nationalist movements in Estonia, Latvia, and Lithuania used the fiftieth anniversary of the Nazi-Soviet nonaggression pact as the occasion to press demands for independence in the three Baltic states. Secret protocols attached to that 1939 treaty cleared the way for Joseph Stalin to seize the three small republics on the Baltic Sea and annex them to the Soviet Union. He and Adolf Hitler agreed to divide Poland and, indeed, all of Eastern Europe into German and Russian spheres of influence. Nine days after the treaty was signed August 23, 1939, Nazi armies invaded Poland and started World War II. The next year, Soviet forces occupied the Baltics.

Exactly fifty years after that signing, popular-front groups in Estonia, Latvia, and Lithuania jointly issued a statement declaring the treaty and annexation illegal. "[W]e remind all the nations of the world that under international law treaties of this kind are criminal and unlawful from the very moment of signing," the document said.

Hundreds of thousands of Estonians, Latvians, and Lithuanians took to the streets that day in a show of solidarity for "independent state-hoods." By prearrangement, they linked hands to form human chains extending nearly 400 miles from Tallinn, the capital of Estonia, across Latvia, to Vilnius, the capital of Lithuania. In Vilnius, the governing council of Sajudis, the Lithuanian popular front, passed a resolution calling for "the creation of an independent, democratic Lithuanian republic, without political, cultural or administrative subordination to the Soviet Union."

The previous day, August 22, a commission appointed by the Lithua-

469

nian legislative body to study the Hitler-Stalin treaty challenged the legitimacy of Soviet rule in Lithuania by declaring that the republic's annexation was illegal. On August 18 the Kremlin for the first time acknowledged the existence of the protocols, which had been among the German documents captured toward the close of World War II.

In Vilnius, Tallinn, and the Latvian capital of Riga many government officials endorsed the declarations despite their affiliations with the Communist party. So strong was the nationalist surge that legislative bodies in Estonia and Lithuania had already asserted the legal right to reject any laws enacted in Moscow. They also restricted the use of the Russian language in favor of native tongues and drew protests from the Russian minority living in the two republics.

The Kremlin's Reaction

Moscow reacted strongly to the turn of events. "Things have gone too far," the Central Committee of the Communist party said in a statement it issued August 26. It added the ominous warning: "The fate of the Baltic peoples is in serious danger." The fate was not specified, but the words raised the fear of Soviet military intervention such as had occurred in Hungary in 1956 and Czechoslovakia in 1968. The Baltics appeared to rely on hope that Soviet leader Mikhail S. Gorbachev would consider military suppression too costly in terms of world opinion—which he assiduously courted for support in seeking to bring about political and economic reforms in the Soviet Union.

Gorbachev, whose reforms had encouraged the Baltic nationalist movement, was away from Moscow on vacation when the Central Committee acted. However, it was reported that he had approved the committee's statement. Upon returning to Moscow, he met with the party and government leaders of the Baltic republics September 13. An official summary of the meeting said Gorbachev warned them of the "ruinous" consequences of pursuing independence but also spoke of the need to work out differences without resorting to confrontation. He spoke in a similar manner four days later in a televised address to a special meeting of the Central Committee. Those statements differed from the praise he expressed in 1987 on a tour of the Baltic republics. At that time he spoke approvingly of "a revolution of expectations" he had found there.

The Soviet constitution affirms the right of the various republics to secede from the Union, but that right had never been tested. Moscow's reaction to the events in the Baltic indicated that attempted secession would not be looked on any more favorably in the Gorbachev era than it had been under his more authoritarian predecessors. Moscow insisted that the secret protocols in the 1939 treaty did not lay a legal basis for the Baltic states to break away.

Defying Moscow's Warning

Leaders of the three movements defied the central committee's August 26 warning. Meeting August 31 in Riga, they called the authors of the

Central Committee statement "younger brothers" of the men who drew up the 1939 pact. "There has been no such sinister and dangerous document for the cause of democracy since the death of Stalin and the events in Czechoslovakia in 1968," the leaders said. Dainis Ivans, president of the Latvian Popular Front, was quoted in the New York Times as saying his group would demand a "special status" for Latvia within the Soviet Union leading to "full economic and political independence."

Several of the leaders, including Ivans, were elected in March to the new Soviet parliament, the Congress of People's Deputies (Remarks on Soviet Election and Perestroika, p. 173). In Lithuania, for instance, thirty-six of the forty-two deputies elected to the People's Congress were candidates from the nationalist movement Sajudis. Moreover, the legislative bodies of the three republics—whose members were elected under the old rules—had become predominantly nationalistic. In Latvia, the Popular Front claimed a membership of 240,000—nearly 60,000 more than the Latvian Communist party—in a country of 2.6 million people.

U.S. Position

In the United States, President George Bush said on June 14 that "the future looks brighter today than at any other time in the Baltic States' post-war experience." Bush made his observation in a "Baltic Freedom Day" proclamation, as was requested by a U.S. Senate resolution. He restated a longstanding U.S. policy of not recognizing the incorporation of Estonia, Latvia, and Lithuania into the Soviet Union, and he expressed "our solidarity with them and call upon the Soviet Union to listen to their calls for freedom and self-determination."

However, the president stopped short of promising U.S. assistance. As long as there was no hope of independence for the "captive nations" of Eastern Europe, the United States could unequivocally advocate their cause. But their new assertions caused Washington to craft its responses with great care. There was belief that any suggestion of direct U.S. involvement might work to the Baltic states' detriment in Moscow and possibly undermine Gorbachev's reform attempts elsewhere.

The impasse between Moscow and the Baltic republics remained unbroken throughout 1989. By the year's end, both Latvia and Lithuania had abolished the Communist party's political monopoly—over Gorbachev's protests. Estonia made plans to follow suit in 1990. The Soviet leader visited Lithuania in mid-January 1990 in an apparently vain attempt to persuade its leaders to stop pushing for Lithuanian autonomy.

> Following are excerpts from a statement issued August 23 by the Baltic nationalist movement, as provided in English translation by the Lithuanian Information Center in Washington, D.C., and from a statement issued August 26 by the Central Committee of the Soviet Communist party, as provided in English translation by the Soviet government:

471

THE BALTIC WAY STATEMENT

August 23, 1939, inflicted wounds to tens of nations and states. Some of these wounds are still bleeding.

The Hitler-Stalin pact unleashed an attack on Poland, which was destroyed and divided between the signatory states. The Hitler-Stalin pact assigned the three Baltic states to the Soviet sphere of interest. Three member states of the League of Nations were occupied by the Red Army; three independent states ceased to exist. The Soviet Union has done everything to remove the republics of Estonia, Latvia, and Lithuania from the memory and map of Europe, from your libraries and textbooks, your sense of justice, your grief and your minds. Many have let their conscience be lulled and put up with the implementation of the Hitler-Stalin pact even during the last decades of [the] millenium.

This is why we, the three Baltic nations, turn to Europe and the world community today, on the 50th anniversary of the deal, in firm conviction that the democratic majority has retained its moral will-power, sense of justice and willingness to share our assessment: the criminal Hitler-Stalin pact has to be voided! The essence of the Hitler-Stalin pact and its secret protocols was imperialist division of the spheres of interest between two great powers. On the basis of this criminal deal the Soviet Union unilaterally violated all the international treaties concluded with the Baltic republics, infringed on the historical right of the Baltic nations to self-determination, presented ruthless ultimatums to the Baltic republics, occupied them with overwhelming military force, and under conditions of military occupation and heavy political terror carried out their violent annexation. The Hitler-Stalin pacts and their still-enforced secret protocols were and are aimed at the destruction of sovereignty and independence of other states.

Today, on the 50th anniversary of the deal, we remind all the nations of the world that under international law treaties of this kind are criminal and unlawful from the very moment of signing. This knowledge, which the apologists of imperialism and red fascists have preferred to overlook, has supported and kept us alive despite the decades-long public terror and systematic genocide. We have remained faithful to democracy and human rights even while the colonial power ... set out to annihilate the Baltic nations physically by means of mass murders, deportations of thousands of people to Siberia, and purposeful denationalization of our towns, villages, factories, schools and culture.

The Hitler-Stalin pact is still shaping the Europe of today, our once-common Europe. Yet we are convinced that the European community and democratic forces in the East will unite their voices in support of the demand of Estonia, Latvia and Lithuania that the pact together with its secret protocol be denounced and declared null and void....

One may close one's eyes to the Baltic problem, but it will not cease to exist. For us, it is a problem of inalienable human rights; for you, it is a problem of double standards and security; but one way or another, we have to solve it together, proceeding from the principles of international law. A common European home can only be set up if all European nations are granted a free right of self-determination. The Baltic nations have sought ways for restoring their independent statehood in a way that would correspond to the interests of Estonia, Latvia and Lithuania, as well as the Soviet Union, and guarantee security in Northern Europe. In our view stability on the shores of the Baltic must be built on a system of treaties such as was in force before the deal of 1939, and which stems from the peace treaties concluded between the Soviet Union and the Baltic States in 1920. We have searched for a solution, and we have called our solution the BALTIC WAY.

The BALTIC WAY is a parliamentary way for the peaceful restoration of our statehood.

The BALTIC WAY does not represent a threat to anyone.

The BALTIC WAY will guarantee social security, civil rights and economic progress to all the people in the Baltic republics regardless of their nationality.

The BALTIC WAY is a way to democracy.

The BALTIC WAY is the only way to freedom, brotherhood and equality on the shores of our common Baltic Sea....

SOVIET PARTY STATEMENT

The current situation in the Baltic republics is the cause of increasing concern. Developments there affect the vital interests of the entire Soviet people, our entire socialist motherland.

Perestroika paved the way for the rapid growth of the national awareness of peoples, made them confident that they can independently solve the problems of their political, social, economic and cultural life. The national revival of every nation in the great Soviet multinational family, with the use of new possibilities for the free and balanced interaction with other nations of the country, brought about by perestroika, lies in the channel of the policy of the Communist party and the Soviet states, is one of the bases for renewing our entire society. The recent crucial measures aimed at strengthening the sovereignty of Union republics and filling them with new and real contents pursue exactly those goals.

The Baltic republics actively joined in the process of deep transformation. Workers' collectives got moving and the intellectual forces of all strata of society became active.

But at a certain stage nationalist, extremist groups took advantage of democracy and openness and gradually began to introduce an unhealthy aspect into the development of events.

Having misappropriated the part of true proponents of the national interests, they, step-by-step, steered the course of affairs toward an alienation of the Baltic republics from the rest of the country and the disruption of long-standing organically formed links with other Soviet nations. Their positions became more and more openly extremist and separatist. The anti-socialist and anti-Soviet nature of their projects became evident very soon. In some places, organizations resembling political formations of the bourgeois period and the time of Nazi occupation sprang up. Actually, parallel bodies of power began to be set up. Intimidation, deception and disinformation became routine, and even moral terror and defamation of all who disagreed, all who remained true to internationalism and the idea of an integral Soviet Union. Some of the mass information media served as sources fostering nationalistic attitudes.

Abusing freedom of international relations, nationalist leaders contacted foreign organizations and centres, seeking to involve them in what was in fact the internal affair of their republics and treating them as consultants and advisers, as if people in the West were better aware of the actual needs of the Baltic nations, as if they were guided not by their own open or concealed projects with respect to our country, but were in fact concerned about the Soviet people's welfare.

It came to direct acts of vandalism, mockery of state insignia, desecration of sacred things viewed as inviolable by any decent individual—monuments to those who fell in the Civil and Great Patriotic Wars.

Soviet people across the country watched and read with astonishment and bitterness about things that in no way agreed with what they knew of Latvian, Lithuanian and Estonian national traditions and would appear insulting to the national character of these people known for their honesty, sober-mindedness and respect for standards of civilized human relationships.

The activity of forces that are destructive, anti-Soviet and anti-national in their core, the atmosphere of nationalism led to the promulgation, at the level of bodies of state authority in the republics, of unconstitutional acts contradicting our state's principles of federation and envisaging discrimination against the non-indigenous population of these republics.

On August 23, 1989, attempts were made to fan up emotions to a point of actual nationalist hysteria. Slogans foisted upon thousands of people were brimful of animosity toward the Soviet Union and the Soviet army...

The activities of the nationalist forces have already led to serious economic losses in the economy of the Baltic republics, as well as to inter-ethnic and social tension. In some places, a real threat of a civil conflict and mass street clashes which will involve grave consequences, has arisen.

Things have gone too far. The fate of the Baltic peoples is in serious danger. People should know into what abyss they are being pushed by the nationalist leaders. The consequences could be disastrous for these peoples if the nationalists managed to achieve their goals. The very viability of the Baltic nations could be called in question.

We should say it openly and with a feeling of responsibility before the Baltic and all Soviet peoples.

Right from the outset the CPSU Central Committee has displayed deep understanding of the specific features of restructuring processes in the Soviet Baltic republics. It saw at proper time the need to renew the republics' leadership by an inflow of fresh forces and helped to act in the spirit of the time, live by the needs and concerns of the people and speed up the solution of urgent socio-economic problems. It seemed that the Baltic leaders managed to find common language with the public and population and gave the right assessment of the possibilities and ways of carrying out transformations with due account of the local national conditions.

It must be said that the leaders of these republics failed to do everything in order to contain the process in the normal channel of perestroika reforms. They failed to stem the negative tendencies, to redress the situation, to uphold the principled positions, to convince people of the harmfulness of the plans and practice of opposition forces. . . .

. . . It is time, in our common interest, to put an end to the fateful course of events, to come to your senses, go over from confrontation to dialogue and a painstaking search for expedient decisions and compromises. . . .

We, communists, are now bearing an extreme responsibility for the fate of our multinational homeland and the Soviet people. Today, as never before, each Communist should have the courage to perform concrete deeds, promote party comradeship, build the unity of forces and increase the joint contribution to restructuring without which no ethnic or inter-ethnic problems can be solved.

The time came for every Communist to take a principled party stand and act so that his honor and conscience be clear before the people now and before the coming generations.

This is our common duty today.

Let's preserve the single family of the Soviet peoples and the unity of the Communist Party of the Soviet Union.

STATEMENTS ON BANNING PETE ROSE FROM BASEBALL
August 24, 1989

The "Pete Rose question"—whether the manager of the Cincinnati Reds bet on baseball games in violation of major league rules—stirred American sports followers as few other matters in 1989. After six months of investigations and legal wrangling, the issue came to a head August 24 in an announcement from A. Bartlett Giamatti, the commissioner of baseball. Saying he was persuaded that Rose had bet on baseball games, including those of the manager's own team, Giamatti declared Rose would be banished from the game "for life." Giamatti's announcement came only eight days before he suffered a fatal heart attack.

Rose, for his part, conceded that he had wagered on sports events but denied that he had bet on baseball games. His lawyers, unable to block Giamatti in the courts, met with the commissioner's legal aides and drew up a carefully worded agreement that made no official finding as to Rose's guilt or innocence as to the betting. The commissioner and manager signed the document, which specified that after a year Rose could apply for reinstatement. However, attorneys for both sides said they had made no deal about reinstatement. It was not automatic or guaranteed, the commissioner said at the time he announced his action against Rose at a New York news conference.

Lifetime suspensions were not revoked for any of the fourteen other players who had drawn them in the past. Rose was considered the most prominent person to be banned from baseball since 1921 when Shoeless Joe Jackson and seven other members of the White Sox team were expelled by the first commissioner, Judge Kenesaw Mountain Landis, for conspiring to fix the 1919 World Series. Rose said he would seek readmission as soon as he became eligible, and "absolutely" expected to return to baseball.

Rose the Legend

Rose had achieved almost legendary status in baseball. In twenty-four seasons as a big league player, he set nineteen records. Before hanging up his glove in 1986 to become a full-time manager, Rose had played in more games than any other big leaguer (3,562), had come to bat the most times (14,053), and collected the most hits (4,256). That last feat, achieved in 1985 during Rose's last full season of play, broke Ty Cobb's record which had stood for fifty-seven years. Three times Rose's batting average led the National League.

Even more than for his records, Rose became the darling of millions of fans for his hard play, determination to win, and versatility on the field. In his rookie season, he earned the nickname "Charlie Hustle" and carried it throughout his career. In sixteen appearances in All Star Games, Rose started at five different positions in the infield and outfield.

Rose's zest for the game sometimes made headlines in unwanted ways. In 1988, Giamatti—then the National League president—suspended him thirty days and fined him $10,000 for pushing an umpire in an argument over a disputed play. On other occasions he was criticized for running the base paths with such abandon that he endangered opposing players. Until the gambling charges surfaced, Rose was considered a shoo-in for membership in baseball's Hall of Fame.

Commissioner's Investigative Report

On March 20, the commissioner's office released a statement that it was investigating "serious allegations against Rose." The previous month, John M. Dowd, a Washington lawyer, had been hired to conduct the inquiry. On the basis of findings by Dowd and his staff, set forth in a 225-page report, Giamatti concluded that Rose had repeatedly bet on sports events—including major league baseball games, and even the Cincinnati Reds, in the 1985, 1986, and 1987 seasons. The report, together with seven volumes of accompanying exhibits, was released June 25 after a Cincinnati judge made it part of the public record in a lawsuit that Rose brought against the commissioner.

"The evidence showed that with few exceptions, Rose did not deal directly with bookmakers but rather placed his bets through others," the report said. It identified a Franklin, Ohio, restaurant owner named Ron Peters as one bookmaker and Tommy Gioiosa, an associate of Rose's, as the intermediary. "Rose's dealings with Gioiosa, and ultimately with Peters, are corroborated by the testimony of others and by Rose's own financial records as well," the report continued. It also named Michael Bertolini as another associate who placed bets for Rose with an unidentified bookie in New York City.

According to the report: "One source of this information is a tape recorded conversation between Bertolini and another of Rose's associates,

Paul Janszen .... [in which Bertolini mentioned] that Rose had incurred substantial debts to Bertolini and the New York bookmaker and that Rose had given Bertolini personal checks which Bertolini had had cashed and the proceeds sent to the New York bookmaker.... Rose acknowledged sending eleven $8,000 checks to Bertolini made out to fictitious payees but said that these checks were loans to Bertolini to be used as payments to athletes for baseball card shows." Rose's debts to a New York bookmaker ran as high as $400,000 during a three-month period in 1987, the report asserted.

Peters had been convicted of distributing illegal drugs and filing false income-tax information. While he awaited a decision by Judge Carl Rubin of the U.S. District Court in Cincinnati, Giamatti wrote the judge on April 18 "to bring to your attention the significant and truthful cooperation Mr. Peters has provided my special counsel [Dowd]" in the Rose investigation.

Rose's Legal Challenge

Soon afterward Rose requested a temporary restraining order to keep Giamatti from holding a hearing. This matter came before Judge Norbert A. Nadel of the Hamilton County (Cincinnati) Common Pleas Court. In granting Rose's request, Nadel said Giamatti had "prejudged Rose" and cited the commissioner's letter to Rubin as evidence. Giamatti's lawyers responded by citing Rose's popularity in his hometown and succeeded in having Rose's lawsuit transferred to another court in another city—to U.S. District Court in Columbus, Ohio. After a federal appeals court on August 17 denied Rose's attempt to have the case sent back to the Cincinnati court, he and the commissioner signed their agreement before a rescheduled hearing could be held.

Giamatti's unexpected death on September 1, at age fifty-one, added still another element of drama to the long-running story. He had been commissioner of baseball only since April 1, when he succeeded Peter Ueberroth. But in preparation for his new duties, Giamatti was involved in the Rose gambling investigation as early as February. His entry into the upper echelon of baseball's officialdom in 1987 as the National League president surprised both professional baseball and the academic community. He was a Renaissance scholar who gave up the presidency of Yale University to take the job—explaining that he did so for his love of the game. On September 13, the major league club owners elected Giamatti's top assistant, Francis T. (Fay) Vincent, Jr., to succeed him as commissioner.

Pervasive Sports Gambling

If the August 23 agreement brought an end to the legal battle between Rose and the commissioner's office, it did not spell an end to his legal problems. Soon afterward, Rose's former associate, Gioiosa, went on trial in federal district court in Cincinnati on tax-fraud charges. Gioiosa cashed a winning ticket at a Kentucky race track and declared it with the

Internal Revenue Service as his own. However, Janszen, also one of the chief witnesses in baseball's investigation of Rose, said that he and Gioiosa each owned only one-eighth of the $2,000 ticket, and that Rose owned the rest. The winnings on the ticket totalled $47,646. The matter was also under grand jury investigation in Cincinnati.

In the press, radio call-in programs, and other forums, Rose's fans often defended him on grounds that sports gambling was pervasive in the United States and it was hypocritical to punish him. The extent of this gambling cannot be measured with any degree of accuracy. However, an organization that attempted to track it, Christiansen/Cummings Associates, estimated that in 1988 Americans bet $56 billion on sports events, only about one-third of it legally. The rest of the betting was conducted by illegal bookies, or between individuals—typically in office pools.

Citing what it said was pervasive illegal betting on pro football games, the Oregon Lottery Commission this year voted to let lottery participants pick winners in the weekly National Football League games. Until the commission took this action on July 27, betting on football games—as well as on many other sports events—was legal only in Nevada. The NFL objected to the commission but to no avail. In 1976 Delaware instituted a football-betting game and the NFL sued to stop it; however, before the courts could decide the issue, revenues from the game fell far below projections and the state abandoned it. The Oregon commission, contending that office football pools and other illegal sports gambling were already common in the state, adopted the plan as a means of providing funds for athletic programs at five of the state's tax-supported universities and colleges.

Following are texts of statements by A. Bartlett Giamatti and Pete Rose, and the agreement they signed August 23, 1989, as issued by the major league baseball commissioner's office in New York City, August 24.

GIAMATTI'S STATEMENT

The banishment for life of Pete Rose from baseball is the sad end of a sorry episode. One of the game's greatest players has engaged in a variety of acts which have stained the game, and he must now live with the consequences of those acts. By choosing not to come to a hearing before me, and by choosing not to proffer any testimony or evidence contrary to the evidence and information contained in the report of the Special Counsel to the Commissioner, Mr. Rose has accepted baseball's ultimate sanction, lifetime ineligibility.

This sorry episode began last February when baseball received firm allegations that Mr. Rose bet on baseball games and on the Reds' games. Such grave charges could not and must not be ignored. Accordingly, I engaged and Mr. Ueberroth appointed John Dowd as Special Counsel to investigate these and any other allegations that might arise and to pursue the truth wherever it took him. I believed then and believe now that such a process, whereby an experienced professional inquires on behalf of the Commissioner as the Commissioner's agent, is fair and appropriate. To pretend that serious charges of any kind can be responsibly examined by a Commissioner alone fails to recognize the necessity to bring professionalism and fairness to any examination and the complexity a private entity encounters when, without judicial or legal powers, it pursues allegations in the complex, real world.

Baseball had never before undertaken such a process because there had not been such grave allegations since the time of [Baseball Commissioner Kenesaw Mountain] Landis. If one is responsible for protecting the integrity of the game of baseball—that is, the game's authenticity, honesty and coherence—then the process one uses to protect the integrity of baseball must itself embody that integrity. I sought by means of a Special Counsel of proven professionalism and integrity, who was obliged to keep the subject of the investigation and his representatives informed about key information, to create a mechanism whereby the integrity we sought to protect was itself never violated. Similarly, in writing to Mr. Rose on May 11, I designed, as is my responsibility, a set of procedures for a hearing that would have afforded him every opportunity to present statements or testimony of witnesses or any other evidence he saw fit to answer the information and evidence presented in the Report of the Special Counsel and its accompanying materials.

That Mr. Rose and his counsel chose to pursue a course in the courts rather than appear at hearings scheduled for May 25 and then June 26, and then chose to come forward with a stated desire to settle this matter is now well known to all. My purpose in recounting the process and the procedures animating that process is to make two points that the American public deserves to know:

First, that the integrity of the game cannot be defended except by a process that itself embodies integrity and fairness.

Second, should any other occasion arise where charges are made or acts are said to be committed that are contrary to the interests of the game or that undermine the integrity of baseball, I fully intend to use such a process and procedure to get to the truth and, if need be, to root out offending behavior. I intend to use, in short, every lawful and ethical means to defend and protect the game.

I say this so that there may be no doubt about where I stand or why I stand there. I believe baseball is a beautiful and exciting game, loved by millions—I among them—and I believe baseball is an important, enduring American institution. It must assert and aspire to the highest principles—of integrity, of professionalism of performance, of fair play within its rules. It will come as no surprise that like any institution composed of human beings, this institution will not always fulfill its highest aspirations. I know of no earthly institution that does. But this one, because it is so much a part of our history as a people and because it has such a purchase on our national soul, has an obligation to the people for whom it is played—to its fans and well-wishers—to strive for excellence in all things and to promote the highest ideals.

I will be told that I am an idealist. I hope so. I will continue to locate ideals I hold for myself and for my country in the national game as well as in other of our national institutions. And while there will be debate and dissent about this or that or another occurrence on or off the field, and while the game's nobler parts will always be enmeshed in the human frailties of those who, whatever their role, have stewardship of this game, let there be no doubt or dissent about our goals for baseball or our dedication to it. Nor about our vigilance and vigor—and patience—in protecting the game from blemish or stain or disgrace.

The matter of Mr. Rose is now closed. It will be debated and discussed. Let no one think that it did not hurt baseball. That hurt will pass, however, as the great glory of the game asserts itself and a resilient institution goes forward. Let it also be clear that no individual is superior to the game.

ROSE'S STATEMENT

I'd like to apologize for this controversy lingering on into the '89 season. I hope it didn't detract from the championship season of the 12 teams in the National League and I hope it didn't detract from the All-Star Game. I know now it won't detract from the upcoming playoffs and the showcase of baseball, the World Series.

I made some mistakes and I think I'm being punished for those mistakes. However, the settlement is fair and especially the wording that says they have no finding that I bet on baseball. It's something I told the commissioner back in February and I've told you people the last four months.

My only regret up to this time is I will not have the opportunity to tell my side of the story. However, I would add, I will tell my side of the story in the very near future.

I'd like to thank you people, as members of the media, for understanding me as a person, for trying to understand me as a manager. I'm hoping that you will give the guy that replaces me the benefit of the doubt as he takes over a very young, banged up baseball team.

My life is baseball. I hope to get back into baseball as soon as I possibly can. I'm looking forward to that. I've never looked forward to a birthday like I'm looking forward to my new daughter's birthday, 'cause two days after that is when I can apply for reinstatement.

THE AGREEMENT

On March 6, 1989, the Commissioner of Baseball instituted an investigation of Peter Edward Rose, the field manager of the Cincinnati Reds

Baseball Club, concerning allegations that Peter Edward Rose engaged in conduct not in the best interests of baseball in violation of Major League Rule 21, including but not limited to betting on Major League Baseball games in connection with which he had a duty to perform.

The Commissioner engaged a special counsel to conduct a full, fair and confidential inquiry of the allegations against Peter Edward Rose. Peter Edward Rose was given notice of the allegations and he and his counsel were generally apprised of the nature and progress of the investigation. During the inquiry, Peter Edward Rose produced documents, gave handwriting exemplars and responded to questions under oath upon oral deposition. During the deposition, the special counsel revealed key evidence gathered in the inquiry to Peter Edward Rose and his counsel.

On May 9, 1989, the special counsel provided a 225-page report, accompanied by seven volumes of exhibits, to the Commissioner. On May 11, 1989, the Commissioner provided a copy of the Report and exhibits to Peter Edward Rose and his counsel, and scheduled a hearing on May 25, 1989 to give Peter Edward Rose an opportunity to respond formally to the information in the Report. Peter Edward Rose received, read and is aware of the contents of the Report. On May 19, 1989, Peter Edward Rose requested, and subsequently received, an extension of the hearing date until June 25, 1989. Peter Edward Rose acknowledges that the Commissioner has treated him fairly in this Agreement and has acted in good faith throughout the course of the investigation and proceedings.

Peter Edward Rose will conclude these proceedings before the Commissioner without a hearing and the Commissioner will not make any formal findings or determinations on any matter including without limitation the allegation that Peter Edward Rose bet on any Major League Baseball game. The commissioner has determined that the best interests of Baseball are served by a resolution of this matter on the following agreed upon terms and conditions:

1. Peter Edward Rose recognizes, agrees and submits to the sole and exclusive jurisdiction of the Commissioner:

A. To investigate, either upon any complaint or upon his own initiative, any act, transaction or practice charged, alleged or suspected to be not in the best interests of the national game of Baseball; and

B. To determine, after investigation, what preventive, remedial or punitive action is appropriate in the premises, and to take such action as the case may be.

2. Counsel for Peter Edward Rose, upon his authority, have executed a Stipulation dismissing with prejudice the civil action that was originally filed in the Court of Common Pleas, Hamilton County, Ohio, captioned *Peter Edward Rose v. A. Bartlett Giamatti*, No. A8905178, and subsequently removed to the United States District Court from the Southern District of Ohio, Eastern Division, Docket No. C-2-89-577.

3. Peter Edward Rose will not avail himself of the opportunity to participate in a hearing concerning the allegations against him, or otherwise offer any defense to those allegations.

4. Peter Edward Rose acknowledges that the Commissioner has a factual basis to impose the penalty provided herein, and hereby accepts the penalty imposed on him by the Commissioner and agrees not to challenge that penalty in court or otherwise. He also agrees he will not institute any legal proceedings of any nature against the Commissioner or any of his representatives, either Major League or any Major League Club.

5. The Commissioner recognizes and agrees that it is in the best interests of the national game of Baseball that this matter be resolved pursuant to his sole and exclusive authority under the Major League Agreement.

THEREFORE, the Commissioner, recognizing the benefits to Baseball from a resolution of this matter, orders and directs that Peter Edward Rose be subject to the following disciplinary sanctions, and Peter Edward Rose, recognizing the sole and exclusive authority of the Commissioner and that it is in his interest to resolve this matter without further proceedings, agrees to accept the following disciplinary sanctions imposed by the Commissioner:

a. Peter Edward Rose is hereby declared permanently ineligible in accordance with Major League Rule 21 and placed on the Ineligible List.

b. Nothing in this Agreement shall deprive Peter Edward Rose of the rights under Major League Rule 15(c) to apply for reinstatement. Peter Edward Rose agrees not to challenge, appeal or otherwise contest the decision of, or the procedure employed by, the Commissioner or any future Commissioner in the evaluation of any application for reinstatement.

c. Nothing in this agreement shall be deemed either an admission or a denial by Peter Edward Rose of the allegation that he bet on any Major League Baseball game.

Neither the Commissioner nor Peter Edward Rose shall be prevented by this agreement from making any public statement relating to this matter so long as no such public statement contradicts the terms of this agreement and resolution.

This document contains the entire agreement of the parties and represents the entire resolution of the matter of Peter Edward Rose before the Commissioner.

Agreed to and resolved this 23rd day of August 1989.

September

Kohl on German Remorse at
  World War II Anniversary 487

Bush's Drug-War Speech,
  Colombian Leader's UN Appeal 499

Navy's Report on the
  USS Iowa Explosion 517

Speeches Marking Poland's
  New Era 523

Smithsonian Agreement to Return
  Indian Bones 539

South African President's
  Inaugural Address 545

Tennessee Court Decision in
  Frozen Embryo Custody 551

Statements at the Education Summit 561

KOHL ON GERMAN REMORSE
AT WORLD WAR II ANNIVERSARY
September 1, 1989

To mark the fiftieth anniversary of the outbreak of World War II, West German chancellor Helmut Kohl addressed a special session of the Bundestag (National Assembly) in Bonn with expressions of remorse for the vast destruction inflicted "by Germans in the name of Germany." He also expressed hope for a "lasting reconciliation" with Poland, "the first victims of the National Socialist [Nazi] war of racism and annihilation." Exactly fifty years earlier, on September 1, 1939, German armies invaded Poland and started World War II.

"The wounds that World War II caused are not yet healed," Kohl said. "They have burnt themselves into the nations' memory, and they have marked people in a personal way—every individual who experienced this time of terror, even as a child." The West German leader, at age sixty, recalled his own wartime childhood filled with terror of night bombings, the destruction of homes, and death in the streets.

He emphasized that the German people also suffered grievously—both from the war's deadly destruction and from the remembrance of their role that enabled it to take place. "It is a burden for us Germans," Kohl declared. While saying that wartime Germans could not deny a special responsibility for what occurred, he nevertheless spoke of mitigating circumstances. "It is part of the tragedy of this time that the loyalty of millions of people and their love of the fatherland were abused for criminal purposes at the front and at home," the West German leader said. Later he added: "Which of us, ladies and gentlemen, could claim with a clear conscience that, faced with evil, he would have the strength to be a martyr?" He went on to name some of the Germans who met death for their underground resistance to Adolf Hitler, which included plots to kill him.

West German leaders typically have felt compelled to acknowledge Nazi crimes committed in the name of the German state and people, but also to portray the Germans as being among the victims of the Nazi tyranny and conquest—as people who lost their freedom, possibly their homes and jobs, and even their lives.

The Guilt Question Debate

Several times the audience interrupted the speech with applause, and generally it was well received in the press in his country and abroad. Kohl did not suffer the fate of Philipp Jenninger, who spoke on the same topic in November 1988 and created a furor, prompting him to resign as president of the Bundestag. That occasion was the fiftieth anniversary observance of Kristallnacht *(crystal night)—named for broken crystal (or glass) amid the debris that littered many German streets after Nazi raids on Jewish homes and businesses during the night of November 9-10, 1938.*

Jenninger's speech was misunderstood by many of his listeners as an apology for the Nazi era. Some walked out, and others denounced it. Ironically, his intent apparently was to rebut the criticism of Germans who saw what was happening but—in his words—"looked away and remained silent." However, some passages that sought to portray German thinking at that time were perceived by the audience as his current thinking. Taken aback by the unexpected and vehement criticism, he resigned his post within twenty-four hours of leaving the podium.

The controversy soon subsided, but it had again called attention to West Germany's longstanding attempts to exorcise the Nazi past without denying that it existed. The country's historians have engaged in lively debate as to whether the Nazi experience was uniquely German. Ernst Nolte, for instance, argued in his 1976 book Germany and the Cold War *and subsequent publications that a "Hitler age" was common to every great power. As others challenged that view, the debate moved from scholarly publications to the mass-circulation newspapers in 1987 and 1988.*

Another debate over the guilt question arose on both sides of the Atlantic in 1985 when President Ronald Reagan placed a wreath at a World War II cemetery in Bitburg, West Germany. It was disclosed after his plans were announced that in addition to two thousand regular German soldiers buried at Bitburg, so were forty-nine members of the Waffen SS, a combat unit of Hitler's elite SS guard, which also ran the concentration camps where millions had perished. Instead of symbolizing the U.S.-West German postwar alliance, Reagan's gesture set off fiery emotions among Jews and American veterans' groups about Nazi atrocities. In a speech at a nearby U.S. air base immediately after the wreathlaying, Reagan said, "We can mourn the German war dead today as human beings crushed by a vicious ideology." (Reagan at Bitburg, Historic Documents of 1985, p. 357)

Reconciliation with Poland

*"We are aware of the bitterness against Germany created in the war—
in Poland, France, and later in the Soviet Union," Kohl said. "Most
European people were suffering immensely. Many of them are today our
partners and even friends." He also expressed gratitude for Americans
"who extended their hands in reconciliation following the war" with food
and reconstruction aid. President George Bush responded in kind, issuing
a "World War II Remembrance Week" proclamation August 29 that read,
in part: "The history of the Federal Republic of Germany is now a moving
testament to the power of democratic ideas, the wisdom of West Germany's postwar leaders, and the talent and resilience of the German People.
Today, the Federal Republic is among America's closest allies, and a
champion of human rights, democracy, and freedom."*

*Most of all, Kohl focused on his hope for good relations with a Polish
government no longer under Communist control. (Speeches Marking
Poland's New Era, p. 523) Speaking of the new Polish prime minister,
Tadeusz Mazowiecki, Kohl said: "We want him to be successful. We want
to do everything possible to support him. . . ." The West German leader
paid a goodwill visit to Poland, and in Warsaw on November 14 signed an
agreement to provide Poland $2.2 billion in economic assistance. That
same day, Kohl traveled into the Polish countryside to place wreaths at
the sites of two Nazi deaths camps, Auschwitz and Birkenau. Before
Kohl's departure from Poland, he and Mazowiecki signed a declaration
that recalled the 1939 invasion and stated that "the large toll of life
exacted by the war warns and exhorts us to achieve a lasting peace
between the two states and peoples."*

> *Following are excerpts from the West German government's
> translation of Chancellor Helmut Kohl's speech at a Bun-
> destag session in Bonn, September 1, 1989, commemorating
> the fiftieth anniversary of the German invasion of Poland
> and the start of World War II. (The bracketed headings have
> been added by Congressional Quarterly to highlight the
> organization of the text.):*

Today in Germany, in Europe, and all over the world we are commemorating the beginning of World War II 50 years ago. As freely elected
representatives of the German people, we have a special duty here. We are
facing this assignment with the seriousness that this day demands of us.

On this day we are full of grief and awareness of the responsibility we
feel when remembering World War II. We have a special responsibility
because of the fact that World War II was unleashed by that criminal
regime which had the power of state and government in Germany at that
time.

We grieve for the suffering caused to individuals and peoples in the
name of Germans and also by German hands. We grieve for the many

innocent victims also found among our own people. According to the will of its originators, this war was a merciless, racial war of destruction. It reached a dimension of horror that was unprecedented and that must never be reached again. It was the ultimate consequence of a totalitarian ideology, which, in its mania, idolized one race.

We owe it to the innocent victims to keep the memory of this alive— above all to the victims of the shoa [holocaust], the unprecedented genocide of European Jews; the Poles, on whom Hitler declared an absolute war of enslavement and eradication; the Sinti and Roma [gyp- sies]; and the many other victims of the Nazi terror regime.

We grieve for the victims of the deprivation of rights and oppression, which Hitler's dictatorship first brought over Germany and then over the world.

We grieve for the innocent victims at the frontlines of the war and at home, for the victims of expulsion.

In our commemoration we also include the millions of soldiers from so many nations who died as prisoners of war or returned home mutilated by war. Who could forget the women who waited in vain for their husbands and the mothers who waited in vain for their sons? How many children lost their fathers and mothers?

Remembering the innocent victims means remembering the horror, making it present in one's mind in the truest sense of the word. It must be an admonishment to us and, therefore, it must not be negotiated away in comparisons. Let us beware of using—either thoughtlessly or with polemic intentions—terms like facism or resistance for topical issues.

There is not only the temptation to negotiate about past events, but those who close their eyes to the suffering of our time are also thoughtless and without feelings. . . .

Ladies and gentlemen, continuity is only acceptable if it consciously continues what is good; and what is good cannot be destroyed. This includes the free and democratic traditions in our people's history, and the ethical substance from which we, above all the founding fathers and mothers, formed the Federal Republic of Germany, the freest and most democratic body politic that has ever existed on German soil.

To be sure, there were still quite a few people after 1945 who were incorrigible and did not want to listen to reason. However, they were resolutely condemned and rejected once and for all by the large majority of those who have survived—and we are grateful for this. These survivors had physically experienced the effect of the old fatal ideology. They knew its disastrous influence too well.

In history, evil does not last, and that makes us hopeful. In his chimera of a racial state, Hitler disregarded every historical experience. History has passed him by. After 12 years, the so-called thousand-year reich lay in ruins.

It is true, too many people in Germany, as well as some people abroad, had been blinded and misled by the tyrant. However, the judgment on the Nazi dictatorship depends solely on its crimes, its destructive war, and the genocide it committed. The wounds that World War II caused are not yet healed, as we know. They have burnt themselves into the nations' memory, and they have marked people in a personal way—every individual who experienced this time of terror, even as a child.

I cannot forget the pictures of 1939—when I was 9 years old—and the following war years. I still remember today the terrors of the bomb nights in my native town, the people killed in the streets, and the destroyed houses. Others still remember today the cattle wagons of the death trains, crowded with people on their way to the concentration camps; the battlefields of the war where millions of soldiers suffered from fear and misery and were killed; the seemingly endless columns of emaciated women, children, and old people fleeing and being expelled; the refugee trains where mothers clung on to their children who had frozen to death; those who were innocent and lost their lives and those who survived the terrors.

They all remind us not to forget that the inalienable dignity of man must remain the yardstick or our action at all times and everywhere. Ladies and gentlemen, the touchstone is always the dignity of the weakest.

[Burden of War Guilt]

In Germany, above all, remembrance of the past must not be lost. It is a burden for us Germans. However, it has also helped us shape our body politic, our Republic, in a responsible way. It remains the prerequisite for our ability to do so.

Unlike the case following World War I, following 1945 there was no discussion about war guilt. Hitler wanted, planned, and unleashed the war. There can be no argument about that. We must resolutely reject any attempt to mitigate this judgment. This is a demand of the truth and of political-moral decency.

Ladies and gentlemen, it is also a demand of a correctly understood patriotism, because Hitler's intention to destroy was finally also aimed at our own people. With total defeat in sight, he intended to drag our own people into the abyss along with him. He talked about the community of the people; however, in reality, he wanted to separate—not include or integrate—many groups of our people. He was dominated by the chimera of race and everything else was subordinated to it, including the idea of own [sic] nation. He talked about providence, but in reality, he intended to destroy religious ties and Christian morality.

... [T]he evil did not start in 1939 but years before, even before 1933. That which at the beginning might have been stopped, became more and more difficult to stop or reverse.

The antecedents of World War II also teach us that power—no matter for which purpose it is granted—can be controlled only by counter-balancing power. The guilt of the Nazi rulers is not whitewashed in any way when we note today that at the time, parts of the social and political elites failed on the domestic front. Too many refused to be loyal to the Weimar democracy. Later on, a great number—some of them to the very end—indulged in the illusion that the fanaticism of the Nazi rulers might be tamed by compromises and cooperation.

It is also true that European powers—often perhaps unwillingly—promoted a development which objectively favored Hitler's plans. They, too, misjudged him.

The widespread desire for, as Neville Chamberlain said after the 1938 Munich Agreement, peace in our time, was understandable for him, but this desire was a bad adviser. At that time, and today too, it was necessary to attentively see through the plans of a dictatorship.

Only a comprehensive balance of power is able to reliably guarantee a lasting peace. True peace, however, requires much more. Therefore, in our Basic Law, we unreservedly support the inviolable and inalienable human rights as the basis of any human community, of peace, and of world justice.

Ladies and gentlemen, from the experiences of the interwar period, we must conclude that a fair settlement is impossible if goodwill exists on one side only. The antecedents of World War II taught the community of free peoples how important it is to be vigilant. This teaching is still true, even though we may witness an extremely fundamental change in the relations with our neighbors in the East and southeast of Europe.

We all hope that the encouraging developments of our time will be lasting and that they will continue. We will do what we can to contribute to this, because we Germans particularly have a special duty to do this.

[Hitler-Stalin Pact]

This is not the least of the consequences of the Hitler-Stalin Pact of 1939. We Germans understand the special responsibility that results for us from the fact that after the conclusion of this pact, which many call the Devil's Pact, Hitler brought war to Poland. Thus, that country became the first victim of the Nazis' racial war of destruction. The agreements made at that time were a shameless neglect of the independence and territorial integrity of Poland, the Baltic states, Finland, and Romania.

Nothing could justify this attack on international law and, not least, on the right to self-determination. We unreservedly condemn it and the subsequent acts of violence.

The FRG [Federal Republic of Germany] has repeatedly stated that the 1939 agreements are not legally valid for the FRG. This also means that we do not consider the pact itself and its additional protocol as any justification for subsequent violations of international law by the German Reich and also by the Soviet Union. The Hitler-Stalin Pact was the product of the cynical cooperation of two dictatorships. One of them perished once and for all in the inferno it unleashed. The Soviet Union is right in the middle of a painful process of self-examination in the spirit new thinking 36 years after Stalin's death.

During World War II a development started that was carried out by force after the end of the war. Our fatherland was divided. For the Germans in the GDR [German Democratic Republic—East Germany] and for many peoples in central, eastern, and southeastern Europe the end of the war became the starting point for the replacement of one dictatorship with another. The division of Germany and of Europe can be partly explained by World War II, but it cannot be justified in any way. Therefore, statements like the ones by [Soviet] General Secretary [Mikhail S.] Gorbachev in Bonn this June, according to which the postwar period is coming to an end, are a sign of hope for all individuals and peoples who are directly suffering under the division of Germany and Europe and wish for the current state of affairs finally to be peacefully overcome.…

[Reconciliation with Poland]

In our common wish for national self-determination we feel particularly linked with the Polish people. Wladyslaw Bartoszewski, who was awarded the Peace Prize of the German Book Trade and who himself had to suffer terrible things under the Nazi terror regime, said in this connection some time ago: Overcoming the division of Germany is also in Poland's interest. We want a democracy to the west of our country.

Professor Bartoszewski, as a friend of the Germans, signed the joint declaration of Polish and German Catholics of September 1989, under the title: For Freedom, Justice, and Peace. The new Polish premier, Tadeusz Mazowiecki, is also one of the signatories.

At this time and in this place I would like to convey to the Polish premier our particularly good and cordial wishes for his difficult office.

We want him to be successful. We want, to do everything possible to support him and I would like to say this also on my own behalf.

… [T]he current political and social changes in the Warsaw Pact open up the historic chance to implement human rights for all Europeans to whom they have been denied over the past decades, and thus also for all Germans. The FRG Government is firmly determined to make use of this opportunity.…

In a future Europe, the most important thing must be self-determination and human rights as well as sovereignty of the peoples, rather than borders and national territories. It is not sovereign states, but sovereign peoples that will eventually complete the building of Europe. Never again must Europe embark on the fatal road from humanity via nationality to bestiality, as the German writer [Franz] Grillparzer had predicted in the last century.

Terrible things were inflicted on the Polish people in the name of the Germans and by the Germans. Who remembers that the concentration camps on Polish soil were also supposed to extinguish this people's elite as well? Reconciliation is only possible if we tell the whole truth. The truth is that over 2 million Germans—innocent people—lost their lives when they were fleeing and being expelled. The loss of their homes has inflicted deep wounds on many millions of our compatriots.

This bitter experience must not be repressed. However, we want to learn from it. What sense would it make for Germans and Poles to mutually square accounts? Some people in our country and in Poland are still doing

493

so. Ladies and gentlemen, the future generations will judge us by what we are doing now for them to live in peace and freedom. The example of German-French reconciliation and friendship proves that trenches that existed for decades and even centuries can be overcome.

The example of our relationship with the state of Israel and Jews throughout the world shows that with goodwill on all sides, even wide differences can be bridged. We want understanding between the German and the Polish peoples. That is our duty, and it also corresponds to both peoples' wish.

This wish that we all have is also expressed in the message sent by the federal president to the Polish president earlier this week. Fifty years after the outbreak of World War II, the time has come for lasting reconciliation. We are aware of the bitterness against Germany created in the war—in Poland, France, and later in the Soviet Union which had to mourn over 20 million victims of the war. Most European peoples were suffering immensely. Many of them are today our partners and even friends.

We are grateful to all those who extended their hands in reconciliation following the war, after the end of the tyranny and the war—primarily the American people who sent us an unforgettable signal of active charity and political farsightedness by providing, very soon, generous food supplies and reconstruction aid. Statesmen such as President Harry S. Truman and George Marshall, as well as very many private citizens contributed their share to such works of peace. . . .

Regarding understanding with Poland, there have been trailblazing steps in recent years. Let me particularly mention here the diverse initiatives in the sphere of the churches. The Warsaw Treaty of 1970, which was signed by colleague Willy Brandt, was another step in this direction. We will continue to keep to the letter and spirit of this treaty. We should not argue about it any further. In its preamble, Poland and the FRG state their willingness to guarantee a peaceful future for the young generation which has grown up in the meanwhile, and—I quote—to create lasting bases of peaceful coexistence and the development of normal and good relations—unquote. . . .

In the long run, prejudices and distrust do not have any chance where borders can be crossed, where information and views are freely exchanged, and where people, particularly young people, can meet in freedom. . . .

[Lessons from Nazi Era]

Hitler's dictatorship and World War II warn us again and again against the alluring power of extremism or totalitarianism. The danger of extremism is always present, also in a liberal society. Therefore, it is essential for a liberal democracy to counter such temptations as early as possible. . . .

. . . [D]emocracy is not an abstract principle. It affects every individual in a very direct manner. . . .

The Nazi regime entangled men of goodwill in a confusing, diabolical net, and it became progressively more difficult to escape from this net. The borderlines between good and evil were increasingly erased. The honesty of the individual became less and less a guarantee for correct behavior....

Until today, we Germans have felt particularly painfully the ambiguous character of human existence in the war unleashed by Hitler. It is part of the tragedy of this time that the loyalty of millions of people and their love for their fatherland were abused for criminal purposes at the front and at home....

On the one hand, there are the soldiers who fought and suffered at the fronts of World War II. Most, really most, of them were sincerely convinced that they were loyally serving their country. There were many examples of courage and human greatness that deserve our respect. Such an attitude does not deserve to be disparaged or mocked, because it involves the experience of death and pain, of fear, and, in many cases, of tormenting doubts of conscience.

On the other hand, there are the crimes of the Nazis. They cannot be removed from the events of the war. Many people had to suffer under this contradiction at that time.

Ladies and gentlemen, when we are speaking of the ruins left by Nazism, we should always be aware of the devastation caused in the hearts and minds of people. They are a psychological burden not only to those who were entangled in this net, they are a burden to the grandchildren and children who have to try to find a just assessment of their parents and grandparents' generation—perhaps they have to try much harder than one sometimes realizes.

We have to be wary of making precipitate judgments from today's point of view. Which of us, ladies and gentlemen, could claim with a clear conscience that, faced with evil, he would have the strength to be a martyr? Which of us can understand what it meant at that time to be aware of the danger and to risk one's own well-being and also the well-being of one's family? People today are not better or worse than the people in the past, but fortunately they are not forced to make a decision under the conditions of a totalitarian dictatorship.

We gratefully remember that even in the darkest period of our history, under the signs of war and dictatorship, it was not possible to destroy the spirit of humanity. There were many moving examples, mostly unknown ones, of helpfulness, of generosity, and humanity—also across the front lines. There were men and women who worked in the resistance, and among them there were many who had first served Hitler's regime until they realized that they, like the majority of the Germans, had been misled, betrayed, and used. They had the strength to turn around, and many of them paid for this with their lives....

...We should remember more often that the great politicians of the postwar period—Kurt Schumacher, chairman of the Social Democratic Party of Germany, and Andreas Hermes, first chairman of the Christian Democratic Union—had all experienced the prisons, concentration camps, and death cells of the Nazi dictatorship....

Let us ... pay tribute to the joiner (Johann Georg Elser), Colonel Claus Graf Schenk zu Stauffenberg, the Kreisau Group around Helmut Graf von

Moltke, the White Rose around the brother and sister Scholl, and great, steadfast personages such as Julius Leber and Karl Goerdeler, and the very many others who courageously resisted tyranny for reasons of conscience. . . .

It is not success or failure that are decisive for the ethical greatness of resistance. The assassination attempt on Hitler had to be ventured—at all costs. Colonel Henning von (Preskow) who had an essential influence on Stauffenberg's acting and thinking from 1943 on made particularly impressive statements. Several hours before he died, he summarized what had been the deepest motives of his action. I quote—I not only consider Hitler the arch enemy of Germany but the arch enemy of the world. When I stand in front of God's judgment seat in a few hours to account for what I have done and for what I have failed to do, I think that I can defend with a clear conscience what I did in the struggle against Hitler. If God promised Abraham that he would not destroy Sodom if there were but ten righteous men in it, I also hope that God will not destroy Germany for our sake. End of quote. We are profoundly grateful to the men and women of the German resistance.

We also highly respect those who rejected the regime of injustice by emigrating or escaping. Among them were people who, out of love for their fatherland, fought against the Hitler dictatorship from outside. Let us think of the writers who tried to stir up the world by the power of their pen and to make the world aware of what was happening in Germany.

. . . [F]or well-founded reasons, I want to recall a man whom I consider one of the great heroes of the 20th century—[Swedish diplomat] Raul Wallenberg. In 1944, at the age of 32, he risked his life to save hundreds of Jews in Budapest from being murdered. In 1945 he was abducted to the Soviet Union. Since then he has been missing. In my talks with General Secretary Gorbachev, I pointed out that the fate of this great, courageous man is unknown, and I hope very much that in this epoch of change, in which the oppressive legacy of Stalinism is being freely discussed in the Warsaw Pact states, the fate of Raul Wallenberg can be convincingly explained. I very much welcome the fact that the Soviet authorities recently invited relatives of Raul Wallenberg to Moscow.

. . . [O]n this 1 September I particularly address the young people in Germany. They do not bear any guilt whatsoever for the dictatorship and the world war—not collectively, because in principle this does not exist, nor individually because their age has saved them from this. Nevertheless, they, too, bear responsibility because the past remains the present. None of us, no German, can escape it. Let us see this not only as the burden of history but also as an opportunity. Those who know the history of this century have a sharp eye for temptations also in our time. Let us resist the temptation to despise the values of love for one's homeland and of patriotism, which were discredited during the Nazi period because they were abused at that time. . . .

Ladies and gentlemen, today we are witness to the beginning of a new epoch in Europe. We have to be willing to participate in decisively shaping this new beginning. Europe, all of Europe, is facing a comprehensive change, a profound change in economy and society. . . .

On this day of remembering, let us direct our gaze forward. Despite all grief that we feel in remembering 1 September 1939, we are aware of our responsibility for the young generations. At one time, these generations, ladies and gentlemen, will judge us as to whether we drew the correct lessons from the experiences with war and dictatorship, whether we lived up to the task of creating a better and more peaceful world.

We have the vision of a future in which the peoples of the world are peacefully united in common freedom and we will not and must not stop working for this.

Remembering 1 September 1939, we know that this is the most important, most valuable legacy we can leave to the coming generations.

BUSH'S DRUG-WAR SPEECH,
COLOMBIAN LEADER'S UN APPEAL
September 5 and 29, 1989

President George Bush outlined to a national television audience September 5 his long-anticipated plan for a national "war on drugs." On September 29, President Virgilio Barco of Colombia appealed to the world community for help in his fight against a flourishing drug cartel in his country. Addressing the United Nations General Assembly, Barco said Colombia was in the "front line" of the drug war and "the casualties of our struggle have been mounting. . . ." Bush's plan called for aid to that country, the source of much of the cocaine entering the United States.

In the first prime-time speech of his presidency, a self-described "heart-to-heart talk with the American people"—including millions of young viewers in their classrooms—Bush said that "the gravest domestic threat to our nation today is drugs." Illegal drugs, he added, "have strained our faith in our system of justice; our courts, our prisons, our legal system are stretched to the breaking point. The social cost of drugs are mounting. In short, drugs are sapping our strength as a nation."

High among the president's goals were reductions in the number of people reporting the use of illegal drugs—by 10 percent within two years and 50 percent within ten years. He also sought equal-size reductions in the same time periods in the estimated amounts of cocaine, marijuana, heroin, and other illegal drugs entering the United States. Bush proposed $717 million in new spending for antidrug programs in fiscal year 1990, bringing the year's total to $7.9 billion—some $2.2 billion more than was being spent in the 1989 fiscal year ending September 30.

The plan was crafted by William J. Bennett, the nation's first "drug czar," a name popularly applied to his position as director of the new

Office of National Drug Control Policy. An outspoken secretary of education in Ronald Reagan's cabinet who attempted to expose the "ills" of the education system, Bennett was chosen by Bush to coordinate the government's various drug-fighting activities, as was required by a law Congress enacted in 1988. Upon announcing Bennett's appointment to the new cabinet-level job February 8, Bush called him a "man with a million ideas" who he chose to make a "very unclear law" workable.

With only minimal opposition, Bennett received the Senate's confirmation March 9 and quickly began devising a national drug strategy. The new law required this of him within six months of assuming the post. That strategy, outlined by Bush in his speech, was fleshed out in greater detail in a 136-page "National Drug Control Strategy" report Bennett sent to Congress the same day the president spoke.

Military Aid for Colombia

That 1988 legislation, the Anti-Drug Abuse Act, also expanded the scope of U.S. military involvement in the interception of illegal drugs coming into the United States. Congress had previously ordered limited military assistance to civilian law-enforcement agencies in trying to control the flow of drugs entering this country from across the Gulf of Mexico and the Rio Grande. In 1988 the lawmakers told a reluctant Pentagon to coordinate all surveillance by federal agencies of air and sea drug-smuggling routes.

Bush sought to enlarge the military role further. On August 25, in response to a plea from President Barco, he ordered $65 million in military equipment be sent to Colombian police and military forces fighting well-organized drug cartels in that country. In his televised address, Bush asked Congress for an immediate increase of $129 million in military aid to Bolivia, Peru, and Colombia, and to consider a long-term, $2 billion program of military and economic aid to those three countries. Those steps constituted a big shift toward a military response to the overseas narcotics trade.

For months, officials in the Bush administration had considered whether to try to enlist Latin American armies in the cocaine wars. The debate was resolved by a crisis that erupted in Colombia in mid-August. Three public officials, including the expected leading candidate in the 1990 presidential elections, Luis Carlos Galan, were slain—presumably on orders from the country's drug lords. On August 19, hours after Galan died, the government cracked down on the drug trade, which operated with relative immunity, especially in and around the city of Medellin.

Colombian authorities rounded up thousands of persons and confiscated property of several major drug dealers. Moreover, reversing a longtime policy, Barco decreed that those who faced charges in the United States would be sent there for trial. The drug lords, in an apparent effort to make the government back down, responded with retaliatory bombings and shootings in several cities. Colombia was fighting the real drug war, and Barco appealed to Washington for help. Bush responded by telling news reporters at his vacation residence in Kennebunkport, Maine: "It's time for the United States and other countries to stand with President Barco during his courageous challenge to these insidious forces that threaten the very fabric of Colombian society."

Question of Funding

The foreign component of Bush's drug plan generated little outright criticism in Congress. Members of both parties expressed support for giving military aid in such situations. The questions on Capitol Hill about Bush's entire drug-fighting strategy focused on money. The president suggested that the needed new funds in 1990 could be raised by trimming half a dozen existing domestic programs. He insisted that no new taxes would be needed.

Republicans generally applauded the plan and said it could be financed by paring existing programs. Democrats generally insisted that there was not enough money in the plan to make it work. House Speaker Thomas S. Foley, D-Wash., said a tax increase would be inevitable. Sen. Joseph R. Biden, Jr., D-Del., chairman of the Senate Judiciary Committee, who represented his party in a televised response to the president's address, summed up the plan as "not tough enough, bold enough, or imaginative enough."

Sen. Robert C. Byrd, D-W.Va., chairman of the Senate Appropriations Committee, tried to put a Democratic stamp on the plan by proposing to double the $2.2 billion increase in antidrug spending that Bush wanted. To pay for the larger amount, Byrd suggested across-the-board cuts of 0.575 percent in domestic and defense programs. In an unusually sharp attack from the White House, presidential press secretary Marlin Fitzwater on September 12 accused Byrd of playing "price-tag politics" with the drug issue. Senate Democratic leaders were incensed and retorted that the White House was engaging in partisan rhetoric. After that the Senate's Democratic and Republican leaders agreed to form a bipartisan task force to work out a compromise.

In September, Senate Republicans and Democrats in negotiations with the White House worked out an agreement that added about $900 million to Bush's request. The House went along with the compromise, which was embodied in legislation Congress passed shortly before its adjournment in November. The new money was to come from cuts of about 0.43 percent in other government programs. In all, federal antidrug spending in fiscal year 1990 would amount to $8.8 billion, 54 percent more than the $5.7 billion expenditure in 1989. About $125 million would be for drug-fighting assistance to Colombia, Bolivia, and Peru.

Public opinion polls taken within a few days of Bush's address indicated that a majority of Americans approved of the president's strategy to fight drugs but they were divided over whether it would succeed. Three *out of four adults who were questioned in a* Washington Post-*ABC News Poll said his proposals did not go far enough in attacking "the real causes of the drug problem." A* New York Times-*CBS News Poll said six of every ten persons who were asked said they thought the plan, if enacted, would significantly reduce the nation's drug problem. Nearly two-thirds of them considered drugs the nation's worst problem.*

> *Following is the address President Bush delivered on national television, outlining his plan for a "war on drugs," and a televised response by Sen. Joseph R. Biden, Jr., D-Del., on behalf of the Democratic party—both on September 5, 1989, and Colombian President Virgilio Barco's address to the United Nations General Assembly, September 29. (The bracketed headings have been added by Congressional Quarterly to highlight the organization of the text.):*

BUSH'S DRUG-WAR SPEECH

Good evening. This is the first time since taking the oath of office that I felt an issue was so important, so threatening, that it warranted talking directly with you, the American people.

All of us agree that the gravest domestic threat facing our nation today is drugs. Drugs have strained our faith in our system of justice; our courts, our prisons, our legal system are stretched to the breaking point. The social costs of drugs are mounting. In short, drugs are sapping our strength as a nation. Turn on the evening news, or pick up the morning paper, and you'll see what some Americans know just by stepping out their front door. Our most serious problem today is cocaine, and in particular, crack.

Who's responsible? Let me tell you straight out: everyone who uses drugs; everyone who sells drugs; and everyone who looks the other way.

Tonight I'll tell you how many Americans are using illegal drugs. I will present to you our national strategy to deal with every aspect of this threat. And I will ask you to get involved in what promises to be a very difficult fight. This—this is crack cocaine, seized a few days ago by drug enforcement agents in a park just across the street from the White House. It could easily have been heroin or PCP. It's as innocent looking as candy. But it's turning our cities into battle zones. And it's murdering our children.

Let there be no mistake: This stuff is poison. Some used to call drugs harmless recreation. They're not. Drugs are a real and terribly dangerous threat to our neighborhoods, our friends, and our families. No one among us is out of harm's way.

When 4-year-olds play in playgrounds strewn with discarded hypodermic needles and crack vials, it breaks my heart. When cocaine, one of the most deadly and addictive illegal drugs, is available to school kids—school kids—it's an outrage.

And when hundreds of thousands of babies are born each year to mothers who use drugs—premature babies born desperately sick—then even the most defenseless among us are at risk. These are the tragedies behind the statistics.

[U.S. Drug Usage]

But the numbers also have quite a story to tell. Let me share with you the results of the recently completed household survey of the National Institute on Drug Abuse. It compares recent drug use to three years ago; it tells us some good news—and some very bad news.

First, the good. As you can see in the chart, in 1985 the government estimated that 23 million Americans were using drugs on a current basis, that is, at least once in the preceding month. Last year that number fell by more than a third.

That means almost 9 million fewer Americans are casual drug users. Good news. Because we changed our national attitude toward drugs, casual drug use has declined. We have many to thank: our brave law enforcement officers, religious leaders, teachers, community activists, and leaders of business and labor. We should also thank the media for their exhaustive news and editorial coverage, and for their air time and space for anti-drug messages.

And, finally, I want to thank President and Mrs. Reagan for their leadership. All of these good people told the truth, that drug use is wrong and dangerous.

But as much comfort as we can draw from these dramatic reductions, there is also bad news—very bad news. Roughly eight million people have used cocaine in the past year, almost one million of them used it frequently, once a week or more.

What this means is that in spite of the fact that overall cocaine use is down, frequent use has almost doubled in the last few years. And that's why habitual cocaine users, especially crack users, are the most pressing immediate drug problem.

[The Bush Plan]

What then is our plan? To begin with, I trust the lesson of experience. No single policy will cut it, no matter how glamorous or magical it may sound. To win the war against addictive drugs like crack will take more than just a federal strategy. It will take a national strategy, one that reaches into every school, every work place, involving every family.

Earlier today, I sent this document, our first such national strategy, to the Congress. It was developed with the hard work of our nation's first drug policy director, Bill Bennett.

In preparing this plan, we talked with state, local and community leaders, law enforcement officials, and experts in education, drug prevention and rehabilitation. We talked with parents and kids. We took a long, hard look at all that the federal government has done about drugs in the past—what's worked, and let's be honest, what hasn't.

Too often, people in government acted as if their part of the problem, whether fighting drug production or drug smuggling or drug demand, was the only problem. But turf battles won't win this war; teamwork will.

Tonight, I'm announcing a strategy that reflects the coordinated, cooperative commitment of all our federal agencies. In short, this plan is as comprehensive as the problem. With this strategy, we now finally have a plan that coordinates our resources, our programs, and the people who run them.

Our weapons in this strategy are: the law and criminal justice system; our foreign policy; our treatment systems and our schools and drug prevention programs. So the basic weapons we need are the ones we already have. What's been lacking is a strategy to effectively use them.

[Greater Law Enforcement]

Let me address four of the major elements of our strategy.

First, we are determined to enforce the law, to make our streets and neighborhoods safe. So to start I am proposing that we more than double federal assistance to state and local law enforcement. Americans have a right to safety in and around their homes, and we won't have safe neighborhoods unless we're tough on drug criminals, much tougher than we are now.

Sometimes that means tougher penalties, but more often it just means punishment that is swift and certain. We've all heard stories about drug dealers who were caught and arrested again and again, but never punished. Well, here the rules have changed: If you sell drugs, you will be caught; and when you're caught, you will be prosecuted; and once you're convicted, you will do time. Caught, prosecuted, punished.

I'm also proposing that we enlarge our criminal justice system across the board at the local, state, and federal levels alike. We need more prisons, more jails, more courts, more prosecutors. So tonight I'm requesting altogether an almost billion-and-a-half-dollar increase in drug-related federal spending on law enforcement.

And while illegal drug use is found in every community, nowhere is it worse than our public housing projects. You know, the poor have never had it easy in this world. But in the past they weren't mugged on the way home from work by crack gangs, and their children didn't have to dodge bullets on the way to school. And that's why I'm targeting $50 million to fight crime in public housing projects, to help restore order and to kick out the dealers for good.

[Beyond Our Borders]

The second element of our strategy looks beyond our borders where the cocaine and crack bought on America's streets is grown and processed. In Colombia alone, cocaine killers have gunned down a leading statesman, murdered almost 200 judges and seven members of their supreme court.

The besieged governments of the drug-producing countries are fighting back, fighting to break the international drug rings. You and I agree with the courageous president of Colombia, Virgilio Barco, who said that if Americans use cocaine, then Americans are paying for murder. American cocaine users need to understand that our nation has zero tolerance for casual drug use. We have a responsibility not to leave our brave friends in Colombia to fight alone.

The $65 million emergency assistance, announced two weeks ago, was just our first step in assisting the Andean nations in their fight against the cocaine cartels. Colombia has already arrested suppliers, seized tons of cocaine, and confiscated palatial homes of drug lords. But Colombia faces a long, uphill battle. So we must be ready to do more.

Our strategy allocates more than a quarter of a billion dollars for next year in military and law enforcement assistance for the three Andean nations of Colombia, Bolivia and Peru. This will be the first part of a five-year, $2 billion program to counter the producers, the traffickers, and the smugglers.

I spoke with President Barco just last week, and we hope to meet with the leaders of affected countries in an unprecedented drug summit, all to coordinate an inter-American strategy against the cartels. We will work with our allies and friends, especially our economic summit partners, to do more in the fight against drugs.

I'm also asking the Senate to ratify the United Nations anti-drug convention concluded last December. To stop those drugs on the way to America, I propose that we spend more than a billion and a half dollars on interdiction. Greater interagency cooperation, combined with sophisticated intelligence gathering and Defense Department technology, can help stop drugs at our borders.

And our message to the drug cartels is this: The rules have changed. We will help any government that wants our help. When requested we will, for the first time, make available the appropriate resources of America's armed forces. We will intensify our efforts against drug smugglers on the high seas, in international air space, and at our borders. We will stop the flow of chemicals from the United States used to process drugs.

We will pursue and enforce international agreements to trap drug money to the front men and financiers. And then we will handcuff these money launderers and jail them, just like any street dealer. And for the drug kingpins, the death penalty.

[Treatment and Prevention]

The third part of our strategy concerns drug treatment. Experts believe that there are two million American drug users who may be able to get off drugs with proper treatment. But right now only 40 percent of them are actually getting help. This is simply not good enough.

Many people who need treatment won't seek it on their own, and some who do seek it are put on a waiting list. Most programs were set up to deal with heroin addicts, but today the major problem is cocaine users. It's time we expand our treatment systems and do a better job of providing services to those who need them.

And so tonight I'm proposing an increase of $321 million in federal spending on drug treatment. With this strategy we will do more. We will work with the states; we will encourage employers to establish employee assistance programs to cope with drug use. And because addiction is such a cruel inheritance, we will intensify our search for ways to help expectant mothers who use drugs.

Fourth, we must stop illegal drug use before it starts. Unfortunately, it begins early—for many kids before their teens. But it doesn't start the way you might think, from a dealer or an addict hanging around a school playground; more often our kids first get their drugs free from friends or even from older brothers or sisters. Peer pressure spreads drug use; peer pressure can help stop it.

I'm proposing a quarter-of-a-billion-dollar increase in federal funds for school and community prevention programs that help young people and adults reject enticements to try drugs.

And I'm proposing something else. Every school, college, and university, and every work place, must adopt tough but fair policies about drug use by students and employees. And those that will not adopt such policies will not get federal funds—period.

The private sector also has an important role to play. I spoke with a businessman named Jim Burke, who said he was haunted by the thought— a nightmare really—that somewhere in America at any given moment there is a teenage girl who should be in school instead of giving birth to a child addicted to cocaine.

So Jim did something. He led an anti-drug partnership, financed by private funds, to work with advertisers and media firms. Their partnership is now determined to work with our strategy by generating educational messages worth a million dollars a day, every day for the next three years, a billion dollars worth of advertising all to promote the anti-drug message.

As president, one of my first missions is to keep the national focus on our offensive against drugs. And so next week I will take the anti-drug message to the classrooms of America in a special television address, one that I hope will reach every school, every young American.

But drug education doesn't begin in class or on TV. It must begin at home and in the neighborhood. Parents and families must set the first example of a drug-free life. And when families are broken, caring friends and neighbors must step in.

[Need for a United America]

These are the most important elements in our strategy to fight drugs. They are all designed to reinforce one another, to mesh into a powerful whole, to mount an aggressive attack on the problem from every angle.

This is the first time in the history of our country that we truly have a comprehensive strategy.

As you can tell, such an approach will not come cheaply. Last February I asked for a $700 million increase in the drug budget for the coming year. And now over the past six months of careful study, we have found an immediate need for another billion and a half dollars.

With this added $2.2 billion, our 1990 drug budget totals almost $8 billion, the largest increase in history. We need this program fully implemented right away. The next fiscal year begins just 26 days from now. So tonight I'm asking the Congress, which has helped us formulate this strategy, to help us move it forward immediately.

We can pay for this fight against drugs without raising taxes or adding to the budget deficit. We have submitted our plan to Congress that shows just how to fund it within the limits of our bipartisan budget agreement.

Now, I know some will still say that we're not spending enough money. But those who judge our strategy only by its price tag simply don't understand the problem. Let's face it: We've all seen in the past that money alone won't solve our toughest problems. To be strong and efficient, our strategy needs these funds. But there is no match for a united America, a determined America, an angry America.

Our outrage against drugs unites us, brings us together behind this one plan of action, an assault on every front. This is the toughest domestic challenge we've faced in decades, and it's a challenge we must face, not as Democrats or Republicans, liberals or conservatives, but as Americans. The key is a coordinated, united effort.

We've responded faithfully to the request of the Congress to produce our nation's first national drug strategy. I'll be looking to the Democratic majority and our Republicans in Congress for leadership and bipartisan support. And our citizens deserve cooperation, not competition. A national effort, not a partisan bidding war.

To start, Congress needs not only to act on this national drug strategy, but also, to act on our crime package, announced last May, a package to toughen sentences, beef up law enforcement, and build new prison space for 24,000 inmates.

You and I both know the federal government can't do it alone. The states need to match tougher federal laws with tougher laws of their own, stiffer bail, probation, parole, and sentencing. And we need your help. If people you know are users, help them. Help them get off drugs.

If you're a parent, talk to your kids about drugs, tonight. Call your local drug prevention program. Be a big brother or sister to a child in need. Pitch in with your local neighborhood watch program, whether you give your time or your talent. Everyone counts.

Every employer who bans drugs from the work place, every school that's tough on drug use, every neighborhood in which drugs are not welcome, and most important, every one of you who refuses to look the other way. Every one of you counts. Of course, victory will take hard work and time.

But together we will win. Too many young lives are at stake.

Not long ago, I read a newspaper story about a little boy named Dooney who, until recently, lived in a crack house in a suburb of Washington, D.C.

In Dooney's neighborhood, children don't flinch at the sound of gunfire. And when they play, they pretend to sell to each other small white rocks that they call crack. Life at home was so cruel that Dooney begged his teachers to let him sleep on the floor at school. And when asked about his future, 6-year-old Dooney answers: "I don't want to sell drugs, but I'll probably have to." Well, Dooney does not have to sell drugs. No child in America should have to live like this.

Together, as a people, we can save these kids. We've already transformed a national attitude of tolerance into one of condemnation. But the war on drugs will be hard won, neighborhood by neighborhood, block by block, child by child.

If we fight this war as a divided nation, then the war is lost. But if we face this evil as a nation united, this will be nothing but a handful of useless chemicals. Victory—victory over drugs is our cause, a just cause. And with your help, we are going to win.

Thank you, God bless you, and good night.

BIDEN'S RESPONSE

Ladies and gentlemen, we have a job to do; we all have a job to do. We speak with great concern about the drug problem in America today, but we fail to appreciate or address it for what it really is—the number one threat to our national security. It affects the readiness of our army, the productivity of our workers, and the achievement of our students, and the very health and safety of our families. America is under attack literally, under attack by an enemy who is well-financed, well-supplied, and well-armed— and fully capable of declaring total war against a nation and its people, as we've seen in Colombia.

Here in America the enemy is already ashore. And for the first time we are fighting and losing a war on our own soil. Every president for the past two decades, Democrat and Republican alike, has declared war on drugs, and each of them has lost that war and lost it miserably.

They lost because they attempted to deal with only part of the drug problem; they lost because their initiatives were pulled apart by bureaucratic squabbling among their advisers; they lost because they always did too little and they did it too late. That's why the Democrats and the Republicans in the Congress got together last year to write the law that required the president to give us a national drug strategy, the one you heard tonight—you heard him deliver it.

[Bush Not Tough Enough]

We don't oppose the president's plan; all we want to do is strengthen it. We don't doubt his resolve; all we want to do is stiffen it. The trouble is that the president's proposals are not big enough to deal with the problem. His rhetoric isn't matched by the resources we need to get the job done. Quite frankly, the president's plan is not tough enough, bold enough, or imaginative enough to meet the crisis at hand.

If you had a child in your family who was seriously ill, I doubt whether you'd call a family meeting to discuss what percentage of the family budget you were willing to spend to make him well. You wouldn't say that we can't afford to spend more than a penny out of every dollar the family has to cure the child.

But that's exactly what the president would have us do: spend one penny—one penny—out of every tax dollar to fight drugs. The Defense Department spends $300 billion a year to prepare for a war we hope we'll never have to fight. But the president says he wants to spend only $8 billion next year on a war we're already fighting and we're losing.

The president says he wants to wage a war on drugs, but if that's true, what we need is another D-Day, not another Vietnam, not another limited war fought on the cheap and destined for stalemate and human tragedy.

Now, I'm going to point out some specific things, six of them that we find inadequate about the president's plan. I think the president has to join us in making a significantly greater commitment to these six areas to stem the rising tide of violence in America, and that's what it is, violence.

First, we have to join together to ensure that drug dealers are punished—swiftly, surely and severely. And in line with what the president is calling for, we have to hold every drug user accountable. Because if there were no drug users, there'd be no appetite for drugs, and there'd be no market for them.

[More Law Enforcement]

Let's take a look at what the real problem is. It's not just how many people are using drugs. As the president said, the number of people using drugs, cocaine in particular, is down in our country. That's true. But the violence associated with drugs is spewing out all over America, and that's terrible.

I know it's hard to believe, but this very day, violent drug offenders will commit more than 100,000 crimes on this day alone. And the sad part is that we have no more police on the streets of our major cities than we had ten years ago. And what the president proposes won't help much. What he proposes is no increase over what the Congress has already approved last year.

In a nutshell, the president's plan doesn't include enough police officers to catch the violent thugs; not enough prosecutors to convict them; not enough judges to sentence them; and not enough prison cells to put them away for a long time. That's why, right now, six out of every 10 criminals who are arrested on drug charges have their cases dropped.

That's why we think the president should triple—triple—the commitment he's made tonight for police, prosecutors and judges for our cities and our states.

[Expanded Education Efforts]

Second, education. The president says he's increasing money for drug education, because he knows what we know: It works. We found out that when students understand how harmful cocaine is, they're five times less likely to even try the drug.

And right now, the drug education message is reaching only 50 percent of the children in this country. And the president's plan, for all the talk, will only increase our efforts by 5 percent. You know, drug education is the only vaccine we have against drug abuse among our young. And can you imagine me sitting before you and saying, we're only going to vaccinate 50 percent of the children against polio or smallpox? We have to do more.

We have to educate our children about the dangers of drugs. And we have to start in kindergarten, because we know that last year one out of every four high school students in America tried drugs, and that the other three were prime targets of drug pushers. We can't afford to lose a generation while we're sorting out the budgetary priorities of this nation. We must do more, and now.

[Protect Our Borders]

Third, we disagree with the president's decision to cut back on our previous commitment to protect against drugs coming across the border, to cut the Customs Service, the Coast Guard and the border patrol. We think we should do more to stem the flow of drugs across our borders, and we think we should go one step further: Let's go after the drug lords where they live with an international strike force. There must be no safe haven for these narco-terrorists. And they must know it.

Fourth, experts tell us there are six and a half million addicts, addicted drug addicts, out there, and that they're committing thousands upon thousands of crimes. And under the president's plan we'll treat only 19 out of 100 addicts.

He talked about pregnant women. Well, his proposal would help only one-quarter of the children under the age of 16 who are addicted and one-quarter of the women who are pregnant and addicted. We can do better than that to prevent the next generation from becoming a generation of violence.

[End Bureaucratic Infighting]

Fifth, the president has to take charge and end the bureaucratic infighting that plagues the anti-drug efforts now.

Last year, for example—and listen to this—last year the Congress approved $5 million to protect Colombian judges, providing the kind of support that the Colombian justice minister, Mrs. De Greiff, recently asked for in Washington, yet not a single penny of that $5 million arrived in Bogota, Colombia, before the justice minister arrived in the United States a couple of weeks ago. And the president's plan does nothing to prevent such fiascos from happening in the future. He must eliminate the duplication among drug-fighting agencies and end the waste. That's one of the main reasons why we created the drug czar in the first place.

[Greater Scientific Investment]

The last thing I'd like to say about the strategy the president proposes is that we have to make a greater investment in the scientific community, the scientific community that's pursuing innovative approaches for fighting the drug crisis, just as we do for cancer and for AIDS and for Alzheimer's. They are already at work.

In a lab in Delaware, scientists are working on new medicines that may block an addict's cravings for drugs, and across the country in Los Alamos Weapons Laboratories other scientists are exploring new state-of-the-art techniques to battle the narco-terrorists. We need more of that kind of scientific enterprise. We need to enlist America's scientific muscle in turning back the drug traffickers.

You know, listening to both of us, this may seem all complicated, very complicated. But it isn't. We know what has to be done. We have to educate our children not to take drugs, reach our children who are on drugs and get them off; we have to lock up the dealers for a long, long time, and we have to attack the source from which the drugs come.

And we have to do that not a piece at a time, but all at once. And we have to do it now. And there's not any reason why we can't do that. We have the power, we have the money, and we have the knowledge.

And we don't have to promise a world without worry or fear. We're not asking for that much. All we have to do together is to keep our promises, and stay together.

To put it in very personal terms for a moment, Joe Biden, me, I would settle for a world in which I could worry about the same kinds of things that my parents worried about; in which I only had to worry about the grades my children got in school, rather than the drugs they're being exposed to; in which I only had to worry about the prices my wife had to pay at the supermarket instead of fearing that she might get mugged by a junkie in the parking lot as she loads her groceries into the car; in which tonight, I could call my mom just to wish her pleasant dreams, not for the purpose of making sure she's safe in her own home.

That's the kind of world I want. That's the kind of world you deserve. And there's no reason we can't have it. Thank you.

BARCO'S UN ADDRESS

... The notion of national sovereignty underlies all our strategic thinking; indeed it is the basis for this United Nations. Yet now we find this newest threat, narcotics, and accompanying terrorism that pays no respect to borders. We, a community of nations, find ourselves under assault from an international criminal enterprise that respects none of our norms of sovereignty, frontiers, or laws.

To meet this new challenge we have to reach back to those core founding values of the United Nations. If we cannot act together in the face of this menace, then we will be abetting the unrestrained growth in the use of drugs and in the violence they generate.

I am certain that Colombia will finally defeat the drug traffickers. But if this effort is not accompanied by a global commitment, then no victory can be achieved.

The recent global outpouring of solidarity and support for Colombia has been a great encouragement to us in these difficult times.

A new era is upon us. A new world war is being waged by an aggressor unrestrained by the traditional rules of engagement or by the responsibilities of national sovereignty. This aggressor is an insidious, global criminal network with enormous power and resources—a criminal enterprise which feeds on the illegal profits from the trafficking of drugs. . . .

The members of these criminal cartels were born in many nations and many of its leaders are called Colombian. But while some may have been born in my country, let me be clear—they are not Colombian in any more than name. They are international fugitives on the run. They have no home.

I am here today to lay out the stark realities of this war against drug trafficking. We are on the front line of this battle. For us this is no war of words. In Colombia the casualties of our struggle have been mounting for some time. A month ago, we suffered the tragic assassination of one of our finest national leaders, Luis Carlos Galan. In many ways, his death has galvanized our nation and focused the attention of the world on this problem. But our war on drugs has been taking its toll for years. We have lost 12 Supreme Court Justices, our Attorney General and Minister of Justice. We have lost Members of Congress and Mayors, scores of journalists, thousands of soldiers and policemen and tens of thousands of Colombian citizens who were committed to the cause of democracy.

Following my announcement last month to enforce drastic measures using executive powers available under a state of siege, the narco-traffickers have continued to engage in a cowardly reign of terror. They have threatened and retaliated against innocent families, they randomly strike at our cities and have bombed institutions like our newspaper El Espectador which dare to speak out against them. In short, in their aim to protect their illegal and criminal activities, they seek to destroy the will of our people and undermine our most precious institutions. Hear me well— they will fail. Colombia—one of the oldest democracies in Latin America— will prevail.

In these past few weeks, we have had some important victories. We are methodically breaking the back of the cartels, but not just by confiscating and destroying many tons of cocaine. Indeed, Colombian authorities capture almost eighty percent of the cocaine seized globally. But our offensive goes beyond that. The assassins of Luis Carlos Galan have already been captured. Many thousands of suspects have been apprehended and millions of dollars in property—processing plants, bank accounts, communication equipment, aircraft, boats, houses and ranches that provide the backbone and the lifestyle for this criminal operation—have been seized.

All these victories, though, will not be nearly sufficient to win this war. That is why I am here today. Only through concerted international action can we hope to defeat the scourge of narcotics. . . .

Many of you, by the way, may not accept that this is a global war; you may believe that it is one of this hemisphere alone—that cocaine is a scourge only of the Americas, produced in the nations of South America and consumed by North America. This is not so, because cocaine's tentacles, even as we meet today, are reaching into Europe and the Far East. The aggressive search for new markets is no more respectful of oceans than it was of borders. Where there are customers there will be suppliers. And indeed cocaine is only one ugly manifestation of a much wider narcotics crisis. Make no mistake, this scourge touches us all.

In solidarity, as a community of nations, this should be our plan of action:

First, we simply must stop demand for these illicit narcotics. It is the insatiable demand for drugs that fuels this terrorism and which is one of the greatest threats to democracy in Latin America. Those who consume cocaine are contributing to the assassination of my people by the criminal drug cartels. No doubt somebody a few blocks from this General Assembly Hall, in one of this city's fashionable neighborhoods, taking cocaine in the civilized calm of his living room, would balk at this description. Yet as surely as if he pulled the trigger he is the slayer of those Colombian judges and policemen who have paid with their lives for trying to uphold the law.

Every tactic and every weapon in the war against narcotics pales into insignificance compared to the need to reduce demand. The illegal profits produced by drug consumption are simply too great. I am sure that in Colombia we will defeat drug traffickers. But someone, in some country, somewhere, will supply the drugs as long as the business remains so profitable. This happened in the case with marijuana. When it became too expensive for drug traffickers to operate in Colombia, because of effective law enforcement, they moved to California, Hawaii and other places. The only law the narco-terrorists do not break is the law of supply and demand.

No society, no matter how rich, can afford to have its sons and daughters poisoned by cocaine, heroin or any other deadly drug. In this regard, President Bush's National Drug Control Strategy is a first step in the right direction. . . .

Second, our efforts to reduce the supply of refined cocaine also depend on international cooperation in stopping the illegal trade in chemicals which are essential to the processing of this drug. Generally, much attention is given to the production and processing of drugs. For example, to countries like Peru and Bolivia where coca leaf is grown. Unfortunately, in contrast, little attention is given to controlling the supply of chemicals which are used to process cocaine and which come mainly from North America and Europe. None of these are manufactured in Colombia—all of them are smuggled into our country. Tightening controls on the manufacture and sale of these chemicals, as well as strengthening sanctions against their illegal shipment, must be one of our highest priorities. It takes more than coca leaf to produce cocaine. Without the chemicals there would be no narcotic. Let us press on the suppliers of these chemicals as firmly as we do on the poor peasant growers of coca leaf.

Third, the weapons used by the cartels to intimidate, maim and kill my people do not come from Colombia. They are found in international arms market where even the most sophisticated weapons are easily and legally bought. Make no mistake, those who sell arms to the narco-terrorists are even more guilty than the addicts whose demand for drugs fuels violence. Last year Colombia presented a draft resolution calling for restrictions in arms sales, but unfortunately, consensus could not be found at the United Nations. We can no longer wait while this deadly trade continues. It is essential to adopt special measures to reduce and control arms sales to drug traffickers and terrorists. I call on all of the nations of the world to stop this madness and to stop it now.

My Government also views with extreme seriousness the activities of foreign mercenaries in training and assisting narco-terrorists in Colombia. The international community must strengthen its condemnation of the murderous association of mercenaries with terrorists and drug traffickers. My Administration has not only condemned the presence of foreign mercenaries in our territory, it has also criminalized their activities and ordered their capture. These developments in Colombia make an urgent and indisputable case for this Assembly to approve the Convention outlawing these activities.

Fourth, international cooperation is an essential element in efforts to halt money-laundering. The drug cartels depend on the international banking system for the transfer of funds. A significant part of the criminal profits are invested in the industrialized nations—in bank accounts and bonds, in properties and in legal businesses. Somehow our sense of justice is warped when a poor farmer who feeds his family by growing coca is seen as the greater villain than the wealthy international banker who illegally transfers millions of dollars of drug money that finances terrorist actions against innocent people. If the international banking system cooperates in cracking down, we can put the cartel out of business.

Fifth, each of us must press for the prompt ratification of the Vienna Convention on narcotics trafficking. Painstakingly negotiated, this Convention includes specific actions on a wide variety of fronts, from penalties for consumption to seizure of ships on the high seas and confiscation of properties. Upon my return to Colombia, I will introduce it to the Colombian Congress for consideration. To be effective, it must be ratified by the community of nations.

In addition, I recommended to this Assembly two other multilateral initiatives: The first is to call a special session of this General Assembly addressed to all aspects of the global drug problem—consumption and production—which would consider urgent actions including those I am suggesting today. The other step, and perhaps the most important way to make concrete progress, is to establish an international working group at ministerial level, which would meet periodically to coordinate and refine specific anti-narcotics actions and to evaluate progress.

Sixth, central to the support for political stability and the maintenance of Colombia's democratic institutions is the strength of its economy. This is why international cooperation to maintain a strong and stable economy is so vital. In spite of the enormous destabilizing power of this international criminal organization, Colombia has been able to remain firm in its will to fight against drug trafficking....

NAVY'S REPORT ON THE USS *IOWA* EXPLOSION
September 7, 1989

A powerful explosion aboard the battleship Iowa *on April 19 resulted in the deaths of forty-seven crew members. At the time the ship was approximately three hundred miles northeast of Puerto Rico during naval exercises in the Atlantic Ocean. The ensuing investigations raised perplexing questions as to whether a sailor who died in the blast might deliberately have caused it, or whether the complexity of the weapons aboard the ship had overwhelmed the men operating them, leading to the explosion.*

The navy released its investigation findings in a 6,330-page report on September 7, concluding that "irrefutable facts" and circumstantial evidence pointed to the likelihood that one of the crewmen, Clayton M. Hartwig, a gunner's mate second-class, was responsible for the tragedy. However, naval officers acknowledged that troubling questions remained unanswered. These questions led to congressional inquiries into the navy's conduct of the investigation, the quality of its weapons-training program, and the feasibility of continuing to keep battleships in U.S. fleets. Criticism of the navy's principal finding—that Hartwig was the culprit—was voiced in Congress, the press, and by relatives of the deceased Iowa *sailors.*

The explosion occurred in the second of the battleship's three gigantic gun turrets, each as tall as a seven-story building and housing three battery guns sixteen inches in diameter at the mouth—the world's largest naval guns. The battleship, built during World War II and afterward decommissioned with other battleships as obsolete, was refitted for sea duty in the early 1980s as part of President Ronald Reagan's defense buildup. New technology was applied to the gun operations.

The big guns on the Iowa *are capable of firing shells weighing up to 2,700 pounds, with a maximum range of twenty-three miles. At the time of the explosion, five 110-pound bags of explosives had been placed in Turret 2 to fire a practice round. The navy concluded that Hartwig probably placed a detonating device between bags of powder in the middle gun of the turret and then guided a ramming device against the barrel to cause a premature explosion.*

Focus on Hartwig

The navy probe focused almost immediately on Hartwig, the gun captain. FBI officials, whose agency assisted with the investigation, described Hartwig as a troubled man "rehearsing all his life for violence and death." It was suggested in press accounts of the investigation that Hartwig had engaged in a homosexual relationship with a shipmate, Kendall Truitt. Hartwig had named Truitt beneficiary of a $100,000 life insurance policy. Truitt, a married man, denied the allegation and was cleared of any complicity in the explosion.

Rear Adm. Richard D. Milligan, who headed the navy's investigation, described its findings in a Pentagon news conference on September 7. Hartwig, he said, was "a loner, a man of low self-esteem who talked of dying in the line of duty, and being buried in Arlington National Cemetery." At the same time, the admiral said, "We have no hard evidence whatsoever of homosexuality in this case." The navy's "compelling evidence" of deliberate action was chemical testing that detected traces of foreign substances on a copper ring that moves through the gun barrel when the gun is fired. Those chemical substances suggested to naval investigators that the explosion was set off by an electric timer and batteries. The FBI also examined a portion of the same copper ring and found the same trace elements but did not concur with the navy's conclusion that they had been left by a homemade detonator.

According to the navy report, Hartwig, as the gun captain, would have been the person in the best position to produce the explosion. The navy concluded that the insertion of a detonating device between two powder bags behind the shell to be fired was the cause of the tragedy and that "Hartwig was the most likely person to have introduced that detonating device."

Questions Remain

Hartwig's relatives expressed outrage over the navy's investigation. Hartwig's sister, Kathy Kubicina, accused the navy of "making him the scapegoat." "It's not fair to let the navy investigate itself," she added in a press interview. "We would like to get an outside opinion from Congress." Several members of Congress and other relatives of the victims also questioned the navy's findings. In addition, letters from some of the Iowa *crewmen as well as interviews with family members disclosed several earlier, less serious accidents involving guns on the ship. The navy did not mention the incidents in its reports.*

"I am not persuaded" that Hartwig intended to commit suicide, said Rep. Nicholas Mavroules, D-Mass., chairman of the House Armed Services Subcommittee on Investigations, in a letter to a congressional colleague October 26. The Iowa's *skipper, Capt. Fred Moosally, testified before the Senate Armed Services Committee on December 11 that he believed someone had deliberately set the explosion but disagreed with the investigation's conclusion that Hartwig was the most likely person.*

Truitt, appearing before Mavroules's subcommittee on December 13, called the navy's report "misleading" and "ridiculous." He reconfirmed the navy's statement that Hartwig did not know he was to be in the turret until just before he was assigned there on the day of the explosion; Truitt contended that Hartwig would not have had time to make plans to detonate the explosives.

Aftermath

The navy ordered light administrative punishment for Moosally and three others aboard the Iowa *for dereliction of duty in failing to train the ship's gun crews adequately before the April 19 explosion. But the navy said that this failure "did not cause or contribute to the explosion in any way."*

In an unprecedented action, the navy announced November 14 that it was suspending routine naval operations for forty-eight hours to review safety procedures. The suspension reflected concern about shipboard accidents. Earlier in the year, a fire aboard an amphibious assault ship injured thirty-one sailors and eight civilians, and an F-14 jet fighter crashed on the aircraft carrier Lexington, *killing five persons.*

The Senate Armed Services Committee opened hearings November 16 on the status of the navy, which were intended to "go way beyond the [Iowa] *explosion," said Chairman Sam Nunn, D-Ga. Some committee members appeared to agree that because battleships required substantial manpower while the pool of qualified personnel might be inadequate, the ships might be too expensive to continue in operation. As 1989 ended, it seemed certain that still more would be heard about the* Iowa *disaster.*

Following are excerpts from the U.S. Navy's report, "Manual of the Judge Advocate General," on the USS Iowa explosion April 19; the passages are in an August 31 memorandum from the chief of naval operations, Adm. Carlisle A. H. Trost, to the judge advocate general, released publicly September 7, 1989:

[1. omitted]

2. On 19 April 1989 a rapid series of three explosions within turret II aboard USS IOWA (BB 61) resulted in the instantaneous deaths of 47 American sailors. A Judge Advocate General's Manual investigation was convened immediately. Every conceivable source of ignition and every aspect of USS IOWA's condition and shipboard routine that might have bearing on the incident were evaluated: procedures, training, safety, manning, and personal conduct. Since the primary explosion was determined to have occurred within the center gun room, the focus of the investigation was properly directed to that location. The tragic loss of personnel within turret II and adjacent ammunition handling spaces precluded a precise causal determination since the personnel most knowledgeable of actions and intentions were those who lost their lives.

3. The initial explosion was caused by premature ignition of five bags of smokeless powder contained within the center gun with the breech open. The point of ignition was most probably between the first and second bags. Exhaustive technical tests have ruled out the following possibilities which constitute the most logical inadvertent causes: burning ember, premature primer firing, mechanical failure, friction, electromagnetic spark, propellant instability, and personnel procedural error. Although deficiencies in training documentation, weapons handling procedures, and adherence to safety procedures were found within the weapons department, the exhaustive tests and duplication of the type of blast that occurred have conclusively demonstrated that these shortcomings did not cause the explosion. Accountability for the identified shortcomings will be addressed in the cases of those officers and petty officers responsible for the associated duties.

4. At the time of the incident, the center gun room of turret II was fully manned with four individuals. Confronted with evidence that brought into question a possible wrongful act, the Naval Investigative Service (NIS) conducted an exhaustive investigation into the backgrounds and recent behavior of not only center gun room personnel but of all relevant USS IOWA crewmembers. . . .

5. The thought of an intentional, wrongful act is repugnant to all professional seagoing men and women; however, this consideration had to be pursued when information surfaced that introduced its possibility. Extensive laboratory tests using optical and electron microscopy revealed the existence of foreign elements not normally present in the 16" [inch] guncharge. An attempt by separate FBI analysis to correlate these elements with material associated with an improvised explosive device proved inconclusive. . . . Additional hard factual evidence such as the position of the projectile/powder rammer and the subsequent delay in retracting the rammer to allow closing of the breech provides credibility to the theory that an intentional human act caused the ignition of the powder charge. The critical controlling station within turret II to allow the

aforementioned factors to occur was that of the center gun captain. These factors, when combined with circumstantial evidence associated with the individual manning that gun captain position at the time of the explosion, strongly suggest that an intentional human act most probably caused the premature ignition.

6. The evidence amassed includes: (1) irrefutable facts on conditions in the center gun room at the instant of the explosion, such as the position of the rammer, (2) the fact GMG2 Clayton M. Hartwig was in the gun captain position, and (3) significant circumstantial evidence documenting the lifestyle and thought patterns of GMG2 Hartwig over a lengthy period of time. The combination of these factors leads me reluctantly to the conclusion that the most likely cause of the explosion was a detonation device, deliberately introduced between powder bags that were being rammed into the breech of the center gun. This caused premature detonation and the subsequent disastrous explosions aboard USS IOWA on 19 April 1989, resulting in the deaths of 47 sailors, including Hartwig. I further concur with the investigating officer and the subsequent endorsers that the preponderance of evidence supports the theory that the most likely person to have introduced the detonation device was GMG2 Hartwig. . . .

SPEECHES MARKING
POLAND'S NEW ERA
September 12 and November 15, 1989

Tadeusz Mazowiecki became prime minister of Poland on August 24, marking a new era. He was the first non-Communist to lead a government in Eastern Europe since it came under Soviet control at the close of World War II. After forty-five years of Communist rule, the transfer of power came about uncertainly but peacefully. Mazowiecki immediately appealed to the Polish people for patience and goodwill while the new government grappled with enormous economic difficulties and completed the transition to democratic rule.

These changes came amid the spreading influence of Mikhail S. Gorbachev's campaign to open up and restructure the Soviet Union's politics and economy (Remarks on Soviet Election and Perestroika, p. 173). The Solidarity labor movement in Poland, long in the forefront of Eastern Europe's opposition to Communist rule, adapted Gorbachev's words to its own cause. Solidarity, directed by Lech Walesa, was outlawed and repressed after its founding in 1979 but was never crushed (Martial Law in Poland, Historic Documents of 1981, p. 881). By 1987, under the twin impact of Gorbachev's reforms and a foundering Polish economy, Gen. Wojciech Jaruzelski, the Polish president, was compelled to soften the Polish government's hard-line position. It accorded Solidarity legal status in 1988 and arranged formal talks with the movement's leaders. These talks led, in June, to the first free elections in any Soviet satellite country. Among the seats contested in the Sejm, the lower house of the National Assembly, only one was won by a Communist candidate.

This situation left Jaruzelski's control so insecure that he yielded to advice from Gorbachev—according to press reports—and agreed to a power-sharing arrangement whereby he would remain as president but turn over the reins of government to Solidarity. By an overwhelming vote, the newly constituted Sejm elected Mazowiecki prime minister. On September 12, the Sejm confirmed his cabinet in which Communists held only four of twenty-three positions.

On that occasion, the new prime minister delivered a speech to the legislative body and the nation—the Polish equivalent of a U.S. State of the Union address—outlining the aims of his government. He spoke of imposing unpopular austerity measures to shrink the soaring inflation rate, expand productivity, and pay interest on a burdensome foreign debt. At the same time, he promised to enlarge and legally guarantee the new political and personal freedoms. Throughout the speech, Mazowiecki emphasized the difficulties that lay ahead for the Polish people and appealed for foreign economic help.

Many political analysts had assumed that Walesa would become prime minister. But by backing Mazowiecki for the post, Walesa implicitly acknowledged that his strength lay in his leadership of the movement rather than in the councils of government. Mazowiecki, at age sixty-two, was a prominent intellectual adviser to Solidarity and a distinguished Catholic layman with close ties to the church's hierarchy. In Poland, the church remained through the long years of Communist rule a strong counterweight to Soviet influences and gave strong support to Solidarity.

Walesa, a hero abroad as well as at home, personally brought the message of Poland's new era to the United States. He made a triumphal seven-day trip to four American cities, highlighted by an address to a joint session of Congress on November 15. Walesa was only the third foreigner who held no official position to be accorded that honor.

Beaming, his eyes moist, his fingers raised in a "V" (for victory) sign, Walesa stood on the dais of the House chambers where presidents and prime ministers normally address Congress. "We the people!" he exclaimed in Polish. The translation into English brought legislators, visiting dignitaries, and other spectators to their feet, cheering wildly. Walesa, who said he was "not fond of speeches," nevertheless talked for fifty minutes while his audience seemed transfixed, repeatedly bursting into applause.

Walesa said an hour later that he, too, was overwhelmed by emotion and that his legs were "still rubbery." He had been in Washington only a few hours when, on November 13, President George Bush presented him with the Presidential Medal of Honor in a White House ceremony. He was acclaimed a hero on November 14 at the annual meeting of the AFL-CIO labor federation, which for a decade had supported Solidarity with money and encouragement. Walesa also received enthusiastic greetings in New York, Chicago, and Detroit.

Much of Walesa's speech to Congress had a hard edge, dwelling on Poland's suffering during and after World War II. He reminded his listeners that the United States bore at least some responsibility for carving Europe into two blocs, one dominated by an "alien" force, the Soviet Union. But he also had words of hope and promise, and those words repeatedly brought the assembled crowd to their feet. As the chamber erupted in cheers, members of the usually reserved diplomatic corps joined in. Among them was Yuri Dubinin, the Soviet ambassador. He, too, stood, tucked his copy of Walesa's speech under his arm, and applauded.

Following are excerpts from speeches by Polish prime minister Tadeusz Mazowiecki to the Sejm (legislative body), September 12, 1989, as translated from Warsaw Television Service by the U.S. State Department; and by Solidarity leader Lech Walesa to a joint session of Congress, November 15, as published in translation in the Congressional Record:

MAZOWIECKI'S SPEECH TO THE SEJM

Mr. Speaker, may it please the House! I wish to present the outline program and composition of the proposed government. I turn to all my countrymen. I am convinced that the decisive majority of Poles similarly understand the goals to which we should be moving, and carry in their hearts the same ideal of the fatherland. We wish to live in dignity in a sovereign and democratic state subject to the rule of law, which everyone, irrespective of world view, ideological and political differentiation, can regard as their own state. We wish to live in a country with a healthy economy, where it is worth working and saving, and where the satisfaction of basic material needs is not associated with trouble and humiliation. We want a Poland that is open to Europe and the world, a Poland without an inferiority complex which makes a contribution to the creation of material and cultural goods, a Poland whose citizens will feel they are welcome guests and not intruders giving trouble to other countries of Europe and the world.

I come as a man of Solidarity, loyal to the August heritage. I conceive it above all as a great, collective call of society for sovereignty, the right to decide the fate of the country, and also as a readiness for solid and decisive action in order to achieve these needs. But the heritage of August is also the ability to overcome disputes and divisions, the ability to seek partnership, the forsaking of thought along the lines of taking revenge for the past, the settling of accounts.

So that the situation could have come about whereby a premier coming from Solidarity could stand before the House, much had to happen. We all had to think through a lot and understand a lot. This fact could not have come about without great shocks which are dangerous to the nation if the main political forces functioning in our country had not shown imagination, good will, and a feeling of responsibility for Poland.

The role of the Church was also irreplaceable in this process. Today, we stand before two main problems for Poland: the political reconstruction of the state, and leading the country out of economic catastrophe. I am aware of the seriousness of the situation. I know how difficult it will be to reconcile both of these aims and simultaneously to implement them. The new government will function under the pressure of the fact that at every moment the construction of democracy in Poland, which has only just begun, could collapse in the event of the breakdown of the economy.

I am convinced that we would only enjoy the regained political freedoms for a short time if we do not succeed in holding back the economic catastrophe. Society will feel the uselessness of democratic institutions if a clear change does not follow in everyday life. We reject the political philosophy that assumes economic reforms can be introduced against society, over its head, laying aside democratic transformations.

Poland can only be raised up by a society of free citizens and the policy of a government that is granted trust by the clear majority of Poles. The transformation of the citizens' attitude in relation to the state is of fundamental importance. The experiences of recent history mean that a significant part of society has not seen in the state shaped after the war [World War II] an institution which serves the nation. The ideal of the state was the organization of the life of society in all its manifestations. The state sought to rule not just over the actions but over the minds of people. This philosophy still resides in the structures and principles of functioning of many institutions of our public life and also in our consciousness and life.

The conditions exist today which allow for overcoming the situation in which the good of the nation was opposed to the interests of the state. The initiative for rebuilding society's trust in the state must, however, above all come from the bodies of state power, and more precisely the government. Our goal is a state which creates a safe framework for individual and collective existence, which specifies only the frontiers of freedom for the individual and social collecties [sic]. Recognizing the value of human activity, I will not however leave the weak and socially incapable without protection.

May it please the House! The logical and necessary consequence of the principles presented on which the state should rest is to seek its construction on the basis of law. The law cannot be an instrument for ruling over citizens by the state apparatus or any other political group. But they, too, should respect the law in force. We will seek to accelerate work on new codifications of the criminal law, especially criminal procedure, and also the law on misdemeanors, which must meet the demands of the international convention of civil and political rights, the right to defense and the right to a trial. Work will be continued on changes in civil law. Reform of the law on the system of courts is urgent. The creation of guarantees of the independence of judges will be served by a government legal initiative on the creation of a National Judicial Council (Krajowa Rada Sadownictwa). We also plan initiatives for the new regulation of the law on assembly. We will seek to include under judicial control all administrative decisions. A matter of great importance is the undertaking of work on a new democratic constitution. The government intends to actively take part in this work.

We also face the exceptionally difficult task of shaping relations between Parliament and the government as—respecting the supreme role of the parliamentary chambers—will allow the efficient functioning of the executive bodies. The basis of our relation to parliament is the conviction that the efficiency of the government will depend not only on the formal acceptance by but also on the moral support of the chambers, on the possibility of drawing on their social authority. The functioning of the government in accordance with social expectations will depend on critical evaluation of its proposals and activities and on the efficient course of legislative work.

The government, within the framework defined by the Constitution, will cooperate with the president. This is demanded by the authority of the state. This is particularly important today for successful implementation of the Polish reforms. The government wishes to cooperate with all the political parties and groups in Parliament. We are in a completely new situation in which all political forces must rethink their role and their attitude to the state and its institutions, in a situation when the state becomes the general and supreme value.

This is not an easy process for everyone, but it is an essential one. It concerns the PZPR (Polish United Worker's Party—FBIS) on one hand, as well as those who so far have been in opposition on the other hand. Departure from the identification of one party with the state is not a once-only act, but a complex process. This process should not be hampered and everything should be encouraged which serves the democratic formula of political life, which creates equal rights and chances for all. . . .

In Poland today, there are many social organizations which have existed for a long time and also those which have been created recently in great numbers thanks to the recovered right of assembly. . . . The government also does not intend to do their work for them. It is a task of great importance to create in Poland authentic territorial self-government. The government will cooperate intensively with the Sejm [lower house of Parliament] and the Senate in the work of creating the legal and material conditions for setting up territorial self-government so that the elections to it can be held sooner than expected. With the creation of self-government we link our hope for a release of great civic energy which has until recently been frustrated by a feeling of impotence due to state red tape and central directorates. . . .

All Polish citizens must have equal rights in seeking access to state service. An important part of the state apparatus are those services whose calling is the supervision of the security of citizens and the state. In the militia we see a service that, within the framework of the law, protects public order, giving citizens a feeling of security. We understand the difficult, often dangerous work of its officials. At the same time, however, we perceive the need for fundamental reforms that should ensue in association with the democratic transformations taking place in the country. The point is, especially, the subjection of militia activities to the supervision of the law and public opinion. From a militia serving to keep society in obedience to a militia protecting the peace of the citizens, this is the road that must be taken to the end. This is also the road to real social recognition of the militia. . . .

The government wants to make permanent the traditional respect in our society for military obligation. We will seek the humanization of military life and service. Both in the armed forces and also in the Ministry of Internal affairs, there should be treated the conditions for the appropriate participation of representatives of various sociopolitical forces in the forming of policy and the evaluation of the activity of its bodies.

. . . The government wants to tell the truth and to make possible the freedom of expression for all sections of public opinion. An open flow of information must be established in both directions between the government and society. We want Polish public opinion to have an influence on state affairs and we will listen to its voice.

The development of the press cannot be administratively regulated and the role of censorship must be limited further. Access to radio and television must be equal to all. Television and radio will have a pluralist character. The era of limitation on the freedom of Polish journalism has passed and the time of its great role in the creation of society's political culture has begun.

There is no free country without free trade unions. The government, respecting their rights, will strive for partnership with different factions of the trade union movement, so that the abilities of the country are reconciled with the employees' needs. In the present very difficult economic situation, it will not be easy. We are expecting understanding on the part of all trade union movements. I promise that the affairs of the working people will be treated with the highest respect by the government. As premier, I will remember my trade union pedigree.

. . . The Polish state can be neither an ideological nor a religious one. It must be a state where no citizen is discriminated against or rewarded for political views or convictions. Religion, which carries with it the motivation to a respected and honest life, which teaches responsibility for neighbors, solidarity with other people—especially those in need—also constitutes a universal value in the social dimension. In the difficult times which we now have, when one has to call for the deepest and noblest human feelings, we feel the significance of religious motivation particularly strongly. The Catholic Church has been fulfilling a significant role in the process of regaining the rights due to the nation and its citizens, as well as in initiating at times of crisis a dialogue between authority and society.

The government wishes to cooperate with the Catholic Church and with all other faiths in Poland. Freedom of religion is a natural and inalienable right of man and every attempt to assault it constitutes an act worthy of condemnation. Poland is a state, a fatherland not only of Poles. We live in this land with the representatives of other nations. We wish that they should feel at home here, that they should cultivate their language, and that they should enrich our community through their culture.

... In all areas of culture and art, our policy will be the same: as few regulations as possible. It is not for the authorities to impose on cultural institutions ideological, artistic, or religious preferences. Recognizing the enormous achievement of Polish literature and art in exile and also the achievements of illegal publication at home, the government will create the conditions in which all the values of culture will become universally accessible.

Polish science represents a great intellectual potential, given the neglected and outdated infrastructure. Its further degradation must not be allowed. The government will be in favor of solutions which will aim at the self-management of science, at shortening the path to promotion, at increasing the scope of creative skills and initiatives. It will also spare no effort to make it easier for scientific establishments to maintain contact with the world of science. However, I expect that work for Poland will remain the ambition of young and talented scientists. We will strive to restore full autonomy to higher education establishments. I expect work on the draft new law will be ended soon and the draft will be approved by the academic milieu. Within the framework of the autonomous higher education establishments there will be room for free development of student organizations.

The state of education arouses the greatest fear. Negligence and lack of investment over many years in the past is taking its toll. The fact that despite those conditions many schools continue to educate their students at a good level is due to the contribution of teachers, people who treat their profession as a vocation and a social service. The new government is fully aware of this debt which society owes the teachers.

Everything that is really important and socially indispensable takes place at the school level. A teacher and a school is for the student, not vice versa. A change in thinking about the role of schools is necessary. Education issues should be regulated by the new education laws.

We realize the dangers which threaten the nation's ecological existence. Ad hoc measures will be taken for the most urgent needs. To solve the health problem, the creation of the foundations for truly social health care based on the principles of cost-effectiveness accounting, independence, and self-management of health service outlets is indispensable....

We realize the bad state of our natural environment. A change of economic strategy, of town and country planning and designing is necessary, so that it is not negatively reflected on the environment in which we live, as well as urgent defining and liquidation of the most serious threats to life and health. It is necessary to create a clear picture of responsibility as far as environmental protection is concerned.

We will be seeking help from the advanced countries of the world in the sphere of environmental protection. Solving the problems of culture, schools, education, the protection of health and national environment demands the help and active participation of the state. The government does not want to avoid this. However, in the dramatic situation of the economy, and especially with the very difficult financial situation of the state, this help will be limited and not equivalent to needs. We rely on the fact that the bold removal of administrative barriers limiting human initiative will awaken authentic social initiatives that will supplement that which the state today cannot itself do for these areas.

... We face the historic task of carrying out breakthrough changes in the economy that will keep pace with the political transformations. However, this task must be carried out in an extremely difficult economic situation. The average standard of living is lower than 10 years ago. The spheres of poverty both in the countryside and in the towns have widened. The economy finds itself in the noose of foreign indebtedness. Productive capital is subject to speedy attrition. The breakdown in housing construction is deepening. The ecological crisis in certain parts of the country has reached catastrophic proportions. For the first time since 1982, a speedy fall in production is beginning. These are but a few elements of the economic drama that the new government is finding. Over the last few months, a prices and wages spiral that is destroying the entire economic mechanism has joined them. We are threatened with enormous inflation, leading to total economic chaos. We have decided to slow this process as quickly as possible and to carry out a breakthrough in the economic system and in the country's economic situation. ... We will ... undertake immediately activities intended to reduce the inflationary pressure. Above all, we intend to propose moves to reduce the budget deficit. It is necessary to decisively increase the discipline of tax receipts. Many enterprises do not fulfill their obligations in relation to the budget, treating tax backlogs as a form of cheap exploitation. Things cannot continue like this. Credits are granted by the bank and not by the budget.

Economics on the expenditures side will also be necessary. They will be based on the further lowering of subsidies, the limitation of investments that are centrally funded, the transfer to civilian purposes a part of the armaments industry, and also the limitation of the range of credit preferences. Activities limiting the growth of money supply in the economy will be indispensable. The government will propose a limitation of investment credits. We will undertake activities that will slow down the fall in the real value of savings and also credit obligations in relation to banks. We will be forced to strictly apply the taxation sanctions in force for the payment of wage awards in enterprises that are not in accord with regulations.

... Simultaneously with current activities aimed at counteracting the process of inflation, the government will take steps to initiate the transfer to a modern market economy, tried and tested by the developed countries. A government plenipotentiary for ownership transformations will be appointed and who, equipped with the appropriate organizational apparatus, will speedily develop a program and principles for the transformation of the ownership structure of our economy. The basic principle will be public and open sale, accessible to all citizens and also institutions interested in the efficiency of management. We are creating solutions which will facilitate the acquisition of shares by the workers of enterprises. There will also be a place for various other economically efficient forms of ownership.

The principle of public and open sale will put an end to the hitherto practice of the appropriation of parts of the national wealth on the basis of informal ties and not economic criteria. We must quickly acquire the legal bases for the stock exchange which is indispensible for ownership transformations. We will also urgently take the appropriate organizational steps in this direction. The suppression of inflation and the abolition of allocation, the introduction of market prices and the exchangability of the zloty [Polish currency], and also the continuation of the process of equalization of the rights and obligations of all sectors will create for state enterprises significantly better conditions ... and will enable them to undertake competitive struggle with enterprises of other sectors....

The organization for countering monopolistic practices will be expanded. It will be separated from the Ministry of Finance and will be vested with the necessary authority. Urgent work on healing the public finance system will be undertaken, among other means by a fundamental reduction in the number of the various specialized funds. They cloud the picture of the entirety of state finances and hamper public control over expenditure from the public coffers.

The preparation of a fundamental reform of the tax system is a matter of great importance. It will embrace the drafting and introduction of an authentic tax on personal incomes. The scale of its progression will not, however, be in conflict with the basic aim of mobilizing the tremendous but currently (?slumbering) resources of human initiative and enterprise in our society.

We shall speed up the creation of a banking system which is imperative for every contemporary market economy. This requires changes in the present banking system in order to raise it to the level existing in economically developed countries. The obstacles to the formation of new commercial banks must be removed.

The steps cited as examples will initiate a process of transferring to a system which, although it is not perfect, is one of known experience. This creates the greatest chance of achieving adequate and better living conditions. It is a system in which, thanks to efficient coordination between its individual cells, people can work at a far more peaceful pace and at the same time far more productively than up to now.

... There is a great barrier on the path to such an economy in the form of galloping inflation ... The steps which we are to take in the coming weeks will not be capable of solving that problem but can only counteract the rise in the pace of price increases. In connection with this, work is already being carried out on a package of more decisive measures whose aim is the control of inflation....

It must, however, be stressed that there is no example in the economic history of the world, where the suppression of such a high rate of inflation has been possible without serious social distress and also in the form of the collapse of some enterprises and the unemployment associated with this....

The possibility of emergence or aggravation of certain social problems will probably place the trade union movement in a difficult position. We realize this and expect that the trade unions, aware of the country's difficult situation and the shortage of easy solutions, will be in favor of reforms. These reforms are, after all, supposed to result in us having more to share. The government will do everything to alleviate the pain connected with the suppression of inflation. We will especially stress the development of employment exchanges as well as institutions which will facilitate changing the qualifications of employees whose enterprises will collapse. We will also create the conditions which will favor the emergence of new workplaces. Insufficient development of services, the retail network, and small-scale manufacturing make it possible for the economy to absorb many working people.

We will also introduce or strengthen other elements of social welfare protection: benefits for those who will lose work included. We must be aware, however, that all this is connected with budget expenditure and may only have such a scope which does not collide with the principal aim of reducing inflation. Such aid will therefore be limited. We see the need to revalorize old age pensions and disability pensions as well as to update the value of other welfare benefits, to prevent the lowering of living standard of the poorest social groups and the widening of the gap between them and the professionally active groups.

There is also a difficult situation in the agriculture and the entire food economy.... Especially troublesome to farmers is high inflation and the market's lack of means of production. Implementation of the presented program aimed at rescuing the economy will remove these problems. This will not take place right away, but the situation where the farmer has money but cannot buy tools for his work will disappear. We also see the need for urgently undertaking additional activities for the sake of the polish countryside. Among them is the liberalization of land transfers, which should as quickly as possible find itself in the hands of those who are capable of making best use of it. The freedom of land transfers will enable an improvement of the agrarian structure....

The action program presented here, having as its aim above all the defeat of inflation, is a road that is difficult but it is the only one.... Money, indexation, and the salaries paid to workers in the public sector already draw after them and will draw after them an increase in prices. At a certain point, this growth in prices can bring about uncontrolled wage increases for productive workers who have the greatest clout. These increases will, in turn, cause an echo in the form of increased payments for farmers and the public sector on the basis of the indexation law. All of this could cause a still greater movement of prices upwards. Meanwhile, prices in August rose by 50 percent and economists predicted a 40 percent rise in September.

If this continues we would have, without the coming year, a rate of inflation of more than 4,000 percent.... At such a high rate of inflation the motivation to produce disappears and farmers don't sell grain which has a greater value for them than money which is falling in value.

The collapse of the system can only, sooner or later, result in sharp social tensions which would only be a step away from general turmoil in Poland. That is the very probable scenario of events if we delay in making these difficult but imperative decisions. If we make them and carry them out to the end, although we will go through a difficult period, we will have a far better chance than today to organize the work of the whole of society.

... I would like to express hope that international financial institutions will give Poland important help in its efforts to radically stabilize the economy and to carry out fundamental institutional reforms. We are also counting on the fact that, in view of the complexity of our situation, friendly governments will make the difficult and socially painful process of reforms easier for Poland by providing financial help. We also hope for understanding and credit facilities from foreign private banks. ...

The renewal of diplomatic relations with the Holy See is a historic fact. I also regard the normalization of relations with other countries, especially with those with which they have been broken off, as important. We need a breakthrough in relations with the FRG. [Federal German Republic (West Germany)] The people of both countries have already gone much further than the government. We count on the clear development of economic relations and we want real reconciliation comparable to that which has taken place between the Germans and the French. It is also in our interest to improve cooperation, especially economic cooperation, with the newly industrialized countries of Asia, Africa, the Pacific, the Middle East, and Latin America.

The development of events directly after the war gave birth to the conviction among Poles that the West had foresaken Poland, agreeing to the limitation of its sovereignty. At the same time, for years—especially during the recent difficult period—we have received from there proof of warm feelings and solidarity. The time has now come for a new approach to mutual relations. The full opening of Poland to the West is impossible without full understanding on the other side of our problems and aspirations. Our indebtedness causes a great problem for our foreign policy. We do not ask for charity, but for investment—capital and technological—commitment of benefit to all. ...

The Polish people must start a new page of their history. Hatred, which could become an enormous destructive force, must be eliminated from mutual relations. As a nation we must break the feeling of hopelessness and jointly take up the challenge of the moment which is facing us: the task of overcoming the economic disaster and the restructuring of the state. The government, which will be appointed by the Sejm today, will take up this double task. We do not promise that it will be easy for everyone. As a nation, however, we do not stand on lost ground if we make an effort, have patience, and the will to act. Let us have trust in the spiritual and material forces of the nation. I believe God will help us to make a giant step on the way which opens before us.

LECH WALESA'S
ADDRESS TO CONGRESS

Mr. Speaker, Mr. President, members of the House and Senate, ladies and gentlemen, "We the People. . . . "

With these words I wish to begin my address. I do not need to remind anyone here where these words come from. And I do not need to explain that I, an electrician from Gdansk, am also entitled to invoke them. "We the People. . . . "

I stand before you as the third foreign non-head-of-state invited to address the joint Houses of Congress of the United States. The Congress, which for many people in the world, oppressed and stripped of their rights, is a beacon of freedom and a bulwark of human rights. And here I stand before you, to speak to America in the name of my nation. To speak to citizens of the country and the continent whose threshold is guarded by the famous Statue of Liberty. It is for me an honor so great, a moment so solemn, that I can find nothing to compare it with.

The people in Poland link the name of the United States with freedom and democracy, with generosity and highmindedness, with human friendship and friendly humanity. I realize that not everywhere in the world is America so perceived. I speak of her image in Poland. This image was strengthened by numerous favorable historical experiences, and it is a very well known thing that Poles repay warmheartedness in kind.

The world remembers the wonderful principle of the American democracy: "government of the people, by the people, for the people."

I too remember these words; I, a shipyard worker from Gdansk, who has devoted his entire life—along with other members of the Solidarity movement—to the service of this idea: "government of the people, by the people, for the people." Against privilege and monopoly, against violations of the law, against the trampling of human dignity, against contempt and injustice.

Such in fact are the principles and values—reminiscent of Abraham Lincoln and the Founding Fathers of the American Republic, and also of the principles and ideas of the American Declaration of Independence and the American Constitution—that are pursued by the great movement of Polish Solidarity; a movement that is effective. I know that Americans are idealistic, but at the same time practical people endowed with common sense and capable of logical action. They combine these features with a belief in the ultimate victory of right over wrong. But they prefer effective work to making speeches. And I understand them very well. I, too, am not too fond of speeches. I prefer facts and work. I treasure effectiveness.

Ladies and gentlemen, here is the fundamental, most important fact I want to tell you about. I want to tell you that the social movement bearing the beautiful name of Solidarity, born of the Polish Nation, is an effective movement. After many long years of struggle it bore fruit which is there for all to see. It pointed to a direction and a way of action which are today affecting the lives of millions of people speaking different languages. It has swayed monopolies, overturning some altogether. It has opened up entirely new horizons.

And this struggle was conducted without resorting to violence of any kind—a point that cannot be stressed too much. We were being locked up in prison, deprived of our jobs, beaten and sometimes killed. And we did not so much as strike a single person. We did not destroy anything. We did not smash a single windowpane. But we were stubborn, very stubborn, ready to suffer, to make sacrifices. We knew what we wanted. And our power prevailed in the end.

The movement called Solidarity received massive support and scored victories because at all times and in all matters it opted for the better, more human, and more dignified solution, standing against brutality and hate. It was a consistent movement, stubborn, never giving up. And that is why after all these hard years, marked by so many tragic moments, Solidarity is today succeeding and showing the way to millions of people in Poland and other countries.

Ladies and Gentlemen, it was 10 years ago, in August 1980, that there began in the Gdansk shipyard the famous strike which led to the emergence of the first independent trade union in Communist countries, which soon became a vast social movement supported by the Polish Nation. I was 10 years younger then, unknown to anybody but my friends in the shipyard, and somewhat slimmer. And I must frankly say, it was important. An unemployed man at that time, fired from my job for earlier attempts to organize workers in the fight for their rights, I jumped over the shipyard wall and rejoined my colleagues who promptly appointed me the leader of the strike. This is how it all began. When I recall the road we have traveled I often think of that jump over the fence. Now others jump fences and tear down walls, they do it because freedom is a human right. . . .

Peacefully and prudently, with their eyes open to dangers, but not giving up what is right and necessary, the Poles gradually paved the way for historic transformations. We are joined along this way, albeit to various extents, by others: Hungarians and Russians, the Ukrainians and people of the Baltic Republics, Armenians and Georgians, and, in recent days, the East Germans. We wish them luck and rejoice at each success they achieve. We are certain that others will also take our road, since there is no other choice. . . .

Things are different in Poland. And I must say that our task is viewed with understanding by our eastern neighbors and their leader, Mikhail Gorbachev. This understanding lays foundations for new relations between Poland and the U.S.S.R. much better than before. These improved mutual relations will also contribute to stabilization and peace in Europe, removing useless tensions. Poles have had a long and difficult history, and no one wants peaceful coexistence and friendship with all nations and countries— and particularly with the Soviet Union—more than we do. We believe that it is only now that the right and favorable conditions for such coexistence and friendship are emerging.

Poland is making an inportant contribution to a better future for Europe, to a European reconciliation—also to the vastly important Polish-German reconciliation—to overcoming of old divisions and to strengthening of human rights on our continent. But it does not come easily for Poland.

In the Second World War Poland was the first country to fall victim to aggression. Her losses in terms of human life and national property were the heaviest. Her fight was the longest; she was always a dedicated member of the victorious alliance; and her soldiers fought in all the war's theaters. In 1945 Poland, theoretically speaking, was one of the victors. Theory, however, had little in common with practice. In practice, as her allies looked on in tacit consent, there was imposed on Poland an alien system of government, without precedent in Polish tradition, unaccepted by the nation, together with an alien economy, an alien law, and alien philosophy of social relations. The legal Polish Government, recognized by the nation and leading the struggle of all Poles throughout the war was condemned, and those who remained faithful to it were subjected to the most ruthless persecution. Many were murdered, thousands vanished somewhere in Russia's east and north. Similar repression befell soldiers of the underground army fighting the Nazis. It is only now that we are discovering their bones in unmarked graves scattered among forests.

These atrocities were followed by persecutions of all those who dared think independently. All the solemn pledges about free elections in Poland that were made in Yalta were broken.

This was the second great national catastrophe, following the one of 1939. When other nations were joyously celebrating victory, Poland was again sinking into mourning. The awareness of this tragedy was doubly bitter, as the Poles realized that they had been abandoned by their allies. The memory of this is still strong in the minds of many.

Nonetheless, the Poles took to rebuilding their devastated country and in the first years following the war they were highly successful. But soon a new economic system was introduced, in which individual entrepreneurship ceased to exist and the entire economy ended up in the hands of a state run by people who were not elected by the nation. Stalin forbade Poland to use aid provided by the Marshall plan, the aid that was used by everyone in Western Europe, including countries which lost the war. It is worth recalling this great American plan which helped Western Europe to protect its freedom and peaceful order. And now it is the moment when Eastern Europe awaits an investment of this kind—an investment in freedom, democracy, and peace—an investment adequate to the greatness of the American Nation.

The Poles have traveled a long way. It would be worthwhile for all those commenting on Poland, often criticizing Poland, to bear in mind that whatever Poland has achieved she achieved through her own effort, through her own stubbornness, her own relentlessness. Everything was achieved thanks to the unflinching faith of our nation in human dignity and in what is described as the values of Western culture and civilization.

Our nation knows well the price of all this.

Ladies and gentlemen, for the past 50 years the Polish nation has been engaged in a difficult and exhausting battle. First to preserve its very biological existence, later to save its national identity. In both instances Polish determination won the day. Today Poland is rejoining the family of democratic and pluralistic countries, returning to the tradition of religious and European values.

For the first time in half a century Poland has a non-Communist and independent government, supported by the nation.

But on our path there looms a serious obstacle, a grave danger. Our long subjection to a political system incompatible with national traditions, to a system of economy incompatible with rationality and common sense, coupled with the stifling of independent thought and disregard for national interests—all this has led the Polish economy to ruin, to the verge of utter catastrophe. The first government in 50 years elected by the people and serving the people has inherited from the previous rulers of the country a burden of an economy organized in a manner preventing it from satisfying even the basic needs of the people.

The economy we inherited after almost five decades of Communist rule is in need of thorough overhaul. This will require patience and great sacrifice. This will require time and means. The present condition of the Polish economy is not due to chance, and is not a specifically Polish predicament. All the countries of the Eastern bloc are bankrupt. The Communist economy has failed in every part of the world. . . .

But Poland entered its new road and will never be turned back. The sense of our work and struggle in Poland lies in our creating situations and prospects that would hold Poles back from seeking a place for themselves abroad, that would encourage them to seek meaning in their work and a hope for a better future in their own country, their own home. . . .

We believe that assistance extended to democracy and freedom in Poland and all of Eastern Europe is the best investment in the future and in peace, better than tanks, warships, and war planes, an investment leading to greater security.

Poland has already done much to patch up the divisions existing in Europe, to create better and more optimistic prospects. Poland's efforts are viewed with sympathetic interest by the West—and for this thanks are in order. We believe that the West's contribution to this process will grow now. We have heard many beautiful words of encouragement. There are appreciated, but, being a worker and a man of concrete work, I must tell you that the supply of words on the world market is plentiful, but the demand is falling. Let deeds follow words now.

The decision by the Congress of the United States about granting economic aid to my country opens a new road. For this wonderful decision, I thank you warmly. I promise you that this aid will not be wasted, and will never be forgotten.

Ladies and gentlemen, from this podium, I'm expressing words of gratitude to the American people. It is they who supported us in the difficult days of martial law and persecution. It is they who sent us aid, they protested against violence. Today, when I am able to freely address the whole world from this elevated spot, I would like to thank them with special warmth.

It is thanks to them that the word "Solidarity" soared across borders and reached every corner of the world. Thanks to them the people of Solidarity were never alone. In this chain of people linked in solidarity there were many, very many Americans. I wish to mention here with warm gratitude our friends from the United States Congress, the AFL-CIO trade unions, from the institutions and foundations supporting freedom and democracy, and all those who lent us support in our most difficult moments. They live in all States, in small and large communities of your vast country. I thank all those who through the airwaves or printed word spread the truth. I also wish to say thank you and to greet all Polish Americans who maintain warm contacts with their old fatherland. Their support was always priceless for us. And the support of American Polish was always tremendously worth it to us.

Wholeheartedly thank the President of the United States and his administration for involvement in my country's affairs. I will never forget the then Vice President George Bush speaking in Warsaw over the tomb of the Reverend Jerzy Popieluszko, the martyr for Poland. And I will not forget President George Bush speaking in Gdansk in front of the monument of the Fallen Shipyard Workers. It's from there that the President of the United States was sending a message of freedom to Poland, to Europe, to the world.

Pope John Paul II once said: "Freedom is not just something to have and to use, it is something to be fought for. One must use freedom to build with it personal life as well as the life of the nation."

I think this weighty thought can equally well be applied to Poland and to America.

I wish all of you to know and to keep in mind that the ideals which underlie this glorious American Republic and which are still alive here, are also living in faraway Poland. And although for many long years efforts were made to cut Poland off from these ideals, Poland held her ground and is now reaching for the freedom to which she is justly entitled. Together with Poland, other nations of Eastern Europe are following this path. The wall that was separating people from freedom has collapsed. And I hope that the nations of the world will never let it be rebuilt.

SMITHSONIAN AGREEMENT TO RETURN INDIAN BONES
September 12, 1989

The Smithsonian Institution reached an agreement with American Indian leaders for the return of the skeletal remains and burial artifacts of thousands of Indians to their modern tribal descendants for reburial. The 18,600 Indian remains in the Smithsonian's research collection, by far the largest of its kind in this country, for years had drawn the wrath of Indian organizations and individuals. They argued that grave-robbing and battlefield-site looting by white men during the past century or more had desecrated the Indians' burial sites and insulted their religious beliefs.

The agreement was essentially concluded in August in Santa Fe, New Mexico, at meetings between Robert McCormick Adams, secretary (chief executive officer) of the Smithsonian Institution, and Indian leaders. They included Rep. Ben Nighthorse Campbell, D-Colo.; Susan Shown Harjo, executive director of the American Congress of American Indians; and Walter Echo-Hawk, an attorney for the Native American Rights Fund. It was formally announced in Washington, D.C., September 12 by Representative Campbell and Secretary Adams.

Influence on Other Museums

At least 160 museums in the United States had Indian bones in their collections—totaling more than 43,000 complete or partial skeletons— according to a 1988 survey by the American Association of Museums. Estimates of total holdings in museums, university laboratories, and private collections ran into the hundreds of thousands. A few universities had already agreed to return some or all of their holdings to Indian tribes

*that sought them. Several anthropologists and Indian spokesmen pre-
dicted that the Smithsonian agreement would persuade many of the
other institutions to follow suit.*

*The Smithsonian "is king of the hill when it comes to setting policy,"
Harjo said at the news conference September 12 at the U.S. Capitol at
which Campbell and Adams announced the agreement. "... [I]t has seen
the trend in the country and decided to go with the national sentiments,"
she said. Bennett Bronson, chairman of anthropology at the Field
Museum in Chicago, which also had a large collection, was quoted as
saying: "We're inclined to be sympathetic and the new policy is a
reasonable one."*

*The no-return policy previously followed by the Smithsonian was an
obstacle to the creation of a National Museum of the American Indian as
part of the Smithsonian complex of museums. The terms of the agreement were added to enabling legislation in Congress. In New Mexico,
Adams acknowledged that there had been congressional pressure on the
Smithsonian to relax its policy. "When this [issue] came to the court of
public opinion," he said, "we were going to lose."*

Scientists Upset

*Many scientists were upset by the change of policy. Some, pointing to a
permanent loss to research, compared reinternment to book burning. A
retired professor of anthropology at Stanford, Bert Gerow, challenged the
university's decision to return the remains of some 550 Indians to the
Ohlone-Costanoan tribe. He said he had collected most of them during his
forty years of teaching and research at Stanford, and he claimed
ownership on behalf of the scientific community. Observing that anthropologists use bones in the same way that other scholars might use a
library, Gerow said they should remain accessible for future scholars to
examine as new questions and new research techniques arise.*

*When Stanford made its decision—more than two months before the
Smithsonian announcement—the director of anthropology at the Smithsonian's National Museum of Natural History expressed concern that the
decision would "forever remove material" that could contribute information of value not only to scientists but also to American Indians
themselves. He said that at the Smithsonian 75 to 150 medical researchers used its collection each year to study everything from facial structures
relevant for reconstructive plastic surgery to the evolution of diseases
among Indian tribes.*

*"We do have some regret," Adams said at the Washington news
conference, "but everyone would acknowledge that when you face a
collision between human rights and scientific study, the scientific values
have to take second place." The Smithsonian made plans to inventory its
collection and, as explained by Campbell: "Those remains that can be
identified, either specifically or by name of tribe, the Smithsonian will
notify the appropriate individuals and tribes and, upon request, will*

repatriate the human remains and associated funerary objects."

Several tribes considered placing the bones in mausoleums where they could receive care appropriate to the tribes' religious reverence for them and yet be accessible to scholars. The Ohlones agreed to consider a delay of transfer of their ancestors' bones to permit further work on specific research projects at Stanford. The bones, 400 to 3,000 years old, were excavated from the tribe's historic place of residence in California, where most of the few hundred remaining members continued to live.

Part of a Trend

Although the Stanford decision was publicly viewed as setting a precedent, it was not the first instance of an institution's return of ancestral remains. The Museum of Anthropology at the University of Michigan at Ann Arbor in the late 1970s returned remains to the Oneida Indians, and in the 1980s the University of Arizona restored remains to several of the tribes in that state. The Stanford decision was followed by similar action at the University of Minnesota.

The Smithsonian's decision was a compromise between the Stanford and Minnesota practices of returning entire collections and the position of the American Anthropological Association, which permitted the return of material only to close relatives. The Smithsonian would return on request any skeletal remains and artifacts that can be linked with "reasonable certainty" to present-day tribes.

Broader Issues

American Indian leaders had long maintained that the removal of skeletal remains and burial artifacts violated Indian religious beliefs, and common standards of decency and respect. Twenty-two states had enacted laws against disturbing Indian burial sites but only one—Nebraska—required the return of Indian remains to their tribes.

In August, more than two hundred archaeologists and representatives of indigenous peoples in Africa, Australia, New Zealand, and India, as well as the United States, met at the University of South Dakota to discuss the treatment of anthropological remains. With near unanimity, the conference approved a resolution calling for a moratorium on research and the development of a code of ethics to guide researchers in this area. Introduced by the International Indian Treaty Council and the American Indians Against Desecration, the resolution insisted that "the anthropologist's primary responsibility is to those he studies."

Following are excerpts from remarks by Rep. Ben Nighthorse Campbell, D-Colo., opening a news conference at the U.S. Capitol on September 12, 1989, and from questions and answers that followed:

Campbell: As many of you are aware, there have been ongoing negotiations between the Smithsonian Institution and representatives of the

American Indian community on an issue that has been generating a lot of emotion and controversy recently—that is the return and the repatriation of Native American skeletal remains held by the Smithsonian. I've very pleased to announce that an agreement has been reached that is suitable to all concerned parties.

Under this agreement, the Smithsonian has agreed to inventory human remains and funerary objects in the possession of the Smithsonian for the purpose of identifying their geographic and tribal origins. Those remains that can be identified either specifically by name or tribe, the Smithsonian will notify the appropriate individuals and tribes and, upon request, will repatriate the human remains and associated funerary objects.

These provisions will be included in the House [of Representatives] bill to establish a National Museum of the American Indian and I am hopeful that by doing so, we will not only witness the fruition of a marvelous new museum paying homage to first Americans, but will bring about closure of an issue that has been an offensive affront to American Indians across the land for quite some time now. . . .

Q. How many remains [does the Smithsonian have]?

Adams: About 18,600.

Q. Does [the Smithsonian Institution] know what tribes they belong to?

Adams: In some cases yes. There are many years of scholarship on the historical distribution of tribes . . . more research needs to be carried out.

Q. Has [the] Smithsonian returned [any] remains? How many remains are there nationwide?

Campbell: Yes, Blackfeet remains, for example. Estimates go as high nationwide as 600,000. . . .

Q. Do we know [the] age of skeletal remains?

Adams: In some cases yes. There are dating techniques . . . but it is a moving target. What is known today about age may be improved in the future [as new techniques become available]. . . .

Echo-Hawk: [This is a] big step for American Indian people and society at large—now Native Americans will be included in the same kinds of legal protections accorded other citizens. . . . The Smithsonian has joined mainstream ethics and I commend Secretary Adams for his strong moral leadership. I hope Congress will be receptive to this legislation.

Q. Could one side have gone further?

Campbell: Indian beliefs are that all remains should be returned, but we have to start somewhere. Many remains cannot be identified by tribal origin. . . . It is important to understand, however, that the Indian belief does not assign a time frame to the burial of ancestors. A mother or father who died today would have to be accorded the same respect as ancestors who died 15 generations ago. . . . We have a long way to go, but this is the best, proper way to go. It will be an ongoing process, for years and years to identify all the remains. . . .

Adams: . . . On the basis of the inventory, tribes will be able to see where they have holdings or sites that are ancestral. . . . The inventory will go far beyond what we have in [the Smithsonian] files now. . . . Army Medical Museum files are incomplete and it will be a long process to pull everything together and make it intelligible. It requires a fresh effort . . . and it will be a collaborative effort.

Q. What percentage of remains will be returned?

Adams: It could be quite a large proportion. . . . My guess would be 5-10 percent at the beginning. We're not saying this far . . . and no further. . . .

Q. Are your scientists upset? What finally persuaded you to change your mind?

Adams: There is a deep scientific concern and a deep sense of loss on the part of many Smithsonian scientists. I don't want to minimize the real sense of loss. What finally persuaded me was many things—dealing with the American Indian leadership and hearing the tale of their own anguish—this becomes a weight that one ultimately cannot carry. [Coming to an understanding] of the sense of what these remains mean in occupying the central place in the attention of American Indian people and what a negative force retaining these remains would have as we seek to participate in the cultural renaissance of American Indians through the new museum—this also persuaded me. And I've been reading more deeply in 19th century history about the barbarous acts, the atrocities, committed against Indian people. The notion that we should suppress that record is unreasonable.

Campbell: We've come a long way, we have a long way to go. Indian people and archaeologists have not seen eye to eye and this has put Secretary Adams in the crossfire. He is to be commended for the position he has taken. . . .

Q. Was it a choice of a new policy or a new museum?

Adams: That was never the case. The new museum could not have gone forward, however, without the central participation of American Indians. . . .

SOUTH AFRICAN PRESIDENT'S INAUGURAL ADDRESS

September 20, 1989

South Africa's new president, F. W. de Klerk, promised in his September 20 inaugural address "a totally changed South Africa . . . free of domination or oppression." De Klerk's Nationalist party in the September 6 election received the sharpest setback in its forty-one-year rule of South Africa. Parties on both the left and right cut into its majority. However, de Klerk called the election "a clear mandate for reform and renewal."

On the day after the balloting, de Klerk noted that a new direction had been endorsed by nearly three-quarters of the nation's white voters. That was the proportion of voters who supported his party, which in June had embraced a vaguely worded reformist "action plan," and the new Democratic party, which called for negotiation with the nation's black majority on South Africa's future. The Democratic party, formed by a coalescing of small liberal parties, made unexpected inroads among whites who formerly voted for the Nationalists.

While de Klerk's inaugural address deliberately avoided "details," its generalities could be translated into a combination of concessions to blacks and assurances to whites. In promising "a new constitutional dispensation in which everyone will be able to participate without domination," the new president confirmed pre-election indications that he would seek to extend the vote to blacks for the first time, but in some form that would preclude black-majority rule.

Election Results

A growing fear that concessions would eventually lead to black rule drew some white voters to the Conservative party. But the election was widely perceived as a defeat for the Conservatives because their gains were less than expected, while those of the Democratic party exceeded expectations. Before the election, the lineup in the white Assembly, the dominant house of Parliament, had been 123 Nationalists, 22 Conservatives, and 21 from liberal parties. After the election, the Nationalists held 93 seats, the Conservatives 39, and the Democratic party 33.

In elections for the smaller, and almost powerless, mixed-race House of Representatives and ethnic Indian House of Delegates, the voter turnout was low. Antiapartheid groups boycotted the polls and workplaces. An estimated three million blacks did not report to work on election day, and many schools in black townships were closed to protest the balloting. Church groups said twenty-five blacks were killed (police confirmed twelve deaths) and more than one hundred injured in election-day violence in black townships around Cape Town.

Conflicting Pressures

De Klerk replaced South Africa's president, P. W. Botha, as head of the Nationalist party after Botha suffered a stroke in January. However, Botha retained the office of president until August 14, when, miffed by de Klerk's planned visit with Zambian president Kenneth Kaunda, he resigned. De Klerk was then named acting president until the election.

In his election campaign, de Klerk gained international attention by calling for negotiations with representatives of all races to plan a new constitution. South Africa's white liberals, unconvinced by his vague rhetoric, remained skeptical. The black majority, even less convinced, challenged de Klerk's reformist intentions. The Mass Democratic Movement, a coalition of antiapartheid groups, launched a "defiance campaign" in which organizations restricted under the government's three-year-old state of emergency held forbidden political gatherings.

The lifting of the ban on organizations such as the African National Congress (ANC), the Pan Africanist Congress, and the United Democratic Front was one of the reformers' demands. Other demands were the repeal of all apartheid legislation and the freeing of political prisoners. On October 10, de Klerk ordered the release of eight leaders of the black movement, including Walter Sisulu, a prisoner since 1963. Sisulu was considered second in importance to Nelson R. Mandela in the movement. Mandela, who entered prison at the same time as Sisulu, was not released.

On October 11, de Klerk met with Archbishop Desmond Tutu and two other black clergymen active in the antiapartheid movement. The three presented the president with preconditions for starting power-sharing talks. These included releasing the remaining political prisoners, lifting bans on political organizations, and removing the state of emergency.

U.S. Pressure

The U.S. government called the election results a "mandate for real change." State Department spokeswoman Margaret D. Tutwiler said that the United States was "committed to supporting negotiations to peacefully bring about a nonracial, democratic South Africa." She listed steps that she said were necessary preliminaries to possible talks between black and white South Africans:

- *freeing all political prisoners, and permitting "political exiles" to return;*
- *lifting the state of emergency and all other restrictions on black political activity and freedom of association;*
- *removing the ban on the ANC and other antiapartheid groups;*
- *ending "violence from all sources."*

De Klerk pledged in his inaugural speech to "take certain initiatives with regard to exactly those matters which so frequently are raised as obstacles by opponents of the government." His promises on each of these issues were couched in vague language, but he hinted at specific actions to come by calling on the international community to "take note of what is happening in South Africa."

De Klerk noted that his party's election campaign had "raised certain expectations" and pledged to "live up to them." He also noted that "unreasonable expectations" had also been aroused, and he could not "accept responsibility for over-enthusiastic or even twisted versions of our policy."

Rep. Howard Wolpe, D-Mich., chairman of the House Foreign Affairs Subcommittee on Africa, said after the election that "the clock is ticking." He said that Congress will be "closely watching President de Klerk in the early policy-making months of his administration." Wolpe expressed confidence that "Congress will demand additional economic sanctions if de Klerk does not take steps to dismantle apartheid by early 1990."

Existing U.S. sanctions, which included a ban on certain imports and exports and on new lending and investment, had been adopted by Congress in 1986 over President Ronald Reagan's veto. The Bush administration contended that these sanctions had been effective, but that further sanctions would not be.

Randall Robinson, executive director of TransAfrica, an organization whose lobbying has influenced many members of Congress, said, "No South African government led by de Klerk or anyone else will be moved to change without the application of greater economic pressure." International bankers, who were under growing pressure not to reschedule the $8 billion South African foreign debt that would start falling due in mid-1990, were also looking for signs that the new government would respond to antiapartheid demands.

Following are excerpts from the inaugural address of President F. W. de Klerk of South Africa, September 20, 1989, as delivered in Pretoria:

In my first public address after my election as leader of the National Party I made the following statement:

> Our goal is a new South Africa:
> A totally changed South Africa;
> A South Africa which has rid itself of the antagonisms of the past;
> A South Africa free of domination or oppression in whatever form;
> A South Africa within which the democratic forces—all reasonable—align themselves behind mutually acceptable goals and against radicalism, irrespective of where it comes from.

In this, my first public address after my inauguration as State President, I repeat that statement. This time I do so, not on behalf of a party, but on behalf of the new, lawfully constituted Government of the Republic of South Africa with a clear mandate for reform and renewal.

Executing this mandate is our highest priority. The new Government will be installed tomorrow. It will start working immediately on the details of practical steps aimed at reaching our objectives. I therefore do not deem it advisable to elaborate today on miscellaneous details.

What is important today is that I commit myself and the Government to the practical and expeditious execution of our mandate. I do so with conviction.

We are determined to turn our words into action. Considerable preparatory work has been done and we fully appreciate the urgency of prompt progress in all fields. We shall pursue that without being guilty of rash or thoughtless action.

We accept that time is of the essence and we are committed to visible evolutionary progress in various fields. This we will endeavour to attain within the framework of the principles of our mandate.

I am aware that we have raised certain expectations during the past months. We intend to live up to them, because we believe in what we advocate.

I am, however, also aware of other unreasonable expectations which have been aroused. In many cases this was done benevolently; in others, less so.

While we are quite prepared to be tested against our undertakings, we cannot accept responsibility for over-enthusiastic or even twisted versions of our policy.

Before turning to the future, I wish to pay homage to my predecessor. He dedicated a lifetime of loyal service to South Africa. It was his unyielding courage that placed our country on the road of reform and renewal. On behalf of South Africa I would like to thank Mr. and Mrs. P. W. Botha for their great contribution over the years in the interests of South Africa.

The mandate of 6 September placed us irrevocably on the road to a new South Africa....

For years progress was hampered by ... lack of cooperation, suspicion and mistrust. And, as critics of the Government would surely want to allege, also by actions and/or failures on the side of the Government.

I do not want to argue about cause and effect on this occasion. We shall not succeed in getting a new South Africa off the ground with accusations and reproaches. An argument about who erred where and when is a dead end. . . . Protest regarding past injustice or alleged injustice does not bring us closer to solutions either. Nor do unrest and violence.

There is but one way to peace, to justice for all: That is the way of reconciliation; of together seeking mutually acceptable solutions; of together discussing what the new South Africa should look like; of constitutional negotiation with a view to a permanent understanding; of participating in a balanced economic plan that will ensure growth and break the back of inflation; of accepting with understanding the sacrifices and adjustments that will be required of everybody. . . .

The time has come for South Africa to restore its pride and to lift itself out of the doldrums of growing international isolation, economic decline and increasing polarisation.

On this day on which I assume the highest office in our country, I want to pledge myself to a quest for peace through fairness and justice. I invite my fellow countrymen and women to join me in this quest.

In particular, I address myself to all the leaders of South Africa, irrespective of their sphere of leadership, be it political, economic, religious, educational, journalistic, or whichever other sphere.

All reasonable people in this country—by far the majority—anxiously await a message of hope. It is our responsibility as leaders in all spheres to provide that message realistically, with courage and conviction. If we fail in that, the ensuing chaos, the demise of stability and progress, will forever be held against us. . . .

I wish today to commit myself and the new Government to an active effort on our part to remove the actual and imagined obstacles on the road to peace and understanding.

Firstly, I should like to convert election promises into definite government commitments. During the term of the new Government we shall concentrate especially on five crucial areas:

1. We shall set everything in motion to bridge the deep gulf of mistrust, suspicion and fear between South Africans. . . . A broad national consensus must be built up around the core values which the large majority of South Africans already shares with one another. Unification and cooperation, with the maintenance of security, is the recipe for the future. . .
2. The negotiation process will, from the start, receive incisive attention. Where necessary, a completely new approach to remove obstacles will be used. . . .
3. We are going to open the door to prosperity and economic growth. We shall do this by breaking out of the international stranglehold which, for political reasons, has been applied to our growth potential. This will be accompanied by the determined and consistent implementation of a comprehensive economic plan which will include strong expenditure discipline by the State, lower taxation, privatisation, deregulation, increased exports and import substitution. . . .

4. We are going to develop a new constitutional dispensation in which everyone will be able to participate without domination. . . . Our constitutional discussion will take a clear direction, domination must be excluded and participation for everyone be assured.

5. We shall continue to deal with unrest, violence and terrorism with a firm hand. . . . We shall not permit the peace process to be disrupted by violence and anarchy.

I believe that in this manner we will break out of the vicious circle of stagnation, distrust, division, tension and conflict and make a breakthrough to a totally new South Africa.

Furthermore, we shall also take certain initiatives with regard to exactly those matters which so frequently are raised as obstacles by opponents of the Government. We shall do this because it is in South Africa's best interest, and not because we buckle to pressure.

We shall work urgently on proposals with regard to the handling of discriminatory legislation. The continued removal of discrimination remains an important objective.

We shall work just as urgently on the formulation of alternative methods of protecting group and minority rights in a non-discriminatory manner. This includes urgent attention to the place and role of a Human Rights Bill and constitutional methods to eliminate domination.

The process of the release of security prisoners, which was started by my predecessor, will be continued. In each case the test will still be whether it would be appropriate on the basis of all the relevant circumstances. . . .

By the strict, but fair, maintenance of law and order, together with the implementation of our action, plan, we shall try to help to create a climate which will make it possible to lift the state of emergency or at least to gradually move away from it.

In Southern Africa the Republic of South Africa is willing to expand the constructive role that it is already playing in this region. On the basis of good neighbourliness, non-intervention and healthy co-operation, Southern Africa can enter into a new era of stability and prosperity. . . .

My call to the international community is: Take note of what is happening in South Africa.

There is a determination amongst millions of South Africans to negotiate fair and peaceful solutions. Use your influence constructively to help us attain that goal.

Now is the time to adopt a positive attitude toward the positive developments in South- and Southern Africa.

And to the leaders and the people of South Africa my appeal is: Help me and the Government to make a breakthrough to peace. . . .

Let us all bow before God Almighty and pray that He give us the wisdom and the strength to face this great challenge.

With all my limitations, I am at the service of the Republic of South Africa and all her people.

TENNESSEE COURT DECISION IN FROZEN EMBRYO CUSTODY
September 21, 1989

The issue of when human life begins—most prominently connected with the abortion controversy—was extended to the question of frozen embryos in a Tennessee state court case. At issue in the case was who should exercise primary rights over the embryos and, by implication, what rights, if any, the embryos should have.

On September 21, Circuit Court Judge W. Dale Young at Maryville ruled that a woman who produced eggs (or ova) that were fertilized outside her body by her husband's sperm had at least temporary guardianship over them. The judge based his decision in large part on a finding that human life begins at conception and that "the best interests of the child" would be served by permitting the mother "the opportunity to bring them [the embryos] to term through implantation." He treated the case as a joint custody suit in which the primary concern was the well-being of the children—in this case, the embryos. Judge Young said his decision and its bearing on the state's role in protecting human life did not specifically address the medical techniques of in vitro fertilization (IVF) and the freezing of the resulting embryos for storage.

The Catholic church and some other religious groups oppose the IFV process and consider the destruction of embryos akin to abortion. The decade-old issue was complicated in the mid-1980s by the introduction of cryogenic preservation—a technique of freezing cells for storage.

About two hundred medical facilities in the United States provided IVF services in 1989 and some four thousand embryos were in frozen storage. The legal status of such embryos remained unclear throughout the decade.

At Issue in the Case

The parties to the Tennessee case were Mary Sue Davis and her estranged husband, Junior Davis. After failing to conceive a child during a nine-year marriage, they turned to IVF. In December 1988 nine eggs were extracted from Mrs. Davis and mixed with her husband's sperm at the Fertility Center of East Tennessee, in Knoxville. Two eggs were implanted in her womb; the other seven were frozen and stored for potential use later. When pregnancy failed to develop, existing strains on the marriage worsened—according to the couple's court testimony—and in February the husband sued for divorce.

The two could not agree on what to do with the seven frozen eggs. Mary Sue Davis claimed ownership, calling them "the beginning of life" and arguing that they represented her only chance of bearing a child. Junior Davis filed for joint custody over the fertilized eggs, insisting that there should be joint agreement over their disposition. He argued that the embryos were not alive and should therefore be treated as marital property.

Junior Davis, the product of a broken home, argued that he did not want to be the father of a child raised by a single parent. "I'm not asking that [the embryos] be destroyed," he testified. "I'm just asking that they not be inserted in Mary" or anyone else. Dr. Ray King, a fertility specialist who attended to Mrs. Davis at the center, suggested to the court that the embryos be anonymously donated if not used by her.

The Ruling and Its Impact

In ruling that life begins at conception and that Mary Sue Davis should have temporary custody of the embryos for implantation purposes, Judge Young relied on a 1988 Florida federal appeals court decision affirming the reliability of DNA profiling in determining a person's individuality—"that the life codes for each special unique individual are resident at conception and animate the new person very soon after fertilization occurs."

"It was the toughest decision of my life as a judge," Young said in a news interview after handing down the ruling. "The full focus of the court in the case of children is on what's in their best interests, not what mom wants, not what dad wants, and not what the grandparents want." In granting Mary Sue Davis temporary custody over the embryos, the judge said that issues of child support, visitation, and final custody would be decided later, if a birth resulted. Junior Davis said he would appeal the decision.

According to Lori Andrews of the American Bar Foundation, existing law did not recognize embryos as having legal rights. The disposition of the Davis case, she said, "may through the back door give a legal identity to the embryo. We may get legal precedents that will later shape how the embryo will be viewed in the abortion context or in the inheritance context."

While the decision did not have "any direct impact" on the current debate on abortion rights, according to Professor Jana B. Singer of the University of Maryland Law School, "The logic of the court's decision does have some disturbing implications for abortion rights and for reproductive rights." In an attempt to resolve these and other uncertainties, an ethics committee of the American Association of Tissue Banks undertook to draft rules for the handling and disposition of frozen embryos.

Following are excerpts from the decision of Judge W. Dale Young in Blount County, Tennessee, Circuit Court, September 21, 1989, granting temporary custody of frozen embryos to the woman from whom the ova were extracted:

No. E-14496

Junior L. Davis, Plaintiff, *v.* Mary Sue Davis, Defendant, *v.* Ray King, M.D., d/b/a Fertility Center of East Tennessee, Third Party Defendant.	In the Circuit Court for Blount County, Tennessee, at Maryville, Equity Division (Division I)

In this domestic relations case, the only issue before the Court is the disposition of seven cryogenically frozen embryos maintained by the Third Party Defendant and the product of in vitro fertilization undertaken by the Plaintiff and the Defendant....

The salient findings, conclusions and the judgment are summarized as follows, to-wit:

(1) Mr. and Mrs. Davis undertook in vitro procedures for the purpose of producing a human being to be their child.

(2) The seven cryogenically preserved embryos are human embryos.

(3) American Fertility Society Guidelines are for intra-professional use, are not binding upon the Court, but are of probative value for consideration by the Court.

(4) The term "preembryo" is not an accepted term and serves as a false distinction between the developmental stages of a human embryo.

(5) From fertilization, the cells of a human embryo are differentiated, unique and specialized to the highest degree of distinction.

(6) Human embryos are not property.

(7) Human life begins at conception.

(8) Mr. and Mrs. Davis have produced human beings, in vitro, to be known as their child or children.

(9) For domestic relations purposes, no public policy prevents the continuing development of the common law as it applies to the seven human beings existing as embryos, in vitro, in this domestic relations case.

(10) The common law doctrine of parens patriae controls children, in vitro.

(11) It is to the manifest best interests of the child or children, in vitro, that they be available for implantation.

(12) It serves the best interests of the child or children, in vitro, for their Mother, Mrs. Davis, to be permitted the opportunity to bring them to term through implantation.

Judgment of the Court: The temporary custody of the seven cryopreserved human embryos is vested in Mrs. Davis for the purpose of implantation. All issues of support, visitation, final custody and related issues are reserved to the Court for consideration and disposition at such time as one or more of the seven human embryos are the product of live birth. . . .

Findings of Fact and Conclusions of Law

The Davises—Their Marriage

Based on the record before it, the Court finds that Mr. Davis is a gentleman; he is 30 years of age, employed as an electrician and a refrigeration technician by the Maryville Housing Authority, Maryville, Tennessee, earning about $17,500.00 annually. Mrs. Davis is a lady; she is 28 years of age who, at the trial, was employed by the Sea Ray Boat Company, Vonore, Tennessee, as a sales representative earning about $18,000.00 annually. Subsequent to the trial, Mrs. Davis has become domiciled in the state of Flordia.

Infertility of Mrs. Davis

Mr. and Mrs. Davis have been married about nine years. They very much wanted to have a family, but after Mrs. Davis suffered five tubal pregnancies, her physician advised and she undertook surgical treatment which rendered her incapable of natural conception. The Court finds that Mrs. Davis suffered significant trauma and pain resulting from the parties' attempts to procure their family by way of natural childbirth. **In vitro** fertilization is the only option now available to her to have her own child.

In Vitro and Adoption Attempts

Remaining committed to having a family, Mr. and Mrs. Davis sought the advice and counsel of Dr. Ray King in the Fall, 1985, became familiar with and participated in the in vitro fertilization program under Dr. King's direction and guidance. Dr. King was assisted by his colleague, Dr. Charles A. Shivers, who performed the necessary laboratory work in connection with the in vitro fertilization program. . . .

After some six attempts by the couple to produce a child through the in vitro fertilization process, resulting in no pregnancy, the parties temporarily suspended their participation in the program and sought to obtain a child through adoption. The adoption process did not work, and the parties abandoned adoption attempts and returned to the in vitro fertilization program conducted by Dr. King.

Cryopreservation Technique

In the Fall, 1988, Mrs. Davis learned of the new cryopreservation program sponsored by King's clinic whereby several ova could be aspirated, inseminated in the laboratory and if the insemination process produced fertilized zygotes, the zygotes could be allowed to mature in the laboratory to a medically accepted point for the purpose of either implantation or cryopreservation for future implantation. Mrs. Davis discussed the new technique with her husband and armed with that information the parties proceeded to re-enter the program with the intent of producing a child or children which would constitute their family.

Further In Vitro Attempts

It is undisputed in the record and the Court finds that in order to prepare her reproductive system to produce quality ova for insemination, Mrs. Davis went through many painful, physically tiring, emotionally and mentally taxing procedures, both before the December, 1988 events and after those events. As a prospective Mother, she spent many hours of anxious moments waiting for word as to whether she would be a Mother. The cryopreservation technique offered Mrs. Davis much welcomed relief from the rigors of the full procedure each time in vitro fertilization was attempted.

It is further undisputed and the Court finds that Mr. Davis donated the sperm for the December, 1988 insemination and resulting fertilization process, that he spent many anxious hours, early in the morning and late at night, waiting at the hospital while Mrs. Davis underwent the aspiration and implant procedures and that he spent many anxious hours, as a prospective Father, awaiting word as to whether he would be a Father.

On December 8, 1988, nine ova were aspirated from Mrs. Davis, nine ova were inseminated with Mr. Davis' sperm by Dr. Shivers in his laboratory and the nine ova were fertilized, producing acceptable zygotes for implantation consideration by Dr. King and Dr. Shivers. The zygotes were permitted to mature under laboratory conditions, variously developing from the four-cell cleavage stage to the eight-cell cleavage stage, all of which were found to be of excellent quality by Dr. Shivers and Dr. King. On December 10, 1988, two of the embryos were implanted in Mrs. Davis, neither of which resulted in pregnancy, and the remaining seven embryos were placed in cryogenic storage for future implantation purposes.

Cryopreservation for Davis Family Only

The Court finds that before their embryos were committed to cryogenic storage, Mr. and Mrs. Davis knew, were aware of and had discussed between themselves (and with at least Dr. Shivers) the fact that reliable medical data indicated the practical storage life of the human embryos would probably not exceed two years. Mr. and Mrs. Davis had discussed the fact that if Mrs. Davis became pregnant as a result of her implant on December 10, 1988, the possibility existed that the remaining seven embryos in cryopreservation could be donated to another infertile couple, but the parties made no decision about the matter.

The Court further finds that during the time between December, 1988 and the filing of the original Complaint in this case (February 23, 1989), Mr. and Mrs. Davis discussed the possibility of and had tentatively planned to implant at least one of the cryopreserved embryos in Mrs. Davis' body in March or April, 1989.

The Intent of Mr. and Mrs. Davis

The Court further finds that Dr. King and Dr. Shivers engaged in a concerted effort with the Davises to help Mr. and Mrs. Davis become parents, both as to the IVF procedures before and after the utilization of the cryopreservation technique; and the Court finds and concludes that Mr. and Mrs. Davis participated in the IVF program, both before and after the employment of the cryopreservation technique, for one purpose: to produce a human being to be known as their child.

The Issues for the Court

There is no fact in the record to persuade the Court that Mr. and Mrs. Davis discussed or had any thought of changing their intent until the Complaint was filed in this case on February 23, 1989 and it must be determined from the proof whether Mr. and Mrs. Davis accomplished their intent. That determination is to be made by the answer to the most poignant question of the case: When does human life begin?

To answer this question, several additional questions must first be asked and answered, based on the record in this case: Are the embryos human? Does a difference exist between a preembryo and an embryo? Are the embryos beings? Are the embryos property that may become human beings?

Human Embryos—The Experts

Of the eight witnesses who gave testimony in this case, five of the witnesses presented themselves possessing the requisite knowledge, special skill, experience and education necessary to establish themselves as experts in their respective fields of professional endeavor. . . .

[Four of the five] expert witnesses . . . offered opinions to assist the Court in determining when human life begins. . . . [A]ll four witnesses agree that the seven cryopreserved embryos are human; that is, "belonging or relating to man; characteristic of man. . . ."

The Court finds and concludes that the seven cryopreserved embryos are human.

Preembryo vs. Embryo: Human Beings

Three of the experts, however, respectfully disagree with Dr. [Jerome] Lejeune [the fourth expert witness] that the human embryos are in "being"; that is, in "existence; conscious existence; as, things brought into being by generation. . . ." or living, alive. The three experts insist the entities are at a stage in development where they simply possess the potential for life. . . .

[The three] . . . rely at least to some degree on the report of the Ethics Committee of The American Fertility Society in forming the basis of their opinions. Each makes a distinction between "embryo" and "preembryo" in conformity to the AFS guidelines. . . .

The AFS guidelines were published by the Society in September, 1986 after the Committee's last deliberation on April 14, 1986 in Norfolk, Virginia. . . .

The Committee . . . defined the word preembryo this way:

"A preembryo is a product of gametic union from fertilization to the appearance of the embryonic axis. The preembryonic stage is considered to last until 14 days after fertilization. This definition is not intended to imply a moral evaluation of the preembryo."

. . . In the Committee's summary of points of special interest, the following is found:

"The Committee finds that the human preembryo is not a person but is entitled to respect because it has the potential to become a person. This view limits the circumstances in which a preembryo may be discarded or used in research. . . ."

The Court finds and concludes that the report of the Ethics Committee of the American Fertility Society constitutes guidelines for those professionals involved in the field of fertility treatment. . . .

[However,] the Court finds and concludes that the guidelines of the AFS do not serve as authority for this Court in making a determination of whether the seven human embryos in question are human beings. . . .

The Court finds and concludes there is no such term as "preembryo"; that to use the term in the context of this case creates a false distinction, one that does not exist. The Court finds and concludes the seven cryopreserved entities are human embryos. . . .

The Court finds and concludes that the cells of human embryos are comprised of differentiated cells, unique in character and specialized to the highest degree of distinction. . . .

. . . [T]he Court accepts his [Dr. Lejeune's] testimony founded on the fact that DNA manipulation of the molecules of human chromosomes reliably detect these features of man; that the life codes for each special, unique individual are resident at conception and antimate [sic] the new person very soon after fertilization occurs.

The argument that the human embryo may never realize its biologic potential, it appears to the Court, is statistically and speculatively true, but is a hollow argument. A newborn baby may never realize its biologic potential, but no one disputes the fact that the newborn baby is a human being. And if it is a part of the logic that an embryo, only a few hours old and perhaps only four cells in development, is not a being because it cannot sustain itself, then we must also reason that a newborn baby (which no one disputes is a human being) can likewise not sustain itself without . . . aid and assistance. . . .

It must be noted that one solution offered for the Court's disposition of the embryos is to allow them to die a passive death. Mrs. Davis reasons that in order to die, one must first live. Her logic is appealing, persuasive and accepted by the Court.

The technical arguments of human genetics aside, Mr. Davis asserts the theory that embryos constitute property jointly owned by the parties; that the embryos do not constitute life, but have the potential for life. . . .

The Court finds and concludes that by whatever name one chooses to call the seven frozen entities—be it preembryo or embryo—those entities are human beings; they are not property. . . .

What then is the legal status to be accorded a human being existing as an embryo, in vitro, in a divorce case in the state of Tennessee?

For the purposes of the Tennessee Wrongful Death Statute, an unborn child is accorded status only if the child is viable at the time of injury; that is: if a child had achieved a stage of development where it could reasonably be expected to be capable of living outside the uterus. For the purposes of the Tennessee Criminal Abortion Statute, the child is accorded no recognized status during the first three months of its Mother's pregnancy. But the legislature for the state of Tennessee has not yet, and to the best of the Court's knowledge, information and belief, no state in the union has, established a public policy declaring the rights to be accorded a human embryo, in vitro, in a divorce case.

In order to give effect to this Court's judgment, it is necessary to establish, in the absence of any authority to give the Court guidance, the status of these unborn human beings in this divorce proceeding.

As my learned colleague in the law, Professor [John A.] Robertson [of the University of Texas], pointed out during his testimony, the recent Webster case leaves open the door for a state to establish its compelling interest in protecting even potential human life by legislation declaring its public policy. Even as to the abortion issue, the Webster Court opined that it saw no reason why the state's interest in protecting potential human life should come into existence only at the point of viability. . . .

This Court finds and concludes that for domestic relations purposes in Tennessee no public policy prevents the continuing development of the common law as it may specifically apply to the seven human beings existing as embryos, in vitro, in this domestic relations case. The Court is of the opinion, finds and concludes that the age-old common law doctrine of parens patriae controls these children, in vitro, as it has always supervised and controlled children of a marriage at live birth in domestic relations cases in Tennessee.

The common law doctrine of parens patriae is defined as that power of the sovereign to watch over the interests of those who are incapable of protecting themselves. . . .

The doctrine . . . is most commonly expressed as the "best interests of the child doctrine" and its sole objective is to achieve justice for the child. . . .

In the case at bar, the undisputed, uncontroverted testimony is that to allow the parties' seven cryogentically [sic] preserved human embryos to remain so preserved for a period exceeding two years is tantamount to the destruction of these human beings. . . .

Mr. Davis strenuously objects to the anonymous donation of the human embryos even for their survival; Mrs. Davis wants to bring these children to term; the human embryos were not caused to come into being by Mr. and Mrs. Davis for any purpose other than the production of their family. Therefore, the Court finds and concludes that it is to the manifest best interest of the children, in vitro, that they be made available for implantation to assure their opportunity for live birth; implantation is their sole and only hope for survival. The Court respectfully finds and concludes that it further serves the best interest of these children for Mrs. Davis to be permitted the opportunity to bring these children to term through implantation.

It is the judgment of the Court that the temporary custody of the parties' seven cryogenically preserved human embryos be vested in Mrs. Davis for the purposes set forth hereinabove, and that all matters concerning support, visitation, final custody and related issues be reserved to the Court for further consideration and disposition at such time as one or more of the seven cryogentically [sic] preserved human embryos are the product of live birth. . . .

STATEMENTS AT THE
EDUCATION SUMMIT
September 28, 1989

Capping a two-day meeting at the University of Virginia in Charlottes-
ville, President George Bush and the nation's governors issued a call for
reforming American education. Bush pledged that his administration
would "follow up in every way possible" the commitments made in the
joint statement released September 28 at the close of the meeting, which
the press and participants labeled an "education summit."

"A social compact begins today ... a compact between parents,
teachers, principals, superintendents, state legislators, governors, and
the administration," the president told the gathering. "Our compact is
founded not on promises, but on challenges—each one a radical depar-
*ture from tradition." (*Report on State of U.S. Education, p. 85)

Govs. Bill Clinton of Arkansas and Carroll A. Campbell of South
Carolina chairmen of the National Governors' Association's (NGA)
education task force, were equally emphatic in their evaluation of the
meeting. They said in a joint statement: "This is the first time a
president and governors have ever stood before the American people and
said: 'Not only are we going to set national performance goals, which are
ambitious, not only are we going to develop strategies to achieve them,
but we stand here before you and tell you we expect to be held personally
accountable for the progress we make in moving this country to a brighter
future.'"

The summit took place six years after the National Commission on
Excellence in Education issued a report, "A Nation at Risk," that deplored
"the rising tide of mediocrity" in American schools. Bush, who promised in
the 1988 election campaign to be an "education president," made clear at

*the meeting that, despite improvements, much work remains to be done.
(Assessing American Education, Historic Documents of 1988, p. 297)
Citing estimates, he said that one-fourth of U.S. high school students drop
out, three-quarters of them cannot write an adequate letter, two-thirds do
not know in which half-century the Civil War was fought, and half of the
students never mastered fractions, decimals, or percentages. (Education
Report: "A Nation at Risk," Historic Documents of 1983, p. 413)*

*"To those who say that money alone is the answer, I say that there is
no one answer," Bush commented. "If anything, hard experience teaches
that we are simply not getting our money's worth in education. Our focus
must no longer be on resources. It must be on results."*

*Some political analysts thought that the president had adroitly shifted
the focus of attention on educational performance back to the states—
and away from the federal government, whose budget constraints leave
little hope for increased funding for education generally.*

Forging an Agreement

*Initially, there had been no commitment to produce a written state-
ment, but by agreeing to do so Bush took "on some measure of political
risk just like the rest of us," said Clinton, a Democrat. "It is amazing the
number of controversial things we were finally able to agree on," noted
Gov. Thomas Kean of New Jersey, a Republican. Only one of the nation's
fifty governors, Rudy Perpich of Minnesota, did not attend the summit.*

*The statement was written by Govs. Clinton, Campbell, and Terry E.
Branstad of Iowa, chairman of the NGA; John H. Sununu, White House
chief of staff; and Roger B. Porter, the president's domestic policy adviser.
Clinton said the main obstacle was overcoming the administration's
reluctance to increase federal funding for early childhood programs. The
final agreement stated that "priority for any further funding increases
[should] be given to prepare young children to succeed in school" and that
the federal government must play "a leading role" in providing greater
assistance to disadvantaged and handicapped children, improving access
to higher education, and increasing educational research.*

The main thrust of the agreement called for initiatives to:

- *increase funding for federal programs, such as Head Start, to
improve the education and health of disadvantaged young children;*
- *establish "clear measures of performance" by 1990 and issue annual
"report cards" measuring performance by "students, schools, the
states, and the federal government";*
- *loosen federal regulations to give states and local school districts
greater freedom in the way they choose to spend federal education
funds, if they agree to meet performance standards; and*
- *work toward "restructuring" the educational system by expanding
authority at the school level, making the curriculum more rigorous,
encouraging parental and community involvement, and enhancing
teachers' responsibility and flexibility.*

Reaction: Mixed Reviews

Although representatives of education organizations were not invited to participate, some attended the closing ceremony on the Lawn, a historic part of the campus that is surrounded by buildings Thomas Jefferson designed in the early nineteenth century. Most of the representatives expressed satisfaction with the outcome. "I think it's terrific," said Albert Shanker, president of the American Federation of Teachers. "Three months ago, you wouldn't have been able to talk about national goals." Dr. Scott Thomson, executive director of the National Association of Secondary School Principals, said that "the successful summit is worth literally hundreds of millions of dollars because it provides inspiration and motivation for teachers and generates a lot of activity on the part of the business community."

Although educators and members of Congress generally supported more local and state flexibility in the use of federal education funds, the House Education and Labor Committee chairman, Augustus F. Hawkins, D-Calif., feared that it might reduce services for disadvantaged students. Several members had reservations about a "national report card" and national goals. "When you start comparing district to district, it's totally unfair—apples and oranges," said Rep. William F. Goodling of Pennsylvania, the committee's ranking Republican.

The harshest comment about the education summit came from William J. Bennett, President Reagan's secretary of education whom Bush chose as national drug-policy director. Bennett commented to news reporters: "There was pap—standard Democratic pap and standard Republican pap. And there was stuff that rhymes with pap on both sides, too." For his comment, Bennett drew a rebuke from Sununu, the White House announced.

> *Following are excerpts from President Bush's address at the University of Virginia September 28, during his meeting with the nation's governors for an "education summit," and the text of the final statement issued by Bush and the governors:*

PRESIDENT'S REMARKS

... I came to Charlottesville with high expectations, and I've got to say, you have exceeded them. So the spirit of our summit is not: "Who will get the credit? " The spirit of this summit is: "How can we get results? " We are here to put progress before partisanship, the future before the moment, and our children before ourselves....

Our educational system is, in many ways, unrivaled in its scale and its diversity, in its commitment to meeting special needs and individual differences. And we're inspired by our best teachers, who give more than we can rightly expect; and from our best students, who surpass our highest expectations. And yet, after two centuries of progress, we are stagnant. While millions of Americans read for pleasure, millions of others don't read at all. And while millions go to college, millions may never graduate from high school.

The national Assessment of Educational Progress estimates that fewer than one in four of our high school juniors can write an adequate, persuasive letter. And only half can manage decimals, fractions, and percentages. And barely one in three can locate the Civil War in the correct half-century. No modern nation can long afford to allow so many of its sons and daughters to emerge into adulthood ignorant and unskilled. The status quo is a guarantee of mediocrity, social decay, and national decline.

Education is our most enduring legacy, vital to everything that we are and can become. And come the next century, just 10 years away, what will we be? Will we be the children of the Enlightenment, or its orphans?

Six years ago, the Committee on Excellence in Education issued its powerful report; and yet today, our nation is still at risk. The educational reform movement has done well in articulating its criticisms. And now it is time to define goals. This is the time for action. I sent my proposals for Federal action in education to Congress last spring, including an increase in funding for Head Start. The Educational Excellence Act of 1989 includes ways to reshape and expand Federal efforts, to recognize excellence, lift the needy, foster flexibility and choice, and measure and reward progress. I remain solidly committed to these principles and I value your advice and ideas as we continue to refine the Federal role.

Some offer a completely different answer: spend more money alone. And at the Federal level, we have asked Congress to provide nearly a half a billion dollars in new funding for 10 worthy programs. Your States may also choose to spend more. But to those who say that money alone is the answer, I say that there is no one answer. If anything, hard experience teaches that we are simply not getting our money's worth in education. Our focus must no longer be on resources. It must be on results.

And this is only the third time in our 200 years as a nation that a President has called a summit with the Governors. . . . And I appreciate the obvious extensive preparations that the Governors have undertaken in the days and weeks leading up to this summit. The Governors have emphasized to me the need for national performance goals and the importance of greater flexibility in the use of Federal funds, while accepting enhanced accountability for the results. And they've also stressed the high priority that helping prepare preschool children should have in Federal spending even in time of fiscal constraint.

And finally, the Governors have articulated eloquently the need to restructure our education system. You already are consulting with State legislators to better our schools. Our teachers already are giving their heart and soul to their jobs. But we've never before worked together—President and principal, Governor and teacher—to achieve results in education.

A social compact begins today in Charlottesville, Virginia—a compact between parents, teachers, principals, superintendents, State legislators, Governors and the administration. Our compact is founded not on promises, but on challenges—each one a radical departure from tradition. I hope that you will join me to define national goals in education for the first time. From this day forward, let us be an America of tougher standards, of higher goals, and a land of bigger dreams.

Our goals must be national, not Federal.... I ask Congress to allow Washington to be more flexible by passing reform legislation. And I ask you, in turn, to ease State restrictions on local bodies. And then we'll judge our efforts not by our intentions, but by our results. So, to get results, we need national goals and more flexibility from Federal and State government. To get results, we will need a new spirit of competition between students, between teachers, and between schools—a report card for all. And to get results, we will need discipline, structure, and goals....

For myself, I envision tradition-shattering reform in five areas.

First, I see the day when every student is literate. But literacy should mean more than the "three R's." We must be a reading nation....

Second, I see a day when our education system will be unafraid of diversity. Of course, all schools in a State will share a core curriculum and minimum standards of achievement. But the means by which that curriculum is taught and those goals met should be as diverse and varied as America itself....

Children also differ in their interests and learning styles and capabilities. And so, third, I see the day when choice among schools will be the norm rather than the exception, when parents will be full partners in the education of their children....

But to be accountable, we need to know just how much progress we're making. So, fourth, I see the day when we use accurate assessments, carefully linked to our educational goals. We need to first know where we are. And this means accepting the bad news along with the good. We've always measured our progress against our past performance. We must now evaluate ourselves on a tougher grading curve—one that includes the other major industrial nations....

Fifth, I see an educational system that never settles for the minimum, in academics or in behavior. Decades of research bear out what the best teachers already know: when standard and expectations are high, everyone does better. And this includes both the unusually gifted and those with special needs and disabilities. But it must also include the student we too often forget, the average student....

The day must come when every young American can know the life of the mind....

In essence, that is why we've gathered here at Mr. Jefferson's school. He was just one man, but look at what one man can do. Imagine what we can do, if we—more than 50 strong—are united by this great cause. So let us dream. And let us talk. And if need be, let us argue. But ... let us walk together on a journey to enlightenment, in the footsteps of Thomas Jefferson....

SUMMIT STATEMENT

The President and the nation's Governors agree that a better educated citizenry is the key to the continued growth and prosperity of the United States. Education has historically been, and should remain, a state responsibility and a local function, which works best when there is also strong parental involvement in the schools. And, as [a] Nation we must have an educated workforce, second to none, in order to succeed in an increasingly competitive world economy.

Education has always been important, but never this important because the stakes have changed: Our competitors for opportunity are also working to educate their people. As they continue to improve, they make the future a moving target. We believe that the time has come, for the first time in U.S. history, to establish clear, national performance goals, goals that will make us internationally competitive.

The President and the nation's Governors have agreed at this summit to:

- establish a process for setting national education goals;
- seek greater flexibility and enhanced accountability in the use of Federal resources to meet the goals, through both regulatory and legislative changes;
- undertake a major state-by-state effort to restructure our education system; and
- report annually on progress in achieving our goals.

This agreement represents the first step in a long-term commitment to reorient the education system and to marshal widespread support for the needed reforms.

National Education Goals

The first step in restructuring our education system is to build a broad-based consensus around a defined set of national education goals. The National Governors' Association Task Force on Education will work with the President's designees to recommend goals to the President and the Nation's Governors. The process to develop the goals will involve teachers, parents, local school administrators, school board members, elected officials, business and labor communities, and the public at large. The overriding objective is to develop an ambitious, realistic set of performance goals that reflect the views of those with a stake in the performance of our education system. To succeed we need a common understanding and a common mission. National goals will allow us to plan effectively, to set priorities, and to establish clear lines of accountability and authority. These goals will lead to the development of detailed strategies that will allow us to meet these objectives.

The process for establishing these goals should be completed and the goals announced in early 1990.

By performance we mean goals that will, if achieved, guarantee that we are internationally competitive, such as goals related to:

- the readiness of children to start school;
- the performance of students on international achievement tests, especially in math and science;
- the reduction of the dropout rate and the improvement of academic performance, especially among at-risk students;
- the functional literacy of adult Americans;
- the level of training necessary to guarantee a competitive workforce;
- the supply of qualified teachers and up-to-date technology; and
- the establishment of safe, disciplined, and drug-free schools.

The Federal/State Partnership

Flexibility and Accountability

The President and the Governors are committed to achieving the maximum return possible from our investments in the Nation's education system. We define maximum return as the following: significant and sustained educational improvement for all children. Nothing less will meet the Nation's needs for a strong, competitive workforce; nothing less will meet our children's needs for successful citizenship and economic opportunity.

Federal funds, which represent only a small part of total education spending, are directed particularly toward services for young people most at risk. Federal laws and regulations control where and for whom states and localities spend this money. State and local laws and regulations control what is taught, and how, for all students.

At present, neither Federal nor State and local laws and regulations focus sufficiently on results, or on real educational improvement for all children. Federal and State executives need authority to waive statutory and regulatory provisions in return for greater accountability for results.

The President and the Governors have agreed:

- to examine Federal regulations under current law and to move in the direction of greater flexibility;
- to take parallel steps in each state with respect to State laws and administrative rules;
- to submit legislation to Congress early next year that would provide State and local recipients greater flexibility in the use of Federal funds, in return for firm commitments to improved levels of education and skill training.

The President and the Governors have agreed to establish a working group of Governors and the President's designees to begin work immediately to accomplish these tasks.

We know that other voices need to be heard in this discussion—voices of educators, parents, and those whose primary interest is the protection of the disadvantaged, minorities, and the handicapped. We need to work with

567

the Congress. The processes we will set up immediately following this conference will involve all parties.

The urgent need for flexibility in using Federal funds can best be illustrated by a few examples.

First, the Federal Vocational Education Act, which mandates specific set-asides that often result in individual awards that are too small to be meaningful and that prohibit the money from being spent to achieve its purpose. One state reported being required to divide $300,000 in aid among far too many categories and set-asides.

Second, similarly, the Chapter 1 program requires that equipment purchased to provide remedial education services cannot be used for non-Chapter 1 institutions in areas such as adult education. Several States report that large numbers of computers purchased by Federal funds are idle at night, while adult education classes that need them either do without or use scarce tax dollars to buy other equipment.

Third, the requirements that children who benefit from Federal funds for compensatory and special education be taught separately often undermines their achievement. Waivers that permit these students to return to regular classes and receive extra help have produced large increases in their test scores. This option should be available for all school districts.

These commitments are historic steps toward ensuring that young people with the greatest needs receive the best our schools and training programs can give them, and that all children reach their highest educational potential.

In a phrase, we want to swap red tape for results.

The Federal Government's Financial Role

State and local Governments provide more than 90 percent of education funding. They should continue to bear that lion's share of the load. The Federal financial role is limited and has even declined, but it is still important. That role is:

- to promote national education equity by helping our poor children get off to a good start in school, giving disadvantaged and handicapped children extra help to assist them in their school years, ensuring accessibility to a college education, and preparing the workforce for jobs;
- and second, to provide research and development for programs that work, good information on the real performance of students, schools, and states, and assistance in replicating successful state and local initiatives all across the United States.

We understand the limits imposed on new spending by the Federal deficit and the budget process. However, we urge that priority for any further funding increases be given to prepare young children to succeed in school. This is consistent with the President's recommendation for an increase in the number of children served by Head Start in this year's budget. If we are ever to develop a system that ensures that our children are healthy and succeed in school, the Federal Government will have to play a leading role.

Further, we urge that the Congress not impose new Federal mandates that are unrelated to children, but that require States to spend state tax money that could otherwise go to education.

Commitment to Restructuring

Virtually every State has substantially increased its investment in education, increased standards, and improved learning. Real gains have occurred. However, we still have a long way to go. We must make dramatic improvements in our education system. This cannot be done without a genuine, national, bipartisan commitment to excellence and without a willingness to dramatically alter our system of education.

The President and the Nation's Governors agree that significant steps must be taken to restructure education in all states. We share the view that simply more of the same will not achieve the results we need. We must find ways to deploy the resources we commit to education more effectively.

A similar process has been going on in American manufacturing industry over the last decade with astonishing results: An increase in productivity of nearly 4 percent a year.

There are many promising new ideas and strategies for restructuring education. These include greater choice for parents and students, greater authority and accountability for teachers and principals, alternative certification programs for teachers, and programs that systematically reward excellence and performance. Most successful restructuring efforts seem to have certain common characteristics:

- a system of accountability that focuses on results, rather than on compliance with rules and regulations;
- decentralization of authority and decision-making responsibility to the school site, so that educators are empowered to determine the means for achieving the goals and to be held accountable for accomplishing them;
- a rigorous program of instruction designed to ensure that every child can acquire the knowledge and skills required in an economy in which our citizens must be able to think for a living;
- an education system that develops first-rate teachers and creates a professional environment that provides real rewards for success with students, real consequences for failure, and the tools and flexibility required to get the job done; and
- active, sustained parental and business community involvement.

Restructuring efforts are now underway in many states. The Nation's Governors are committed to a major restructuring effort in every state. The Governors will give this task high priority and will report on their progress in one year.

Assuring Accountability

As elected chief executives, we expect to be held accountable for progress in meeting the new national goals and we expect to hold others accountable as well.

When goals are set and strategies for achieving them are adopted, we must establish clear measures of performance and then issue annual report cards on the progress of students, schools, the states, and the Federal Government.

Over the last few days we have humbly walked in the footsteps of Thomas Jefferson. We have started down a promising path. We have entered into a compact—a Jeffersonian compact to enlighten our children and the children of generations to come.

The time for rhetoric is past; the time for performance is now.

October

Nobel Peace Prize,
  Dalai Lama's Speech................... 573

Congress Impeaches Two Federal
  Judges.............................. 583

Amnesty International's Report on
  Human Rights 597

NOBEL PEACE PRIZE, DALAI LAMA'S SPEECH

October 5 and December 10, 1989

The Norwegian Nobel Committee awarded its 1989 peace prize to the Dalai Lama, the spiritual and political leader of the Tibetan people. Both the committee, in its October 5 announcement, and the Dalai Lama, in his December 10 acceptance speech, called attention to China's occupation of Tibet since 1950. Fearing for his life, the Dalai Lama fled to India in 1959 and set up a government in exile. From the Indian city of Dharmsala, high in the Himalayan mountains, he has ministered to fellow Buddhist refugees from Tibet and traveled the world pleading for international support to free their country from Chinese control by nonviolent means.

"This policy of non-violence is all the more remarkable," the committee said in a statement preceding the Dalai Lama's speech, "when it is considered in relation to the sufferings inflicted on the Tibetan people during the occupation of their country." The Dalai Lama told his audience in Oslo, the Norwegian capital, that one-sixth of Tibet's 6 million people had died as a "direct result of the Chinese invasion and occupation."

Soon after seizing control of China, the country's Communist leaders directed an invasion of their neighbor, the isolated mountain kingdom of Tibet. The invaders overthrew the Buddhist theocracy, claiming Tibet as a part of "historic" China. The Dalai Lama remained virtually a prisoner in Lhasa, the capital, until 1959 when a Tibetan uprising resulted in a severe crackdown marked by massive bloodshed. It was then that he and many close followers escaped to India.

The award also called attention to the Chinese government's brutal suppression of student-led freedom demonstrations in Peking in June 1989. (Statements on China's Protest and Repression, p. 275) *Egil Aarvik, chairman of the Norwegian Nobel Committee, said that the award was not politically motivated. But in announcing it, Aarvik acknowledged to the press that the decision to honor the Dalai Lama could be construed as a signal of encouragement for China's democracy movement.*

The Chinese government apparently saw the Dalai Lama's selection in that light. The Norwegian News Agency quoted a Chinese embassy official in Oslo as saying: "It is interference in China's internal affairs. It has hurt the Chinese people's feelings. Tibet's affairs are wholly and purely China's own business." The official further said that the Dalai Lama was not simply a religious leader but also a political figure whose purpose was to "divide the mother country and undermine national unity." China's ambassador to Norway, Li Baocheng, left the Oslo awards ceremony as the Dalai Lama rose to speak. The ceremony was attended by King Olav, Norwegian government officials, and many foreign dignitaries.

Political Focus of Peace Prize

The Nobel Peace Prize is one of six awards bearing the name of Alfred Nobel, a Swedish industrialist and maker of dynamite. The other prizes—for literature, physics, chemistry, medicine or physiology, and economics—are granted by Swedish committees and awarded at annual ceremonies in Stockholm. The economics prize was first given in 1969; the others in 1901. The peace prize—consisting of a diploma, gold medal, and Swedish crowns bearing a 1989 value of $455,000—was the only one provided by Nobel's will. It is generally considered the most prestigious, and often focuses on an oppressive situation in some part of the world. Among the recipients of the prize in the 1980s were Lech Walesa, leader of the anti-Communist Solidarity movement in Poland, and Bishop Desmond Tutu, an outspoken foe of racial separation (apartheid) in South Africa.

The Western press tended to view the 1989 award as another recognition of the fight against oppression. The Wall Street Journal, *for instance, saw the Dalai Lama as a "symbol" of the struggle for freedom in China. In his Nobel acceptance speech, the Dalai Lama had a message of hope for China's prodemocracy students; he did not believe that their demonstrations were in vain "because the spirit of freedom has been rekindled among the Chinese people."*

The Dalai Lama reported that protests were continuing in Tibet despite intensified repressive measures by Chinese authorities since 1987. In response to the increased repression, the Dalai Lama proposed a peace plan under which the whole country would be declared a "peace zone," neutral in outlook and free of soldiers. His plan also envisaged a halt to a Chinese immigration so sizable that Tibetans may become a minority in their own country. *Speaking to the European Parliament in June 1988, the Dalai Lama modified his proposal. He said he recognized that China, as an Asian power, had strategic interests in Tibet, and thus he was willing to let China direct Tibet's military and defense policy if Tibetans could regain internal autonomy under international guarantees. Several national assemblies, including the U.S. Congress, formally expressed support for his proposal as a negotiating policy but it did not lead to formal negotiations with China.*

A "Simple Monk"

Before his audience in Oslo, the Dalai Lama returned to his idea of a demilitarized Tibet—a buffer zone between China and India, and a model for all mankind. Wearing the scarlet robe of a Buddhist monk—a "simple monk" he called himself—the Dalai Lama began his speech with a brief Buddhist chant and a few remarks in his own language before switching to English. He extolled passive resistance as the proper response to violent adversaries and paid homage to his "mentor," Mahatma Gandhi. The former Indian spiritual leader, he said, "is an inspiration to so many of us."

The Norwegian Nobel Committee, noting that the Dalai Lama considered himself one of Gandhi's successors, observed that people "have occasionally wondered why Gandhi himself was never awarded the Nobel Peace Prize, and the present Nobel Committee can with impunity share this surprise, while regarding this year's award of the prize as in part a tribute to the memory of Mahatma Gandhi."

According to Mayahana Buddhist belief, the Dalai Lama—meaning literally "Ocean of Wisdom"—is more than a leader in the traditional sense. For Tibetan believers, he symbolizes the whole nation and is imbued with the attributes of a deity. According to the Buddhist tradition of Tibet, every Dalai Lama is an earthly reincarnation of Avalokiteshvara, the Lord of Compassion. When the thirteenth Dalai Lama died in 1935, religious authorities immediately began a search for the new reincarnation; oracles and learned lamas were consulted and certain signs observed. The signs pointed to a farm in eastern Tibet. There a visiting delegation found a two-year-old boy, Tenzin Gyatso, whose performance of inexplicable acts persuaded the religious authorities that they had discovered the fourteenth Dalai Lama.

In his autobiography, My Life and My People, *he tells of receiving rigorous training in Buddhist lore but having no political experience when, at age sixteen, he assumed the authority that the title Dalai Lama bestowed. As a Buddhist monk, it was his duty never to harm any living creature and to show compassion for all life. In later life, especially after he fled to India, his education broadened to comprehend the ways of the the secular world. He continued to insist that "non-violence is for us [Tibetans] the only way. . . . [In] our case violence would be tantamount to suicide."*

Following are the text of the Norwegian Nobel Committee's announcement October 5, 1989, that the Dalai Lama had been awarded the Nobel Peace Prize; and excerpts from the Dalai Lama's speech in Oslo on December 10, accepting the prize. (The bracketed headings have been added by Congressional Quarterly to highlight the organization of the text):

NOBEL PRIZE ANNOUNCEMENT

The Norwegian Nobel Committee has decided to award the 1989 Nobel Peace Prize to the 14th Dalai Lama, Tenzin Gyatso, the religious and political leader of the Tibetan people.

The Committee wants to emphasize the fact that the Dalai Lama in his struggle for the liberation of Tibet consistently has opposed the use of violence. He has instead advocated peaceful solutions based upon tolerance and mutual respect in order to preserve the historical and cultural heritage of his people.

The Dalai Lama has developed his philosophy of peace from a great reverence for all things living and upon the concept of universal responsibility embracing all mankind as well as nature.

In the opinion of the Committee the Dalai Lama has come forward with constructive and forward-looking proposals for the solution of international conflicts, human rights issues, and global environmental problems.

DALAI LAMA'S NOBEL LECTURE

... Because we all share this small planet earth, we have to learn to live in harmony and peace with each other and with nature. That is not just a dream, but a necessity. We are dependent on each other in so many ways, that we can no longer live in isolated communities and ignore what is happening outside those communities. We need to help each other when we have difficulties, and we must share the good fortune that we enjoy. I speak to you as just another human being; as a simple monk. If you find what I say useful, then I hope you will try to practice it.

I also wish to share with you today my feelings concerning the plight and aspirations of the people of Tibet. The Nobel Prize is a prize they well deserve for their courage and unfailing determination during the past forty years of foreign occupation. As a free spokesman for my captive countrymen and -women, I feel it is my duty to speak out on their behalf. I speak not with a feeling of anger or hatred towards those who are responsible for the immense suffering of our people and the destruction of our land, homes and culture. They too are human beings who struggle to find happiness and deserve our compassion. I speak to inform you of the sad situation in my country today and of the aspirations of my people, because in our struggle for freedom, truth is the only weapon we possess.

The realization that we are all basically the same human beings, who seek happiness and try to avoid suffering, is very helpful in developing a sense of brotherhood and sisterhood; a warm feeling of love and compassion for others. This, in turn, is essential if we are to survive in this ever shrinking world we live in. . . .

We feel a sense of sadness when children are starving in Eastern Africa. Similarly, we feel a sense of joy when a family is reunited after decades of separation by the Berlin Wall. Our crops and livestock are contaminated and our health and livelihood threatened when a nuclear accident happens miles away in another country. Our own security is enhanced when peace breaks out between warring parties in other continents. . . .

Peace, in the sense of the absence of war, is of little value to someone who is dying of hunger or cold. It will not remove the pain of torture inflicted on a prisoner of conscience. It does not comfort those who have lost their loved ones in floods caused by senseless deforestation in a neighboring country. Peace can only last where human rights are respected, where the people are fed, and where individuals and nations are free. . . .

Material progress is of course important for human advancement. In Tibet, we paid too little attention to technological and economic development, and today we realize that this was a mistake. At the same time, material development without spiritual development can cause serious problems. In some countries too much attention is paid to external things and very little importance is given to inner development. I believe both are important and must be developed side by side so as to achieve a good balance between them. . . .

I am very encouraged by the developments which are taking place around us. . . . Serious efforts to bring peace to war-torn zones and to implement the right to self-determination of some peoples have resulted in the withdrawal of Soviet troops from Afghanistan and the establishment of independent Namibia. Through persistent non-violent popular efforts dramatic changes, bringing many countries closer to real democracy, have occurred in many places, from Manila in the Philippines to Berlin in East Germany. With the Cold War era apparently drawing to a close, people everywhere live with renewed hope. Sadly, the courageous efforts of the Chinese people to bring similar change to their country was brutally crushed last June. But their efforts too are a source of hope. The military might has not extinguished the desire for freedom and the determination of the Chinese people to achieve it. I have particularly admired the fact that these young people who have been taught that "power grows from the barrel of the gun," chose, instead, to use non-violence as their weapon.

What these positive changes indicate is that reason, courage, determination, and the inextinguishable desire for freedom can ultimately win. In the struggle between forces of war, violence and oppression on the one hand, and peace, reason and freedom on the other, the latter are gaining the upper hand. This realization fills us Tibetans with hope that some day we too will once again be free.

The awarding of the Nobel Prize to me, a simple monk far away from Tibet, here in Norway, also fills us Tibetans with hope. It means that, despite the fact that we have not drawn attention to our plight by means of violence, we have not been forgotten. It also means that the values we cherish, in particular our respect for all forms of life and the belief in the power of truth, are today recognized and encouraged. It is also a tribute to my mentor, Mahatma Gandhi, whose example is an inspiration to so many of us. . . .

[China's Suppression of Tibet]

As you know, Tibet has, for forty years, been under foreign occupation. Today, more than a quarter of a million Chinese troops are stationed in Tibet. Some sources estimate the occupation army to be twice this strength. During this time, Tibetans have been deprived of their most basic human rights, including the right to life, movement, speech, worship, only to mention a few. More than one sixth of Tibet's population of six million died as a direct result of the Chinese invasion and occupation. Even before the Cultural Revolution started, many of Tibet's monasteries, temples and historic buildings were destroyed. Almost everything that remained was destroyed during the Cultural Revolution. I do not wish to dwell on this point, which is well documented. What is important to realize, however, is that despite the limited freedom granted after 1979, to rebuild parts of some monasteries and other such tokens of liberalization, the fundamental human rights of the Tibetan people are still today being systematically violated. In recent months this bad situation has become even worse.

If it were not for our community in exile, so generously sheltered and supported by the government and people of India and helped by organizations and individuals from many parts of the world, our nation would today be little more than a shattered remnant of a people. Our culture, religion and national identity would have been effectively eliminated. As it is, we have built schools and monasteries in exile and have created democratic institutions to serve our people and preserve the seeds of our civilization. With this experience, we intend to implement full democracy in a future free Tibet. Thus, as we develop our community in exile on modern lines, we also cherish and preserve our own identity and culture and bring hope to millions of our countrymen and -women in Tibet.

The issue of most urgent concern at this time is the massive influx of Chinese settlers into Tibet. Although in the first decades of occupation a considerable number of Chinese were transferred into the eastern parts of Tibet—in the Tibetan provinces of Amdo (Chinghai) and Kham (most of which has been annexed by neighboring Chinese provinces)—since 1983 an unprecedented number of Chinese have been encouraged by their government to migrate to all parts of Tibet, including central and western Tibet (which the PRC refers to as the so-called Tibet Autonomous Region). Tibetans are rapidly being reduced to an insignificant minority in their own country. This development, which threatens the very survival of the Tibetan nation, its culture and spiritual heritage, can still be stopped and reversed. But this must be done now, before it is too late.

The new cycle of protest and violent repression, which started in Tibet in September 1987 and culminated in the imposition of martial law in the capital, Lhasa, in March of this year, was in large part a reaction to this tremendous Chinese influx. Information reaching us in exile indicates that the protest marches and other peaceful forms of protest are continuing in Lhasa and a number of other places in Tibet, despite the severe punishment and inhumane treatment given to Tibetans detained for expressing their grievances. The number of Tibetans killed by security forces during the protest in March and of those who died in detention afterwards is not known but is believed to be more than two hundred. Thousands have been detained or arrested and imprisoned, and torture is commonplace.

It was against the background of this worsening situation and in order to prevent further bloodshed, that I proposed what is generally referred to as the Five Point Peace Plan for the restoration of peace and human rights in Tibet. I elaborated on the plan in a speech in Strasbourg [France] last year. I believe the plan provides a reasonable and realistic framework for negotiations with the People's Republic of China. So far, however, China's leaders have been unwilling to respond constructively. The brutal suppression of the Chinese democracy movement in June of this year, however, reinforced my view that any settlement of the Tibetan question will only be meaningful if it is supported by adequately international guarantees.

[Five Point Plan]

The Five Point Peace Plan addresses the principal and interrelated issues, which I referred to in the first part of this lecture. It calls for (1) transformation of the whole of Tibet, including the eastern provinces of Kham and Amdo, into a zone of Ahimsa (non-violence); (2) Abandonment of China's population transfer policy; (3) Respect for the Tibetan people's fundamental human rights and democratic freedoms; (4) Restoration and protection of Tibet's natural environment; and (5) Commencement of earnest negotiations on the future status of Tibet and of relations between the Tibetan and Chinese peoples. In the Strasbourg address I proposed that Tibet become a fully self-governing democratic political entity.

I would like to take this opportunity to explain the Zone of Ahimsa or peace sanctuary concept, which is the central element of the Five Point Peace Plan. I am convinced that it is of great importance not only for Tibet, but for peace and stability in Asia.

It is my dream that the entire Tibetan plateau should become a free refuge where humanity and nature can live in peace and in harmonious balance. It would be a place where people from all over the world could come to seek the true meaning of peace within themselves, away from the tensions and pressures of much of the rest of the world. Tibet could indeed become a creative center for the promotion and development of peace.

The following are key elements of the proposed Zone of Ahimsa:

- the entire Tibetan plateau would be demilitarized;
- the manufacture, testing, and stockpiling of nuclear weapons and other armaments on the Tibetan plateau would be prohibited;
- the Tibetan plateau would be transformed into the world's largest natural park or biosphere. Strict laws would be enforced to protect wildlife and plant life; the exploitation of natural resources would be carefully regulated so as not to damage relevant ecosystems; and a policy of sustainable development would be adopted in populated areas;
- the manufacture and use of nuclear power and other technologies which produce hazardous waste would be prohibited;
- national resources and policy would be directed towards the active promotion of peace and environmental protection. Organizations dedicated to the furtherance of peace and to the protection of all forms of life would find a hospitable home in Tibet;
- the establishment of international and regional organizations for the promotion and protection of human rights would be encouraged in Tibet.

Tibet's height and size (the size of the European Community), as well as its unique history and profound spiritual heritage make it ideally suited to fulfill the role of a sanctuary of peace in the strategic heart of Asia. It would also be in keeping with Tibet's historical role as a peaceful Buddhist nation and buffer region separating the Asian continent's great and often rival powers.

In order to reduce existing tensions in Asia, the President of the Soviet Union, Mr. [Mikhail S.] Gorbachev, proposed the demilitarization of [the] Soviet-Chinese border and their transformation into "a frontier of peace and good-neighborliness." The Nepal government had earlier proposed that the Himalayan country of Nepal, bordering on Tibet, should also become a zone of peace, although that proposal did not include demilitarization of the country.

For the stability and peace of Asia, it is essential to create peace zones to separate the continent's biggest powers and potential adversaries. President Gorbachev's proposal, which also included a complete Soviet troop withdrawal from Mongolia, would help to reduce tension and the potential for confrontation between the Soviet Union and China. A true peace zone must, clearly, also be created to separate the world's two most populous states, China and India.

The establishment of the Zone of Ahimsa, would require the withdrawal of troops and military installations from Tibet, which would enable India and Nepal also to withdraw troops and military installations from the

Himalayan regions bordering Tibet. This would have to be achieved by international agreements. It would be in the best interest of all states in Asia, particularly China and India, as it would enhance their security, while reducing the economic burden of maintaining high troop concentrations in remote areas.

[Sinai and Costa Rica]

Tibet would not be the first strategic area to be demilitarized. Parts of the Sinai's peninsula, the Egyptian territory separating Israel and Egypt, have been demilitarized for some time. Of course, Costa Rica is the best example of a demilitarized country.... Two examples [of "peace parks"] are in the La Amistad park, on the Costa Rica-Panama border and the Si A Paz project on the Costa Rica-Nicaragua border.

When I visited Costa Rica earlier this year, I saw how a country can develop successfully without an army, to become a stable democracy committed to peace and the protection of the natural environment. This confirmed my belief that my vision of Tibet in the future is a realistic plan, not merely a dream.

Let me end with a personal note of thanks to all of you and our friends who are not here today. The concern and support which you have expressed for the plight of the Tibetans has touched us all greatly, and continues to give us courage to struggle for freedom and justice: not through the use of arms, but with the powerful weapons of truth and determination. I know that I speak on behalf of all the people of Tibet when I thank you and ask you not to forget Tibet at this critical time in our country's history....

CONGRESS IMPEACHES
TWO FEDERAL JUDGES
October 20 and November 3, 1989

Within a two-week time span, the United States Senate voted to remove two federal judges from office on impeachment charges submitted by the House of Representatives. As mandated by the Constitution, the House served as prosecutor and the Senate as jury in the proceedings.

The judges removed were Alcee L. Hastings of Florida, on October 20, and Walter L. Nixon, Jr., of Mississippi, on November 3. Hastings, appointed by President Jimmy Carter in 1979, was the first black to serve on the federal bench in Florida. Nixon was appointed to the federal judiciary in 1968 by President Lyndon B. Johnson.

The Senate found Hastings guilty of conspiring to accept a bribe in return for lenience toward two defendants in a racketeering case. Nixon was convicted on two articles of impeachment charging him with perjury. He had already been convicted in court of lying to a grand jury that was investigating allegations he intervened in a drug-smuggling case against the son of a business associate.

Hastings and Nixon became the sixth and seventh federal officials—all judges—to be removed from office by Congress through the impeachment process since the first case in 1789. In that time, six other officials— including President Andrew Johnson—were tried on impeachment charges but not convicted. The last federal official to be removed from office through impeachment in Congress was Judge Harry E. Claiborne of Nevada in 1986. His was the first ouster in fifty years, since the removal of Halsted L. Ritter from the bench in 1936. (Impeachment of Judge Claiborne, Historic Documents of 1986, p. 847)

Hastings Case

The Hastings case was unique in that the judge had been acquitted in 1983 by a federal jury of conspiracy and bribery charges that were related to his impeachment. But the articles of impeachment against Hastings included charges that he gave false testimony at his 1983 trial, by denying under oath that he had agreed to take a bribe. The articles also accused him of fabricating documents submitted as evidence in the trial. Hastings was specifically charged with engaging in a conspiracy with a Washington lawyer, William A. Borders, Jr., to obtain $150,000 from two defendants in a case before him in return for imposing lighter sentences.

Following his 1983 acquittal, a panel of his fellow judges concluded after a long investigation that Hastings had participated in the bribery conspiracy and lied repeatedly about it at his trial. But Hastings's defense said that his impeachment after the court acquittal amounted to double jeopardy, which is unconstitutional. Hastings attributed his troubles to racism and his outspoken nature.

In the House, the Criminal Justice Subcommittee of the Judiciary Committee held several days of hearings on the matter. Rep. John Conyers, Jr., D-Mich., a black subcommittee member, said he was convinced that racism was not involved in the charges. He took the lead in urging the House Judiciary Committee to vote for impeachment. It did, and the House approved the committee's recommendation to bring seventeen articles against Hastings. The vote was 413-10. The Senate considered eleven of the articles and found Hastings guilty in eight of them.

A vote of 69-26 for conviction on the first article was critical to the outcome of the case. Conviction required approval by two-thirds of the senators present and voting, and some senators were troubled over trying Hastings in the Senate after his courtroom acquittal. The other votes for conviction were of a similar margin.

Hastings immediately lost his judgeship and $89,500 salary. He said he planned to set up a law practice in Florida and run for governor as a Democrat in 1990.

Nixon Case

When Judge Nixon was tried in the Senate, he was still serving a five-year sentence for perjury, imposed in 1986 after a federal jury found him guilty. The charges on which he was convicted were similar to those in the articles of impeachment. After the Supreme Court on January 19, 1989, refused to review Nixon's conviction, the Fifth Circuit Court of Appeals, which includes Mississippi, and the U.S. Judicial Conference, which administers the federal judicial system, recommended his impeachment.

Nixon was found guilty of lying to the federal grand jury that investigated his oil and gas investments with a rich Mississippi business-man, Wiley Fairchild, and his alleged intervention on behalf of the businessman's son, Drew, the defendant in a drug-smuggling case. Nixon consistently denied discussing the case with the local prosecutor who was handling it, or intervening with the prosecutor, a friend, on Drew Fairchild's behalf.

The House Judiciary Committee voted 34-0 on April 25 to charge Nixon with two counts of lying under oath and one count of undermining the integrity of the judiciary. The House approved the committee's action May 10, by a vote of 417-0. House prosecutors told the Senate that Nixon's 1986 conviction was "fully justified" by "overwhelming evidence against him." His conviction and removal from the bench came November 3, 1989, by Senate votes of 89-8 and 78-19.

Calls for Change

Faced with the long and troubling task of removing three judges in three years, many members of Congress pointed to what they believed were shortcomings in the impeachment system. Sen. Jeff Bingaman, D-N.M., chairman of a special committee that considered the Hastings matter, was quoted in the press as saying the Founding Fathers never expected the federal judiciary to be so large as it had become. Bingaman, who voted to acquit Hastings in the Senate, also said, "We should look seriously at a constitutional amendment to see that the Senate is not overrun [by impeachment cases]."

In the House, Rep. Robert W. Kastenmeier, D-Wis., introduced a bill to establish a commission to study problems related to life-tenured judges and propose alternatives to the impeachment process. Many have suggested that the federal judiciary discipline its own members. In 1980, Congress authorized judicial councils in the twelve circuits to take action short of removal.

Rep. Don Edwards, D-Calif., chairman of the House Judiciary Subcommittee on Civil and Constitutional Rights, defended the impeachment process, saying that the removal of an official from office should be difficult. Sen. Patrick J. Leahy, D-Vt., was quoted as saying that the impeachment process "is made purposefully cumbersome to preserve the Constitution. The proposals [for change] are a threat to the very independence of the judiciary." The New York Times commented editorially October 24 that Hastings's removal "vindicated the Constitution's admittedly inefficient method for purging those who dishonor their offices."

> Following are passages from a statement to the Senate by
> Sen. Arlen Specter, R-Pa., on the Hastings case, printed in
> the Congressional Record, October 20, 1989; and from Senate
> proceedings in the Nixon case giving portions of Rep. Don
> Edwards's summation of House impeachment articles and of
> Judge Walter L. Nixon's defense argument, November 1, as
> printed in the Congressional Record:

STATEMENT OF SENATOR ARLEN SPECTER

Introduction

The impeachment trial of federal Judge Alcee Hastings represents a landmark in our constitutional history. In the 202 years since the adoption of the Constitution, this is the first time that any federal official has been impeached after being tried and acquitted by a jury. In essence, the House's 1988 impeachment of Judge Hastings asks the Senate in 1989— eight years after the events in question, and six years after the jury verdict—to reconsider a jury decision on charges and evidence that, if not identical to those before the jury, certainly are substantially the same. The case thus presents the Senate with unsettled issues touching on the applicability in an impeachment trial of legal concepts such as double jeopardy, collateral estoppel and undue delay.

Moreover, these issues arise here in the *Hastings* case in the context of a factually complicated matter. The 17 Impeachment Articles encompass events that center on Judge Hastings' handling of a criminal trial in 1981; his testimony at his own criminal trial in 1983; and his actions as supervising judge over an FBI wiretap in 1985. To consider fairly all these issues, the Impeachment Trial Committee in the *Hastings* impeachment heard 18 full days of testimony between July 10 and August 3, 1989. It heard 54 live witnesses (including one, William Borders, who was jailed for his refusal to testify), and two videotaped depositions; it had its record supplemented with the testimony of 25 additional witnesses from prior proceedings, including the criminal trials of Judge Hastings and William Borders. The Committee received 365 exhibits and 155 stipulations of uncontested facts into its record. Its full printed record is over 6,000 pages. The very factual complexity of the matter makes the decision that each Senator must make about the appropriate standard of proof a critical issue.

In my view, the factual and legal complexities of the matter render it a case where a just decision can be made only after extensive study and reflection. After having served as Vice Chairman of the Impeachment Trial Committee, having had the opportunity to discuss the evidence and legal issues with my colleagues on the Committee, having reviewed the briefs and considered the arguments of the parties, and with the benefit of time for my own reflection on the issues, I have decided to announce my decision on the matter of Judge Hastings' impeachment at this time with the hope that by doing so now and in this way I may assist my Senate colleagues in the difficult task of judging this historic matter. This Statement sets forth my thinking and analysis of the evidence and issues raised by this case. Recognizing that this is a matter in which significant evidence and substantial arguments may be marshalled on both sides, I have attempted to discuss the case in its entirety, with recognition of the strengths and weaknesses of both sides.

Background

The Constitution delegates the trial of impeached federal officials exclusively to the Senate. The impeachment of a federal judge involves an especially significant aspect of this fundamental Constitutional duty because of the importance that our Founders recognized, and our history has confirmed, of an independent federal judiciary. It is essential that federal judges be preserved in office, possessed of freedom to exercise independent judgment without fear of the momentary passions or possible partisanship of either the Executive or the Legislature. But it is equally important, because of the inevitable potential for corruption in those who hold office permanently, that there be a fair and just mechanism to remove judges from office if they become corrupt. . . .

In terms of the public perception of this proceeding, perhaps the most frequently asked question is how can it be fair to try impeachment articles against someone who has already been acquitted by a jury? In that regard, the full Senate last March considered Judge Hastings' contention that the impeachment proceedings should not go forward because they were barred by the constitutional prohibition against double jeopardy. The matter was argued to the full Senate by both Judge Hastings personally and his counsel, and by all six Managers from the House. After deliberation in closed session, the Senate voted 92-1 to deny Judge Hastings' motion to dismiss. At that time, although I voted with the majority, I expressed the opinion that while double jeopardy should not be an absolute bar to impeachment, nonetheless as a matter of fundamental fairness Judge Hastings' prior acquittal might well be entitled to substantial consideration after the evidence had been heard. . . .

[I]n both the *Claiborne* and *Hastings* impeachments, the Senate has expressed the clear view that it will not be bound in impeachment matters by the determinations of the judicial branch. But that is not necessarily the end point of the inquiry here; the novel issue that remains is whether principles of double jeopardy, collateral estoppel, due process or fundamental fairness require that the jury's verdict acquitting Judge Hastings, even if not preclusive of impeachment, nonetheless be given weight or deference. At the same time we should also be mindful that the Judicial Council of the Eleventh Circuit conducted an extensive inquiry, resulting in a 4909-page record, and urged impeachment. Beyond that, the House of Representatives impeached Judge Hastings on 17 Articles by a vote of 413-3.

Committee Proceedings

Before turning to a discussion of the evidence and legal principles, I note that the Impeachment Trial Committee has taken its assignment on this matter with a seriousness appropriate to the gravity of the constitutional task before it. Even before the hearings commenced in early July, a number of significant issues required decision. The Committee considered and established procedures to assure evidentiary hearings that would center on important issues on genuine dispute; it guided the parties through a stipulation process and urged their reliance on testimony from prior proceedings where the issues were either marginal or not really in dispute, so that the Committee was able to focus its attention on the heart of the controversy.

After extensive consideration, the Committee also decided to grant Judge Hastings' request for pre-hearing discovery. It authorized three depositions on his behalf over which I as Vice Chairman presided, and one such examination by the House, which did not occur. Although no precedent existed for these examinations, this authorization reflected the Committee's determination that Judge Hastings—and, for that matter, the House—be given ample opportunity to develop all evidence necessary to the case. In that vein, the committee also directed its staff to work with the Department of Justice and the FBI to assure that no documents in the files of those agencies material to the case were withheld.

My distinguished colleague, Senator Jeff Bingaman of New Mexico, chaired the proceedings with care, courtesy, and deliberateness. There were significant differences of opinions among the 12 senators at various stages, and the Chairman showed patience and consideration in hearing out all points of view before calling for Committee decisions. . . .

After the completion of prehearing procedures, on July 10, 1989 our Committee commenced hearing evidence. We received evidence over approximately 120 hours of hearings in the course of 18 hearing days, concluded our proceedings shortly after 10:00 p.m. on August 3. . . .

Summary of the Articles

There were 17 articles of impeachment which we considered. Briefly summarized, the articles charged:

That in 1981 Judge Hastings conspired with William Borders, a Washington, D.C. attorney, to solicit a $150,000 bribe from two defendants who were being tried before Judge Hastings on racketeering charges (Article I);

That in his 1983 trial on the bribery conspiracy, Judge Hastings lied repeatedly in securing his acquittal (Articles II-XV);

That is [sic] 1985 Judge Hastings revealed secret material to a Miami politician that Judge Hastings had learned in his capacity as supervising judge over an FBI wiretap (Article XVI); and

That by virtue of all of the foregoing, Judge Hastings undermined confidence in the integrity of the judiciary. (Article XVII). . . .

Evidence on the Wiretap Disclosure Article

Article XVI charged Judge Hastings with ruining an FBI undercover investigation by revealing to one of the subjects, Dade County Mayor Steven Clark, confidential information that Judge Hastings had learned in his capacity as supervising judge of the wiretap. The evidence on this charge was weak, and the charge itself insubstantial. . . .

Evidence on the Bribery/Conspiracy and Perjury Articles

As I have said, the central Article in the case involves charges of conspiracy to solicit a bribe and perjury. Judge Hastings was charged with agreeing with a Washington attorney, William Borders, to fix a racketeering case involving two brothers, Tom and Frank Romano, who were to be sentenced by Judge Hastings. In the House's view, soon after the *Romano* case was assigned to Judge Hastings, he in conjunction with Borders began attempting to solicit a bribe from the Romanos. As the House argued, Judge Hastings in May of 1981 continued the Romanos' sentencing solely for the purpose of demonstrating to them the necessity of paying him a bribe; in July of 1981 Judge Hastings sentenced the Romanos, who were elderly, in bad health and had no criminal history, to substantial jail terms in order to coerce them to participate in a bribe; as a further coercion, Judge Hastings throughout the summer of 1981 refused to follow binding precedents of the U.S. Court of Appeals for the Fifth Circuit that would have required him to return over $800,000 of forfeited property to the Romanos. In the House's view, only after Judge Hastings believed that the Romanos were prepared to pay a $150,000 bribe, and after the first $25,000 of that bribe was paid to Borders, did Judge Hastings finally issue the order returning the Romanos' property that the law required.

Judge Hastings denied all of this categorically, as he did in his 1983 trial. . . .

The House Case Against Judge Hastings

The evidence presented by the House against Judge Hastings was circumstantial in the sense that there was no "smoking gun": that is, no admission of guilt by Judge Hastings, and no witness who directly testified that he had paid money to Judge Hastings or saw or heard Judge Hastings agree to accept a bribe or participate in a scheme with Borders. The fact that the case was entirely circumstantial, however, does not necessarily mean that it was weak or insubstantial. The law has consistently recognized that circumstantial evidence—meaning evidence that involves facts from which inferences are drawn rather than direct observation of the fact at issue—may be as good or better than direct evidence; indeed it is possible to convict someone of first-degree murder based entirely on circumstantial evidence.

However, what the fact that the case against Judge Hastings is entirely circumstantial does mean is that a meticulous scrutiny of the record is required. We must be sure that the facts which comprise the circumstantial case have been established; that the inferences which the House seeks to have drawn from those facts are appropriate; that there are not other equally appropriate inferences consistent with innocence to be drawn from those same facts; and that the chain of circumstantial evidence presented is in its entirety sufficient to lead to a conclusion of guilt. . . .

NIXON CASE

MR. EDWARDS: We deal here with a Federal judge who committed perjury. A man who lied to law enforcement officials in an interview, and then lied again in sworn testimony before a grand jury. A man who was properly convicted of perjury by a jury of his peers. A man who was sentenced to prison and who has exhausted his appellate rights, all the way to the Supreme Court. A man who, despite his crimes, demands the high privilege of remaining on the Federal bench.

From the beginning, we in the House recognized the gravity of impeachment proceedings. As chairman of the subcommittee assigned to investigate this matter, I felt that a felony conviction, in and of itself, is not enough to remove a judge from office.

Even in this day and age, a prominent official might be unfairly convicted because of race, politics, or overreaching by prosecutors. In part because of my subcommittee's hearings on such matters as Abscam, Cointelpro, and our general oversight of the Department of Justice and FBI, we wanted to make sure that Judge Nixon had been treated fairly.

We chose to investigate this matter thoroughly, no matter how long it took. Our counsel spent weeks in Mississippi tracking down every possible lead that might exonerate the Judge. We held the equivalent of a trial in the House. We required all the key witnesses to come forward and testify under oath, subject to unlimited cross-examination. We gave Judge Nixon every possible opportunity to present evidence and argue his cause. Notwithstanding the perjury convictions, we had to be convinced that very serious misconduct had taken place.

We discovered that the jury verdict was fully justified. The evidence against Judge Nixon is overwhelming. Sadly, the evidence shows that Judge Nixon lied to a Federal grand jury under oath, and to Federal investigators during an interview.

After carefully investigating the facts and hearing all the evidence, the House voted 417 to 0 in favor of three articles of impeachment. Accordingly, you must now grapple with the same question we faced in the House. Is a man who repeatedly lied fit to hold the high office of Federal judge? I hope you agree that the answer is obvious. To preserve the integrity of the judiciary, to maintain public respect for law and order, Judge Nixon must be removed from the bench.

You have learned that following a divorce and remarriage, and with a growing family, Judge Nixon felt strapped by his judicial salary. Believing himself to be in need of supplemental income, he met with Carroll Ingram. Mr. Ingram is a friend of Judge Nixon and an attorney who regularly practiced before him. Mr. Ingram represented Wiley Fairchild, an oil and construction millionaire. Even though he did not know Mr. Fairchild personally, Judge Nixon solicited an investment. Judge Nixon asked Ingram to ask Wiley Fairchild to put him in an oil deal.

Mr. Ingram approached his client, and Wiley Fairchild did as Judge

Nixon requested. Fairchild gave Judge Nixon a lucrative oil investment that was not available to the general public, on very favorable terms.

Wiley Fairchild financed the investment completely. Fairchild gave Judge Nixon a $9,500 loan at an interest rate 5 points below the market rate, so that Judge Nixon was never out of pocket any money at all. Judge Nixon's other outside investments either barely were profitable or lost money. But the Fairchild investment was different. The $9,500 Fairchild investment paid off handsomely, generating more than $73,000 in income to Judge Nixon.

Judge Nixon was grateful for the investment. He knew he owed Wiley Fairchild a favor and told him, "If I can ever help you I will, and if I can't I'll just tell you I can't." Those were Judge Nixon's exact words. And with large royalty checks coming in, Judge Nixon was eager for other investments with Fairchild, to obtain even more income.

The time came when Judge Nixon had an opportunity to return the favor. As fate would have it, Wiley Fairchild's son, Drew, committed a crime. Drew was one of the managers at the Hattiesburg airport. Drew became involved in a conspiracy to smuggle a planeload of marijuana into the United States.

But the plot failed. The airplane was seized and Drew was ultimately indicted on State drug charges. The local prosecutor who handled Drew's drug smuggling case—this is the local district attorney—was Bud Holmes. Holmes has been a very close friend of Judge Nixon for 30 years. They hunt, and fish, together.

Wiley Fairchild did not like the way State prosecutor Holmes was handling his son's drug case. Even though Drew had agreed to plead guilty in return for a sentence of no jail time, a fine and 5 years probation, the case was dragging on with no resolution.

Worse, Wiley Fairchild thought his son was the victim of unequal justice. Robert Royals, Drew's partner at the airport, was also guilty but had never been prosecuted. Wiley thought Holmes was blackmailing him, that Drew had been prosecuted only because his father was wealthy.

Wiley Fairchild knew Holmes was a close friend of Judge Nixon. He also believed Judge Nixon owed him a favor because of the investment. So Wiley Fairchild complained to Judge Nixon about how Holmes was handling the drug case.

Mr. Fairchild told Judge Nixon that his son Drew was guilty, but that Royals was guilty too and should be prosecuted. Fairchild did not beg the judge for help. He did not need to ask. Even Judge Nixon admits the message was loud and clear. Fairchild was calling in the favor, and wanted Judge Nixon to talk with Bud Holmes, the local district attorney, about Drew's drug case.

Grateful for the investment and hopeful for other deals, Judge Nixon did exactly what Wiley Fairchild wanted. The very same afternoon after meeting with Fairchild, Judge Nixon spoke with Bud Holmes about the drug case. Judge Nixon told Holmes he was happy with the investment and was thinking of doing some more deals with Fairchild. And he told Bud Holmes that Wiley Fairchild had asked him to put in a good word for Drew in the drug case.

Holmes was willing to help his old friend Judge Nixon solidify the financial relationship and pick up some brownie points with Fairchild. So Holmes told Judge Nixon he would pass the drug smuggling case to the file.

What does it mean in Mississippi procedure to pass a case to the file? It means that the case becomes inactive, notwithstanding Drew's guilty plea. With his case passed to the file, Drew Fairchild would suffer no fine, no probation, no adverse consequences of any kind. The case goes nowhere, as if there had never been a prosecution.

After Holmes told him that the Drew Fairchild case would be passed to the file, Judge Nixon telephoned Wiley Fairchild. The judge told Wiley that he had talked with Holmes, and that the case would be taken care of to Wiley's satisfaction. Fairchild thanked Judge Nixon for speaking with Holmes about the handling of the drug case and told Judge Nixon, "I'm satisfied." Bud Holmes then took the telephone from Judge Nixon and told Fairchild, "when this man—Judge Nixon—asks me to do something, I don't ask questions. I just go ahead and do it."

Shortly thereafter, in a continuing effort to score points with Wiley Fairchild, Judge Nixon told Fairchild's attorney, Carroll Ingram, about his involvement in the drug case. After discussing the possibility of more investments, Judge Nixon took credit for helping Drew. Judge Nixon's telephone conversation with Ingram is important evidence.

Judge Nixon told Ingram he had spoken with Bud Holmes, the district attorney, about the Drew Fairchild drug case, with "positive"—that is his words—results. That telephone conversation was a confession by Judge Nixon; a confession that he had talked with Holmes about the case; a confession that he had influenced the case, by achieving positive results with Holmes.

In December 1982, the Drew Fairchild drug smuggling case was passed to the file upon motion by District Attorney Holmes. This was unprecedented. Everyone agrees that never before had there been a case passed to the file, when the defendant had already pled guilty like Drew.

Wiley Fairchild and Bud Holmes have both testified that but for Judge Nixon's involvement, the Drew Fairchild case would not have been passed to the file. Carroll Ingram also associates the passing of the case to the file with Judge Nixon's involvement.

Fortunately, a new local judge assumed the bench, noticed that the case has been passed to the files, and complained publicly about the handling of the case. In January 1983, Holmes, the district attorney, reinstated the case to the active docket.

Acting upon information supplied by one of Wiley Fairchild's employees, in late 1983 Federal law enforcement authorities began to investigate the Nixon-Fairchild drug case. Early in the investigation, in April 1984, the

FBI and the Department of Justice interviewed Judge Nixon to find out if he knew anything about the drug case. But during the interview Judge Nixon did not disclose his contacts with Holmes, Fairchild, and Ingram about the drug case. Judge Nixon was given every chance in this interview to be truthful and forthcoming. Instead, Judge Nixon categorically denied any involvement in the case, over and over again.

Three months later, in July 1984, a federal grand jury was empaneled to investigate the handling of the Drew Fairchild drug smuggling case. Again, during his testimony before the grand jury, Judge Nixon did not disclose his involvement, but instead swore that he never discussed the case with Holmes. Judge Nixon swore that he never talked to anyone about the case.

This false grand jury testimony led to his conviction on two counts of perjury following a lengthy criminal trial in February 1986.

The three articles of impeachment brought to you by the House are simple and straightforward.

Article I deals with Judge Nixon's statement under oath to the grand jury that District Attorney Bud Holmes never discussed the Drew Fairchild case with Judge Nixon. This specific statement was found by the jury to be false, and led to Judge Nixon's first perjury conviction.

This sworn statement by Judge Nixon was obviously false or misleading as charged. The evidence shows that Judge Nixon in fact discussed the Drew Fairchild case with Holmes. Even in Judge Nixon's own version of the events, he talked with Holmes about the case.

Article II deals with part of Judge Nixon's answer in the grand jury to the simple question, "All right, Judge. Do you have anything you want to add?"

The jury found the following part of Judge Nixon's answer to be false:

> Now I have had nothing whatsoever officially or unofficially to do with the Drew Fairchild criminal case in Federal court or State court.... I never handled any part of it, never had a thing to do with it at all, and never talked to anyone, State or Federal, prosecutor or judge, that in any way influenced anybody with respect to this case.

This quoted testimony led to Judge Nixon's second perjury conviction, and is the basis for article II.

This statement in article II was clearly false, as proven by the collective testimony of Bud Holmes, Wiley Fairchild and Carroll Ingram. Judge Nixon did have unofficial involvement in the drug case. He did talk with Wiley Fairchild, the defendant's father, about the case. He did talk with Bud Holmes, the State prosecutor, about the case.

And four witnesses prove that Judge Nixon influenced the matter. Bud Holmes and Wiley Fairchild have both testified that the drug case was passed to the file because of Judge Nixon's involvement. Carroll Ingram described Judge Nixon's admission to him that he had spoken to Holmes about the case, with positive results. And Judge Nixon himself has stipulated that in the telephone conversation from the farm, Fairchild thanked him for speaking with Holmes about the case and told Judge

Nixon, "I'm satisfied."

That brings us to article III. Some of you may wonder, why a third article of impeachment? Judge Nixon was found guilty on only two counts of perjury. Why expand the charges beyond the criminal conviction?

The answer is simple. Judge Nixon made many more false statements beyond those that put him in prison.

Judge Nixon committed a serious crime by lying to law enforcement officials during the interview. In our system of justice, a citizen has a constitutional right to remain silent when Federal investigators ask questions. You don't have to cooperate. But if you agree to an interview, you have to tell the truth. That is the law. If you conceal information or lie, you ... commit a felony.

We listened closely to the tape of his interview. I urge you to do the same. Judge Nixon was repeatedly asked during the interview whether he knew anything about the Drew Fairchild drug case. His interview answers were riddled with falsehoods. Judge Nixon told the interviewers that he never discussed with Wiley Fairchild anything about Wiley's son's case; that Wiley Fairchild never brought up his son's case; that he had no knowledge of the case and didn't even know Drew Fairchild existed, except what he read in the newspaper; that nothing was ever mentioned about Wiley Fairchild's son; that he had never heard about the case; that he had nothing to do with the case; and that Bud Holmes never talked to him about the case.

These interview statements are just as false as the grand jury testimony in articles I and II, that led to his perjury convictions. We could not ignore these false interview answers. These lies were the start of a long pattern of deceit and coverup by Judge Nixon.

The testimony of Wiley Fairchild, Bud Holmes and Carroll Ingram proves these interview statements are false. Even Judge Nixon has grudgingly conceded that many of his interview answers were false. He admits that Drew was mentioned. He admits that he knew Drew existed, from his conversation with Fairchild and Holmes. He admits Wiley brought up his son's case. He admits he heard about the case from Wiley Fairchild and Bud Holmes. In his own current version of the events, Judge Nixon proves that his interview answers are false.

The deceit and concealment continued when Judge Nixon appeared before the grand jury. Article III again goes beyond the jury verdict, because there were additional sworn statements by Judge Nixon in his grand jury testimony that are just as false as the testimony that put him in prison. We could not ignore these lies, either.

For example, Judge Nixon swore to the grand jury that he did not know of any reason he would have met with Wiley Fairchild after the investment was finalized in February 1981. Yet, Judge Nixon has admitted that at the time he made this statement, he specifically recalled his meeting when Fairchild complained about the handling of the drug deal. You simply can not reconcile Judge Nixon's own testimony.

Judge Nixon swore to the grand jury that he had given them all the information that he had, and had withheld nothing. Yet Judge Nixon told us last year in the House that he deliberately withheld his conversations with Holmes and Fairchild, because he thought it would be "irresponsible" to "blabber" about "rumors" that had "been resolved." Again, Judge Nixon proves himself to be a liar.

Judge Nixon swore to the grand jury, without qualification, that he never talked to anyone about the drug case. This statement was patently false.

We could not ignore these additional false statements. We had conclusive evidence of a continuing pattern of deceit and falsehood. So, in article III we allege that Judge Nixon concealed the truth. First, by one or more false or misleading statements in his interview, then by one or more false or misleading statements in his grand jury testimony.

Judge Nixon has broken the law, tainted the integrity of the judiciary and brought disrepute on the courts. By his misconduct, he has forfeited his privilege of serving on the Federal bench....

JUDGE NIXON.... I have been unjustly and wrongfully convicted. Otherwise, I assure you that I would have long ago resigned and not subjected my wife and children to this emotionally physically and financially draining ordeal.

I very much value the integrity of the Federal judiciary. I have done nothing to impugn the integrity of this great branch of Government and would do nothing to impugn it....

The investigation of my case was begun on false premises, and pursued for the wrong reasons. From the very beginning, the goal of the Federal prosecutors was to get the Federal judge no matter what it took. And it took plenty—threats of indictments of some, and indictments of others on charges which the prosecutor later admitted before the House subcommittee that he probably could not have proved. Then, following these indictments came promises, threats and deals with the witnesses. The basis for the investigation was the charge that I received some illegal benefit in return for my actions as a judge.

There never was any basis for that charge and I was acquitted of it. In fact, during my trial the prosecutor told two newspaper reporters covering the trial that he probably could not prove the illegal gratuity charge and, after the trial, he admitted to another reporter that he had not proved that charge.

By including that false allegation, however, the prosecutor was able to taint the trial, to taint my character before the jury and secure the compromise verdict of conviction on two of the four charges against me.

You may well wonder what our basis is for saying that I was not afforded a fair trial. First, I would not have been convicted had the jury not been prejudiced against me by the prosecution of the unfounded, and unsupported, illegal gratuity charge of corruption.

Second, I would not have been convicted if the jury had known that one of the two principal prosecution witnesses, Wiley Fairchild, gave false testimony against me at my trial in order to please the prosecutor and benefit himself, as he later admitted in the postconviction hearing before the U.S. district court in Jackson, MS, last year. . . .

Third, while testifying before the House subcommittee and also here before your trial committee, Bud Holmes, the State district attorney, the second of the two principal prosecution witnesses, finally acknowledged that when he tried to discuss the Drew Fairchild case with me at his farm on the night of March 11, 1983, the night in question, that I prevented him from discussing that case with me when he attempted to tell me about it that night. Those are his words. Twice he testified to that before the House subcommittee and before your trial committee. That goes directly to count 1. . . .

Senators, my wife, children, and I have suffered and lost so much over the past 5½ years—our peace of mind, damage to reputation, our ability to be together, and my freedom, but we have not lost faith and trust in God or in our system of justice. We ascribe the wrong that has been done to those who administer the system. We hope and pray that justice and right will now prevail.

We know that it is difficult to look beyond the fact of my conviction to the underlying true facts of this case. We know that it may be politically more difficult to vote not guilty. Many have said that these problems cannot be overcome, but we have disagreed, and we do so now, very strongly. We have great faith that each of you will have the insight and the courage to vote your conscience based upon the evidence. . . .

In closing, I wish to thank you for the opportunity to speak to you today. I have paid a debt that I did not owe by serving 20 months in prison. I ask you now to right this wrong, and I can assure each of you that if rightfully given the privilege of continuing to serve my country as a Federal judge, I absolutely can and will do so in the same fair and dedicated way that I have in the past.

May Almighty God give you the courage to vote your conscience and may your conscience guide each of you in your deliberations and vote this week.

Thank you.

AMNESTY INTERNATIONAL'S REPORT ON HUMAN RIGHTS
October 24, 1989

Amnesty International, the human rights organization, reported Octo-
ber 24 that it had documented thousands of killings by government
agents in at least two dozen countries during 1988. Most of the victims
died because of their political or religious beliefs, their ethnic identifica-
tion, or simply because they associated with people considered enemies of
the authorities.

The organization further reported that in 1988 it had documented
cases of "prisoners of conscience"—people imprisoned for the nonviolent
exercise of their basic rights—in eighty countries. Unfair trials, torture,
and other methods of ill treatment were reported in dozens of countries;
political prisoners were detained in more than half of the 133 countries
investigated, many of them without charge or trial Amnesty Internation-
al's latest annual report, a 310-page volume, corroborated many of the
findings made public earlier in the year by the U.S. State Department in
its annual worldwide human rights survey. (State Department's Human
Rights Report, p. 57)

A concern of Amnesty International was the use of the death penalty
in fifty-eight countries, including the United States. In particular, the
report cited China, where 126 executions were recorded but possibly
many more occurred. Iran announced 142 executions, but the human
rights organization said it learned of at least 1,200 that occurred secretly.
Hundreds were believed to have been executed in Iraq, at least 85 in
Nigeria, and at least 117 in South Africa. In the United States, 11
prisoners were put to death, but at the end of the year 2,182 inmates in
thirty-four states were under death sentences.

Some of the year's worst violence occurred in Burundi. Thousands of unarmed civilians, members of the majority Hutu community, were killed by members of the armed forces, dominated by the minority Tutsi community, after Hutu villagers had attacked and killed Tutsi living in the northeast section of the country.

Amnesty International reported renewed activity by "death squads" in El Salvador. The squads, presumably composed of regular troops, police, and gunmen working with security forces, were responsible for the murder, "disappearance," torture, and mutilation of scores of people perceived to be opponents of the government. Massacres and summary executions by military forces in Peru were said to have "largely replaced imprisonment and trial by the courts" in large areas of that country.

In Israel and the Occupied Territories, more than 300 Palestinian civilians were killed in 1988, and thousands were victims of punitive beatings by security forces, the organization reported. Elsewhere in the Middle East, the armed forces of Iraq attacked ethnic Kurds with chemical weapons, killing some 6,000 men, women, and children. Survivors of chemical attacks were often summarily executed, the report further stated.

The report noted that human rights workers themselves were frequently victims of government terror and abuse. The victims included leaders of local and national human rights commissions, human rights lawyers, and members of religious orders who were working actively for human rights. Some were killed in El Salvador, Guatemala, Colombia, and the Philippines. Others were the object of death threats or survived assassination attempts.

Following are excerpts from "Amnesty International Report 1989 on global human rights violations, released October 24, 1989:

Introduction

Tens of thousands of people were deliberately killed in 1988 by government agents acting beyond the limits of the law. They were victims of executions that evaded the judicial process.

Killing grounds were many and varied. Some alleged opponents of governments, or people targeted because of their religion, ethnic group, language or political beliefs were killed in full public view; others in secret cells and remote camps. Some victims were shot down near battlefields, others in mosques and churches, hospital beds, public squares and busy city streets. Prison cells and courtyards, police stations, military barracks and government offices were all sites of political killing by agents of the state. Many people were killed in their own homes, some in front of their families.

Victims were assassinated by snipers, blown up by explosive devices or gunned down in groups by assailants using automatic weapons. Others were stabbed, strangled, drowned, hacked to death or poisoned. Many were tortured to death. In Colombia, Guatemala, El Salvador, Syria and the Philippines victims were often severely mutilated before they were killed. Their bodies were burned or slashed, ears and noses were severed and limbs amputated.

A state of armed conflict was frequently the pretext, as well as the context, for government campaigns of extrajudicial execution against those they considered undesirable. Warfare makes it easier to evade accountability; not only is access by independent observers limited but the dead can be characterized as combatants killed in encounters or as the unavoidable civilian casualties of war. In Afghanistan forces of the Afghan Government and the USSR summarily killed civilians and captive guerrillas. In one incident a mosque was demolished, killing nine of the 12 captured guerrillas held within. In Ethiopia troops combating guerrilla movements in Eritrea and Tigray carried out mass executions of civilians accused of supporting the guerrillas. On one occasion hundreds of people were reportedly forced into a shallow ditch and then crushed by army tanks. In Burma measures to control the people in areas of insurgency included instant, illegal executions of those found outside their communities or in possession of quantities of food or other goods. In Peru massacres and summary executions largely replaced imprisonment and trial by the courts in counter-insurgency zones under the control of the military.

Many people became victims simply because they lived in an area where the population as a whole was seen as the enemy. In Iraq the Kurdish population was attacked with chemical weapons; survivors were arrested and summarily executed—in one town over 1,000 executions were reported. In Somalia government forces bombarded and strafed fleeing refugees in the north, killing thousands, and executed hundreds of other members of the Issaq clan, which was associated with a guerrilla opposition movement.

In Sri Lanka, both Sri Lankan and Indian troops used deliberate killings of non-combatants in their efforts to suppress armed opposition groups. They were also responsible for "disappearances"—secret, unacknowledged arrests which often resulted in execution.

Mass killings were also carried out outside the immediate context of armed conflict. In Burundi tensions between the dominant Tutsi minority and the Hutu community—which makes up over 80 per cent of the population—led to the reported massacre by Tutsi-dominated troops of thousands of unarmed Hutu. In Guatemala people were killed each month for their political beliefs. During the 1980s tens of thousands of Guatemalan civilians have been killed by agents of the government's security services. Among those executed, apparently because they were deemed subversive, have been teachers, community leaders, trade unionists, human rights workers and peasant farmers active in community life.

In many countries prisoners died as a consequence of torture. Many governments used methods of torture that were inherently life-threatening, such as beating, electric shocks, drugs, immersion and hanging. In

1988 deaths after torture were reported in Turkey, El Salvador, Indonesia, Iraq, China, Syria and Burma.

Some prisoners died as a result of deliberate neglect—by being denied medical attention, by exposure, or from starvation. In Chad a journalist held in secret detention without charge reportedly died as a result of illness brought on by harsh conditions and ill-treatment. In Mauritania four political prisoners in the remote desert prison of Oualata also died after being held in harsh conditions. In Burma at least 41 students arrested during demonstrations suffocated to death in a police van....

The violence of non-governmental entities often provided the background to extrajudicial executions by government forces. Violent opposition groups and sectarian movements in many countries were responsible for the random killing and maiming of civilians on a large scale and tortured and killed their captives. Many government troops and police involved in these conflicts were themselves tortured or killed after capture or while incapacitated by wounds. The torture and murder of captives by non-governmental groups in Afghanistan, Sri Lanka, Peru, Colombia and elsewhere were a grim part of the context of gross human rights abuse....

Government denials and measures to muzzle or eliminate local witnesses were often combined with efforts to exclude outsiders. In Burundi the authorities denied reports of a pogrom of the Hutu majority and refused to allow an international commission of inquiry to investigate how thousands of civilians had died. The Government of Iraq refused a request by the United Nations Secretary-General to permit on-site investigation of the reported killings of members of the Kurdish population.

Suppression of evidence can extend to silencing a government's institutions established to investigate disputed killings. In India a government-established committee investigating the "disappearance" of several dozen Muslims in 1987 was not allowed to make public its findings, which reportedly implicated the provincial police.

Governments' methods of murder often help them evade accountability. Killings are carried out at night, when the victims are alone, or in remote rural areas where even large-scale troop movements can be undertaken unobserved. In urban areas specialized squads are trained to function in secrecy and are authorized to conduct operations in areas under curfew and police control.

Some of those killed are among the "disappeared", although efforts at concealment may break down. In Colombia, El Salvador, Guatemala, Peru, the Philippines and elsewhere the bodies of "disappeared" prisoners were periodically found in remote mass graves and dumping grounds—in sandpits, overgrown ravines, caves and abandoned wells—or washed up on beaches....

International awareness of extrajudicial executions as a major human rights issue has grown dramatically in the 1980s. The strengthening of human rights monitoring at a local level in many countries and concerted efforts by international human rights organizations—both governmental and non-governmental—have helped turn this awareness into action....

The 1980s have been marked by an extraordinary level of mass killings and individual assassinations by government forces and by a significant change in the way they are viewed by international public opinion. The international community receives more and better information and is readier to cut through the fog of secrecy and deceit that cloaks illicit government actions.

It is common practice for governments to attribute state-sponsored killings to independent "death squads", vigilantes or uncontrollable intercommunal violence but it is increasingly obvious that this may merely be a device to deflect public criticism from those in authority.

Killings continue but the fact that reports of extrajudicial executions now rapidly become known around the world is a new element in international relations. In the 1990s the impact of public opinion and the remedial action of the international community should make it more difficult for governments that aim to carry out killings which are murder by any other name. . . .

Burundi

. . . Major Pierre Buyoya, who took power in a military coup in September 1987, continued to head the *Comité militaire de salut national* (CMSN), the Military Committee for National Salvation, which was composed entirely of officers belonging to the minority Tutsi community which dominates the army. In October, following the intercommunal violence, the Hutu community was given stronger representation in the government and a prominent Hutu leader, Adrien Sibomana, was appointed Prime Minister.

In August intercommunal killing involving the Hutu and Tutsi communities broke out. . . . Many people, including women and children, were said by eye-witnesses to have been killed by soldiers while fleeing and others were reported to have been killed after being herded into huts which were then set on fire. Medical examinations of Hutu civilians who sought refuge in Rwanda revealed that many had bayonet or gunshot wounds in the back, apparently caused by weapons of a type used in Burundi only by the armed forces.

In the wake of the killings several thousand Hutu fled to Rwanda; some also sought refuge in Tanzania and Zaire. Three days after the killings began the government estimated the number of dead at 5,000 and implied that most were Tutsi who had been killed by Hutu. Other sources suggested that as many as 20,000 people had been killed, the majority of them Hutu. . . .

Ethiopia

Several hundred unarmed civilians were said to have been extrajudicially executed by government forces in Eritrea and Tigray, where there was intensified fighting between government and opposition forces and where the government imposed a new state of emergency. Here and in other parts of the country, hundreds of people were arrested for suspected links with opposition groups. Seven members of the former royal family who had been detained since 1974 were released in May. However, many people arrested in previous years for political reasons, including prisoners of conscience, remained in detention without trial or had "disappeared". Torture of political prisoners continued to be reported and conditions in most prisons—particularly special security and military prisons—were harsh. . . .

Somalia

Large numbers of unarmed civilians were extrajudicially executed in the north by government forces after opposition attacks in May. Hundreds of Issaq clan members living in the north, whom the government suspected of opposition activities or sympathies, were arrested and detained without trial. Many other suspected government opponents arrested before 1988, including prisoners of conscience, remained in prison throughout the year. One of them had been held for virtually all the government's 19 years in power. At least 30 death sentences were imposed but it was not known if there were any executions. Two former members of parliament and six others were sentenced to death after an unfair trial before the National Security Court. Although these sentences were commuted, the two, and four other former members of parliament acquitted of capital offences, were placed under house arrest until their release in October. Torture of political prisoners was widespread and prison conditions were extremely harsh. . . .

South Africa

Thousands of people, including many prisoners of conscience, were detained without trial under state of emergency regulations or other security laws on account of their actual or suspected activities in opposition to *apartheid*. Many others were jailed for alleged political offences after trials which may have been unfair—defendants and uncharged detainees required to testify against them under threat of further imprisonment alleged that they had been tortured or ill-treated while held incommunicado in prolonged pre-trial detention. There were new deaths in custody of political detainees in suspicious circumstances. The death penalty continued to be used at a high rate: 117 people were hanged at Pretoria Central Prison and further executions were believed to have been carried out in Transkei and other nominally independent "homelands". Death sentences imposed on the "Sharpeville Six" and others, including four white police officers convicted of murdering prisoners, were commuted by State President P. W. Botha.

There was continued armed opposition to the government, in particular by the military wing of the banned African National Congress (ANC), which was reportedly responsible for various bombings and other acts of sabotage, some of which caused civilian deaths. A number of alleged ANC guerrillas were arrested or brought to trial during the year. In contrast, those responsible for a series of sabotage attacks directed at organizations critical of the government were not identified or apprehended. Such attacks included a bomb explosion which destroyed the Johannesburg headquarters of the South African Council of Churches (SACC) and an arson attack which destroyed the offices of the Southern African Catholic Bishops' Conference (SACBC) in Pretoria. The SACC and SACBC have long been critical of the government.

In June the government renewed for a further year the nationwide state of emergency which has been continuously in force since 12 June 1986. In February it had invoked its emergency powers to restrict drastically the activities of 18 political, community and other organizations. These included two human rights groups—the Detainees' Parents' Support Committee and the Detainees' Support Committee—which had actively monitored and campaigned against the use of detention without trial, torture and other human rights violations. Subsequently, the activities of over a dozen other non-violent organizations, including the End Conscription Campaign (ECC), were similarly restricted. . . .

Police torture and ill-treatment of uncharged political detainees was also reported from the "homelands". In July and August students and others . . . in the Venda "homeland" were reported to have been severely abused by local police, in particular by being beaten on the body and soles of their feet with *sjamboks,* a type of whip. In Transkei a former university student, Aga Khan Tiya, was reported to have been suffocated with a wet towel and stabbed in the throat while under interrogation by security police. His condition came to light only when he was moved to hospital under police guard and admitted to an intensive care unit. . . .

Colombia

Widespread and systematic violations of human rights continued against a background of escalating civil conflict. Over 1,500 apparent extrajudicial executions were carried out and 250 people were reported to have "disappeared". There were scores of multiple killings by paramilitary "death squads" which resulted in the deaths of hundreds of civilians. Further evidence emerged that "death squads" responsibile for the majority of killings acted as part of or in coordination with regular armed forces. There were renewed reports of torture and ill-treatment of prisoners, particularly detainees arrested under new anti-terrorist legislation and held illegally in military installations. Hundreds of people, many of whom were believed to be prisoners of conscience, were detained under special decree laws and tried by summary procedures which failed to conform to international standards of impartiality and fairness.

Armed forces counter-insurgency operations were intensified to combat the country's . . . guerrilla groups. Such groups were responsible for an increasing number of bomb attacks and ambushes of government forces, some of which resulted in civilian deaths. The government ceded civilian authority in several areas of the country, which were placed under the control of senior army commanders appointed by decree laws issued under the state of siege legislation in force since 1984. The principal victims of political violence continued to be the civilian population. . . .

An alarming development during 1988 was a series of multiple killings on non-combatant civilians apparently suspected of having left-wing sympathies or of supporting anti-government guerrillas. Amnesty International received information on over 30 massacres carried out by paramilitary "death squads" in which some 350 people died.... Although military authorities frequently attributed multiple killings to anti-government guerrillas, in several cases judicial investigations established that particular killings had been carried out or coordinated by army personnel and financed by land-owners or drug-traffickers....

In addition to these multiple killings, there was a dramatic increase in the number of apparent extrajudicial executions, over 1,500 of which were reported to Amnesty International. The victims appeared to have been targeted because they were active in left-wing political parties, trade unions and community movements....

There was also a significant increase in "disappearances". The bodies of some people initially reported to have "disappeared" reappeared days or weeks later, many showing signs of torture. According to local human rights groups, over 200 people who "disappeared" after detention in the first 10 months of 1988 remained unaccounted for....

El Salvador

There was increased activity by so-called "death squads", which the government said were outside their control but which were widely alleged to be composed of police and military personnel operating both in uniform and in plain clothes. They were responsible for abductions, "disappearances" and politically motivated killings of suspected opponents of the government, including former political prisoners, trade unionists and human rights activists. The authorities took little action to investigate such violations. There were reports of torture and of one death in detention, apparently as a result of torture.

Throughout the year the government of President Napoleón Duarte—who was seriously ill—continued to face armed opposition from the *Frente Farabundo Marti para la Liberación Nacional* (FMLN), Farabundo Marti National Liberation Front. The FMLN was accused by local human rights groups and others of abducting and killing civilians whom they suspected of supporting or collaborating with the authorities.

It remained difficult to identify those responsible for many apparently politically motivated killings. However, in a number of cases there was persuasive evidence that abductions and killings were carried out by "death squads" composed of police or military personnel, and that their actions were condoned or encouraged by the authorities....

There were several hundred "disappearance" cases reported....

There were allegations that security forces posed as anti-government guerrillas in order to implicate the guerrillas in apparent abuses. One such alleged case occurred in October, when soldiers from the Second Infantry Brigade posing as FMLN guerrillas visted the hamlet of San Antonio La Junta, Metapán, Santa Ana department, and abducted five people. Two of the peasants were members of the National Association of Agricultural Workers; none has been seen since. Villagers said they recognized some of the men as soldiers who had participated in a military operation in the area a few days before. . . .

Guatemala

There was an escalation in human rights violations against suspected critics and opponents of the government. Hundreds of people were "disappeared" or extrajudicially executed and scores of others faced death threats from the security forces, sometimes acting in uniform, sometimes clandestinely in the guise of "death squads". Civil patrols formed under military order and operating under them were also allegedly responsible for such abuses. . . .

It was difficult to assess the full extent of human rights violations, not least because of the manner in which many were carried out—often by armed men in plain clothes using vehicles with darkened windows and no licence plates. The gross human rights violations which occurred during military rule in the early 1980s had destroyed organizations that were trying to carry out human rights work and also made victims and witnesses reluctant to come forward and report violations for fear of the consequences.

Nevertheless, during the year information was received about numerous cases in which peasants living in areas affected by conflict between government forces and armed opposition groups were abducted and either "disappeared" or were found dead. . . .

Various official mechanisms established to investigate human rights violations since the present government came to power in 1986 continued to prove ineffective. . . .

Nicaragua

Many critics and opponents of the government, including some believed to be prisoners of conscience, were detained in connection with protest demonstrations and strike activity. Some received prison sentences from police magistrates appointed by the Ministry of the Interior under a procedure which did not provide for a judicial hearing or right of appeal; others were tried on criminal charges. Approximately 3,200 political prisoners remained in prison at the end of the year. They included some 1,700 convicted of crimes committed as members of the National Guard of the previous President, Anastasio Somoza Debayle, and approximately 1,500 prisoners convicted of belonging to, or assisting, armed opposition forces. The majority had been convicted by special courts which failed to meet international standards of fairness and impartiality; some were believed to be prisoners of conscience. There were new allegations of extrajudicial executions and "disappearances" by government forces in areas affected by the armed conflict. In many cases little progress appeared to have been made by the authorities in investigating reports of politically motivated killings and "disappearances" by government forces in previous years. . . .

Peru

Over 300 people "disappeared" after arrest by army and navy counter-insurgency forces in zones under a state of emergency. Hundreds more were victims of extrajudicial execution. In July attacks of a new kind began against critics of the government and the armed forces. These were said by the authorities to have been carried out by an independent anti-terrorist revenge group. People whose roles in public life may previously have protected them—including journalists, lawyers, academics and human rights activists—were threatened or killed. In the emergency zones evidence emerged that linked these attacks directly to armed forces "political-military commands" effectively responsible for local administration. Torture continued to be reported in both criminal and political cases. An estimated 630 political prisoners, including prisoners of conscience, were being held at the end of the year, all charged with terrorism, although few had been convicted. Others, including prisoners of conscience, were held for short periods.

Inflation of almost 2,000 per cent, proliferating violence and recurrent rumours of an imminent military coup contributed to a situation of extreme political tension. President Alan García Pérez resigned his position as head of the ruling *Alianza Popular Revolucionaria Americana* (APRA), American Popular Revolutionary Alliance, in December after calls from his own party that he step down from the presidency and bring forward elections scheduled for April 1990. The human rights situation deteriorated as a long-standing pattern of "disappearances" and extrajudicial executions extended beyond the mountain areas to which it had been confined. These practices, first reported in 1983 in seven provinces, extended to other regions as they too came under armed forces' control. By the end of the year 56 of Peru's 181 provinces were under state of emergency, with all but the provinces of Lima and Callao administered by armed forces political-military commands.

The *Partido Comunista del Perú "Sendero Luminoso"*, Communist Party of Peru "Shining Path", continued to wage a nationwide campaign of attacks on government property, on the communications and electricity network, on state-run cooperative farms and on private businesses. It carried out scores of execution-style killings, some after torture and mutilation of those it had seized. The Senate Commission on National Pacification, citing Defence Ministry statistics, reported 289 police and military personnel killed in political violence in 1988, many of them after capture or while incapacitated by wounds. The number of "subversives" killed was put at 667, although some may have been non-combatant civilians. The Commission reported that 1,030 civilians were killed in 1988. The total toll of 1,986 dead was nearly three times that in 1987. . . .

Afghanistan

Many hundreds of real or suspected opponents of the government were believed to be imprisoned, including possible prisoners of conscience. In September the government announced that they were holding 2,125 political prisoners, and that more than 7,600 others, most of whom had been held for political reasons, had been released since the beginning of 1988. Amnesty International could not confirm these figures but received reports suggesting that many of those released were transferred directly to military service. Some political prisoners were sentenced after trials by Special Revolutionary Courts which did not conform to international standards. There were reports of torture and ill-treatment of prisoners, although on a lesser scale than in previous years. There were also reports of extrajudicial executions by Afghan security forces and Soviet troops.

On 14 April the Geneva accords to settle the Afghan conflict were signed by the governments of Afghanistan, Pakistan, the United States of America and the Union of Soviet Socialist Republics. The accords provided for the withdrawal of half the Soviet troops in Afghanistan by 15 August and the remainder by 15 February 1989. They also required the governments of Afghanistan and Pakistan to refrain from using force and engaging in subversive activities across each other's frontiers. The Afghan armed opposition groups, the Mujahideen, however, were not a party to the accords and refused to be bound by them. Consequently, despite the phased withdrawal of Soviet troops, the conflict continued unabated with arms supplied to the Mujahideen by the USA and Pakistan, and to the Afghan Government by the USSR. Between January and July over 100,000 Afghans were reported to have fled the fighting and entered Pakistan, although the government said almost 40,000 returned to Afghanistan between January and August under the official policy of national reconciliation. At the end of the year, over five million Afghans remained in exile, mostly in Pakistan and Iran. They constituted the largest refugee group in the world.

Information about human rights violations continued to be difficult to obtain and corroborate as a result of the war and social dislocation. However, Professor Felix Ermacora, the United Nations Special Rapporteur on human rights in Afghanistan, was allowed to visit a number of detention centres and prisons, including Pul-e-Charkhi Prison in Kabul, during his two visits to Afghanistan in January and September. The visits formed the basis of a report submitted to the UN Human Rights Commission in March and of an interim report to the UN General Assembly in October. . . .

Burma

Thousands of people were killed and thousands more arrested during widespread protests against military rule. Many detainees were freed but several hundred, including possible prisoners of conscience, were still held at the end of the year. Some detainees were reportedly tortured or ill-treated. More than 50 prisoners were killed when security personnel opened fire on rioting inmates at Insein Prison. Five executions were reported and at least 62 prisoners remained under sentence of death. There were reports of torture and extrajudicial killing of civilians belonging to Burma's ethnic minorities during army counter-insurgency operations.

In March security forces violently broke up student demonstrations in Rangoon, and the rest of the year was marked by widespread civil unrest, violent clashes between security forces and demonstrators, and frequent changes of heads of government....

There were thousands of arrests and deaths during demonstrations, allegedly a result of the actions of riot police and army personnel. In June protests in Rangoon resulted in a dusk-to-dawn curfew and an announcement by the government that anyone "gathering, making speeches, marching, instigating, encouraging, protesting, rioting and breaking the curfew" would face "serious action". The unrest spread to other cities, including Mandalay, Taunggyi and Pegu. By August it had become nationwide, with protesters demanding an end to military rule and the establishment of parliamentary democracy.

In early August, after the authorities had responded to small street demonstrations by imposing a state of emergency and martial law, hundreds of thousands of people demonstrated repeatedly and peacefully in Rangoon and other cities. Some 8,000 troops were dispatched to suppress the demonstrations; they included soldiers normally assigned to counter-insurgency operations and from units responsible for unlawful killings and torture of members of ethnic minorities.

The security forces repeatedly intervened in demonstrations which were overwhelmingly peaceful. During the March demonstration in Rangoon, many people were reportedly beaten unconscious by riot police and some of them allegedly drowned in Inya Lake. A further 41 died from suffocation in a police van—a fact acknowledged in June in a report by a government commission of inquiry into the events....

Between March and July an estimated 200 protesters and prisoners were killed but the death toll increased dramatically following the demonstrations in August. Official reports stated that 12 people were killed and hundreds were wounded, but unofficial sources put the number of dead at up to 1,000. These sources alleged that most demonstrators were unarmed and had conducted themselves peacefully but that troops appeared to be under orders to shoot protesters. There were similar allegations after demonstrations in September when hundreds of peaceful protesters, including children, were reportedly shot. In Sagaing eye-witnesses said that troops had killed several dozen demonstrators. The authorities stated that 450 people had been killed between 18 September and mid-October, and the official radio station continued to report sporadic killings of "looters", "undisciplined elements" and "people bent on violence". Unofficial sources estimated that 1,000 people had been killed in the month after the coup and that the majority of victims had again been non-violent demonstrators.

In late September the government announced that it had suppressed "strike centers" in over 100 townships. In the process, it said, 180 demonstrators had been killed. The centres, which had been established throughout the country, had organized demonstrations and in some cases had functioned as a local administration.

The repeated waves of unrest resulted in thousands of arrests. . . .

At the end of September the goverment announced that 1,376 people had been arrested since the military resumed power earlier that month. Although it said that none of them were political prisoners, other sources claimed that the majority had been detained for their participation in the protest demonstrations. By December most detainees had been released after initial investigations had been conducted but a few remained in custody, including possible prisoners of conscience. . . .

Ill-treatment in prisons and detention centres was said to be widespread. Some of those held after the March protests were allegedly beaten by prison staff. Victims included several dozen factory workers of Indian descent held in Tharawaddy. Several female students confirmed after their release that they had been raped and at least four detainees reportedly died from suffocation after several dozen of them were crammed into a small cell at Insein Prison.

Human rights violations were also committed by counter-insurgency troops deployed in remote and mountainous areas where armed opposition groups were active. Army units executed and tortured civilians suspected of supporting the opposition. Most of the victims were members of Burma's ethnic minorities. . . .

November

Long-Term Study on Fitness
  and Health 613

U.S. Catholic Bicentennial
  Observed in Baltimore 619

Statements on Berlin Wall and
  German Reunification 625

Communist Concessions in
  Czechoslovakia 635

LONG-TERM STUDY ON FITNESS AND HEALTH
November 3, 1989

Americans do not have to emulate marathon runners to achieve some health benefits from exercise. Even those who exercise only modestly, perhaps by walking briskly thirty minutes a day, improve their chances of escaping death from cancer and heart disease. That was the strong message of a study published in the November 3 Journal of the American Medical Association *and described by its authors as the largest study ever undertaken to test the relationship of physical fitness to health. It was conducted by the Institute for Aerobics Research and the Cooper Clinic, in Dallas, Texas, with the aid of a U.S. Public Health Service grant from the National Institute on Aging, in Bethesda, Maryland.*

Dr. Steven N. Blair, the study's chief author, and a group of medical colleagues charted the correlation between physical fitness and death rates among 10,344 men and 3,120 women for an average of eight years. This study added up to 110,482 person-years (the study of one person for one year is a person-year), making it about five times the size of previous studies of the same question. However, the participants were not representative of the nation as a whole; about 70 percent were college graduates, and most of them held professional, executive, or other white-collar jobs. More than 99 percent of them were white. They ranged in age from their twenties to beyond sixty.

All the participants took medical exams at the Cooper Clinic between 1970 and 1981 and were pronounced basically healthy, although not necessarily in good physical condition. Their performances on the tread-mill exercise test, adjusted for different expectations for age and sex, placed them in one of five fitness categories—ranging from the superbly fit to the wretchedly unfit. At the time of testing, none of the participants had personal histories of heart attack, high blood pressure, stroke, or diabetes, and none of their tests showed heartbeat abnormalities.

During the years in which their lives were tracked by the research team, 240 men and 43 women died of various causes. The study showed that the age-adjusted death rate per ten thousand person-years was 64.0 percent among the least-fit group of men—those who were first to drop out of the treadmill test—and only 18.3 percent among the most fit. Among women, the comparable rates were 39.5 and 8.5 percent. Even more striking, at least to some health experts, was the finding that men in the middle categories of fitness—those who typically exercised but not regularly and strenuously—showed a death rate of 27.1 percent. Their rate was closer to the fittest group than to the least-fit group. This was also true for the women but less dramatically so; the middle-fitness group of women had a death rate of 20.5 percent.

Those findings were considered particularly significant because other studies had indicated that only about every tenth adult American exercised vigorously and regularly despite two decades or more of "exercise awareness" in the United States. This study showed that among the fitter participants, the drop in the death rate was chiefly associated with heart disease and cancer. Dr. Blair said that the study was the first one measuring fitness to detect a lower death rate for cancer. But he declined to make any recommendations in regard to that finding until more information became available. Some medical researchers previously noted a low prevalence of colon cancer among athletes; one explanation was that exercise increased bowel motility.

The linkage between heart disease and exercise had been more firmly established over the years. This study indicated that in several cases men who had high blood pressure or high cholesterol levels but otherwise were physically fit were less at risk than physically unfit men with low blood pressure or cholesterol.

> *Following are excerpts from the study, "Physical Fitness and All-Cause Mortality," conducted by Dr. Steven N. Blair and colleagues at the Institute for Aerobics Research and Cooper Clinic, in Dallas, and published November 3, 1989, in the* Journal of the American Medical Association:

Physical activity is inversely associated with morbidity and mortality from several chronic diseases. The apparently protective effect of a more active life is seen for occupational activity and death from cardiovascular disease and colon cancer, and for leisure-time physical activity and cardiovascular disease. Higher levels of leisure-time physical activity are associated with increased longevity in college alumni. These associations of sedentary habits to health appear to be independent of confounding by other well-established risk factors. Furthermore, the relationship of physical fitness (an attribute) to physical activity (a behavior) and disease rates is controversial, and it is uncertain whether physical activity sufficient to increase physical fitness is required for health benefits.

In contrast to physical activity, published studies on physical fitness and mortality are few, typically with fewer than 20,000 person-years of follow-up, and usually limited to men. Physical activity is an important determinant of physical fitness; so to some extent, fitness is an objective marker for habitual physical activity. Physical fitness can be measured more objectively than physical activity, and thus may be more useful clinically. Research studies that include the measurement of physical fitness may provide additional insight into the contribution of a physically active way of life to decreased risk of morbidity and mortality.

Here, we report all-cause and cause-specific mortality by physical fitness categories in men and women followed up for 110,482 person-years, or an average of more than 8 years.

Subjects and Methods

Subjects

The 13,344 study participants comprised 10,224 men and 3,120 women who received a preventive medical examination at the Cooper Clinic in Dallas, Tex, during 1970 to 1981. Patients were included in the study if they were residents of the United States at their first clinic visit, had a complete examination, and achieved at least 85% of their age-predicted maximal heart rate on a treadmill exercise test at the baseline clinic visit. . . .

Patients were assigned to physical fitness categories based on their age, sex, and maximal time on the treadmill test. Treadmill-time quintiles were determined for each age and sex group. Individuals with a treadmill time in the first quintile were assigned to the low-fit group. Those with scores in the second through the fifth quintiles constituted fitness groups 2 through 5, respectively. Thus, assignment to a fitness category was based on age and sex norms of treadmill performance rather than by an absolute fitness standard. . . .

Cigarette-smoking status was determined from the medical questionnaire. Patients who reported smoking at present or within the 2 years preceding the baseline examination were designated as current smokers. This conservative definition for smoking was adopted because many smokers may have quit temporarily in preparation for their preventive medical examination, and mortality risk for recent quitters is similar to continuing smokers. Results from the smoking analyses were essentially unchanged when current smoking was defined as cigarette smoking at baseline or during the year preceding the examination.

Height and weight were measured on a standard physician's scale, and body mass index was calculated (kilograms per meter squared). Blood pressure was measured by the auscultatory method with a mercury sphygmomanometer, diastolic pressure being recorded as the disappearance of sound. Serum samples were analyzed for cholesterol and glucose by automated techniques.

Mortality Surveillance

Study subjects were followed up for mortality from their first clinic visit through 1985. The average length of follow-up was slightly more than 8 years, and the total follow-up experience for the cohort was 110,482 person-years. Several follow-up methods were used. Decedents were identified by reports from family, friends, and business associates; responses to appointment reminders; and other mailings from the clinic. The entire cohort was sent a case-finding and disease-identifying questionnaire in 1982. Nonrespondents were followed-up via the Social Security Administration files, the Department of Motor Vehicles in the subject's state of residence, and a nationwide credit bureau network. The National Death Index has been used since it was established in 1979 to search for possible matches in this cohort. Finally, individuals with unknown vital status and with a Dallas-area address were checked in local telephone directories. Follow-up has been difficult since patients come from all 50 states and are mobile and since a significant portion of the follow-up occurred prior to the establishment of the National Death Index. Despite these limitations, vital status has been ascertained for 95% of the cohort. . . .

Data Analysis

A total of 283 deaths were identified in the cohort over the average of approximately 8 years of follow-up. Mortality rates per 10,000 person-years of follow-up were computed for each of the five fitness categories and age-adjusted by the direct method, using the total experience in the population as the standard. Age differences were adjusted by the following groups: 20 to 39, 40 to 49, 50 to 59, and 60 or more years. These rates were then used to compute relative risks (RR) of death for each fitness quintile as well as for examination of the role other variables played in confounding the relationship between fitness and mortality. Attributable risk percentages (etiologic fractions) for those groups exposed to adverse characteristics were calculated as were population-based estimates of attributable risks. . . .

Results

Patients in this study are from middle to upper socioeconomic strata; approximately 70% are college graduates. Most are employed in professional, executive, or white-collar positions. More than 99% are white. . . . Decedents were somewhat older, less physically fit, and had less favorable risk profiles. . . . Less-fit individuals had a higher risk of death than the more-fit men and women. Increased RR for all-cause mortality was significantly higher for the least-fit quintile in men, and for the two least-fit quintiles in women. . . . The findings show an increased risk, as expected, for all variables except body mass index, which shows a trend in the expected direction only in women.

Multiple logistic analyses were done to estimate RR of death in the fitness categories while adjusting for potential confounding. . . .

Subclinical disease could cause poor performance on the treadmill and also lead to elevated death rates in patients presumed to be healthy at baseline. Mortality rates in both short- and long-term follow-up were examined to test the hypothesis that preexisting disease was confounding the relationship between fitness and mortality. . . .

Increased risk of death in low-fit men and women is clearly illustrated . . . and this pattern generally holds across risk strata for the other variables. In several cases . . . high-fit [male] patients at the highest level of either blood pressure or cholesterol have a lower risk than unfit patients with low blood pressure or cholesterol level. For example, fit but hypercholesterolemic men have double the risk (death rate of 27 per 10,000 person-years compared with 14 per 10,000 person-years) of the fit men with lower cholesterol levels, but these fit, hypercholesterolemic men have only a little more than one third the risk (death rate of 27 per 10,000 person-years compared with 68 per 10,000 person-years) of unfit men with low cholesterol levels. . . .

The results presented here support the hypothesis that a low level of physical fitness is an important risk factor for all-cause mortality in both men and women. . . . If all unfit persons became fit, reductions in death rates of 9.0% in men and 15.3% in women might be expected.

Comment

The results presented herein show a strong and graded association between physical fitness and mortality due to all causes, cardiovascular disease, and cancer. The findings are consistent for men and women and hold after adjustment for age, serum cholesterol level, blood pressure, smoking habit, fasting blood glucose level, family history of CHD [coronary heart disease], and length of follow-up. Strengths of the study are a maximal exercise test, participants free of known chronic disease at baseline, wide range of physical fitness, objective end points (mortality), a large sample (13,344 men and women) with extensive follow-up experience (85,049 person-years of observation for men and 25,433 for women), and a large enough sample of women to permit meaningful analyses. We believe that this is the only study of physical fitness and health that meets all these criteria. . . .

U.S. CATHOLIC BICENTENNIAL OBSERVED IN BALTIMORE
November 5, 1989

American Catholic bishops and other dignitaries gathered in Baltimore on November 5 to observe the bicentennial of the Diocese of Baltimore. Established in 1789, it was the first Catholic diocese in the United States, which at that time comprised only the thirteen original states. A decree formally creating the diocese was signed in Rome by Pope Pius VI that November 6—two hundred years, less one day before the commemorative ceremony in Baltimore.

The pontiff named John Carroll, descendant of an old-line Maryland family, bishop of the new diocese, thereby giving him spiritual authority over forty thousand Catholics clustered mainly in Maryland and Pennsylvania, which alone among the American colonies had welcomed Catholics. Maryland's first Catholics arrived in 1634 aboard two small, crowded ships, the Ark *and the* Dove, *to settle a vast tract of land along the Chesapeake Bay.*

Charles I, a monarch with Catholic tendencies, had granted Lord Baltimore the land. Lord Baltimore died before the charter became official, but his son Cecil, the second Lord Baltimore, shared the father's vision of Maryland as a refuge for fellow Catholics and the source of a new family fortune. Cecil stayed in England to fight off political intrigues, but his brothers Leonard and Philip went to the new colony. Leonard, the colony's first governor, ordered the ships to delay their landing at St. Clement's Island until March 25, "the day of the Annunciation of the Most Holy Virgin Mary." Coming ashore, Jesuit priests offered a mass of thanksgiving, which historians believe was the first Catholic mass said in British North America.

619

*At that time, the Catholic church was already well established in areas
that would later be added to the United States—notably Florida and the
Southwest, colonized by the Spanish; and the upper Midwest, inhabited
by the French. St. Augustine, Florida, and Santa Fe, New Mexico, both
claim the oldest existing churches in the United States. However, the
Baltimore diocese—later archdiocese—took a leadership role in expanding American Catholicism and its concerns as the frontier advanced, and
its seniority continued to be acknowledged by the American church.*

*An expression of that seniority was the November 5 gathering in
Baltimore. The National Conference of Bishops, which normally meets
each autumn in Washington, D.C., scheduled its 1989 meeting in Baltimore instead, to coincide with the bicentennial events. The bishops,
joined by other religious figures and civil officials, attended a mass at the
Basilica of the Assumption in Baltimore. The Most Rev. William H.
Keeler, the archbishop of Baltimore, recalled in his homily some of the
ways in which the historic see had helped to shape American Catholicism
during the past two centuries.*

*Following are excerpts from Archbishop William H. Keeler's
homily at the bicentennial mass celebrated in Baltimore's
Basilica of the Assumption, November 5, 1989:*

On November 5, 1831, exactly 158 years ago today, perhaps the most
astute and influential observer of this nation and its ways, a young
Frenchman, Alexis de Tocqueville, was in Baltimore and went to pay a
visit. He called on Maryland's senior citizen, the last surviving signer of the
Declaration of Independence, Charles Carroll of Carrollton.

De Tocqueville found a man of 94, standing straight and tall, clear-
minded and rejoicing in his memories of having risked life and fortune for
his nation at its birth. In Charles Carroll, a Catholic and a patriot, the
foreign visitor saw personified the unique way in which religious faith
could be separate from and yet undergird the free institutions of the
United States of America.

And today we celebrate Charles Carroll's cousin and collaborator, John.
We do this guided by the word of God. The author of the Book of Wisdom
recalls God's loving care for all creation and asks a question, "How could a
thing remain, unless you willed it; or be preserved, had it not been called
forth by you? "

What has remained and been preserved and what we remember with
praise and thanks to God is the Catholic Church in the United States of
America. We do so with a sentiment common to John Carroll and those
who came after him, a sentiment which sees God's provident and loving
care in the evolution of this land and in the opportunities for religious
freedom it affords.

We rejoice that leading us in our celebration is one come from Rome, His
Eminence Agostino Cardinal Casaroli, the Secretary of State of the Holy

Father and his close collaborator in the care of all the Church. . . . In your presence we recall with thanks how, two hundred years ago tomorrow, Pope Pius VI signed at the Basilica of St. Mary Major in Rome the decree whereby he established the Diocese of Baltimore and appointed John Carroll its first bishop.

The flock then was not large—some 40,000 people, most of them in Maryland and Pennsylvania, with some scattered throughout the other eleven colonies.

When, many months later, official word of this decision came to him, John Carroll wrote to affirm his personal, loyal and loving attachment to the Holy Father. Your Eminence, as we greet you we ask you to carry from the spiritual descendants of John Carroll and his early collaborators that same pledge of fidelity and love and prayer to our Holy Father.

Now, with Archbishop [John] May [of St. Louis], the president of our Conference, [former] Archbishop [William D.] Borders [of Baltimore], national chairman of the Bicentennial Committee and chief architect of this observance, and all God's people in this historic See, I welcome also the cardinals, archbishops and bishops who come from diocesan churches grown from the one diocese of 1789, as well as others who have come from Rome and elsewhere. We are deeply grateful for your presence.

And we bishops, all of us, greet with joy representatives of other Christian churches and of the Jewish faith. Your presence bespeaks a Maryland tradition going back to John Carroll.

We welcome civic leaders of the United States government and of this state and city, grateful for the heritage of freedom and justice which you uphold and serve.

We greet distinguished guests from far and near. We are especially delighted that so many national Catholic organizations are represented. We welcome priests, deacons, religious men and women, and our laity, happy to acknowledge through you some fifty-five million members of the Church in the nearly 20,000 parishes of our 188 diocesan families. . . .

One hundred years ago this week, our predecessors gathered here to mark the first centennial of the Church. They came twice to this, the first cathedral of the land, and heard two addresses. First, Archbishop Patrick Ryan of Philadelphia preached at the end of the Jubilee Mass and recalled how, amid many trials, the Church in the United States had grown from the mustard seed of Carroll to some nine million members in a century. He painted a dark picture of the crosses carried in often harsh and hostile days of discrimination and of the Church's need to preach to its people and to its neighbors a call to simplicity and holiness in the face of a materialistic society. He spoke, it seems, for at least an hour.

That same Sunday evening, the cathedral was thronged again for solemn vespers. Archbishop John Ireland of St. Paul took the pulpit. He looked toward a brighter future, full of opportunities in which he hoped the promise of American initiative in action would be complemented and elevated through the gospel preached by the Church. He foresaw and sought understanding and support from other churches and faith groups.

621

He, too, spoke for more than an hour. . . .

Let me rather recall a few events related to the history of the See of Baltimore, events which touched and helped to shape the life of the Catholic Church in this land. . . .

An early "work of faith" for which John Carroll labored with intensity was that of education: He founded the first Catholic college at Georgetown just two hundred years ago; with the Sulpicians, the first seminary and college in Baltimore came soon afterwards. De Tocqueville would learn on his visit that "the best institutions of education in Maryland are Catholic" and serve both men and women well.

In those early days, just a few blocks from here, with Archbishop Carroll's encouragement, St. Elizabeth Ann Seton began her school, later transferred to Emmitsburg [Maryland]. Here, in 1829, Mother Mary Elizabeth Lange launched the Oblate Sisters of Providence, the first religious community to serve especially the spiritual needs of Black Catholic children.

Meanwhile, yet other "works of faith" grew apace: throughout the colonies priests and people cooperated to form parish communities. The Carmelite nuns came to Maryland in 1791 to found the first contemplative monastery.

As the decades of the first hundred years went on, religious congregations of men and women came from Europe or were founded in the United States to begin hospitals, orphanages, and other endeavors to minister the healing and the love of Jesus.

To serve and lead the people in all these "works of faith," successive popes responded by establishing new diocesan churches and appointing bishops for them. While this first cathedral was still rising, John Carroll ordained in small churches not far away the first bishops of Philadelphia, Boston and Bardstown. In time, in this church, the gift of the Spirit in ordination was conferred on 35 other bishops to serve in dioceses and vicariates apostolic from New York City and Hartford to Santa Fe and Tucson, from Florida, Mobile and Savannah, to Detroit, Chicago, and beyond to Idaho.

The gift of the Spirit for "works of faith" was implored as well when all the bishops of this country were called to assemble in this cathedral, first for six provincial councils of the one province of the United States. Then, when new provinces were formed, they met here in plenary council to chart a common course for the Church throughout the land. Three times they gathered in Baltimore for such councils, beginning and concluding each with solemn sessions here.

One participant at the First Plenary Council in 1852 had been ordained a bishop less than two months earlier, just a block from here at St. Alphonsus Church. His name was John Neumann. The Council urged the establishment of parish schools. St. John Neumann went on to Philadelphia where he set about on doing just that with enormous zeal. Later, the Third Plenary Council (1884) was to move from exhortation to mandate regarding parish schools as the bishops considered how best to prepare immigrant children for lives of faith and civic usefulness in a new land. . . .

Today we invoke the memories of the Carrolls, John and Charles, and we pray again for our America, the America they loved. May the continued blessings of freedom which meant so much to them be used responsibly, with renewed reverence for God, God's ways and God's creation. . . .

In this celebration of the Eucharist, there are precious reminders of the past: John Carroll's pastoral staff and the altar stone he used; the chalice Pope Pius VII gave to Archbishop Marechal, used at the dedication of this cathedral and in the Masses of the Provincial and Plenary Councils.

There is this great church itself, which John Carroll wished dedicated to Mary under the title of her Assumption. May her powerful prayer be with us now as, beneath the signs of bread and wine, we acknowledge the Lord Jesus Himself, acting in the Eucharist. Victor over sin and death, He renews His promise of new hope and strength. Thus given courage, may we together, faithfully, prepare ourseves to begin a third century as the organized family of faith here; prepare ourselves to begin the third milennium of the Church on earth.

We pray with the Apostle John, "Come, Lord Jesus, come!" Come with the Spirit's gifts of faith and hope and love to sustain us for Your work on earth. Amen.

STATEMENTS ON BERLIN WALL
AND GERMAN REUNIFICATION
November 9, 28, and 29, 1989

In a year of swift and far-reaching political changes in Eastern Europe, none was more dramatic than a besieged East German government's decision to open the Berlin Wall, which for twenty-eight years had been the visible symbol of a divided Germany and the Cold War. On November 9, immediately after East Germany lifted emigration and other travel restrictions on its people, Berliners from East and West surged through border crossings that once held them apart. They took part in a massive, impromptu celebration that involved many of Berlin's 4 million residents. Millions of others, in Germany and abroad, remained in front of their television sets for hours on end watching the joyous frenzy in Berlin.

East Germany said officially that, although opened, the wall would not be dismantled immediately. However, thousands of individual Germans—with only hammers and hands—tore big gaps in it during the next few days, showing their extreme distaste for the barrier, which was erected in 1961 by the Communist government of East Germany to halt an exodus of its citizens to the West. An initial twenty-nine miles of cinder blocks and barbed wire went up that August 21, splitting the Soviet-controlled sector of Berlin (East Berlin) from the rest of the city, which was placed under American, British, and French control at the end of World War II. The wall later was extended around all of West Berlin, sealing it off from East Germany. Both states were created in the breakup of wartime Germany.

In little more than two months, East Germany had changed from a hard-line Communist state to the focal point of a reform movement sweeping the Soviet bloc. A lid on the people's aspirations, long held in place by the firm hand of the Soviet Union, had burst off when Soviet leader Mikhail S. Gorbachev loosened the grip. East Germans, aware of political liberalization in Poland and Hungary, took to the streets protesting their government's repressive measures. They had long looked westward across the Iron Curtain to the prosperity and freedom their fellow Germans enjoyed.

The "German Question"

The "German question"—how and when East and West Germany might end their forty-two-year-old division and reunite as a single country—emerged with a new urgency from the East European reform movement of 1989. During the previous four decades of East-West tension, the question of German reunification had been superseded by more pressing concerns over Western security and West Germany's key role in the North Atlantic Treaty Association (NATO). But as the Cold War fizzled out on the streets of Eastern Europe, pressure to resolve the German question was felt once again.

The call for German reunification came directly from demonstrators in the streets of Leipzig, East Berlin, and other East German cities at the center of that country's anti-Communist revolution. In May, when Hungary removed the barbed-wire fences along its border with Austria, East German citizens began streaming across the opened border to the West. The exodus grew in size and became an expression of popular rejection of the country's system of government. Finally, it produced a political crisis that on October 18 forced Erich Honecker, the longtime East German Communist party leader and head of state, to step down.

Honecker's successor, former security police chief Egon Krenz, purged the party leadership and lifted travel restrictions, hopeful that reforms could save the regime that had governed East Germany for the past four decades. But it was not enough. On November 4, half a million East Berliners took to the streets to demand free elections and freedom of travel. East Germans in other cities followed suit. On November 9, Krenz opened the Berlin Wall. Political pressure continued in the streets of East German cities. Krenz and members of the Communist party's ruling Politburo and Central Committee resigned, leaving the party to negotiate with opposition groups on the future of East Germany's political system. As a result, free, multiparty elections were scheduled for May 6, 1990.

Allied Concern over Reunification

The rapid pace of East Germany's anti-Communist revolution raised red flags among Western leaders whose memory of Nazi Germany tempered their enthusiasm for the democratic reforms being introduced in Berlin. British prime minister Margaret Thatcher and French president François Mitterrand were among those NATO leaders who expressed concern that a reunified Germany might be less committed to the Western alliance than West Germany currently was. Reiterating a longstanding U.S. policy of support for eventual German reunification, President George Bush said on October 24 that he did not share those fears. But the opening of the Berlin Wall less than three weeks later caught him by surprise. At a news conference on November 9, shortly after word of the wall's opening reached Washington, Bush dodged reporters' efforts to pin him down to an official U.S. position on the German question, saying, "It's way too early to speak on that."

It would take policy makers in Washington another three weeks to formulate a position. On November 29, Secretary of State James A. Baker III identified four "principles," or conditions of U.S. support, that must govern any future move toward German reunification. While the United States would not attempt to define the extent to which the two Germanys should merge, Baker said, a united Germany must be allied with the West, should come about gradually, and should observe the terms of the Helsinki Final Act. That declaration, signed in 1975 by thirty-five nations, including all European countries, Canada, and the United States, ratified the existing borders of all participating nations.

Kohl's Ten-Point Plan

The previous day, West German chancellor Helmut Kohl outlined a ten-point plan for reunification. He envisioned that, after free elections in East Germany, a period of increasing rapprochement between the two Germanys would culminate in a kind of "confederation." During this period, the two states would retain their sovereignty and membership in their respective military alliances. According to Kohl's plan, a unified German federation would emerge from the confederation.

Kohl's plan initially was greeted as a constructive guideline for eventual reunification of the two Germanys. But it quickly became the target of criticism both at home and abroad. West German opposition leaders accused Kohl of trying to capitalize on the issue in view of national elections to be held in 1990. West Germany's allies were miffed by Kohl's failure to consult with them before issuing a proposal on a question of obvious consequence to the military alliance. They also were alarmed by his failure to mention the status of a confederated Germany's borders, specifically East Germany's eastern border with Poland along the Oder and Neisse rivers. Poland, which gained the German provinces of Silesia and Pomerania after World War II, feared that a reunified Germany might try to regain this territory. Because no peace treaty was ever signed by wartime Germany—an entity that no longer exists—the Oder-Neisse Line was never unequivocally recognized until the Helsinki Act of 1975.

> *Following is the East German government's announcement on November 9, 1989, as reported by the official news agency ADN, that it would open border crossings to the West, including the Berlin Wall; excerpts from the White House transcript of President George Bush's reaction to that news,*

627

*as expressed to reporters in the Oval Office, November 9;
from an English-language translation of Chancellor Helmut
Kohl's televised speech to the West German Budestag
(National Assembly), November 28; and the response by
Secretary of State James A. Baker III to Kohl's speech,
November 29.:*

EAST GERMAN TRAVEL DECISION

The Government spokesman told ADN [the official East German news
agency] the Council of Ministers of East Germany has decided immediately to set in force the following stipulations for private journeys and
permanent emigration until a corresponding parliamentary law comes into
effect:

1. Private journeys into foreign countries can be applied for without
   fulfilling preconditions (reasons for travel, relatives). Permission will
   be given at short notice.
2. The relevant passport and registration offices of the regional offices
   of the People's Police in East Germany have been ordered to issue
   visas for permanent emigration immediately without the present
   preconditions for permanent emigration having been fulfilled. Application for permanent emigration is also possible as before at departments of internal affairs.
3. Permanent emigration is allowed across all border crossing points
   between East Germany and West Germany and West Berlin.
4. Because of this the temporary issuing of permits in East German
   missions abroad and permanent emigration using East German
   identity cards through third countries will no longer apply.

BUSH'S NEWS CONFERENCE

The President. We just wanted to make a brief statement here. I've
just been briefed by the Secretary of State and my national security
adviser on the latest news coming out of Germany. And of course, I
welcome the decision by the East German leadership to open the borders
to those wishing to emigrate or travel. And this, if it's implemented fully,
certainly conforms with the Helsinki Final Act, which the GDR [German
Democratic Republic] signed. And if the GDR goes forward now, this wall
built in '61 will have very little relevance. And it clearly is a good
development in terms of human rights. And I must say that after
discussing this here with the Secretary of State and the national security
adviser, I am very pleased with this development....
    Q. Is this the end of the Iron Curtain, sir?
    The President. Well, I don't think any single event is the end of what

you might call the Iron Curtain, but clearly this is a long way from the harshest Iron Curtain days—a long way from that.

Q. Mr. President, what do you think the implications are for the Warsaw Pact now? I mean, can we say that this may be an indication that they're headed toward a loosening or even a dismantling of the Warsaw Pact?

The President. I think you have to say what you mean by Warsaw Pact. I mean, it seems to me that it's certainly a loosening up in terms of travel. It concurs with the Helsinki Final Act, and it is a very good development.

Our objective is a Europe whole and free. And is it a step towards that? I would say yes. Gorbachev talks about a common home. Is it a step towards that? Probably so....

Q. What's the danger here of events just spinning out of control? Secretary Baker commented earlier about how rapid the pace of change has been in Eastern Europe. Nobody really expected this to happen as quickly as it did. Is there a danger here that things are accelerating too quickly?

The President. I wouldn't want to say this kind of development makes things to be moving too quickly at all. It's the kind of development that we have long encouraged by our strong support for the Helsinki Final Act. So, I'm not going to hypothecate that anything goes too fast.

Q. So, you don't see—

The President. But we are handling it in a way where we are not trying to give anybody a hard time. We're saluting those who can move forward with democracy. We are encouraging the concept of a Europe whole and free. And so, we just welcome it. But I don't like to go into a lot of hypotheses about too much change or too rapid change or what I'd do, what our whole team here would do if something went wrong. I think it's been handled by the West very well; and certainly we salute the people in East Germany, the GDR, whose aspirations for freedom seem to be a little further down the road now.

Q. Mr. President, do you think now that East Germany appears to be moving in the direction of Poland and Hungary that the rest of the Eastern bloc can continue to resist this? I'm thinking of Czechoslovakia, Bulgaria, Romania? Will they be the next?

The President. No, I don't think anyone can resist it, in Europe or in the Western Hemisphere....

Q. Did you ever imagine anything like this happening?

Q. On your watch?

The President. We've imagined it, but I can't say that I foresaw this development at this stage. Now, I didn't foresee it, but imagining it, yes. When I talk about a Europe whole and free, we're talking about this kind of freedom to come and go, this kind of staying with and living by the Helsinki Final Act, which gives the people the rights to come and go.

Q. In what you just said, that this is a sort of great victory for our side in the big East-West battle, but you don't seem elated. And I'm wondering if you're thinking of the problems.

The President. I am not an emotional kind of guy.

Q. Well, how elated are you?

The President. I'm very pleased. And I've been very pleased with a lot of other developments. . . .

KOHL'S REUNIFICATION PLAN

. . . We are all overjoyed about the newly won freedom of movement for those living in divided Germany. We, along with those Germans in the GDR [German Democratic Republic—East Germany], are happy that the wall and border blockades could finally, after decades, be overcome peacefully. . . .

We, in the free part of Germany, stand in solidarity alongside our fellow countrymen. . . .

Chances are arising to overcome the division of Europe and that of our fatherland. The Germans, who are reuniting in the spirit of freedom, will never pose a threat to, but will rather be an asset for, a Europe which is growing together.

The move to change, which we are currently experiencing, is primarily the deserts of the people who are so impressively demonstrating their will for freedom. It is also, however, the result of the many political developments of past years. We have, with our policy, substantially contributed to this.

Decisively important was the fact that we initially conducted this policy based on the solid foundation of our integration in the community of free democracies. The uniformity and steadfastness on the part of the alliance during the difficult test of 1983 have paid off. We have strengthened the backbone of the reform movement in central, eastern and south-eastern Europe by pursuing our clear course within the Atlantic Alliance and in the European Community.

We have, with the transition to new stages of economic and political integration within the European Community, successfully further developed the model for the free coalition of European peoples, which has attractive powers far beyond the community.

On the other hand, [Soviet] General Secretary [Mikhail S.] Gorbachev's reform policy within the Soviet Union and the new way of thinking in Soviet foreign policy were a decisive prerequisite. Without the recognition of the rights of peoples and countries to choose their own way, the reform movements in other countries of the Warsaw Pact would not have been successful.

The dramatic occurrences in the GDR would not have taken place if Poland and Hungary had not led the way with far-reaching political, economic and social reforms. I welcome the fact that changes are also becoming apparent in Bulgaria, and the USSR. . . .

The CSCE [Helsinki Accords] process also played an important role, whereby we, together with our partners, have always insisted on the dismantling of sources of tension, on dialogue and co-operation, and most particularly on the respect of human rights.

Thanks to the continual summit diplomacy of the major powers and the numerous intensive East-West meetings of heads of state and government, a new trust was able to develop in East-West relations. The historical breakthrough in disarmament and arms control is a visible expression of this trust.

The broadly based contractual policy of the federal government towards the Soviet Union and all other Warsaw Pact states has made considerable contributions to the development of East-West relations and has given them important impulses. . . .

Since 1987, millions of fellow countrymen from the GDR have visited us, amongst them many young people. Our "small step policy" has, in difficult times, kept awake and sharpened the consciousness for the unity of the nation, and has deepened the Germans' sense of togetherness. . . .

Today, we have a greater sense of understanding and community in Germany and Europe than has ever been felt since the end of World War II. . . .

As everyone can see, we have reached a new epoch in European and German history, an age which points beyond the status quo, and beyond the former political structures in Europe. . . .

All who carry responsibility in and for Europe have to make allowance for the will of people and nations. We are all called upon to design a new architecture for the house of Europe and for a permanent and just order of peace on our continent as both General Secretary Gorbachev and I reaffirmed in our common declaration of June 13th this year. . . .

I have offered to extensively extend our aid and co-operation should fundamental change of the political and economic system in the GDR be firmly agreed upon and put irrevocably into effect. By irrevocable, we mean that the East German leadership comes to an understanding with opposition groups concerning constitutional change and a new electoral law.

We support the demands for free, equal and secret elections in the GDR which incorporates independent and non-socialist parties. The power monopoly of the SED [East German Communist Party] must be lifted.

The introduction of constitutional state conditions means, above all, the abolition of laws concerning political crimes.

Economic aid can only be effective if fundamental reforms within the economic system take place. Former experience with all Comecon [Communist bloc] states proves this. The bureaucratic planned economy must be dismantled.

We do not want to stabilize conditions which have become indefensible. Economic improvement can only occur if the GDR opens its doors to Western investment, if conditions of free enterprise are created and if private enterprise becomes possible. There are already examples of this in Hungary and Poland, examples which can be used by the GDR for orientation. Under these conditions, joint-ventures would soon be possible. There is already a large degree of willingness to undertake such ventures both at home and abroad.

These are not official preconditions but factual prerequisites needed before our aid can take effect. . . .

[East German] Prime Minister [Hans] Modrow spoke in his governmental declaration of a contractual community. We are prepared to accept these thoughts. The proximity and the special nature of the relationships between our two states in Germany demand an increasingly close-knit network of agreements in all sectors and at all levels.

This co-operation will also increasingly demand common institutions. Commissions which already exist can be given new tasks and further commissions can be called into being. Here I am particularly thinking of the economic, transport, environmental, scientific and technical, health and cultural sectors. It goes without saying that Berlin will be fully included in these co-operative efforts.

I call upon all social groups and institutions to actively participate in the development of such a contractual community.

. . . We are also prepared to take a further decisive step, namely, to develop confederative structures between the two states in Germany with the goal of creating a federation, a federal state order in Germany. A legitimate democratic government within the GDR is [an] unrelinquishable prerequisite.

We can envisage that after free elections the following institutions be formed:

- A common governmental committee for permanent consultation and political harmonization,
- Common technical committees,
- A common parliamentary gremium [forum].

Previous policy with reference to the GDR had to essentially concentrate itself on small steps, these strove to alleviate the results of being a divided nation and uphold and sharpen the consciousness for the unity of the nation. If in the future, a democratically legitimized, that is a freely elected government becomes our partner, totally new perspectives are available.

New forms of institutional co-operation could be created and further developed in stages. Such a coming together is in the interest of the continuation of German history. State organizations within Germany are always confederations or federations. At this time, we can once again make use of this historical precedence.

Nobody knows how a reunified Germany will look. I am however sure that it will come, if unity is wanted by the German nation.

. . . The development of inner-German relations remains bedded in the pan-European process and in East-West relations. The future structure of Germany must fit into the future architecture of Europe as a whole. The West has to provide pace-making aid here with its concept for a permanent and just European order of peace.

In our common declaration of June this year, the Soviet leader Gorbachev and I speak of the building components of a "common European house." I can name, for example,

- The unlimited respect of the integrity and safety of each state. Each state has the right to choose its own political and social system.
- The unlimited respect of the principles and standards of international law, particularly respect for the peoples' right of self-determination.
- The realization of human rights.
- Respect for, and the upholding of the historically based cultures of the people of Europe.

With all of these points, as Mr. Gorbachev and I prescribed, we want to link onto the historically based European traditions and help to overcome the divisions in Europe.

... The powers of attraction and the aura of the European community is and remains a constant feature in the pan-European development. We want to strengthen this further.

The European Community is now required to approach the reform-oriented states in central, eastern, and southern Europe with openness and flexibility. This was ascertained unanimously by the heads of state and government of the EEC member states during their recent meeting in Paris....

We understand the process leading to the recovery of the German unity to be of European concern. It must, therefore, be considered together with European integration. In keeping with this, the European Community must remain open to a democratic GDR and to other democratic countries from central and south-eastern Europe. The EC must not end on the Elba [River], but must remain open to the East....

If the countries of central and south-eastern Europe fulfill the necessary prerequisites, we would also greet their entrance into the European Council, especially into the convention for the protection of human rights and fundamental freedoms.

... The CSCE process is and remains a crucial part of the total European architecture and must be further advanced....

The surmounting of the separation of Europe and the division of Germany demands far-reaching and speedy steps pertaining to disarmament and arms control. Disarmament and arms control must keep step with political developments and therefore, might have to be accelerated.

This is particularly true of the negotiations in Vienna for the dismantling of conventional armed forces in Europe and for the agreement upon measures to establish trust, such as the worldwide ban of chemical weapons. This also demands that the nuclear potential of world powers be reduced to a strategic minimal level....

We can only peacefully overcome the division of Europe and Germany together and in an atmosphere of mutual trust.

...Every successful reform step means more stability and increased freedom and security for all of Europe.

BAKER ON REUNIFICATION

On the question of German reunification, let me simply say that I think that our position on that should essentially embrace four principles, if you will. First of all, that self-determination must be pursued without prejudice as to its outcome; that is, we really shouldn't endorse or exclude any particular vision of unity. Unity can mean a lot of things. It can mean a single federal state; it can mean a confederation; or it could mean something else.

If there is unification—the second principle, I think—if there is unification, it should occur in the context of Germany's continued alignment with NATO [North Atlantic Treaty Organization] and an increasingly integrated European Community; that is, there should be no trade of neutralism for unity, and there should be no dilution of the Federal Republic of Germany's liberal democratic character.

Third principle: In the interests of general European stability, I think I would prefer to see moves toward unification be peaceful, gradual, and part of a step-by-step process.

And lastly, with respect to the question of borders, which was not addressed in Chancellor Kohl's speech, I think we should reiterate our support for the principles of the Helsinki Final Act, recognizing the inviolability where I said, "We are of the view that we should seize the opportunity where we can and where it is to the mutual advantage of the United States and Soviet Union, seize the opportunity to engage." That would include political engagement. It would include military and arms control engagement. And it would certainly include economic engagement. What's really needed here, it seems to me, more than anything else on the economic side, is that we give them technical economic cooperation. They are, after all, talking about changing a system that has existed for 70 years and that is totally foreign to our most basic concepts of free market economics.

COMMUNIST CONCESSIONS
IN CZECHOSLOVAKIA
November 28, 1989

Communism's long rule in Czechoslovakia began to crumble in November under the weight of massive street demonstrations by Czechs demanding political freedom. The critical event occurred November 28, when the embattled Communist government pledged to share power with the rising opposition. By the year's end, the country's leadership had passed into the hands of once-beleaguered dissidents, leaving communism virtually powerless in a country where its control had been pervasive and often harsh during most of the past forty-one years.

The events in Czechoslovakia were part of a pattern in Eastern Europe. In Poland, Hungary, East Germany, Romania, and Bulgaria—the other countries of the so-called Soviet bloc—the old order was also cast out. Soviet president Mikhail S. Gorbachev, whose own liberalization in the Soviet Union had ignited freedom demands in the satellite countries, declined to rescue the faltering governments.

Without Gorbachev's help, those governments could not withstand the popular outpouring of pent-up grievances and frustrations. In country after country, Communist attempts to invoke half-hearted reform measures were met with scorn. Hungary's Communist party disbanded and Poland's became a minority faction in a new Solidarity-led government. Romania's communist dictator Nicolae Ceaucescu lost his life. East Germany pushed toward reunification with West Germany. In Czechoslovakia, the people demanded a transformation of the political system. (Hungary's Belated Eulogy for 1956 Uprising Heroes, p. 339; Gorbachev's Vision of a Common Europe, p. 399; Speeches Marking Poland's New Era, p. 523; Statements on Berlin Wall and German Reunification, p. 625;

Bucharest's Announcement of Romanian Ruler's Execution, p. 709)

Czech Regime's Hard-Line Stand

Amid the turmoil sweeping Eastern Europe, the Czechoslovakian regime had attempted to stand fast. Milos Jakes, general secretary of the Czech Communist party, told a youth conference as late as November 12 that the party would not tolerate street protests or relax its control over the country. Only five days later, tens of thousands of university students took to the streets of Prague, the capital, to mark the fiftieth anniversary of the Nazi murder of Czech student demonstrators in 1939. In an apparent attempt to frighten the latter-day students into obedience, the government showed little restraint in suppressing the rally.

Thomas Omestad, an editor of Foreign Policy *magazine, reported from Prague: "The zeal with which security forces bloodied unarmed students shocked Czechoslovaks more than any other event since Soviet tanks rolled over the Prague Spring reforms of 21 years earlier." In April 1968, Communist reformers led by Alexander Dubcek introduced extensive reforms that incurred Moscow's wrath. Soviet tanks and troops later entered Prague and crushed the movement. At that time, Jakes was placed in charge of purging Dubcek and half-a-million other liberal members from the Communist party, dooming them to low-paid, menial jobs, and sometimes jail or house arrest.*

In November 1989, Soviet tanks and troops were nowhere to be seen. This time Jakes and fellow Communist hard-liners became the political casualties. The bloody student crackdown incited tens of thousands of Czechs to take to the streets November 19 to denounce police brutality. That same day, several opposition groups formed an umbrella organization, Civic Forum, to coordinate their activities. On the following days, the protests grew much bigger and spread to other cities besides Prague. Crowds numbering in the hundreds of thousands shouted their demands for free elections and the resignation of Communist leaders. A general strike was called to show that the political opposition could paralyze the country at will.

Communists Yield Control

Jakes, joined by twelve other members of the ruling Politburo, did step down November 24. According to the official press agency CTK, his resignation was accompanied by a self-critical speech to his colleagues. Jakes was quoted as saying, "We have underestimated completely the processes taking place in Poland, Hungary and especially recently in East Germany and their effect and influence on our society." Karel Urbanek, a little-known party official, replaced him as general secretary.

Hours before the resignations were announced, Dubcek made his first public appearance in Prague since 1968. The white-haired former leader stepped to the railing of a balcony overlooking historic Wenceslas Square and addressed a flag-waving crowd below. In remarks frequently :inter-

rupted by cheers and cries of "Svabodu!" (freedom), Dubcek recalled that a wise old man had said, "If there once was light, why should there be darkness?" Dubcek then told the crowd, "Let us act in such a way to bring the light back again." For twenty-one years Dubcek had lived under what amounted to house arrest. His name and picture had been banned in the Czech press and television.

To celebrating Czechs, the other hero of the hour was Vaclav Havel, a writer who had gone to prison three times for his outspoken opposition to the Communist regime. Havel had recently been thrust into the leadership of the Civic Forum. But witnesses to the public demonstrations insisted that the real leadership came from the demonstrators themselves, especially the university students.

Threats of new protests and strikes kept pressure on the Communist government. Gustav Husak, one of the Eastern bloc's remaining old-time leaders, was forced to resign as president of the country on December 9 and permit the formation of a coalition government in which Communists would hold only ten of the twenty-one Cabinet posts.

An obscure Communist bureaucrat, Marian Calfa, became prime minister, replacing Ladislav Adamec, but the balance of power had clearly shifted to the opposition. Parliament soon named Havel president and Dubcek chairman of the legislative body. Both were due to serve until June 1990, when national elections determine the makeup of a fully democratic government.

Following are excerpts in English translation from statements issued in Prague on November 29, 1989, by the Communist government and by the political opposition— the Civic Forum and a counterpart organization, Public Against Violence—spelling out the terms of an agreement between the two sides on a political restructuring in Czechoslovakia:

Government Statement

Delegations of the Central Committee of the Czechoslovak National Front and the Czechoslovak Government, headed by Prime Minister Ladislav Adamec, and the Civil Forum, led by the playwright Vaclav Havel, met today. . . .

It was agreed by the Prime Minister that a new government should be formed by Dec. 3, 1989, composed mainly of experts and professionals. It is expected that this will be a broad coalition government with representatives of other political parties and of course representatives of the Communist Party.

The Government will propose to the Federal Assembly to change three articles in the Czechoslovak Constitution: to leave out the provision on the leading role of the Czechoslovak Communist Party in society; to leave out the provision that the National Front is closed to other parties and the leading role of the Czechoslovak Communist Party in this organization; and to leave out the provision that education is carried out in the spirit of Marxism-Leninism.

This concept will be replaced by the formulation that education is carried out in harmony with scientific knowledge and at the same time with the principles of humanity and humanism.

The Czechoslovak Prime Minister promised to ask the national committee of the capital, Prague, to provide necessary facilities for the activity of the Civil Forum.

Opposition Statement

The Prime Minister promised the C.F. [Civil Forum] and P.A.V. [Public Against Violence] delegation that by Dec. 3, 1989 he will present a newly composed and reorganized Cabinet.

The Prime Minister notified the C.F. and P.A.V. delegation that tomorrow he will submit to the Federal Assembly the draft of a constitutional law which will delete from the Czechoslovak Constitution those articles which deal with the leading role of the Communist Party of Czechoslovakia and with Marxism-Leninism as the state ideology.

The Prime Minister promised the C.F. and P.A.V. delegation that he will immediately discuss with the Municipal National Committee of Prague and with other institutions that the C.F. and P.A.V. have access to the communication media, as well as conditions for the publication of a daily newspaper.

The Prime Minister informed the C.F. and P.A.V. delegation that he has already submitted to the President of the Republic the suggestion that all the political prisoners whose names were submitted by the C.F. to the Prime Minister at their last meeting be pardoned. The C.F. intends to appeal to the President that he do so before Dec. 10. . . . The C.F. is receiving information that its list was incomplete and therefore the C.F. and P.A.V. reserve the right to extend this list. . . .

The Presidium of the Federal Assembly will tomorrow . . . suggest the setting up of a special committee to investigate the brutal intervention against a peaceful demonstration of Prague students on Nov. 17 of this year. Representatives of the C.F., especially students, will be invited to participate in the work of this committee.

The delegation of the C.F. and P.A.V. requested of the Prime Minister that the changed Cabinet, as speedily as possible, issue the outlines of its program declaration which would make it plain that the Government is prepared to create the legal prerequisites for the holding of free elections, assuring freedom of assembly and association, freedom of speech and the press, the abolition of government supervision of the churches and change in the defense law, as well as others. . . .

The delegation made it plain to the Prime Minister that if the public is not satisfied with the program declaration of the Government and its transformation into specific measures, the C.F. and P.A.V. will, at the end of this year, ask the Prime Minister and his Cabinet to resign and the President of the Republic to name a new Prime Minister, which if the President considers it suitable, will be drafted by the C.F. and P.A.V.

The C.F. and P.A.V. will on Nov. 29, 1989, appeal in writing to the president, Dr. Gustav Husak, to resign before Dec. 10, 1989.

The C.F. and P.A.V. delegation proposed to the Prime Minister that the Government of Czechoslovakia submit to the Federal Assembly the draft of a constitutional law, according to which those deputies of the Federal Assembly, the Czech National council, the Slovak national council and national committees at all levels who have betrayed their oaths as deputies and have not taken into account the will and interests of the people have their mandate revoked. The method of holding by-elections will be drafted by the C.F. and P.A.V. shortly.

The C.F. and P.A.V. appeal to the Government and the Federal Assembly to immediately condemn the occupation of the country by the Warsaw Pact armies in 1968. . . .

The C.F. and P.A.V. are of the opinion that these results of the negotiations are sufficient for it to appeal to all citizens to continue in their work while maintaining a permanent strike alert. . . .

The C.F. and P.A.V. will appeal to the public that it assess the situation and results we have so far achieved in our negotiations and make its opinion known to the C.F. and P.A.V. in all available ways.

December

Bush-Gorbachev on Malta,
   Bush on NATO....................... 643

Relief Effort in Hurricane,
   Earthquake Disasters 667

Congressional Report on
   "Discarded" Children................. 671

Navigation Foundation Backs
   Peary's North Pole Claim 687

Army Denies Medal to
   Veteran for 1942 Combat 697

Bush Announces Invasion
   of Panama 701

Bucharest's Announcement of
   Romanian Ruler's Execution 709

BUSH-GORBACHEV ON MALTA, BUSH ON NATO
December 3 and 4, 1989

President George Bush and Soviet president Mikhail S. Gorbachev held shipboard "nonsummit" meetings off the Mediterranean island of Malta, December 2-3, in preparation for a full-scale summit in the United States in June 1990. This was Bush's first personal encounter as U.S. president with the Soviet leader. However, as president-elect, Bush accompanied incumbent Ronald Reagan to a December 1988 meeting with Gorbachev in New York City, where the Soviet leader addressed the United Nations General Assembly. (Gorbachev's Speech to the United Nations, Historic Documents of 1988, p. 927)

At Malta, aboard the Soviet cruise ship Maxim Gorky, *anchored in Marsaxlokk Bay, the two leaders cleared away much of the ideological debris left over from the Cold War and put relations between the two superpowers on friendlier footing. Their plans for meetings aboard two nearby battle cruisers, the Soviet* Slava *and USS* Belknap, *were scratched in favor of the larger passenger liner because of high winds and pounding waves. The tempest kept the two leaders virtually prisoners aboard their own warships for hours at a time, causing the cancellation of a dinner meeting the first evening.*

Despite the foul weather, the two leaders held long sessions and scheduled an ambitious diplomatic agenda—including accelerated negotiations on the entire range of arms control issues—to be completed in time for the June summit. At a joint news conference closing the Malta meetings, Bush said: "We stand at the threshold of a brand new era of U.S.-Soviet relations." Gorbachev saw the joint news conference—the first to be held after a meeting of U.S. and Soviet leaders—as an "important symbol."

An improvement in ties between the United States and the Soviet Union "is to be valued in and of itself, but it also should be an instrument of positive change," Bush said. Gorbachev declared that the Cold War "epoch" had ended. "We are just at the very beginning of our road, a long road, to a long-lasting peaceful period," he said.

Democratic Criticism Quieted

The American president's performance at the meeting went a long way toward quieting criticism about his cautious approach in world affairs. Most Democratic leaders in Congress—including those who had lambasted his "timidity"—congratulated Bush on his performance at Malta. However, Bush's warm embrace of Gorbachev at least temporarily regenerated fears on the Republican right about moving too quickly to dismantle Cold War defenses against Soviet expansionism.

Conservatives were especially unhappy that Bush failed to persuade Gorbachev to halt all Soviet support for leftist regimes and guerrilla movements in the Western Hemisphere. While praising Bush's actions, Vice President Dan Quayle was among the conservatives who expressed concern about the course of U.S.-Soviet relations. Quayle was quoted in the Washington Post *on December 4 as saying that the Soviet Union had not moderated its aggressive behavior in foreign affairs.*

After months of agonizing about how to deal with Moscow, Bush decided that it was in America's interest to support Gorbachev's uphill efforts to reform the Soviet economic and political systems. For the first time, Bush pledged trade concessions and offered to help the Soviet Union enter the world economy. Bush said he made up his mind after watching Gorbachev allow, and even encourage, the breakup of the Soviet empire.

Events in Eastern Europe

The astonishing events in Eastern Europe tended to upstage the Malta meetings. Under extraordinary public pressure, the entire leadership of the East German Communist party resigned on December 3 as Bush and Gorbachev were winding up their talks. The next day, mass protests in Czechoslovakia forced concessions from that country's teetering Communist leadership.

The fast pace of change in Eastern Europe demonstrated the limits of power wielded by the United States and the Soviet Union. Bush acknowledged that while the United States was enthusiastic about the changes taking place in Eastern Europe, and willing to help the reformers, it was unable to exercise much control. Gorbachev had in effect relinquished a direct Soviet political role in Eastern Europe when he declared that each state was free to act in its own best interests. (Gorbachev's Vision of a Common Europe, p. 399)

In a comment on Eastern Europe that could have been taken from the speeches of any Western politician, Gorbachev said he was impressed by "the desire of these peoples to ennoble their societies, to make them more democratic, humanitarian, to open them up to the rest of the world. So I'm encouraged and inspired by all these processes, and I'm sure this is the way they are understood and appreciated by other peoples."

Agreements at Malta

Bush and Gorbachev had said that the Malta meeting was not intended to produce major decisions, and indeed they signed no treaty documents and made no significant declarations altering their fundamental policies. But they agreed to speed up negotiations on arms control and economic issues—in effect keeping superpower relations on a par with the pace of political upheavals in Eastern Europe. Other agreements included:

- *Secretary of State James A. Baker III and Soviet foreign minister Eduard A. Shevardnadze would meet in Moscow in January to lay the groundwork for an agreement at the June summit on a strategic arms reduction treaty (START) halving each superpower nuclear arsenal. Both Bush and Gorbachev said they hoped to sign the treaty some time in 1990 and to conclude a treaty on the reduction of conventional forces in Europe (CFE) that would limit the number of troops, tanks, warplanes, and other nonnuclear forces arrayed by the North Atlantic Treaty Organization (NATO) and its Communist counterpart, the Warsaw Pact.*
- *Both sides would hasten their work on an international treaty to ban the use and possession of chemical and biological weapons.*
- *Work would begin immediately to fashion a U.S.-Soviet trade agreement—the first such accord since one was negotiated in the early 1970s but never carried out. Bush said that once the Supreme Soviet (parliament) enacted laws guaranteeing freedom of emigration, he would waive a 1974 U.S. law that prevented the Soviet Union from receiving a favored trade status. He also said he would discuss with Congress the question of allowing the U.S. Export-Import Bank to issue loans and guarantees to finance exports to the Soviet Union.*

Gorbachev sought Bush's backing for convening a meeting in 1990 of the thirty-five nation Conference on Security and Cooperation in Europe to discuss Eastern Europe—and specifically the issue of unifying East and West Germany, which the Soviet Union opposes. (The conference, which meets periodically, in 1975 produced an agreement in Helsinki, Finland, calling for greater adherence to human rights standards.) Bush appeared to rebuff the suggestion, but Gorbachev later won an endorsement of the idea from French president François Mitterrand.

NATO-Warsaw Pact Questions

Immediately after the Malta sessions, both leaders left for meetings with their allies. Bush traveled to Brussels, where he dined privately with

Chancellor Helmut Kohl of West Germany on December 3, and briefed him and fellow NATO leaders the next day. Gorbachev returned to Moscow for a Warsaw Pact meeting December 4—a meeting that would have been inconceivable only a few months earlier.

Among those sitting at a large table in the Kremlin were the new non-Communist prime minister of Poland, reform-minded representatives from Hungary, and Communist party officials from East Germany and Czechoslovakia who were still in office but whose grasp of political power was under assault from daily demonstrations. In fact, East German leader Egon Krenz was forced to resign his government post just two days later. The Warsaw Pact representatives issued a statement condemning the 1968 Soviet invasion of Czechoslovakia as illegal.

Some Western analysts said that the Warsaw Pact meeting was the first of a new era in which Moscow could no longer dictate alliance policy. Gorbachev himself signaled a move to reshape the functions of the Warsaw Pact, an alliance formed in 1955 by the Soviet Union and its East European satellite countries in response to West Germany's entry into NATO. He said the pact should become "more of a political organization and not so much a military alliance."

In Brussels, Western leaders also grappled with the meaning of their alliance in view of a fast-changing Europe, and particularly with the possibility that the two Germanys might merge. (Statements on Berlin Wall and German Reunification, p. 625)

Bush seemed eager to play down speculation that NATO might shed its military functions in response to the collapse of the Warsaw Pact. At a December 4 news conference at NATO headquarters, he said that the Atlantic alliance was "the bedrock of peaceful change in Europe." As he had done on a trip to Brussels in June, Bush assured America's allies that the United States would not unilaterally withdraw its troops from Europe. (NATO's Fortieth Anniversary, p. 297)

Eight days later Secretary of State Baker was in Europe outlining a set of proposals for transforming NATO from a primarily military alliance to a primarily political one. He spelled out his thoughts in a speech to the West Berlin Press Club on December 12 and immediately left for East Germany to confer with its government and opposition leaders—marking the first time in forty-five years that an American secretary of state had consented to visit that country.

> *Following are excerpts from White House transcripts of a news conference held jointly by U.S. president George Bush and Soviet president Mikhail S. Gorbachev at the conclusion of their meeting at Malta, December 3; and from a news conference Bush conducted December 4 at NATO headquarters in Brussels:*

JOINT NEWS CONFERENCE

Bush's Statement

PRESIDENT BUSH: Ladies and gentlemen, President Gorbachev has graciously suggested I go first, and I don't think anyone can say that the saltwater get-together was anything other than an adventure, at least out in the harbor here. First, I want to thank Prime Minister [Eddie Fenech] Adami and the people of Malta and others for their warm and gracious hospitality. I want to thank the captain and crew of *Belknap* [Bush's base ship] for the great support that they have given us—I think they were wondering if I was about to become a permanent guest. And a special thanks to the captain and crew of *Gorky* [Gorbachev's base ship] for their hospitality, and also thanks to the captain and crew of *Slava*, who have been so hospitable to many on the American side.

I first approached Chairman Gorbachev about an informal meeting of this kind after my trip to Europe last July. Amazing changes that I witnessed in Poland and in Hungary—hopeful changes—led me to believe that it was time to sit down with Chairman Gorbachev face to face to see what he and I could do to seize the opportunities before us to move this relationship forward. He agreed with that concept of a meeting. And so we got rapid agreement, and I think that the extraordinary developments in Europe since the time that the meeting was proposed only reinforced the importance of our getting together. And so I'm especially glad we had this meeting. And we did gain a deeper understanding of each other's views. We set the stage for progress across a broad range of issues, and while it is not for the United States and the Soviet Union to design the future, for Europeans or for any other people, I am convinced that a cooperative U.S.-Soviet relationship can, indeed, make the future safer and brighter. And there is virtually no problem in the world, and certainly no problem in Europe, that improvement in the U.S.-Soviet relationship will not help to ameliorate. A better U.S.-Soviet relationship is to be valued in and of itself, but it also should be an instrument of positive change for the world.

For 40 years, the Western alliance has stood together in the cause of freedom, and now with reform under way in the Soviet Union, we stand at the threshold of a brand new era of U.S.-Soviet relations. And it is within our grasp to contribute, each in our own way, to overcoming the division of Europe and ending the military confrontation there. We've got to do more to ameliorate the violence and suffering that afflicts so many regions in the world and to remove common threats to our future—the deterioration of the environment, the spread of nuclear and chemical weapons, ballistic missile technology, the narcotics trade—and our discussions here will give greater impetus to—to make real progress in these areas. There's also a great potential to develop common opportunities. For example, the Soviet Union now seeks greater engagement with the international market economy, a step that certainly I'm prepared to encourage in every way I can.

As I leave Malta for Brussels and a meeting with our NATO allies, I am optimistic that as the West works patiently together and increasingly cooperates with the Soviet Union, we can realize a lasting peace and transform the East-West relationship to one of enduring cooperation. And that is a future that's worthy of our peoples, and that's the future that I want to help in creating, and that's the future that Chairman Gorbachev and I began right here in Malta. Thank you, sir, for your hospitality.

Gorbachev's Statement

PRESIDENT GORBACHEV: Ladies and gentlemen, comrades, there are many symbolic things about this meeting, and one of them—it has never been in the history that the leaders of our two countries hold a joint press conference. This is also an important symbol. I share the view voiced by President Bush that we are satisfied in general with the results of the meeting. We regard this informal meeting—it was—the idea of it was an informal meeting, and the idea belongs to President Bush, and I supported it—that we would have this informal meeting without restricting it to any formal agenda to have a free exchange of views, because the time makes great demands to our countries, and this increases the responsibility and the role of our two countries, and I can assure you that in all our discussions—and our discussions lasted for eight hours in general—this responsibility on both sides was present. Our meeting was characterized by openness, by full scope of the exchange of views. Today it is even difficult, and perhaps there is no sense to explain the entire range of issues that we have discussed.

I wish to say right away nevertheless that on all major issues we attempted in a frank manner, using each side's arguments, to explain our own positions, both with regard to the assessment of the situation and the current changes in the world, in Europe and as regards disarmament issues. We addressed the Geneva negotiating process, the Vienna process and also negotiations on the elaboration of the convention on the chemical weapons ban. All those questions were considered thoroughly. The president and I, myself, also felt it necessary to exchange views on our perception, both from Moscow and Washington, of the hot points on our planet, and this exchange of views was very significant and thorough. We reaffirmed our formal positions that all those issues, acute issues, must be resolved by political methods. And I consider that this was a very important statement of fact.

We not only discussed problems and explained our positions; I think that both sides had many elements which, if they are taken into account in our future activities, activities of both governments, then we can count on progress. This concerns the subject of the reduction of strategic offensive arms by 50 percent, and we have an optimistic assessment of the possibility to move even next year to the conclusion of the Vienna treaty. We both are in favor, and this is our position—naturally, we can be responsible only for our position—we are in favor of signing this document at the summit meeting.

This time we discussed much bilateral relations, and I on my part, would like to note many positive elements and points which were contained in statements and words by President Bush. Thus, I would say that in all directions of the political dialogue of our discussion, including bilateral relations, we not only confirmed the consistency of our political course, the continuity of our political course—and I should say it, although we had an informal meeting, we met only for the first time with President Bush in his capacity. And the confirmation of the continuity of the course is an important element. What is also important is that during this informal meeting, we have laid the foundation for increasing this capital. And I believe that in the first place, it serves the interest of our both countries and also the interest of the entire world community.

Well, we have made our contact, a good contact. The atmosphere was friendly, straightforward, open, and this enabled us to have—to make good work. In our position, the most dangerous thing is to exaggerate. And it is always that we should preserve elements of cautiousness—and I use the favorite word by President Bush. Our world and our relations are at a crucial juncture. We should be highly responsible to face up to the challenges of today's world. And the leaders of our two countries cannot act as a fire brigade, although fire brigades are very useful. We have to keep it in mind, also. This element was also present.

I would like once again to thank the president for the idea of holding this meeting, with which we are satisfied, I hope, and I would like to thank the people and the government of Malta and to express the words of appreciation and gratitude for the hospitality. Thank you, Mr. President, for your cooperation.

[The Cold War]

Q: Chairman Gorbachev, President Bush called on you to end the cold war once and for all. Do you think that has been done now?

GORBACHEV: In the first place, I assured the president of the United States that the Soviet Union would never start a hot war against the United States of America, and we would like our relations to develop in such a way that they would open greater possibilities for cooperation. Naturally, the president and I had a wide discussion, or rather we sought the answer to the question [of] where we stand now. We stated, both of us, that the world leaves one epoch of cold war and enters another epoch. This is just the beginning; we are just at the very beginning of our road, a long road, to a long-lasting peaceful period. Thus we were unanimous in concluding about the special responsibility of such countries as the United States and the Soviet Union.

Naturally, we had a rather long discussion, but this is not for the press conference; that is, we shouldn't explain our discussion regarding the fact that the new era calls for a new approach and that many things that were characteristic of the cold war should be abandoned, both the stake on force, the arms race, mistrust, psychological and ideological struggle and all that. All that should be things of the past.

[Central America]

Q: President Gorbachev—what are the hot spots, President Gorbachev, that you spoke about? There's El Salvador. Were you able to assure President Bush that the Soviet Union would use its influence on either Cuba or Nicaragua to stop the arms shipments? And President Bush, were you satisfied with President Gorbachev's response?

GORBACHEV: This question is addressed to me? This subject has been thoroughly discussed. We have reaffirmed once again to the president that we have ceased arms shipment to Central America. We also reaffirmed our position that we're sympathetic with the political process that is going on there regarding the settlement of the situation. We are in favor of free elections with the representatives of the United Nations and other Latin American countries to determine the fate of Nicaragua. We understand the concerns of the United States. We listened carefully to the arguments by President Bush in this respect, and we assured him that our position in principle is that we are in favor of a political settlement of the situation in Central America. I believe—and now I wouldn't like to explain everything that we discussed on the subject—but to sum up, I would say that there are possibilities to have peace in that area—tranquillity, in the interests above all of the peoples of that region, which does not run counter to the interests of the people of the United States.

Q: Question to President Bush from the *Izvestia* newspaper.

BUSH: I think I owe him a short answer, and then we'll come over there. Please ask the question.

Q: The question was: Were you, Mr. President, satisfied with President Gorbachev's response on the question about arms to El Salvador?

BUSH: My answer is that we had an in-depth discussion on these questions, as President Gorbachev said. I will not be satisfied until total self-determination takes place through verifiably free elections in Nicaragua. And the chairman gave me every opportunity to express in detail the concerns I feel about that region. He indeed has cited his concerns. So I can't say there are no differences between us, but we had a chance to talk about them. And if there are remaining differences, I like to think they have been narrowed. But you know, all you from the United States, the concerns we feel that the Nicaraguans go through with certifiably free elections and that they not export revolution into El Salvador. So we had a big, wide-ranging discussion, and I would simply say that I feel we have much more understanding between the parties as a result of that discussion.

[Business Contacts]

Q. (through translator): The *Izvestia* newspaper, to President Bush, and if these were comments from Comrade Gorbachev, we would welcome

it. There has been a long-standing issue of expanding economic cooperation between the United States and the Soviet Union. It is a very acute
problem, taking into account our economic reforms and our economic
difficulties. To what degree [has] that issue been discussed during your
meeting, and what is the position of your administration, Mr. President,
regarding the expanding of your economic cooperation and whether U.S.
business would like to promote contacts with the Soviet Union?

BUSH: We had a long discussion about the—on economic matters. We
took some specific—made some specific representations about how we can
work close—more closely on the economic front with the Soviet Union, and
we've made certain representations that we—that I will now follow
through with, in terms of observer status [for the Soviet Union at the
General Agreement on Tariffs and Trade], and I think one of the most
fruitful parts of our discussion related to the economy, and I would like to
have a climate in which American businessmen can help in what Chairman
Gorbachev is trying to do with reform, and obviously with *glasnost*. But, I
think the climate, as a result of these talks, for investment inside the
Soviet Union, and for certain things we can do to help the Soviet Union,
and, indeed, other countries, seek common ground with these multilateral
organizations related to finance—all of that's a big plus. It was an
extraordinarily big plus as far as I'm concerned.

GORBACHEV: I would like to comment [on] the answer. First of all, I
confirm what I've said, what the president said. And the second point, the
things that have taken place at the meeting could be regarded as a political
impetus, which we were lacking for our economic cooperation to gain
momentum and to acquire forms and methods which would be adequate to
our contemporary life. Well, as to the future course of this process, this will
depend on the Soviet actions, whether legal or economic. You understand
that today we try to turn drastically our economy toward cooperation with
other countries so that it would be part and parcel of the world economic
system. Therefore we think and hope that that which has happened during
the meeting on this subject of the agenda—well, let's call it the agenda—
these are of principal importance.

[Lebanon]

Q: With the tense situation in Lebanon—how did you discuss the
military option in Lebanon? And what have you decided on the Middle
East in general? How did you discuss it? The question is to both President
Bush and President Gorbachev.

GORBACHEV: We couldn't but address this Lebanese conflict,
because both the U.S. and the Soviet people are sympathetic with the
grave situation and sufferings of that people. We explained our views—we
shared our views on assistance in this respect, and agreed to continue the
exchange of views so that each, according to his possibilities—and I think
everyone has his own possibilities—well, President Bush thought that we
had more possibilities, and I thought that we had equal possibilities—in

order to resolve positively this conflict.

Q. (through translator): May I ask a question to President Bush, please?

BUSH: May I finish? Our aspirations, shared in by President Gorbachev, [are] to see a peaceful resolution of the question regarding Lebanon. We support the tripartite agreement; he has supported it very actively. We do not want to see any more killing in Lebanon. The chairman agrees with us—we're in total agreement on that. And so Lebanon was discussed in detail, and we would like to see a return to a peaceful democratic Lebanon. And everybody in the United States, I think, shares the agony that I feel about the turmoil in Lebanon. But we're going to try to help. We're trying any way we can to help.

Q. (through translator): My question is to President Bush—Gennady Vassiliev of Pravda. You, as president of the United States, participate for the first time at the summit meeting, but you were the vice president of the previous administration and took part in forming foreign policies. So what is your assessment of the course that our two countries have passed since Geneva to Malta?

[Progress From Past Summits]

BUSH: That's what we call a slow ball in the trade. It's an easy question because I really think they are improving dramatically. There is enormous support in our country for what Chairman Gorbachev is doing inside the Soviet Union. There is enormous respect and support for the way he has advocated peaceful change in Europe. And so this meeting accomplished everything that I had hoped it would. It was a no-agenda meeting, and yet it was a meeting where we discussed, as the chairman said, many, many subjects. So I think, if a meeting can improve relations, I think this one has.

[Arms Control]

Q: Did you reach any actual understandings or instructions or timetables or deadlines to negotiators on chemical weapons, nuclear weapons, conventional arms?

GORBACHEV: Well, you know, we devoted much time to the discussion of concrete issues related to disarmament negotiations on different types of arms. And just as an example, to show you that this was a substantive discussion, I'll tell you that in the near future our foreign ministers will meet, which have been instructed to do some specific work to move the positions closer. In connection with new interesting proposals by President Bush regarding chemical weapons, which have the goal of a global ban and provides for certain phases and movement towards this global ban, then we have the possibility of a rapid movement towards it. As to strategic offensive arms, the analysis of the situations and the instructions that have been given regarding the preparation of that treaty demonstrate that we may be able, by the second half of June—and we agreed on the formal meeting at that time—to do the necessary work to agree on the basic provisions of this treaty, which then later in the coming months would be ready for signature. Therefore I highly assess and evaluate what we have done here.

Well, of course there are questions which would require detailed discussion so that there will be no concerns on both sides. As to our concerns, they are—as regards strategic offensive arms and the preparation of the treaty on the 50 percent cuts of such weapons, they concern SLCMs [submarine-launched cruise missiles]. Well, and in general, we raised a question with the president that when we have advanced along different directions on the reduction of nuclear arms and conventional forces, when we move towards a defensive doctrine—that is, we, the Soviet Union—we are interested in having new elements in the military doctrines of the NATO countries. And therefore, the time has come when we should begin discussing naval forces. We should discuss this problem also. Thus, I would also like to confirm, and I think that the president would confirm it, that our discussions were very thorough, which encourages—and therefore we can count on success. This was a salute.

Q. (through translator): Can I ask you a question? Mr. President, will you tell us, President Gorbachev, will you tell me why you were so cautious at the beginning of the negotiations? The Soviet side was very optimistic, and now you have voiced certain optimistic elements. What is the reason for it? Maybe that optimism was not justified. This is Portuguese television to President Gorbachev.

BUSH: This is for you. Go ahead.

GORBACHEV: Well, I would say that there were elements of optimism and pessimism here, and I wouldn't dwell into the details.

Q: Could you just—

GORBACHEV: Well, the core of the question is that, if I read you correctly, is that to what degree we can speak of optimism or pessimism regarding the results of this meeting. Or perhaps I didn't understand you correctly. Did I get you right? Yes. Well, you know, on the eve of the meeting, both sides were restrained, and had, well-balanced position, a cautious one. I would say it again. This did not mean, however, that we were pessimists. That meant that we were highly responsible. Today, now that the meeting has taken place and we have summed up the results together with the president, I can tell you that I am optimistic about the results and the prospects that are open now. This is dialectics.

Q: President Bush, may I refer to the question of naval forces, please, that President Gorbachev raised just a moment ago? Can you respond to your feeling and exactly what you've told President Gorbachev about your disposition toward reducing naval forces, NATO's disposition in that regard? And if in fact the Soviets are prepared to move to a defensive posture, is not it time to consider some cuts in this regard?

BUSH: The answer is that this is not an arms control meeting in the sense of trying to hammer out details. We still have differences with the

Soviet Union—he knows it and I know it—as it relates to naval forces. But the point is we could discuss these things in a very constructive environment, and certainly the chairman knows that I could not come here and make deals in arms control, and I'm disinclined to think that that is an area where we will have immediate progress. But we talked about a wide array of these issues, but we have no agreement at all on that particular question of naval arms control.

But the point is he knows that and I know that. The point is he had an opportunity to let me know how important it is, and I can, as a part of an alliance, have an opportunity to discuss a wide array of armament questions, disarmament questions, with our allies. So it's exactly the kind of climate for a meeting that I had visualized, that I had envisioned and that he had envisioned. We can sit there and talk about issues of which we've had divisions over the years, try to find ways to narrow them, and we did narrow them in some important areas. And there are still some differences that exist—there's no point in covering that over.

[Military Alliances]

Q: Did you discuss the Soviet proposal on Helsinki II? And an adjoining question, are you prepared to take a joint initiative with the Soviet Union about the Middle East crisis?

BUSH: Is that to me?

Q: Yes—to both.

Q: President Gorbachev, did you assure President Bush that you will not—

Q: A question to Chairman Gorbachev from Globo TV Brazil—

BUSH: The question—I think I owe this gentleman—

GORBACHEV (not translated; translated afterward by the White House): The first question is regarding Helsinki II. I think that we have found during this meeting—we have come to a common understanding of the CSCE process—the results that have made it possible to respond with deep changes in Europe and the world as well, as Europe has a great influence on the world due to certain reasons. Both the president and myself are in favor of developing the CSCE process in accordance with the new requirements that are required by our times so that we could think of and build a new Europe on the basis of common elements among the European countries. We reaffirmed that this a common affair for all the European countries that signed the Helsinki Act, including the whole EC [European Community]. And it was—this element was present everywhere whenever we discussed Europe and other parts of the world with the active and constructive participation of the United States and Canada. Thus, we are in favor of the process' gaining in strength and in force. The transformation of the CSCE-Helsinki institutions at this stage should be such that their nature would change, or rather would be adequate to the current changes.

Take, for example, NATO and the Warsaw Pact. They should not remain military alliances, but rather military-political alliances, and later on, just political alliances, so that their nature would change in accordance with the changes on that continent. We are also entitled to expect that the relations—that when the Common Market and the CMEC would also change in respect of greater openness, with the active participation in economic processes of the United States. Thus we think that the time has come for us to act step by step, in a thorough manner, in accordance with the requirements of the times, taking full responsibility without damaging the balance and security in this way. This was the manner of our discussion. And I believe that the president can only nod and say that we have coincidence of views on this.

[Naval Arms]

Q: The meeting took place at the center of the Mediterranean. How did you discuss the problem of the reduction in the military presence of the size in the Mediterranean?

BUSH: This to me? Well, first, on the reduction, we did not have specific figures in mind. The chairman raised the question of naval arms control, and I was not particularly positive in responding on naval arms control. But we agree that we want to move forward and bring to completion this CFE [Conventional Forces in Europe] that does affect Italy and other countries in the sense that they are part of our—a strong part of our NATO alliance. So we didn't get agreements—crossing the t's, dotting the i's—on some of these issues. But that's not what we were trying to do. May I respond to this gentleman's last half? The question was Soviet and U.S.—please repeat.

Q: Joint initiative.

[The Middle East]

BUSH: It doesn't require joint initiatives to solve the Middle East question, but we have found that the Soviet Union is playing a constructive role in Lebanon in trying throughout the Middle East to give their support for the tripartite agreement, which clearly the U.S. has supported. And so there's common ground there. That may not always have been the case in history, and that may not always have been the way the United States looked at it as to whether—how constructive the role the Soviets might play. But I can tell you that after these discussions and after the discussions between Jim Baker [Secretary of State James A. Baker III] and [Soviet Foreign Minister Eduard A.] Shevardnadze, there is a constructive role that the Soviets are implementing. And again I cite the tripartite agreement. I'm sure that they share our view, after these talks, in terms of peaceful resolution of these questions in the Middle East, be it Lebanon or on the—in West Bank questions. So I don't think we're very far apart on this.

Q: President Gorbachev, did you assure President Bush that the Soviet Union will—

GORBACHEV (not translated; translated afterward by the White House): Well, my opinion on the Middle East in terms of discussions at the meeting—I can only add to what President Bush has said, that we have just discussed very thoroughly this subject. And I believe that we have come to an understanding that we should use our possibilities and interact in order to promote a solution to this protracted conflict, which affects negatively the entire world situation. As it seemed to me, we also agreed that, as a result of the sides' progress, we have approached the point when we have a realistic chance to start the settlement process. Therefore, it is important not to lose this chance, because the situation is changing very rapidly. Therefore, we think we will contribute to this.

[The Future of Reform]

Q: I'm from the group of Czechoslovak journalists. President Gorbachev, did you assure President Bush that the changes in Eastern Europe are irreversible and that the Soviet Union has forsaken the right to intervene there militarily? And President Bush, similarly, as a result of this meeting, are you now more trusting that the Soviets have indeed renounced the Brezhnev doctrine?

GORBACHEV: I wouldn't like you to consider me here or to regard me as a full-fledged representative of all European countries. This wouldn't be true. We are a part of Eastern Europe, of Europe. We interact with our allies in all areas, and our ties are deep. However, every nation is an independent entity in world politics, and every people has the right to choose its own destiny, the destiny of its own state. And I can only explain my own attitude.

I believe that those changes, both in the Soviet Union and in the countries of Eastern Europe, have been prepared by the course of the historic evolution itself. No one can avoid this evolutionary process, and those problems should be resolved on a new basis, taking into account the experience and the potential of those countries, opening up possibilities for utilizing anything positive that has been accumulated by the—by mankind. And I believe that we should welcome the thrust of those processes, because they are related to the desire of the people to make those societies more democratic, more humane, and to face the world. Therefore, I'm encouraged by the thrust of those processes, and I believe that this is highly assessed by other countries.

I also see deep, profound changes in other countries, including Western European countries, and this is also very important, because this is a reciprocal movement so that the people would become more close around the continent, and preserving at the same time the—the identity of one's own people. This is very important for us to understand.

Q. (through translator): I ask a question on the part of the Czechoslovak journalists. We are discussing the future of Europe—

BUSH: May I just respond briefly? There is no question that there is dramatic change; nobody can question it. And as President Gorbachev talks about democratic change and peaceful, that certainly lays to rest previous doctrines that may have had a different approach. And so we are—he knows that not just the president, but all the people in the United States would like to see this peaceful democratic evolution continue. And so I think that's the best way to answer the question, because the change is so dramatic and so obvious to people. But I will say we had a very good chance to discuss it in considerably more detail than I think would be appropriate to discuss it here.

[Central America]

Q: President Bush, you have accused the Soviet Union for sending arms to El Salvador, to Central America. And President Gorbachev, you have denied those charges. Now, both of you sit here together. Who is right?

BUSH: Maybe I ought to take the first shot at that one. I don't think we accused the Soviet Union of that. What we did say is arms were going in there in an unsatisfactory way. My view is that not only did the Nicaraguans acquiesce in it, but they encouraged in it—encouraged that to happen. And the evidence is demonstrable. But I'm not challenging whether—the word of the foreign minister [Shevardnadze]. He and Jim Baker talked about that, and President Gorbachev and I talked about it. All I know is that—and he said it earlier—elections, free elections, should be the mode. And I also reported to him what Mr. Oscar Arias [president of Costa Rica] called me about—blaming [Cuban President Fidel] Castro and the Sandinistas for exporting revolution and for just tearing things up there in Central America. So we may have a difference on that one, but I want to be careful when you say I accuse them of sending these weapons. I did not, because Mr. Shevardnadze made a direct representation to Mr. Baker. And everyone knows that there's a wide international arms flow out there. But whatever it is, however it comes, it is unsatisfactory for countries in the region that want to see the evolution toward democracy continue.

GORBACHEV: I believe I have to say a few words on this. The president explained correctly the discussion on the subject. We were never accused, and we didn't have to accept or reject anything. We informed the president that we had firm assurances from Nicaragua that no arms, including those aircraft, are being used. And the president took our arguments and agreed to them. As regards the fact of principle—I have mentioned it—is that we are—we are for free elections, so that this conflict would be resolved by political means and the situation was kept normal.

BUSH: Well, that's what we agreed on. I agree that that's the assessment. I still feel that arms are going into El Salvador. We've seen clear evidence of it. But I can't argue with the factual presentation made here. But we have a difference. I don't believe that the Sandinistas have told the truth to our Soviet friends. And why? Because we know for fact certain that arms have gone in there. I'm not saying they're Soviet arms—they've said they aren't shipping arms, and I'm accepting that. But they're going in there, and I am saying that they have misled Mr. Shevardnadze when they gave a specific representation that no arms were going from Nicaragua into El Salvador. So we have some differences in how we look at this key question. And the best way to have those differences ameliorated is to have these certifiably free elections in Nicaragua. And Castro—I have no influence with him whatsoever, and maybe somebody is yelling that question at President Gorbachev. But, look, we've got some differences in different places around the world.

Q: What about Cuba?

GORBACHEV: What do you mean?

Q: Oscar Arias apparently called President Bush and told him that Cuba was really creating the situation in the region by commenting—

GORBACHEV: We discussed the situation in Latin America and Central America and explained our assessments. On the basis of our analysis, on our own analysis and our assessments, I told the president that there were conditions emerging for improving the situation for the better, as different countries had the desire to change the situation and normalize the situation, both in the United States and in other countries.

Q: Will you give, Mr. President, an answer?

BUSH: I'd be glad to. Someone had better tell me what the question was if I'm going to answer. The question of Germany?

[German Reunification]

Q: Whether the German issue was discussed, and your attitude to the Kohl plan [West German Chancellor Helmut Kohl's proposal for an interim "confederation" of East and West Germany, leading to reunification]?

BUSH: The United States, as part of NATO, has had a longstanding position. Helsinki [the European human-rights agreement] spells out a concept of permanent borders. We—I made clear to President Gorbachev that we for our part do not want to do anything that is unrealistic and causes any country to end up going backwards or end up having its own people in military conflict, one with the other. And so I think we have tried to act with the word that President Gorbachev has used, and that is "with caution"—not to go demonstrating on top of the Berlin Wall to show how happy we are about the change. We are happy about the change. And the German question—I've heard many leaders speak about the German question, and I don't think it is the role of the United States to dictate the rapidity of change in any country. It's a matter for the people to determine themselves. So that's our position. And the last word goes to the chairman on this one.

GORBACHEV: Yes, and the president wrote a note in to me in English. I don't read English, but I answered in Russian—he doesn't read Russian. But we agreed on it anyway.

I'll be brief. In the past few days, I already answered a few times on the question. I can only confirm what I said before, that we approach this subject on the basis of the Helsinki process, which summed up the results of the Second World War and consolidated the results of the war, and this is—those are realities. And the reality is such that we have today's Europe with two German states, the Federal Republic of Germany and the German Democratic Republic, which are both members of the United Nations and sovereign states. This was the decision of history, and I always revert to this subject or thesis, which saves me.

Indeed, in order to remain realists, we should say that history itself decides the processes and fates on the European continent and also the fates of those two states. I think this is a common understanding shared by anyone. And every—any artificial acceleration of the process would only exacerbate and make it more difficult to change in many European countries those changes that are taking place now in Europe. Thus, we wouldn't serve that process by an artificial acceleration or prompting of the process, in processes that are going on in all sorts of countries. Well, I think that we can thank the media for their cooperation. We are not yet aware of what they will write about us.

BUSH: No matter what it says.

Q: The answer is it's all right.

BUSH: Reserve the right to thank them afterward—after they've written?

GORBACHEV: I think we should thank them in advance so they'll do a better story. I would like to thank you, Mr. President, for your cooperation.

BUSH: We're going to have to leave at 1:20 p.m. Should we each take one more question or not? Last one—last one for me right here. No rebuttal, no back-up questions—last one.

[Bush, Gorbachev Relationship]

Q: What's your personal relationship now between you two leaders, and would regular contacts that would perhaps no longer be called summits be helpful?

BUSH: I had known President Gorbachev before, and I'd let him speak for himself, but I think we have a good personal relationship, and I believe that helps each side be frank, point out the differences as well as the areas we—we agree on. And that is a very, very important ingredient, I think, because of the standing of the two powers, and because of the dramatic change that is taking place. And I am not saying that if he likes me, he is going to change long-held policies. And I am going to say, if I like him, we're not going to change long-held policies. But what we've been able to do here is to get together and talk about the differences without rancor and frankly as possible, and I think it's been very constructive. So I couldn't have asked for a better result out of this non-summit summit.

The question is regular meetings? I'm open for—to see him as much as it requires to keep things moving forward. We've already set a summit meeting. That summit meeting will drive the arms control agenda, and that's a good thing, because I represented to him that we wanted to see a START agreement, a CFE agreement and, hopefully, a chemical agreement. That's a very ambitious agenda. But I think if we hadn't sat here and talked, we might not have understood how each other feels on these important questions.

GORBACHEV: I would like to confirm what President Bush has said, that we had known each other for a long time. But I would also add, and I have not agreed on it with the president in advance, but this is no secret, that we have had changes, considerable exchanges of views in previous contacts, and we had an understanding of the positions of each other. And we would only mention the Governor's Island, or our discussion in the car [in Gorbachev's previous visit to the United States], and then we would understand what we're talking about. Then we exchanged letters, and our today's meeting boosts our contacts to a higher level.

I'm satisfied with the discussions and meetings we had, including our two private discussions. I share the view of the president that personal contacts are an important—very important element in the relations between two—between leaders of states, the more so we are talking about the leaders of such countries as the United States and the Soviet Union, and I welcome those personal relations. And the president was quite correct in saying that this didn't mean that we would sacrifice our long-held positions at the expense of our personal ties or that we forget our responsibility. I think that our personal contacts help us implement our responsibilities and help us better interact in the interests of our two nations and in the interests of the entire world community, and I myself would like to thank the president for cooperation, for this meeting, for the cooperation in a very important joint Soviet-U.S. endeavor. And our capital, our share, is 50/50.

BUSH: Well, I guess we're going to fly away to Brussels.

BUSH'S BRUSSELS NEWS CONFERENCE

[Europe's Future]

The President. I have a statement, and then I'll be glad to respond to your questions.

This year the people of the East made fundamental choices about their destiny, and governments there began to honor the citizen's right to choose. What these changes amount to is nothing less than a peaceful revolution. And the task before us, therefore, is to consolidate the fruits of this peaceful revolution and provide the architecture for continued peaceful change, to end the division of Europe and Germany, to make Europe whole and free.

Great choices are being made. Greater opportunities beckon. The political strategy for NATO [North Atlantic Treaty Organization] that we agreed upon last May makes the promotion of greater freedom in the East a basic element of alliance policy. Accordingly, NATO should promote human rights, democracy, and reform within Eastern countries as the best means of encouraging reconciliation among the countries of Eastern and Western Europe.

Although this is a time of great hope—and it is—we must not blur the distinction between promising expectations and present realities. We must remain constant with NATO's traditional security mission. I pledge today that the United States will maintain significant military forces in Europe as long as our allies desire our presence as part of a common defense effort. The U.S. will remain a European power, and that means that the United States will stay engaged in the future of Europe and in our common defense.

Many of the values that should guide Europe's future are described in the Final Act of the Conference on Security and Cooperation in Europe [CSCE]. These values encompass the freedom of people to choose their destiny under a rule of law with rulers who are democratically accountable. I think we can look to the CSCE to play a greater role in the future of Europe. The 35 nations of the CSCE bridge both the division of Europe and the Atlantic Ocean. It's a structure that should be able to contribute much to the future architecture of Europe.

I also appreciate the vital role that the EC [European Communities] must play in the new Europe. And it's my belief that the events of our times call both for a continued, perhaps even intensified, effort of the 12 to integrate, and a role for the EC as a magnet that draws the forces of reform toward Eastern Europe. And that's why I was exceptionally pleased that we agreed at the Paris economic summit on a specific role for the EC in that Group of 24 [leading industrial nations] effort to assist Poland and Hungary.

We stand on the threshold of a new era. And we know that we are contributing to a process of history driven by the peoples determined to be free. The people of Europe, especially the brave citizens of the East, are illuminating the future. And yet the outcome is not predestined. It depends on our continued strength and our solidarity as an alliance.

Our transatlantic partnership can create the architecture of a new Europe and a new Atlanticism, where self-determination and individual freedom everywhere replace coercion and tyranny, where economic liberty everywhere replaces economic controls and stagnation, and where lasting peace is reinforced everywhere by common respect for the rights of man.

I now would be glad to respond to some questions. And we've got to be out of here about a little after quarter of.

[U.S. Role in Europe and Defense Budget Cuts]

Q. Mr. President, I have a two-part question. You've made it clear that you are going to stay in Europe. But in view of the dramatic reduction in tensions and the obvious weakening of the Warsaw Pact, what will be the real American role? And two: Will there now be more money for the poor, the homeless, public housing—the nation's really badly-in-need-of-repair-infrastructure?

The President. We have a lot of demands at home, and there's no question about that. But I think it is premature to speak, as some are at home, about a "peace dividend": Take a lot of money out of defense and put it into other worthy causes. And so, as I started over the budget figures for the next budget cycle, we are under a tremendous burden to get our total spending down in order to meet the Gramm-Rudman targets.

In terms of the U.S. role, I think I said it out here pretty well. We will continue to play a very active role in NATO. I see nothing that diminishes the importance of the United States. And I might say that I gathered from our interlocutors there—the other heads of state and governments—that they want us fully involved. And thinking back on my talks with Mr. Gorbachev, I don't see any conflict there either.

[Reunification of Germany]

Q. Mr. President, Vernon Walters, your trusted adviser and the Ambassador to Bonn, said that he envisions a—he says that Germany East and West will be reunited within 5 years. Do you think that's possible? And what would be the implications for NATO and the Warsaw Pact?

The President. I am not into the predicting of time on the question of Germany. I don't know whether the Secretary General read you these points. Let me just read the four points that represent the U.S. position on reunification. Self-determination must be pursued without prejudice to its outcome, and we should not at this time endorse any particular vision. Secondly, unification should occur in the context of Germany's continued commitment to NATO and an increasingly integrated European Community, and with due regard for the legal role and responsibilities of the allied powers. Third, in the interest of general European stability, moves toward unification must be peaceful, gradual, and part of a step-by-step basis. And lastly, on the question of borders, we should reiterate our support for the principles of the Helsinki Final Act. . . .

[U.S. Role in Europe]

Q. To go back to what Helen [Helen Thomas, United Press International] asked you about, you said we would remain an Atlantic power.

The President. Keep talking. I'm just going to get some water.

Q. After World War II, the Europeans needed our money with the Marshall plan. They needed our military backing because of the Soviet threat. But now, if the Soviet military threat does recede—and I know it's early days yet—maybe this is a question that one of your successors will have to deal with eventually: What are they going to need from us? What role will we really have to play here?

The President. Well, we have a tremendous interaction if you want to hypothetically project to that guaranteed peaceful time. I would say interaction with the United States on student exchanges, cultural exchanges, economic matters. I mean, there's a tremendous potential for a Soviet Union that is in accord with us on these democratic values. It's a tremendous market, for example, but it needs the economic reform. So, what we've got to do is be sure that we conduct ourselves in such a way that the changes, the political reforms, can keep going forward there in Eastern Europe; that the Soviet Union can do what Mr. Gorbachev is trying to do internally. And then there's just enormous potential for living at peace with that tremendous power.

Q. Sir, maybe I misstated my question. What I really mean is: Why do West Europeans need us once the military threat recedes? The West Europeans? Why would there have to be a NATO? This is a political and military alliance, and truly a political alliance because of the military need.

The President. You mean, why will there always have to be a U.S. presence?

Q. Why will there always have to be a NATO?

The President. Well, if you want to project out 100 years or take some years off of that, you can look to a utopian day when there might not be. But as I pointed out to them, that day hasn't arrived; and they agree with me. And so, the United States must stay involved.

What we don't want to do is send the signal of the decoupling of the United States and Canada from NATO, particularly at this highly sensitive time. And Mr. Gorbachev understood that. He made that point to me.

[Ethnic Dissent in the Soviet Union]

Q. Did President Gorbachev ask your forbearance in case he decided to crack down on dissidents? And if so, what did you say? Or what role did the question of ethnic and Baltic dissent have in your meeting?

The President. The answer to the first part is no. And the answer to the second part is: I asked him to describe for me the nationality problems inside the Soviet Union. And he did it in considerable detail.

[Chairman Gorbachev]

Q. Mr. President, you had mentioned that you got some insight into President Gorbachev at this point. I wonder if the insights included any sense of internal—did he behave as if a man operating from a strong position or a man who seemed to be in jeopardy, or how did you assess that?

The President. I thought he seemed very much in control. You could tell the way he interacted with his own top people there. And he felt very confident in discussing without notes a wide array of subjects with me. He did have a little notebook that he referred to. It was written in his own handwriting, the best I could see. [Laughter.] And once having seen it, I couldn't read it. [Laughter.] And so, he seemed in control. He seemed—subdued is the wrong word, but I would say determined and unemotional about it. The most emotion we saw was at that press conference yesterday. But it was a wonderful presentation. And the climate for—leave out the weather—the climate for the discussions was really good.

[Reunification of Germany]

Q. Mr. President, again as part of the insights you gained, what is your understanding about Secretary General Gorbachev's view of unification of Germany? Do you think he's as opposed as he's said in public, or do you think he accepts the fact that—

The President. I think his view was one of—if I could use a word that's unfamiliar to many—caution. And I really believe that. I think he recognizes the rapidity of change. He has very constructively talked about peaceful change. And I think his hope is that people don't try to set up some artificial calendar date by which that reunification should happen. And I think he feels that if there were outside forces setting dates on something like that, that would complicate the way in which he is helping manage the change in the Pact. . . .

[East German Reforms and the Reunification of Germany]

Q. Mr. President, on East Germany, as you know, the Communist Party structure has collapsed there. It's unclear who's running the Government. I wonder if you talked about that, if you personally think that it's a dangerous situation, that that moves unification up in the timetable at all? And secondly, what Gorbachev said to you when you said to him unification of Germany would have to be in the NATO context?

The President. No, I don't think it's a dangerous situation. I don't think anybody here in this room, including myself, has been able to predict the rapidity of the change, the totality of the change. But I don't see it as dangerous as long as the Soviet leader and the Germans and the West conduct themselves the way I've been urging.

What was the second part?

Q. Well, what Mr. Gorbachev said to you when you said unification, but only in the NATO context. He keeps saying it has to be in the Warsaw Pact context.

The President. No, we were—I don't think we went into that in real depth, Lesley [Lesley Stahl, CBS News].

Q. Well, what do you think he'd think of that? I mean, obviously—

The President. That's too hypothetical. I've got trouble figuring it out on our side with all our experts, rather than knowing what he might think about something he hadn't thought about, maybe. [Laughter]

[Chairman Gorbachev]

Q. Mr. President, you seem to have traveled some distance between what you were saying about Mr. Gorbachev a year or so ago and some of the things you said yesterday. Could you please talk in a little bit more detail about the evolution in your thinking that you mentioned yesterday:

how that happened and what persuaded you along the—

The President. As I watched the way in which Mr. Gorbachev has handled the changes in Eastern Europe, it deserves new thinking. It absolutely mandates new thinking. And when I see his willingness to give support to a CFE agreement that calls for him to disproportionately reduce his forces and that is there on the table, I think that mandates new thinking. When I hear him talk about peaceful change and the right of countries in the Warsaw Pact to choose, that deserves new thinking.

And so, I approach this, and I think in step with our allies, with a certain respect for what he's doing. And thus we want to try to meet him on some of the areas where he needs help. I'm thinking of a few suggestions I had in the economic area. But I also believe that the West must remain strong and together and try to be helpful where we can in a united way, but not be imprudent.

[Meeting With Chairman Gorbachev]

Q. Mr. President, you mentioned earlier that there was some tension during the meeting and earlier reported you had said that there was no personal rancor. Could you outline the moments of tension and tell us a little bit about the moments where you felt there was tension between you and the Soviet leader?

The President. Well, I think where you don't have agreement some slight tension might result. I don't want to imply there was great, dramatic moments of tension. Please let me clarify it if that's the impression I left.

But we have a big difference on how we look at Central America. And I would like to see him use his influence with Mr. [Fidel] Castro [President of Cuba] and, if he's got any left, with Mr. [Daniel] Ortega [President of Nicaragua] to facilitate democratic change in the Western Hemisphere. And I made clear this isn't just the view of the United States, but it's the view of many Americans. . . .

[NATO and the Warsaw Pact's Future]

Q. Mr. President, what is your reaction to Chairman Gorbachev's proposal that NATO and the Warsaw Pact should not remain just military alliances but rather become military-political alliances and later on just political alliances? Can you envisage in the future a new form of cooperation between the two alliances?

The President. Well, I can see an economic interaction. And I hope that NATO will—along with the EC and along with OECD [Organization for Economic Cooperation and Development] and these other areas—will take more of an active East-West role in the economy, in helping each other in terms of systems. But he did not press that point with me at all. I think he envisions an active U.S. presence in Europe, one way or another.

[Meeting With Chairman Gorbachev]

Q. Mr. President, after 5 hours of talks on Saturday, despite extremely treacherous seas—you even had trouble getting to the talks—you got back on your launch and got back on your ship. Mr. President, why did you do that?

The President. Because I wanted to go back in time to receive him for dinner.

Q. But didn't you understand you were risking the summit, number one? And number two, what do you think Gorbachev thinks of your judgment?

The President. Maureen, [Maureen Doud, *New York Times*] you've been to Maine. Don't tell me that that little chop was—[laughter]—risking anything. Frankly, I haven't had that much fun in a long time either. But the fact that we got out there and the seas kicked up even more—the winds were up to 60 miles an hour, 50 knots, which is a big wind. And along with it came a swell, and along with it came a chop. But we didn't miss a beat. In fact, we had a very relaxed evening out there. And then showed up, and we got 8 hours of talks in. So, that was a nonissue. And I didn't feel there was any risk in getting in a little safe launch like that and going back out to the ship; it was sheer pleasure. Really.

Q. It wasn't hot-dogging?

The President. Hot-dogging? No. [Laughter] Well, you know, these charismatic, macho, visionary guys. They'll do anything. [Laughter]. This is the last question. I've go to go. I've got to go home.

Central America

Q. Mr. President, a few moments ago you questioned whether Gorbachev had any influence at all over Danny Ortega. Yet in his news conference yesterday, Chairman Gorbachev indicated that there may be an opportunity now for peace in the region. Did he indicate to you in any way whether, one, he had any control over Ortega or, two, whether there was something in the works that may lead to some kind of peaceful political—

The President. No, he didn't. He didn't indicate whether he had any control over him. What he did indicate was that there were going to be free elections. . . .

RELIEF EFFORT IN HURRICANE, EARTHQUAKE DISASTERS
December 4, 1989

Occurring less than a month apart, two natural disasters—one on the East Coast and the other on the West Coast—caused enormous destruction and claimed the lives of ninety-five Americans. The first, Hurricane Hugo, hit the U.S. mainland September 21, after devastating islands in the Caribbean. The second, an earthquake, struck the San Francisco area October 17. Damage estimates ran to $7 billion for the earthquake and to $4 billion for the hurricane, making each disaster the costliest of its kind on record. The American Red Cross announced on December 4 that over a two-month period it had raised $98 million for disaster relief, also a record amount.

Hurricane Hugo

After sweeping through the Caribbean, Hugo hit Charleston, South Carolina, late in the evening of September 21, then headed north through the Carolinas, dissipating over Virginia, West Virginia, Ohio, and New York the following day. With winds of 135 miles an hour and a seventeen-foot tidal surge, Hugo was the worst storm to strike the South Carolina coast in thirty-five years—since Hurricane Hazel left a path of destruction and ninety-five deaths in 1954. According to the National Hurricane Center in Miami, Hugo was the tenth strongest storm to strike the United States this century.

Although Hugo was the costliest hurricane in terms of destruction, it was far from the deadliest. Hugo caused 28 deaths, far fewer than several of its predecessors. Hurricane Camille, for instance, left a death toll of 256 when it struck Louisiana and nearby coastal regions in 1969. The

Galveston (Texas) hurricane of 1900, the deadliest of this century in the United States, claimed 6,000 lives.

Extensive damage also occurred in the Caribbean. Winds of 160 miles an hour battered St. Croix, destroying or damaging more than 90 percent of the buildings on the tiny island. Responding to the breakdown of civil authority and widespread looting on St. Croix, an American territory, President George Bush sent 1,100 military police to the island. He declared the American Virgin Islands and the Commonwealth of Puerto Rico disaster areas, allocating $25.3 million in emergency relief for the U.S. Caribbean and $11 million for Puerto Rico. On September 28 Congress approved $1.1 billion in aid for the Virgin Islands, Puerto Rico, and South Carolina.

Waterfront communities were hardest hit in South Carolina. The historic downtown district of Charleston, a showcase of antebellum architecture, was damaged but left largely intact. However, some 50,000 inhabitants of Charleston were displaced. Forewarned of the storm, about 500,000 people along the coast from Jacksonville, Florida, to Cape Hatteras, North Carolina, fled inland for safety.

In the aftermath of the hurricane, the federal relief effort drew sharp criticism from Charleston mayor Joseph P. Riley, Jr. "I'm not sure the extent of the damage from Hugo is understood yet at the federal level," Riley said a week after the storm hit his city. Riley said he asked the Federal Emergency Management Agency (FEMA) for supplies, including generators to provide electric power for 760,000 people, and the agency responded by requesting a cost assessment. "Holy cow! The lights are out. We don't have time to do an assessment," Riley commented.

President Bush traveled to South Carolina September 29 to view the damage and defend the government's relief measures.

California Earthquake

With a force of 7.1 on the Richter scale, the October 17 earthquake was the sixth deadliest in the nation's history, leaving in its wake damage that spread across a 100-mile area in and around San Francisco. Tremors were felt as far as Los Angeles, 350 miles to the southeast, and Reno, Nevada, 225 miles to the northeast. The quake resulted in sixty-seven deaths and 2,500 injuries. It left 10,000 people homeless; the American Red Cross estimated that 14,000 families received temporary shelter, clothes, blankets, and food.

Most of the deaths occurred when a 1.2-mile section of the double-decker Nimitz Freeway (Interstate 880) collapsed in Oakland, crushing more than forty motorists traveling on the lower level during the evening rush hour; the quake struck at 5:04 p.m. PDT, and lasted fifteen seconds. A section of the Bay Bridge connecting Oakland and San Francisco also buckled, killing two motorists and closing the bridge.

Fires created by leaking gas from broken pipes destroyed a block of apartment buildings and damaged many others in San Francisco's affluent Marina District. More than 100,000 buildings were damaged in the region, but only about 1,200 in San Francisco itself. By early 1990, nearly 70,000 claims had been filed with FEMA in the San Francisco Bay area for temporary housing assistance, home and business loans, and other kinds of federal relief aid.

The Loma Prieta area in Santa Cruz County, about seventy-five miles south of the city, was the epicenter of the earthquake. Six persons died in nearby towns and cities, and large portions of downtown Santa Cruz were destroyed. In neighboring Santa Clara County, the quake destroyed much of the Los Gatos business center, disrupted water-treatment facilities, and caused 647 injuries and three deaths. One death and 20 injuries were reported in San Mateo County, south of San Francisco.

Millions of baseball fans across the United States and beyond, watching a telecast of preparations for the third game of the World Series, quickly became aware of the earthquake. ABC-TV crews at Candlestick Park in San Francisco were preparing to televise the game between the San Francisco Giants and the Oakland Athletics; they quickly turned to coverage of the earthquake. The stadium, filled with sixty thousand people, swayed but did not collapse, frightening but not seriously injuring any spectators or players.

Contrast to 1906 Earthquake

The 1989 earthquake was far less destructive than the famous one that wrecked San Francisco in 1906. The earlier earthquake was sixty times more powerful, measuring 8.3 on the Richter scale. It left between 500 and 3,000 dead and 250,000 homeless. Fires caused by that quake destroyed 28,000 buildings.

Carl B. Koon, San Francisco's emergency planning coordinator, said: "We have been planning for [a major earthquake] and anticipating it for years." Within two hours of the first shock waves, at least three hundred off-duty firefighters had reported to work. Key officials—including the mayor and police chief—went to the city's Emergency Operations Center and coordinated the rescue effort. Police and firefighters were aided by scores of bystanders. Rescue workers combed through collapsed structures for survivors; Oakland residents rushed to the freeway to lend assistance. Strict building codes and earthquake-resistant designs, developed in the 1960s, saved hundreds of modern structures. In contrast, the Interstate 880 collapse was attributed to the absence of special structural fitting. The collapsed section had been built in 1955. The Bay Bridge was completed in 1936.

Although as many as 100,000 homes initially were without gas and electricity, the utilities were restored relatively quickly. The Bay Area Rapid Transit System (BART) resumed full service October 18. The interrupted World Series resumed in Candlestick Park on October 27.

> Following is the text of the December 4, 1989, American Red Cross announcement describing its relief efforts in the aftermath of Hurricane Hugo and the California earthquake:

The American Red Cross today thanked the American public and announced that its two-month disaster fund campaign has reached $98 million, a milestone that finally surpasses its unprecedented disaster expenses for Hurricane Hugo, the California earthquake and other recent disasters. The money is two-and-a-half times more than the Red Cross has ever raised for disasters. . . .

The Red Cross estimates it will spend about $94 million on relief efforts for Hugo, the earthquake, and smaller disasters in Kentucky, Texas, Louisiana and Alabama. Red Cross disaster relief estimates for Hugo now stand at $72 million—almost three times the cost of any single disaster in Red Cross history. The costliest Red Cross disaster had been the Ohio-Mississippi flood in 1937, which reached $25 million.

Red Cross relief expenses for the California earthquake are expected to reach $16 million. . . .

Since Hurricane Hugo roared into the Caribbean Sept. 18, the Red Cross has sheltered 188,000 people, served 12 million meals and given financial assistance to 143,000 families and individuals. Some 17,000 Red Cross workers have been helping with relief efforts. . . . [T]he Red Cross gives immediate assistance to help people purchase food, clothing, household and medical items, and other emergency needs. The organization will also assist with rent or temporary repairs. . . .

The Red Cross, which responds to 50,000 disasters every year, has launched similar fund campaigns this decade. In 1985, the Red Cross raised $38 million for a series of six hurricanes that pummeled America's coastlines. About $30 million was raised in 1984 for the African famine. . . .

CONGRESSIONAL REPORT
ON "DISCARDED" CHILDREN
December 11, 1989

A large and growing number of American children live in foster homes, detention centers, shelters, mental health facilities, and hospitals. They are the homeless victims of family breakups, abandonment, poverty, child abuse, and other misfortune. As portrayed in a lengthy report issued December 11 by a congressional committee, they are "discarded children"—cast adrift by family and inadequately cared for by an overwhelmed and underfunded network of child welfare, juvenile justice, and mental health services. Nearly 500,000 children under eighteen years of age fell into this category, according to the report's estimates. By 1995, it added, their ranks could rise to 850,000.

The report, titled "No Place to Call Home: Discarded Children in America," was prepared and released by the House Select Committee on Children, Youth, and Families. This committee based its findings mainly on evidence it had gathered from families, children, and their care providers. They testified at various hearings the committee had conducted, sometimes on its own and sometimes jointly with the House Ways and Means Committee.

In 1980 Congress enacted legislation—the Adoption Assistance and Child Welfare Act—to guarantee support for children in troubled families. This support was to take place in the children's homes and in the communities. If removing children from their homes became necessary, Congress assured them high-quality services, with the hope of eventually reuniting them with their families. If eventually it was determined that the children could not rejoin their families, the law included a commitment to find them permanent homes.

Democratic-Republican Disagreement

The select committee's chairman, Rep. George Miller, D-Calif., said in the report's foreword that the panel wanted to learn if the law's intent was being fulfilled. The answer, as approved by Miller and his fellow Democrats who constituted the committee's majority, was that the problem of caring for these children had grown faster than the government's response. The committee's Republican members, while not disagreeing entirely with that assessment, insisted that some aspects of the problem were overstated.

"Our findings are alarming," Miller said. "Over and over again, witnesses describe agencies in crisis, and services that are failing families and children. The promise extended ten years ago has not been kept, and children are paying the price for this failure."

In their separate statement, the Republican members said that "even with dedicated professionals working in the social welfare system, some families cannot withstand the hurricane force waves of abuse, drugs, sexual exploitation, and violence." The report's information, "while dramatic, and in some cases, overly dramatic, might help us describe the problem, but gives us little direction as to appropriate policy responses," the minority statement continued.

Moreover, it asserted that despite Democratic claims of underfunding, federally supported care programs for homeless children had grown substantially in the 1980s under Republican presidents. According to the committee's figures, federal outlays for five major service programs, including foster-care maintenance and child-welfare services, rose from $1.1 billion in 1981 to $1.35 billion in 1989, as calculated in terms of 1989 buying power.

Tales of Unmet Need

Regardless of how the government's response could properly be characterized, there was no disagreement that the problem was big, and a burden to the care services. An array of witnesses had pictured the care givers typically as shorthanded and underfunded. We "skim the surface of the need," a social service worker testified. Another told the committee: "The only way a lot of these kids can be assured of getting halfway adequate social services is by being locked up.... I've seen concerned police or probation officers incarcerate a kid just to see to it that kid gets a couple of nutritious meals every day ... [and] some basic medical services."

Among the homeless, the report said, families with children have been among the fastest growing groups. It cited a recent survey by the U.S. Conference of Mayors that showed an 18 percent rise during 1988 in the number of requests for shelter by homeless families. Studies by the Department of Housing and Urban Development indicated that on any given night families accounted for about 40 percent of the people using shelters in 1988, in contrast to 21 percent in 1984.

Following are excerpts from the report, "No Place to Call Home," issued December 11, 1989 by the House Select Committee on Children, Youth, and Families, describing the plight of nearly 500,000 children in the United States:

Findings

1. More Children Placed Outside of Their Homes

Dramatic increases in the numbers of children placed outside their homes have occurred during the decade of the 1980s, and are continuing to occur in the child welfare, juvenile justice and mental health systems:

- Nearly 500,000 children are currently estimated in out-of-home placement. If current trends continue, by 1995, that population is projected to increase by an estimated 73.4% to more than 840,000 children.
- In the child welfare system, the number of children in foster care has risen by an estimated 23% between 1985 and 1988 in contrast to a 9% decline between 1980 and 1985, according to new data collected by the Select Committee on Children, Youth, and Families.
    - There were an estimated 340,300 children in foster care in 1988, compared to 276,300 in 1985.
    - In California, which has one in five of the nation's children in foster care, the number of foster children increased by 44% during that period; in Michigan by 34%; in New York by 29%; and in Illinois by 19%. By contrast, in New Jersey and North Carolina, the number of foster children declined by 5% and 7% respectively.
- In the juvenile justice system, the number of youth held in public and private juvenile facilities in 1987 had increased by 27% since 1979, 10% between 1985-87 alone. There were 91,646 juveniles in custody in 1987, compared with 83,402 in 1985 and 71,922 in 1979. In 1987, 353 juveniles per 100,000 were in custody compared with 313 per 100,000 in 1985 and 251 per 100,000 in 1979, a 41% increase in custody rates during this decade.
- In the mental health system, there was a 60% increase in the number of children under 18 in care as inpatients in hospitals, in residential treatment centers or in other residential care settings between 1983 and 1986. At the end of 1986, 54,716 children were in care, compared with 34,068 in 1983.

2. More Children Experience Repeat Placements

- Between 1983 and 1985, the number of children placed in foster care more than once nearly doubled, from 16% to 30%.
- There has been no significant progress in reducing the average length of stay of children in foster care. In 1985, the percentage of children in care more than 2 years stood at 39%, relatively unchanged from 1983.

3. Younger Children Entering Out-of-Home
Placement at Increasing Rate

- In 1988, a greater proportion—42%—of the children who entered foster care were under six years old, compared with those who entered in 1985 (37%), according to a Select Committee survey.
  - In Missouri, nearly one out of every two children entering the Division of Family Services placement system is between birth and six years of age.

4. Minority Children Disproportionately Represented

- While the majority of children in foster care is white, in 1985, minority children comprised 41% of the children in foster care; by 1988, that proportion is estimated to have increased to approximately 46%— more than twice the proportion of minority children in the nation's child population.
- The median length of stay for black children in care is one-third longer than the national median, according to a recent study of 1,000 black children in care.

5. Drug and Alcohol Abuse Contribute Substantially
to Increased Out-of-Home Placements

- The number of infants born drug-exposed—an estimated 375,000 nationwide in 1988—has nearly quadrupled in the last three years in hospitals across the country. Many ... are abandoned or neglected, often becoming "boarder babies" in hospitals, or foster children.
- State and local child services systems report the serious impact of substance abuse on their caseloads:
  - New York: In 1988, crack use was identified in nearly 9,000 cases of child neglect, over three times the number of such cases in 1986;
  - District of Columbia: more than 80% of the reported cases of child abuse and neglect involved substance abuse;
  - Florida: 33% of all reported cases of child abuse were substance-abuse-related;
  - California: up to 60% of drug-exposed infants have been placed in foster care;
  - Illinois: the number of infants requiring placement out of home for substance-abuse-related reasons totalled 1,223 in 1988, a 132% increase over 1987.

6. Other Deteriorating Social Conditions Jeopardize
Child Safety, Fuel Child Placement Explosion

- Between 1981-1988, reports of abused or neglected children rose 82%, reaching 2.2 million. In 1988, deaths from child abuse exceeded

1,200—more than a 36% increase since 1985.

- The U.S. Conference of Mayors reports an 18% increase in requests for shelter by homeless families between 1987 and 1988. Many cities cannot accommodate homeless families with children, resulting in family break-up and the entry of children into substitute care. Homelessness was a factor in over 40% of the placements into foster care in New Jersey in 1986, and in 18% of the placements, it was the sole precipitating cause of placement.

7. Child Services Systems Overwhelmed

- An estimated 70-80% of emotionally disturbed children get inappropriate mental health services or no services at all.
- Foster family homes—for decades the mainstay of out-of-home care resources—are far too few to meet the demand. In California between 1986 and 1988, the number of foster family homes increased by 11%, while the number of foster children increased by 28%.
- Excessive caseloads overburden the system's ability to provide minimal care and appropriate services.
  - In Los Angeles, the average foster care worker caseload in 1988 was between 75 and 78 children.
  - In California, juvenile probation officers carried average caseloads of between 65 and 80.
  - In large urban areas, one judge may hear as many as 100 abuse and neglect proceedings a day.
  - As of September 1989, the District of Columbia's child welfare system had not completed investigations on a reported backlog of more than 700 cases involving some 1,200 children.
- In 1985, adoption was the goal for approximately 36,000 of the 276,300 children in foster care; more than 16,000 were awaiting adoption; and 79% of them had been waiting more than six months.

8. Failures of Federal Leadership, Funding and Oversight Impede Effective Services for Children and Families in Crisis

- Despite soaring increases in the number of children in state care, federal funding has not kept pace:
  - Funding for child welfare services that provide prevention and reunification support has not yet reached the 1980 authorized level of $266 million.
  - While the number of youth in juvenile facilities increased 27% between 1979 and 1987, funding for the federal Juvenile Justice and Delinquency Prevention Act has declined from $100 million in 1979 to $70 million in 1981, to $66.7 million in 1989.
  - Despite new data demonstrating that millions of children need mental health services, the principal federal support for mental

health services, the Alcohol, Drug Abuse and Mental Health Block Grant, provided $503 million in FY 1989, $17 million less than the sum of the categorical programs prior to consolidation into the Block Grant in 1981. There is no separate funding for children's mental health services, and only since 1988 has 10% of the mental health share of the Block Grant been set aside for community-based mental health services for seriously disturbed children and youth.

- Federal reimbursements to the states under Title IV-E of the Social Security Act (foster care maintenance program) have grown from $546.2 million in 1985 to $891 million in 1988. States have expanded permanency planning services and claimed federal funds more thoroughly under federal law and regulations to serve an estimated 122,949 children who were in IV-E foster care in 1988, up 17% from 1981, and up 13% from 1985. While states have utilized changes in definitions to claim additional federal support, the definitions in the law do not provide for precise accounting about the use of these monies.

- Funding mechanisms create disincentives to keeping families together and maintaining children in the community. For example:
  - Open-ended federal matching funding is provided to the states for expenditures under the Title IV-E foster care maintenance program at an average of 53% of eligible costs; only very limited funding is available for placement prevention and family preservation.
  - In Minnesota, the mandatory mental health and chemical dependency health insurance laws provide financial incentives favoring inpatient over outpatient care.

- Weak federal monitoring and oversight have undermined implementation of protections and services under P.L. 96-272, the Adoption Assistance and Child Welfare Act of 1980. The Department of Health and Human Services (DHHS) fails to monitor the requirement to make "reasonable efforts" to prevent the need for placement and to make it possible for a child to return home, and fails to assess whether states' Title IV-B child welfare services programs are adequate to meet the needs of the children and families served. The Office of Juvenile Justice and Delinquency Prevention conducts little monitoring of state activity under the juvenile justice law.

- There are no complete and accurate national data on children in publicly-funded substitute care. This seriously compromises planning and service-delivery by the states and the federal government.

9. Prevention and Early Intervention Programs Show Great Program Benefits and Cost Effectiveness

- Family preservation programs which provide intensive in-home services to families at risk of having a child removed have demonstrated success:

- In family preservation programs in Washington and Utah, 68% of children who received services remained in their own homes or with relatives. By contrast, 69% of children who did not receive services were placed out-of-home.
- Only 2% of the families served under Maryland's Intensive Family Services' program required out-of-home placement, at an estimated cost saving of $6,174 in averted foster care costs per child.
- In Virginia's family preservation effort, only 7% of participating families during 1986 experienced placement; 69% showed improved family functioning; the intervention cost $1,214 per child compared with $11,173 for foster care and $22,025 for residential care.

- Administrators, providers and advocates agree that future help for children must reverse current funding patterns, provide earlier support for both children and their families, and forge a comprehensive service system that responds to individual needs.

Chapter I. Children and Families in Crisis

... New data collected by the Select Committee on Children, Youth, and Families indicate that there are more children in care today than before passage of P.L. 96-272.... In 1980, the foster care population numbered approximately 302,000. That number reportedly dropped to 267,000 in 1982 and was reported at 269,000 in 1983 for the 50 states and the District of Columbia. The most recently published national survey reported more than 276,000 children in foster care at the end of 1985, and experts consider that count conservative.

By all accounts, since 1985 the placement rate has surged. To determine the extent of this increase, the Select Committee conducted a telephone survey of the 10 most populous states to obtain the most recent data on the number of children in substitute care. The states surveyed were California, Florida, Illinois, Michigan, New Jersey, New York, North Carolina, Ohio, Pennsylvania and Texas. (Together these states accounted for 52% of the total 1980 foster care population and 51% of the 1985 foster care population.) Recent available data for Missouri, the 15th most populous state, were also included in calculating estimates of the total foster care population, bringing the proportion of the total foster care population that was accounted for to 54%.

The 10 surveyed states were variously able to respond to the committee's request for information. All provided some data on the numbers of children in care through 1988. Nine of the 10 were able to report data by age, race, time in care and/or outcome for one or more years after 1985.

Based on this survey, the Committee estimates that approximately 340,300 children were in foster care at any point in 1988, representing an increase of 23% since 1985, in dramatic contrast to the 9% decline seen from 1980 to 1985....

Youth in public and private youth facilities in 1987 totaled 91,646, up 10% from 83,402 in 1985 and 27% from 71,922 in 1979. The number of juveniles held in publicly run facilities in 1987 totalled 53,503, the highest number since the Department of Justice conducted the first *Children In Custody* census in 1971, representing an 8% increase over 1985, and a 24% increase since 1979. The number of youth in private facilities was 38,143 in 1987, up 12% from 1985, and 33% from 1979.

Of these children, more than 35,000 individuals were confined in long-term, public juvenile institutions, the majority of which are state-operated. Approximately 60% of the juveniles and young adults in these long-term institutions were between the ages of 15 and 17; 12% were younger and 27% were older....

Corresponding growth has occurred in the number of public and private facilities housing children served by the juvenile justice system. The census found that states or local government agencies operated 1,107 facilities in 1987, or 9% more than they operated in 1979 and 6% more than 1985. The number of private facilities grew from 1,561 in 1979 to 1,996 in 1985 and 2,195 in 1987....

The number of children in placement as a result of emotional problems also has risen dramatically over the last few years. According to the end-of-year census conducted by the National Institute of Mental Health, in 1983 there were 34,060 children under 18 in care as inpatients in hospitals, in a residential treatment center or other residential care setting. The count at the end of 1987 had increased more than 60% to 54,716.

Over a year period, the total number of children in such facilities is much higher, approximately 100,000 children. In addition, about 2 million children receive mental health treatment in out-patient settings....

More children and their families are now living in precarious economic circumstances. Nearly three million more U.S. children fell into poverty over the last decade and today, one in five children (13 million) lives in poverty....

Changing family demographics have also profoundly affected children's living situations. For example, while one in 10 children lived with only one parent in 1960, currently nearly one in four lives in a single-parent family. Between 1970 and 1988, the percentage of children with working mothers has increased by 54%....

Perhaps the major problem fueling the increasing numbers of children in care has been the rapid growth in the numbers of children reported as abused and neglected. A 1988 Department of Health and Human Services report ... documented a 64% increase over 1980 in the number of children reported, and using a revised definition agreed upon by experts in the field, a 150% increase in actual child abuse and neglect victims. This report is consistent with the findings of the Select Committee's 1986 study on child abuse that documented a 55% increase in reports of abuse and neglect between 1981 and 1985 and the more than 11% average annual increase during the first half of the decade noted by the American

Association for Protecting Children.

The absolute number of reports behind these percentages is very large. There were 2.2 million reports of maltreatment filed in 1988, according to the National Committee for the Prevention of Child Abuse. This represents an increase of 82% from the 1.2 million children reports recorded for 1981 by the American Humane Association and a 17% increase above the number of reports recorded by the Select Committee in its 1986 study of child protective and child welfare services. . . .

Children in the growing numbers of homeless families are at risk of placement into substitute state care. One-third of the homeless population, estimated to number up to 2.2 million, are families with children. Estimates of the number of children in the United States who are homeless on any given night range from 50,000 to 500,000. . . .

Among the homeless, families with children have been among the fastest growing groups. . . . Studies by the Department of Housing and Urban Development indicate that, on any given night, the proportion of shelter-using homeless who are family members has increased from 21% in 1984 to 40% in 1988. . . .

The epidemic of drug and alcohol abuse has placed increasing numbers of vulnerable children, families and communities in crises, resulting in more reports of child abuse and neglect, and greater need for care and out-of-home placements. . . .

According to the National Committee for the Prevention of Child Abuse and Neglect, 33% of all reported cases of child abuse in the State of Florida are related to substance abuse. In the District of Columbia, almost 25% of the 6,000 cases of child abuse and neglect reported to Child and Family Services Division of the City's Department of Human Services in 1985 involved alcohol abuse and emotional problems, generally related to other forms of substance abuse. By fiscal year 1988, that percentage had grown to more than 80%. The National Black Child Development Institute's study of black children in foster care found that drug abuse by parents was reported as a contributing factor to placement in 36% of the 1,000 cases studied. . . .

The problems of substance abuse are increasingly pervasive, affecting children at younger and younger ages in all systems of care. As one witness told the Committee,

> Alcohol and drug abuse are appearing very early. We're seeing nine- and ten-year-old kids who are heavy drinkers and who are beginning to abuse crack. . . .

Increasing numbers of infants are being born drug-exposed placing them at particular risk of multiple problems that lead to out-of-home care. An estimated 375,000 infants were born drug-exposed in 1988. A recent Select Committee survey of public and private metropolitan hospitals in 15 major U.S. cities documented the devastating impact of substance abuse-related problems for pregnant women, infants and families. The survey reported a three- to fourfold increase in perinatal drug exposure between 1985 and 1988. . . .

Authorities further report that the drug trade and the nationwide spread of youth gangs involved in the drug trade have stimulated a sharp increase in the level of violence associated with juvenile crime that also brings youth into the juvenile justice system. The number of juveniles arrested for violent crime (homicide, rape, robbery, and aggravated assault) increased between 1984 and 1986, after a 20% decline between 1974 and 1984. . . .

The children in care today are children who have been abused and/or neglected; children who suffer a variety of mental health problems; children who have been exposed to drugs perinatally and/or throughout their lives; children who have committed crimes or otherwise run afoul of the law; adolescents with little schooling and no job skills, pregnant teens and teens with babies; and children whose chaotic and distressed family lives due to poverty, homelessness, mental illness and a cluster of other contributing factors bring them into state care. . . .

In the juvenile justice system, a disproportionate number of children also have a history of multiple problems, including child abuse, learning disabilities, severe emotional disturbance, school failure, behavioral disorders, and family problems. . . .

The fact that so many children have multiple needs means that traditional divisions between child welfare, juvenile justice and mental health may no longer make sense and may create barriers to appropriate services for individual children. . . .

The picture that emerges is one in which children entering state care today typically exhibit far more difficult and often multiple problems, have been in care before, and often move from one service system to another rather than returning to their families permanently. . . .

Two groups of children comprise the major new entrants into substitute care under public responsibility: one, infants and young children, many with medical complications resulting in actual or potential physical and mental limitations; two, many older children who continue through the revolving doors of state care.

In 1988, a greater proportion—42%—of the children who entered foster care were under six years old, compared with those who entered in 1985 (37%), according to the Select Committee's 10-state survey. The largest change appeared in the number of very young children entering the system.

The increased proportion of young children entering the foster care system is due to both demographic and social factors. Nationally, the Census Bureau estimates that this population of children will have increased by 17% between 1980 and 1990, while the adolescent population will have decreased by 14%. . . .

Widespread substance abuse appears to be the other major factor contributing to the increasing numbers of young children entering placement. . . .

In addition to increasing numbers of younger children entering systems of care, particularly foster care, there remains a high proportion of older children in state care.

> Over the last decade, we've been successful returning younger children to their homes more quickly; the foster care population has increasingly come to consist of older, seriously troubled children. . . . The preponderance of teen-agers in the child welfare system has produced a new set of problems; teens are much more likely than younger children to be delinquents or status offenders. Serious long-standing family problems often require out-of-home placement, but traditional foster home settings are ill-equipped to respond to their needs. Further an older child's family situation may prove so difficult to resolve that reunification can never occur. . . .

> The patients we now see are showing behavioral changes. They're more apt to present us with a long history of police and correctional contacts as well as residential treatment as well as previous psychiatric history. They are more apt to experience academic and vocational failure. They're very likely to have had an experience of a mixture of alcohol and poly drug abuse. . . .

While the majority of children placed away from their homes are white, minority and low-income children are disproportionately represented in out-of-home state care.

In 1985, minority children comprised 41% of the children in foster care. Based on the Select Committee's recent survey of substitute care in 10 states, the proportion of minority children entering foster care has increased slightly to 46%. The proportion of minority children in foster care is more than twice the proportion of minority children to the nation's child population, estimated to be about 19%. . . .

The increasing overrepresentation of minority children and youth is even more skewed in the juvenile justice system. The number of white juveniles held in public facilities decreased slightly between 1985 and 1987, while the number of black and Hispanic juveniles increased 15% and 20%, respectively. In 1987, 56% of the juveniles in custody were a racial and/or ethnic minority. . . .

At worst, the children entering care are not helped—and are often hurt—by the very system that has been designed to protect them. Increasingly, many of the children who die as a result of maltreatment are known to the public service agencies charged with protecting and serving them.

Many witnesses before the Committee submitted that in the end, children may be traumatized as much or more by the failure of agencies that are supposed to help than by the problems that brought them to the attention of public child welfare agencies in the first place. . . .

Chapter II. Children's Services in Crisis

A. State and Local Agencies, Courts Overwhelmed

1. Services Are in Short Supply.

In many cases, effective services are in short supply, "skim-[ming] the surface of the need." Regardless of the system, the lament is the same:

where services exist, they are generally ineffective, inappropriate, or inefficient.

> The range of services [is] frequently unavailable, there is very little coordina-
> tion among the systems that are mandated to serve our children and there is
> usually no plan to determine which agencies should be responsible for serving
> a particular child. Consequently, our children are unserved, underserved or
> served inappropriately.

The shortage and inappropriateness of services are common within and across care systems. Shortages of preventive services, family foster care placements, group home placements, reunification services, health care, mental health treatment, rehabilitative services, crisis and respite services, educational programs and transitional services are increasingly common.

Across the country, children who are at risk of developing an emotional illness, of being abused or neglected, or of breaking the law, often remain undiagnosed or are placed on waiting lists for evaluation and treatment.

**a. Most acute shortages occur in prevention and early inter-
vention programs.** Witnesses repeatedly told the Committee that needy children and families get attention and services only after the fact—after abuse has occurred, after a crime has been committed, or after a child has died.

> The problems of these children go unnoticed or misdiagnosed through a
> troubled and troublesome school career until after repeated contacts with the
> juvenile justice system they are finally 'discovered.' Even then there [is] often
> no remediation or habilitation available.

> Seven years have passed since the passage of P.L. 96-272 which mandates
> preventive services, and recent research has shown that services are being
> offered unevenly at best. There is some indication that they [services] still may
> be triggered more by placement than offered in preventing placement.

> The flow of dollars still favors out-of-home care, at the expense of alternatives
> designed to preserve families or prepare children in care who cannot return
> home for adoption or independent living.

Services that reach and serve individuals with problems of substance abuse—currently one of the major factors leading to out-of-home place-ment—remain largely unavailable and terribly inadequate where they do exist. In the Select Committee's survey on drug-addicted infants and their mothers, two-thirds of the hospitals surveyed reported that they had no place to send pregnant women for drug treatment. . . .

Mental health services also seldom get to children in need. . . .

An estimated 70% to 80% of emotionally disturbed children receive inappropriate mental health services or no services at all. . . .

The juvenile justice system reflects a similar scarcity of services and treatment, whether community-based or not. . . .

> . . . [S]ome witnesses suggested that the juvenile justice system is often used
> inappropriately because no other services are available. The juvenile justice

system becomes the social service agency of first resort. The only way a lot of these kids can be assured of getting halfway adequate social services is by getting locked up. . . . I've seen concerned police or probation officers incarcerate a kid just to see to it that kid gets a couple of nutritious meals every day, gets some basic medical services, and has someone to keep them from hurting themselves or damaging their brains with chemicals, at least for the time being. . . .

The foster care system has traditionally relied on families and service agencies in a community to provide homes for children whose biological families cannot care for them. . . .

Yet, the reality of today's foster care system falls short of this ideal in almost every way. The number of available foster parents is inadequate and shrinking. This reflects the fact that the pool of families potentially available to be foster families has been reduced because of the changing demographic profile of American families in which both parents work. Consequently, there are fewer families available to assume the responsibility of being foster or adoptive parents. . . .

In addition, there has been insufficient assistance to foster parents to enable them to support and properly care for these children, many of whom have special needs. . . .

Even when services exist, they are not organized or designed in a fashion which responds comprehensively to the needs of the child or the family. . . .

Administrators and practitioners concur that almost nothing has been done "to make structural linkages between education, health, mental health, developmental disabilities, juvenile justice, and legal systems." In fact, structure, "turf" issues and categorical program design were cited repeatedly as principal barriers to delivering needed services to troubled children and families. . . .

> Children in one system are often ineligible for services from another. Labels are attached to children who enter public systems—some are 'abused,' 'neglected,' 'dependent' or 'emotionally disturbed'; others are 'runaways' or 'adjudicated youths'—but the labels tell nothing about the children's special service needs. Rather, they only indicate to which public agency responsibility for a child has fallen and the restrictions that will apply to the child's care. . . .

Chapter III. Promising Programs to Prevent Placement

. . . The Select Committee's continuing examination of children in state care has revealed numerous effective and promising programs that assist vulnerable children and families. From health care to social service needs, from infancy through adulthood, researchers and providers increasingly recommend efforts that emphasize early rather than late intervention. They also advocate providing services to children in a coordinated, comprehensive fashion, and in a home setting whenever possible.

A wide range of child welfare experts testified to the value of prevention and early intervention in eliminating or reducing problems that, left unattended, became much more complex, difficult and costly. . . .

Testimony emphasized that effective prevention and early intervention strategies are not just limited to efforts with infants and young children. . . .

> Family based services are a fairly new, rapidly growing area of child welfare services in which the focus is on the whole family, not on individual members of the family; in which services are provided intensively, that is at least 1 to 2 hours a week, minimum, face-to-face contact with the family; which are generally short-term, lasting no longer than 3 to 6 months and which are enabled by low caseloads averaging about 10. . . .

A number of states and local communities have begun to develop and expand these programs with impressive results so far. . . .

While many states and local communities have developed interest in and begun to support model efforts, very little federal funding has been available to states for these activities. . . .

No Place To Call Home: Discarded Children in America Dissenting Views

The increase in children placed in the care of the state is a reflection of what is happening in our society—the devaluation of human life. The report is an admission that even with dedicated professionals working in the social welfare system, some families cannot withstand the hurricane force waves of abuse, drugs, sexual exploitation, and violence which have unleashed their destruction on society. Thus, this report is a challenge to us all.

This report "from the front" paints a Dickens-like picture of children in state care who are "traumatized" by the very systems designed to help them. But to assume that the Select Committee report can be relied upon to help make policy would be a mistake. The anecdotes presented here are not a substitute for basic national information about what the state and locals are doing in child welfare. This information, while dramatic, and in some cases, overly dramatic, might help us describe the problem, but gives us little direction as to appropriate policy responses. . . .

Problems With Projections

While we agree that the growing numbers of children in substitute care concern us all, we strongly reject the projected data the Majority would have us adopt. We cannot agree with the "finding" that "out-of-home placement" will increase by over 70 percent to more than 840,000 children. . . .

Federal/State Responsibility

While the report faults the federal government for weak compliance standards, the facts are that, as weak as they are, the states have not been able to comply even with these admittedly weak guidelines.

Ten years after the enactment of federal legislation designed to provide protections for children in out-of-home care, we find that we still don't know how many children are in care; how many are waiting to be adopted;

how many have realistic goals of going back home, etc. Clearly, additional nation-wide information on adoption and foster care is needed.

Republican members of the Select Committee on Children, Youth, and Families have ordered four different GAO reports, which provide convincing evidence that at present the procedures and protections put in place by the federal government to protect children have not been implemented by the states. . . .

Drugs Driving Increase in Out-of-Home Placements

Although the Committee Republicans disagree with the size of the increase in out-of-home placements based on a ten-state survey, we are in complete agreement that an increase of some proportion is happening. There is no question that drug-related behaviors are driving the increase in out-of-home placements. Questions abound, however, in terms of appropriate policy response.

Traditionally, the child welfare system has only reluctantly considered termination of parental rights. With increasing recognition of the effects of parental drug abuse on children, coupled with high rates of recidivism among patients in drug treatment centers, doubts are raised about the extent to which permanent placement plans can be made for children of substance abusers without increased attention to adoption options. . . .

Child Abuse

While the number of child abuse allegations continues to climb, the Republicans hesitate to equate this increase with a rise in the number of incidents. . . .

Contributing to the confusion surrounding the interpretation of child abuse numbers are the following factors: each state defines child abuse, neglect and sexual abuse differently; and there are different reportable conditions. Thus, the wide variance in definitions makes any across-state or nationwide data less meaningful.

Homelessness

Homelessness does place children at increased risk for substitute care. The numbers that estimate the size of the problem, however, should be read with caution. . . . No family in America ought to be without a "place to call home"; the tragedy lies not with the spirit of the American people reflected in government policies, but in the tragic breakdown of human relationships.

Funding

The rhetoric of the majority on support for child welfare programs sometimes does not match reality. Our federal, state and local governments indeed provide many forms of assistance to our children in foster care. The funding for the Title IV-E Foster Care program has increased in constant dollar terms every year since 1980 and now totals nearly $1.1 billion. In addition, many foster care children are eligible for Medicaid. . . .

The Challenge for the 1990s

The pressures of a materialistic, "have it all, have it now" society can threaten families. The question of the times is, "can we master the technological age while keeping our values intact in today's world?" It is a challenge to the "mediating structures" in our society, including churches, to recognize that physical abuse is a sign of spirituality in crisis. The children who have been abandoned by their parents must be assured that they have not been abandoned by the extended family of our society.

NAVIGATION FOUNDATION BACKS PEARY'S NORTH POLE CLAIM

December 11, 1989

Robert E. Peary, accompanied by four Eskimo companions and his black assistant, Matthew Henson, staked the American flag in the arctic ice on April 6, 1909, and announced to the world his discovery of the North Pole. "Stars and stripes nailed to the Pole!" Peary wired American news services upon returning from the frozen wasteland. Unfortunately for him, however, a rival named Frederick Cook telegraphed from the Shetland Islands a few days earlier that he and two Eskimos had reached the pole nearly a year earlier, on April 21, 1908. Whoever was first would be ensured fame and fortune, and the gratitude of his country. In that era, polar exploration held a popular fascination akin to space travel at a later time.

The world, so to speak, chose sides. Peary had his loyal backers and fierce detractors, but many people chose to believe Cook, an affable surgeon. He did not personally contest Peary's claim but charitably asserted that "two records are better than one." Peary's sponsoring organization, the National Geographic Society, examined his claim and pronounced it valid. Peary, then a captain in the U.S. Navy, submitted himself and his expedition records to a congressional subcommittee that was considering a bill to bestow on him the "Thanks of Congress" and retire him with the honorary rank and pay of a rear admiral. Ultimately the bill was passed, but not before a lineup of witnesses questioned the authenticity of his records—whether he had indeed been at or near the North Pole.

This controversy was never stilled entirely. Another congressional inquiry followed in 1916. Cook's claim was discredited in later years, although he never ceased to find champions of his cause. The arguments over Peary's claim flared up periodically into the 1980s, usually following the publication of one book or another that questioned it. In 1988 a Baltimore professor of astronomy, Dennis Rawlins, announced in the Washington Post *that he had discovered a long-suppressed document containing calculations by Peary that proved the explorer had faked his claim and was actually more than one hundred miles from the pole. National attention was focused on Rawlins, who had already cast doubt on the claim in his 1973 book,* Peary at the North Pole: Fact or Fiction? *(Peary's Polar Notes, Historic Documents of 1988, p. 831)*

The National Geographic Society asked the Navigation Foundation (formally the Foundation for the Promotion of the Art of Navigation), a Maryland-based group dedicated to preserving the art of navigation, to examine Rawlins's charges and study Peary's records anew. The foundation's book-length report, titled "Robert E. Peary at the North Pole", was released December 11, 1989. It reported that the document upon which Rawlins based his analysis was in fact unrelated to Peary's whereabouts. Instead of being calculations for compass variation, which Rawlins presumed, they were serial numbers on Peary's chronometer watches, the report concluded.

The Navigation Foundation's study went further, examining all the evidence it could muster from Peary's diary, notes, and other records. It turned for help to fields such as arctic oceanography, bathymetry, and forensic photography (photoprogrammetric analysis). For example, a picture taken at Peary's camp on April 7, 1909, depicting two men in front of a flag atop a pile of snow, enabled forensic photography experts to calculate that the sun angle in the photograph was 6.8 degrees. They concluded that the scene was very close to the pole, because the sun angle at the pole that day, as determined by astronomy, was 6.8 degrees. Other types of sophisticated calculations also provided evidence to justify Peary's assertions, the report recounted.

"The ultimate question addressed in this our final report is whether Peary arrived at his intended goal or whether he faked his journey," said Thomas D. Davis, a retired rear admiral who heads the foundation, in the report's introduction. "We realized with a jolt at the beginning of our inquiry that there is no middle ground. . . . He was either an out-and-out impostor like Dr. Frederick Cook, or a genuine American hero who deserved the honors bestowed on him in his lifetime, and now deserves far more respect than he has been accorded by the media. We feel that the time has come to determine once and for all how Robert E. Peary will go down in the history books."

That determination was expressed in the report in these words: "[W]e can categorically say that Peary realized his lifelong goal of attaining the Pole on the last of his many expeditions. Certainly we turned up no evidence to the contrary."

Gilbert M. Grosvenor, president of the National Geographic Society, wrote in the January 1990 issue of the society's National Geographic *magazine that the report "seems unimpeachable." He added that "unless something better comes along, I consider this the end of a historic controversy and the confirmation of due justice to a great explorer." But the controversy did not end. Rawlins contended that it was impossible to establish Peary's positions with the accuracy that the report purported. "There are large errors running around in the analysis," he said. Charles Cowall, an astronomer at the Space Telescope Science Institute in Baltimore, said: "What I resent is the way the [National] Geographic is trying at all costs to be an advocate of Peary. That's not the proper stance for an educational or scientific organization."*

Following is the text of the "Summary and Conclusion" section of the report by the Foundation for the Promotion of the Art of Navigation entitled "Robert E. Peary at the North Pole," issued December 11, 1989, supporting the accuracy of Peary's claim to have reached the North Pole:

We, the directors of the Navigation Foundation, are pleased to report that we have unanimously concluded that Robert E. Peary, Matt Henson and their four Eskimo companions reached the North Pole on April 6, 1909. Our analysis of the data Peary brought back from his journey—his celestial sights, his diary, his ocean soundings and his photographs—has convinced us that their final camp, named Camp Jesup, was no more than five miles from the Pole, allowing for some inaccuracy in their instruments. Thus our study confirms the decision of the original three-man committee of experts appointed by the National Geographic Society in 1909 to examine and pass upon Peary's claim.

Our conclusion is based upon a year of intensive research by members of the Foundation who have combed through 225 cubic feet of papers at the National Archives, and have reviewed materials from the archives of the American Geographical Society, the National Geographic Society, the Explorers Club of New York, the Library of Congress, the Smithsonian Institution, the Peary-MacMillan Arctic Studies Center at Bowdoin College, Maine, and many other public and private institutions. In addition, we have had access to bathymetric and other data provided by government agencies, including the Department of Defense Mapping Agency, the Naval Observatory, the Office of Naval Research, the Naval Oceanographic Office, the Navy Polar Oceanographic Command and the NOAA Snow and Ice Data center.

To our surprise we found that remarkably little new information relating to Peary's claim has been introduced in the succession of critical books and articles that have appeared in the seven decades since the explorer's death in 1920, and few new issues have been raised since the Congressional hearings of 1911 and 1916. We determined that in our study we would not merely scrutinize the charges that have been brought against him by those who label his claim a hoax, but that we would examine the proofs he brought back from his journey in the light of all applicable scientific data and techniques. We have now done so, as is explained below.

At the outset, however, in Part I, "Peary's Role in Arctic Exploration," we review the story of Peary's life and his achievements against the background of what had been accomplished by courageous arctic explorers who had preceded him. In their day we must realize that these men were tantamount to the astronauts of the 1960's whose goal was to reach the moon. We touch upon Peary's early explorations in Greenland, which took him over the great interior ice cap to the uncharted east coast of northern Greenland, and eventually enabled him to determine the insularity of Greenland. And we take note of his early futile attempts to reach the North Pole via bases in northern Greenland or Ellesmere Island, one of which nearly cost him his life and did cost him the loss of eight toes. Though the experience might have deterred a less determined explorer, Peary persisted and in 1906 established a new "farthest north" record of latitude 87-06, which meant that he had come closer to the top of the world than any explorer before him.

Then finally in 1909, on a journey in which fortune smiled on him by favoring him with good weather, relatively smooth ice surfaces, and few open water leads, he claimed to have reached the Pole at last. He came home, however, to find that most Americans had already accorded the honor of being first at the Pole to his rival, Dr. Frederick Cook. When the Cook-Peary controversy was finally resolved, Peary emerged as the sole contender for the prize. Though he eventually attained public recognition and the honors he deserved, his enjoyment of them was diminished by the ensuing battles with hostile Congressmen, spurred on by his enemies, among whom was General Adolphus Greely whose own arctic expedition had ended disastrously. The story of Peary's life and career is therefore one of bitter irony.

In Part II, "Peary's Navigation," we show that the explorer's method of navigation, which he described to the Congressional committee as "dead reckoning" corrected by noon observations of the sun, was entirely adequate for polar latitudes. It was, in fact, the method used by Roald Amundsen on his successful trip to the South Pole in 1911. There was no need for longitude observations and none were taken—a factor which has evoked unwarranted criticism from persons who have not grasped his techniques. His method called for finding the direction of the Pole from the sun as often as feasible. By always heading straight for the Pole itself, however he had been diverted, he compensated as he went along for the effects of ice drift, changing magnetic variation, and detours to the east or west due to open water leads and unsurmountable pressure ridges. His was a zigzag course with his heading intermittently corrected to true north, not a beeline up a given meridian.

Peary's compass always pointed to the magnetic pole and not true north. However, he was able to set his compass course by the sun, which, when visible on the trip north, lay exactly due south at "local apparent noon," the moment at which the sun reaches its highest altitude above the horizon. To make an observation for apparent noon, he used a sextant to measure the angle between the sun and the horizon. Since the frozen Arctic Ocean with its ice ridges does not provide a clean horizon, he used an instrument called an artificial horizon—a small wooden pan covered with glass and filled with liquid mercury. The mercury acts as a perfectly level mirror, and the sextant measures the angle between the sun and its reflected image.

When taking a sun sight, he would note the time of culmination on his watch, and it is important to note that the time indicated by the watch did not have to be the "correct" time. Much has been made of the fact that the *Roosevelt*'s chronometers were fast when Peary set his watches from them upon starting for the Pole. We have determined that the most probable error of the watches was less than one minute, but whatever the error was, it did not matter, since the time of the sun's maximum altitude determined the time of local noon. Whatever his watch read when the maximum altitude was achieved was regarded as local noon on subsequent days when noon sights were not taken, but the direction of the noon sun was used whenever it was visible. We are persuaded that Peary's system of navigation was adequate to get him to the near vicinity of the Pole, without taking longitude observations along the way.

We also examined the patterns of ice drift in the Arctic Ocean, and the expedition members' accounts of winds and ice movements experienced, and concluded that Peary was able to maintain a relatively direct course to the Pole up the 70th meridian. We determined that the initial drift westward noted by the explorer Wally Herbert, in his *National Geographic Magazine* article (September 1988) and in his book, *The Noose of Laurels* (1989) was offset by a subsequent rapid eastward movement of the ice that he apparently overlooked.

Herbert's conjecture as to Peary's track (which places him west of the Pole for his entire journey) is based upon a westward drift of the ice just north of Cape Columbia of about 20 miles in the first three days, caused by easterly winds. He asserts that from the outset of the polar assault Peary was always west of where he thought he was because he had failed to take this phenomenon into account. However, Herbert overlooked the fact that after returning to the land base for supplies, expedition members Ross Marvin and George Borup recorded that westerly winds (also noted by Peary) were moving the ice rapidly back eastward. To their surprise the outbound trail, which earlier had been driven 15 miles west of Cape Columbia, had drifted back almost to its original position. We have thus concluded that during the entire northward trip, Peary would have experienced only a slight westward drift due to the net effect of the wind.

Moreover, available modern data indicate that he would have experienced a slight *eastward* ice movement as he got closer to the Pole. In sum, from our study of ice drifts caused by winds and currents, we think that the net effect of ice movements within the time span of Peary's polar journey was negligible.

Since Peary's critics have unanimously denounced as "faked" the celestial observations he brought back from the Pole, we minutely examined those sights for mistakes that a faker would be likely to make. Our examination led us to conclude that the sights are indeed genuine, as determined by the National Geographic Society's board of experts in 1909. Among other things, the pattern of "random scatter"—the fingerprint of the field observer—is completely consistent with other sights Peary made on previous expeditions. In short, we are satisfied that the observations of the sun that Peary took over a period of 24 hours after arriving at his northernmost camp, Camp Jesup, were not faked, and that he was essentially where his sights showed him to be when he "nailed" the Stars and Stripes to the Pole.

In Part III, "Peary's Sledging Speeds and Distances," we consider the critics' contentions that the speeds and distances Peary claimed to have attained on his final dash to the Pole and back, when his sole witnesses were Henson and the Eskimos, are incredible. As for the distances in controversy, we specify them, as did Peary, as "nautical miles made good." The polar party covered about 270 miles (excluding excursions Peary made at the Pole) round-trip from 5 a.m. April 2, when they departed from Camp Bartlett (where Captain Bartlett turned back) to 30 minutes after midnight on April 10, when they returned to the same camp after spending 30 hours in the vicinity of the Pole.

Peary covered the distance to the Pole in five marches averaging about 27 miles per march, at an average speed of about 2.5 miles per hour. Peary's return trip, from 4 p.m. on April 7 to 12:30 a.m. on April 10, is more frequently the basis of skepticism. This trek was made in three forced marches of about 45 miles per march, following the party's old trail and using previously built igloos, totalling about 48 hours of sledging at an average speed of about 2.8 miles an hour with nine hours of stops for food and rest. Peary's rapid progress on the return trip was attributable more to the duration of his extended marches than to the small increase in speed. Both factors are understandable when one considers that every hour of delay increased the party's chance that their southward travel would be hindered by winds that would obliterate the trail or open leads that could be slow to freeze over, leaving them to face starvation on the ice.

We examined the distances and speeds of a number of sled travellers in the Arctic, including Peary himself on his earlier expeditions. From the accumulated data, it is clear that skilled drivers of dogs and sledges have often maintained or exceeded the claimed speeds of Peary's polar party; thus we do not consider them incredible. To give but one example, Gunnar Isachsen, captain of the *Fram* under the Norewgian explorer Otto Sverdrup, wrote in *Geographical Review* in 1929: "On our sledging trips we were not content with marches under 15 miles. We often made 20 to 30 miles, and marches of over 30 miles were not rare."

Speed in sledging is determined by a number of variables—the ability and determination of drivers, the strength of dogs, the configuration and weight of sledges and, of course, ice conditions. Peary's Eskimo drivers were unsurpassed; Ootah's sledging skills had made him a hero among his people, and Matt Henson, after long years in the Arctic, was almost his equal. The north Greenland dogs were conceded to be superior to those of other Eskimo tribes. Peary's dogs for the final dash were the pick of 133 that had started the trek and were well fed in preparation for the final assault.

Except for Peary's own accounts in his journal—which reported better than usual ice conditions for the last five marches—we cannot know what ice conditions were at the time. But Will Steger reported that on his 1986 trek to the Pole in Peary's footsteps, he encountered a smoothing of the ice and the presence of north-south leads that provided an improved surface for sledge travel in the near vicinity of the Pole. Similarly, Colonel Gerry Pitzl, navigator on Ralph Plaisted's snowmobile expedition to the Pole in 1968, reported that for the last two weeks before reaching the Pole travel was "practically unrestricted. . . . In many cases the lead direction was north, affording us the luxury of effortless travel."

Lastly, while on the subject of Peary's speeds and distances, we note that his critics who place him 50 miles east, west or south of the Pole as a result of his alleged miscalculated distances combined with faulty navigation, have failed to explain why upon discovering his error when he took his observations at Camp Jesup, he did not continue on for those relatively few additional miles. To assume that this persistent and fearless explorer would have turned back when so close to achieving his lifetime goal, even though he had supplies enough for approximately another forty days, in favor of faking observations upon his return to the *Roosevelt* makes no sense whatsoever. Yet that he did just that is the untenable premise upon which the "hoax" theory espoused by Dennis Rawlins and Wally Herbert, among others, rests.

In Part IV, "Peary's Soundings," we analyze the measurements of the ocean depths taken by Peary on his trek from Cape Columbia (on the northern coast of Ellesmere Island at the 70th meridian) to the Pole, and find that they contribute significantly to the question of where his course lay. These data were of no help to Peary in proving his case in 1909, since a profile of the Arctic Ocean in the vicinity of the 70th meridian did not exist. Now of course it does.

The Defense Mapping Agency made available to the Foundation a number of relevant bottom depths obtained by U.S. submarines operating under the arctic ice, and these were used to refine a chart of the area issued by the Office of Naval Research. A computer-generated model based on these data shows that if Peary's track was close to the 70th meridian, he would twice have crossed over a major feature of the ocean bottom, the Lomonosov Ridge, during the trek to the Pole. Sure enough, a series of deep-shallow-deep soundings by Marvin indicates that the party passed over a southern leg of the ridge. A later sounding made by Bartlett at 87°-15′ north indicates that they were over the canyon just west of the ridge. And a sounding by Peary at 89°-55′ indicates that the ridge had been crossed again. We realize that some of the soundings showing "no-bottom" are less informative than they might be. Yet taken together, the series of soundings shows that Peary was essentially on the track he claimed he was on enroute to the Pole. At least the soundings rule out one of the suggested tracks that Wally Herbert defines in his *National Geographic Magazine* article, which happens to be the *single* track he decided was the correct one in his book.

In Part V, "Shadows on the North Pole Photographs," we present the results of our final and most conclusive examination of the data Peary brought back from the Pole—the photographs taken near Camp Jesup. Since an inadequate attempt by merchant captain Thomas Hall in *Did Peary Reach The Pole?* (1917), no one has attempted to analyze Peary's photographs; accordingly, our efforts represent new evidence.

Techniques of photographic analysis that were pioneered during World War II developed into a fine craft afterward with the advent of satellite observation. One technique, called photogrammetric rectification, can produce the angle of the elevation of the sun from shadows in pictures. The angle can be compared with the sun angle calculated from the *Nautical Almanac* to confirm a specific location and time. There are, however, certain prerequisites that must be met. There must be shadows that begin and end within the frame of an uncropped negative; there must be a horizon to determine the orientation of the camera; and the focal length of the camera must be known. Thus not every photograph can be analyzed, but we found that several from Peary's North Pole collection could be.

The technique is one based on simple perspective. Imaginary lines drawn through each object and the end of its shadow would be, in the real world, parallel to the sun's rays. Such lines drawn on a two-dimensional picture converge at a vanishing point (often outside the picture). This vanishing point is also the point at which a ray of sunlight through the camera would cast a shadow of the camera. Thus the vanishing point defines the angle of the sun's rays relative to the optical axis of the camera, which may be pointing up or down, as shown by the horizon.

The mathematical method used to fix these relationships is spherical trigonometry, much like that used in the reduction of a navigation sight. The *Nautical Almanac* gives the declination of the sun at the Pole for the date, and the time (taken from Peary's account of his activities at the Pole) tells which meridian the sun is on. The altitude of the sun measured from the photograph is used to establish a rough "line of position."

We were able to analyze several pictures taken in the vicinity of Camp Jesup and concluded that they place Peary within four or five miles of his reported position and certainly no more than fifteen miles away.

We regard the photogrammetric analysis of the photographs as the most innovative and significant contribution thus far made to the dispute over the attainment of the Pole because while sights can, at least in theory, be faked, the natural shadows in the photographs cannot be falsified. To quote Captain Hall: "Shadows are nature's witnesses. They never lie and they testify on other subjects besides that of altitudes." Here since they place Peary and his party in the near vicinity of the Pole, they reinforce our conclusion that the sights are genuine.

In Part VI, "Ancillary Matters," we digress to consider some of the extraneous matters that critics have raised in their efforts to prove that Peary faked his attainment of the Pole. We address oft-repeated allegations (1) that Peary's 1906 "farthest north" record is dubious, and may also have been faked; (2) that on the 1906 expedition he faked the discovery of non-existent new land, which he called "Crocker Land," in order to be able to name territory after a financial backer, George Crocker; (3) that his 1909 diary entries are suspiciously incomplete or irregular; and (4) that he deceived his faithful Negro assistant, Matt Henson, about the location of Camp Jesup, thereby making it easier to pull off his hoax of having attained the Pole.

To summarize: *First,* we determined that Peary *did* set a new "farthest north" record in 1906 by reaching latitude 87°-06'. He brought back a photograph which we assumed was taken at that latitude in the early afternoon of April 21—on the basis of his account in his *Nearest The Pole*—that when subjected to the photogrammetric technique we utilized in analyzing his Camp Jesup photographs showed him to be at least at latitude 87°-06' or perhaps a little further north. In short, we used forensic photography.

Second, we are persuaded that Peary honestly believed that he had seen distant "new land" when he viewed "Crocker Land" because he told a member of his expedition, Dr. Wolf, of having seen it, as Dr. Wolf records in his diary. He did not, as his critics claim, first mention his discovery upon his return to the United States. If he believed in the existence of "Crocker Land" there is nothing reprehensible in his having named it for George Crocker who was a sponsor of the 1906 expedition. He followed a common practice of explorers from time immemorial. We believe that what Peary actually saw was either a mirage or a floating ice island as other persons have speculated.

Third, we discount the discrepancies with regard to Peary's diary that have led critics to speculate that it was fabricated in whole or in part, these include: (1) the lack of a destination (which presumably would have read "the North Pole") on the cover; (2) some pages left blank on the return trip; and (3) the fact that the entry "The Pole at last!!!" is written on a loose page. We found that the incomplete cover is typical of virtually every journal of Peary's that is preserved in the Archives. One must bear in mind that his diaries were never intended for publication but as an aid in preparing books or articles; accordingly proper form was of little concern to him. As for the missing pages on the return journey, we accept Peary's explanation to the Congressional committee that he was sometimes "too busy" to write in his diary. We know that he was racing for the safety of land, and keeping a complete diary was necessarily secondary to survival. As for the loose page on which he scribbled his "The Pole at last!!!" entry, we offer two possible explanations. First, that he tore the page from a notebook similar to the diary notebook—from which he tore pages to send messages to expedition members—that perhaps was closer at hand. Or, second, that he intentionally scrawled the dramatic entry which, unlike the rest of the diary, *was* intended to be published, on a separate sheet of paper. If indeed he faked his 1909 diary, it seems to us that he would have filled in the blank pages, would have completed the cover destination, and would have made sure that all the pages were attached.

Fourth, we are distressed by the allegations of critics Rawlins and Herbert that Peary deceived Matt Henson as to the location of Camp Jesup while he formulated Machiavellian plans for deceiving the world as to his discovery of the Pole. The claims are premised on innocuous but unreliable ghost-written accounts of Henson's experiences at the Pole which can be construed to suggest that relations were strained between Peary and himself at the end of the journey. We do not pretend to know whether this was true or not, but even if it was, it affords no basis for presuming that Peary was engaged in carrying out a sinister plot. As for ourselves, we remain convinced that Peary, Matt Henson and the four Eskimos went to the Pole together, just as they all maintained for the rest of their lives.

In Part VII, "Peary's Track," which concludes our report, we present in graphic form our version of how Peary and his party proceeded from Cape Columbia to the Pole. The track integrates the information we developed with regard to ice movements during the early part of the trip, Peary's method of navigation, and his and other expedition members' celestial observations and soundings.

In sum, in the light of all the data we accumulated and assimilated, we feel that we can say categorically that Peary realized his lifelong goal of attaining the Pole on the last of his many expeditions. Certainly we turned up no evidence to the contrary.

We should also like to say that after perusing hundreds of boxes of Peary's private papers, his correspondence and his journals, we are convinced of the man's integrity. We can appreciate Roald Amundsen's statement: "I know Admiral Peary reached the Pole. The reason that I know it is that I know Peary."

We sincerely hope that this report will help to set the record straight and perhaps put an end to the long process of vilification of a courageous American explorer.

ARMY DENIES MEDAL TO VETERAN FOR 1942 COMBAT

December 15, 1989

For two years the U.S. Army investigated the contention that religious bias had denied the nation's highest military award to David S. Rubitsky, a Jewish combat soldier in World War II. At the inquiry's conclusion, a military review board in Washington reported on December 15 that it had found "insufficient evidence" to support Rubitsky's assertion of unheralded heroism—that in a singlehanded defense of a machinegun position in the New Guinea jungles he killed five hundred to six hundred attacking Japanese soldiers during one night's action.

Nor could the board substantiate the claim of Rubitsky's company and battalion commanders that they recommended him for the Medal of Honor but were blocked by a superior officer who scoffed at the notion of a Jew receiving the decoration. The medal, authorized by Congress and sometimes called the congressional Medal of Honor, is awarded for gallantry in action at the risk of life above and beyond the call of duty.

Rubitsky, a communications sergeant in the Thirty-second Infantry Division, started to pursue his claim more than four decades after he returned from the war and upon his civilian retirement after thirty years service as a merchant seaman. He was supported by the Vietnam Veterans of America, several members of Congress, and the Anti-Defamation League of B'nai B'rith, a Jewish organization.

Several veterans who had served with Rubitsky were quoted as saying they were surprised to learn at a 1986 reunion of the 128th Regiment that he was never awarded the medal. By then, Rubitsky had returned in retirement to his home state, Wisconsin. The ranks of the division, including the regiment, were filled largely by Wisconsin National

Guardsmen called to duty in World War II.

The former sergeant told an interviewer in 1988 that for years he had attempted to put his battle experience out of mind but that he finally decided, in the interest of justice, to press his claim to the medal. "I don't want this to happen to anyone else, black, white, Jewish or otherwise," Rubitsky said on that occasion. In a broadcast on National Public Radio in October 1989, he gave a graphic account of the military action in question.

He said that on December 1, 1942, near the village of Buna, New Guinea, Japanese infantrymen attacked a forward machinegun nest. Some GI's fled, Rubitsky recounted, but he remained. Rubitsky said he had a clear field of fire that enabled him to slaughter enemy troops in their attack as they emerged from the jungle into a narrow clearing. He said he repeatedly switched from one weapon to another—a machinegun, rifle, and carbine—to keep the attackers from realizing that he was alone.

As dawn came, he saw a mind-boggling sight. Japanese bodies, he said, "were lying there, on branches, roots, piled like cordwood, atop one another. Some were alive. Some I just hit in the shoulder and couldn't move, some in the legs. So I would just shoot them and bayonet them, shoot them and bayonet them. I was completely an insane man."

Assertion of Religious Bias

Many combat veterans were reported to be incredulous that one infantry soldier could account for so many enemy casualties. But J. H. Stehling, a captain commanding E Company in which Rubitsky served, vouched for his former sergeant's story. Stehling, who retired from military service as a brigadier general, said in a sworn statement in October 1987 that he inspected the battle scene immediately after the fighting and witnessed more than five hundred slain enemy soldiers.

Stehling said in his affidavit that he immediately recommended Rubitsky for the Medal of Honor, "but nothing came of it, the reason being the religion of Sergeant Rubitsky." The retired general asked that the Army reconsider the decoration and "do not let religion stand in the way this time."

The Army also obtained a statement from Herbert A. Smith, a retired major general, before his death in 1989. In 1942, Smith commanded the battalion to which E Company was assigned. Smith said he promptly forwarded Stehling's recommendation to Col. John Mott, the division's chief of staff. According to Smith: "Colonel Mott's answer was, 'You mean a Jew for the Congressional Medal of Honor?'" Smith further recalled that Mott "just laughed and walked away." Mott, having died in the intervening time, could not respond to the allegation.

Another piece of evidence supporting Rubitsky's claim was a handwritten message discovered on the back of a yellowing photograph that purportedly had been removed from the body of a Japanese officer in New Guinea. The officer, identified only as Colonel Yamamoto, wrote that he was committing suicide to atone for the slaughter of six hundred Japanese soldiers by "a solitary American soldier."

Army's Rejection of the Medal

Sen. Herb Kohl of Wisconsin, Rubitsky's home state, asked Secret Service experts to appraise the document's authenticity. They reported that the ink and paper were consistent with materials used in 1942; they had no reason to believe it was "anything other than genuine," the senator's office reported.

Kohl, a Democrat, and some other lawmakers—including Sen. Robert W. Kasten, R-Wis., Rep. Les Aspin, D-Wis., and Rep. Nita M. Lowey, D-N.Y.—pressed Rubitsky's case with the Army. Shortly before the Army review board announced its findings on December 15, Army investigators met with the lawmakers and their congressional aides. At the meeting's conclusion, the group issued a statement saying: "The investigation establishes as conclusively as possible that there was no mass killing of Japanese attackers at Buna in New Guinea in 1942."

The board's formal recommendation was exceptionally brief and offered no details on the findings of the investigation. However, Lt. Col. Terrence Adkins, the officer in charge of the inquiry, was quoted as saying that American and Japanese military records, and interviews with both American and Japanese survivors of combat action near Buna, indicated that the "action did not occur as alleged."

As for the enemy officer's message, Edward J. Drea, an American military historian fluent in Japanese, called it "spurious" and "fraudulent." He said the handwriting was not that of a native, and contained improper forms of Japanese names and other mistakes a native would not make. Drea surmised that it had been written by a second-generation Japanese-American as a wartime propaganda ploy. Presumably the message was planted on the body in the hope it would be found by other Japanese and demoralize them.

Army officials and the interested lawmakers appeared careful not to indicate that Rubitsky or his backers had engaged in deceit and fraud. The legislators said in a statement they issued after their meeting with Army officials: "What we are dealing with here is not a lie fabricated by the generals [Stehling and Smith] and Mr. Rubitsky. It is simply the unfortunate result of the passage of many years, the fogging of many ... difficult memories from a war long past."

New Look at Other Cases

The delicacy with which the Rubitsky case was discussed probably reflected a military sensitivity to questions of discrimination in the awarding of medals in two world wars. In 1988 the Army said it would review the records of all black soldiers in both wars to determine if any were denied high honors they deserved. No black soldiers and only two Jews were among the 297 Medals of Honor winners in World War II, the

Defense Department reported.

The review board's recommendation against Rubitsky's claim was endorsed by top Pentagon officials, including Secretary of the Army Michael P. W. Stone. The outcome did not satisfy Rubitsky or some of his advocates. Abraham H. Foxman, national director of the Anti-Defamation League, called the ruling "unconscionable" because the board did not release the report on which its decision was based. "If the facts are sufficiently clear to convince members of Congress, why can't they be made public?" he asked.

From his home in Milton, Wisconsin, Rubitsky released a statement, saying: "It did happen. I think there is some sort of coverup." General Stehling, speaking from his home in Oshkosh, Wisconsin, continued to back his former sergeant. "The Army can say what it wants," Stehling commented, "but let me say this: the stench of those decaying bodies that day in the jungle stayed with me for years."

> *Following is the Army's review board recommendation denying a Medal of Honor to David Rubitsky, as issued December 15, 1989, by the Army Public Affairs Office in the Pentagon:*

For the past two years, the United States Army reviewed Mr. David Rubitsky's eligibility for the award of the Medal of Honor based on his alleged action in New Guinea during World War II.

There are two essential factors required by law and regulation to support a claim for the Medal of Honor. First, Department of Army records must contain incontestable proof that the action in question occurred as claimed. Second, there must be conclusive evidence that a recommendation for the award was submitted within two years of the action.

The Army conducted extensive research into the circumstances involving Mr. Rubitsky in New Guinea in 1942. After an exhaustive effort, the review has been completed. Based on a thorough examination of detailed information from numerous sources, there is insufficient evidence to substantiate either that the event reported by Mr. Rubitsky occurred or that the Medal of Honor was recommended on his behalf within the stipulated period. Since neither of the two essential criteria has been met, the Army cannot support the award of the Medal of Honor for Mr. Rubitsky.

BUSH ANNOUNCES
INVASION OF PANAMA
December 20, 1989

On the morning of December 20, President George Bush announced in a broadcast televised from the White House that U.S. military forces had invaded the Republic of Panama. He said his goals were to protect the lives of Americans in Panama, restore democracy to that country, ensure the security of the Panama Canal, and bring to justice Panamanian military dictator Manuel Antonio Noriega, with whom the Reagan and Bush administrations had feuded for more than two years. General Noriega had been indicted in 1988 by federal grand juries in Miami and Tampa on drug trafficking charges. (Grand Jury Indictments of General Noriega, Historic Documents of 1988, p. 81)

The 15,000-man Panamanian Defense Forces (PDF) were overwhelmed within two days by the invaders' superior numbers and firepower. Some 24,500 U.S. troops were backed by tanks and aircraft, including technologically advanced F-117 fighter-bombers. Sporadic resistance and sniper fire from scattered pockets of Noriega's paramilitary units continued for nearly a week, and looting broke out in Panama City, the capital.

During the first few days, Noriega eluded capture by the invading forces, which posted a $1 million reward for information leading to his apprehension. Constantly on the move in Panama City, Noriega finally sought refuge in the Papal Nunciature, on Christmas Eve. U.S. troops surrounded the nunciature—equivalent to a Vatican embassy—and at one point bombarded the compound with loud rock music.

While U.S. diplomatic and military officials negotiated with Monsignor José Sebastian Laboa, the papal nuncio, Noriega remained holed up in a sparsely furnished room in the nunciature. Then, faced with a threat by Laboa to withdraw the Vatican's protective asylum, and with a hostile crowd of up to twenty thousand Panamanians outside the gates, Noriega surrendered to U.S. authorities on the evening of January 3, 1990. He was immediately taken by helicopter to nearby Howard Air Base, a U.S. installation in the Canal Zone; less than an hour later, he was placed aboard a military transport plane and flown to Miami. Laboa later denied press reports that he had issued an ultimatum to Noriega; he said he had used "psychology" to persuade Noriega to give himself up.

Arraigned on drug-trafficking charges the next day, Noriega argued through his American lawyers that his seizure in Panama was illegal and that the court had no jurisdiction over him. He was detained without bond in a Miami jail pending trial.

Celebrations in Panama

Raucous celebrations erupted in the streets of Panama City at the news of Noriega's surrender. Panamanians honked car horns, banged pots and pans, and hailed U.S. troops as liberators. By the morning of January 4, relative calm had returned to the city. Government workers returned to their offices, some of which had been heavily damaged by fighting and looting. Shopkeepers began cleaning up the debris left by looters. The damage was estimated at between $500 million and $2 billion. Hundreds of retail stores and other commercial establishments were stripped bare. Buildings were destroyed by mortar and heavy artillery fire. A slum area called Chorillo, near the headquarters of the Panamanian Defense Forces, was virtually destroyed by fire.

A new Panamanian civil government—the first in twenty-one years— was installed by the United States even before the invasion began. President Guillermo Endara and Vice Presidents Ricardo Arias Calderon and Guillermo Ford, the apparent victors in a presidential election held May 1989, took the oath of office at a U.S. military base. Noriega had nullified the results of the election.

Costs of the Invasion

The physical damage to Panama resulting from the invasion was extensive. The long-term losses to the Panamanian economy brought on by U.S. economic sanctions over the previous two years were even more severe, analysts have said, running into billions of dollars. As part of its campaign against Noriega, the United States froze Panamanian funds deposited in American banks, cut off Panama's sugar quota, excluded Panama from duty-free privileges under U.S. trade preference programs, and suspended payments to the Panamanian government, including Panama Canal tolls.

As tension mounted between the United States and Panama, foreign banks fled the country. Offshore banking had been a mainstay of the Panamanian economy. Panama's economic output dwindled and unemployment doubled to include a quarter of the working population. As an *emergency measure, the United States transferred $70 million in blocked funds to the Endara government at the end of December. President Bush said U.S. sanctions were being lifted and that at least $400 million in frozen funds would be turned over to the government.*

American casualties were relatively light: 23 soldiers were killed and 323 wounded, according to the Pentagon. Two soldiers died in noncombat situations and two civilians were killed. A number of American civilians were taken by the Panamanian Defense Forces but were released unharmed. Panamanian casualties were higher, but estimates remained imprecise even after calm returned to Panama. The Pentagon put the number of Panamanian dead at about six hundred, half of whom were said to be civilians. Hospital reports indicated that thousands more were injured.

Foreign Criticism

Numerous foreign governments bitterly criticized the invasion, although U.S. State Department officials said that many foreign diplomats had privately expressed relief that Noriega was removed from the world scene. The Permanent Council of the Organization of American States (OAS) voted 20 to 1 to censure the United States. The American delegation cast the sole negative vote. The United Nations General Assembly by a vote of 75 to 20 "strongly deplored" the U.S. intervention and demanded an immediate cease-fire and withdrawal of the U.S. invading force.

Diplomats in Washington said the censure votes would make it more difficult for the Endara government to obtain diplomatic recognition and economic assistance from the international community. The government of Peru, for example, applauded Noriega's decision to surrender to the United States, but it called Endara "the Panamanian Judas."

The invasion may have hampered recent improvements in U.S.-Soviet relations. A Soviet Foreign Ministry spokesman, Gennadi Gerasimov, condemned the seizure of Noriega. "No state has the right to take the law into its own hands," Gerasimov said. "That's basically lynch law."

The United States also drew criticism when U.S. troops forcibly entered the residence of the ambassador of Nicaragua in Panama City in search of weapons. Under international law, foreign embassies and the homes of diplomats have immunity against such intrusion. Nicaragua retaliated by expelling twenty U.S. diplomats from Managua.

Reacting to the international criticism, President Bush, in a news conference January 5, said that U.S. intervention in Panama would set no precedent for future U.S. action in this hemisphere. He announced that he would send Vice President Dan Quayle on a mission to several Latin American countries to try to repair U.S. relations. "I want to assure all of the countries of Latin America that United States policy remains one of a friendly, supportive and respectful neighbor." But, the president observed, "given the history of the use of U.S. force," the Latin

American reaction was "predictable." Bush also announced that a withdrawal of U.S. troops from Panama had begun and would continue until only the twelve thousand U.S. soldiers permanently stationed in Panama remained.

The invasion marked a first for U.S. armed forces: the direct involvement of female military personnel in armed combat. Army Capt. Linda L. Bray, in command of a military police (MP) platoon, was assigned to lead a raid on an attack dog kennel of the PDF. Shots were exchanged but no one was killed. Dozens of other female MPs were also involved in fighting the PDF. Defense regulations forbid direct combat roles for women, but military police units are classified as support forces not intended for combat action.

Background of the Invasion

The triggering event for the invasion was the shooting death December 16 of an off-duty Marine Corps lieutenant, Robert Paz, at a road block by Panamanian Defense Forces. In the same incident a U.S. Navy lieutenant and his wife were arrested and physically abused by members of the PDF before being released four hours later. Relations between Panama and the United States had been strained long before that, however.

Noriega had been an asset of the U.S. intelligence community for three decades or more, according to numerous reports. As he rose through the ranks of the Panamanian military, he lent valuable assistance to the Central Intelligence Agency (CIA) and to the Pentagon. During the Reagan administration, for example, Noriega supported U.S. efforts to supply the anti-Sandinista contra forces in Nicaragua, and once offered to attempt to assassinate the leaders of Nicaragua's government. Somewhere along the line, it is charged, he became involved in drug dealing and money laundering. At the same time, he forged close links with foreign figures hostile to the United States, including Cuba's Fidel Castro and Libya's Muammar Qaddafi.

In 1970, under the military government of Gen. Omar Torrijos, Noriega became chief of intelligence of the Panamanian National Guard, the country's principal military body. After the death of Torrijos in a plane crash in 1981, Noriega formed part of an unofficial triumvirate of de facto military rulers of Panama. In 1983 he engineered the merger of the national guard with other military and police units in the Panamanian Defense Forces, with Noriega as commander.

Noriega eventually eliminated challenges to his leadership of the military and the government. One of the officers who opposed Noriega, Col. Roberto Diaz Herrera, in 1987 publicly accused him of drug-related activities and murder, including involvement in arranging the plane crash that killed Torrijos. Under heavy pressure, Diaz Herrera recanted and went into exile. By then civilian opposition to Noriega had mounted and the PDF began moving against street demonstrations, detaining

704

leading political figures, and closing the opposition news media. Panama had entered a stage of muted civil war, according to observers of the country.

In February 1988, two U.S. federal grand juries returned indictments against Noriega, among other things charging him with accepting a $4.6 million bribe from Colombia's Medellin drug cartel to permit the use of Panama as a transshipment point for cocaine and other drugs headed for the United States.

The next month, President Ronald Reagan imposed the first of a series of economic sanctions against Panama. In May 1989, Noriega nullified the results of a presidential election that impartial observers said was won overwhelmingly by Guillermo Endara. Members of the opposition slate were physically beaten in front of television cameras by goon squads said to be directed by Noriega.

An attempted coup against Noriega failed in October 1989. U.S. forces in Panama took some limited steps to aid the anti-Noriega plotters, mostly members of the PDF, but Bush was criticized for not doing more. At this point, according to unofficial accounts, planning for a U.S. invasion of Panama began in earnest. Attempts to enlist the cooperation of Latin American and Caribbean governments in the effort proved futile.

The die was cast when the Panamanian legislature, appointed by Noriega, declared on December 15 that Panama was in a "state of war" with the United States, and it named Noriega as chief of the Panamanian government. The following day, PDF forces killed Lieutenant Paz. U.S. and Panamanian forces went on a state of alert, and the United States began airlifting heavy combat equipment, including armored vehicles, into its air bases in Panama. From then on, the invasion was but a matter of timing.

Following is the text of President George Bush's televised address to the nation on the morning of December 20, 1989, from the White House, announcing the U.S. invasion of Panama:

My fellow citizens. Last night, I ordered U.S. military forces to Panama. No president takes such action lightly. This morning, I want to tell you what I did and why I did it.

For nearly two years, the United States, the nations of Latin America and the Caribbean have worked together to resolve the crisis in Panama. The goals of the United States have been to safeguard the lives of Americans, to defend democracy in Panama, to combat drug trafficking and to protect the integrity of the Panama Canal treaty.

Many attempts have been made to resolve this crisis through diplomacy and negotiations. All were rejected by the dictator of Panama, General Manuel Noriega, an indicted drug trafficker.

Last Friday, Noriega declared his military dictatorship to be in a state of war with the United States and publicly threatened the lives of Americans in Panama. The very next day, forces under his command shot and killed an unarmed American serviceman, wounded another, arrested and brutally beat a third American serviceman, and then brutally interrogated his wife, threatening her with sexual abuse. That was enough.

General Noriega's reckless threats and attacks upon Americans in Panama created an imminent danger to the 35,000 American citizens in Panama. As president, I have no higher obligation than to safeguard the lives of American citizens.

And that is why I directed our armed forces to protect the lives of American citizens in Panama and to bring General Noriega to justice in the United States.

I contacted the bipartisan leadership of Congress last night and informed them of this decision. And after taking this action, I also talked with leaders in Latin America, the Caribbean and those of other U.S. allies.

At this moment U.S. forces, including forces deployed from the United States last night, are engaged in action in Panama. The United States intends to withdraw the forces newly deployed to Panama as quickly as possible.

Our forces have conducted themselves courageously and selflessly. And as commander-in-chief, I salute every one of them and thank them on behalf of our country. Tragically, some Americans have lost their lives in defense of their fellow citizens, in defense of democracy. And my heart goes out to their families. We also regret and mourn the loss of innocent Panamanians.

The brave Panamanians elected by the people of Panama in the elections last May, President Guillermo Endara and Vice Presidents Calderon and Ford, have assumed the rightful leadership of their country.

You remember those horrible pictures of newly elected Vice President Ford, covered head to toe with blood, beaten mercilessly by so-called dignity battalions. Well, the United States today recognizes the democratically elected government of President Endara. I will send our ambassador back to Panama immediately.

Key military objectives have been achieved. Most organized resistance has been eliminated. But the operation is not over yet. General Noriega is in hiding. And nevertheless, yesterday a dictator ruled Panama and today constitutionally elected leaders govern.

I've today directed the secretary of the Treasury and the secretary of state to lift the economic sanctions with respect to the democratically elected government of Panama and, in cooperation with that government, to take steps to effect an orderly unblocking of Panamanian government assets in the United States.

I am fully committed to implement the Panama Canal Treaties and turn over the canal to Panama in the year 2000. The actions we have taken and the cooperation of a new democratic government in Panama will permit us to honor these commitments. As soon as the new government recommends a qualified candidate—Panamanian—to be administrator of the canal as called for in the treaties, I will submit this nominee to the Senate for expedited consideration.

I am committed to strengthening our relationship with the democratic nations in this hemisphere. I will continue to seek solutions to the problems of this region through dialogue and multilateral diplomacy. I took this action only after reaching the conclusion that every other avenue was closed and the lives of American citizens were in grave danger.

I hope that the people of Panama will put this dark chapter of dictatorship behind them and move forward together as citizens of a democratic Panama with this government that they themselves have elected. The United States is eager to work with the Panamanian people in partnership and friendship to rebuild their economy.

The Panamanian people want democracy, peace and the chance for a better life in dignity and freedom. The people of the United States seek only to support them in pursuit of these noble goals.

Thank you very much.

BUCHAREST'S ANNOUNCEMENT OF ROMANIAN RULER'S EXECUTION

December 25, 1989

Romania's president Nicolae Ceausescu and his wife, Elena, died at the hands of a firing squad on Christmas Day, three days after their capture by Romanians in revolt against his oppressive Communist regime. The first news of the execution promptly reached Romanians, and the outside world, in a terse announcement on Bucharest radio. It said the Ceausescus had been condemned to death that day by a military tribunal for "crimes against the Romanian people and Romania."

Within a few hours fascinated television viewers witnessed filmed scenes from the trial and graphic views of the former ruling couple in death. In the televised portrayal of the trial, the two were defiant to the end. His last audible words, upon hearing the death sentence, were: "I refuse to recognize this court." Hers were a refusal to stand up, as ordered. She said, in an aside to her husband: "No, dear, we will not rise."

Mme. Ceausescu was not only the wife of the seventy-one-year-old dictator, but officially his first deputy in a government in which their kinsmen held several high positions. It was later learned that the new provisional government, the Council of National Salvation, decided to execute them quickly—and show the Romanian people that they were dead—in an attempt to defuse the armed opposition of an elite security force (the Securitate) still loyal to Ceausescu.

That plan appeared to have the intended effect. Within a day street violence subsided in Bucharest, the capital, and other sizable Romanian cities. Many members of the large (180,000-member) and well-equipped Securitate surrendered voluntarily or were hunted down by soldiers and armed civilians. The Romanian army had turned against Ceausescu in

the preceding days of civil strife, and it used tanks and troops to bring
about his downfall. Military commanders, like masses of other Romanians, had been shocked into rebellion by his bloody crackdown on
protest demonstrators.

Alone among leaders of East European countries within the Soviet
bloc, Ceausescu refused to yield to the democratic changes taking place in
that region. Since the late summer, the ruling Communist regimes in
Poland, Hungary, Czechoslovakia, East Germany, and Bulgaria had been
forced to share power with newly recognized opposition parties. Poland's
new government was led by a non-Communist prime minister, and in
Hungary the Communist party disbanded, taking on a new name and
espousing reformist ideas in preparation for multiparty national elections in 1990. (Speeches Marking Poland's New Era, p. 523) But in
Romania an unyielding Ceausescu continued to rule with an iron hand
until he was driven from power in an uprising that developed so fast it
caught him and the entire world by suprise.

Revolt Sparked by a Massacre

Analysts of the revolt agreed that its catalyst was the large-scale
killing beginning December 17 of demonstrators in Timisoara, Romania's
fourth largest city (325,000 population). The previous night crowds had
taken to the streets to protest the forcible transfer of a popular,
outspoken Lutheran clergyman, Laszlo Tokes. They shouted insults
against Ceausescu and fed bonfires with his books and portraits. He
responded by telling regional Communist leaders on closed-circuit television, according to a transcript the new provisional government later
issued, "Anyone who does not obey orders should be shot."

Hundreds—perhaps thousands—of people in Timisoara were indeed
shot and killed. The size of the massacre could not be known with
certainty; security forces removed many of the fallen victims—men,
women, and children—from the scene of the massacre in the city's central
square and tossed their bodies into mass graves in a futile attempt to hide
the evidence. However, relatives and friends later exhumed many of the
bodies. The transcript made clear that Ceausescu received direct reports
from the scene while the killings were taking place in the city's central
square.

Confident that the situation was under control, Ceausescu left December 18 on a long-planned state visit to Iran. In his absence, word of the
massacre spread throughout Romania—often through foreign broadcasts
secretly heard. When Ceausescu returned December 20, he learned of
widespread unrest and sought to counteract it with a mass rally of
support on December 21. As usual, Communist leaders in local factories
called out the workers, put placards in their hands, and transported them
to Palace Square in Bucharest to cheer.

From a balcony of the party's headquarters facing the square,
Ceausescu addressed the dutifully assembled crowd and a national

television audience. At first the cheers came on cue, as usual, but soon booing could also be heard. As it grew louder, he appeared perplexed. He hesitated, took a step back from the microphone, and television engineers cut off the broadcast for three minutes. When it resumed, the actual crowd sounds had been replaced with canned applause. But the damage had already been done.

Many Romanians later told Western correspondents that this had been the moment of truth—that Ceausescu no longer appeared powerful, but confused and vulnerable.

New Provisional Government Formed

The rally for Ceausescu was replaced by anti-Ceausescu demonstrations, in which soldiers were prominent. The next morning a crowd broke through the lines of guards outside the party building and entered it in search of the dictator just as he and his wife escaped from the rooftop by helicopter. The craft was overloaded and forced to land in the countryside, where farmers recognized and captured the occupants, turning them over to the army. At a military base fifty miles northwest of Bucharest, they were held prisoner inside an armored car whose guards had orders to shoot them if rescuers came near. Units of the security forces did attack the garrison but were repelled. Fearful that another attack might succeed, the leaders of the provisional government met on Christmas Eve and decided that the trial had to be held promptly. It came the next day, at the base, and lasted two hours. Five minutes later the Ceausescus were dead.

The new government was organized in the same building in Bucharest that the dictator and his wife had fled only hours before. There was no single heroic figure, such as Lech Walesa in Poland or Vaclev Havel in Czechoslovakia, for the people to rally around. Ion Iliescu, a former high-ranking Communist who ran afoul of Ceausescu in 1971 and became a political outcast, was named the country's provisional president. Petre Roman, a professor of hydrology, was chosen as prime minister. One of the new government's first acts was to schedule national elections in April, in the hope that Romania could develop democratic traditions with which it had little direct experience, either during or before four decades of Communist rule. For the past twenty-four years, the Communist rule had been directed by Ceausescu.

Romania's interim leaders quickly won favor with the people by emptying warehouses of food intended for export and distributing it to the people who long had suffered from food shortages. Romanians, living in a country rich in petroleum and farm goods, had been deprived of ample food and heating fuel because of Ceausescu's insistence on large-scale exports to pay off $10 billion in foreign debts. The United States and several other Western nations, as well as the Soviet Union, quickly granted the new government formal recognition. Several countries promised economic assistance.

Following is the text of a Bucharest radio announcement
December 25, 1989, as reported in translation by the West-
ern press, that Romanian president Nicolae Ceausescu and
his wife, Elena, had been tried by a military court and
executed for crimes against Romania and its people:

On Dec. 25, 1989, the trial of Nicolae Ceausescu and Elena Ceaucescu
was held before an extraordinary military tribunal. The charges were:

1. Genocide. More than 60,000 victims.
2. Undermining of the state power through organization of armed
   actions against the people and the state power.
3. Destruction of public property through destruction and damaging of
   buildings and numerous explosions in cities, etc.
4. The undermining of the national economy.
5. The attempt to flee the country by taking advantage of more than $1
   billion deposited in foreign banks.

For these crimes against the Rumanian people and Rumania, the
culprits Nicolae Ceausescu and Elena Ceausescu were condemned to death
and the confiscation of their wealth.

The sentence was definitive and was carried out.

CUMULATIVE INDEX, 1985-1989

A

Abortion. *See also Birth control*
Economic Summit Meeting (Paris), 430
(1989)
Presidential Debates on, 722, 723, 736-738,
766-767 (1988)
Reagan Remarks to Right-to-Life March-
ers, 53-56 (1985)
Republican Party Platform on, 642 (1988)
State of the Union, 65 (1988)
Supreme Court Decisions
Thornburgh Case, 559-580 (1986)
Webster Case, 365-389 (1989)
Acquired immune deficiency syndrome (AIDS)
AMA Report, 817-832 (1987)
Center for Disease Control Report on
AIDS in the Workplace, 733-747 (1985)
Democratic Party Platform on, 564 (1988)
FDA Approval of AZT (azidothymidine),
327-330 (1987)
Institute of Medicine Report, 887-908
(1986)
PHS Report on Aids Education, 319-326
(1987)
Presidential Commission Report, 415-446
(1988)
Presidential Debates on, 730-731 (1988)
Reagan's Budget Message, 9 (1987); 150,
155 (1988)
Republican Party Platform on, 638 (1988)
Supreme Court on Victims of Contagious
Disease, 245-252 (1987)
Urban League Report, 55-58 (1987)
Adams, Robert McCormick
Smithsonian Agreement on Indian Bones
and Burial Artifacts, 539-543 (1989)
Adoption
House Report on Discarded Children in
America, 671-686 (1989)
Republican Party Platform on, 635-636
(1988)

Affirmative action
Black America Report, 58 (1987)
Kerner Report Updated, 189-190, 193
(1988)
Supreme Court Decisions, 651-678 (1986);
331-349 (1987); 321-332 (1989)
Afghanistan
Amnesty International Human Rights Re-
port, 607 (1989)
Negotiated Settlement Agreements, 257-
266 (1988)
Reagan-Gorbachev Summit Meeting, 991,
993 (1987); 356, 358, 361 (1988)
State of the Union, 66 (1988)
UN Report on Human Rights, 919-936
(1986)
Africa. *See also specific countries*
Democratic Party Platform on, 68 (1988)
Pope John Paul II's Trip, 499-514 (1985)
Republican Party Platform on, 685-686
(1988)
Aged. *See also Medicaid and Medicare*
Economic Advisers' Report, 99-101 (1985)
Republican Party Platform on, 639-640
(1988)
Supreme Court Decision on Mandatory
Retirement, 397-407 (1985)
Agriculture. *See also Food supply*
Bishops' Report on Economic Justice,
1002-1005 (1986)
Democratic Party Platform on, 564-565
(1988)
Economic Report, 124, 126-127 (1987)
Gorbachev at 27th Party Congress, 146,
156-157 (1986)
Gorbachev Farm Policy, 145-152 (1989)
OTA Report on Biotechnology, 287-306
(1986)
Presidential Debates on, 751-752 (1988)
Reagan on Farm Subsidies, 10, 526 (1987);
393 (1988)
Reagan's Budget Message, 10 (1987); 157
(1988)

713

Republican Party Platform on, 660-664 (1988)

Vice Presidential Debate on, 812-813 (1988)

Sweden's Farm-Animal Rights Law, 347-351 (1988)

Aguilar v. Felton, 433-461 (1985)

Aid to Families with Dependent Children (AFDC)

Kerner Report Updated, 189, 193 (1988)

Revision of Welfare System, 847-852 (1988)

AIDS. *See Acquired immune deficiency syndrome*

Air pollution. *See Pollution*

Airline deregulation. *See also Regulatory reform; Transportation*

Aviation Safety Report, 267-276 (1988)

Economic Advisers' Report, 85-87 (1986); 118, 144-148 (1988)

GAO Report on Air Traffic Safety, 253-266 (1986)

President's Commission on Privatization Report, 233 (1988)

State of the Union Address, 60 (1986)

Ake v. Oklahoma, 207-209 (1985)

Akhromeyev, Marshal Sergei F.

Congressional Testimony, 439-444 (1989)

Alaskan Oil Spill Hearings, 225-237 (1989)

Albania

Enver Hoxa death, 325-331 (1985)

Alcoholism. *See also Drug abuse*

Report on Black and Minority Health, 686-687, 698-702 (1985)

Supreme Court on Alcoholism and Veterans' Benefits, 277-285 (1988)

Alzheimer's disease

OTA Report, 391-406 (1987)

Amendments, Constitutional. *See Constitution, U.S.*

American Bar Association

Legal Professionalism Report, 767-778 (1986)

Tort Reform Recommendations, 165-181 (1987)

American Indians. *See Native Americans*

American Israel Public Affairs Committee

Baker Address on Middle East Policy, 289-296 (1989)

American Medical Association

AIDS Report, 817-832 (1987)

America's Cup Race, Court Rulings on, 183-193 (1989)

Americas Watch Nicaragua Reports, 255-269 (1985)

Amnesty International

Human Rights Report, 883-889 (1988); 597-609 (1989)

Amundsen, Roald, 833 (1988)

Angola-Namibia Peace Accord, 947-950 (1988)

Aquino, Corazon C.

Philippine Cease-fire Agreement, 1037-1046 (1986)

Philippine Change of Government, 307-314 (1986)

Philippine Coup Attempt Thwarted, 843-854 (1987)

Arab states. *See Middle East*

Arafat, Yasir, 905, 907-908 (1988)

Arctic Expedition of 1909

Navigation Foundation Report on Peary's Claim, 687-696 (1989)

Peary's Polar Notes, 831-833 (1988)

Argentina

Human Rights Report, 148-149 (1985); 98-100 (1988)

Arias Sanchez, Oscar

Central American Peace Agreement, 637-648 (1987); 241-243 (1988)

Nobel Peace Prize Speech, 1007-1011 (1987)

Tela Declaration, 161, 168-172 (1989)

Armed forces. *See also Defense Department; Military; Veterans*

Joint Chiefs of Staff Reorganization, 681, 684-685 (1986)

Pentagon Report on Sexual Harassment, 671-679 (1987)

Republican Party Platform on, 697 (1988)

Arms control. *See also Defense; Intermediate-range Nuclear Forces; Space; Strategic Arms Limitation Treaty; Strategic Arms Reduction Talks; Strategic Defense Initiative*

ABM Treaty Interpretation, 289-317 (1987); 330 (1988)

Bush-Gorbachev Malta Meeting, 652-655 (1989)

Bush Proposal for Conventional Arms Cuts, 297-304 (1989)

Democratic Party Platform on, 566-567 (1988)

Former Security Officials' Paper on Defense Strategy, 782-784, 789-790 (1986)

Gorbachev, Mikhail S.

27th Party Congress Address, 163-166 (1986)

U.S.-Soviet INF Treaty Statement, 945, 947-950 (1987)

Paris Declaration on Chemical Weapons, 25-30 (1989)

Reagan-Gorbachev New Year's Messages, 3-8 (1986)

Reagan-Gorbachev Summit Meetings

(Geneva), 749-761 (1985)

(Moscow), 353-373 (1988)

(Reykjavik), 875-885 (1986)

(Washington, D.C.), 995-999 (1987)

Republican Party Platform on, 692-693 (1988)

Soviet Marshal Akhromeyev's Congressional Testimony, 439-444 (1989)

State of the Union, 114-115 (1985); 46-47 (1986); 57-58, 67 (1988)
U.S.-Soviet INF Treaty, 945-989 (1987); 57-58, 67 (1988)
Arts and humanities
Humanities Education Report, 681-696 (1987)
Republican Party Platform on, 653 (1988)
State of the Humanities Report, 517-527 (1988)
Asians
Alcoholism and, 701-702 (1985)
California Vote on English as Official Language, 959 (1986)
Association for Supervision and Curriculum Development (ASCD), 597-608 (1987)
Association of American Colleges, 127-144 (1985)
Attorneys. *See also American Bar Association*
ABA Commission on Legal Profession, 767-778 (1986)
Supreme Court on Independent Counsel, 465-478 (1988)
Austria
Pope John Paul's Visit, 405-414 (1988)
Waldheim's Inaugural Address, 743-750 (1986)
Aviation Safety Commission Report, 267-276 (1988)

B

Baby M, In Matter of, 373-387 (1987); 71-80 (1988)
Baker, James A., III
Bipartisan Accord on Central America, 163-166 (1989)
German Reunification Statement, 627, 634 (1989)
IMF-World Bank Conference, 643-652 (1985)
Middle East Policy Address, 289-296 (1989)
Balanced Budget and Emergency Deficit Control Act. *See Gramm-Rudman-Hollings Act*
Baldus, David C., 464-476 (1987)
Baltic Nationalist Movement, 469-475 (1989)
Banks and banking. *See also Credit; Stock Market*
Economic Advisers' Report, 90-91 (1985); 89-91 (1986)
IMF-World Bank Conference, 643-652 (1985)
Savings and Loan Bailout Bill, 463-468 (1989)
Savings and Loan Crisis, 913-918 (1988)
Barbie, Klaus, 517-524 (1987)
Barco, Virgilio
UN Address, 499, 511-515 (1989)
Barnes, Michael D., D-Md., 558 (1988)
Baseball
Banning of Pete Rose, 477-484 (1989)

Ueberroth on Drugs, 169-175 (1986)
Batson v. Kentucky, 409-433 (1986)
Belgium
Pope John Paul II's Visit, 365, 374-376 (1985)
Bender Foundation
Assessing American Education, 297-306 (1988)
Elementary Education Report, 803-817 (1986)
Meese Investigation, 507-509 (1988)
Teaching and Learning Report, 217-238 (1986)
Bennett, William J., 499-500 (1989)
Bentsen, Lloyd, D-Tex.
Acceptance Speech, 533, 542-546 (1988)
Presidential Debates on, 750-751 (1988)
Vice Presidential Debate, 799-829 (1988)
Berlin Wall
Anniversary, 791-799 (1986)
Opening, 627, 628 (1989)
Bernadin, Joseph, 910 (1986)
Bethel School District v. Fraser, 731-742 (1986)
Biaggi, Mario, D-N.Y., 498-499 (1988)
Biden, Joseph R., Jr., D-Del.
Bush's Drug War Speech, 502, 508-511 (1989)
Bingaman, Jeff, D-N.M., 850, 853-856 (1986)
Bioethics. *See also Ethics*
Frozen Embryo Custody Court Decision, 551-559 (1989)
New Jersey Court on Surrogates, 71-80 (1988)
OTA Reports on Biotechnology, 351-372 (1987)
Rights of Surrogates, 373-387 (1987)
Vatican Report, 267-287 (1987)
Birth control. *See also Abortion*
Pope John Paul II on, 363 (1985); 25, 35-37 (1986); 170 (1988)
Population Institute Report, 439-462 (1987)
Report on Teenage Pregnancy, 1057-1064 (1986)
Vatican on Bioethics, 267-287 (1987)
Blackmun, Harry A.
Abortion, 561, 562-571 (1986); 367, 379-387 (1989)
Alcoholism and Veterans' Benefits, 279, 284-285 (1988)
Employment Discrimination, 328-329, 331-332 (1989)
Federal and State Powers, 167-187 (1985)
Labor Union Membership, 415-429 (1985)
Mandatory Budget Cuts, 707, 728-730 (1986)
Sodomy and Privacy, 602-603, 608-614 (1986)
Blacks. *See also Civil and political rights; Equal opportunity; Minority groups*
Alcoholism, 699-700 (1985)

College Athletes, 213-223 (1989)
Diabetes, 702-703 (1985)
Employment
Economic Advisers' Report, 140 (1988)
President's Economic Report, 119
(1988)
Episcopal Church on First Woman Bishop,
49-54 (1989)
Kerner Report Updated, 185-194 (1988)
National Research Council Report, 445-
459 (1989)
President Botha's Manifesto for the Fu-
ture, 515-527 (1985)
Report on Black and Minority Health,
685-706 (1985)
South Africa, 99, 102, 369-381 (1986)
Supreme Court Decisions
Affirmative Action, 651-678 (1986); 331-
349 (1987); 332, 329, 330 (1989)
Death Penalty and Race, 463-476 (1987)
Urban League Report, 27-37 (1985); 43-60
(1987)
Blair, Steven N., 613-617 (1989)
Bobovikov, Ratmir S., 178-179 (1989)
Boff, Rev. Leonardo, 317, 757 (1986)
Boggs, Lindy, D-La.
Congressional Bicentennial Commemora-
tion Remarks, 125-126 (1989)
Bork, Robert H.
Supreme Court Confirmation Battle, 717-
744 (1987)
Botha, P. W., 515-527 (1985); 370, 582 (1986)
Bowen, Otis R., 483-484, 1025-1035 (1986);
319-326 (1987)
Bowen v. American Hospital Association, 541-
558 (1986)
Bowers v. Hardwick, 601-614 (1986)
Bowman, Isaiah, 832 (1988)
Bowsher v. Synar, 705-730 (1986)
Boyer, Ernest L., 939-958 (1986)
Brady, Nicholas F.
World Debt Relief Plan, 137-144 (1989)
Brady Commission Report, 9-11, 13-33 (1988)
Brazil
Discovery of Mengele, 409-414 (1985)
Presidential Elections, 3-12 (1985)
Brennan, William J., Jr.
Abortion, 379-387 (1989)
Address on Role of Supreme Court, 653-
666 (1985)
Adult Theaters, 133-134, 140-144 (1986)
Affirmative Action, 654-676 (1986); 332-
333, 335-344 (1987)
Contagious Diseases, 246-250 (1987)
Creation Science, 566-571 (1987)
Death Penalty and Race, 463, 465, 473-476
(1987)
Disruptive Handicapped Students, 47-56
(1988)
Employment Discrimination, 328-329,
331-332 (1989)
Flag Burning, 346-350 (1989)

Labor Union Membership, 415, 424-429
(1985)
Media Libel Law, 364 (1986)
Miranda Rule, 225, 233, 236-250 (1985)
PAC Spending Limits, 279-280, 283-291
(1985)
Public School Teachers in Parochial
Classes, 433, 436-448, 450-453 (1985) Se-
crecy of CIA Sources, 333, 342-344 (1985)
Student Newspaper Censorship, 45-46
(1988)
Student Searches, 15, 23-26 (1985)
Students' Free Speech, 739 (1986)
Uncompensated Takings and Land Use,
533-534, 549-553 (1987)
Brezhnev doctrine, 399-400, 656 (1989)
British-Irish Accord on Northern Ireland, 723-
732 (1985)
Brokaw, Tom, 806-807, 813-814, 819-820,
826-827 (1988)
Brown, Harold, 781-790 (1986)
Browning, Rt. Rev. Edmond L., 49-54 (1989)
Budget, Federal. See also Gramm-Rudman-
Hollings Act; International debt
Balanced Budget Bill, 803-808 (1985)
Bipartisan Budget Agreement, 72, 83-84
(1989)
Deficit, 53-54 (1986); 124, 126, 128-129
(1988)
Economic Report, 71-104 (1985); 124-125
(1988); 10-11 (1989)
Packard Commission Report on Defense
Management, 679-695 (1986)
Presidential Debates on, 726-728, 756-758
(1988)
President's Budget Message, 71-78 (1985);
49-58 (1986); 3-15 (1987); 149-163 (1988);
71-82 (1989)
State of the Union, 111-113 (1985); 40, 43-
44 (1986); 106, 111 (1987); 58, 61-63
(1988)
Supreme Court on Mandatory Budget
Cuts, 705-730 (1986)
Vice Presidential Debate on, 813-814, 825-
826 (1988)
Burger, Warren E.
Federal and State Powers, 167-187 (1985)
Legal Professionalism, 767 (1986)
Mandatory Budget Cuts, 706, 708-718
(1986)
Peremptory Challenge, 425-433 (1986)
Public School Teachers in Parochial
Classes, 433-461 (1985)
Resignation, 591-599 (1986)
Secrecy of CIA Sources, 333-342 (1985)
Silent Prayer, 379-395 (1985)
Sodomy and Privacy, 602, 607 (1986)
Students' Free Speech, 732, 733-739 (1986)
Use of Deadly Force, 303-315 (1985)
Burma
Amnesty International Human Rights Re-
port, 607-609 (1989)

State Department Human Rights Report, 64-65 (1989)

Burundi
Amnesty International Human Rights Report, 601 (1989)

Bush, George
Congressional Bicentennial Commemoration Speech, 133-135 (1989)
Defense
  Conventional Arms Cuts Proposal, 297-304 (1989)
Domestic Affairs
  Drug War Speech, 499-508 (1989)
  Education, 75-76, 87 (1989)
  Education Summit, 561-570 (1989)
Economic Affairs
  Bipartisan Budget Agreement, 72, 83-84 (1989)
  Budget Message, 71-82 (1989)
  Economic Summit Meeting (Paris), 411, 414, 422, 424-430 (1989)
  Savings and Loan Bailout Bill, 463-468 (1989)
Foreign Affairs
  Central American Bipartisan Accord, 161-168 (1989)
  Chinese Student Protests and Repression, 277-278, 281-286 (1989)
  European Trip to Hungary, Poland and the Netherlands, 411-424, 430-437 (1989)
  Hirohito Funeral Tribute, 99-103 (1989)
  Lebanese Hostage Situation, 319-320 (1989)
  Malta Meeting with Gorbachev, 643-660 (1989)
  Panama Invasion, 701-707 (1989)
  Paris News Conference on European Trip and Economic Summit, 420-424 (1989)
  Soviet Elections, 176, 179-181 (1989)
Inaugural Address, 41-48 (1989)
Politics
  Acceptance Speech, 589-591, 604-613 (1988)
  Postelection Statements, 891-904 (1988)
  Presidential Debates, 721-783 (1988)
  Transfer of Presidential Power, 491-495 (1985)
  Victory Statement, 893-894 (1988)

Business and industry. *See also Foreign trade; Privatization of government services; Small business*
Bhopal Gas Poisoning, 295-302 (1985)
Corporate Management, 971-981 (1986)
Corporate Takeovers, 921-925 (1988)
President's Commission on Organized Crime, 200-210 (1986)
President's Economic Report, 89-90, 101, 104 (1985); 61, 68, 88-89 (1986)
Supreme Court Decisions
  Mandatory Retirement, 397-407 (1985)

Union Membership, 415-429 (1985)

Byrd, Robert C., D-W.Va.
Congressional Bicentennial Commemoration, 126-127 (1989)

C

Cabinet. *See Executive branch*
California
Earthquake Disaster, 667-670 (1989)
Vote on English as Official Language, 959-962 (1986)
California Federal Savings and Loan v. Guerra, 17-27 (1987)
Cambodia
Human Rights Report, 103-104 (1988)
Cameroon
Disaster Aid Report, 61-77 (1987)
Pope John Paul II's Trip, 500, 504-509 (1985)
Campaign financing. *See Government ethics*
Campbell, Ben Nighthorse, D-Colo.
Smithsonian Agreement on Indian Bones and Burial Artifacts, 539-543 (1989)
Canada
Economic Summit, 347-355 (1985); 391-397 (1988)
Trade Pact, 571-578 (1988)
Cancer
Black and Minority Health Report, 686, 697-698 (1985)
Cigarette Smoking, 1079, 1084-1085 (1986)
Interferon Approval, 481-484 (1986)
Radon Report, 3-8 (1988)
Capital punishment. *See Death penalty*
Carlucci, Frank C.
Appointment, 1049 (1986)
Downing of Iranian Airliner, 703-717 (1988)
Military Base Closings, 951-954 (1988)
Carnegie Foundation
Higher Education Report, 583-602 (1985)
Teaching Profession Report, 457-485 (1986)
Undergraduate Colleges Report, 939-958 (1986)
Urban Schools Report, 195-219 (1988)
Carpenter v. United States, 881-889 (1987)
Catholic church. *See also Religion*
Apostolic Letter on Women, 785-792 (1988)
Bishops on Economic Justice, 983-1011 (1986)
Bishops' Report to the Vatican, 571-581 (1985)
Excommunication of Archbishop Lefebvre, 489-494 (1988)
Pope John Paul II's Journeys, 57-67, 363-376, 499-514 (1985); 23-37, 639-649 (1986); 555-564, 699-716 (1987); 405-414 (1988)
Pope John Paul II's Visit to Rome Syna-

gogue, 339-346 (1986)
Synod of Catholic Bishops, 765-780 (1985)
Theology of Liberation, 317-338, 640-641, 646-649 (1986)
U.S. Catholic Bicentennial in Baltimore, 619-623 (1989)
Vatican Disciplining of Father Curran, 757-765 (1986)
Vatican on Bioethics, 267-287 (1987)
Vatican on Pastoral Care of Homosexuals, 909-918 (1986)
CBS/Westmoreland Controversy, 159-165 (1985)
Ceausescu, Elena and Nicolae, Execution of, 709-712 (1989)
Censorship
Rushdie's Death Sentence, 95-98 (1989)
Student Newspaper Censorship, Supreme Court on, 37-46 (1988)
Central America. *See also Latin America; specific countries*
Americas Watch Reports on Nicaragua, 255-269 (1985)
Arias Nobel Peace Prize Speech, 1007-1011 (1987)
Bipartisan Accord, 163-166 (1989)
Bush-Gorbachev Malta Meeting, 650, 657-658 (1989)
Bush Statement on, 166-168 (1989)
Central American Cease-Fire Agreement, 241-245 (1988)
Central American Peace Agreement, 637-648 (1987)
Democratic Party Platform on, 567-568 (1988)
Republican Party Platform on, 675-676 (1988)
State of the Union, 66 (1988)
Tela Declaration, 161, 168-172 (1989)
Vice Presidential Debate on, 807-808 (1988)
Central Intelligence Agency. *See also Iran-contra affair*
Americas Watch Reports on Nicaragua, 256-257, 259 (1985)
Iran Arms Deal and Contra Funding, 1013-1024 (1986)
Secrecy of Sources, 333-344 (1985)
Challenger Space Shuttle
Accident Commission Report, 515-539 (1986)
Discovery Tribute, 795-798 (1988)
Chazov, Dr. Yevgeny I., 781-785 (1985)
Chemical weapons
Paris Declaration on, 25-30 (1989)
Cheney, Dick, R-Wyo.
Defense Secretary Confirmation, 107 (1989)
Cheney, Lynne V., 517-527 (1988)
Chernenko, Konstantin U.
Death of, 271-274 (1985)
Children. *See also Education; Family and*

marital issues
Bishops on Economic Justice, 999 (1986)
Child Survival Program, 686 (1988)
Democratic Party Platform on, 560-561 (1988)
Frozen Embryo Custody Court Decision, 551-559 (1989)
House Report on "Discarded" Children in America, 671-686 (1989)
Infant Mortality Report, 147-165 (1987)
Republican Party Platform on, 634-636, 638-639, 686 (1988)
Supreme Court on Sustaining Handi-capped Infants, 541-558 (1986)
Urban Institute Child Poverty Report, 877-880 (1988)
Children's Defense Fund (CDF) Infant Mortality Report, 147-165 (1987)
Chile
Human Rights Report, 149-150 (1985); 102-103 (1986); 193-194 (1987); 100-101 (1988)
China, People's Republic of
Dalai Lama's Nobel Peace Prize, 573-581 (1989)
Student Protest and Repression, 275-288 (1989)
Chirac, Jacques
French Antiterrorist Plan, 829-838 (1986)
Cholesterol, 779-790 (1987)
Chun Doo Hwan, 583-586, 590-594 (1987)
Church and state
Creation Science, 565-576 (1987)
Pope John Paul II on, 57-67 (1985)
Supreme Court Decisions, 379-395, 433-461 (1985); 565-576 (1987)
Vatican on Theology of Liberation, 317-338, 640-641, 646-649 (1986)
CIA v. Sims and Wolfe, 333-344 (1985)
Cicippio, Joseph James, 315-317 (1989)
Ciparick, Carmen Beauchamp
America's Cup Race State Supreme Court Ruling, 185-188 (1989)
Cities. *See State and local government*
City of Richmond v. J. A. Croson Co., 323-324 (1989)
Civil and political rights. *See also Affirmative action; Equal opportunity; Human rights*
Black America Report, 31-32, 33, 35 (1985) 43-45, 47, 51-52, 58 (1987)
Domestic Partnerships Ordinances, 305-311 (1989)
Kerner Report Updated, 185-194 (1988)
Republican Party Platform on, 642-649 (1988)
Supreme Court Decisions
Affirmative Action, 651-678 (1986); 331-349 (1987)
Civil Rights Rulings, 321-332 (1989)
Indigents' Rights to Psychiatric Aid, 207-219 (1985)
Private Clubs, 399-403 (1988)

Student Searches, 13-26 (1985)
Suspects' Rights, 223-253 (1985)
Use of Deadly Force, 303-315 (1985)
Claiborne, Harry E.
Impeachment, 849-857 (1986)
Clausen, A. W., 860 (1986)
Cocaine. *See also Drug abuse*
President's Commission on Organized
Crime, 181, 183-187 (1986)
Cold War, 649-650 (1989). *See also Demo-
cratic reforms*
Colleges and universities
Black College Athletes, 213-223 (1989)
Higher Education Report, 583-602 (1985)
Undergraduate Colleges Report, 939-958
(1986)
U.S. College Curriculum, 127-144 (1985)
Colombia
Amnesty International Human Rights Re-
port, 603-604 (1989)
Barco United Nations Address, 499, 511-
515 (1989)
John Paul II's Trip, 639-649 (1986)
President's Commission on Organized
Crime, 185-189 (1986)
Commission on Civil Rights
Urban League Report, 45 (1987)
**Commission on Minority Participation in Edu-
cation and American Life**
Kerner Report Updated, 185-187 (1988)
Commission on the Cities
Kerner Report Updated, 185-194 (1988)
**Commission on Wartime Relocation and In-
ternment of Civilians,** 288-289 (1988)
Common Market. *See European Community
(EC)*
**Commonwealth of Nations Report on South
Africa,** 581-590 (1986)
Communications
FCC on Fairness Doctrine, 625-636 (1987)
Supreme Court Decisions
Media Libel Law, 355-368 (1986)
Communists. *See individual communist
countries*
Compton, Ann, 756-757, 764-765, 772-773,
781 (1988)
Conable, Barber, 861 (1986)
Congress. *See also Government ethics;
House of Representatives; Senate*
Balanced Budget Bill, 803-808 (1985)
Bicentennial Commemorations, 123-135
(1989)
Defense Budget Process, 693-695 (1986)
Reagan's Post-Geneva Summit Address,
751, 756-761 (1985)
Soviet Marshal Akhromeyev Testimony,
439-444 (1989)
Congressional Budget Office (CBO)
Grace Commission, Report on, 231 (1988)
Constitution, U.S.
Bicentennial Observance, 765-775
(1987)

1st (First Amendment)
Adult Theaters, 131-144 (1986)
Church and State, 379-395, 433-461
(1985); 565-576 (1987)
FCC on Fairness Doctrine, 625-636
(1987)
Flag Burning, 343-354 (1989)
Media Libel Law, 355-368 (1986)
Obscenity, 479-490 (1987)
Press Freedom, 175-182 (1988)
Private Clubs, 399-403 (1988)
Religion in Curriculum, 597-608 (1987)
School Prayer, 379-395 (1985)
Student Newspaper Censorship, 37-46
(1988)
Students' Free Speech, 731-742 (1986)
4th (Fourth Amendment)
Sodomy and Privacy, 601-614 (1986)
Student Searches, 13-26 (1985)
Use of Deadly Force, 303-315 (1985)
5th (Fifth Amendment)
Suspects' Rights, 223-253 (1987)
Uncompensated Takings and Land Use,
531-553 (1987)
6th (Sixth Amendment)
Jury Selection in Capital Cases, 445-456
(1986)
Peremptory Challenge, 409-433 (1986)
8th (Eighth Amendment)
Death Penalty and Race, 463-476 (1987)
Preventive Detention, 491-508 (1987)
10th (Tenth Amendment)
Independent Counsel, 465-478 (1988)
Mandatory Budget Cuts, 705-730 (1986)
Republican Party Platform on, 647
(1988)
14th (Fourteenth Amendment)
Death Penalty and Race, 463-476 (1987)
Jury Selection in Capital Cases, 445-456
(1986)
Political Gerrymandering, 615-635
(1986)
Preventive Detention, 491-508 (1987)
Uncompensated Takings and Land Use,
531-553 (1987)
25th (Twenty-fifth Amendment)
Transfer of Presidential Power, 491-495
(1985)
Contadora Agreement
Administration Reports on Nicaragua,
257, 266-267 (1985)
Central American Peace Agreement, 637-
648 (1987)
Contras. *See Central America; Iran-Contra
affair; Nicaragua*
Cook, Frederick A., 832-833 (1988); 687-688,
690 (1989)
Cooper Clinic Fitness and Health Report, 613-
617 (1989)
**Coordinating Committee on Multilateral Ex-
port Controls (CoCom)**
National Security Export Controls, 29-42
(1987)

Costa Rica
Central American Peace Agreement, 637-648 (1987)
Vice Presidential Debate on, 807 (1988)
Council of Economic Advisers
Annual Economic Report, 80, 88-104 (1985); 59, 70-92 (1986); 117-119, 125-144 (1987); 126-148 (1988); 3-5, 12-14 (1989)
Council of Europe
Gorbachev Address on a Common Europe, 399-409 (1989)
Courts, U.S. *See also Supreme Court*
America's Cup Race Rulings, 183-193 (1989)
Frozen Embryo Custody Decision, 551-559 (1989)
Impeachment of Federal Judges, 583-596 (1989)
Indigents' Rights to Psychiatric Aid, 207-219 (1985)
Jury Selection in Capital Cases, 445-456 (1986)
Peremptory Challenge, 409-433 (1986)
PLO Office Closing, 479-485 (1988)
Sentencing Commission Report, 407-426 (1987)
Surrogates' Rights, 373-387 (1987); 71-80 (1988)
Covey, Col. Harvey O., 798 (1988)
Credit. *See also Banks and banking*
Economic Advisers' Report, 89-91 (1986)
Federal Credit Programs, 11-12 (1987)
OTA Report on Biotechnology, 292-294 (1986)
Crime and law enforcement. *See also Courts, U.S.; Supreme Court*
Black Americans, NRC Report on, 456 (1989)
Budget Message, 155 (1988)
Cuban Detainee Agreements, 929-937 (1987)
Democratic Party Platform on, 562 (1988)
Meese Criticism of Supreme Court, 480-481, 485-486 (1985)
Philadelphia Police Raid on MOVE Group, 239-251 (1986)
President's Commission on Organized Crime, 179-216 (1986)
President's Commission on Privatization Report, 234 (1988)
Republican Party Platform on, 655-656 (1988)
Sentencing Commission Report, 407-426 (1987)
State of the Union, 114 (1985)
Supreme Court Decisions
Death Penalty and Race, 463-476 (1987)
Miranda Ruling, 223-253 (1985)
Preventive Detention, 491-508 (1987)
Student Searches, 13-26 (1985)
Use of Deadly Force, 303-315 (1985)
U.S.-U.K. Extradition Treaty, 751-756 (1986)

Crowe, Adm. William J., 703-717 (1988)
Cuba
Angola-Namibia Peace Accord, 947-950 (1988)
Cuban Detainee Agreements, 929-937 (1987)
International Terrorism, 471-472 (1985)
Cuellar, Javier Perez de, 610-611 (1987); 531-532 (1988)
Curran, Charles E.
Vatican Disciplining of, 757-765 (1986)
Czechoslovakia
Communist Concessions, 635-639 (1989)

D

Dalai Lama, 573-581 (1989)
Daniloff, Nicholas S., 819-827 (1986)
Darman, Richard G., 971-981 (1986)
Davis v. Bandemer, 615-635 (1986)
Death penalty
Amnesty International, 597 (1989)
Presidential Debates on, 723, 736-737 (1988)
Supreme Court Decisions, 463-476 (1987)
Debates. *See Presidential election; Vice presidency*
Defense. *See also Arms control; Defense Department; Foreign affairs; Foreign aid; Strategic Arms Limitation Treaty; Strategic Defense Initiative*
ABM Treaty Interpretation, 289-317 (1987); 330 (1988)
Budget, 51, 55 (1986); 4, 9-10, 14 (1987); 79-80, 661-662 (1989)
Conventional Arms Cuts Proposal, 297-304 (1989)
Democratic Party Platform on, 566-567 (1988)
Intelligence
Iran-Contra Reports, 891-928 (1987)
Pentagon Report on Soviet Espionage, 603-614 (1985)
Republican Party Platform on, 698-699 (1988)
Tower Commission Report, 205-242 (1987)
Westmoreland/CBS Controversy, 159-165 (1985)
MX Missile Production, 4 (1987)
National Security Export Controls, 29-42 (1987)
National Security Strategy, 781-790 (1986)
Packard Commission on Defense Management, 679-695 (1986)
Presidential Debates on, 741-744, 761-764, 767-769, 778-781 (1988)
President's Budget Message, 80-82 (1989)
Republican Party Platform on, 688-702 (1988)
Science Board Panel on Strategic Missile Defense, 323-331 (1988)

Soviet Marshal Akhromeyev's Congressional Testimony, 439-444 (1989)
State of the Union, 106-107 (1985); 40, 44 (1986); 57-58, 60, 66-67 (1988)
USS Stark Attack, 791-816 (1987)
Vice Presidential Debate on, 827 (1988)
Defense Department
Downing of Iranian Airliner, 703-717 (1988)
Joint Chiefs of Staff Reorganization, 679 (1986)
Military Base Closings, 951-954 (1988)
National Security Export Controls, 29-42 (1987)
Packard Commission on Defense Management, 679-695 (1986)
SDI Milestone Panel on Strategic Missile Defense, 323-331 (1988)
Senate Armed Services Report on the Pentagon, 669-683 (1985)
Sexual Harassment Report, 671-679 (1987)
Tower Defense Secretary Nomination Rejection, 105-120 (1989)
Deficits. See Budget, Federal
De Klerk, F. W.
South African President's Inaugural Address, 545-550 (1989)
Delvalle, Eric Arturo, 81 (1988)
Democratic party
Convention
Bentsen Acceptance Speech, 533, 535, 542-546 (1988)
Dukakis Acceptance Speech, 533-542 (1988)
Jackson Address, 534-535, 546-556 (1988)
Platform, 557-569 (1988)
Democratic reforms
Baltic Freedom Statements, 469-475 (1989)
Bush-Gorbachev Malta Meeting, 656-657 (1989)
Chinese Student Protests and Repression, 275-288 (1989)
Czechoslovakian Communist Concessions, 635-639 (1989)
German Reunification Statements, 625-634, 658-659 (1989)
Gorbachev Addresses
19th All-Union Soviet Party Conference, 447-464 (1988)
Council of Europe on a Common Europe, 399-409 (1989)
Plenary Session of Soviet Party Congress, 79-104 (1987)
Kennan on Cold War, 207-212 (1989)
Poland's New Era
Mazowiecki Speech to Polish Sejm, 523-533 (1989)
Walesa Address to U.S. Congress, 523-525, 534-538 (1989)
South Korean Leaders Speeches, 583-594 (1987)

Soviet Elections, 173-181 (1989)
Deng Xiaoping
Chinese Student Demonstrations, 287-288 (1989)
Desegregation. See Civil and political rights; Equal opportunity; Education; Housing
Developing countries. See also Foreign aid; United Nations; and specific countries
Bishop's Letter on Economic Justice, 1005-1010 (1986)
Brady World Debt Relief Plan, 137-144 (1989)
Child Survival Program, 686 (1988)
Economic Advisers' Report, 78-83 (1986)
Economic Summit Meetings
(Bonn), 353-354 (1985)
(Paris), 425-526 (1989)
(Toronto), 391, 396-397 (1988)
Environmental Defense Fund on World Bank Project, 859-873 (1986)
IMF-World Bank Conference, 643-652 (1985)
Pope's Encyclical on Social Concerns, 165-174 (1988)
Population Institute Report, 439-462 (1987)
Vatican on Theology of Liberation, 317-338 (1986)
Diabetes
Black and Minority Health Report, 686, 697-698 (1985)
Disabled persons. See Handicapped persons
Disarmament. See Arms control
Disasters
California Earthquakes, 667-670 (1989)
Cameroon Aid Report, 61-77 (1987)
Hurricane Hugo, 667-670 (1989)
Discovery Space Shuttle Tribute to Challenger Victims, 795-798 (1988)
Discrimination. See Affirmative action; Civil and political rights; Equal opportunity; Human rights; Pregnancy Discrimination Act
Dixon, Alan, D-Ill., 850, 856-857 (1986)
Dole, Robert, R-Kan.
Congressional Bicentennial Commemoration, 131-132 (1989)
Donaldson, Sam, 1093-1095 (1986)
Drug abuse. See also Acquired immune deficiency syndrome
Barco's UN Address, 499, 511-515 (1989)
Budget Message, 150, 155 (1988); 76-77 (1989)
Bush's Drug War Speech, 499-511 (1989)
Democratic Party Platform on, 562 (1988)
Economic Summit
(Paris), 429-430 (1989)
(Toronto), 394-395 (1988)
Jackson Address to Democratic National Convention, 552-553 (1988)
Nicotine Addiction Report, 309-322 (1988)

Noriega Indictments, 81-92 (1988)
Presidential Commission on the Human Immunodeficiency Virus Epidemic, 416, 435-436 (1988)
Presidential Debates on, 725-726 (1988)
President's Commission on Organized Crime, 180-200 (1986)
Reagan's Executive Order on Drug Testing, 839-846 (1986)
Republican Party Platform on, 656-657, 679-680 (1988)
Ueberroth on Drugs in Baseball, 169-175 (1986)
Vice Presidential Debate on, 814-815 (1988)
Due process. See Constitution, U.S., Fourteenth Amendment
Dukakis, Michael S.
Acceptance Speech, 533-542 (1988)
Postelection Statement, 900-904 (1988)
Presidential Debates, 721-783 (1988)
Duvalier, Jean-Claude "Baby Doc," 98-99, 106-107 (1986)

E

Echo-Hawk, Walter, 539, 542 (1989)
Economic policy. See also Budget, Federal; Inflation; Monetary policy
Bishops on Economic Justice, 983-1011 (1986)
Brady World Debt Relief Plan, 137-144 (1989)
Budget Message, 71-78 (1985); 49-58 (1986); 3-15 (1987); 149-163 (1988)
Council of Economic Advisers Report, 3-5, 12-14 (1989)
Democratic Party Platform on, 559-560 (1988)
Economic Sanctions in Panama, 81 (1988)
Economic Summit Meetings
(Bonn), 347-355 (1985)
(Paris), 411, 414, 422, 424-430 (1989)
(Tokyo), 437-444 (1986)
(Toronto), 391-397 (1988)
(Venice), 512, 525-530 (1987)
Gorbachev's Address to 27th Soviet Party Congress, 145-146, 152-160 (1986)
IMF-World Bank Conference, 643-652 (1985)
Plunge of the Dollar, 523-530 (1985)
President's Economic Report, 79-104 (1985); 59-92 (1986); 117-144 (1987); 3, 5-12 (1989)
Republican Party Platform on, 619-621, 632-633 (1988)
State of the Union, 105-117 (1985); 38-45 (1986); 111 (1987)
Stock Market Crash, 833-842 (1987); 9-36 (1988)
Vice Presidential Debate on, 813-814 (1988)

Education
Assessing American Education, 297-306 (1988)
Black America Report, 30, 36-37 (1985)
Black Americans, NRC Report on, 454-455 (1989)
Black College Athletes, 213-223 (1989)
Budget Message, 150, 154 (1988); 75-76 (1989)
Democratic Party Platform on, 561-562 (1988)
Department of Education Report on Teaching and Learning, 217-238 (1986)
Education Summit, 561-570 (1989)
Elementary Education, 803-817 (1986)
Higher Education Report, 583-602 (1985)
Humanities Education Report, 681-696 (1987)
Kerner Report Updated, 190-191, 193 (1988)
Math and Science Education Reports, 377-390 (1988)
National Assessment of Educational Progress Report, 85-94 (1989)
President's Commission on Privatization Report, 233 (1988)
Religion in Curriculum, 597-608 (1987)
Republican Party Platform on, 649-653 (1988)
State of the Humanities Report, 517-527 (1988)
State of the Union, 63-64 (1988)
Supreme Court Decisions
Alcoholism and Veterans' Benefits, 277-285 (1988)
Creation Science, 565-576 (1987)
Disruptive Handicapped Students, 47-56 (1988)
Public School Teachers in Parochial Classes, 433-461 (1985)
School Prayer, 379-395 (1985)
Student Newspaper Censorship, 37-46 (1988)
Student Searches, 13-26 (1985)
Students' Free Speech, 731-742 (1986)
Teaching Profession, 457-485 (1986)
Undergraduate Colleges Report, 939-958 (1986)
U.S. College Curriculum, 127-144 (1985)
Urban Schools Report, 195-219 (1988)
Educational Testing Service
Report on U.S. Education, 85-94 (1989)
Edwards, Don, D-Calif.
Impeachment of Judge Walter L. Nixon, 585, 590-596 (1989)
Edwards v. Aguillard, 565-576 (1987)
Egypt
Arab Summit Communique, 869-874 (1987)
Eighth Amendment. See Constitution, U.S.
El Salvador. See also Central America
Amnesty International Human Rights Re-

port, 604-605 (1989)
Central American Peace Agreement, 637-648 (1987)
Human Rights Report, 146, 150-151 (1985); 103-104 (1986); 194-195 (1987)
Elderly. *See Aged*
Elections. *See also Voting*
Court on Closed Party Primaries, 1065-1073 (1986)
Democratic Party Platform on, 565 (1988)
Employment and unemployment
Bishops on Economic Justice, 996-998 (1986)
Black America Report, 27-37 (1985)
Economic Advisers' Report, 143-144 (1987); 118, 126, 139-142 (1988)
Economic Summit (Bonn), 351-352 (1985)
Kerner Report Updated, 187-188, 193 (1988)
NRC Report on Black Americans, 453-454 (1989)
President's Economic Report, 63 (1986); 118, 119-121 (1988); 8-9 (1989)
Republican Party Platform on, 621-623 (1988)
Sex Segregation in the Workplace, 789-801 (1985)
Smoking in the Workplace, 809-822 (1985)
Supreme Court Decisions
Affirmative Action, 651-678 (1986); 321-332 (1989)
Labor Union Membership, 415-429 (1985)
Mandatory Retirement, 397-407 (1985)
Women in the Labor Force, 143-144 (1987)
Energy policy
Democratic Party Platform on, 565 (1988)
Republican Party Platform on, 665-668 (1988)
English language
California Vote on English as Official Language, 959-962 (1986)
Environment. *See also "Greenhouse effect"; Pollution*
Alaskan Oil Spill Hearings, 225-237 (1989)
Bhopal Gas Poisoning, 295-302 (1985)
Chernobyl Nuclear Accident, 384, 401-404 (1986)
Democratic Party Platform on, 564 (1988)
Economic Summit Meetings
(Bonn), 354-355 (1985)
(Paris), 427-429, 432 (1989)
(Toronto), 397 (1988)
Energy Secretary Watt's Environmental Plan, 355-362 (1989)
Environmental Defense Fund on World Bank Project, 859-873 (1986)
EPA Report on "Greenhouse Effect," 861-866 (1988)
Interagency Report on Forest-Fire Policy, 941-946 (1988)
Nuclear War Effects, 541-554 (1985)

OTA Report on Biotechnology, 295-296 (1986)
Ozone Treaty and Scientific Study, 745-764 (1987); 221-228, 397 (1988)
Presidential Debates on, 776-777 (1988)
President's Budget Message, 77 (1989)
Republican Party Platform on, 668-671 (1988)
Supreme Court Decisions
Uncompensated Takings and Land Use, 531-553 (1987)
Vice Presidential Debate on, 805-806, 817-818 (1988)
Environmental Protection Agency (EPA)
"Greenhouse Effect" on America's Climate, 861-866 (1988)
Equal opportunity. *See also Civil and political rights*
Democratic Party Platform on, 563 (1988)
Republican Party Platform on, 622-623 (1988)
Supreme Court Decisions
Affirmative Action, 651-678 (1986)
Civil Rights Rulings, 321-332 (1989)
Estonia
Baltic Nationalist Movement, 469-475 (1989)
Ethics. *See also Bioethics; Government*
ABA Report on Legal Professionalism, 767-778 (1986)
Bishops on Economic Justice, 990-994 (1986)
Wright Investigation, 239-271 (1989)
Ethiopia
Amnesty International Human Rights Report, 601-602 (1989)
State Department Human Rights Report, 151-152 (1985); 99-101 (1986); 191-192 (1987)
Europe. *See specific countries*
European Community (EC)
Economic Summit Meetings
(Tokyo), 437-444 (1986)
(Venice), 525-530 (1987)
Evans, Daniel J., D.-Wash., 292-293 (1988)
Executive branch. *See also Government reorganization*
Cabinet nomination rejections, 107 (1989)
Supreme Court Decision on Mandatory Budget Cuts, 705-730 (1986)
Tower Defense Secretary Nomination Rejection, 105-120 (1989)
Transfer of Presidential Power, 491-495 (1985)
Exxon Valdez Oil Spill Hearings, 225-237 (1989)

F

Fabius, Laurent, 631-634 (1985)
Fabrikant, Jacob I.
NRC Radon Report, 3-8 (1988)

Fairness doctrine. *See Constitution, U.S.,*
First Amendment
Falwell, Jerry
  Supreme Court on Freedom of the Press,
  175-177 (1988)
Family and marital issues. *See also Children*
  Black America Report, 27-37 (1985)
  Black Americans, NRC Report on, 456-457
  (1989)
  Domestic Partnerships Ordinances, 305-
  311 (1989)
  Frozen Embryo Custody Court Decision,
  551-559 (1989)
  House Report on Discarded Children in
  America, 671-686 (1989)
  Pope John Paul II on, 25, 35-37 (1986)
  Population Institute Report, 439-462
  (1987)
  Republican Party Platform on, 633-636
  (1988)
  State of the Union, 41, 43, 45-46 (1986); 59,
  63-65 (1988)
  Surrogates' Rights, 373-387 (1987); 71-80
  (1988)
  Vice Presidential Debate on, 806-807
  (1988)
Family planning. *See Abortion; Birth control*
Family Support Act of 1988, 847-852 (1988)
Farmers and farming. *See Agriculture*
Federal Aviation Administration (FAA)
  Air Traffic Safety, 253-266 (1986)
  Aviation Safety Commission Report, 267-
  276 (1988)
Federal Communications Commission (FCC)
  Fairness Doctrine, 625-636 (1987)
Federal Communications Commission v.
League of Women Voters of California, 626-
627 (1987)
Federal Deposit Insurance Corporation (FDIC)
  Savings and Loan Crisis, 913-918 (1988)
Federal Election Commission v. National Con-
servative Political Action Committee, 277-294
(1985)
Federal Reserve System
  Economic Advisers' Report, 72-73 (1986);
  117-118, 129-131 (1988)
  Greenspan Appointment, 511-516 (1987)
  Volcker Resignation, 511-516 (1987)
Fellay, Bernard, 490-492 (1988)
Fifth Amendment. *See Constitution, U.S.*
Financial Institutions Reform, Recovery, and
  Enforcement Act of 1989, 463-468 (1989)
Financial policy. *See Economic policy; Infla-*
tion; Monetary policy
First Amendment. *See Constitution, U.S.*
First English Evangelical Lutheran Church of
Glendale v. County of Los Angeles, 531-546
(1987)
Flag Burning
  Supreme Court Ruling on, 343-354 (1989)
Fogarty, Rear Adm. William M., 703-717
(1988)

Foley, Thomas S., D-Wash.
  Congressional Bicentennial Commemora-
  tion, 130-131 (1989)
Food
  Cholesterol Report, 779-790 (1987)
Food and Drug Administration (FDA)
  AZT (azidothymidine) approval, 327-330
  (1987)
  TPA (tissue plasminogen activator) ap-
  proval, 875-879 (1987)
Food supply
  Bishops on Economic Justice, 1002-1005,
  1009 (1986)
  Economic Advisers' Report, 83-84 (1986)
  Gorbachev at 27th Party Congress, 146,
  156-157 (1986)
  Hunger in America, 189-205 (1985)
  Nuclear War Effects, 543, 551-554 (1985)
Foreign affairs. *See also Arms control; For-*
eign aid; Foreign trade; Human rights; In-
ternational debt; Iran-contra affair; Sum-
mit conferences; Treaties and agreements
  Americas Watch/Administration Reports
  on Nicaragua, 255-269 (1985)
  Democratic Party Platform on, 566 (1988)
  Gorbachev at 27th Party Congress, 163-
  167 (1986)
  Republican Party Platform on, 673-688
  (1988)
  State of the Union, 115-116 (1985); 40, 47
  (1986); 60, 65-66 (1988)
  U.S. Reduction of Soviet UN Mission, 267-
  272 (1986)
  U.S.-U.K. Extradition Treaty, 751-756
  (1986)
  U.S. Withdrawal from World Court Juris-
  diction, 637-641 (1985)
  USS Stark Attack, 791-816 (1987)
Foreign aid
  Child Survival Program, 686 (1988)
  Haiti, 939-941 (1987)
  State of the Union, 115-116 (1985)
Foreign trade. *See also General Agreement*
on Tariffs and Trade (GATT); Interna-
tional debt
  Canada-U.S., 58, 65-66, 123; 571-578
  (1988)
  Democratic Party Platform on, 561 (1988)
  Economic Advisers' Report, 95-99 (1985);
  117-118, 126 (1987); 118, 142-144 (1988);
  13 (1989)
  Economic Summit Meetings
    (Bonn), 354 (1985)
    (Paris), 425 (1989)
  Japan-U.S. Trade Dispute, 427-437 (1987)
  Mexico-U.S., 58, 66 (1988)
  Nakasone Speech, 319-323 (1985)
  National Security Export Controls, 29-42
  (1987)
  Poland, Lifting Trade Sanctions Against,
  183-188 (1987)
  President's Economic Report, 68-69

(1986); 117-118, 122-123 (1987); 123, 125 (1988); 10 (1989)
Reagan Trade Bill Vetoes, 339-346 (1988)
Republican Party Platform on, 630-632 (1988)
State of the Union, 115-116 (1985); 44-45 (1986); 58, 65-66 (1988)
Forest fires. *See Environment*
Fourteenth Amendment. *See Constitution, U.S.*
Fourth Amendment. *See Constitution, U.S.*
France
Chirac on French Antiterrorist Plan, 829-838 (1986)
Economic Summit (Bonn), 347-355 (1985)
Economic Summit (Paris), 411, 414, 422, 424-430 (1989)
Greenpeace Affair, 631-634 (1985)
Group of Five Communique on the Dollar, 523-530 (1985)
Frank, Barney, D-Mass., 336-337 (1989)
Free speech. *See Constitution, U.S., First Amendment*
Free trade. *See Foreign trade*
Freedom of Information Act. *See also Press*
Secrecy of CIA Sources, 333-344 (1985)
Fuel. *See Energy policy*

G

Galarreta, Alfonso de, 490-492 (1988)
Gambling
Banning of Pete Rose from Baseball, 477-484 (1989)
Gandhi, Mahatma, 24, 26-28 (1986)
Gandhi, Rajiv, 615-622 (1987)
Garcia, Robert, D-N.Y., 499 (1988)
Gases, Asphyxiating and poisonous.
Bhopal Gas Poisoning, 295-302 (1985)
Cameroon Disaster Aid Report, 61-77 (1987)
Gay rights. *See Homosexuals*
General Accounting Office (GAO)
Grace Commission Report, 231 (1988)
Report on Air Traffic Safety, 253-266 (1986)
General Agreement on Tariffs and Trade (GATT), 142-143, 631 (1988). *See also Foreign trade*
Genetic engineering. *See also Bioethics*
Interferon Approval, 484-485 (1986)
OTA Report on Biotechnology, 287-288, 296 (1986); 352-353, 356-358 (1987)
Genocide Convention
Senate Ratification of, 115-130 (1986)
Geneva Protocol of 1925
Paris Declaration on Chemical Weapons, 25-30 (1989)
Germany, East
German Reunification Statement, 625-634, 658-659 (1989)

Germany, Federal Republic of
Berlin Wall Anniversary, 791-799 (1986)
Berlin Wall Opening, 627, 628 (1989)
Economic Summit (Bonn), 347-355 (1985)
German Reunification Statements, 625-634, 658-659 (1989)
Group of Five Communique on the Dollar, 523-530 (1985)
Kohl on German Remorse at World War II Anniversary, 487-497 (1989)
Reagan at Bitburg, 357-362 (1985)
Gesell, Gerhard A., 391-397 (1989)
Giamatti, A. Bartlett
Banning of Pete Rose, 477, 479, 480-482 (1989)
Ginsburg, Douglas H., 720 (1987)
Goldwater, Barry, R-Ariz., 669 (1985); 682 (1986)
Goode, W. Wilson, 239-241 (1986)
Gorbachev, Mikhail S.
Afghanistan Agreements, 257-258 (1988)
All-Union Soviet Party Congress, 447-464 (1988)
Arms Control Proposal, 9-20 (1986)
Beijing Visit, 276-277 (1989)
Bolshevik Anniversary Speech, 857-868 (1987)
Chernenko Death, 271-274 (1985)
Council of Europe Address on a Common Europe, 399-409 (1989)
Democratic Reforms, 79-104 (1987); 447-464 (1988)
Economic Summit Meetings, 431-432, 433-434 (1989)
Farm Policy, 145-152 (1989)
INF Treaty Statement, 945, 947-950 (1987)
Malta Meeting with Bush, 643-660 (1989)
New Year's Message to U.S., 3-6 (1986)
Soviet Elections, 173-178 (1989)
Soviet Party Congress, 145-168 (1986); 79-104 (1987)
Summit Meetings
(Geneva), 749-761 (1985)
(Moscow), 353-373 (1988)
(Reykjavik), 875-885 (1986); 866-867 (1987)
(Washington, D.C.), 991-1006 (1987)
United Nations Address, 927-940 (1988)
Government ethics
Meese Investigation, 495-516 (1988)
PAC Spending Limits, Supreme Court on, 277-294 (1985)
Presidential Debates on, 781-782 (1988)
Republican Party Platform on, 647-649 (1988)
Vice Presidential Debate on, 808-809, 810, 816-817 (1988)
Government regulations. *See Regulatory reform*
Government reorganization
Budget Message, 54-58 (1986); 157-158 (1988)

Reagan's Reform '88 Program, 152, 159-161 (1988)
Government spending. *See also Budget*
Packard Commission Report on Defense Management, 679-695 (1986)
President's Economic Report, 66 (1986); 121-122 (1987); 124-125 (1988)
Republican Party Platform on, 629-630 (1988)
State of the Union, 111-113 (1985); 61 (1988)
Grace Commission, 231 (1988)
Gramm-Rudman-Hollings Act. *See also Budget, Federal*
Balanced Budget Bill, 803-808 (1985)
Budget Message, 49-58 (1986); 3-15 (1987); 153, 154 (1988)
Economic Advisers' Report, 74, 76 (1986)
President's Economic Report, 66 (1986); 124 (1988)
State of the Union, 43-44 (1986); 63 (1988)
Supreme Court Decision, 705-730 (1986)
Vice Presidential Debate on, 826 (1988)
Grand Rapids School District v. Ball, 433-461 (1985)
Gray, Nellie J., 53-56 (1985)
Great Britain
British-Irish Accord on Northern Ireland, 723-732 (1985)
Economic Summit Meetings (London), 355-364 (1986)
Group of Five Communique on the Dollar, 523-530 (1985)
U.S.-U.K. Extradition Treaty, 751-756 (1986)
"Greenhouse effect"
EPA Report on Global Climate Change, 861-866 (1988)
Vice Presidential Debate on, 817-818 (1988)
Greenpeace affair, 631-634 (1985)
Greenspan, Alan, 511-516 (1987)
Grenada, 808, 814 (1988)
Groer, Anne, 729-730, 736-737, 744-745, 751 (1988)
Grosz, Paul, 409-411 (1988)
Group of Five Communique on the Dollar, 523-530 (1985)
Guatemala
Amnesty International Human Rights Report, 605 (1989)
Central American Peace Agreement, 637-648 (1987)
State Department Human Rights Report, 152 (1985); 104-106 (1986); 195-196 (1987)

H

Habib, Philip C., 308 (1986)
Haiti
AIDS Report, 735 (1985)

Elections, 939-941 (1987)
Human Rights Report, 98-99, 106-107 (1986); 191, 196-197 (1987); 101-103 (1988)
Hale, Mother, 117 (1985)
Handicapped persons
Republican Party Platform on, 644-645 (1988)
Supreme Court Decisions
Contagious Diseases, 245-252 (1987)
Disruptive Handicapped Students, 47-56 (1988)
Sustaining Handicapped Infants, 541-558 (1986)
Harris, Rev. Barbara Clementine, 49-54 (1989)
Hartwig, Clayton M., 517-521 (1989)
Harvard Commission on the Presidential Press Conference, 835-845 (1988)
Harvard University Report on Medicare Reform, 273-285 (1986)
Hastings, Alcee L.
Impeachment of, 583-589 (1989)
Hauck, Capt. Frederick H., 795, 798 (1988)
Hazardous wastes
Energy Secretary Watkins' Environmental Plan, 355-362 (1989)
Toxic Waste Treaty, 153-160 (1989)
Health. *See also Acquired immune deficiency syndrome; Cancer; Heart disease; Medical care; Medicaid and Medicare; Radiation; Smoking*
Alzheimer's Disease Report, 391-406 (1987)
Black and Minority Health Report, 685-706 (1985)
Black Americans, NRC Report on, 455-456 (1989)
Cholesterol Report, 779-790 (1987)
Contagious Diseases, Supreme Court on, 245-252 (1987)
Fitness and Health Report, 613-617 (1989)
Frozen Embryo Custody Court Decision, 551-559 (1989)
Health Costs of Smoking, 615-622 (1985)
Hospital Length of Stay Report, 333-337 (1988)
Interferon Approval, 481-484 (1986)
Involuntary Smoking, 1079-1090 (1986)
Nicotine Addiction Report, 309-322 (1988)
Republican Party Platform on, 636-639, 686 (1988)
Smoking in the Workplace, 809-822 (1985)
Health and Human Services Department
AIDS, 733-747 (1985); 887-889 (1986); 319-326 (1987)
AZT Approval, 327-330 (1987)
Catastrophic Illness Expenses, 1025-1035 (1986)
Interferon Approval, 481-485 (1986)
Health insurance
Presidential Debates on, 729-730 (1988)

Heart disease
Black and Minority Health Report, 686, 697-698 (1985)
Cholesterol Report, 779-790 (1987)
FDA Approval of TPA, 875-879 (1987)
Heckler, Margaret, 685-687 (1985)
Helms, Jesse, R-N.C., 289, 293 (1988)
Henson, Matthew, 687, 693, 696 (1989)
Higgins, Lt. Col. William R., 315-316 (1989)
Hills, Carla A., 335 (1989)
Hilmers, David C., 797 (1988)
Hirohito (Emperor) Funeral Tributes, 99-103 (1989)
Hispanics. *See also Minority groups*
Alcoholism, 700 (1985)
California Vote on English as Official Language, 959 (1986)
Diabetes, 703-704 (1985)
Employment
Economic Advisers' Report, 140 (1988)
President's Economic Report, 119 (1988)
Pope John Paul II's Visit to U.S., 700, 705-707 (1987)
Hollings, Ernest F., D.-S.C.
Alaskan Oil Spill Hearings, 228-230 (1989)
Holocaust
Mengele Discovery, 409-414 (1985)
Pope John Paul in Austria, 405-414 (1988)
Wiesel Nobel Peace Prize, 1075-1078 (1986)
Wiesel Testimony at Klaus Barbie Trial, 517-524 (1987)
Homeless persons
Presidential Debates on, 734-736 (1988)
Republican Party Platform on, 640-642 (1988)
Vice Presidential Debate on, 806 (1988)
Homosexuals
AIDS, 733-736 (1985); 887 (1986)
Domestic Partnerships Ordinances, 305-311 (1989)
Vatican on Pastoral Care of Homosexuals, 909-918 (1986)
Honduras
Central American Peace Agreement, 637-648 (1987)
Honig v. Doe, 47-56 (1988)
Hospitals
For-Profit Hospitals, 487-513 (1986)
PHS Report on Length of Hospitalization, 333-337 (1988)
House of Representatives. *See also Congress; Senate*
Discarded Children in America Report, 671-686 (1989)
Iran-Contra Reports, 891-928 (1987)
Wright Investigation, 239-257 (1989)
Wright Farewell Speech, 242, 257-271 (1989)
Housing
Democratic Party Platform on, 563 (1988)

Kerner Report Updated, 190, 193 (1988)
Presidential Debates on, 734-736 (1988)
President's Commission on Privatization Report, 231-232 (1988)
Republican Party Platform on, 628-629 (1988)
Housing and Urban Development Department (HUD)
Watt on Influence Peddling, 333-337 (1989)
Hoxha, Enver, 325-331 (1985)
Human immunodeficiency virus (HIV). *See Acquired immune deficiency syndrome*
Human rights. *See also Civil and political rights*
Americas Watch, Administration Reports on Nicaragua, 255-269 (1985)
Amnesty International Report, 883-889 (1988); 597-609 (1989)
Commonwealth Group on South Africa, 581-590 (1986)
Democratic Party Platform on, 568 (1988)
Reagan-Gorbachev Summit, 355-356, 359, 371 (1988)
Senate Ratification of Genocide Convention, 115-130 (1986)
South African Pass Laws, 369-381 (1986)
South African Violations, 515-527, 531-540 (1985)
State Department Reports, 145-157 (1985); 97-113 (1986); 189-204 (1987); 93-115 (1988); 57-70 (1989)
UN Report on Afghanistan, 919-936 (1986)
Humanities. *See Arts and humanities*
Hume, Brit, 808-810, 815-816, 821-822 (1988)
Hungary
Bush Trip, 411-413, 416-420 (1989)
Commemoration for Uprising of 1956, 339-342 (1989)
Hunger in America Report, 189-205 (1985)
Hunthausen, Raymond G., 757, 985-986 (1986)
Hussein, King of Jordan
West Bank Speech, 579-585 (1988)
Hussein, Saddam of Iraq
869-874 (1987); 529-530 (1988)
Hustler Magazine v. Falwell, 175-182 (1988)

I

Iceland Summit, 875-885 (1986); 866-867 (1987)
Illegal aliens. *See Immigration; Refugees*
Immigration. *See also Refugees*
Cuban Detainee Agreements, 929-937 (1987)
Economic Advisers' Report, 91-93 (1986)
Immigration Reform and Control Act, 963-969 (1986)
Republican Party Platform on, 647 (1988)
Supreme Court on Political Asylum, 253-265 (1987)

Immigration and Naturalization Service v. Luz Marina Cardoza-Fonseca, 253-265 (1987)
Impeachments
    Claiborne, Harry E., 849-857 (1986)
    Hastings, Alcee L., 583-589 (1989)
    Mecham, Gov. Evan, 249-256 (1988)
    Nixon, Walter L., Jr., 583-585, 590-596 (1989)
Inaugurals. *See Presidential inaugurations*
India
    Bhopal Gas Poisoning, 295-302 (1985)
    Indo-Sri Lankan Accord, 615-622 (1987)
    Pope John Paul II's Trip, 23-37 (1986)
Indians, American. *See Native Americans*
Indictments
    Marcos, Ferdinand and Imelda, 867-872 (1988)
    Noriega, Manuel Antonio, 81-92 (1988)
Indochina
    Environmental Defense Fund on World Bank Project, 859-873 (1986)
INF. *See Intermediate-range Nuclear Forces*
Infant mortality
    Black and Minority Health Report, 686-687, 705-706 (1985)
    CDF Report on Infant Mortality, 147-165 (1987)
Inflation. *See also Monetary policy*
    Budget Message, 70-73 (1986); 151 (1988)
    Democratic Party Platform on, 70-73 (1986)
    Economic Advisers' Report, 90-91 (1985)
    President's Economic Report, 79-87 (1985); 63-64 (1986)
    Republican Party Platform on, 626 (1988)
    State of the Union, 108 (1987)
Inouye, Daniel K., D-Hawaii, 289, 290-291 (1988)
Insider trading. *See Stock market*
Institute for Aerobics Research Fitness and Health Report, 613-617 (1989)
Intelligence. *See Central Intelligence Agency (CIA); Defense*
Intercontinental Ballistic Missile (ICBM)
    Former Security Officials on Defense Strategy, 785-786 (1986)
Interest rates. *See Monetary policy*
Intermediate-range Nuclear Forces (INF)
    Democratic Party Platform on, 566-567 (1988)
    Reagan-Gorbachev Summit, 353-355, 358, 367-369 (1988)
    State of the Union, 57-58, 67 (1988)
    U.S.-Soviet INF Treaty, 945-989 (1987)
International Association of Firefighters v. City of Cleveland, 651-678 (1986)
International Court of Justice
    Genocide Convention Ratification, 116, 121 (1986)
    Pope John Paul II's Speech, 365, 369-371 (1985)
    U.S. Withdrawal from Jurisdiction of, 637-641 (1985)

International debt. *See also Foreign trade*
    Brady World Debt Relief Plan, 137-144 (1989)
    Economic Advisers' Report, 78-79, 82-83 (1986); 4 (1989)
    Economic Summit Meeting (Paris), 426-427 (1989)
    Reagan's Budget Message, 149 (1988)
    Vice Presidential Debate on, 818-819 (1988)
International Monetary Fund (IMF)
    Brady World Debt Relief Plan, 138, 141-143 (1989)
    Economic Advisers' Report, 79-80 (1986)
    IMF-World Bank Conference, 643-652 (1985)
International Physicians for the Prevention of Nuclear War, 781-787 (1985)
Iowa, USS
    Navy Report on Explosion, 517-521 (1989)
Iran. *See also Khomeini, Ayatollah Ruhollah*
    Arab Summit Communique, 869-874 (1987)
    Downing of Iranian Airliner, 703-717 (1988)
    Economic Summit Meeting (Venice), 527, 530 (1987)
    Human Rights Report, 67-68 (1989)
    International Terrorism, 470-471 (1985)
    Iran-Iraq Truce, 529-532 (1988)
    Rushdie's Death Sentence, 95-98 (1989)
    UN on Iran-Iraq War, 609-613 (1987)
    U.S.-Iran Relations, 315-320 (1989)
Iran-Contra affair
    Iran Arms Deal and Contra Funding, 1013-1024, 1049-1055 (1986)
    Iran-Contra Reports, 891-928 (1987)
    North Sentencing, 391-397 (1989)
    State of the Union, 106, 109-110 (1987)
    Tower Commission Report, 205-242 (1987)
    Vice Presidential Debate on, 807-808 (1988)
Iraq
    Arab Summit Communique, 869-874 (1987)
    Attack on USS Stark, 791-816 (1987)
    Chemical Weapons, Paris Declaration on, 27 (1989)
    Economic Summit Meeting (Venice), 527, 530 (1987)
    Human Rights Report, 68-69 (1989)
    Iran-Iraq Truce, 529-532 (1988)
    UN on Iran-Iraq War, 609-613 (1987)
Ireland, 723-732 (1985). *See also Northern Ireland*
Israel
    Baker's Middle East Policy Address, 289-296 (1989)
    Human Rights Report, 112-113 (1986); 113-115 (1988); 69-70 (1989)
    Hussein's West Bank Speech, 579-585 (1988)

Obeid kidnapping, 315-317, 319 (1989)
Italy
Economic Summit (Bonn), 347-355 (1985)

J

Jackson, Jesse L., 27, 32 (1985)
Democratic National Convention Address, 535, 546-556 (1988)
Democratic Party Platform, 557-558 (1988)
Urban League Report, 27, 32 (1985)
Japan
Economic Summit Meetings
(Bonn), 347-355 (1985)
(Tokyo), 437-444 (1986)
Group of Five Communique on the Dollar, 523-530 (1985)
Hirohito Funeral Tributes, 99-103 (1989)
Nakasone Speech on Foreign Trade, 319-323 (1985)
Nakasone Visit, 427, 429, 433-437 (1987)
U.S.-Japan Trade Dispute, 427-437 (1987)
Japanese-American Internees Reparations, 287-295 (1988)
Jaruzelski, Wojciech, 555 (1987)
Jayewardene, Junius, 615-622 (1987)
Jennings, Peter, 731-733, 738-740, 746-747 (1988)
Jett v. Dallas Independent School District, 323 (1989)
Jews. *See also Holocaust*
Army Denial of Medal of Honor, 697-700 (1989)
Pope John Paul II
Austria Trip, 405-414 (1988)
Miami Address to Jewish Leaders, 699-700, 702-705 (1987)
Rome Synagogue Visit, 339-346 (1986)
Jobs. *See Employment and unemployment*
John Paul II
Apostolic Letter on Women, 785-792 (1988)
Encyclical on Social Concerns, 165-174 (1988)
Excommunication of Archbishop Lefebvre, 489-494 (1988)
Journeys, 57-67, 363-376, 499-514 (1985); 23-37, 639-649 (1986); 555-564 (1987); 699-716 (1987); 405-414 (1988)
Vatican on Theology of Liberation, 317 (1986)
Visit to Austria, 405-414 (1988)
Visit to Rome Synagogue, 339-346 (1986)
Johnson v. Transportation Agency, Santa Clara, California, 331-349 (1987)
Jordan
Hussein's West Bank Speech, 579-585 (1988)
Judiciary. *See Courts, U.S.; Supreme Court*

K

Kassal, Bentley
America's Cup Race Appellate Division Opinion, 193 (1989)
Kasten, Bob, R-Wis., 860 (1986)
Kauffman, Bruce W., 240-241, 248-251 (1986)
Keeler, Archbishop William H., 619-623 (1988)
Kennan, George F.
Cold War, 207-212 (1989)
Kennedy, Anthony M.
Flag Burning, 350-351 (1989)
Supreme Court Nomination, 720-721 (1987)
Kerner Commission Report Update, 185-194 (1988)
Khamenei, Ali, 531-532 (1988)
Khomeini, Ayatollah Ruhollah
Death of, 315, 318 (1989)
Iran-Iraq Truce, 529-531 (1988)
Rushdie's Death Sentence, 95-98 (1989)
Kohl, Helmut
Berlin Wall Anniversary, 791-799 (1986)
German Remorse at World War II Anniversary, 487-497 (1989)
German Reunification Plan, 627, 630-634 (1989)
Koop, C. Everett
Antismoking Campaign, 31-40 (1989)
Involuntary Smoking Report, 1079-1090 (1986)
Nicotine Addiction Report, 309-322 (1988)
Korea. *See North Korea; South Korea*

L

Labor. *See also Employment and unemployment*
Pope John Paul II's South America Trip, 59-61 (1985)
President's Commission on Organized Crime, 200-210 (1986)
Supreme Court Decisions
Affirmative Action, 651-678 (1986); 331-349 (1987)
Union Membership, 415-429 (1985)
Land Use and Uncompensated Takings
Supreme Court on, 531-553 (1987)
Lantos, Tom, D-Calif., 335-336 (1989)
Latin America. *See also Central America; specific countries*
Human Rights Report, 102-108 (1986)
Pope John Paul II's Journeys, 57-67 (1985)
Republican Party Platform on, 675-677 (1988)
State of the Union, 66 (1988)
Latvia
Baltic Nationalist Movement, 469-475 (1989)
Law enforcement. *See Crime and law enforcement*

Lebanon
Bush-Gorbachev Malta Meeting, 651-652 (1989)
Hostages, 315-329 (1989)
Lefebvre, Archbishop Marcel
Excommunication, 489-494 (1988)
Legislative branch. *See Congress*
Lehrer, Jim, 724-754 (1988)
Lehn, Kenneth, 921-925 (1988)
Liability. *See Tort reform*
Libel
Sharon Libel Verdict, 47-52 (1985)
Westmoreland/CBS Controversy, 159-165 (1985)
Supreme Court Decisions
Media Libel Law, 355-368 (1986)
Libya
Human Rights, 203-204 (1987)
Reagan on International Terrorism, 470-471 (1985)
U.S. Air Strike, 347-354 (1986)
Lillestrand, Robert, 832-833 (1988)
Lithuania
Baltic Nationalist Movement, 469-475 (1989)
Lobbying
Watt on Influence Peddling, 333-337 (1989)
Local government. *See State and local government*
Lockhart v. McCree, 445-456 (1986)
Lounge, John M., 797 (1988)
Lown, Dr. Bernard, 781-787 (1985)

M

Mack, John P., 241-242, 270 (1989)
Mallerais, Bernard Tissier de, 490-492 (1988)
Mallick, George, 250-257, 262-265 (1989)
Malone, James, 571-581 (1985)
Mandela, Nelson, 582, 586-587 (1986)
Marcos, Ferdinand, 98, 110-111, 307, 1037 (1986); 867-872 (1988)
Marcos, Imelda, 867-872 (1988)
Margolis, Jon, 804-805, 810-812, 817-818, 823-825 (1988)
Marijuana. *See Drug abuse*
Marital issues. *See Family and marital issues*
Marshall, Thurgood
Abortion, 379-387 (1989)
Closed Party Primaries, 1065, 1066, 1068-1071 (1986)
Employment Discrimination, 328-329, 331-332 (1989)
Indigents' Rights to Psychiatric Aid, 208, 210-217 (1985)
Jury Selection in Capital Cases, 454-456 (1986)
Labor Union Membership, 415, 424-429 (1985)
Maternity Leave, 20-26 (1987)
Miranda Rule, 225, 236-250 (1985)

PAC Spending Limits, 279, 290-291 (1985)
Peremptory Challenge, 421-425 (1986)
Preventive Detention, 491-494, 502-508 (1987)
Secrecy of CIA Sources, 333, 342-344 (1985)
Student Searches, 15, 23-26 (1985)
Students' Free Speech, 733, 739-740 (1986)
Martin v. Wilks, 322, 329-332 (1989)
Mashek, John, 726-727, 734-735, 741-742, 749 (1988)
Maternity leave, 17-27 (1987)
Matsunaga, Spark M., D.-Hawaii, 289-291 (1988)
Mauthausen (Austria)
Pope John Paul's Visit, 406-409 (1988)
Mazowiecki, Tadeusz
Speech to the Polish Sejm, 523-533 (1989)
McCleskey v. Kemp, 463-476 (1987)
McCullough, David
Congressional Bicentennial Commemoration, 132-133 (1989)
McFarlane, Robert, 1015-1016, 1050 (1986)
McKay, James C.
Ethics Investigation of Edwin Meese III, 495-516 (1988)
McKelvey v. Turnage, 277-285 (1988)
Mecham, Gov. Evan, 249-256 (1988)
Media. *See Communications; Press*
Medicaid and Medicare
Catastrophic Illness Expenses, 1025-1035 (1986)
Harvard Report on Medicare Reform, 273-285 (1986)
Hospital Length of Stay Report, 333-337 (1988)
President's Commission on Privatization Report, 235 (1988)
Reagan's Budget Message, 152, 157 (1988)
Medical care
AIDS in the Workplace, 733-747 (1985)
Catastrophic Illness Expenses, 1025-1035 (1986)
Court on Sustaining Handicapped Infants, 541-558 (1986)
Democratic Party Platform on, 563-564 (1988)
For-Profit Hospitals, 487-513 (1986)
Hospital Length of Stay Report, 333-337 (1988)
Medicare. *See Medicaid and medicare*
Meese, Edwin, III, 479-490 (1985); 1014, 1023-1024 (1986); 495-516 (1988)
Melnikov, Vladmir I., 178 (1989)
Mengele, Josef, 409-414 (1985)
Mexican-Americans. *See Hispanics*
Mexico
Brady Debt Relief Plan, 138-139 (1989)
Middle East. *See also specific countries*
Arab Summit Communique, 869-874 (1987)
Baker's Middle East Policy Address, 289-296 (1989)

Bush-Gorbachev Malta Meeting, 655-656 (1989)

Democratic Party Platform on, 567-568 (1988)

Iran Arms Deal, 1013-1024, 1049-1055 (1986)

Republican Party Platform on, 683-685 (1988)

UN Resolution on Iran-Iraq War, 609-613 (1987)

Vice Presidential Debate on, 820-821 (1988)

Military. *See also Defense; Defense Department*

Joint Chiefs of Staff, 669-683 (1985)

Military Base Closings, 951-954 (1988)

Organized Crime Commission, 181, 194-195 (1986)

Military aid. *See Foreign aid*

Miller, George, D-Calif., 672 (1989)

Minority groups. *See also specific groups*

Affirmative Action, 651-678 (1986)

Bishops' Letter on Economic Justice, 999 (1986)

Black and Minority Health Report, 685-706 (1985)

Educational equity, 88-89 (1989)

Employment

Economic Advisers' Report, 140 (1988)

President's Economic Report, 119 (1988)

Kerner Report Updated, 185-194 (1988)

Smoking and, 36-37 (1989)

Mitchell, Andrea, 761-762, 769-771, 777-779 (1988)

Mitchell, George, D-Maine

Congressional Bicentennial Commemoration, 129-130 (1989)

Mitchell, Mark L., 921-925 (1988)

Mitterrand, François

Economic Summit (Bonn), 348-349 (1985)

Statue of Liberty's Centennial, 697, 702-703 (1986)

Monetary policy. *See also Economic policy; Inflation*

Economic Advisers' Report, 91 (1985); 59-60, 76-78 (1986); 117, 128-131 (1988); 3-5, 12-14 (1989)

Economic Summit Meetings

(Bonn), 354 (1985)

(Venice), 512 (1987); 525-530 (1987)

Greenspan Appointment, 511-516 (1987)

IMF-World Bank Conference, 643-652 (1985)

Plunge of the Dollar, 523-530 (1985)

President's Economic Report, 87 (1985); 3, 5-12 (1989)

Stock Market Crash, 833-842 (1987); 9-36 (1988); 132-135 (1988)

Volcker Resignation, 511-516 (1987)

Morocco

Pope John Paul II's Visit, 500, 509-514 (1985)

Morrison v. Olson, 465-478 (1988)

Moslems

Rushdie's Death Sentence, 95-98 (1989)

MOVE Raid in Philadelphia, 239-251 (1986)

Mulroney, Brian, 571-574 (1988)

MX Missile

Former Security Officials on Defense Strategy, 782-783 (1986)

N

Nagy, Imre, 339-342, 417 (1989)

Nakasone, Yasuhiro, 319-323 (1985); 427, 429, 433-437 (1987)

Namibia

Angola-Namibia Peace Accord, 947-950 (1988)

UN Resolution on, 356 (1988)

Narcotics. *See Drug abuse*

National Academy of Sciences (NAS)

AIDS Report, 887-908 (1986)

For-Profit Hospitals, 487-513 (1986)

National Security Export Controls Report, 29-42 (1987)

Sex Segregation in the Workplace, 789-801 (1985)

Teenage Pregnancy, 1057-1064 (1986)

National Advisory Commission on Civil Disorders

Kerner Report Updated, 185-194 (1988)

National Aeronautics and Space Administration (NASA)

Challenger Accident Commission Report, 515-539 (1986)

Discovery Tribute to Challenger Victims, 795-798 (1988)

Ozone Depletion Report, 221-228 (1988)

Ride Commission Report, 649-669 (1987)

National Assessment of Educational Progress (NAEP)

Educational Testing Service Report, 85-94 (1989)

Math and Science Education Reports, 377-390 (1988)

National Center for Health Services Research and Health Care Technology Assessment

Report on Length of Hospitalization, 333-337 (1988)

National Collegiate Athletic Association (NCAA)

Report on Black College Athletes, 213-223 (1989)

National Commission on the Public Service Report, 196-202 (1989)

National Conference of Catholic Bishops

Pastoral Letter on Economy, 983-1011 (1986)

National Endowment for the Humanities (NEH)

Humanities Education Report, 681-696 (1987)

State of the Humanities Report, 517-527 (1988)

National Geographic Society
Peary's Arctic Expedition Controversy, 687-689 (1989)
National Institutes of Health (NIH)
Cholesterol Report, 779-790 (1987)
Reagan's Budget Message, 150, 155 (1988)
National Museum of the American Indian, 540, 542 (1989)
National Research Council (NRC)
Black Americans, 445-459 (1989)
Radon Report, 3-8 (1988)
National Security Council (NSC). *See also Defense*
Iran-Contra Reports, 891-928 (1987)
Tower Commission Report, 205-242 (1987)
National Urban League
Black America Report, 27-37 (1985); 43-60 (1987)
Kerner Report Updated, 185-186 (1988)
Nation's Report Card Project. *See National Assessment of Educational Progress*
Native Americans
Alcoholism, 700-701 (1985)
Diabetes, 703 (1985)
Reagan-Gorbachev Summit, 365-366 (1988)
Republican Party Platform on, 645 (1988)
Smithsonian Agreement on Indian Bones and Burial Artifacts, 539-543 (1989)
Natural disasters. *See Disasters*
Navigation Foundation Report on Peary's Claim, 687-696 (1989)
Navy, U.S.
Pentagon on Sexual Harassment, 671-679 (1987)
Report on USS Iowa Explosion, 517-521 (1989)
Report on USS Stark Attack, 791-816 (1987)
Nelson, George D., 798 (1988)
Netherlands
Bush Visit, 435-437 (1989)
Pope John Paul II's Visit, 363-374 (1985)
Neves, Tancredo, 3-12 (1985)
New Jersey v. T.L.O., 13-26 (1985)
New York State Club Assn., Inc. v. City of New York, 399-403 (1988)
Newman, Frank, 583-602 (1985)
Nguyen, Jean, 116-117 (1985)
Nicaragua. *See also Central America*
Americas Watch Administration Reports, 255-269 (1985)
Amnesty International Human Rights Report, 605-606 (1989)
Bush Statement on Central American Bipartisan Accord, 161-163, 166-168 (1989)
Central American Bipartisan Accord, 163-166 (1989)
Central American Cease-Fire Agreement, 241-245 (1988)
Central American Peace Agreement, 637-648 (1987)

Iran Arms Deal and Contra Funding, 1013-1024, 1049-1055 (1986)
Iran-Contra Reports, 891-928 (1987)
Reagan on International Terrorism, 472 (1985)
State Department Human Rights Report, 146, 153 (1985); 107-108 (1986); 197-198 (1987); 61-62 (1989)
State of the Union, 66 (1988)
Tela Declaration on Central America, 161, 168-172 (1989)
Tower Commission Report, 205-242 (1987)
U.S. Withdrawal from World Court Jurisdiction, 637-641 (1985)
Vatican on Theology of Liberation, 318 (1986)
Nicotine Addiction Report, 309-322 (1988)
Niskanen, William A., 80 (1985)
Nixon, Walter L., Jr., 583-585, 590-596 (1989)
Nobel Peace Prize
Arias Speech, 1007-1011 (1987)
Dalai Lama's Speech, 573-581 (1989)
International Physicians for the Prevention of Nuclear War Speech, 781-787 (1985)
Wiesel Speech, 1075-1078 (1986)
Nofziger, Lyn (Franklyn C.), 495, 499 (1988)
Nollan v. California Coastal Commission, 531, 533-534, 547-553 (1987)
Noriega, Gen. Manuel Antonio
Grand Jury Indictments, 81-92 (1988)
Panama Invasion, 701-707 (1989)
Vice Presidential Debate on, 814-815 (1988)
North, Oliver L. *See also Iran-Contra Affair*
Iran-Contra Affair, 1015-117, 1050-1052 (1986); 217-218, 225-226, 232-233 (1987)
Sentencing of, 391-397 (1989)
North Atlantic Treaty Organization (NATO)
Bush Brussels News Conference, 645-646, 660-666 (1989)
Bush Conventional-Arms Cuts Proposal, 297-304 (1989)
Republican Party Platform on, 680-681, 694 (1988)
North Korea
Human Rights Report, 198-199 (1987)
Reagan on Terrorism, 471 (1985)
Roh Tae Woo's UN Address, 853-859 (1988)
Northern Ireland
British-Irish Accord on Northern Ireland, 723-732 (1985)
Human Rights Report, 112-113 (1988)
U. S.-U. K. Extradition Treaty, 751-756 (1986)
Nuclear energy. *See also Energy policy; Radiation*
Chernobyl Nuclear Accident, 383-407 (1986)
Republican Party Platform on, 667 (1988)
Nuclear weapons. *See also Arms control; Treaties and agreements*

Effects of Nuclear War, 541-554 (1985)
Former Security Officials on Defense
Strategy, 781-790 (1986)
Nobel Peace Prize speech, 781-787 (1985)
Nunn, Sam, D-Ga.
ABM Treaty Interpretation, 289-317
(1987)
Tower Defense Secretary Nomination Re-
jection, 105-120 (1989)

O

Obeid, Sheik Abdul Karim, 315-317, 319
(1989)
Obscenity. *See Pornography*
Occupational safety
AIDS in the Workplace, 733-747 (1985)
Energy Secretary Watkins' Environmental
Plan, 355-362 (1989)
Health Costs of Smoking, 615-622 (1985)
Vice Presidential Debate on, 810-812
(1988)
O'Connor, Sandra Day
Abortion, 562, 579-580 (1986); 367, 376-
378 (1989)
Affirmative Action, 676 (1986); 332-333,
340, 346 (1987)
Federal and State Powers, 169, 182-187
(1985)
Flag Burning, 351-353 (1989)
Media Libel Law, 356-364 (1986)
Miranda Rule, 223-236 (1985)
Political Gerrymandering, 617, 629-63
(1986)
Private Clubs, 403 (1988)
Public School Teachers in Parochial
Classes, 433, 448-449, 455-461 (1985)
Silent Prayer, 380, 387-392 (1985)
Sustaining Handicapped Infants, 544-558
(1986)
Use of Deadly Force, 304, 312-315 (1985)
Office of Technology Assessment (OTA)
Alzheimer's Disease, 391-406 (1987)
Biotechnology Reports, 287-306 (1986);
351-372 (1987)
Health Costs of Smoking, 615-622 (1985)
Ownership of Human Tissues and Cells,
351-372 (1987)
Oil. *See also Energy policy*
Economic Adviser's Report, 118, 127-128
(1987)
Republican Party Platform on, 665-666
(1988)
Okun, Herbert S., 267-272 (1986)
O'Neill, Thomas P., Jr., D-Mass., 39, 42, 753
(1986)
Oregon v. Elstad, 223-253 (1985)
OTA. *See Office of Technology Assessment*

P

Packard Commission on Defense Management
Report, 679-695 (1986)

Republican Party Platform on, 696 (1988)
PACs. *See Political Action Committees*
Pakistan
Afghanistan Agreements, 257-261 (1988)
Palestine Liberation Organization (PLO)
Hussein's West Bank Speech, 579-585
(1988)
Office Closing, 479-485 (1988)
Palestine Statehood, 291 (1989)
Palestinian Elections, 290 (1989)
PNC Declaration of Independence, 905-
908 (1988)
Palestine National Council (PNC)
Declaration of Independence, 905-911
(1988)
Palestinians
Baker's Middle East Policy Address, 289-
296 (1989)
Human Rights Report, 69-70 (1989)
Panama
Noriega Indictments, 81-92 (1988)
Panama Invasion, 701-707 (1989)
Republican Party Platform on, 677 (1988)
*Pattern Makers League of North America
(AFL-CIO) v. National Labor Relations
Board,* 415-429 (1985)
Patterson v. McLean Credit Union, 322-323
(1989)
Peacemaking efforts. *See also Arms control;
Nobel Peace Prize; Treaties and
agreements*
Arab Summit Communique, 869-874
(1987)
Central American Cease-Fire Agreement,
241-245 (1988)
Central American Peace Agreement, 637-
648 (1987)
Indo-Sri Lankan Accord, 615-622 (1987)
Reagan-Gorbachev New Year's Messages,
3-8 (1986)
State of the Union, 114-115 (1985)
UN on Iran-Iraq War, 609-613 (1987)
UN World Conference on Women, 567-570
(1985)
Peary, Robert E., 831-833 (1988); 687-696
(1989)
People's Republic of China (PRC). *See China,
People's Republic of*
Peres, Shimon, 498 (1988)
Perestroika. *See Democratic reforms;
Gorbachev, Mikhail S.; Soviet Union*
Peru
Amnesty International Human Rights Re-
port, 606 (1989)
Pope John Paul II's Visit, 57, 58, 62-67
(1985)
State Department Human Rights Report,
62-64 (1989)
Philadelphia
Investigation of Police Raid on MOVE
Group, 239-251 (1986)
Philadelphia Newspapers Inc. v. Hepps, 355-
368 (1986)

Philippines
Aquino Speech on Coup Attempt, 843-854 (1987)
Cease-Fire Agreement, 1037-1046 (1986)
Change of Government, 307-314 (1986)
Human Rights Report, 154-155 (1985); 98, 110-112 (1986); 190-191, 201-202; 106-108 (1988)
Marcos Indictment, 867-872 (1988)
Physicians Task Force on Hunger in America, 189-205 (1985)
Platforms, Political. *See Democratic party; Republican party*
Poindexter, John, 1016, 1049-1050 (1986); 208, 216, 218, 222, 232 (1987). *See also Iran-contra affair*
Poland
Bush European Trip, 412-413, 414-416 (1989)
Human Rights Report, 153-154 (1985)
Kohl at Fiftieth Anniversary of German Invasion of Poland, 487-497 (1989)
Lifting Trade Sanctions, 183-188 (1987)
Mazowiecki Speech to Polish Sejm, 523-533 (1989)
Pope John Paul II's Visits, 555-564 (1987)
Sentencing of Popieluszko's Slayers, 119-126 (1985)
Walesa Address to U.S. Congress, 523-525, 534-538 (1989)
Polar exploration. *See Arctic Expedition of 1909*
Political Action Committees (PACs)
Spending Limits, 277-294 (1985)
Vice Presidential Debate on, 808-809 (1988)
Political activism
Black America Report, 28, 33 (1985)
Pope John Paul II's Journey to South America, 57, 65-67 (1985)
Pollution. *See also Environment*
Alaskan Oil Spill Hearings, 225-237 (1989)
Radon Report, 3-8 (1988)
Poole, William, 80 (1985)
Pope v. Illinois, 479-490 (1987)
Pope John Paul II. *See John Paul II*
Popieluszko, Jerzy, 119-126 (1985); 557 (1987)
Population
Population Institute Report, 439-462 (1987)
Pornography
Court on Adult Theaters, 131-144 (1986)
Court on Obscenity, 479-490 (1987)
Republican Party Platform on, 636 (1988)
Postal Service, U.S.
Economic Advisers' Report, 88-89 (1986)
President's Commission on Privatization Report, 231, 233-234 (1988)
Poverty. *See also Homeless persons; Welfare and social services*
Bishops on Economic Justice, 984, 998-1002 (1986)

Black Americans, NRC Report on, 458 (1989)
Hunger in America, 189-205 (1985)
Kerner Report Updated, 185-194 (1988)
Pope John Paul II on, 23-37 (1986)
Republican Party Platform on, 657-659 (1988)
Urban Institute Child Poverty Report, 877-880 (1988)
Vatican on Theology of Liberation, 317-338 (1986)
Vice Presidential Debate on, 806-807 (1988)
Powell, Lewis F., Jr.
Creation Science, 566, 572-574 (1987)
Death Penalty, 463-473 (1987)
Federal and State Powers, 168-169, 182-187 (1985)
Labor Union Membership, 415-424 (1985)
Peremptory Challenge, 410, 412-421 (1986)
Political Asylum, 253-255, 262-265 (1987)
Political Gerrymandering, 617, 632-633 (1986)
Retirement, 577-581 (1987)
Sodomy and Privacy, 602, 607-608 (1986)
Pregnancy and childbirth. *See also Abortion; Birth control*
CDF Infant Mortality Report, 147-165 (1987)
Maternity Leave, 17-27 (1987)
Surrogates' Rights, 373-387 (1987); 71-80 (1988)
Teenage Pregnancy, 1057-1064 (1986)
Vatican on Bioethics, 267-287 (1987)
Pregnancy Discrimination Act
Supreme Court Decisions, 17-27 (1987)
Presidency. *See also individual names*
Harvard Commission on the Presidential Press Conference, 835-845 (1988)
Transfer of Presidential Power, 491-495 (1985)
Vice Presidential Debate on, 809-810, 815-816, 819-820 821-825 (1988)
Presidential Commission on the Human Immunodeficiency Virus Epidemic, 415-446 (1988)
Presidential Commission on the Space Shuttle Challenger Accident, 515-539 (1986)
Presidential election, 1988
Bush-Quayle Acceptance Speeches, 589-591, 601-613 (1988)
Debates, 721-783 (1988)
Democratic Party Platform, 557-569 (1988)
Dukakis-Bentsen Acceptance Speeches, 533-546 (1988)
Postelection Statements, 891-904 (1988)
Republican Party Platform, 615-702 (1988)
Presidential inaugurations
Bicentennial Commemorations, 123-135 (1989)
Bush Inaugural Address, 41-48 (1989)

Presidential Task Force on Market Mechanisms (Brady Commission), 9-11, 13-33 (1988)

President's Blue Ribbon Commission on Defense Management (Packard Commission), 679-695 (1988)

President's Commission on Organized Crime, 179-216 (1986)

President's Commission on Privatization, 229-239 (1988)

President's Private Sector Survey on Cost Control (Grace Commission), 231 (1988)

Press
  Daniloff Arrest in Moscow, 819-827 (1986)
  Harvard Commission on the Presidential Press Conference, 835-845 (1988)
  Sharon Libel Verdict, 47-52 (1985)
  Supreme Court Decisions
    Freedom of Press, 175-182 (1988)
    Westmoreland/CBS Controversy, 159-165 (1985)

Prisons. See Crime and law enforcement

Privacy, Right of, 601-614 (1986)

Privatization of government services. See also Business and industry
  Economic Advisers' Report, 88-89 (1986)
  Presidential Debates on, 740 (1988)
  President's Commission on Privatization Report, 229-239 (1988)
  President's Economic Report, 61, 68 (1986); 123-124 (1987); 121-122 (1988)
  Reagan's Budget Message, 150, 152, 158-159 (1988)
  Republican Party Platform on, 627 (1988)

Public Health Service (PHS)
  Aids Education Report, 319-326 (1987)
  Length of Hospitalization Report, 333-337 (1988)

Public service
  Judiciary Pay Raises, 195-204 (1989)
  National Commission on the Public Service Report, 196-202 (1989)

Puerto Rico
  Democratic Party Platform on, 565 (1988)
  Republican Party Platform on, 646 (1988)

Q

Qaddafi, Muammar
  Reagan on U. S. Air Strike Against Libya, 347-354 (1986)
  Reagan on Terrorism, 464-471 (1985)

Quayle, Dan
  Acceptance Speech, 590-591, 601-604 (1988)
  Presidential Debates on, 749-750 (1988)
  Vice Presidential Debate, 799-829 (1988)

R

Radiation. See also Nuclear energy
  Energy Secretary Watkins' Environmental
  Plan, 355-362 (1989)
  Nuclear War Effects, 541-554 (1985)
  Radon Report, 3-8 (1988)

Rafsanjani, Hojatolislam Hashemi, 317-319 (1989)

Ratzinger, Cardinal Joseph
  Bioethics, 267-287 (1987)
  Letter to Charles E. Curran, 758-762 (1986)
  Liberation Theology, 319-338 (1986)
  Pastoral Care of Homosexuals, 909-918 (1986)

Rawl, L. G.
  Alaskan Oil Spill Hearings, 233-237 (1989)

Rawlins, Dennis, 831-833 (1988)

Reagan, Ronald
  Constitution Bicentennial Observance, 765-775 (1987)
  Defense
    Budget Message, 4, 9-10, 14 (1987); 152, 156 (1988)
    Department of Veterans Affairs, 873-876 (1988)
    INF Treaty Statement, 945, 947-950 (1987)
    MX Missile Basing, 4 (1987)
    Terrorism Policy, 463-477 (1985)
  Domestic Affairs
    Administration Policy on Black America, 27-37 (1985)
    Executive Order on Drug Testing, 839-846 (1986)
    Family Support Act, 847-852 (1988)
    Immigration Bill, 963-969 (1986)
    Remarks to Right-to-Life Marchers, 53-56 (1985)
  Economic Affairs
    Balanced Budget Bill, 803-808 (1985)
    Budget Message, 71-78 (1985); 49-58 (1986); 3-15 (1987); 149-163 (1988)
    Economic Report, 79-87 (1985); 59, 62-69 (1986); 117-124 (1987); 117-125 (1988); 3, 5-12 (1989)
    Economic Summit Meetings: (Toronto), 392-393 (1988); (Venice), 525-530 (1987)
    Greenspan Appointment, 511-516 (1987)
    Stock Market Crash, 837-839 (1987); 9-36 (1988)
    Trade Bill Vetoes, 339-346 (1988)
    U.S.-Japan Trade Dispute, 427-437 (1987)
    Volcker Resignation, 511-516 (1987)
  Farewell Address, 15-23 (1989)
  Foreign Affairs
    Administration Reports on Nicaragua, 255-258, 260-269 (1988)
    Air Strike Against Libya, 347-354 (1986)
    Bitburg Visit, 357-362 (1985)
    Canada-U.S. Trade Pact, 571-578 (1988)
    Iran Arms Deal and Contra Funding, 1013-1024, 1049-1055 (1986)

New Year's Message to Soviets, 3-5, 7-8 (1986)
South Africa Sanctions, 531-540 (1985)
Summits with Gorbachev: (Geneva), 749-761 (1985); (Moscow), 353-373; (Reykjavik), 875-885 (1986); (Washington, D.C.), 991-1006 (1987)
Terrorism Policy, 463-477 (1985)
Trade Bill Vetoes, 339-346 (1988)
United Nations Address, 707-719 (1985)
U.S.-Japan Trade Dispute, 427-437 (1987)
Politics
  Republican National Convention Address, 589-590, 592-601 (1988)
State of the Union, 105-117 (1985); 39-48 (1986); 105-115 (1987); 47-56 (1988)
Statue of Liberty's Centennial, 697-698, 700-702 (1986)
Supreme Court
  Appointments, 591-599 (1986); 720 (1987)
  Bork Confirmation Battle, 717-744 (1987)
Transfer of Presidential Power, 491-495 (1985)
Refugees. *See also Immigration*
Cuban Detainee Agreements, 929-937 (1987)
Supreme Court on Political Asylum, 253-265 (1987)
Regional government. *See State and local government*
Regulatory reform. *See also Airline deregulation*
Budget Message, 12 (1987); 158 (1988)
Economic Advisers' Report, 85-89 (1986)
President's Economic Report, 86-87 (1985); 67-68 (1986); 122 (1988)
Republican Party Platform on, 626-627 (1988)
State of the Union, 60-61 (1986)
Rehnquist, William H.
Abortion, 369-375 (1989)
Adult Theaters, 132, 134-140 (1986)
Affirmative Action, 677-678 (1986)
Appointment to Chief Justice, 591-599 (1986)
Contagious Diseases, 246, 250-252 (1987)
Employment Discrimination, 329-331 (1989)
Federal and State Powers, 169, 182-187 (1985)
Flag Burning, 351-353 (1989)
Freedom of Press, 175-182 (1988)
Independent Counsel, 465, 469-477 (1988)
Indigents' Rights to Psychiatric Aid, 209, 217-219 (1985)
Judiciary Pay Raises, 195-197, 202-204 (1989)
Jury Selection in Capital Cases, 446-454 (1986)

PAC Spending Limits, 278-290 (1985)
Preventive Detention, 491, 494-502 (1987)
Public School Teachers in Parochial classes, 433, 449-450, 455, 458-462 (1985)
Uncompensated Takings and Land Use, 532-540 (1987)
Use of Deadly Force, 304, 312-315 (1985)
Reilly, William K.
Alaskan Oil Spill Hearings, 231-233 (1989)
Religion. *See also Catholic church*
Apostolic Letter on Women, 785-792 (1988)
Bishops on U.S. Economy, 983-1011 (1986)
Episcopal Church on First Woman Bishop, 49-54 (1989)
Meese Criticism of Supreme Court, 479-480, 486-490 (1985)
Pope John Paul II, 363-376, 499-514 (1985); 23-37, 339-346, 639-649 (1986); 555-564; 699-716 (1987)
Reagan-Gorbachev Summit, 358-359 (1988)
Rushdie's Death Sentence, 95-98 (1989)
School Curriculum and, 597-608 (1987)
School Prayer, 112-113 (1987)
Supreme Court Decisions
  Public School Teachers in Parochial Classes, 433-461 (1985)
  School Prayer, 379-395 (1985)
Synod of Catholic Bishops, 765-780 (1985)
U.S. Bishops Report to the Vatican, 571-581 (1985)
U.S. Catholic Bicentennial in Baltimore, 619-623 (1989)
Vatican on Theology of Liberation, 317-338 (1986)
Republican party
Convention
  Bush Acceptance Speech, 590-591, 604-613 (1988)
  Quayle Acceptance Speech, 590-591, 601-604 (1988)
  Reagan Address, 589, 592-601 (1988)
Party Platform, 615-702 (1988)
Ride, Sally K., 649-669 (1987)
Rifkin, Jeremy, 228 (1986)
Roh Tae Woo
Statement on Democratic Reforms, 583-590 (1987)
UN Address, 853-859 (1988)
Romania
Ceausescu Execution, 709-712 (1989)
Rose, Pete, 477-484 (1989)
Rubitsky, David S., 697-700 (1989)
Rural development. *See Agriculture*
Rushdie, Salman, 95-98 (1989)

S

Sakharov, Andrei D.
Release from Exile, 1091-1095 (1986)
Salerno, Anthony (Fat Tony), 491-508 (1987)

SALT. *See Strategic Arms Limitation Treaty*

Saudi Arabia
Arab Summit Communique, 869-874 (1987)

Savings and loan institutions (S&Ls). *See Banks and banking*

Scalia, Antonin
Abortion, 378-379 (1989)
Affirmative Action, 333-334, 346-349 (1987)
Appointment to Supreme Court, 591-599 (1986)
Closed Party Primaries, 1065, 1067, 1072-1073 (1986)
Contagious Diseases, 246, 250-252 (1987)
Creation Science, 567, 574-576 (1987)
Disruptive Handicapped Students, 49, 56 (1988)
Independent Counsel, 468, 477-478 (1988)
Obscenity, 479-481, 484-485 (1987)
Private Clubs, 399, 403 (1988)
Uncompensated Takings and Land Use, 533, 547-549 (1987)

School Board of Nassau County, Florida v. Arline, 245-252 (1987)

Schools. *See Education*

Schwebel, Stephen, 638 (1985)

Science and technology. *See also Space*
Economic Summit (Bonn), 355 (1985)
Gorbachev at 27th Party Congress, 154-155 (1986)
Math and Science Education Reports, 377-390 (1988)
National Security Export Controls, 29-42 (1987)
Nuclear War Effects, 541-554 (1985)
OTA Report on Biotechnology, 287-306 (1986)
Reagan's Budget Message, 155 (1988)
Report on Soviet Espionage, 603-614 (1985)
Republican Party Platform on, 653-654 (1988)

Search and seizure
Student Searches, 13-26 (1985)

Securities and Exchange Commission (SEC)
Corporate Takeovers Report, 921-925 (1988)

Segregation. *See Civil and political rights; Education; Housing*

Senate
Armed Services Committee Pentagon Report, 669-683 (1985)
Bork Confirmation Battle, 717-744 (1987)
Impeachment of Judge Claiborne, 849-857 (1986)
Iran-Contra Reports, 891-928 (1987)
Ratification of Genocide Convention, 115-130 (1986)
U.S.-U.K. Extradition Treaty, 751-756 (1986)

Sentencing Commission Report, 407-426 (1987)

Separation of Powers. *See Constitution, U.S., Tenth Amendment*

Sex discrimination
Pentagon on Sexual Harassment, 671-679 (1987)
Segregation in the Workplace, 789-801 (1985)
Supreme Court Decisions
Maternity Leave, 17-27 (1987)
Private Clubs, 399-403 (1988)

Shamir, Yitzhak
Sharon Libel Verdict, 47-52 (1985)
Palestinian Election Proposal, 290 (1989)

Shaw, Bernard, 754-783 (1988)

Shcharansky, Anatoly Borisovich, 93-96 (1986)

Sheet Metal Workers' International Association v. Equal Employment Opportunity Commission, 651-678 (1986)

Sher, Neal, 409-414 (1985)

Shultz, George P.
Iran Arms Sales, 1015, 1051 (1986)
U.S. Withdrawal from World Court Jurisdiction, 637-641 (1985)

Simpson, Alan K., R-Wyo., 288, 289, 294-295 (1988)

Sisulu, Walter, 546 (1989)

Skinner, Samuel K.
Alaskan Oil Spill Hearings, 230-231 (1989)

Sixth Amendment. *See Constitution, U.S.*

Small business.
Republican Party Platform on, 623-624 (1988)

Smithsonian Institution
Agreement on Indian Bones and Burial Artifacts, 539-543 (1989)

Smoking
Antismoking Campaign, 31-40 (1989)
Health Costs Report, 615-622 (1985)
Involuntary Smoking, 1079-1090 (1986)
Nicotine Addiction Report, 309-322 (1988)
Smoking in the Workplace, 809-822 (1985)
Teenage Smoking Survey, 35-36 (1989)

Social Security. *See also Welfare and social services*
Economic Advisers' Report, 100-101 (1985)
Presidential Debates on, 769-771 (1988)
Vice Presidential Debate on, 804-805 (1988)

Social services. *See Welfare and social services*

Sofaer, Abraham D., 49, 639 (1985); 752-753 (1986); 289 (1987)

Solar energy. *See Energy policy*

Solidarity Labor Movement
Religious Freedom and, 556-557 (1987)
Walesa Address to U.S. Congress, 523-525, 534-538 (1989)

Solovyev, Yuri F., 177-178 (1989)

Somalia
Amnesty International Human Rights Re-

port, 602 (1989)

South Africa. *See also Angola; Namibia*
Amnesty International Human Rights Report, 602-603 (1989)
Angola-Namibia Peace Accord, 947-950 (1988)
Apartheid government, 43, 50 (1987)
Botha's Manifesto for the Future, 515-527 (1985)
Commonwealth Group Report, 581-590 (1986)
De Klerk's Inaugural Address, 545-550 (1989)
Democratic Party Platform on, 568 (1988)
Pass Laws, 369-381 (1986)
Reagan Sanctions, 531-540 (1985)
State Department Human Rights, 146-147, 155-156 (1985); 99, 101-102 (1986); 190, 192-193 (1987); 94-96 (1988); 60-61 (1989)

South Korea
Human Rights Report, 109-110 (1986); 199-201 (1987); 104-106 (1988)
Roh Tae Woo's UN Address, 853-859 (1988)
South Korean Leaders on Democratic Reforms, 583-594 (1987)

Soviet Union
Afghanistan Agreements, 257-266 (1988)
Akhromeyev Testimony Before U.S. Congress, 439-444 (1989)
Baltic Nationalist Movement, 469-475 (1989)
Chernenko Death, 271-274 (1985)
Chernobyl Nuclear Accident, 383-407 (1986)
Daniloff Arrest in Moscow, 819-827 (1986)
Economic Summit Meetings
    (Paris), 431-432, 433-434 (1989)
    (Venice), 526, 528 (1987)
Elections, 173-181 (1989)
Gorbachev, Mikhail S.
    Address to 19th All-Union Conference, 447-464 (1988)
    Address to 27th Soviet Party Congress, 145-168 (1986)
    Arms Control Proposal, 9-20 (1986)
    Bolshevik Anniversary Speech, 857-868 (1987)
    Council of Europe Address on a Common Europe, 399-409 (1989)
    Democratic Reforms Speech, 79-104 (1987)
    Farm Policy, 145-152 (1989)
Human Rights Report, 98, 111-112 (1986); 190, 202-203 (1987); 93-94, 110-112 (1988); 66-67 (1989)
Kennan on Cold War, 207-212 (1989)
Paris Declaration on Chemical Weapons, 26-28 (1989)
Presidential Debates on, 744-745 (1988)

Reagan-Gorbachev
    INF Treaty Statement, 945, 947-950 (1987)
    New Year's Messages, 3-8 (1986)
    Summit Meetings, 749-761 (1985); 875-885 (1986); 991-1006 (1987); 353-373 (1988)
Reagan on International Terrorism, 474-475 (1985)
Republican Party Platform on, 677-679 (1988)
Sakharov Release from Exile, 1092-1095 (1986)
Shcharansky Release, 93-96 (1986)
Soviet Espionage, 603-614 (1985)
State of the Union, 109-111 (1987)
U.S. Reduction of Soviet UN Mission, 267-272 (1986)
U.S. Relations, 707-709, 712-718 (1985)
U.S.-Soviet INF Treaty, 945-989 (1987); 57-58, 67 (1988)

Space
Budget Message, 155 (1988)
Challenger Accident Commission Report, 515-539 (1986)
Discovery Tribute to Challenger Victims, 795-798 (1988)
Missile Defense
    Iceland Summit, 875-885 (1986)
    Security Officials on Defense Strategy, 782, 784, 786-788 (1986)
Republican Party Platform on, 654-655, 693-694 (1988)
Ride Commission Report to NASA, 649-669 (1987)
State of the Union, 113 (1985)

Specter, Arlen, R-Pa.
Impeachment of Judge Alcee Hastings, 585-589 (1989)

Sprinkel, Beryl W., 4 (1989)

Sports
Banning of Pete Rose from Baseball, 477-484 (1989)
Black College Athletes, 213-223 (1989)
Ueberroth on Drugs in Baseball, 169-175 (1986)

Sri Lanka Accord with India, 615-622 (1987)

Star Wars. *See Strategic Defense Initiative*

Stark, USS
Navy Reports on Attack on, 791-816 (1987)

START. *See Strategic Arms Reduction Talks*

State and local government
Philadelphia Police Raid on MOVE Group, 239-251 (1986)
Supreme Court Decisions
    Adult Theaters, 131-144 (1986)
    Affirmative Action, 651-678 (1986)
    Federal Intervention, 167-187 (1985)
    Redistricting, 615-635 (1986)

State Department
Human Rights Reports, 145-157 (1985);

97-113 (1986); 189-204 (1987); 93-115
(1988); 57-70 (1989)
Republican Party Platform on, 688 (1988)
U.S. Withdrawal from World Court Juris-
diction, 637-641 (1985)
State of the Union, 105-117 (1985); 39-48
(1986); 105-115 (1987); 57-68 (1988)
Statue of Liberty's Centennial, 697-703 (1986)
Stehling, J.H., 698-700 (1989)
Stern, William, 373-387 (1987); 71-80 (1988)
Stevens, John Paul
Abortion, 387-389 (1989)
Address on Role of Supreme Court, 653-
654, 666-668 (1985)
Affirmative Action, 332-334, 345-346
(1987)
Employment Discrimination, 328-329,
331-332 (1989)
Flag Burning, 354 (1989)
Mandatory Budget Cuts, 707, 718-723
(1986)
Mandatory Retirement, 397-407 (1985)
Media Libel Law, 364-368 (1986)
Miranda Rule, 226, 233, 250-253 (1985)
Obscenity, 479, 485-490 (1987)
Political Asylum, 253-254, 256-261 (1987)
Silent Prayer, 379-380, 382-387 (1985)
Student Searches, 15, 23-26 (1985)
Students' Free Speech, 740-742 (1986)
Sustaining Handicapped Infants, 543, 545-
554 (1986)
Uncompensated Takings and Land Use,
532-533, 541-546 (1987)
Stevens, Ted, R-Alaska, 291-292 (1988)
Stock market
Economic Advisers' Report on Stock Mar-
ket Crash, 132-135 (1988)
Stock Market Crash, 833-842 (1987); 9-36
(1988)
Supreme Court on Insider Trading, 881-
889 (1987)
Strategic Arms Limitation Treaty (SALT), 354
(1988)
Security Officials on Defense Strategy,
783, 788-789 (1986)
Strategic Arms Reduction Talks (START)
Reagan-Gorbachev Summit, 353-355, 372-
373 (1988)
State of the Union, 58, 67 (1988)
Tower role in, 106, 109, 111, 113-114
(1989)
Strategic Defense Initiative (SDI). *See also*
Space
Economic Summit (Bonn), 349 (1985)
Iceland Summit, 875-885 (1986); 110
(1987)
Presidential Debates on, 745-746 (1988)
Republican Party Platform on, 690, 692
(1988)
Science Board Panel on Strategic Missile
Defense, 323-331 (1988)
Security Officials on Defense Strategy,
782-790 (1986)

State of the Union, 58, 60, 67 (1988)
Substance abuse. *See Alcoholism; Drug*
abuse; Smoking
Sullivan, Joseph P., Jr.
America's Cup Race Appellate Division
Opinion, 188-193 (1989)
Summit conferences
Economic summit meetings
(Bonn), 347-355 (1987)
(Paris), 411, 414, 422, 424-430 (1989)
(Tokyo), 437-444 (1986)
(Toronto), 391-397 (1988)
(Venice), 525-530 (1987)
Reagan-Gorbachev Summit Meetings
(Geneva), 749-761 (1985)
(Moscow), 353-373 (1988)
(Reykjavik), 875-885 (1986)
(Washington, D.C.), 991-1006 (1987)
Supreme Court. *See also Supreme Court*
cases
Abortion, 559-580 (1986); 365-389 (1989)
Adult Theaters, 131-144 (1986)
Affirmative Action, 651-678 (1986); 331-
349 (1987)
Alcoholism and Veterans' Benefits, 277-
285 (1988)
Appointments, 591-599 (1986); 717-744
(1987); 772-773 (1988)
Bork Confirmation Battle, 717-744 (1987);
772 (1988)
Civil Rights Rulings, 321-332 (1989)
Closed Party Primaries, 1065-1073 (1986)
Contagious Diseases, 245-252 (1987)
Creation Science, 565-576 (1987)
Death Penalty, 463-476 (1987)
Disruptive Handicapped Students, 47-56
(1988)
Federal and State Powers, 167-187 (1985)
Flag Burning, 343-354 (1989)
Freedom of the Press, 175-182 (1988)
Independent Counsel, 465-478 (1988)
Indigents' Rights to Psychiatric Aid, 207-
219 (1985)
Insider Trading, 881-889 (1987)
Judiciary Pay Raises, 195-204 (1989)
Jury Selection in Capital Cases, 445-456
(1986)
Justices on Role of Supreme Court, 653-
668 (1985)
Labor Union Membership, 415-429 (1985)
Mandatory Budget Cuts, 705-730 (1986)
Mandatory Retirement, 397-407 (1985)
Maternity Leave, 17-27 (1987)
Media Libel Law, 355-368 (1986)
Meese Criticism, 479-490 (1985)
Obscenity, 479-490 (1987)
PAC Spending Limits, 277-295 (1985)
Peremptory Challenge, 409-433 (1986)
Political Asylum, 253-265 (1987)
Political Gerrymandering, 615-635 (1986)
Powell's Retirement, 577-581 (1987)
Preventive Detention, 491-508 (1987)
Private Clubs, 399-403 (1988)

Public School Teachers in Parochial
Classes, 433-461 (1985)
School Prayer, 379-395 (1985)
Secrecy of CIA Sources, 333-344 (1985)
Sodomy and Privacy, 601-614 (1986)
Student Newspaper Censorship, 37-46
(1988)
Student Searches, 13-26 (1985)
Students' Free Speech, 731-742 (1986)
Suspects' Rights, 223-253 (1985)
Sustaining Handicapped Infants, 541-558
(1986)
Uncompensated Takings and Land Use,
531-553 (1987)
Use of Deadly Force, 303-315 (1985)
Supreme Court cases
Aguilar v. Felton, 433-461 (1985)
Ake v. Oklahoma, 207-219 (1985)
Batson v. Kentucky, 409-433 (1986)
Bethel School District v. Fraser, 731-742
(1986)
Bowen v. American Hospital Association,
541-558 (1986)
Bowers v. Hardwick, 601-614 (1986)
Bowsher v. Synar, 705-730 (1986)
Carpenter v. United States, 881-889
(1987)
*California Federal Savings and Loan v.
Guerra*, 17-27 (1987)
CIA v. Sims and Wolfe, 333-344 (1985)
City of Richmond v. J. A. Croson Co., 323-
324 (1989)
Davis v. Bandemer, 615-635 (1986)
Edwards v. Aguillard, 565-576 (1987)
*Federal Election Commission (FEC) v.
National Conservative Political Action
Committee (NCPAC)*, 277-294 (1985)
*First English Evangelical Lutheran
Church of Glendale v. County of Los
Angeles*, 531-546 (1987)
*Garcia v. San Antonio Metropolitan
Transit Authority*, 167-187 (1985)
Grand Rapids School District v. Ball, 433-
461 (1985)
Hazelwood School District v. Kuhlmeier,
37-46 (1988)
Honig v. Doe, 47-56 (1988)
*Immigration and Naturalization Service
v. Luz Marina Cardoza-Fonseca*, 253-265
(1987)
*International Association of Firefighters
v. City of Cleveland*, 651-678 (1986)
*Jett v. Dallas Independent School Dis-
trict*, 323 (1989)
*Johnson v. Transportation Agency, Santa
Clara, California*, 331-349 (1987)
Lockhart v. McCree, 445-456 (1986)
Martin v. Wilks, 322, 329-332 (1989)
McCleskey v. Kemp, 463-476 (1987)
McKelvey v. Turnage, 277-285 (1988)
Morrison v. Olson, 465-478 (1988)
New Jersey v. T. L. O., 13-26 (1985)

*New York State Club Association, Inc. v.
City of New York et al.*, 399-403 (1988)
Nollan v. California Coastal Commission,
531, 533, 547-553 (1987)
Oregon v. Elstad, 223-253 (1985)
*Pattern Makers' League of North Amer-
ica (AFL-CIO) v. National Labor Rela-
tions Board*, 415-429 (1985)
Patterson v. McLean Credit Union, 322-
323 (1989)
Philadelphia Newspapers Inc. v. Hepps,
355-368 (1986)
Pope v. Illinois, 479-490 (1987)
Renton v. Playtime Theatres Inc., 131-144
(1986)
*School Board of Nassau Co., Florida v.
Arline*, 245-252 (1987)
*Sheet Metal Workers' International Asso-
ciation v. Equal Employment Commis-
sion*, 651-678 (1986)
*Tashjian v. Republican Party of Connect-
icut*, 1065-1073 (1986)
Tennessee v. Garner, 303-315 (1985)
Texas v. Johnson, 343-354 (1989)
*Thornburgh v. American College of Obste-
tricians and Gynecologists*, 559-580
(1986)
Traynor v. Turnage, 277-285 (1988)
United States v. Salerno, 491-508 (1987)
Wallace v. Jaffree, 379-395 (1985)
Wards Cove Packing Co. v. Atonio, 321-
322, 324-329 (1989)
Webster v. Reproductive Health Services,
365-389 (1989)
Western Air Lines Inc. v. Criswell et al.,
397-407 (1985)
Surgeon general's report
Antismoking Campaign, 31-40 (1989)
Involuntary Smoking, 1079-1090 (1986)
Nicotine Addiction Report, 309-322 (1988)
Smoking in the Workplace, 809-822 (1985)
Surrogate mothers. *See Bioethics; Pregnancy
and childbirth*
Sweden
Farm-Animal Rights Law, 347-351 (1988)

T

Tashjian v. Republican Party of Connecticut,
1065-1073 (1986)
Taxes
Corporate Management, 971-981 (1986)
Economic Advisers' Report, 133-135
(1987)
Presidential Debates on, 756-758 769-771
(1988)
President's Economic Report, 86 (1985);
66-67 (1986); 121-122 (1987); 9 (1989)
Republican Party Platform on, 624-626
(1988)
State of the Union, 110 (1985); 40, 44
(1986)

Technology. *See Science and technology*
Teenage pregnancy, 1057-1064 (1986)
Television
    Westmoreland/CBS Controversy, Su-
       preme Court Decision on, 159-165 (1985)
Tennessee v. Garner, 303-315 (1985)
Terrorism
    Chirac's Statement on French Antiterror-
       ist Plan, 829-838 (1986)
    Economic Summit Meetings
       (Tokyo), 438-439, 443-444 (1986)
       (Toronto), 394 (1988)
       (Venice), 526-527, 528-529 (1987)
    Gorbachev's Address to 27th Soviet Party
       Congress, 146, 166-167 (1986)
    Lebanese Hostages, 315-320 (1989)
    Organized Crime Commission, 181, 187-
       189 (1986)
    Palestine Liberation Organization (PLO)
       Office Closing, 479-485 (1988)
    Presidential Debates on, 746-747 (1988)
    Reagan on International Terrorism, 463-
       477 (1985)
    Reagan on U.S. Air Strike Against Libya,
       347-354 (1986)
    Republican Party Platform on, 687-688
       (1988)
    U.S.-U.K. Extradition Treaty, 751-756
       (1986)
Texas v. Johnson, 343-354 (1989)
Thatcher, Margaret
    British-Irish Accord, 723-732 (1985)
Third World. *See Developing countries; For-
eign aid; Foreign trade; United Nations*
Thornburgh, Dick
    Abortion, 367 (1989)
    Flag Burning, 345 (1989)
*Thornburgh v. American College of Obstetri-
cians and Gynecologists,* 559-580 (1986)
Tibet
    Dalai Lama's Nobel Peace Prize Speech,
       573-581 (1989)
Time Magazine
    Sharon Libel Verdict, 47-52 (1985)
Togo
    Pope John Paul II's Visit, 500, 501-504
       (1985)
Tort reform
    American Bar Association Report, 165-181
       (1987)
    Economic Adviser's Report, 142-143
       (1987)
Tower, John
    Defense Secretary Nomination Rejection,
       105-120 (1989)
Tower Commission Report, 205-242 (1987)
Toxic Waste Treaty, 153-160 (1989)
Trade. *See Foreign trade*
Transportation. *See also Airline deregulation*
    Aviation Safety Commission Report, 267-
       276 (1988)
    Economic Advisers' Report, 85-87 (1986)

GAO Report on Air Traffic Safety, 253-
   266 (1986)
President's Report on Privatization, 230-
   231, 233, 235, 236 (1988)
Republican Party Platform on, 671-673
   (1988)
Traynor v. Turnage, 277-285 (1988)
Treaties and agreements. *See also Arms control; Peacemaking efforts; United Nations*
    Afghanistan Agreements, 257-266 (1988)
    ABM Treaty Interpretation, 289-317
       (1987)
    Angola-Namibia Peace Accord, 947-950
       (1988)
    Hazardous Wastes Treaty, 153-160 (1989)
    Ozone Treaty and Scientific Study, 745-
       764 (1987); 221-228 (1988)
    Paris Declaration on Chemical Weapons,
       25-30 (1989)
    Senate Ratification of Genocide Conven-
       tion, 115-130 (1986)
    Toxic Waste Treaty, 153-160 (1989)
    U.S.-Soviet INF Treaty, 945-989 (1987)
    U.S.-U.K. Extradition Treaty, 751-756
       (1986)
Turkey
    Human Rights Report, 156-157 (1985);
       108-110 (1988)
Twenty-fifth Amendment. *See Constitution,
U.S.*

U

Ueberroth, Peter V., 169-175 (1986)
Uganda
    Human Rights Report, 97-98 (1988)
Union Carbide Corp., 295-302 (1985)
Union of Soviet Socialist Republics. *See So-
viet Union*
United Kingdom. *See Great Britain*
United Nations
    Afghanistan Agreements, 257-259, 264-265
       (1988)
    Angola-Namibia Peace Accord, 947-950
       (1988)
    Barco Address, 499, 511-515 (1989)
    Gorbachev Address, 927-940 (1988)
    Human Rights in Afghanistan, 919-936
       (1986)
    Iran-Iraq War Resolutions, 609-613 (1987);
       529-532 (1988)
    PLO Office Closing, 479-485 (1988)
    Reagan Address to General Assembly, 707-
       719 (1985)
    Senate Ratification of Genocide Conven-
       tion, 115-130 (1986)
    South Korean President's UN Address,
       853-859 (1988)
    U.S. Reduction of Soviet Mission, 267-272
       (1986)
    World Conference on Women, 555-570
       (1985)

United States v. Salerno, 491-508 (1987)
Urban affairs. *See also State and local government*
  Republican Party Platform on, 659-660 (1988)
Urban Institute, 877-880 (1988)
Urban League. *See National Urban League*
Urbanization and South African Pass Laws, 369-381 (1986)

V

Vatican. *See also Catholic church; John Paul II*
  Bioethics, 267-287 (1987)
  Excommunication of Archbishop Lefebvre, 489-494 (1988)
  Pastoral Care of Homosexuals, 909-919 (1986)
  Synod of Bishops, 765-780 (1985)
  Theology of Liberation, 317-338 (1986)
  U.S. Bishops' Report, 571-581 (1985)
Venezuela
  Pope John Paul II's Visit, 57, 58, 59-61 (1985)
Ver, Fabian C., 307-308 (1986)
Veterans
  Army Denial of Medal of Honor, 697-700 (1989)
  Department of Veterans Affairs (DVA), 873-876 (1988)
  Republican Party Platform on, 697-698 (1988)
  Supreme Court on Alcoholism and Veterans' Benefits, 277-285 (1988)
Vice presidency
  Bentsen Nomination Acceptance Speech, 542-546 (1988)
  Quayle Nomination Acceptance Speech, 601-604 (1988)
  Vice Presidential Debate, 799-829 (1988)
Vincennes, USS (Ship)
  Downing of Iranian Airliner, 703-717 (1988)
Volcker, Paul A., 511-516 (1987)
Voting. *See also Elections; Presidential election*
  Supreme Court on Redistricting, 615-635 (1986)

W

Waldheim, Kurt
  Inaugural Address, 743-750 (1986)
  Pope John Paul's Visit to Austria, 405-406 (1988)
Walesa, Lech
  Address to U.S. Congress, 523-525, 534-538 (1989)
  Solidarity movement, 556-557 (1987)
Wallace v. Jaffree, 379-395 (1985)
Wallach, E. Robert, 497-516 (1988)

Walsh, Lawrence E., 632 (1986)
Wards Cove Packing Co. v. Atonio, 321-322, 324-329 (1989)
Warner, Margaret, 758, 760-768, 774, 776 (1988)
Warsaw Pact, 645-646 (1989)
Washington, George, 123-125 (1989)
Watkins, James D.
  Environmental Plan, 355-362 (1989)
Watt, James
  Influence Peddling, 333-337 (1989)
Webster v. Reproductive Health Services, 365-389 (1989)
Wedtech Corp., 496-516 (1988)
Welbilt Corp. *See Wedtech Corp.*
Welfare and social services. *See also Medicaid and Medicare*
  Bishops on Economic Justice, 1000-1002 (1986)
  CDF Infant Mortality Report, 161-165 (1987)
  Family Support Act, 847-852 (1988)
  House Report on Discarded Children in America, 671-686 (1989)
  Presidential Debates on, 738-741, 773-775 (1988)
  President's Budget Message, 78-79 (1989)
  Republican Party Platform on, 657-659 (1988)
  State of the Union, 112 (1987); 64 (1988)
  Welfare System Revision, 847-852 (1988)
West Bank. *See Israel*
Western Air Lines Inc. v. Criswell et al., 397-407 (1985)
Westmoreland, William C., 159-165 (1985)
White, Byron R.
  Abortion, 561, 571-579 (1986)
  Affirmative Action, 667-676 (1986)
  Alcoholism and Veterans' Benefits, 277-284 (1988)
  Discrimination in Employment, 325-327 (1989)
  Flag Burning, 351-353 (1989)
  Freedom of Press, 182 (1988)
  Insider Trading, 884-889 (1987)
  Mandatory Budget Cuts, 707, 724-728 (1986)
  Maternity Leave, 9, 25-27 (1987)
  Obscenity, 479-483 (1987)
  PAC Spending Limits, 279, 290-294 (1985)
  Private Clubs, 399-403 (1988)
  Public School Teachers in Parochial Classes, 433, 449 (1985)
  Redistricting, 617, 618-619 (1986)
  Student Newspaper Censorship, 37-44 (1988)
  Student Searches, 14-23 (1985)
  Sustaining Handicapped Infants, 544, 554-558 (1986)
  Use of Deadly Force, 303-311 (1985)
Whitehead, Mary Beth, 373-387 (1987); 71-80 (1988)

Wiesel, Elie
Nobel Peace Prize, 1075-1078 (1986)
Testimony at Klaus Barbie Trial, 517-524 (1987)
Wilentz, C. J., 72-80 (1988)
Will, George, 1092-1095 (1986)
Williamson, Richard, 490-492 (1988)
Winans, R. Foster, 881-889 (1987)
Women
Apostolic Letter on Women, 785-792 (1988)
Bishops on Economic Justice, 999 (1986)
Episcopal Church on First Woman Bishop, 49-54 (1989)
Pentagon Report on Sexual Harassment, 671-679 (1987)
Republican Party Platform on, 643 (1988)
Sex Segregation in the Workplace, 789-801 (1985)
Smoking and, 36 (1989)
UN World Conference, 555-570 (1985)
Woodruff, Judy, 799-829 (1988)
Working Group on Financial Markets, 9-12, 34-36 (1988)
World Bank
Brady World Debt Relief Plan, 138, 141-143 (1989)
Environmental Defense Fund on World Bank Project, 859-873 (1986)
IMF-World Bank Conference, 643-652 (1985)

World Court. *See International Court of Justice*
World debt. *See International debt*
World War II
Army Denial of Medal of Honor, 697-700 (1989)
Emperor Hirohito's Role, 99-103 (1989)
Japanese-American Internees Reparations, 287-295 (1988)
Kohl on German Remorse at 50th Anniversary of Polish Invasion, 487-497 (1989)
Mengele Discovery, 409-414 (1985)
Pope John Paul's Visit to Austria, 405-411 (1988)
Wiesel Testimony at Klaus Barbie Trial, 517-524 (1987)
Wright, Betty, 260-262 (1989)
Wright, Jim, D-Tex.
Congressional Bicentennial Commemoration, 127-129 (1989)
Farewell Speech, 242, 251-271 (1989)
House Ethics Committee Reports, 239-271 (1989)

Y

Young, Frank E., 484-485 (1986)
Young, W. Dale
Frozen Embryo Custody Court Decision, 551-559 (1989)
Youth. *See Children; Education*